HANDBOOK OF COGNITIVE LINGUISTICS AND SECOND LANGUAGE ACQUISTION

Cognitive Linguistics (CL) is an approach to the study of language informed by both linguistics and psychology. It describes how language interfaces with cognition, and how it adapts in the course of language usage, phylogenetically in language evolution, ontogenetically in language acquisition, and moment-to-moment in situated, on-line language processing and performance. Second Language Acquisition (SLA) involves the study of the cognitive representations and mechanisms of second language processing, their time-course of acquisition, and, where possible and feasible, their relevance to instruction.

The Handbook of Cognitive Linguistics and Second Language Acquisition brings these two areas of theory and research together. It provides in nine chapters making up Part II, "Cognitive Linguistics and cognition," up-to-date coverage of theoretical and empirical issues in the rapidly developing domain of CL research. The nine chapters in Part III, "Cognitive Linguistics, Second Language Acquisition, and L2 instruction" demonstrate the relevance of these basic CL concepts, and theoretical frameworks for researching them, to the fields of SLA and language pedagogy. The chapters are written by acknowledged experts in the fields of psychology, linguistics, and SLA, and an extensive agenda for future research linking them is proposed both in individual chapters and in synthesis in the final chapter. This handbook, thus, provides a new appreciation of the relationships between cognitive theory, first and second language acquisition research, and their pedagogic applications.

Peter Robinson is Professor of Linguistics and SLA in the Department of English, Aoyama Gakuin University, Tokyo. His books include *Consciousness, Rules and Instructed Second Language Acquisition* (1996), Lang; *Cognition and Second Language Instruction* (2001), Cambridge University Press; and *Individual Differences and Instructed Language Learning* (2002), Benjamins.

Nick C. Ellis is Professor of Psychology and Research Scientist in the English Language Institute at the University of Michigan. His research interests include psycholinguistic, neuroscientific, applied cognitive, and emergentist aspects of second language acquisition. He edited *Implicit and Explicit Learning of Languages* (1994), Academic Press and co-edited *Handbook of Spelling: Theory, Process and Intervention* (1994), Wiley.

HANDBOOK OF COGNITIVE LINGUISTICS AND SECOND LANGUAGE ACQUISITION

Edited by

Peter Robinson
Aoyama Gakuin University, Japan

and

Nick C. Ellis
University of Michigan, U.S.A.

Routledge
Taylor & Francis Group

NEW YORK AND LONDON

First published 2008
by Routledge
270 Madison Ave, New York, NY 10016

Simultaneously published in the UK
by Routledge
2 Park Square, Milton Park, Abingdon, Oxon OX14 4RN

Routledge is an imprint of the Taylor & Francis Group, an informa business

© 2008 Taylor & Francis

Typeset in Goudy by
RefineCatch Limited, Bungay, Suffolk
Printed and bound in the United States of America on acid-free paper
by Sheridan Books, Inc.

Library of Congress Cataloging in Publication Data
Robinson, Peter
Handbook of cognitive linguistics and second language acquisition / by
Peter Robinson and Nick C. Ellis.
p. cm.
Includes index.
ISBN 978–0–8058–5351–3 – ISBN 978–0–8058–5352–0
ISBN 978–0–203–93856–0
1. Cognitive grammar. 2. Second language acquisition. 3. Language
and languages – Study and teaching. I. Ellis, Nick C. II. Title.
P165.R63 2008
410–dc22
2007026713

ISBN10: 0–805–85351–0 (hbk)
ISBN10: 0–805–85352–9 (pbk)
ISBN10: 0–203–93856–9 (ebk)

ISBN13: 978–0–805–85351–3 (hbk)
ISBN13: 978–0–805–85352–0 (pbk)
ISBN13: 978–0–203–93856–0 (ebk)

CONTENTS

CONTENTS

CONTENTS

FIGURES

TABLES

CONTRIBUTORS

Michel Achard Rice University, U.S.A.

Joan Bybee University of New Mexico, U.S.A.

Teresa Cadierno University of Southern Denmark, Denmark.

Devin Casenhiser Princeton University, U.S.A.

Kenny R. Coventry Northumbria University, U.K.

Nick C. Ellis University of Michigan, U.S.A.

Adele E. Goldberg Princeton University, U.S.A.

Stefan Th. Gries University of California, Santa Barbara, U.S.A.

Pedro Guijarro-Fuentes University of Plymouth, U.K.

Marianne Gullberg Max Planck Institute for Psycholinguistics, Netherlands.

Richard Hudson University College London, U.K.

Ronald W. Langacker University of California, San Diego, U.S.A.

Elena Lieven Max Planck Institute for Evolutionary Anthropology, Germany.

Brian MacWhinney Carnegie Mellon University, U.S.A.

Terence Odlin Ohio State University, U.S.A.

William O'Grady University of Hawaii, U.S.A.

Peter Robinson Aoyama Gakuin University, Japan.

Leonard Talmy University at Buffalo, State University of New York, U.S.A.

John R. Taylor University of Otago, New Zealand.

Michael Tomasello Max Planck Institute for Evolutionary Anthropology, Germany.

Andrea Tyler Georgetown University, U.S.A.

Part I

INTRODUCTION

1

AN INTRODUCTION TO COGNITIVE LINGUISTICS, SECOND LANGUAGE ACQUISITION, AND LANGUAGE INSTRUCTION

Nick C. Ellis and Peter Robinson

Cognitive Linguistics (CL) is about language, communication, and cognition. They are mutually inextricable. Cognition and language create each other. Language has come to represent the world as we know it; it is grounded in our perceptual experience. Language is used to organize, process, and convey information, from one person to another, from one embodied mind to another. Learning language involves determining structure from usage and this, like learning about all other aspects of the world, involves the full scope of cognition: the remembering of utterances and episodes, the categorization of experience, the determination of patterns among and between stimuli, the generalization of conceptual schema and prototypes from exemplars, and the use of cognitive models, of metaphors, analogies, and images in thinking. Language is used to focus the listener's attention to the world; it can foreground different elements in the theatre of consciousness to potentially relate many different stories and perspectives about the same scene. What is attended is learned, and so attention controls the acquisition of language itself. The functions of language in discourse determine language usage and language learning. Cognition, consciousness, experience, embodiment, brain, self, and human interaction, society, culture, and history are all inextricably intertwined in rich, complex, and dynamic ways in language. Yet despite this complexity, there are patterns everywhere. Patterns that are not pre-ordained by god, by genes, by school curriculum, or by other human policy, but patterns that emerge—synchronic patterns of linguistic organization at numerous levels (phonology, lexis, syntax, semantics, pragmatics, discourse genre, . . .), dynamic patterns of usage, diachronic patterns of language change (linguistic cycles of grammaticization, pidginization, creolization, . . .), ontogenetic developmental patterns in child language acquisition, etc. CL investigates these patterns, the cross-linguistic and panchronic generalities as well as the more specific patterns of particular languages, cultures, times, individuals, and places. As a discipline, it is a relatively new area of linguistic and psycholinguistic enquiry, dating back perhaps to 1990, when the first journal, *Cognitive Linguistics*, dedicated to this approach was published.

CL shares many of the assumptions of more broadly defined functional linguistics, which sees the processing conditions of language performance, and the communicative goals and intentions of language users as shaping influences on language structure, but CL seeks to go beyond these functional explanations of linguistic form to further explain how language mutually interfaces with conceptual structure as this becomes established during child L1 development and as it becomes available for change during adult L2 language learning. As Langacker notes, "However great its functional motivation, the structure of a language cannot be predicted in full and precise detail on the basis of the motivating factors" (1999, p. 19). The additional cognitive commitment of CL is to specify the interface of linguistic representation (grammatical factors), which can be used to communicative effect in producing utterances, with other aspects of conceptual structure (e.g., semantic factors, such as our concepts of time, and spatial location), as well as with the constraints imposed by the architecture of cognitive processes, and the structure of cognitive abilities (e.g., psychological factors, such as those involved in the allocation and inhibition of attention).

Because CL holds that the basic units of language representation are *constructions*—form-meaning mappings, conventionalized in the child L1 learner and adult L2 learner speech communities, and gradually entrenched as language knowledge in the child L1 or adult L2 learner's mind—work within this approach links and builds with that in a range of research areas within Cognitive Science:

- *Functional analyses* of language which hold that constructions are symbolic, their defining properties of morphological, syntactic, and lexical form being associated with particular semantic, pragmatic, and discourse functions (Croft, 2001; Croft & Cruise, 2004; Gonzálvez-García & Butler, 2006; Halliday, 1985, 1987; Langacker, 2000; Taylor, 2002).
- *Perception and Attention analyses* of the ways our embodiment and perceptuo-motor systems govern our representation of the world and the ways that language can guide our attention to these representations (Barsalou, 1999; Coventry & Garrod, 2004; Mandler, 2004; Talmy, 1988, 2000a, 2000b).

- *Usage-based theories* of language acquisition which hold that we learn constructions while engaging in communication (Barlow & Kemmer, 2000; Hopper, 1998), the "interpersonal communicative and cognitive processes that everywhere and always shape language" (Slobin, 1997).
- *Constructionist theories* of child language acquisition where dense longitudinal corpora chart the emergence of creative linguistic competence from children's analyses of the utterances in their usage history and from their abstraction of regularities within them (Goldberg, 2006; Tomasello, 1998, 2003).
- *Cognitive theories* of categorization and generalization whereby schematic constructions are abstracted over less schematic ones that are inferred inductively by the learner in acquisition (Harnad, 1987; Lakoff, 1987; Schank & Abelson, 1977; Taylor, 1998).
- *Construction Grammar and Phraseological theories* of language demonstrating that much of communication makes use of fixed expressions memorized as formulaic chunks, that language is rich in collocational and colligation restrictions and semantic prosodies, and that the phrase is the basic level of language representation where form and meaning come together with greatest reliability (N. C. Ellis, 1996; Goldberg, 1995, 2003; Granger & Meunier, in press; Pawley & Syder, 1983; Sinclair, 1991, 2004; Vygotsky, 1980, 1986; Wray, 2002).

CL holds that language is learned from usage, and this assumption involves natural interplay with investigations of language usage and language processing and computational and statistical simulations of acquisition:

- *Corpus Linguistic analyses* of large collections of language which show how there are recurrent patterns of words, collocations, phrases, and constructions, that syntax and semantics are inextricably linked, and that grammar cannot be described without lexis, nor lexis without grammar (Biber, Conrad, & Reppen, 1998; Biber, Johansson, Leech, Conrad, & Finegan, 1999; Hoey, 2005; McEnery & Wilson, 1996; Sinclair, 1991, 2004). Distributional analyses of language also show the importance of Zipf's law at all levels in determining the structure and network characteristics of linguistic systems and the effects of these properties on learning (N. C. Ellis, in press b; Ferrer i Cancho & Solé, 2001, 2003; Ferrer i Cancho, Solé, & Köhler, 2004).
- *Psycholinguistic theories* of the mental representation of language which show that fluent language users are sensitive to the relative probabilities of occurrence of different constructions in the language input and to the contingencies of their mappings to meaning (Altman, 1997; Gernsbacher, 1994).
- *Probabilistic and frequency-based theories* of language which analyze

how frequency and repetition affect and ultimately bring about form in language and how probabilistic knowledge drives language comprehension and production (Bod, Hay, & Jannedy, 2003; Bybee & Hopper, 2001; N. C. Ellis, 2002a, 2002b; Jurafsky, 2002; Jurafsky & Martin, 2000).

- *Connectionist, Competition model,* and *Rational models* of language which demonstrate the ways in which generalizations emerge from the conspiracy of memorized instances, the ways in which different cues and their cue reliabilities compete for activation, and the ways in which these representations provide the best model of language that is available from the learner's sample of experience, one that is optimized in its organization for usage (Anderson, 1989; Anderson & Schooler, 2000; Bates & MacWhinney, 1987; Chater, 2004; Chater & Manning, 2006; Christiansen & Chater, 2001; N. C. Ellis, 2006; Elman et al., 1996; MacWhinney, 1987, 1997).

- *Dynamic Systems Theory (DST)* which analyses language as a complex dynamic system where cognitive, social and environmental factors continuously interact, where creative communicative behaviors emerge from socially co-regulated interactions, where flux and individual variation abound, and where cause-effect relationships are nonlinear, multivariate and interactive in time (de Bot, Lowie, & Verspoor, 2007; N. C. Ellis, in press b; N. C. Ellis & Larsen Freeman, 2006a, 2006b; Port & Van Gelder, 1995; Spivey, 2006; van Geert, 1991).

- *Sociocultural theory* which analyses how language learning takes place in a social context, involving action, reaction, collaborative interaction, intersubjectivity, and mutually assisted performance (Lantolf, 2006; Lantolf & Pavlenko, 1995; Lantolf & Thorne, 2006; van Geert, 1994), and how individual language learning is an emergent, holistic property of a dynamic system comprising many dialectic influences, both social, individual, and contextual, involving the learner in a conscious tension between the conflicting forces of their current interlanguage productions and the evidence of feedback, either linguistic, pragmatic, or metalinguistic, that allows socially scaffolded development (Kramsch, 2002; Lantolf & Pavlenko, 1995; Lantolf & Thorne, 2006; Norton, 1997; Swain, 2000; Vygotsky, 1980, 1986).

- *Emergentist and Chaos/Complexity Theory (CCT)* where language is neither a genetic inheritance, largely prescribed by innate linguistic universals in a modularized Language Acquisition Device, nor a collection of rules and target forms to be acquired, but rather a by-product of communicative processes. CCT analyses how complex patterns are emergent from the interactions of many agents, how each emergent level cannot come into being except by involving the levels that lie below it, and how at each higher level there are new and emergent kinds of relatedness not found below (N. C. Ellis, 1998; N. C. Ellis & Larsen Freeman, 2006a; MacWhinney, 1999).

One purpose of this Handbook is to summarize current Cognitive Linguistic perspectives on patterns of language, patterns of language use, and patterns of child language acquisition, and this is the focus of the chapters in Part II of the volume. These chapters concern how language draws on other, more basic cognitive systems and abilities, such as perception, attention allocation, memory and categorization, and how it cannot be separated from these as a distinct, modularized, self-governed entity; how knowledge of language is integrated with our general knowledge of the world; and how, in usage-based child language acquisition, attention to input controls the products of learning, the increasingly productive frames, schemata and constructions that reflect and in turn enable the development of fluent, and complex, language use.

The other focus of this Handbook is Second Language Acquisition (SLA). There are many essential patterns of SLA, too (Doughty & Long, 2003; R. Ellis, 1994; Kaplan, 2002; Kroll & De Groot, 2005; Long, 1990; Perdue, 1993). For illustration, consider an agreed list of summary essentials of SLA gathered by Long (1990) as "the least a second language acquisition theory needs to explain":

- There are common patterns in development in different kinds of learner under diverse conditions of exposure. These systematicites of interlanguage—regular developmental sequences as well as systematic production of non-targetlike forms—indicate that learners do not simply echo input but instead go through successive stages of cognitive analysis and representation of the input.
- There are systematic differences in the problems posed learners of different L1 backgrounds by certain kinds of L1/L2 configuration and by other qualitative features of the input such as the salience of certain linguistic features. These patterns suggest that L1 cognition transfers to that of the L2, sometimes facilitating L2 development, sometimes interfering with it.
- Children and adults learning under comparable conditions differ in their rate of acquisition (adults initially learn faster) and in their level of attainment (children achieve greater ultimate proficiency).
- Learners' aptitude, attitude and motivation are all systematically related to rate of progress and ultimate attainment, but affective factors are subordinate to more powerful cognitive developmental and maturational factors.
- Some aspects of an L2 require awareness and/or attention to language form—implicit learning is not sufficient for successful SLA and focus on form improves rate and ultimate L2 attainment.

- Some aspects of the L2 are unlearnable for positive evidence alone—exposure to samples of comprehensible input is necessary for SLA but not sufficient, and some forms of negative feedback and correction are necessary.
- Development is gradual and U-shaped acquisition profiles occur, suggesting that learners gradually construct their system of L2 representation over considerable periods of time and language usage.

These systematicities of Second Language Acquisition are all, in essence, issues of second language cognition. The adult's language learning task is clearly different from the child's. As Slobin notes, "For the child, the construction of the grammar and the construction of semantic/pragmatic concepts go hand-in-hand. For the adult, construction of the grammar often requires a revision of semantic/pragmatic concepts, along with what may well be a more difficult task of perceptual identification of the relevant morphological elements" (1993, p. 242). In cases where the forms lack perceptual salience and so go unnoticed by learners (Robinson, 1995, 1996; Schmidt, 1990, 2001), or where the semantic/pragmatic concepts available to be mapped onto the L2 forms are unfamiliar, additional "Focus on Form" (attention to form in communicative context: Doughty & Williams, 1998; N. C. Ellis, 2005; R. Ellis, 2001; Lightbown, Spada, & White, 1993; Long, 1991; Long & Robinson, 1998; Robinson, 2001, 2002, 2003, in press 2007a, 2007b) is likely to be needed in order for the mapping process to be facilitated. Thus, the second aim of this volume is the development of a Cognitive Linguistics of SLA and L2 pedagogy. This is why many of the authors of the chapters in Part II, primarily from the fields of linguistics and psycholinguistics, have been asked to make links between their own work and SLA, and why the issues they raise are then taken up and expanded upon in the Part III by authors from the fields of SLA and SL pedagogy.

Chapter overviews

Part II. Cognitive Linguistics and cognition

Chapters 2–5 represent classic *Cognitive Linguistics*: cognitive semantics, the ways language controls listener attention, the grounding of language in cognition, the prototype structure of linguistic construction categories, the interrelation of linguistic and other information in semantic networks, and the interplay of language and usage. Chapter 6 supplements these with a more *Psycholinguistic* investigation of how the perceptual systems interface with language—introspection is a good start to the understanding of cognition, but psychological experimentation is necessary, too. Chapter 7 focuses upon *Language Processing* and how the functions of a limited-capacity working memory system in language parsing constrain the types of structure that emerge in language and their orders of acquisition. Finally, this section moves to *Acquisition*, with chapters 8 and 9 presenting construction grammar perspectives on child language acquisition, and chapter 10 focusing on the ways in which type and token frequency of usage affect language structure, language change, and language learning.

In chapter 2, Talmy presents an overview of research in Cognitive Semantics and describes his analysis of the *Attentional System of Language*. In a speech situation, a hearer may attend to the linguistic expression produced by a speaker, to the conceptual content represented by that expression, and to the context at hand. But not all of this material appears uniformly in the foreground of the hearer's attention. Rather, various portions or aspects of the expression, content, and context have different degrees of salience. Such differences are only partly due to any intrinsically greater interest of certain elements over others. More fundamentally, language has an extensive system that assigns different degrees of salience to the parts of an expression, reference, or context. This system includes some fifty basic factors, its "building blocks." Each factor involves a particular linguistic mechanism that increases or decreases attention on a certain type of linguistic entity. Although able to act alone, the basic factors also regularly combine and interact to produce further attentional effects. Thus, several factors can converge on the same linguistic entity to reinforce a particular level of salience, making it especially high or especially low. Or two factors can conflict in their attentional effects, with the resolution usually either that one factor overrides the other, or that the hearer's attention is divided or wavers between the two claims on it. Or a number of factors can combine in the production of higher-level attentional patterns, such as that of figure-ground assignment, or that of maintaining a single attentional target through a discourse. Learning a language involves the learning of these various attention-directing mechanisms of language, and this, in turn, rests upon L1 learners' developing attentional systems and L2 learners' attentional biases. Because languages achieve these attention-directing outcomes in different ways, Talmy proposes that such cross-linguistic differences must affect L2 learning, making it easier where languages use them in the same way, and more difficult when they use them differently, themes which are taken up empirically in later chapters by Cadierno, Gullberg, Ellis, MacWhinney, and Odlin.

In chapter 3, Taylor describes how an important impetus to the development of Cognitive Linguistics from the 1980s onwards came from cognitive psychological theories of *Prototype Categorization*. These offered a radical alternative to the, till then, dominant "checklist" models of categories. The liberating effect of the prototype concept was felt, most obviously and most immediately, in lexical semantics. Subsequently, prototype theories permeated other areas of language study—morphology, syntax, phonology—as well as the study of language change and language acquisition. This chapter first summarizes the reception and development of prototype theories in linguistics, highlighting some of the more problematic and contentious issues surrounding the prototype concept, including (a) the different ways in which "prototypes" can be understood, and (b) the properties of so-called "prototype categories," in interaction with such matters as the taxonomic "level" of categorization (with special reference to the basic level), the distinction between natural and nominal categories, the polysemy vs. monosemy debate, and the role of Idealized Cognitive Models (ICMs) in categorization. Taylor illustrates these points primarily with examples from lexical semantics, though he also shows their relevance in the study of word classes and syntactic constructions, as well as phonological categories. Prototype effects apply throughout linguistic knowledge, its acquisition, and deployment, and Taylor considers how "bottom-up," exemplar-based models of categorization from usage might underpin the induction of these categories, themes taken up in later chapters by Goldberg, Lieven and Tomasello, Bybee, and Gries.

In chapter 4, Langacker summarizes *Cognitive Grammar* and considers how this offers a natural and promising basis for language instruction. The most obvious reason is that it advances a conceptually grounded account of linguistic meaning. By showing in detail how alternate expressions construe the same situation in subtly different ways, it renders comprehensible the varied means of expression a language provides. A second reason is that this conceptual semantics is not confined to lexicon but also supports the characterization of grammar. Since every grammatical element or grammatical construction imposes a particular construal on the situation being described, grammar can be presented as an array of meaningful options whose ranges of application are in large measure predictable. A third reason is the usage-based nature of Cognitive Grammar. Language structure emerges by abstraction from expressions that occur in usage events, embracing all dimensions of how they are understood by interlocutors in the social, cultural, and discourse context. This interactive grounding has a number of implications for language learning: the importance of non-descriptive modes of speech; the need to actually produce and understand appropriate expressions in a natural context; and the great extent to which fluent speech depends on mastery of a vast array of complex fixed expressions and conventional ways of phrasing things, out of all the ways a language in principle makes available. Langacker's proposals are analyzed, implemented for SLA, and evaluated in chapters in Part III by Achard, and Tyler.

In chapter 5, Hudson outlines *Word Grammar*, and considers the consequences of its major components for second-language learning and teaching. Firstly, language is just knowledge, and thus learning a language is just like other kinds of learning, with the same need for a balance between instruction and practice. Secondly, language is a (symbolic) network, and this is true not only of the vocabulary but also of the more general patterns of morphology and syntax, and thus L2 is also a network which grows inside the L1 network and interacts with it (e.g., by sharing its word classes). Thirdly, categories show prototype effects, with some members more typical than others, and thus learners benefit from experiencing typical examples before exceptions. Fourthly, knowledge of language is declarative, and we match both produced and perceived tokens with it; thus, learners will maximize the value of their existing knowledge by using L1 for guessing unknown L2 patterns; this should be encouraged so long as it does not prevent learning. Fifthly, the grammar includes the lexicon in a single homogeneous lexico-grammar; thus, grammar and vocabulary are likely to follow a very similar pattern of acquisition. Sixthly, meanings are embedded in culture, so there is no clear boundary between the learning of language and the learning of culture. Finally, language is based on usage, and masses of detailed patterns of usage—including relative frequencies—are stored in language, and this is why it is so important for classroom L2 teaching to include as rich as possible a diet of L2 usage. These various themes of L1 and L2 usage-based acquisition, transfer, and instruction resonate through Part III of this volume.

In chapter 6, Coventry and Guijarro-Fuentes present a *Functional Geometric Framework of Spatial Language*. Although early CL theories argued that the distinction in visual science between the so-called "what" and "where" systems maps fairly directly onto differences between syntactic categories in language, with closed class categories such as spatial prepositions relating more to the output of the "where" system and open class terms such as nouns relating more to the "what" system, subsequent studies demonstrated that the comprehension and production of spatial prepositions have to do with *what plus where*. The chapter reviews the empirical evidence for the importance of the three components of the framework: geometric routines, extra-geometric dynamic-kinematic routines, and object knowledge. It then describes computational, developmental, and cross-linguistic considerations of these components. The computational work involves the implementation of this framework as a connectionist model that grounds spatial language understanding directly in visual processing. The developmental contribution explores the various non-verbal understandings of space which the child brings to language acquisition and considers how language acquisition in different languages might be coordinated with such knowledge. Cross-linguistic contrasts of spatial language in English and Spanish along these lines make various predictions of whether there would be transfer from L1 or not. Coventry and Guijarro-Fuentes present some initial empirical tests of these predictions, and there is further evidence in the existing empirical literature on Second Language Acquisition of spatial language reviewed by Cadierno, Gullberg, and Odlin in later chapters. Whatever the detailed findings now and from future research, this chapter, like that of Langacker, presents a clear interim conclusion that SLA instruction must provide grounded, contextualized, and communicative opportunities where language maps properly onto relations in a spatial world rather than taking place through the translation equivalents of an existing L1 system.

In chapter 7, O'Grady presents an *Emergentist* theory of *Syntactic Computation* that proposes that key properties of human language follow from more basic non-linguistic forces rather than from a grammar, as traditionally assumed. The basic idea is that the mechanisms that are required to account for the traditional concerns of syntactic theory (e.g., the design of phrase structure, pronoun interpretation, agreement, and structure dependence) are identical to the mechanisms that are independently required to account for how sentences are processed from "left to right" in real time. The key proposal involves an efficiency-driven linear computational system that operates from "left to right," building structure by combining words and resolving their lexical requirements at the first opportunity. As the chapter explains, such a computational system is nothing but a processor that seeks to minimize the burden on working memory (the pool of operational resources that holds representations and supports computations on them). O'Grady explores the implications of this perspective for both first and second language acquisition.

In chapter 8, Lieven and Tomasello consider *Child Language Acquisition* from a usage-based perspective. Whereas traditional accounts of L1A use as analytic tools adult-like syntactic categories and grammars, with little concern for whether they are psychologically real for young children, recent research within a cognitive-functional framework has demonstrated that children do not operate initially with such abstract linguistic entities but instead operate on the basis of item-based, form-meaning constructions. Children construct more abstract linguistic constructions only gradually on the basis of linguistic experience. The chapter reviews naturalistic studies demonstrating that children's ability to deal with more general and abstract categories, for instance of argument structure and inflectional marking, changes radically between the ages of 2;0–4;0. It supports these with empirical studies showing how construction generalization depends upon type and token frequency, consistency of form-function mapping, and complexity of form, giving examples of these processes in three aspects of child language acquisition: morphological development, the development of the transitive construction in English, and in the development of more complex sentences. The chapter closes with an emphasis on the ways in which contextual and processing factors can affect success with a construction, for example forced-choice recognition between known alternatives is much easier than productive generalization. Thus, they argue, the best account of first language acquisition is provided by a usage-based model in which children process the language they experience in discourse interactions with other persons, relying explicitly and exclusively on social and cognitive skills that children of this age are known to possess.

In chapter 9, Goldberg and Casenhiser present a detailed *Construction Grammar* analysis of the ways that form–function pairings (constructions) are learned on the basis of frequencies in the input. The chapter summarizes studies involving training child and adult subjects on a novel construction which indicate that subjects can in fact learn to recognize the form and meaning of a novel construction with quite minimal training. Morphological marking of the construction is not necessary for it to be learned. When overall type and token frequencies are held constant, input that is skewed such that one type of example accounts for the preponderance of tokens results in more accurate generalization than input that is more representative. Skewed input is also present in the natural Zipfian frequency distributions for constructions in naturalistic language. In addition, if the skewed examples are presented first, there is further facilitation in learning the generalization. On the other hand, input that is noisier inhibits generalization. These themes resonate with the analyses of natural language constructions made earlier by Taylor, and with the evidence of the differential effects of type and token frequency in child language acquisition reviewed by Lieven and Tomasello. Goldberg and Casenhiser conclude by outlining implications for second language learning and pedagogy, implications which Bybee also develops in the following chapter.

In chapter 10, Bybee considers the effects of *Usage Frequency*, analyzing the separate effects of token frequency and type frequency on construction learning, structure, and productivity, providing examples from morphology, syntax, and grammaticization. Experience with language shapes the cognitive representations of language users, just as language use leads to the creation of grammar: high-frequency constructions have stronger mental representations and are easier to access and less susceptible to change; patterns with high type frequency are more productive; repetition of sequences of linguistic units leads to representation at a higher level as a single unit, with fluent language users making use of these prefabricated chunks of language; and extremely high levels of use lead to the development of grammaticized forms and constructions. There is no unitary "grammar" of language but rather a continuum of categories and constructions ranging from low frequency, highly specific, and lexical to high frequency, highly abstract, and general. The chapter examines three points along the continuum: first, the pervasive use of specific prefabricated word combinations; second, limited scope patterns generalized from pre-fabricated constructions; and, third, fully grammaticized constructions. Bybee pays particular attention to the interaction of type and token frequency on productivity and categorization, and considers the question of to what extent exposure to a second language in a classroom situation should mirror exposure in more natural situations. The suggested answer is that an exact parallel to natural situations is not necessary, but attention to issues of token and type frequency remains important, with there being plenty of opportunity for communicative, grounded, authentic usage of language which mirrors the natural Zipfian frequency distributions, whilst additionally providing privileged practice of lower-frequency prefabs and formulas embedded in an approach that also teaches general morphosyntactic constructions.

Part III. Cognitive Linguistics, SLA, and L2 instruction

Chapters 11–13 analyze the classic *Cognitive Linguistic* issues of linguistic relativity and "thinking for speaking" as they affect SLA—to what extent is there transfer, with cross-linguistic differences between the L1 and the L2 facilitating acquisition where the L1 and L2 are typologically similar, and interfering where they are different? Chapters 14 and 15 present *Psychological* accounts of the competition between different linguistic constructions, within and between languages, in processing language, and the ways that fundamental properties of associative learning such as construction frequency, salience, redundancy, and exposure order affect learners' attention to language, thereby affecting the course and level of ultimate attainment in the L2. Chapter 16 provides a *Corpus Linguistic* analysis of construction grammar, demonstrates its potential for studying the second language acquisition of constructions and their potential applications in language teaching. Chapters 17 and 18 develop and evaluate a *Cognitive Linguistic Pedagogy*, focusing on classroom teaching and the nature and scope of a pedagogic grammar informed by the tenets and descriptive procedures of CL. Chapter 19 summarizes the major themes of the volume and looks to *Future Developments*.

In Chapter 11, Cadierno discusses how cognitive semantics informs investigation of adult language learners' *Expression of Motion Events in a Foreign Language*. Talmy's (2000a, 2000b) typological framework for describing the linguistic encoding of motion events distinguishes between languages that are verb-framed and those that are satellite-framed. Cadierno reviews support for this typology from analyses of novels and novel translations, cross-linguistic first language acquisition studies, and cross-linguistic studies of gesture and language. Slobin (2004) argues that these typological differences between languages lead their speakers to experience different "thinking for speaking" and thus to construe experience in different ways. Cadierno develops hypotheses motivated by these theories to examine the extent to which typologically different L1s influence how motion events are construed and filtered through the resources a language has available to describe them. The major issue for SLA research is that of transfer. Cadierno presents a thorough review of the existing experimental evidence for what Slobin (2004) has called "thinking for speaking" in studies of the use of preferred lexicalization patterns for referring to motion events in L2 narrative production. While the studies do demonstrate effects of transfer, there are qualifications that depend upon such factors as the particular motion verbs studied, learner proficiency, and assessment task. The chapter concludes by outlining the ways in which this research needs to develop to include studies of learners at early and intermediate stages of language acquisition to examine whether the influence of the L1 thinking patterns at these stages is stronger than at more advanced levels, and bi-directional studies to compare the expression of motion events by learners of satellite-framed languages (e.g., Spanish learners of English) and learners of verb-framed languages (e.g., English learners of Spanish) in order to determine similarities and differences in both acquisitional processes.

In chapter 12, Gullberg shows how the study of *Gestures* provides an additional window on *Second Language Cognition and Acquisition*. Gestures, the symbolic movements speakers perform while they speak, are systematically related to speech and language at multiple levels, and they reflect cognitive and linguistic activities in non-trivial ways. The chapter first outlines current views on the relationship between gesture, speech, and language, and establishes that there is both cross-linguistic systematicity and variation in gestural repertoires. Next it considers what gestures can contribute to the study of a developing language system—both to a particular L2 and to the developing L2 system in general. With regard to particular L2s, gestures open new avenues for exploring cross-linguistic influences in that learners' gestures allow us to glean information about L1/L2 interactions at the level of semantic-conceptual representations and their interfaces with information structure, beyond surface forms. With regard to L2 development generally, evidence of systematically parallel change in gesture and speech at a given point in development allows the interactions between communicative and cognitive process-related constraints on learner varieties to be investigated. Gullberg also addresses the effect of gestures on learning more generally, and reviews findings that suggest that both the perception and production of gestures facilitates SLA. The chapter concludes by discussing some implications of these findings for L2 acquisition and instruction, specifically regarding the relationship between underlying representations and surface forms, and the notion of native-likeness.

In chapter 13, Odlin considers *Semantic Extensions and the Problem of*

Conceptual Transfer in SLA. There is more to language than the encoding of space and time, and this chapter considers broader issues of linguistic relativity, the hypothesized influence of language upon thought, as it relates more generally to conceptual transfer and Second Language Acquisition. Starting from the opposing historical perspectives on linguistic relativity of von Humbolt and Whorf, Odlin surveys relativistic research using monolinguals (cross-linguistic differences in cognitive processing by speakers of different native languages) and bilinguals (SLA research on "conceptual transfer" of meanings related to space and time). The chapter then focuses upon a particular problem: the fact that L1 structures involving space and time often have additional meanings which can and do affect the acquisition of L2 structures. For example, the tense forms in Quechua and Turkish code not only temporal meanings but evidential ones (i.e., meanings involving the source of information for an assertion), and studies of Quechua influence on Peruvian Spanish and Turkish influence on L2 English show interlanguage forms with evidential and not just temporal information. Such cases clearly involve meaning transfer from either the semantic or pragmatic system of a native language. Odlin considers whether they reflect conceptual transfer, too—whether the "habitual thought" of individuals depends somewhat on their native languages and whether grammar itself plays an especially important role in habitual thought.

In chapter 14, MacWhinney outlines his *Unified Competition Model of SLA*, an information-processing model of language acquisition which holds that first and second language acquisition share the same goals (the learning of the norms of the target linguistic community) and the same structures, processes, and learning mechanisms. In both cases, learning involves the tuning of a core system of device competition. The input to this core system comes from self-organizing neural network associative maps for syllables, lexical items, and constructions. The central competitive processor integrates information stored in map-based buffers. Processes of chunking and resonance promote learning and fluency. The chapter presents information processing descriptions of the learning mechanisms involved in first and second language construction acquisition, embodied meaning, language and attention focusing, and thinking and rethinking for language. In this view, what separates First and Second Language Acquisition are the abilities and experiences that older second language learners bring to this task that are very different from those of young children. For the second language learner, L1 entrenchment leads to interference and transfer, and the limitations typical of L2A are not age-related changes but instead arise from entrenchment in associative maps.

In chapter 15, Ellis provides a psychological overview of the *Associative Learning of Linguistic Constructions*. The chapter first describes the aspects of associative learning that affect both L1A and L2A: frequency, contingency, competition between multiple cues, and salience. It explains each of these from within associative learning theory, and illustrates each with examples from language learning. This section concludes by illustrating the combined operation of these factors in First and Second Language Acquisition of English grammatical morphemes, a particular illustration of a broader claim that they control the acquisition of all linguistic constructions. The second half of the chapter considers why usage-based SLA is typically much less successful that L1A, with naturalistic SLA stabilizing at end-states far short of native-like ability. It describes how "learned attention" explains these effects. The fragile features of L2A, those aspects of the second language that are not typically acquired, are those which, however available in the input, fall short of intake because of one of the factors of contingency, cue competition, salience, interference, overshadowing, blocking, or perceptual learning, all shaped by L1 entrenchment. Each phenomenon is explained within associative learning theory and exemplified in language learning. The chapter concludes with evidence of L1/L2 differences in morpheme acquisition order, illustrating these processes as they contribute to transfer and "learned attention." That the successes of L1A and the limitations of L2A both, paradoxically, derive from the same basic learning principles provides a non age-invoked biological explanation for why usage-based L2A stops short while L1A does not. These processes also explain why form-focused instruction is a necessary component of L2A, and why successful L2A necessitates a greater level of explicit awareness of the L2 constructions.

In chapter 16, Gries provides a *Corpus Linguistic* analysis of *Construction Grammar*: the nature of the symbolic units within the constructicon, the ways in which usage frequency and reliability of mapping results in elements of various degrees of schematicity, and the ways these affect First and Second Language Acquisition. Usage-based theories are based on the evidence that distributional information—frequencies of occurrence and frequencies of co-occurrence—plays a vital role for the acquisition, processing, and representation of language. Thus, the quantification of corpus linguistics is necessary to properly describe this distributional information. At a basic level, corpus analyses can identify the token frequency of instances of a linguistic schematic unit, which contributes to its entrenchment, routinization, and speed of access in language learning and use. It can also identify type frequency, the number of different instances which conform to the schema, which is important to the development of productive and abstract constructions. Using data from the International Corpus of Learner English, Gries describes three corpus linguistic methods (frequency lists and collocational analyses, colligation and collostruction analyses, concordancing), and demonstrates their potential for studying the Second Language Acquisition of constructions, as well their potential applications in language teaching. This chapter closes with a review of methodological issues in analyzing and using corpora for research and teaching purposes.

In chapter 17, Achard describes *Cognitive Pedagogical Grammar*, an approach to second language pedagogy based on Cognitive Grammar (CG). This chapter complements Langacker's overview of CG in Part II by considering issues of how grammar instruction should proceed in practice. Achard argues that the CG position that the grammar of a language is composed of a "structured set of conventionalized symbolic units" validates grammatical instruction on a par with lexical instruction, a highly desirable outcome for second language teachers because it allows for a kind of grammatical presentation fully congruent with the methods and principles of communicative models of instruction. CG takes the position that linguistic production is mostly a matter of speaker construal, i.e., her/his desire to structure a given scene in a specific way for purposes of linguistic description. This focus on speaker choice rather than on the nature of the linguistic system has profound ramifications for the teaching of grammatical expressions because it calls into question the time-honored way of presenting those expressions as patterns of lexical association. Rather, a CG-inspired grammar lesson shows that constructions are best seen as conventionalized ways of matching certain expressions to specific situations. Achard illustrates a CG-informed teaching of construal by distinguishing the meaning of two constructions, VV and VOV, as they are affected by the use of French causation/perception verbs. The key for the instructor is to precisely isolate and clearly present the various conditions that motivate speaker choice. Pedagogic proposals based on the theoretical and descriptive principles described are then made in the final section, which involves a grammatical presentation of the French definite and partitive articles and recommendations for teaching.

In chapter 18, Tyler explores the *Cognitive Linguistics of Second Language Instruction* by outlining several principles foundational to the CL enterprise, their contributions to a more complete, systematic description of language, and the subsequent implications for second language teaching. A central point is that whatever instructional approach a teacher chooses, teaching is well served by CL analyses of the language being taught. A review of current ELT texts and grammars, which teachers rely on for instructional activities, materials, and curriculum, reveals that these texts and grammars fail to provide accurate, complete explanations of many key points of the English language. The discussion then focuses on modals, a notoriously difficult area of English which has long been represented as highly idiosyncratic and hence as largely immune to any kind of learning strategy other than rote memorization. The chapter demonstrates that under Sweetser's (1990) cognitive analysis, much of the apparent arbitrariness falls away. Recognizing that having a better description does not automatically translate into more effective learning, Tyler presents example materials, based on these analyses, which can be used for explaining modals to advanced learners of English as a second language. She then describes the findings of two effects-of-instruction studies examining the learning of appropriate use of English modals, the first a pretest-posttest study comparing a feedback plus CL instruction treatment with a minimal feedback group over the course of 10 weeks' instruction, the second a longitudinal analysis of six students in an AB single-subject design as they received two days' baseline followed by three days' CL feedback. These small-scale studies suggest that providing a cognitive explanation in conjunction with several interactive tasks does indeed result in significant learner gains in their appropriate use of modals in comparison to instruction which either relies solely on task-based instruction or incidental learning. The chapter concludes by pointing to CL analyses of other patterns of relevance, and describes the ways in which teaching materials can be developed that are based upon these analyses.

Finally, in chapter 19, we, Robinson and Ellis, summarize the main themes of the book as we see them and we look to *Future Directions*. We identify important issues that future SLA research should address, adopting many of the principles and approaches to CL described by authors in Part II, and developing many of the ideas presented by authors of chapters in Part III.

Bibliography

Altman, G. T. (1997). *The ascent of Babel*. Oxford: Oxford University Press.

Anderson, J. R. (1989). A rational analysis of human memory. In H. L. I. Roediger & F. I. M. Craik (Eds.), *Varieties of memory and consciousness: Essays in honour of Endel Tulving* (pp. 195–210). Hillsdale, NJ: Lawrence Erlbaum Associates.

Anderson, J. R., & Schooler, L. J. (2000). The adaptive nature of memory. In E. Tulving & F. I. M. Craik (Eds.), *The Oxford handbook of memory* (pp. 557–570). London: Oxford University Press.

Barlow, M., & Kemmer, S. (Eds.) (2000). *Usage-based models of language*. Stanford, CA: CSLI Publications.

Barsalou, L. W. (1999). Perceptual symbol systems. *Behavioral and Brain Sciences, 22*, 577–660.

Bates, E., & MacWhinney, B. (1987). Competition, variation, and language learning. In B. MacWhinney (Ed.), *Mechanisms of language acquisition* (pp. 157–193).

Biber, D., Conrad, S., & Reppen, R. (1998). *Corpus linguistics: Investigating language structure and use*. New York: Cambridge University Press.

Biber, D., Johansson, S., Leech, G., Conrad, S., & Finegan, E. (1999). *Longman grammar of spoken and written English*. Harlow, UK: Pearson Education.

Bod, R., Hay, J., & Jannedy, S. (Eds.) (2003). *Probabilistic linguistics*. Cambridge, MA: MIT Press.

Bybee, J., & Hopper, P. (Eds.) (2001). *Frequency and the emergence of linguistic structure*. Amsterdam: John Benjamins.

Chater, N. (2004). What can be learned from positive data? Insights from an "ideal learner." *Journal of Child Language, 31*, 915–918.

Chater, N., & Manning, C. (2006). Probabilistic models of language processing and acquisition. *Trends in Cognitive Science, 10*, 335–344.

Christiansen, M. H., & Chater, N. (Eds.) (2001). *Connectionist psycholinguistics*. Westport, CO: Ablex.

Coventry, K. R., & Garrod, S. C. (2004). *Saying, seeing and acting. The psychological semantics of spatial prepositions*. Hove and New York: Psychology Press.

Croft, W. (2001). *Radical construction grammar: Syntactic theory in typological perspective*. Oxford: Oxford University Press.

Croft, W., & Cruise, A. (2004). *Cognitive linguistics*. Cambridge: Cambridge University Press.

de Bot, K., Lowie, W., & Verspoor, M. (2007). A dynamic systems theory to second language acquisition. *Bilingualism: Language and Cognition, 10*, 7–21.

Doughty, C., & Long, M. (Eds.) (2003). *The handbook of second language acquisition*. Oxford: Blackwell.

Doughty, C., & Williams, J. (Eds.) (1998). *Focus on form in classroom second language acquisition*. New York: Cambridge University Press.

Ellis, N. C. (1996). Sequencing in SLA: Phonological memory, chunking, and points of order. *Studies in Second Language Acquisition, 18*(1), 91–126.

Ellis, N. C. (1998). Emergentism, connectionism and language learning. *Language Learning, 48*(4), 631–664.

Ellis, N. C. (2002a). Frequency effects in language processing: A review with implications for theories of implicit and explicit language acquisition. *Studies in Second Language Acquisition, 24*(2), 143–188.

Ellis, N. C. (2002b). Reflections on frequency effects in language processing. *Studies in Second Language Acquisition, 24*(2), 297–339.

Ellis, N. C. (2005). At the interface: Dynamic interactions of explicit and implicit language knowledge. *Studies in Second Language Acquisition, 27*, 305–352.

Ellis, N. C. (2006). Language acquisition as rational contingency learning. *Applied Linguistics, 27*(1), 1–24.

Ellis, N. C. (in press, a). The dynamics of language use, language change, and first and second language acquisition. *Modern Language Journal*.

Ellis, N. C. (in press, b). Optimizing the input: Frequency and sampling in usage-based and form-focussed learning. In M. H. Long & C. Doughty (Eds.), *Handbook of Second and Foreign Language Teaching*. Oxford: Blackwell.

Ellis, N. C., & Larsen Freeman, D. (2006a). Language emergence: Implications for applied linguistics. *Applied Linguistics, 27*(4), whole issue.

Ellis, N. C., & Larsen Freeman, D. (2006b). Language emergence: Implications for applied linguistics (Introduction to the special issue). *Applied Linguistics, 27*(4), 558–589.

Ellis, R. (1994). *The study of second language acquisition*. Oxford: Oxford University Press.

Ellis, R. (2001). Introduction: Investigating form-focused instruction. *Language Learning, 51*(Suppl 1), 1–46.

Elman, J. L., Bates, E. A., Johnson, M. H., Karmiloff-Smith, A., Parisi, D., & Plunkett, K. (1996). *Rethinking innateness: A connectionist perspective on development*. Cambridge, MA: MIT Press.

Ferrer i Cancho, R., & Solé, R. V. (2001). The small world of human language. *Proceedings of the Royal Society of London, B., 268*, 2,261–2,265.

Ferrer i Cancho, R., & Solé, R. V. (2003). Least effort and the origins of scaling in human language. *Proceedings of the New York Academy of Sciences, 100*, 788–791.

Ferrer i Cancho, R., Solé, R. V., & Köhler, R. (2004). Patterns in syntactic dependency networks. *Physical Review, E69*, 0519151–0519158.

Gernsbacher, M. A. (1994). *A handbook of psycholinguistics*. San Diego, CA: Academic Press.

Goldberg, A. (1995). *Constructions: A construction grammar approach to argument structure*. Chicago: University of Chicago Press.

Goldberg, A. (2003). Constructions: a new theoretical approach to language. *Trends in Cognitive Science, 7*, 219–224.

Goldberg, A. (2006). *Constructions at work: The nature of generalization in language*. Oxford: Oxford University Press.

Gonzálvez-García, F., & Butler, C. S. (2006). Mapping functional-cognitive space. *Annual Review of Cognitive Linguistics, 4*, 39–96.

Granger, S., & Meunier, F. (Eds.) (in press). *Phraseology: An interdisciplinary perspective*. Amsterdam: John Benjamins.

Halliday, M. A. K. (1985). *An introduction to functional grammar*. London: E. Arnold.

Halliday, M. A. K. (1987). Spoken and written modes of meaning. In R. Horowitz & S. J. Samuels (Eds.), *Comprehending oral and written language* (pp. 55–82). San Diego/London: Academic Press.

Harnad, S. (Ed.) (1987). *Categorical perception: The groundwork of cognition*. New York: Cambridge University Press.

Hoey, M. P. (2005). *Lexical priming: A new theory of words and language*. London: Routledge.

Hopper, P. J. (1998). Emergent grammar. In M. Tomasello (Ed.), *The new psychology of language: Cognitive and functional approaches to language structure* (pp. 155–176). Mahwah, NJ: Erlbaum.

Jurafsky, D. (2002). Probabilistic modeling in psycholinguistics: Linguistic comprehension and production. In R. Bod, J. Hay, & S. Jannedy (Eds.), *Probabilistic Linguistics* (pp. 39–96). Harvard, MA: MIT Press.

Jurafsky, D., & Martin, J. H. (2000). *Speech and language processing: An introduction to natural language processing, speech recognition, and computational linguistics*. Englewood Cliffs, NJ: Prentice-Hall.

Kaplan, R. B. (Ed.). (2002). *The Oxford handbook of applied linguistics*. Oxford: Oxford University Press.

Kramsch, C. (Ed.). (2002). *Language acquisition and language socialization: Ecological perspectives*. London: Continuum.

Kroll, J. F., & De Groot, A. M. B. (Eds.). (2005). *Handbook of bilingualism: Psycholinguistic approaches*. Oxford: Oxford University Press.

Lakoff, G. (1987). *Women, fire, and dangerous things: What categories reveal about the mind*. Chicago: University of Chicago Press.

Langacker, R. W. (1999). *Grammar and Conceptualization*. Amsterdam: Walter De Gruyter.

Langacker, R. W. (2000). A dynamic usage-based model. In M. Barlow & S. Kemmer (Eds.), *Usage-based models of language* (pp. 1–63). Stanford, CA: CSLI Publications.

Lantolf, J. (2006). Sociocultural theory and L2: State of the Art. *Studies in Second Language Acquisition, 28*, 67–109.

Lantolf, J., & Pavlenko, A. (1995). Sociocultural theory and second language acquisition. *Annual Review of Applied Linguistics, 15*, 38–53.

Lantolf, J., & Thorne, S. (2006). *Sociocultural theory and the genesis of second language development*. Oxford: Oxford University Press.

Lightbown, P. M., Spada, N., & White, L. (1993). The role of instruction in second language acquisition. *Studies in Second Language Acquisition, 15 (Special issue)*.

Long, M. H. (1990). The least a second language acquisition theory needs to explain. *TESOL Quarterly, 24*, 649–666.

Long, M. H. (1991). Focus on form: A design feature in language teaching methodology. In K. de Bot, R. Ginsberg & C. Kramsch (Eds.), *Foreign language research in cross-cultural perspective* (pp. 39–52). Amsterdam: John Benjamins.

Long, M. H., & Robinson, P. (1998). Focus on form: Theory, reasearch and practice. In C. Doughty & J. Williams (Eds.), *Focus on form in classroom second language acquisition*, pp. 1–32. New York: Cambridge University Press.

MacWhinney, B. (1987). The Competition Model. In B. MacWhinney (Ed.), *Mechanisms of language acquisition* (pp. 249–308).

MacWhinney, B. (1997). Second language acquisition and the Competition Model. In A. M. B. De Groot & J. F. Kroll (Eds.), *Tutorials in bilingualism: Psycholinguistic perspectives* (pp. 113–142). Mahwah, NJ: Erlbaum.

MacWhinney, B. (Ed.) (1999). *The emergence of language*. Hillsdale, NJ: Erlbaum.

Mandler, J. (2004). *The foundations of mind: Origins of conceptual thought*. Oxford: Oxford University Press.

McEnery, T., & Wilson, A. (1996). *Corpus linguistics*. Edinburgh, UK: Edinburgh University Press.

Norton, B. (1997). Language, identity, and the ownership of English. *TESOL Quarterly, 31*, 409–430.

Pawley, A., & Syder, F. H. (1983). Two puzzles for linguistic theory: Nativelike selection and nativelike fluency. In J. C. Richards & R. W. Schmidt (Eds.), *Language and communication* (pp. 191–225). London: Longman.

Perdue, C. (Ed.). (1993). *Adult language acquisition: Crosslinguistic perspectives*. Cambridge: Cambridge University Press.

Port, R. F., & Van Gelder, T. (1995). *Mind as motion: Explorations in the dynamics of cognition*. Boston MA: MIT Press.

Robinson, P. (1995). Attention, memory and the 'noticing' hypothesis. *Language Learning, 45*, 283–331.

Robinson, P. (1996). *Consciousness, rules, and instructed second language acquisition*. New York: Lang.

Robinson, P. (2001). (Ed.), *Cognition and second language instruction*. Cambridge: Cambridge University Press.

Robinson, P. (2002). Learning conditions, aptitude complexes and SLA: A framework for research and pedagogy. In P. Robinson (Ed.), *Individual differences and instructed language learning*, pp. 95–112. Amsterdam: John Benjamins.

Robinson, P. (2003). Attention and memory during SLA. In C. Doughty & M. H. Long (Eds.), *Handbook of second language acquisition*, (pp. 631–678). Oxford: Blackwell.

Robinson, P. (2007 a). Attention and awareness. In J. Cenoz & N. Hornberger (Eds.), *Encylopedia of language and education Vol. 6: Knowledge about language*. New York: Springer Academic.

Robinson, P. (2007 b). Task complexity, theory of mind and intentional reasoning: Effects on speech production, interaction, uptake and perceptions of task difficulty. In P. Robinson & R. Gilabert (Eds.), *Task complexity, the Cognition Hypothesis and second language instruction (Special issue), International Review of Appied Linguistics*. Berlin: Mouton DeGruyter.

Schank, R. C., & Abelson, R. P. (1977). *Scripts, plans, goals, and understanding: An inquiry into human knowledge structures*. Hillsdale, NJ: Erlbaum.

Schmidt, R. (1990). The role of consciousness in second language learning. *Applied Linguistics, 11*, 129–158.

Schmidt, R. (2001). Attention. In P. Robinson (Ed.), *Cognition and second language instruction* (pp. 3–32). Cambridge: Cambridge University Press.

Sinclair, J. (1991). *Corpus, concordance, collocation*. Oxford: Oxford University Press.

Sinclair, J. (2004). *Trust the text: Language, corpus and discourse*. London: Routledge.

Slobin, D. I. (1993). Adult language acquisition: A view from child language study. In C. Perdue (Ed.), *Adult language acquisition: cross-linguistic perspectives* (pp. 239–252). Cambridge: Cambridge University Press.

Slobin, D. I. (1997). The origins of grammaticizable notions: Beyond the individual mind. In D. I. Slobin (Ed.), *The crosslinguistic study of language acquisition* (Vol. 5, pp. 265–323). Mahwah, NJ: Erlbaum.

Slobin, D. I. (2004). The many ways to search for a frog: Linguistic typology and the expression of motion events. In S. Strömqvist & L. T. Verhoeven (Eds.), *Relating events in narrative: Vol. 2: Typological and contextual perspectives* (pp. 219–257).

Spivey, M. (2006). *The continuity of mind* (Vol. Oxford University Press). Oxford.

Swain, M. (2000). The output hypothesis and beyond: Mediating acquisition through collaborative dialogue. In J. Lantolf (Ed.), *Sociocultural theory and second language learning* (pp. 97–114). Oxford: Oxford University Press.

Sweetser, E. (1990). *From etymology to pragmatics: Metaphorical and cultural aspects of semantic structure*. Cambridge: Cambridge University Press.

Talmy, L. (1988). The relation of grammar to cognition. In B. Rudzka-Ostyn (Ed.), *Topics in cognitive linguistics* (pp. 166–205). Amsterdam: John Benjamins.

Talmy, L. (2000a). *Toward a Cognitive Semantics: Concept-structuring systems*. Cambridge MA: MIT Press.

Talmy, L. (2000b). *Toward a Cognitive Semantics: Typology and process in concept structuring*. Cambridge MA: MIT Press.

Taylor, J. R. (1998). Syntactic constructions as prototype categories. In M. Tomasello (Ed.), *The new psychology of language: Cognitive and functional approaches to language structure* (pp. 177–202). Mahwah, NJ: Erlbaum.

Taylor, J. R. (2002). *Cognitive grammar*. Oxford: Oxford University Press.

Tomasello, M. (Ed.) (1998). *The new psychology of language: Cognitive and functional approaches to language structure*. Mahwah, NJ: Erlbaum.

Tomasello, M. (2003). *Constructing a language*. Boston, MA: Harvard University Press.

van Geert, P. (1991). A dynamic systems model of cognitive and language growth. *Psychological Review, 98*(3–53).

van Geert, P. (1994). Vygotskian dynamics of development. *Human Development, 37*, 346–365.

Vygotsky, L. S. (1980). *Mind in society: The development of higher mental processes*. Boston, MA: Harvard University Press.

Vygotsky, L. S. (1986). *Thought and language*. Cambridge, MA: MIT Press.

Wray, A. (2002). *Formulaic language and the lexicon*. Cambridge: Cambridge University Press.

Part II

COGNITIVE LINGUISTICS
AND COGNITION

2

ASPECTS OF ATTENTION IN LANGUAGE

Leonard Talmy

1 Introduction

1.1 *Content of the study*

This chapter introduces new work on the fundamental attentional system of language (Talmy, forthcoming), while in part providing a framework in which prior linguistic work on attention can be placed. In a speech situation, a hearer may attend to the linguistic expression produced by a speaker, to the conceptual content represented by that expression, and to the context at hand. But not all of this material appears uniformly in the foreground of the hearer's attention. Rather, various portions or aspects of the expression, content, and context have differing degrees of salience. Such differences are only partially due to any intrinsically greater interest of certain elements over others. More fundamentally, language has an extensive system that assigns different degrees of salience to the parts of an expression or of its reference or of the context. In terms of the speech participants, the speaker employs this system in formulating an expression; the hearer, largely on the basis of such formulations, allocates his or her attention in a particular way over the material of these domains.

This attentional system in language includes a large number of basic factors, the "building blocks" of the system, with over fifty identified to date. Each factor involves a particular linguistic mechanism that increases or decreases attention on a certain type of linguistic entity. The mechanisms employed fall into some ten categories, most with subcategories. The type of linguistic entity whose degree of salience is determined by the factors is usually the semantic referent of a constituent, but other types occur, including the phonological shape of a constituent, or the vocal delivery of the utterance. Each factor contrasts a linguistic circumstance in which attention is increased with a complementary circumstance in which it is decreased. A speaker can use a factor for either purpose—or in some cases for both at the same time. For some factors, increased attention on a linguistic entity is regularly accompanied by additional cognitive

27

effects, such as distinctness, clarity, and significance, while decreased attention correlates with such converse effects as meldedness, vagueness, and ordinariness. The bulk of this chapter, section 2, presents in highly excerpted form some of the attentional factors in their taxonomy.

Although able to act alone, the basic factors also regularly combine and interact—whether in a single constituent, over a sentence, or through a discourse—to produce further attentional effects. Several such factor patterns are abbreviatedly presented in section 3. Finally, section 4 briefly discusses differences in the attentional system across languages, and points to the implications of such differences for first language (L1) and second language (L2) acquisition.

1.2 Context of the study

Much previous linguistic work has involved the issue of attention or salience. Areas within such work are familiar under terms like topic and focus (e.g., Lambrecht, 1994), focal attention (e.g., Tomlin, 1995), activation (e.g., Givón, 1990; Chafe, 1994), prototype theory (e.g., Lakoff, 1987), frame semantics (e.g., Fillmore, 1976, 1982), profiling (e.g., Langacker, 1987), and deictic center (e.g., Zubin & Hewitt, 1995). My own research on attention has included: the relative salience of the "Figure" and the "Ground" in a represented situation (Talmy, 2000a, chapter 5); the "windowing" of attention on one or more selected portions of a represented scene, with attentional backgrounding of the "gapped" portions (Talmy, 2000a, chapter 4); the attentional backgrounding vs. foregrounding of concepts when expressed by closed-class (grammatical) forms vs. by open-class (lexical) forms (Talmy, 2000a, chapter 1); the "level" of attention set either on the whole of a scene or on its componential makeup (Talmy, 2000a, chapter 1); the differential attention on the Agonist and the Antagonist, the two entities in a force–dynamic opposition (Talmy, 2000a, chapter 7); "fictive motion," in which a hearer is linguistically directed to sweep his focus of attention over the contours of a static scene (Talmy, 2000a, chapter 2); the backgrounding vs. foregrounding of a concept when it is expressed in the verb complex vs. by a nominal complement (Talmy, 2000b, chapter 1); the backgrounding vs. foregrounding of a proposition when it is expressed by a subordinate clause vs. by a main clause (Talmy, 2000a, chapter 6); the conscious as against unconscious processes in the acquisition, manifestation, and imparting of cultural patterns (Talmy, 2000b, chapter 7); and attentional differences between spoken and signed language (Talmy, 2003).

However, the present study may be the first with the aim of developing a systematic framework within which to place all such prior findings—together with a number of new findings—about linguistic attention. In fact, this study is perhaps the first to recognize that the linguistic phenomena across this whole range do all pertain to the same single cognitive system of attention.

2 Some linguistic factors that set strength of attention

To give an idea of the basic tier of the attention system in language, one attentional factor from each of eight domains is presented in this section. The following are the domains to be illustrated:

- Domain A: factors involving properties of the morpheme
- Domain B: factors involving morphology and syntax
- Domain C: factors involving forms that set attention outside themselves
- Domain D: phonological factors
- Domain E: factors involving properties of the referent
- Domain F: factors involving the relation between reference and its representation
- Domain G: factors involving the occurrence of representation
- Domain H: factors involving properties of temporal progression

2.1 Domain A: Factors involving properties of the morpheme

A morpheme is here quite generally understood to be any minimal linguistic form with an associated meaning. This thus includes not only simplex morphemes but also idioms like *turn in*, *go to sleep*, and constructions like the English auxiliary-subject inversion meaning "if," as in *had I known her*.

One factor from the subdomain of "formal properties of the morpheme" concerns the lexical category of a morpheme. A concept tends to be more or less salient in accordance with the lexical category of the form representing the concept. First, open-class categories in general lend more salience than closed-class categories. Further, within open-class categories, nouns may tend to outrank verbs while, within closed-class categories, forms with phonological substance may tend to outrank forms lacking it. Accordingly, lexical categories may exhibit something of the following salience hierarchy:

open-class (N > V) > closed-class (phonological > aphonological)

Only the open-/closed-class contrast is illustrated here. Consider a case where essentially the same concept can be represented both by a closed-class form and by an open-class form. Thus, English tense is typically represented for a verb in a finite clause by a closed-class form, either an inflection or a modal, as in (1a.–b.) with an *-ed* for the past and an *-s* or *will* for the future. But a nominal in a prepositional phrase cannot indicate tense in that way. If relative time is to be indicated here, one must resort to open-class forms, as in (2a.–b.) with the adjectives *previous* to mark the past and *upcoming* to mark the future. The concepts of relative time seem much more salient when expressed by adjectives than by closed-class forms (Talmy, 2000a, chapter 1).

1a. When he arriv*ed*, . . .
1b. When he arriv*es/will* arrive, . . .
2a. On his *previous* arrival, . . .
2b. On his *upcoming* arrival, . . .

2.2 Domain B: Factors involving morphology and syntax

While Domain A dealt with individual morphemes one at a time, the present domain treats attentional properties present in combinations of morphemes. One factor from the subdomain of "constructional properties" pertains to a morpheme's positioning within a sentence. Each language may have certain locations within a sentence—e.g., initial position or pre-verbal position—that tend to foreground the referent of a constituent placed there. Such added salience usually accompanies or facilitates a further cognitive effect, such as making that referent the target of a conceptual contrast. Many properties of topic and focus, as these have been regarded in the literature, are often engaged by such special positioning. To illustrate, a sentence like (3a.) has its constituents in their basic locations. But the initial position of the temporal referent in (3b.) foregrounds that referent and suggests a contrast: some other time would be all right. And the initial position of the Patient referent in (3c.) foregrounds *that* referent and suggests a new contrast: another kind of music would be all right.

3a. I can't stand this kind of music right now.
3b. Right now I can't stand this kind of music.
3c. This kind of music I can't stand right now.

2.3 Domain C: Factors involving forms that set attention outside themselves

The attentional factors outside the present category generally involve properties of a linguistic unit that set the level of attention for that unit itself. For example, by the factor presented under Domain A, a morpheme's lexical category affects the attentional strength of its own referent. By contrast, in the factors of the present category, a certain linguistic unit sets attention for some linguistic unit or nonlinguistic phenomenon fully outside itself.

One factor in the subdomain of "specific linguistic forms with an outside attentional effect" establishes some attribute of a constituent, other than its direct reference, as the object of attention. Examples of such attributes are the phonological shape of the constituent, its vocal delivery, its exact composition, and its shape-referent linkage. In directing some attention away from the direct referring function of the constituent—its default function—such forms establish a certain degree and kind of meta-linguistic awareness of the constituent.

For example, the linguistic form *be called* (compare the monomorphemic German form *heiss[en]*) as in (4a.) directs the hearer to attend not just to the referent of the following constituent but especially to the phonological shape of that constituent and to the linkage of that shape with that referent. By contrast, when the same constituent appears in a sentence like (4b.) without a form like *be called*, its presence has the hearer attend simply to its referent.

4a. This gadget is called a pie segmenter.
4b. Please hand me that pie segmenter.

For another example, the current colloquial expression *be like*, as in (5), though often frowned on, is actually unique in English. It presents the expression that follows as an enactment of an utterance—either an actual utterance or what likely would be the utterance if the subject's state of mind were verbalized. The particular intonation pattern and vocal tones of the expression's delivery are necessarily divergent from a neutral delivery. The form thus directs a hearer's attention not only to the overall referent of the utterance but also to its style of delivery and, hence, to the affective state of the subject inferable from that style, as in (5).

5. So then I'm like: Wow, I don't believe this!

2.4 Domain D: Phonological factors

This domain of factors covers all phonological properties within an utterance, including those of individual morphemes (not covered in Domain A). In the subdomain of "phonological properties of intrinsic morphemic shape" one factor involves morphemic length. The phonological length of a morpheme or word tends to correlate with the degree of salience that attaches to its referent. One venue in which this correlation is evident is where basically the same concept is expressed by morphemes or words of different lengths. Here, a longer form attracts more attention to the concept, while a shorter form attracts less attention. Thus, roughly the same adversative meaning is expressed by the English conjunctions *nevertheless* and *but*. Despite this, apparently the greater phonological length of

31

nevertheless correlates with its fully imposing and prominent effect on narrative structure, while the brevity of *but* correlates with its light backgrounded touch, as in (6).

6. They promised they would contact me. Nevertheless/But they never called back.

2.5 Domain E: Factors involving properties of the referent

All the factors outside the present domain raise or lower attention on an object "regardless" of its identity or content. The factors in this domain raise or lower attention on an object "because" of its identity or content. One factor deals with referential divergence from norms. A referent's divergence from certain norms tends to foreground it. Such norms, and deviations from them, include: ordinariness vs. unusualness; neutral affect vs. affective intensity; and genericness vs. specificity.

To illustrate, relative to cultural and other experiential norms, a more unusual referent tends to attract greater attention than a more ordinary referent, as the referent of *hop* does relative to that of *walk*, as in (7a.). Similarly, a referent with greater affective intensity tends to evoke greater attention than one with lesser intensity, as the referent of *scream* does relative to that of *shout*, as in (7b.). And a more specific referent tends to attract greater attention than a more general referent, as the referent of *drown* does relative to that of *die*, as seen in (7c.).

7a. He hopped/walked to the store.
7b. She screamed/shouted to him.
7c. He drowned/died.

2.6 Domain F: Factors involving the relation between reference and its representation

The factors in this domain all rest on what appears to be a general attentional bias in language users toward content over form. One factor establishes that: More attention goes to the concept expressed by a linguistic form than to the shape of that form. This holds for forms ranging from a single morpheme to an expression (or to an extended discourse, for that matter). For example, at the single morpheme level, if a wife says (8a.) to her husband, the occurrence of the morpheme *sick* is likely to direct the husband's attention more to its referent "sickness" than to its phonological representation consisting of the sound sequence [s]-[ɪ]-[k]. This same phonological point can be made at the level of the whole expression in (8a.). In addition, though, if the "representation" of an expression as covered by the present factor can be taken also to include the particular words and constructions selected to constitute the expression, a further observation follows. The husband in this example is later more likely to remember the general reference of the sentence than its specific wording. Thus, he might well be able to recall that his wife telephonically learned from her sister of her illness earlier that day, but he might not be able to recall whether this conception was represented, say, by (8a.), (8b.), or (8c.) (here, knowing that "Judy" is her sister's name). If the pattern of memory of an event correlates at least in part with the pattern of attention on an event during its occurrence, then findings like the present type would be evidence for greater attention on a reference than on its representation.

8a. My sister called and said she was very sick this morning.
8b. My sister called this morning to tell me that she was feeling really sick.
8c. Judy said she was very ill when she called today.

2.7 Domain G: Factors involving the occurrence of representation

The salience of a concept can depend on the occurrence of representation for it in a language's lexicon, or on its simple inclusion in discourse. By one factor of this last subdomain, the presence within discourse of overt linguistic forms explicitly referring to a concept foregrounds the concept. And the absence of forms referring to a concept that might otherwise be represented backgrounds that concept. This is the factor underlying the whole of the "windowing of attention" analysis in Talmy (2000a, chapter 4).

As background for the present factor, a speaker in communicating can have a certain conceptual complex that she wants to cause to become replicated in the addressee's cognition. The conceptual complex is typically too rich to capture in full scope and detail in a brief enough interval for any cognitively feasible system of representation. For this problem, one of the solutions that seems to have emerged in the evolution of language is a cognitive process of "abstractive representation." By this process, the speaker selects only a subset out of the multiplicity of aspects in her more extensive conceptual complex for explicit representation by the linguistic elements of her utterance. By a complementary cognitive process of "reconstitution," the hearer then uses this partial explicit representation to reconstitute or "flesh out" a replete conceptual complex sufficiently close to the original one in the speaker. In this reconstitution process, the hearer must assume or infer the inexplicit material, mostly through contextual or background knowledge.

To illustrate, consider the case in which I am a guest in the house of a host, we are both sitting near an open window, and I am feeling cold. Here, my extended conceptual complex includes general background knowledge, for example, physical knowledge, such as that air is typically colder out-side a house than inside and can enter through an aperture; psychological knowledge, such as that a person can feel uncomfortable from contact with colder air; and socio-cultural knowledge, such as that a guest typically does not act directly on the property of a host other than that assigned for his use.

As noted, even just this most immediately relevant conceptual complex cannot be explicitly represented briefly by language. Instead, by the prin-ciple of abstractive representation, I must select a subset of concepts in the complex for overt expression, for example, by saying (9a.) or (9b.). My host will then reconstitute much of the remainder of my conceptual complex.

9a. Could you please close the window?
9b. It's a bit chilly in here.

Where the present factor comes in is that the selection of concepts for explicit expression is not an attentionally neutral act but rather one that foregrounds the selected concepts relative to those in the conceptual complex remaining unexpressed. Moreover, the explicitly represented concepts tend to determine the center of a gradient of attention: greatest at the explicitly represented concepts, less over the remaining concepts within the conceptual complex, and radially decreasing over the rest of one's skein of knowledge. Thus, (9a.) will tend to direct my host's atten-tion most on the window and its closing; somewhat less on the likelihood of my feeling cold or on her need to get up from where she is sitting to walk over to the window; and quite little on how her window compares with other window designs. Utterance (9b.) will place the center at a dif-ferent conceptual location.

2.8 Domain H: Factors involving properties of temporal progression

This domain covers attentional effects due to the arrangement of expressed concepts through time in a discourse. Its subdomains include the recency of an expressed concept, the cumulative amount of reference to a particular concept, the sequencing of certain concepts, and setting up expectations for a particular concept. One factor in the first subdomain is the recency of the last reference to a particular concept. Under this factor, the more recently a phenomenon has been referred to or has occurred, the more hearer attention that remains on that phenomenon or the more readily that her attention can be directed back to it. This factor corresponds to the "referential distance" component within the "referential accessibil-ity" described by Givon (1990). He observes that, as the recency of a referent lessens, a speaker refers back to it by selecting a type of linguistic form located progressively further along a certain hierarchy, from a zero form through an unstressed pro-form through a stressed pro-form to a full lexical form. Although treatment of this behavior in the functionalist discourse tradition has seemingly dealt only with the case of prior linguistic reference to a phenomenon, we note that the nonlinguistic occurrence of a phenomenon evokes the same reflex. For example, let us say you are visiting me in my office and a man enters, says a few words to me, and leaves. I can refer to that man using a pronoun if I speak to you within a few minutes after his departure, saying for example, *He's the director of our lab*. But after a while, I would need to use a full lexical phrase, as in *That man who came in and spoke to me was the director of our lab*.

3 Attentional effects resulting from combining factors

When the basic attentional factors combine and interact, the further attentional effects that result include incremental gradation, convergence, and conflict.

3.1 *Gradation in strength of attention through factor combination*

Factors can be incrementally added to produce a gradation in the degree of attention directed to some particular linguistic entity. To illustrate, this linguistic entity can be the concept of "agency." Attention on agency incrementally increases by the successive addition of factors in the following series of otherwise comparable sentences. These sentences are all taken to refer to the same scene in which a group of diners—the agents—hand a goblet of wine from one to another as they sit around a banquet table. In (10a.), a minimal backgrounded sense of agency is pragmatically inferable from the context by a factor in Domain C pertaining to the attentional effects of context, though not specifically represented by the linguistic forms themselves. Agency is slightly more salient in (10b.), where the intransitive verb *pass* includes indirect reference to an agent within its lexicalization in Domain A pertaining to semantic components. Still more attention is on agency in (10c.), whose passive syntax (in construction with a now transitive verb *pass*) directly represents the presence of an agent by a factor in Domain A pertaining to grammatical meaning. A sharp rise in attention on the agent occurs when it is explicitly referred to by an overt pronoun, the oblique *them* in (10d.) by the factor described above under Domain G. The agency is further foregrounded by the occurrence of this pronoun as subject in initial position in (10e.) by syntactic factors in Domain B. And finally, replacement of the pronoun by a full lexical noun as in (10f.), through the factor described above under Domain A, foregrounds the agent to the greatest degree.

10a.   The goblet slowly went around the banquet table.
10b.   The goblet slowly passed around the banquet table.
10c.   The goblet was slowly passed around the banquet table.
10d.   The goblet was slowly passed around the banquet table by them.
10e.   They slowly passed the goblet around the banquet table.
10f.   The diners slowly passed the goblet around the banquet table.

3.2 Reinforcement of an attentional pattern through factor convergence

Several factors can converge on the same linguistic entity to reinforce a particular level of salience, making it especially high or especially low. The grammar of a language is often organized so as to facilitate certain convergences. Consider the sentence in (11a.). Here, the concept of "aircraft" is relatively foregrounded in the constituent "plane" through the convergence of four factors. It is expressed in the lexical category highest on the attentional hierarchy, a noun through the factor described above under Domain A. It is the sole concept expressed in its morpheme by a factor in Domain A pertaining to a concept's share of a morpheme's total meaning. It is in the prominent sentence-final position by a factor in Domain B. And it receives the heavy stress standard for such a final constituent by a phonological factor in Domain D. By contrast, the same concept of aircraft is relatively backgrounded within the constituent "flew." It is backgrounded there through the convergence of the same four factors. It appears in a lexical category lower on the attentional hierarchy, a verb. It is joined there by other concepts, namely "go" and "by means of." It is in a sentence position non-prominent in English. And it receives the relatively low stress of that position.

11a.   I went to Key West last month by plane.
11b.   I flew to Key West last month.

3.3 Attentional resultants of factor conflict

Two factors can conflict in their attentional effects, with the resolution usually either that one factor overrides the other, or that they are in competition, with the hearer's attention divided or wavering between the two claims on it. For an example of override, consider again the last example sentence, now shown in (12a.). As just seen, the concept of "aircraft" is backgrounded in the verb *flew*. In fact, an English speaker may tend to hear this sentence as mainly conveying the fact of the journey per se to Key West, and as including the idea of aeronautic means only as an incidental piece of background information. However, the further application of extra heavy stress to the verb by a phonological factor in Domain

D, as in (12b.), now undoes the backgrounding effects of the four convergent factors. It overrides them and forces the foregrounding of the "aircraft" concept.

12a. I flew to Key West last month.
12b. I FLEW to Key West last month.

4 Conclusion

Most of the attention system illustrated by the above excerpts, it appears, is basic to the language faculty and hence common across languages. But the extensiveness of some factors differs across languages, and the way most of the factors are realized certainly differs across them.

As for extensiveness, a phonological factor involving the use of extra heavy stress on a constituent to direct attention to its referent is freely and flexibly used in a language like English, whereas it is minimal in a language like French. On the other hand, a syntactic or other type of factor involving the use of topicalization to direct attention to the most topical element of a conception is minimal in English but extensive in a language like Japanese.

And, as noted, even a universal factor is realized differently in each language. For example, concerning the factor discussed for Domain A, although every language backgrounds the concepts represented by its closed-class forms, each language has a different set of such concepts. And while every language licenses the obligatory representation of certain concepts under certain conditions—in accordance with a factor from Domain G not treated above—each language has a different set of concepts requiring such explicit indication.

These cross-linguistic differences in attentional effects presumably have implications for L1 and L2 acquisition. For example, it might prove to be that the non-universal aspects of attentional allocation take longer for a child to acquire in her native language than the universal aspects. And attention-assigning mechanisms in an L2 that differ from those in an adult's L1 might prove more difficult to learn. The present study of the attention system in language might provide the groundwork for investigation into the acquisition of attentional competence in language.

Bibliography

Chafe, W. (1994). *Discourse, consciousness and time*. Chicago: University of Chicago Press.

Fillmore, C. J. (1976). Frame semantics and the nature of language. In *Annals of the New York Academy of Sciences: Conference on the Origin and Development of Language and Speech*, 280, pp. 20–32.

Fillmore, C.J. (1982). Frame semantics. In Linguistic Society of Korea (Ed.), *Linguistics in the morning calm*, pp. 111–137. Seoul: Hanshin Publishing Co.

Givón, T. (1990). *Syntax: A functional-typological introduction*. Amsterdam/ Philadelphia: John Benjamins.

Lakoff, G. (1987). *Women, fire and dangerous things: What categories reveal about the mind*. Chicago: University of Chicago Press.

Lambrecht, K. (1994). *Information structure and sentence form: A theory of topic, focus and the mental representations of discourse referents*. Cambridge: Cambridge University Press.

Langacker, R. (1987). *Foundations of cognitive grammar, Volume 1: Theoretical prerequisites*. Stanford: Stanford University Press.

Talmy, L. (2000a). *Toward a cognitive semantics, Volume 1: Concept-structuring systems*. Cambridge, MA: MIT Press.

Talmy, L. (2000b). *Toward a cognitive semantics, Volume 2: Typology and process in concept structuring*. Cambridge, MA: MIT Press.

Talmy, L. (2003). The representation of spatial structure in spoken and signed language. In I. K. Emmorey (Ed.), *Perspectives on classifier constructions in sign language*. Mahwah, NJ: Erlbaum.

Talmy, L. (forthcoming). *The attention system of language*. Cambridge, MA: MIT Press.

Tomlin, R. (1995). Focal attention, voice, and word order: An experimental, cross-linguistic study. In P. Downing & M. Noonan (Eds.), *Word order in discourse*, pp. 517–554. Amsterdam/Philadelphia: John Benjamins.

Zubin, D. A., & Hewitt, L. (1995). The deictic center: A theory of deixis in narrative. In J. F. Duchan, G. A. Bruder & L. Hewitt (Eds.), *Deixis in narrative: A cognitive science perspective*, pp. 129–155. Mahwah, NJ: Erlbaum.

3

PROTOTYPES IN COGNITIVE LINGUISTICS

John R. Taylor

> If linguistics can be said to be any one thing it is the study of
> categories: that is, the study of how language translates mean-
> ing into sound through the categorization of reality into discrete
> units and sets of units.
>
> Labov, 1973, p. 342

1 Introduction

A major impetus for the emergence of Cognitive Linguistics, from the
early 1980s onwards, was Eleanor Rosch's work on categorization. Rosch
addressed the question of the relation between words and the range of
things in the world that the words can be used to refer to. The standard
view of the matter had been (and in certain quarters still is) that an entity
can be named by a word if, and only if, it exhibits each of the features
which collectively define the meaning of the word. This so-called "classical" theory of categories entails (a) that word meanings can be defined
in terms of sets of features, (b) that the features are individually necessary
and jointly sufficient, (c) that words pick out categories of entities which
exhibit each of the features, (d) that all members of a category have equal
status within the category, and (e) that membership in a category is a
clear-cut, all-or-nothing matter.

In a series of papers published between 1971 to 1978, Rosch argued
that this view of the relation between a word and its referents (and the
view of word meaning which it entailed) simply does not hold up. While
she continued to be sympathetic to the role of features (or "attributes")
in the characterization of categories, her research indicated that these
features, taken individually, need not be necessary, nor is the presence
of a certain set of features always sufficient for category membership.
Importantly, she demonstrated that categories have an internal structure,
in the sense that some members might be "better," or "more representative" (i.e., more "prototypical") examples of the category than others.

Another important finding was that many categories lacked clear-cut boundaries.

Rosch's findings on prototype categorization were quickly taken up by the newly emerging trend of Cognitive Linguistics. They found an application, most obviously, in the study of word meanings, both synchronic and diachronic, and proved especially fruitful in the investigation of polysemy (Blank & Koch, 1999; Croft & Cruse, 2004; Geeraerts, 1989, 1997; Lakoff, 1982, 1987; Taylor, 2003a [1989]; Tsohatzidis, 1990; Ungerer & Schmid, 1996; Violi, 1997). The approach was also extended to a study of the meanings of elements other than words, such as bound morphemes, clause types, and constructions. Indeed, prototype categorization is now a *locus communis* of the cognitive linguistics literature, having found applications, not only in the study of categories designated by linguistic expressions but also in the study of the categories of language itself. These include the lexical categories (noun, adjective, etc.), clause types, syntactic constructions, and even phonological categories such as the phoneme.

In this chapter, I first review the evidence for prototype effects, then consider the implications of these effects for lexical semantics. The last part of the chapter addresses the application of prototype categorization to the categories of language itself.

2 Prototype effects

Rosch's work uncovered the "internal structure" of categories. Reviewing her earlier work on color (Heider, 1971, 1972), she surmised that:

> [c]olor categories are processed by the human mind (learned, remembered, denoted, and evolved in languages) in terms of their internal structure; color categories appear to be represented in cognition not as a set of criterial features with clear-cut boundaries but rather in terms of a prototype (the clearest cases, best examples) of the category, surrounded by other colors of decreasing similarity to the prototype and of decreasing degree of membership.
>
> Rosch, 1975b, p. 193

Her subsequent work was to demonstrate a comparable state of affairs for categories denoted by common everyday words, such as *fruit, bird, vehicle,* and *furniture.* Her basic experimental paradigm was very simple. Subjects were given a category name, such as *furniture, bird,* or *clothing,* and a list of up to 60 possible examples of the categories. They were then invited to rate, on a 7-point scale, "the extent to which each instance represented their idea or image of the meaning of the category name"

(Rosch, 1975b, p. 198). For each of the categories investigated, it turned out that goodness-of-example ratings ranged from "very good" (such as *pants* and *shirt*, for the clothing category) through to "very poor" (as with *cane* and *bracelet*). These ratings were highly reliable for the given population sample.

Goodness-of-example ratings were also shown to have a bearing on a number of other experimental effects (Rosch, 1978, pp. 38–39). These include speed of verification (the speed with which subjects evaluate a statement that X *is a* Y correlates with the degree to which X is independently rated as a good example of Y), priming effects (exposure to a category name facilitates processing of more prototypical members), and list effects (when asked to name members of a category, subjects tend to mention more prototypical members first).

Prototype effects—the finding that members of a category can be rated in terms of how good they are—are now very well documented. They pertain to natural-kind terms (*bird*, *tree*, etc.), names of artifacts (*furniture*, *vehicle*), emotion concepts (Fehr & Russel, 1984), as well as artificial categories (such as displays of dots, or sequences of letters and numbers). They show up on "ad hoc categories" (such as "things that can fall on your head": Barsalou, 1983) and goal-oriented categories ("things to pack in a suitcase": Barsalou, 1991). While most research has focused on categories designated by nominals, prototype effects have also been reported for verbal (Pulman, 1983) and adjectival (Dirven & Taylor, 1988) categories. Most spectacularly, they show up even with categories which arguably do have a classical definition, such as "odd number" (Armstrong, Gleitman, & Gleitman, 1983).

3 Prototypes and semantic categories

While the pervasiveness of prototype effects is not in dispute, not all scholars share the view that these effects need to be incorporated into a theory of word meaning (and into a semantic theory more generally). Hummel (1994) and Coseriu (2002) maintain that prototype effects emerge because of the frequently imperfect match between the conceptual categories which constitute word meanings and states of affairs in the world. Goodness-of-example ratings would thus reflect the structure of the world, not the structure of our concepts. In the case of a word such as *bald*, it may be difficult to know whether the appellation would truly apply to an individual, even though the meaning of the word is reasonably clear. It could be similarly argued that words such as *fruit* and *furniture* have perfectly clear-cut meanings; what is not clear-cut is the applicability of the words to specific referents. Another variation on this theme is that prototype effects reflect psychological processes of deciding whether an entity belongs to a category or not. Thus, Osherson and Smith (1981) propose to distinguish between the "core" (or "linguistic") meaning of a word and "identification procedures" which are used "to make rapid decisions about membership" (p. 57). Wierzbicka (1990), taking a different tack, claims that appeal to prototypes is simply a way for lazy semanticists to avoid having to formulate rigorous definitions.

Skepticism about the linguistic-semantic relevance of prototype effects might have some force in the case of concepts which arguably do have clear-cut definitions, such as "odd number" and "bald." The argument loses much of its force, however, when we turn to a word like *fruit*. Uncertainly as to whether olives and pumpkins are fruit would appear to be due, not to the imperfect fit of the concept to the world, but to the inherent fuzziness of the concept itself. Geeraerts (1997, pp. 13–16) critically examined Wierzbicka's (1985) supposedly "rigorous" definition of the word, and concluded that the various components of her definition (these include "Before they are good to eat they are green or greenish outside" and "They are good to eat cooked with sugar, or cooked as part of some things which have sugar in them") failed to pick out all and only the things that we would want to call fruit. For this word—and no doubt for many others—prototype effects cannot simply be relegated to the imperfect fit between words and the world but must derive from the semantic structure of the words themselves. Some approaches to this latter issue are discussed below.

3.1 Categories as prototypes

Some of Rosch's statements (especially if taken out of context) are liable to encourage the view that a category may be represented simply in terms of its prototype. In Heider (1971), she surmises that "much actual learning of semantic reference, particularly in perceptual domains, may occur through generalization from focal exemplars" (p. 455). Later, she writes of "conceiving of each category in terms of its clear cases rather than its boundaries" (Rosch, 1978, pp. 35–36), and states that "categories tend to become defined in terms of prototypes or prototypical instances" (p. 30).

One approach to the relation of prototypes to word meanings, then, would be to claim that the prototypical category member *is* the word's meaning and that the referential potential of a word is a function of similarity to the prototype. The boundaries of the category would be set by the presence of neighboring, contrasting categories. There are some categories for which this account may have some plausibility, such as the basic color categories, and perhaps also the vessels (cups, bowls, and vases) studied by Labov (1973). As a vessel morphs from a prototypical cup into a prototypical bowl, categorization as cup gradually decreases, offset by increased categorization as bowl.

This approach presupposes a "structuralist" view of word meanings, whereby word meanings divide up conceptual space in a mosaic-like manner, such that the denotational range of one term is restricted by the presence of neighboring, contrastive terms (Geeraerts, Grondelaers, & Bekema, 1994, p. 119). It also predicts (correctly, in the case of colors and Labov's cups and bowls) that membership will be graded, in that an entity may be judged to be a member of a category only to a certain degree depending on its distance from the prototype. The category, as a consequence, will have fuzzy boundaries, and degree of membership in one category will inversely correlate with degree of membership in a neighboring category. The redder a shade of orange, the less it is orange and the more it is red.

In general, however, the view that a category can be defined solely in terms of its prototype raises a number of problems. First, for many sets of words, the mosaic metaphor is not applicable. This is most obviously the case with near synonyms, that is, words whose usage ranges overlap, sometimes considerably, but which nevertheless can be associated with distinct prototypes. Take the pair *high* and *tall* (Taylor, 2003b). *Tall* applies prototypically to humans (*tall man*), *high* to inanimates (*high mountain*). Yet the words do not mutually define each other at their boundaries. Many entities can be described equally well as *tall* or *high*. Similar problems arise in connection with some of the senses of *over*. In the sense "vertical to, not in contact with," *over* competes with *above*, while in the sense "from one side to the other" (*the bridge over the river*) the word overlaps with *across* (Taylor, 2003a, p. 121).

A second problem concerns the notion of resemblance. The prototypical bird is a small songbird, such as robin or sparrow. But it seems absurd to claim that the prototype is all there is to the bird concept—that the meaning of *bird* is "robin" (Kleiber, 1990, p. 59) and that creatures are called birds simply on the basis of their similarity to the prototype. While a duck may be similar to a robin in some respects (and this would be the basis for the categorization of both as birds), we could just as well appeal to the similarity as evidence that ducks should be called robins. And while penguins may not be very representative of the bird category, they are birds nonetheless, not birds to a certain degree. The bird category certainly exhibits prototype effects (understood as goodness-of-example ratings), but the boundaries of the category are not fuzzy.

Fodor's sustained criticism of the role of prototypes in semantic theory (e.g. Fodor, 1980, 1998; Fodor & Lepore, 1996) appears to be based on the (mis-)understanding of prototypes as being the categories. Fodor drew attention to the fact that complex expressions typically fail to inherit the prototypes of their constituents. We may well have an image of a prototypical grandmother (say, as a kindly, frail old lady with gray hair), but the prototype plays no role in our understanding of the expressions *my grandmother*, or *grandmothers most of whose grandchildren are married to dentists* (Fodor, 1980, p. 197). If one equates the concept "fish" with its prototype (e.g. a herring), and the concept "pet" with a poodle, then one would predict that a pet fish would be some sort of hybrid between a herring and a poodle, which, of course, is nonsense (Osherson & Smith, 1981).

In the case of categories like bird (and even fruit), the prototype is clearly insufficient as a category representation. We need to know what kinds of things are likely to be members of the category, how far we can generalize from the prototype, and where (if only approximately) the boundaries lie. Moreover, in order to account for the ways in which concepts combine, we need some more abstract, generic representation of the category. The approach outlined in the following section addresses these issues.

3.2 Categories as sets of weighted attributes

I mentioned at the beginning of the preceding section that Rosch's views, if taken out of context, are liable to encourage the view that equates a word meaning with its prototype. The cited passage from Rosch continues as follows: "categories tend to become defined in terms of prototypes or prototypical instances *that contain the attributes most representative of items inside and least representative of items outside the category*" (1978, p. 30, my italics). For Rosch, then, the prototype is a category member which exhibits a maximum number of attributes which are diagnostic of the category, in that these attributes are shared by the largest number of members of the category but tend not to be shared by members of contrasting categories. The category itself comes to be defined as a set of attributes which are differentially weighted according to their importance in diagnosing category membership, and an entity belongs in the category if the cumulative weightings of its attributes achieve a certain threshold level. Category members need not share the same attributes, nor is an attribute necessarily shared by all category members. Rather, the category hangs together in virtue of a "family resemblance" (Rosch & Mervis, 1975), in which attributes "criss-cross," like the threads of a rope (Wittgenstein, 1978, p. 32). The more similar an instance to all other category members (this being a measure of its family resemblance), the more prototypical it is of the category.

An example of the weighted attribute view may be found in Coleman and Kay's (1981) well-known study of the verb *to lie*. They identified three characteristic traits of a lie—it is factually incorrect, the speaker believes it to be incorrect, and the speaker intends to deceive the hearer. If all three features are present, a statement is viewed as a good example of lying, otherwise there may be doubts as to whether a lie has been told or not. Coleman and Kay found that the three features were not equally weighted. The speaker's belief that the statement is factually incorrect was the most important, factual incorrectness itself was the least important (p. 35).

The weighted attribute view of categories proposes "summary representations" which, as on the classical theory, "somehow encompass an entire concept" (Murphy, 2002, p. 49). Indeed, a classical category would simply be a limiting case where each of the defining attributes has maximal weighting. Moreover, the weighted attribute approach, by encompassing more than simply the prototype, offers a way to handle the problem of conceptual combination (Hampton, 1987, 1991). It also is able to account for the intriguing finding that subjects are able to identify the prototype of a category they have learned, even though they have not been previously exposed to the prototype (Posner & Keele, 1968).

The weighted feature approach requires that the appropriate features be identified. As Murphy (2002, p. 216) notes, there is an open-ended list of features which could enter into the representation. For example, "less than 100 years old" and "does not own a raincoat" are possible features of "dog." Clearly, we need some measure of the importance, or relevance, of the features (Ortony, Vondruska, Voss & Jones, 1985). Rosch's (1978) answer was to propose a measure of "cue validity." Cue validity is an estimate of the probability that possession of a feature will confer membership in the category. For example, given that an entity flies, what is the probability that this entity will be a bird? (Quite high, one should imagine, though nowhere near 100 percent, since we may be dealing with a flying insect, a bat, or even an airplane). On the other hand, being less than 100 years old will have very low cue validity for the bird category. Although this attribute might be exhibited by just about all birds, it is also shared by countless other kinds of entity, and thus has little predictive value.

A major problem with any feature-based approach is that in some cases the features cannot reasonably be identified independently of the category which they are supposed to define. Rosch became aware of this problem. She (1978, p. 42) observed that while "has a seat" may be a characteristic feature of "chair," knowing what it means for something to "have a seat" rests on a prior understanding of what it means for something to be a chair-like object. The problem is probably very widespread. Characteristic features of birds, such as having a beak and being covered with feathers, derive from our knowledge of birds. It is implausible that our bird concept is assembled from its characteristic features which are available independently of the concept itself. On the contrary, it is the category itself which provides the background knowledge for a proper understanding of its features. It is as if we must first have some global, gestalt representation of category instances before we are able to identify the features which define it. The features emerge as dimensions of similarity between known instances (Langacker, 1987, p. 22).

3.3 Categories as exemplars

A radical alternative to feature-based approaches construes a category simply as a collection of instances. Knowledge of a category consists in a memory store of encountered exemplars (Medin & Schaffer, 1978; Smith & Medin, 1981). Categorization of a new instance occurs in virtue of similarities to one or more of the stored exemplars. In its purest form, the exemplar theory denies that people make generalizations over category exemplars. Mixed representations might also be envisaged, however, in that instances which closely resemble each other might coalesce into a generic image which preserves what is common to the instances and filters out the idiosyncratic details (Ross & Makin, 1999).

On the face of it, the exemplar view, even in its mixed form, looks intuitively implausible. The idea that we retain specific memories of previously encountered instances would surely make intolerable demands on human memory. Several factors, however, suggest that we should not dismiss the exemplar theory out of hand. First, computer simulations have shown that exemplar models are able to account for a surprising range of experimental findings on human categorization, including, importantly, prototype effects (Hintzman, 1986; Kruschke, 1992; Nosofsky, 1988). Second, there is evidence that human memory is indeed rich in episodic detail (Schacter, 1987). Even such apparently irrelevant aspects of encountered language, such as the position on a page of a piece of text (Rothkopf, 1971), or the voice with which a word is spoken (Goldinger, 1996), may be retained over substantial periods of time. Moreover, we are exquisitely sensitive to the frequency with which events, including linguistic events, have occurred (Ellis, 2002), and frequency is now recognized as a major determinant of linguistic performance, language acquisition, and language change (Bybee, 2001). The very notion of grammaticality might simply be frequency by another name (Bybee & Hopper, 2001).

A focus on exemplars ties in with the basic principles of usage-based models of grammar (Barlow & Kemmer, 2000; Tomasello, 2003). It is axiomatic, in a usage-based model, that linguistic knowledge is acquired on the basis of encounters with actual usage events. While generalizations may be made over encountered events, the particularities of the events need not thereby be erased from memory (Langacker, 1987, p. 29). Indeed, it is now widely recognized that a great deal of linguistic knowledge must reside in rather particular facts about a language, such as its phraseologies, idioms, and collocations (Moon, 1998; Wray, 2002). Moreover, the frequency with which certain events (or types of events) have been encountered would itself form part of linguistic knowledge, and be a crucial factor in future performance (Bybee, 2001).

3.4 Prototypes as category defaults

Another approach to prototypes and categorization is the view that prototypes constitute the default value of a category, activated in the absence of more specific information. Thus, on hearing mention of "birds," one would assume that the creatures in question possess the typical attributes of the category, for example, that they fly, perch on trees, and so on. Rosch (1977) showed that a statement involving birds tends to make sense if the statement is changed to one referring to a prototypical member of the category, such as robins, but becomes ludicrous if reference is changed to a non-prototypical member, such as turkeys.

If prototypes are defaults, we should expect that attributes of the prototype may be overridden as more specific information becomes available. The notion of a "wooden spoon" overrides the size specification of the prototypical spoon (Hampton, 1987). As Fodor's grandmother example shows, the more one knows about the specific grandmother(s) in question, the less relevant the prototype may be.

The notion of what is prototypical can also vary according to background knowledge and the task in hand (Barsalou, 1987). If asked to take a Chinese perspective, American subjects rate swan and peacock as typical exemplars of the bird category, whereas robin and eagle are taken as typical from an American perspective (pp. 106–107). This does not, of course, mean that Chinese subjects *would* rate swans and peacocks over robins and eagles, only that the judgments of the American subjects were influenced by their background assumptions.

3.5 Categories as theories

Why is it that certain configurations of properties (or certain sets of exemplars) come to constitute a category? Rosch (1975b, p. 197) suggested that these may reflect the "correlational structure of the environment," in that categories "follow the natural correlation of attributes, those that maximize the correlation and thus the predictability of attributes within categories." This approach would make the (manifestly incorrect) prediction that different languages will zoom in on essentially the same categories, also that categories will only change if the environment changes (MacLaury, 1995, p. 251). Rosch herself came to accept a more nuanced view, in which categories and their attributes are mediated by the culture of a language community (Rosch, 1978). This approach was developed by Murphy and Medin (1985), who argued that a category is coherent to the extent that it plays a role in wider scenarios, in causal relations, or in deeply held beliefs. A category such as "geometrical figure that is either green or a square" (on the use of such categories in psychologists' "concept formation experiments," see Fodor, 1980, pp. 266–267) is not one that is likely to be lexicalized in any human language, for the reason that the category plays no role in any established knowledge configuration.

The role of background knowledge in categorization is exemplified in Sweetser's (1987) reanalysis of Coleman and Kay's (1981) study of the verb *to lie*. Sweetser proposes that lying should be understood against an idealized model of communication, in which information is deemed to be true if one has reasons to believe it, the transfer of true information is believed to benefit the hearer, and communication is supposed to be cooperative. Given these background assumptions, making a statement one believes to be false entails conveying information which is factually incorrect, and this can only be done with the intention of harming the hearer. If the background assumptions hold, a lie is a prototypical lie. Borderline judgments arise if the background assumptions do not hold, for example, when we seek to capture an audience by telling tall stories, when teasing people by pulling their leg, or when making compliments as part of a social routine.

4 Prototypes and the basic level

Let us return to an issue raised at the beginning of this chapter, namely, the relation between words and things in the world. It will be apparent that the relation can be approached from two perspectives. We can ask, for this word, what are the things that the word can be used to refer to? We can also reverse the perspective, and ask, for this thing, what are the words most likely to be used to name it?

The first perspective goes from word to thing; it is a referential, or semasiological perspective. This is the methodology used by Rosch, and it underlies the notion of prototype. Thus, the prototype might be characterized as the entity (or kind of entity) that is most likely to be referred to by a word. The second perspective goes from thing to word; it is a naming, or onomasiological perceptive. This is the perspective employed in much color research, as when, for example, subjects are shown a series of color chips which they are asked to name. The onomasiological perspective underlies the notion of basic level term. The basic level is the level in a taxonomy at which things are normally named (in the absence of reasons to the contrary), for example, as a chair, rather than as furniture, or as a kitchen chair. A number of factors conspire to render the basic level salient. In particular, it is at this level that categories are maximally contrastive with respect to the cue validity of their attributes (Murphy, 2002, Ch. 7).

The notions of prototype and basic level are often twinned, the former having to do with the "horizontal" organization of categories, the latter with their "vertical" organization in taxonomies (Rosch, 1978). The interplay between these two perspectives was systematically investigated by Geeraerts, Grondelaers & Bakema (1994). In order to pursue both perspectives, it was necessary to select a domain in which words could be reliably matched to their referents, and vice versa. They chose to examine terms for outer clothing garments and their illustration in fashion magazines. One of their findings was that the basic level was by no means uniform within a taxonomy. Basic-level terms for articles of clothing include *jacket, shirt, pullover*, and *trousers*. Jeans would be a subcategory of trousers, though by no means the most prototypical. Yet jeans are commonly referred to as such, not as trousers. It seems that more marginal members of a basic-level category tend to be referred to by name, precisely because they are distinctive vis-à-vis more prototypical members. For example, if there are starlings and sparrows in the garden, I might comment on the "birds" that we have. But if I see ducks and geese waddling over the lawn, I would name them as such.

5 Polysemy

A particularly fruitful application of the prototype notion concerns the treatment of polysemy, that is, the situation in which a linguistic form (whether word, bound morpheme, syntactic construction, or whatever) typically has a range of distinct meanings. When we use the word *fruit* to refer, first, to apples and bananas, and then to coconuts and olives, we should probably want to say that the word has a constant meaning. But when we speak of *the fruits of my labor*, or say that *my work bore fruit* (Geeraerts, 1997, p. 16), we are not dealing with marginal members, or indeed members at all, of the biological category, but with distinct, extended senses of the word. The word *fruit* is polysemous, that is, it has more than one identifiable meaning.

It is tempting to impose a prototype structure on a polysemous word like *fruit*. Lakoff (1987, pp. 416–419) discusses polysemy in just such terms. The various meanings of a polysemous item constitute a "category of senses," which center on a "prototypical," or "most representative" sense, from which the others may be derived. This radial network approach to polysemy has enjoyed considerable popularity (Taylor, 2003a, Ch. 6; for a particularly well worked-out example, see Fillmore & Atkins, 2000). Some caveats are, however, called for.

First, we need to bear in mind that when we speak of a "category of senses" (as in the case of *over* as discussed in Lakoff, 1987), or of the "prototypical" sense of a polysemous word, we are using the terms "category" and "prototypical" rather differently from how they are used with reference to the kinds of studies that Rosch pursued. In the one case, the category consists of distinct senses; in the other, we are dealing with different instances of one and the same concept. Each of the identifiable senses of a polysemous word will itself constitute a category, with its own internal structure, prototypical instances, and so on. And whereas Rosch substantiated the prototype notion by a variety of experimental techniques, linguists applying the prototype model to polysemous items rely mostly on intuition and appeals to descriptive elegance, identifying the prototype as that sense to which the others can most reasonably, or most economically, be related. Typically, a spatial sense is taken as more central than non-spatial senses, on the basis of what is supposed to be a very general conceptual metaphor which maps spatial notions onto non-spatial domains. For Lakoff (1987, pp. 416–417), the spatial sense of *long* (as in *a long stick*) is "more central" than the temporal sense (*a long time*).

While we may agree that olives are not representative of the fruit category, it is by no means obvious in what way the temporal sense of, e.g. *long*, is to be regarded as "less representative," or a "less good" example of the polysemous category than the spatial sense. A competent speaker of English needs to have mastered both senses, and from this point of view each of the senses is equally central. On Lakoff's radial model, the senses of *over* exhibited in *over here*, *over the weekend*, and *fall over* would have to be regarded as fairly marginal. Yet these are well entrenched uses of the word, and are in fact amongst the earliest uses to be acquired by children (Hallan, 2001; see also Rice, 2003). Experimental evidence, such as it is, would suggest that radial category networks might actually have very little psychological reality for speakers of the language (Sandra & Rice, 1995).

Secondly, in the case of some polysemous words, it seems highly counterintuitive to speak of a "category of senses" at all. Take Jackendoff's (2002, p. 340) example of *cardinal*. It is not difficult, with the aid of the *Oxford English Dictionary*, to track the polysemization of this word, from an original sense "principal" (retained in *cardinal sins*), through to a church official, to the color of his robes, then to a bird of that color. Although the links can be perceived, these disparate senses hardly constitute a coherent, even less, useful category.

At the other end of the spectrum are cases where it is difficult to determine whether two uses of a word exemplify two distinct senses or one and the same sense, and the various criteria for the distinction that have been proposed sometimes do not give an unequivocal answer (Geeraerts, 1993). To be sure, there are cases where it is quite clear that we are dealing with distinct senses, as with the example of *fruit* just cited, but there are others in which a decision is by no means obvious. Is the same sense of *paint* exemplified in *paint a portrait* and *paint white stripes on the road* (Tuggy, 1993)? Recently, a number of scholars have queried whether it is legitimate in principle to try to identify *the* senses of a word (Allwood, 2003; Zlatev, 2003).

Perhaps the most reasonable conclusion to draw from the above is that knowing a word involves learning a set (possibly, a very large and open-ended set) of established uses and usage patterns. Whether, or how, the speaker of the language perceives these uses to be related may not be very relevant to the speaker's proficiency in the language. The notion of prototype in the Roschean sense might not therefore be all that applicable. The notion of prototype, and extensions therefrom, might, however, be important in the case of novel, or creative utterances. In this connection, Langacker (1987, p. 381), speaks of "local" prototypes. Langacker construes a language as an inventory of conventionalized symbolic resources (p. 57). Mostly, the conceptualization that a speaker wishes to symbolize on a particular occasion will not correspond exactly with any of the available resources. Inevitably, some extension of an existing resource will be indicated. The existing resource constitutes the local prototype and the actual usage an extension from it. If the extension is used on future occasions, it may become entrenched and will itself acquire the status of an established unit in the language and become available as a local prototype for further extensions.

6 Beyond semantics

So far, this chapter has focused on the role of prototypes in linguistic semantics. The prototype notion has, however, been fruitfully applied to the structural elements of language. This section reviews three such applications.

6.1 Phonological categories

Phonology is the area of linguistic theory which has been most thoroughly pervaded by the classical theory of categories. Almost all modern theories of phonology presuppose the existence of a small set of (usually binary) features, and phonetic segments are defined as sets of these features. Phonological rules, generalizations, and constraints are also usually stated in terms of such features. Inevitably, the phonological representations abstract away from the fine phonetic detail and the variation which exist in actual pronunciations. A phonology based on classical categories thus tends to ignore sociophonetic dimensions of speech (Kristiansen, 2003); it is also difficult to reconcile with evidence that phonological units—words in the first instance, but also syllables and segments—might be stored in their full phonetic forms, indeed, that much episodic information might also be retained (Johnson, 1997; Lachs, McMichael, & Pisoni, 2000).

Classical definitions, with their necessary and sufficient conditions for category membership, can quickly run into difficulties when we consider the range of possible realizations of a phonological unit such as a phoneme. This is because the features which enter into the definition may be overridden in actual pronunciations. The phoneme /t/ in English is particularly instructive in this respect. This phoneme is remarkable for its rich and varied set of allophones. These include the aspirated, unaspirated, glottalized, and ejective variants, alveolar and dental realizations, both voiced and voiceless sounds, as well as flaps, approximants, and, increasingly in many dialects, the glottal stop. Phonetically, these sounds lack any common defining features. This prompted Taylor (2003a), following Nathan (1986), to propose a radial category analysis for these variants. Fig. 3.1 displays these sounds as radiating out from a central member, where the solid lines link up pairs of sounds which are minimally different.

The format of Fig. 3.1 is similar to that proposed for the related senses of polysemous items. The figure thus presupposes a view of the phoneme as a "family of sounds" (Jones, 1964, p. 49), in contrast with the standard view, whereby /t/ would be defined by a feature matrix, and allophonic realizations would be derived by dedicated rules. Even so, each of the supposedly defining features of the phoneme will be defeated in at least some of the realizations of the phoneme.

Closer in spirit to Rosch's work on conceptual categories is research by Kuhl and her associates on phoneme prototypes, especially vowels (summarized in Kuhl, 2000). In many respects, her research constitutes a phonetic-acoustic extension of Rosch's early work on the categorization of color. Exactly paralleling Rosch's methodology on goodness-of-example ratings, Grieser and Kuhl (1989) and Kuhl (1991) found that subjects were able to judge a range of synthesized vowel sounds as good or less good examples of a vowel phoneme. Fuzzy boundary effects were

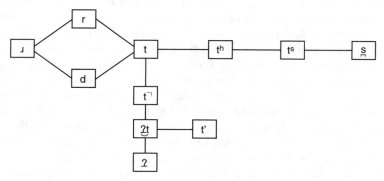

Figure 3.1 A network for allophones of the phoneme /t/.

also observed, as tokens of one vowel gradually came to be categorized as tokens of a neighboring vowel.

The vowel space is in many interesting respects comparable to color space. Color space may be described in terms of three parameters—hue, saturation, and brightness. The space itself contains no obvious lines of demarcation, and languages differ with respect to the number, and the boundaries, of their color terms (Gleason, 1955, p. 4). However, the human visual system is especially responsive to certain focal colors, such as pure red and pure yellow (Kay & McDaniel, 1978), and one of the findings of Rosch's early work was that even though different languages might carve up the color space differently, speakers of different languages tend to agree on the focal reference of their respective color terms.

Vowel space is traditionally described in terms of formants, minimally F1 and F2. These correspond (indirectly) to parameters of articulation, in particular, the relative size of the pharyngeal and oral cavities. Like color space, vowel space contains no obvious lines of demarcation, though certain regions of the space—roughly, the so-called point vowels, /i, a, u/ —have been claimed to have special status, in that a relatively stable vowel quality can be achieved with relatively varied articulations (Stevens, 1972). Perhaps even more than with colors, however, languages differ widely in the number of vowel categories that they recognize. Moreover, unlike with colors, there is considerable variation with respect to the focal values. Thus, /i/ in English by no means corresponds to /i/ in French (not to mention the considerable variation in the different regional varieties of English).

Research on infants' speech perception has shown that up to the age of about six months infants possess a remarkable ability to discriminate different vowel qualities (Jusczyk, 1997). Kuhl, in a series of ingenious experiments (Kuhl, 1991; Kuhl & Iverson, 1995) demonstrated that with ongoing exposure to the ambient language the vowel space is restructured, or warped. Initially, the vowel categories are seeded by exposure to the particularly clear, prolonged articulations typical of infant-directed speech. Once these vowel qualities are established as the prototypes of the emerging vowel phonemes, neighboring sounds are drawn in towards the prototype. Kuhl refers to this as the "perceptual magnet effect," whereby the perceptual distance between the prototype and its neighbors is reduced (an effect also observed, in different domains, by Ortony, Vondruska, Voss & Jones, 1985; Rips, 1975; Rosch, 1975a; and Tversky, 1977; see also MacLaury, 1995). At the same time, the perceptual distance between sounds which straddle the boundary between categories is increased. The result is that the vowel sounds of a language tend to be perceived categorically, that is, as members of their respective phoneme categories, within-category differences being underestimated. This mechanism probably underlies the subjective impression (for native speakers of a language) that all members of a phoneme category (for example, all instances of English /i/), are essentially "the same." Bloomfield (1933, p. 79), in fact, speculated that advances in acoustic science would one day discover the invariant acoustic properties definitional of each of the phonemes of a language. Subsequent research, as is well known, showed Bloomfield's hope to be chimerical.

In terms of the theories of prototypes summarized in section 3, Kuhl's findings would be compatible with the simplest of these, that is, that vowel phonemes are represented as their prototypes. A vowel sound would be judged to be /i/, /e/, or whatever, in virtue of its closeness to the prototype, whereby the boundaries of any one category would be set by the presence of neighboring categories. Her findings would also be consistent with an exemplar theory, in which a speaker's mental representation of a vowel consists of memory traces of previously encountered instances. An exemplar theory of phoneme categories has been pursued by Pierrehumbert (2001, 2002). There are also implications for the learning of the sound categories of foreign languages. It would be appropriate to place the emphasis, initially, on seeding the new categories through the best examples, rather than on training learners to discriminate borderline cases (McClelland, Fiez, & McCandliss, 2002; see also Avrahami et al., 1997; Ellis & Anderson, 1984).

6.2 Syntactic categories

The use of diagnostic tests is standard practice in syntactic analysis. There are tests for determining whether a group of words make up a syntactic constituent; whether a constituent is a noun phrase, verb phrase, or whatever; whether a noun phrase is the subject of a verb; whether a particular word is noun or adjective, and, if a noun, whether it is a count noun or a mass noun, and so on. There are also tests for whether a particular phonological form constitutes a word, or whether it is better analyzed as a bound morpheme, a clitic, or a group of words (Taylor, 2003a, pp. 202–208). Mostly, these tests have to do with distribution and substitutabilty and can be seen as identifying the features, or attributes, of the categories in question, while the categories themselves are able to be defined in terms of their features. In many cases, to be sure, the tests converge on an unambiguous result. There can be no doubt about the status of *the cat*, in *The cat sat on the mat*, as a noun phrase and as the subject of the verb. In these cases we would be entitled to speak of prototypical instances of the respective categories. Often, however, an item fails to pass all of the relevant tests, in which case it would count as a more marginal member of the category. Consider, for example, the status of *there*, as noun phrase and as subject, in *There's a man at the door* (Taylor, 2003a, p. 215) and in *There's a man been shot* (Taylor, 2003a, p. 203).

The existence of goodness-of-example ratings does not necessarily entail fuzziness of category boundaries (recall the example of the bird category). Aarts (2004) has argued that degrees of representativity are quite well documented with respect to grammatical and lexical categories but finds little convincing evidence of fuzzy boundaries between categories. Some noun phrases might be less noun-phrasy than others, but they are still nominal in character, not verbal or adjectival. Probably, Aarts is being too dogmatic on this point. There does seem to be a genuinely gray area between nouns, adjectives, and the so-called nominal adjectives in Japanese (Uehara, 2003), and even in English, the status of the modifying element in nominals such as *apple pie, gold watch*, and *Shakespeare play* may be open to question (Taylor, 1998). Another potential area of fuzziness is the distinction between prenominal (or determinative) possessives, of the kind *[a man]'s skull*, and compound (or descriptive) possessives, of the kind *a [man's skull]* (Taylor, 1996).

6.3 Constructions

An important development within Cognitive Linguistics has been the status accorded to constructions. As is to be expected, we find disagreement on what, precisely, is to come under the purview of the concept (Taylor, 2004). For our purposes, we can take constructions to be patterns for the combination of smaller linguistic units, such as words, morphemes, and phrases. Generative theories take constructions to be the output of rule applications and constraints; on a usage-based perspective, constructions are what speakers of a language infer from the input and which sanction their linguistic productions. Constructions, thus understood, can be described both from the semantic perspective (what is the meaning conveyed by the construction?) and from the formal perspective (what kinds of items are likely to occur in the construction, and in what kind of configuration?). Both of these aspects are liable to give rise to prototype effects.

The applicability of the prototype notion to constructions may be illustrated by Verhagen's recent discussion of long-distance Wh-extraction. An initial question word (such as *who* or *what*) may correspond to a constituent within the same clause (as in *Who did you meet?*) or to a constituent in a more distant, subordinate clause (as in *Who did you say that you met?*). The acceptability of long-distance extraction is known to vary considerably, and various pragmatic explanations have been proposed to account for these effects (Deane, 1991; Goldberg, 2006, Ch. 7). One of the few scholars who has conducted a corpus-based analysis of the phenomenon, however, is Verhagen (2005). His observations pertain mainly to Dutch, but they are likely to generalize also to English.

In the small, 720,000 word Eindhoven corpus, Verhagen (2005, pp. 121–122) found only six examples of long-distance extraction, and only 11 in the one million word Brown corpus of English. (The construction, therefore, is not particularly frequent.) Remarkably, all six Dutch examples had *denken* "think" as their main verb which occurred with a second person singular subject (*je* or *u*). Ten of the English examples also had *think* as their main verb and nine had *you* as subject. Analysis of a larger Dutch corpus confirmed the dominance of *denken* as main verb (34 out of 43 examples), also of second person subjects (36 examples). The data, then, point to a very clear prototype for the construction. Especially interesting is the fact that examples which did not conform to the prototype deviated in only one feature: If the verb was not *denken*, the subject was second person; if the subject was not second person, the verb was *denken* (p. 126). The data, then, point not only to the existence of a prototype but also to the fact that minimal deviation from the prototype is tolerated.

According to Verhagen, the salience of the prototype is due to the fact that the main clause, with "did/do you think," does not in fact bear the main information content; on the contrary, it functions pragmatically as an appeal to the hearer, not too dissimilar, in fact, to an epenthetic phrase such as *in your opinion*, as in *Who (do you think) pays the rent?* Diessel and Tomasello (2001) report that main clauses in children's first complex sentences have just such a pragmatic function. According to Verhagen, a prototype approach to the construction is to be favored, not only because of its descriptive adequacy but because it offers an explanation for why the prototype should be as it is.

The example of Wh-extraction demonstrates the association between a construction and the items that are likely to occur in it. Let us say that the construction constitutes a category and its lexical material is the features, or attributes, of the category. We can study the association from two perspectives. One perspective we have already mentioned, that of the cue validity of a feature:

(1.) <u>Cue validity</u>: Given that entity *e* exhibits property *p*, what is the probability that *e* is a member of category C?

Having wings and being able to fly would have rather high cue validity for membership in the bird category; having a liver or living underground would have rather low cue validity.

Reversing the perspective, we can enquire into the probability that a member of category will possess a certain feature; this constitutes category validity (Murphy, 2002, p. 215):

(2.) <u>Category validity</u>: Given that entity *e* is a member of category C, what is the probability that *e* will exhibit property *p*?

If something is a bird, we can infer with some degree of confidence that it will be able to fly and that it has a liver, but not that it lives underground. It would seem that "successful" categories—ones that people find useful to construct and operate with—combine both kinds of validity. It is useful if categorization of an entity is able to generate expectations about its likely properties; conversely, if we learn that an entity has a certain property it is helpful if we are able to generate expectations as to its likely categorization (which in turn will generate expectations about further properties).

Let us now apply these notions to constructions and the items which occur in them. The perspective of cue validity may be stated as follows:

(3.) <u>Cue validity of words vis-à-vis constructions</u>: Given an occurrence of word *w*, what is the probability that *w* is part of construction C?

High cue validity in this sense would occur with so-called cranberry words (Taylor, 2002, p. 550), that is, words which are virtually restricted to occurring in certain constructions. Take as an example the word *dint*. The British National Corpus (BNC) records 73 instances of *dint*, of which 67 (= 92%) occur in the context *by dint of*. Of the six recalcitrant examples, one would appear to be a dialectal rendering of *didn't* while four would seem to involve confusion with *dent* (*she made a little dint in the ground*). Only one example—*with dint of great effort*—would appear to be a genuine case of an extended use of the noun *dint* in a slightly different lexico-syntactic environment.

While the occurrence of *dint* is highly predictive of the construction in which it occurs, the occurrence of *by * of* is by no means predictive of the word *dint*. There are 11,748 instances of *by * of* in the BNC, involving 1,000 different types. Of these, the most frequent are *by means of* (1,553, or 15.53% of all instances), *by way of* (1,383, or 13.83%), and *by virtue of* (965, or 9.65%). These three types account for almost one third (33.21%) of all instances of *by * of*. In contrast, *by dint of* accounts for only about half of 1% (0.57) of these instances.

By examining a construction with an eye on the kinds of items which occur in it, we are invoking the notion of category validity:

(4.) <u>Category validity of constructions vis-à-vis the words that occur in them</u>: Given the occurrence of construction C, what is the probability that word *w* features as part of C?

The Dutch Wh-extraction construction has high category validity, in that an occurrence of this construction very strongly predicts the occurrence of the main verb *denken*. On the other hand, *denken* is a rather frequent word in Dutch, with 920 instances in the Eindhoven corpus. Whereas the occurrence of the construction strongly predicts the use of the verb, the occurrence of the verb has virtually no predictive power vis-à-vis the construction.[1]

The examples discussed (*dint* and Wh-extraction) exhibit striking asymmetries with respect to cue and category validity. It is perhaps no accident that both examples would be regarded as fairly marginal to the languages in question (both, in fact, have very low absolute frequencies). Of special interest would be cases where both cue and category validity converge on moderately high values. These cases, we might presume, would constitute the productive and dynamic core of a language.

The mutual association of words and constructions has been studied by Stefanowitch and Gries (2003; see also Gries & Stefanowitch, 2004) in terms of "collostructions." Their program involves examining constructions with respect to the words that occur in them, and, simultaneously, examining the words with an eye on the constructions that they occur in. An early example of collostructional analysis (though it was not so called) may be found in Renouf and Sinclair's (1991) discussion of the *a * of* construction. A ten million word corpus of written English contained 25,416 instances of this construction, with as many as 2,848 different items occurring in it. The construction would not seem to be particularly choosy with respect to the items which it selects. However, as many as 14% of all instances are accounted for by only four different items, *lot* (1,322 tokens), *kind* (864), *number* (762) and *couple* (685). What is interesting is that for some items, their occurrence in the construction accounts for a large percentage of their tokens. The highest degree of association between word and construction is exhibited by *couple*. 62% of all tokens of this word occurred in the *a * of* construction; corresponding percentages for *lot*, *number*, and *kind* are 53%, 30%, and 21%.

The interaction of words and constructions has also been pursued by Goldberg (2006; see also Goldberg, Casenhiser & Sethuraman 2004, 2005). Goldberg focused on three verb phrase constructions in English, the intransitive motion construction [V PP] (*go into the room*), the caused motion construction [V NP PP] (*put the book on the shelf*), and the ditransitive construction [V NP NP] (*give Chris a book*). She examined the incidence of these constructions in the speech of children and their adult caregivers and found that, while a fair number of different verbs were used by both children and adults, there was, for each construction, a single verb which accounted for "the lion's share" of its instances, *go* in the case of intransitive motion, *put* for caused motion, and *give* for ditransitives. These are verbs which seem to encapsulate the prototypical meanings of the constructions.

In the case of these three constructions, then, the occurrence of the construction was fairly predictive of the verbs which occur in them. Concerning the cue validity of the verbs vis-à-vis the constructions, we learn (Goldberg, 2006, p. 109) that 99 out of 114 occurrences of *put* in the corpus were associated with the caused motion construction, while 11 out of the 14 (p. 112) occurrences of *give* were in the ditransitive construction. Here we observe a quite remarkable convergence of cue and category validity, where the construction strongly favors a particular word, while most occurrences of the word occur in the construction.

Goldberg discusses cue and category validity in slightly different terms from the one presented here, in that she takes the category to be, not the syntactic construction, but the semantics of the designated event (her approach thus introduces the onomasiological perspective, mentioned earlier), the features of the semantic category being both the construction and its head verb. There are some obvious difficulties associated with this approach, in particular, how to reliably identify the intended semantics of an utterance independent of its verbal expression. Moreover, the semantic categories (e.g. "transfer" in the case of the ditransitive) are not clear-cut (in fact, a prototype approach may well be indicated: Goldberg, 1992). Goldberg's analyses are, however, suggestive. She claims (2006, p. 111) that 61% of occurrences of the ditransitive construction in her corpus encoded "literal transfer," while 33% encoded "metaphorical transfer." The occurrence of the construction is therefore highly predictive of the semantic notion of transfer, broadly construed.

The picture that emerges from these studies is that the syntax and lexicon of a language are closely intertwined and interdependent. This links up with an important theme in Rosch's work. One of Rosch's "principles of categorization" is that an organism perceives a "correlational structure" in the world:

> the perceived world is not an unstructured total set of equiprobable co-occurring attributes. Rather, the material objects of the world are perceived to possess [. . .] high correlational structure. [. . .] [C]ombinations of what we perceive as the attributes of real objects do not occur uniformly.
>
> Rosch, 1978, p. 29

It is this correlational which underlies the viability, and indeed the very *raison d'être* of a category. Language exhibits a similar correlational structure; like the external environment, language does not present itself to us as an unstructured set of equiprobable elements. Words tend to select their contexts, constructions tend to select their lexical content, and semantic structures tend to select their syntactic and lexical realizations. Goldberg (2006) argues that languages are learnable precisely because of this interplay of categories and their features.

The quotation from Labov which heads this chapter states that the linguistic encoding of a situation involves the categorization of the situation in accordance with the available linguistic resources. Our discussion has suggested that categorization may play an even more fundamental role in language. The very structure of language itself is a matter of categorization. Rosch's discoveries regarding the internal structure of categories are no less relevant to the category *of* language than they are to the categories symbolized *by* language.

Note

1 In order to calculate cue and category validities we need information on the overall frequency of the features, the categories, and the occurrence of the features in the categories. For semantic categories, these data are simply not obtainable. (How could we ever determine the number of times we have encountered "flying things" along with data on the number birds, and flying birds, that we have encountered?) Such data is, however, readily derivable from language corpora with respect to the occurrence of constructions and their constituents. Thus, Gries (2003) was able to apply the notion of cue validity in order to characterize the prototypes of two contrasting constructions in English, namely the ditransitive [V NP NP] and its prepositional alternative [V NP to/for NP]. The "features" of the constructions involved such aspects as the animacy of the NPs, their length, their definiteness, and their status as given or new.

Bibliography

Aarts, B. (2004). Modelling linguistic gradience. *Studies in Language*, 28, 1–49.

Allwood, J. (2003). Meaning potentials and context: Some consequences for the analysis of variation in meaning. In Cuyckens, H., Dirven, R., & Taylor, J. (Eds.) (2003). *Cognitive approaches to lexical semantics* pp. 29–65. Berlin: Mouton de Gruyter.

Armstrong, S. L., Gleitman, L. R., & Gleitman, H. (1983). What some concepts might not be. *Cognition*, *13*, 163–308.

Avrahami, J., Kareev, Y., Bogot, Y., Caspi, R., Dunaevsky, S., & Lerner, S. (1997). Teaching by examples: Implications for the process of category acquisition. *Quarterly Journal of Experimental Psychology*, *50A*, 586–606.

Barlow, M., & Kemmer, S. (Eds.) (2000). *Usage-based models of language*. Stanford: CSLI Publications.

Barsalou, L. (1983). Ad hoc categories. *Memory & Cognition*, *11*, 211–227.

Barsalou, L. (1987). The instability of graded structure: Implications for the nature of concepts. In U. Neisser (Ed.) *Concepts and conceptual development: Ecological and intellectual factors in categorization* (pp. 101–140). Cambridge: Cambridge University Press.

Barsalou, L. (1991). Deriving categories to achieve goals. In G. H. Bower (Ed.), *The Psychology of learning and motivation, Vol. 27* (pp. 1–64). New York, Academic Press.

Blank, A. & Koch, P. (Eds.) (1999). *Historical semantics and cognition.* Berlin: Mouton de Gruyter.

Bloomfield, L. (1933). *Language.* London: George Allen & Unwin.

Bybee, J. (2001). *Phonology and language use.* Cambridge: Cambridge University Press.

Bybee, J., & Hopper, P. (Eds.) (2001). *Frequency and the emergence of linguistic structure.* Amsterdam: John Benjamins.

Coleman L., & Kay, P. (1981). Prototype semantics: The English word "lie." *Language, 57,* 26–44.

Coseriu, E. (2002). Structural semantics and "cognitive" semantics. *Logos and Language, 1,* 19–42.

Croft, W. & Cruse, D. A. (2004). *Cognitive linguistics.* Cambridge: Cambridge University Press.

Deane, P. (1991). Limits to attention: A cognitive theory of island phenomena. *Cognitive Linguistics, 2,* 1–63.

Diessel, H., & Tomasello, M. (2001). The acquisition of finite complement clauses in English: A corpus-based analysis. *Cognitive Linguistics, 12,* 97–141.

Dirven, R., & Taylor, J. R. (1988). The conceptualization of vertical space in English: The case of *tall.* In B. Rudzka-Ostyn (Ed.), *Topics in cognitive linguistics* (pp. 379–402). Amsterdam: John Benjamins.

Ellis, N. (2002). Frequency effects in language processing. A review with implications for theories of implicit and explicit language acquisition. *Studies in Second Language Acquisition, 24,* 143–188.

Ellis, R., & Anderson, J. R. (1984). The effects of information order and learning mode on schema abstraction. *Memory and Cognition, 12,* 20–30.

Fehr, B., & Russel, J. A. (1984). Concept of emotion viewed from a prototype perspective. *Journal of Experimental Psychology: General, 113,* 464–486.

Fillmore, C. & Atkins, B. (2000). Describing polysemy: The case of "crawl". In Y. Ravin & C. Leacock (Eds.), *Polysemy: Theoretical and computational approaches* (pp. 91–110). Oxford: Oxford University Press.

Fodor, J. (1980). The present status of the innateness controversy. In *Representations: Philosophical essays on the foundations of cognitive science* (pp. 257–316). Cambridge, MA: MIT Press.

Fodor, J. (1998). *Concepts: Where cognitive science went wrong.* Oxford: Oxford University Press.

Fodor, J., & Lepore, E. (1996). The red herring and the pet fish: Why concepts still can't be prototypes. *Cognition, 58,* 253–270.

Geeraerts, D. (1989). Prospects and problems of prototype theory. *Linguistics, 27,* 587–612.

Geeraerts, D. (1993). Vagueness's puzzles, polysemy's vagaries. *Cognitive Linguistics, 4,* 223–272.

Geeraerts, D. (1997). *Diachronic prototype semantics: A contribution to historical lexicology.* Oxford: Oxford University Press.

Geeraerts, D., Grondelaers, S., & Bakema, P. (1994). *The structure of lexical variation: Meaning, naming, and context.* Berlin: Mouton de Gruyter.

61

Gleason, H. A. (1955). *An introduction to descriptive linguistics.* New York: Holt, Rinehart & Winston.

Goldberg, A. (1992). The inherent semantics of argument structure: The case of the English ditransitive construction. *Cognitive Linguistics, 3,* 37–74.

Goldberg, A. (2006). *Constructions at work. The nature of generalization in language.* Oxford: Oxford University Press.

Goldberg, A., Casenhiser, D., & Sethuraman, N. (2004). Learning argument structure generalizations. *Cognitive Linguistics, 15,* 289–316.

Goldberg, A., Casenhiser, D., & Sethuraman, N. (2005). The role of prediction in construction-learning. *Journal of Child Language, 32,* 407–426.

Goldinger, S. D. (1996). Words and voices: Episodic traces in spoken word identification and recognition memory. *Journal of Experimental Psychology: Learning, Memory, and Cognition, 22,* 1,166–1,183.

Gries, S. Th. (2003). Towards a corpus-based identification of prototypical instances of constructions. *Annual Review of Cognitive Linguistics, 1,* 1–18.

Gries, S. Th., & Stefanowitch, A. (2004). Extending collostructional analysis: A corpus-based perspective on "alternations." *International Journal of Corpus Linguistics, 9,* 97–129.

Grieser, D., & Kuhl, P. (1989). Categorization of speech by infants: Support for speech-perception prototypes. *Developmental Psychology, 25,* pp. 577–588.

Hallan, N. (2001). Paths to prepositions? A corpus-based study of the acquisition of a lexico-grammatical category. In J. Bybee & P. Hopper (Eds.), *Frequency and the emergence of linguistic structure* (pp. 91–120). Amsterdam: John Benjamins.

Hampton, J. (1987). Inheritance of attributes in natural concept conjunctions. *Memory and Cognition, 15,* 55–71.

Hampton, J. (1991). The combination of prototype concepts. In P. Schwanenflugel (Ed.), *The psychology of word meanings* (pp. 91–116). Hillsdale, NJ: Lawrence Erlbaum.

Heider, E. R. (1971). "Focal" color areas and the development of color names. *Developmental Psychology, 4,* 447–455.

Heider, E. R. (1972). Universals in color naming and memory. *Journal of Experimental Psychology, 93,* 10–20.

Hintzman, D. (1986). "Schema abstraction" in a multiple-trace memory model. *Psychological Review, 93,* 328–338.

Hummel, M. (1994). Regard critique sur la sémantique du prototype. *Cahiers de lexicologie, 65,* 159–182.

Jackendoff, R. (2002). *Foundations of language: Brain, meaning, grammar, evolution.* Oxford: Oxford University Press.

Johnson, K. (1997) Speech perception without speaker normalization: An exemplar model. In K. Johnson & J. W. Mullennix (Eds.), *Talker variability in speech processing* (pp. 145–165). San Diego: Academic Press.

Jones, D. (1964). *An outline of English phonetics.* Cambridge: Heffer. First published 1918.

Jusczyk, P. (1997). *The discovery of spoken language.* Cambridge, MA: MIT Press.

Kay, P., & McDaniel, C. K. (1978). The linguistic significance of the meanings of basic color terms. *Language, 54,* 610–646.

Kleiber, G. (1990). *La sémantique du prototype: Catégories et sens lexical.* Paris: PUF.

Kristiansen, G. (2003). How to do things with allophones: Linguistic stereotypes as cognitive reference points in social cognition. In R. Dirven, R. Frank, & M. Pütz (Eds.), *Cognitive models in language and thought: Ideology, metaphors and meanings* (pp. 69–120). Berlin: Mouton de Gruyter.

Kruschke, J. K. (1992). ALCOVE: An exemplar-based connectionist model of category learning. *Psychological Review, 99*, 22–44.

Kuhl, P. (1991). Human adults and human infants show a "perceptual magnet effect" for prototypes of speech categories, monkeys do not. *Perception and Psychophysics, 50*, 93–107.

Kuhl, P. (2000). A new view of language acquisition. *Proceedings of the National Academy of Sciences, 97* (no. 22), 11,850–11,857.

Kuhl, P., & Iverson, P. (1995). Linguistic experience and the "perceptual magnet effect." In W. Strange (Ed.), *Speech perception and linguistic experience: Issues in cross-language research* (pp. 121–154). Timonium, MD: York Press.

Labov, W. (1973). The boundaries of words and their meanings. In C.-J. Bailey & R. W. Shuy (Eds.), *New ways of analyzing variation in English* (pp. 340–372). Washington, DC: Georgetown University Press. Reprinted in Aarts et al. (2004), 67–89.

Lachs, L., McMichael, K., & Pisoni, D. B. (2000). Speech perception and implicit memory: Evidence for detailed episodic encoding of phonetic events. *Research on Spoken Language Processing, Progress Report*, No. 24 (pp. 149–167). Speech Research Laboratory, Indiana University, Bloomington.

Lakoff, G. (1982). Categories: An essay in cognitive linguistics. In The Linguistic Society of Korea (Ed.), *Linguistics in the morning calm: Selected papers from SICOL-1981* (pp. 139–193). Seoul: Hanshin.

Lakoff, G. (1987). *Women, fire, and dangerous things: What categories reveal about the mind.* Chicago: University of Chicago Press.

Langacker, R. W. (1987). *Foundations of cognitive grammar, vol. 1: Theoretical prerequisites.* Stanford: Stanford University Press.

MacLaury, R. (1995). Vantage theory. In J. Taylor & R. MacLaury (Eds.), *Language and the cognitive construal of the world* (pp. 231–276). Berlin: Mouton de Gruyter.

McClelland, J., Fiez, J., & McCandliss, B. (2002). Teaching the /r/-/l/ discrimination to Japanese adults: Behavioral and neural aspects. *Physiology and Behavior, 77*, 657–662.

Medin, D. L., & Schaffer, E. J. (1978). Context theory of classification learning. *Psychological Review, 85*, 207–238.

Moon, R. (1998). *Fixed expressions and idioms in English: A corpus-based approach.* Oxford: Oxford University Press.

Murphy, G. (2002). *The big book of concepts.* Cambridge, MA: MIT Press

Murphy, G., & Medin, D. (1985). The role of theories in conceptual coherence. *Psychological Review, 92*, 289–316.

Nathan, G. (1986). Phonemes as mental categories. *Proceedings of the Berkeley Linguistics Society, 12*, 212–223.

Nosofsky, R.M. (1988). Exemplar-based accounts of relations between classification, recognition, and typicality. *Journal of Experimental Psychology: Learning Memory, and Cognition, 14*, 700–708.

Ortony, A., Vondruska, R., Voss, M., & Jones. L. (1985). Salience, similes, and the asymmetry of similarity. *Journal of Memory and Language, 24*, 569–594.

Osherson, D., & Smith, E. (1981). On the adequacy of prototype theory as a theory of concepts. *Cognition, 9*, 35–58.

Pierrehumbert, J. (2001). Exemplar dynamics: Word frequency, lenition and contrast. In Bybee & Hopper (2001), pp. 137–157.

Pierrehumbert, J. (2002). Word-specific phonetics. In C. Gussenhoven & N. Warner (Eds.), *Laboratory phonology 7* (pp. 101–139). Berlin: Mouton de Gruyter.

Posner, M. L. & Keele, S. W. (1968). On the genesis of abstract ideas. *Journal of Experimental Psychology, 77*, 353–363.

Pulman, S. G. (1983). *Word meaning and belief*. London: Croom Helm.

Renouf, A. & Sinclair, J. (1991). Collocational frameworks in English. In K. Aijmer & B. Altenberg (Eds.), *English corpus linguistics* (pp. 128–143). London: Longman.

Rice, S. (2003). Growth of a lexical network: Nine English prepositions in acquisition. In Cuyckens, H., Dirven, R., & Taylor, J. (Eds.) (2003). *Cognitive approaches to lexical semantics* pp. 243–280. Berlin: Mouton de Gruyter.

Rips, L. J. (1975). Inductive judgments about natural categories. *Journal of Verbal Learning and Verbal Behavior, 14*, 665–681.

Rosch. E. (1975a). Cognitive reference points. *Cognitive Psychology, 7*, 532–547.

Rosch, E. (1975b). Cognitive representations of semantic categories. *Journal of Experimental Psychology: General, 104*, 192–233.

Rosch, E. (1977). Human categorization. In N. Warren (Ed.), *Studies in cross-cultural psychology. Vol. 1* (pp. 3–49). London: Academic Press.

Rosch, E. (1978). Principles of categorization. In E. Rosch & B. Lloyd (Eds.), *Cognition and categorization* (pp. 27–48). Hillsdale, NJ: Lawrence Erlbaum. Reprinted in Aarts et al. (2004), pp. 91–108.

Rosch, E., & Mervis, C. B. (1975). Family resemblances: Studies in the internal structure of categories. *Cognitive Psychology, 7*, 573–605.

Ross, B. H., & Makin, V. S. (1999). Prototype versus exemplar models. In R. J. Steinberg (Ed.), *The nature of cognition* (pp. 205–241). Cambridge, MA: MIT Press.

Rothkopf, E. Z. (1971). Incidental memory for location of information page. *Journal of Verbal Learning and Verbal Behavior, 10*, 608–613.

Sandra, D., & Rice, S. (1995). Network analyses of prepositional meaning: Mirroring whose mind—the linguist's or the language user's? *Cognitive Linguistics, 6*, 89–130.

Schacter, D. (1987). Implicit memory: History and current status. *Journal of Experimental Psychology: Learning, Memory, and Cognition, 13*, 501–518.

Smith, E. E., & Medin, D. L. (1981). *Categories and concepts*. Cambridge, MA: Harvard University Press.

Stefanowitch, A., & Gries, S. Th. (2003). Collostructions: Investigating the interaction between words and constructions. *International Journal of Corpus Linguistics, 8*, 209–243.

Stevens, K. (1972). The quantal nature of speech: Evidence from articulatory-acoustic data. In E. E. David & P. D. Denes (Eds.), *Human communication: A unified view* (pp. 51–66). New York: McGraw-Hill.

Sweetser, E. (1987). The definition of *lie*: An examination of the folk models underlying a semantic prototype. In D. Holland & N. Quinn (Eds.), *Cultural models in language and thought* (pp. 43–66). Cambridge: Cambridge University Press.

Taylor, J. R. (1996). *Possessives in English*. Oxford: Oxford University Press.

Taylor, J. R. (1998). Syntactic constructions as prototype categories. In M. Tomasello (Ed.), *The new psychology of language: Cognitive and functional approaches to language structure* (pp. 177–202). Mahwah, NJ: Lawrence Erlbaum.

Taylor, J. R. (2002). *Cognitive grammar*. Oxford: Oxford University Press.

Taylor, J. R. (2003a). *Linguistic categorization*. Oxford: Oxford University Press. First edition: 1989.

Taylor, J. R. (2003b). Near synonyms as co-extensive categories: "High" and "tall" revisited. *Language Sciences, 25*, 263–284.

Taylor, J. R. (2004). Why construction grammar is radical. *Annual Review of Cognitive Linguistics, 2*, 321–348.

Tomasello, M. (2003). *Constructing a language: A usage-based theory of language acquisition*. Cambridge, MA: Harvard University Press.

Tsohatzidis, S. (Ed.) (1990). *Meanings and prototypes: Studies on linguistic categorization*. London: Routledge.

Tuggy, D. (1993). Ambiguity, polysemy, and vagueness. *Cognitive Linguistics, 4*, 273–290.

Tversky, A. 1977. Features of similarity. *Psychological Review, 84*, 327–352.

Uehara, S. (2003). A diachronic perspective on prototypicality: The case of nominal adjectives in Japanese. In Cuyckens, H., Dirven, R., & Taylor, J. (Eds.) (2003). *Cognitive approaches to lexical semantics* pp. 363–391. Berlin: Mouton de Gruyter.

Ungerer, F., & Schmid, H.-J. (1996). *An introduction to cognitive linguistics*. London: Longman.

Verhagen, A. (2005). *Constructions of intersubjectivity: Discourse, syntax, and cognition*. Oxford: Oxford University Press.

Violi, P. (1997). *Significato ed esperienza*. Milan: Bompiani. [*Meaning and experience*, Trans. Jeremy Carden, 2001, Bloomington: Indiana University Press]

Wierzbicka, A. (1985). *Lexicography and conceptual analysis*. Ann Arbor, MI: Karoma.

Wierzbicka, A. 1990. "Prototypes save": On the uses and abuses of the notion of "prototype" in linguistics and related fields. In Tsohatzidis (1990), pp. 347–367. Reprinted in Aarts, B., Denison, D., Keizer, E., & Popova, G. (Eds.) (2004). *Fuzzy grammar: A reader* pp. 461–478. Oxford: Oxford University Press.

Wittgenstein, L. (1978). *Philosophical investigations*. Translated by G. E. M. Anscombe. Oxford: Blackwell.

Wray, A. (2002). *Formulaic language and the lexicon*. Cambridge: Cambridge University Press.

Zlatev, J. (2003). Polysemy or generality? Mu. In Cuyckens, H., Dirven, R., & Taylor, J. (Eds.) (2003). *Cognitive approaches to lexical semantics* pp. 447–494. Berlin: Mouton de Gruyter.

4

COGNITIVE GRAMMAR AS A BASIS FOR LANGUAGE INSTRUCTION

Ronald W. Langacker

Few would maintain that language instruction is easy. Nor can the advice of linguists always be counted on to make it any easier. Unless they are themselves experienced language teachers, the advice of linguists on language pedagogy is likely to be of no more practical value than the advice of theoretical physicists on how to teach pole vaulting. What they can offer, *qua* linguists, is insight into the structure of particular languages and the properties of language in general. But even when limited in this fashion, the input of linguists cannot necessarily be trusted. They quarrel with one another about the most fundamental issues, suggesting that some of them (at least) must be fundamentally wrong. It is therefore unsurprising that the impact of linguistic theory on language pedagogy has been less than miraculous and sometimes less than helpful.

It remains to be seen whether language teaching will fare any better when guided by notions from cognitive linguistics. There are, however, grounds for being optimistic. Compared to other approaches, cognitive linguistics offers an account of language structure that—just from the linguistic standpoint—is arguably more comprehensive, revealing, and descriptively adequate (certainly I have argued this, e.g. in Langacker 1995a). More to the point, the present discussion will focus on three basic features of Cognitive Grammar (Langacker 1987a, 1990, 1991, 1999a) that suggest its potential utility as a basis for language instruction: the centrality of meaning, the meaningfulness of grammar, and its usage-based nature. Although extensive pedagogical application remains a long-term goal, I regard its effectiveness in language teaching to be an important empirical test for the framework.

1 The centrality of meaning

If generative linguistics views syntax as being central to language, Cognitive Linguistics accords this honor to meaning. The latter seems far more natural from the perspective of language users. When ordinary people speak and listen, it is not for the sheer pleasure of manipulating syntactic form—their concern is with the meanings expressed. This does not of course imply that grammar is unimportant in language or in language teaching. It is, however, helpful to realize that grammar subserves meaning rather than being an end in itself.

The centrality of meaning is reflected in a fundamental claim of Cognitive Grammar (henceforth CG), namely that lexicon and grammar form a continuum consisting solely in assemblies of symbolic structures. A **symbolic structure** is nothing more than the pairing of a **semantic structure** and a **phonological structure**. It follows from this claim that grammar itself is meaningful, just as lexical items are. Grammatical meanings are generally more abstract than lexical meanings. This is, however, a matter of degree, so there is no clear line between lexicon and grammar.

Over the years, progress in describing meanings was greatly impeded by certain assumptions which, from the standpoint of cognitive semantics, were simply gratuitous. First is the notion that a given element, such as a lexical item, has just a single linguistic meaning. A glance at any comprehensive dictionary makes this seem quite dubious. Although many details have yet to be resolved (Allwood 2003; Langacker 2006; Sandra & Rice 1995; Zlatev 2003), the basic point that lexical items are frequently **polysemous**—having multiple, related senses—has been established through numerous case studies (e.g. Brugman 1981; Lindner 1982; Tuggy 2003; Tyler & Evans 2003). The polysemy of lexical items is a special case of the general cognitive linguistic claim, also well established, that linguistic categories are usually **complex**: their full description takes the form of a network of related variants (Lakoff 1987; Langacker 1987a; Taylor 2004).

A second standard but gratuitous assumption is that a lexical item's meaning is circumscribed and distinct from general knowledge. Metaphorically, it is like a dictionary entry: a short definition in a special format, capturing everything speakers know about the entities denoted just by virtue of knowing the language. The problem, *pace* Wierzbicka (1995), is the absence of any non-arbitrary way to draw the line (Haiman 1980). Instead of being distinct from general knowledge, lexical meanings recruit and exploit it, representing particular ways of viewing it and making it accessible for linguistic purposes. Though some specifications are clearly more central and frequently accessed than others, virtually any aspect of our knowledge of the entities denoted can be invoked for linguistic purposes (Langacker 1987a, 2003).

   More basic is the assumption that meaning resides in correspondences with the world: the set of entities a word denotes, or the conditions under which a sentence is true. In stark contrast to the objectivist tradition, where the mind is left out of the loop, cognitive semantics views meaning as a mental phenomenon. It resides in conceptualizing activity, whereby we engage the world at many levels: physical, mental, social, cultural, emotional, and imaginative. Crucially, we have the capacity to conceive and portray the same situation in alternate ways. While there may be defaults, there is no completely neutral way to describe situations—expressions necessarily **construe** them in a certain manner. An expression's meaning is therefore only partly determined by objective properties of the situation described (if, indeed, it has any objective existence at all).

   One dimension of construal is **specificity**, i.e. degree of precision and detail. It is reflected in lexical hierarchies like *thing > creature > animal > dog > poodle*, or *do > act > move > run > sprint*. Within such a hierarchy, there is usually a **basic level** (in this case *dog* or *run*) at which we tend to operate lacking any reason to be more specific or more schematic (Rosch 1978). For a given lexical choice, greater specificity can always be achieved through modifiers and more elaborate descriptions. One measure of success in language learning is facility in moving away from basic-level descriptions.

   A second dimension of construal is **prominence**, of which there are various sorts. Two are especially important: profiling and the focal prominence of relational participants. An expression's **profile** is what it designates, i.e. its referent within the array of conceptual content it evokes as the basis for its meaning. For instance, *roof* evokes the conception of a building, within which it profiles the structural portion that covers it on top. *Nephew* designates a male individual who occupies a particular position in a kinship network relative to a reference individual. The word *key* invokes the conception of locks and how they function, profiling an object characterized most essentially by its role in their operation. In diagrams, heavy lines indicate profiling, as in Fig. 4.1(a.).

   Expressions profile either **things** or **relationships**, given very general definitions of those terms (Langacker 1987b). In the case of relational expressions, a second kind of prominence comes into play: the degree of salience conferred on the participants in the profiled relationship. There is generally a primary focal participant, called the **trajector** (tr), and often a secondary focal participant, called the **landmark** (lm). The trajector is the entity being described, located, or otherwise characterized. As shown in Fig. 4.1(b.), *on* profiles a relationship where (prototypically) the trajector is in contact with the upper surface of the landmark, which supports it (double-headed arrow). The verb *move* has two basic senses, sketched in diagrams (c.) and (d.). The intransitive *move* profiles a relationship wherein

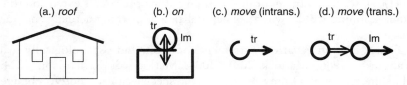

Figure 4.1 Profiling of things and relationships.

the trajector successively occupies a series of locations (single arrow). As a transitive verb, its trajector is characterized as acting on the landmark (double arrow) and thereby causing its motion.

Let us note just one more dimension of construal, namely **perspective**, which is also multifaceted. Among its facets are **vantage point** and **orientation**, implicated in the various interpretations of *Jack was sitting to the left of Jill*. Another facet is the contrast between a **local** and a **global** perspective. For example, (1)(a.) is the sort of thing one would say while actually traveling along the road. What counts as *this road* is then the portion one can see at a given moment. Use of the progressive (*is winding*) indicates that the road (so characterized) changes position through time vis-à-vis the mountains (Langacker 1987b). On the other hand, (1)(b.) is the sort of thing one would say when the entire configuration of road and mountain is apprehended as a single gestalt (e.g. in looking at a map). Use of the simple present tense (*winds*) indicates that their relationship is stable through time.

> (1)(a.) *This road is winding through the mountains.*   [local view]
>   (b.) *This road winds through the mountains.*   [global view]

The pervasive importance of construal shows clearly that linguistic meaning does not reside in the objective nature of the situation described but is crucially dependent on how the situation is apprehended. Indeed, the situation in question is very often a **mental construction** which has no objective existence in the first place. Much of what we express linguistically is **imaginative** in nature, even in talking about actual occurrences. The sentences in (1), for instance, can both be used in reference to an actual configuration of road and mountain. They nonetheless involve what is known as **fictive** (or **virtual**) **motion**: although the road is really stationary, we describe it with expressions (like *wind* and *through the mountains*) normally used for movement along a path:

> (2) *A snake was winding through the grass.*   [actual motion]

In (1)(a.), we construct a sense of motion by imagining distinct road segments (the portions successively in view) as being a single moving entity.

In (1)(b.), we do so by **mentally scanning** along the road's extension (the same scanning we do when conceptualizing something actually moving along it).

Fictive motion is varied, extremely common, and psychologically real (Langacker 1986; Matlock 2001, 2004; Matlock & Richardson 2004; Matsumoto 1996a; Talmy 1996). It is a special case of **fictive change** (Dapremont 2001; Matsumoto 1996b; Sweetser 1997), some further examples of which are given in (3). The president who defies the laws of nature is a fictive entity analogous to the road in (1)(a.). We mentally construct this person by treating different instantiations of the role as if they were a single individual. Past participles like *broken, scattered*, and *sunken* normally designate the situation resulting from a change-of-state process, e.g. a *broken pencil* is one that has undergone the process of breaking. The uses cited, however, do not involve any actual change—*scattered villages* have never been clustered together, nor has a *sunken bathtub* ever actually sunk. The change implied is only virtual, representing the conceived departure of the situation described from the one regarded as canonical.

(3)(a.)   *The company's president keeps getting younger.*
  (b.)   *broken line* (cf. *broken pencil*); *scattered villages* (cf. *scattered marbles*); *sunken bathtub* (cf. *sunken ship*).

Everyday language is replete with references to fictive entities, often invoked for describing actual situations. If we take the sentences in (4) as truthful statements of what the world is actually like, the nominals in bold nevertheless have referents which are only virtual—they are "conjured up" as parts of mental constructions that relate to actuality in various ways. In sentence (a.), a sister is conjured up precisely in order to specify what is not the case. The novel referred to in (b.) exists only in the hypothetical situation introduced by *if*. A generic statement like (c.) represents a generalization about the world's essential structure. As such, it does not refer to any actual kitten or its tail but rather to fictive instances of these types which correspond to open-ended sets of actual ones. Similarly, (d.) makes a generalization about a delimited set of actual boys. The entities directly expressed linguistically are only virtual, however: *each boy* is not any actual boy, nor does *a frog* designate a specific frog; these virtual entities are invoked to describe a virtual relationship taken as corresponding to a contextually determined set of actual ones. Despite their fictivity, these nominals all have referents in the linguistically relevant sense. Observe that the pronoun *it* refers back to the novel in (b.), and to the kitten in (c.).

(4)(a.)   *He doesn't have **a sister**.*
  (b.)   *If she writes **a novel**, she will try to publish **it**.*

(c.) *A **kitten** likes to chase **its tail.***
(d.) ***Each boy** was holding **a frog.***

Much of what we talk about is constructed **metaphorically** (Kövecses 2005; Lakoff & Johnson 1980; Lakoff & Núñez 2000; Turner 1987). In (5), for instance, achieving a goal is metaphorically construed as hitting a target (*aim at*), drug dependency as captivity (*free from*), and the lure of drugs as fishing (*hooked*). Even the preposition *on* is metaphorical: to be *on drugs* is to be in contact with them and require them for support.

(5) *The therapy is aimed at freeing him from the drugs he is hooked on.*

Metaphor is a special case of **blending** (Fauconnier & Turner 2002), where selected elements of two conceptions are projected and integrated to form a third, which is often purely imaginative but nonetheless real as an object of thought. One such case is a cartoon character, e.g. a dog that behaves like a person and thinks in English. *Brunch* is a blend of breakfast and lunch (both conceptually and phonologically). Blending in turn is a special case of **mental space** configurations (Fauconnier 1985, 1997; Fauconnier & Sweetser 1996). In both thought and discourse, we divide our mental world into separate representational "spaces," which are connected to one another in particular ways but nonetheless retain a measure of autonomy. In (4)(b.), *if* introduces a hypothetical space distinct from reality. Generic statements like (4)(c.) pertain to a space representing the world's essential nature (Goldsmith & Woisetschlaeger 1982; Langacker 1999b). In (5), *aim at* implies a goal and thus a person who entertains that goal. The goal is a special mental space within the space representing that person's thoughts.

Though generally implicit, these various kinds of mental constructions are crucial to both the form and meaning of expressions. They are facets of an elaborate **conceptual substrate** that supports and makes coherent the notions overtly expressed. This substrate gives us the freedom to be selective in what we explicitly code linguistically, knowing that the listener can fill in the gaps. It also gives us the freedom to focus on what is salient or easily expressed, at the expense of full accuracy. This is the basis for **metonymy**, in which some entity is invoked by overtly mentioning another, associated entity which calls it to mind (Kövecses & Radden 1998; Langacker 1993; Panther & Radden 2004). Metonymy is utterly pervasive in language. A few examples are given in (6):

(6)(a.) ***I'm** parked down the street.*   [*I* → my car]
　　(b.) ***Chicago** made the playoffs.*   [*Chicago* → team from Chicago]
　　(c.) *She heard **a truck.***   [*a truck* → sound emitted by a truck]

> (d.) ***The omelet*** *is impatient.*   [*the omelet* → the customer who ordered the omelet]
>
> (e.) *I* ***phoned*** *my lawyer.*   [*phoned* → talked to on the phone]

Since language is all about meaning, the findings of cognitive semantics are clearly relevant to language teaching. Most broadly, they show the blatant inadequacy of standard metaphors employed in thinking and talking about language itself: meaning is conceived metaphorically as a substance (*meaning* is a mass noun); words are containers (cf. *empty words*) which hold only limited quantities of this substance; expressions holding ideas are conveyed from the speaker to the hearer (*get the idea across*); so understanding an expression is just a matter of opening the containers and combining the thoughts they hold (Reddy 1979). But it is simply not true that an expression's meaning is "in" its words. Words are merely prompts for an elaborate process of meaning construction that draws on the full range of our mental resources. An appreciation of their richness and flexibility would seem essential for effective language instruction, especially at advanced levels. It is also a worthy educational goal, even for first language instruction.

More specific pedagogical implications are limited only by the availability of cogent and detailed analyses. For example, Kövecses (2001) has suggested—and to some extent shown empirically—that the learning of idioms is facilitated by apprehension of their metaphorical motivation. Along the same lines, Kurtyka (2001) reports positive results in using cognitive semantic descriptions as a basis for teaching phrasal verbs. It stands to reason that the teaching and/or learning of these verb + particle combinations would be aided by the realization that the choice of particle, rather than being arbitrary, virtually always has a semantic rationale (Lindner 1982; Rudzka-Ostyn 2003). It is likewise pertinent to realize that a particular element does not have a single, fixed meaning but rather an array of senses related in principled ways to its prototypical value. Consider *on*. Prototypically it designates a physical relationship in which the trajector is supported by the landmark and in contact with its upper surface (e.g. *the cat on the mat*). Other uses are then obtained by suspending one or more of its specifications: that the surface be an upper one (*the painting on the wall*); the notion of support (*the spots on that cow*); or that of contact (*the accent marks on these vowels*). Still other uses can be seen as metaphorical applications of these same features (e.g. contact and support for *on drugs*).

The basic point is that conventional usage almost always has conceptual motivation. Though it has to be learned, it represents a particular way of construing the situation described. With proper instruction, the learning of a usage is thus a matter of grasping the semantic "spin" it imposes, a far more natural and enjoyable process than sheer memorization. The pedagogical challenge is then to determine the optimal means of leading students to this understanding.

2 The meaningfulness of grammar

A conceptualist semantics that properly accommodates construal makes possible a symbolic account of grammar. Like lexicon, with which it forms a gradation, grammar reduces to form-meaning pairings. All the elements correctly invoked in grammatical description should thus have semantic import, however schematic they might be in terms of conceptual content. The meaningfulness of grammar must obviously be recognized in devising strategies for teaching it.

From the CG perspective, the first order of business in analyzing grammar is to ascertain the meanings of grammatical structures and the elements invoked to describe them. These include both general descriptive notions (e.g. noun, verb, subject, object, clause) and the grammatical formatives (markers or function words) of particular languages. Semantic characterizations are possible when it is recognized that such elements are often polysemous, that their meanings are usually quite abstract, and that meaning resides in conceptualization (not in correspondences with the world).

These points invalidate standard arguments for the doctrine—found in almost every linguistics textbook—that basic grammatical notions like noun, verb, subject, and object cannot be semantically characterized. It is presupposed that the only possible characterizations would be notions like "(physical) thing," "event," "agent," and "patient," pertaining to objective properties of the entities involved. The arguments then consist in showing that such definitions are inappropriate for many instances, e.g. a noun like *explosion* (which refers to an event) or the subject of a passive (which is non-agentive). But this is comparable to looking for your car keys under the street light instead of where you dropped them. Any general definition would have to be considerably more abstract, and would have to be based on conceptual factors rather than objective properties. The characterizations proposed in CG are based on factors justified independently as being necessary for semantic description.

Briefly, an expression's basic category depends on the nature of its profile (not its overall conceptual content). A verb profiles a **process**, characterized schematically as a relationship followed sequentially in its evolution through time. *Move* is thus a verb, as it profiles the change through time in a spatial relationship. On the other hand, *mover* is a noun, even though it evokes the same conceptual content. It is a noun because it profiles a **thing**, specifically the trajector of the verb it derives from, as shown in Fig. 4.2. A thing is defined abstractly as any product of two (a.) *move* (verb)   (b.) *mover* (noun)

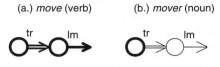

Figure 4.2 Contrasting profiles.

fundamental conceptual operations, namely grouping and reification. Many nouns designate groups: *team, stack, herd, set, convoy,* etc. Reification is the treatment of a group as a unitary entity for higher-level cognitive purposes (e.g. in assessing a *herd* as large, even when all the animals constituting it are small). In the case of physical objects, the prototype for nouns, these operations occur automatically at a low level of processing, leaving us unaware of constitutive entities.

Likewise, the correlation of subject and object with the semantic roles agent and patient, or subject with discourse topic, is at best only prototypical. Schematic characterizations valid for all instances have to be independent of specific conceptual content and discourse status. From the CG standpoint, they find a natural basis in the focal prominence of relational participants: a subject specifies the trajector of a profiled relationship, and an object specifies the landmark. It is further suggested that this primary and secondary focal prominence resides in the participants being invoked as initial and subsequent **reference points** in building up to the full conception of the profiled relation (Langacker 1993, 1999c, 2001a, 2001b). This dynamic characterization meshes with Chafe's description of a subject as the "starting point" for apprehending a clause (Chafe 1994).

The conceptual definability of basic grammatical notions makes evident the meaningfulness of grammatical formatives. Among these are derivational elements, such as *-er*, which combines with a verb to derive a noun. Since these categories are meaningful, so are elements effecting a change of category membership. What *-er* contributes semantically to a form like *mover* is an aspect of construal: the specification that it profiles the verb stem's trajector—a thing—rather than the overall process it designates. Similarly, any elements affecting the choice of subject or object are meaningful by virtue of conferring focal prominence on particular relational participants. For instance, a passive marker confers trajector status on what would otherwise be a clausal landmark.

Conceptual characterizations have been offered in CG for numerous parade examples of "purely grammatical" markers. For example, the auxiliary verb *do* is semantically equivalent to the schematic description of the verb class: it profiles a process, i.e. a relationship tracked through time. Since it does not specify any particular kind of process, it is used as a "pro form" for clauses, referring back to a previously mentioned process (just as a pronoun refers back to a nominal referent): *She does; They did.* The preposition *of* indicates that the relationship between its trajector and landmark is somehow intrinsic rather than contingent (Langacker 1992). Thus it is used for part–whole relations (*the sole of my foot*), for identity (*the month of January*), to specify the participants in a reified process (*the shooting of the hunters*), etc. Note that we say *the color of the lawn* but *the brown spot in (*of) my lawn*, the difference being that the spot is not supposed to be there. Another case is the (non-reflexive) *se* that occurs with many Spanish verbs: *sentarse* "sit," *caerse* "fall," *lavarse* "wash," *enojarse* "get mad," *ahogarse* "drown," etc. Though polysemous, it has been shown by Maldonado (1988, 1999) to be consistently meaningful. Its various senses are natural extensions from a prototype that is intermediate between a prototypical transitive and a prototypical intransitive (hence the term "middle voice"). While the trajector has patient-like properties, there is also a notion of force or agentivity, without however invoking an agent distinct from the trajector.

Grammar consists primarily in patterns for combining simpler expressions into more complex ones. Complex expressions are called **constructions**, and the patterns they instantiate are **constructional schemas**. In CG, a construction is simply an assembly of symbolic structures linked by **correspondences**. Consider expressions where a prepositional phrase modifies a noun: *the table by the window, a cabin in the woods, the roof on that house,* etc. The schema for such expressions is sketched in Fig. 4.3. Two levels of organization are shown. At the lower level, a preposition (P) combines with a nominal expression (N) to form a prepositional phrase (P+N); P and N are **component structures** at this level, while P+N is the **composite structure** resulting from their combination. At the higher level of organization, the component structures N and P+N combine to yield the composite structure N P+N. The two nominal expressions

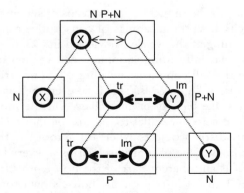

Figure 4.3 A constructional schema.

profile things (represented as circles), with X and Y abbreviating their additional semantic content. The preposition designates a relationship (shown as an arrow) between two things characterized only schematically.

Correspondences, given as dotted lines, indicate how component structures at each level are conceptually integrated to form the composite structure. At the lower level, the nominal profile corresponds to the preposition's landmark. The composite structure results from merging the specifications of the corresponding elements while preserving the profile of the preposition. Because it inherits its profile from the preposition (which is thus the **head** at this level), the composite expression is a prepositional phrase (rather than a nominal). This prepositional phrase then modifies the other nominal element at the higher level of organization. Here the nominal profile corresponds to the schematic trajector of the prepositional relation. At this level it is the nominal that imposes its profile (making it the head), so the overall expression is nominal rather than relational. Taken as a whole, for example, *the roof on that house* profiles the roof.

The various aspects of construal needed for describing lexical meanings also figure in the description of complex expressions. In particular, profiling and trajector/landmark organization are pivotal in grammatical constructions. *On that house* is a prepositional phrase because it profiles a relationship rather than a thing, and *that house* is the prepositional object because its profile corresponds to *on*'s landmark. Similarly, the overall expression is nominal rather than prepositional because it profiles a thing, and the head noun *roof* is the subject of the prepositional phrase because its profile corresponds to the latter's trajector. The profiling and correspondences in Fig. 4.3 are specified by the constructional schema describing this grammatical pattern, hence they are characteristic of all the expressions which instantiate it. They constitute the **constructional meaning** of the pattern, which particular instantiations elaborate based on the lexical elements chosen.

Constructional schemas can also be thought of as patterns of **semantic composition**, since they specify how the meanings of constitutive elements combine to form the meaning of the whole. As viewed in CG, however, semantic structure is only **partially compositional**, since we draw on many resources in arriving at the full composite meaning—it is not true than an expression's meaning is "in" its words. This is so even for seemingly straightforward examples like *the roof on that house*. On the most likely interpretation, it is not precisely parallel to *the vase on that table*, since the vase and the table are distinct objects, whereas the roof and the house are not. Based on our knowledge of typical scenarios in everyday life, we presume that the roof is an inherent part of the house, not that the roof from some other building is resting on the house's own roof. (Given a proper context, e.g. in describing the aftermath of a hurricane, this default assumption may of course be overridden.) Just because the trajector and landmark are non-distinct, this usage of *on* is non-prototypical. We would normally say *the roof of the house*, recognizing the intrinsic nature of their part–whole relationship. By using *on* instead, we highlight the role of the house in supporting the roof, as well as suggesting that their relationship is non-intrinsic (i.e. the roof in question is not the only one the house might have had—it is considered in relation to other possible sorts of roof).

On the CG account, therefore, grammar consists in patterns for assembling not just complex expressions but also complex meanings. It incorporates particular ways of construing conceptual content and symbolizing the construal imposed on it. Besides the sorts of prominence already indicated, the construal embodied in grammar includes the related factors of perspective and sequentiality in the evocation of conceived entities. A local vs. a global perspective was exemplified in (1). Another difference in perspective is whether a situation is viewed in terms of interacting participants or in terms of how the scene is organized. Illustrating the latter are numerous constructions that first introduce a setting or location and then indicate what is found there. In some of these constructions the setting or location is focused as trajector, making it the grammatical subject:

(7)(a.) **The streets** *were lined with spectators.* [cf. *Spectators lined the streets.*]

(b.) **This year** *has seen some big events.* [cf. *Some big events have occurred this year.*]

(c.) **It** *appears that she's quite smart.* [cf. *She appears to be quite smart.*]

(d.) **There** *are problems with that theory.* [cf. *That theory has problems.*]

The setting in (7)(b.) is temporal rather than spatial. The *it* in (7)(c.) is an abstract setting, something like the scope of awareness for the following judgment (Langacker 2004). In (7)(d.), *there* is an abstract realm of existence.

If not the grammatical subject, a setting or location can nonetheless be initial in terms of word order:

(8) **On the mat** *was a lazy cat.* [cf. *A lazy cat was on the mat.*]

This represents the discourse strategy of first directing attention to a known location as a way of introducing a new participant found there. It exemplifies sequentiality as a dimension of construal. Another, more striking example is the contrast in (9):

(9)(a.) *The cookies are in the pantry, on the bottom shelf, in a plastic container.*

(b.) *The cookies are in a plastic container, on the bottom shelf, in the pantry.*

Both sentences use the same locative phrases to describe exactly the same spatial configuration. They are nevertheless semantically distinct by virtue of imposing different ways of mentally accessing it: the conceptual experience is that of "zooming in" vs. "zooming out." This is just one of many grammatical phenomena whose essential import resides in sequence of mental access (Langacker 1993, 2001b).

These brief examples merely hint at the conceptual richness embodied and reflected in grammatical structure. The fact that grammar is meaningful, not an autonomous formal system, creates the potential for new and different approaches in teaching and learning it. Being conventionally determined, the proper form of expression does of course require instruction. Learning grammar does not, however, have to be the soulless internalization of arbitrary restrictions. If properly analyzed, every grammatical element makes a semantic contribution and every grammatical distinction has conceptual import. Awareness of these factors offers a basis for effective language instruction aimed at their full exploitation in thought and communication. How can this be achieved? Not being qualified to make specific pedagogical recommendations, I will limit myself to some general considerations.

A point not yet mentioned is the extensive **iconicity** of grammar (Givón 1991; Haiman 1983, 1985). The symbolic nature of grammar does not imply that the form–meaning pairings are simply arbitrary. On the contrary, the symbolization of grammatical notions invariably has some kind or degree of conceptual motivation. Usually, for example, the more tenuous meanings of grammatical elements are paralleled by their more tenuous phonological realizations: the latter tend to be shorter than lexical items, and are often affixes or inflections rather than independent words. A well-known iconic principle is that elements which belong together semantically generally occur together phonologically. To state this more precisely in CG terms, the conceptual integration effected by grammatical constructions tends to be symbolized by phonological adjacency. With respect to Fig. 4.3, the semantic relationship between a preposition and its object is symbolized by placing the object nominal directly after the preposition. Likewise, a prepositional phrase is placed directly after the nominal expression it modifies to symbolize that relationship. A further dimension of iconicity is the tendency for the sequencing of words to mirror the sequence of events or some other conceptual ordering (Langacker 2001b). In (8), word order implements the discourse strategy of using a known location to anchor the introduction of a new participant. The contrasting orders in (9) represent alternate natural paths for arriving at the full conception of a complex spatial configuration. However it might be exploited pedagogically, the iconicity of grammar is an important factor in its learnability.

Cognitive linguistic notions are also potentially helpful in showing connections among the varied uses of a grammatical element or construction. Why should possessives, for instance, be used in expressions like *Lincoln's assassination* (since Lincoln was hardly the "owner" of this event, even metaphorically)? The answer lies in the conceptual characterization of *'s* and the possessive construction (Langacker 1995b, 2001a; Taylor 1996). Their wide range of conventional usage, exemplified in (10), covers far more than ownership, part–whole, and kinship relationships, which all have some claim to prototypicality:

(10) *Sam's house; my neck; the girl's mother; our town; the cat's fleas; your bus; the store's location; their anxiety; Zelda's problem; his height; the year's biggest event; my driving; anyone's guess; Booth's assassination [of Lincoln]; Lincoln's assassination [by Booth].*

The prototypical senses are special cases of a schematic characterization based on a mental operation rather than any specific conceptual content. Possessives manifest our capacity for invoking one conceived entity as a **reference point** in establishing mental contact with another, i.e. for mentally accessing a **target** via and in relation to the reference point. Out of all the houses in the world, *Sam's house* directs attention to a particular instance of that type, namely the one mentally accessible via Sam. This would typically be the house he lives in, but given the proper context it might also be the house he owns and rents out, the one he dreams of owning someday, the one he designed, the one he is scheduled to paint next week, etc. Recall now that the focal prominence of trajector and landmark was ascribed to their functioning as conceptual reference points for purposes of building up to the full conception of a profiled relationship. On this account both the agent and the patient of *assassinate* are reference points for purposes of conceptualizing (mentally accessing) the profiled event. For this reason either one can be coded as possessor of the derived noun *assassination*, obtained from *assassinate* by conceptual reification: *Booth's assassination; Lincoln's assassination.*

More generally, it is helpful to realize that grammatical elements of any sort are likely to be polysemous, having a prototypical meaning as well as an array of other, less central values possibly susceptible to schematic characterization. It may not be true that the possessive construction carries the meaning of ownership, but neither is it appropriate to ignore the centrality of this particular kind of reference point relationship (nor that of part–whole and kinship relations). Indeed, full mastery of the construction implies awareness of a wide range of usage possibilities like those in (10), since there is no assurance that every type of usage that conforms to the schematic meaning is conventionally exploited in the language. Similarly, while it is important to realize that nouns are not simply the names for physical objects, and that subjects are agents only prototypically, it is also useful to know that these notions are indeed central to the categories, a conceptual core which is grounded in physical experience and provides a basis for extension to more abstract or less typical values.

Finally, grammar is less mysterious when it is recognized that the form of expressions is shaped by an elaborate, multifaceted conceptual substrate. Grammatical peculiarities are commonly the visible trace of tacit, often imaginative mental constructions which are readily grasped by native speakers even when they fail to cross the threshold of explicit awareness. A simple example concerns the prepositional phrase in (11):

(11) *It's pretty through that valley.*

Normally a *through*-phrase modifies a motion verb and specifies the path traversed (as in (2)). But (11) has no such verb—indeed, *it's pretty* describes a static situation. So what does *through the valley* modify? Instead of modifying an overt element, it itself evokes the conception of someone traveling through the valley and observing its appearance. Moreover, this travel scenario may be entirely fictive. It cannot be identified with ongoing movement by the current speaker (as it might if *that* were changed to *this*). Nor is it necessarily based on memory or knowledge of any specific journey. It may be just an imagined journey, on the part of an imagined representative viewer, conjured up as a way of describing the valley.

The general point is that an expression's semantic and grammatical coherence is often dependent on imagined scenarios or other tacit conceptions. As one more example, this is the key to understanding non-present uses of the English present tense (Langacker 2001c), as in (12):

(12)(a.) *I come home last night and a stranger opens the door.*
   (b.) *The children leave for camp next week.*
   (c.) *A kitten is born with blue eyes.*

Inter alia, the so-called present tense is used for past events (the "historical present"), anticipated future occurrences, and "timeless" statements (such as generics). The label is not really a misnomer, however. These uses are based on particular mental constructions in the context of which an instance of the profiled process coincides with the time of speaking. The coincident process is not, however, actual but rather virtual—a fictive occurrence that serves as a representation of one or more actual ones. In

(12)(a.), the profiled events belong to a mental "replay" of a previous episode. Sentence (12)(b.) does not refer directly to the actual event of leaving (as would be the case with the future *will*); it amounts instead to "reading off" an entry on a conceptual plan or schedule, where each entry represents a planned future occurrence. Invoked in (12)(c.) is something like a "blueprint," a supposed representation of the world's essential nature. In this generic expression, the kitten and the process of its being born are virtual entities, corresponding to an open-ended set of actual instances. These sentences are in the present tense because the profiled occurrences are part of a mental construction—the replay, the schedule, or the blueprint—immediately available at the time of speaking.

3 A usage-based approach

A final aspect of CG that makes it relevant for language teaching is its **usage-based** nature (Barlow & Kemmer 2000; Langacker 2000). A language comprises an immense inventory of conventionally established elements (lexical items, formatives, grammatical constructions, sound patterns, etc.) which fluent speakers learn as **units**, i.e. they are thoroughly mastered and can thus be employed in largely automatic fashion. Conventional units are abstracted from **usage events**: actual instances of language use, in their full phonetic detail and contextual understanding. A crucial factor in this process is the reinforcing of features that recur across a sufficient number of such events. Since every usage event is unique at the level of fine-grained detail, the recurring commonalities are apparent only at a certain level of abstraction. To some extent, therefore, all linguistic units—even the most specific—are schematic relative to the usage events in which they figure. Fine-grained differences fail to be reinforced and are therefore filtered out as units emerge.

The emphasis is thus on actual learning. Whatever might be its innate basis, mastering a language requires the specific, usage-based learning of a vast array of conventional units. This itself has pedagogical implications (which may seem obvious but are not so in every linguistic theory). It suggests the importance of providing the learner with sufficient exposure to representative uses of a given unit. Ideally, moreover, this exposure should occur in the context of meaningful exchanges approximating socially and culturally normal usage events. In this respect the usage-based approach resonates with the natural approach to language teaching (Achard 2004).

From a usage-based perspective, a basic question is the degree of abstraction relative to usage events. Given that all units derive from such events by schematization, it remains to determine just how schematic they might be. There is no real doubt that linguistic units run the gamut from highly specific to highly schematic. We have noted this in regard to the meanings of lexical items (e.g. *do* > *act* > *move* > *run* > *sprint*). In CG, grammatical structures are schematic relative to instantiating expressions: the constructional schema in Fig. 4.3, for example, is a schematized representation of particular expressions like *a cabin in the woods, the roof on that house,* etc. Phonologists find good reason to characterize sounds at different levels of abstraction, for instance [i] < [HIGH VOWEL] < [VOWEL] < [SEGMENT].

In the case of grammar, degree of abstraction figures in several contentious theoretical issues. The first is whether—as claimed in CG—grammatical structures are in fact simply schematized representations of complex expressions. On this account they consist in assemblies of symbolic structures fully reducible to form–meaning pairings. With certain qualifications (Langacker 2005a, 2005b), CG shares this outlook with Construction Grammar (Fillmore, Kay, & O'Connor 1988; Goldberg 1995). It is not, however, standard linguistic doctrine. A second issue is the relative importance of higher- versus lower-level schemas, and a third is whether we learn both schemas and specific instantiations of them. These latter issues pertain to the abstractness and hence the generality of linguistic knowledge. Theorists have a natural tendency to look for the broadest generalizations, corresponding to highly schematic descriptions. Broad generalizations should of course be sought. Still, it cannot be taken for granted that speakers have the same proclivity. One aspect of the usage-based approach is the notion that speakers rely extensively on low-level schemas and specific learned expressions, even when these conform to general patterns.

The learning of specific forms is obviously necessary in cases of irregularity or limited productivity. At the extreme we find the student's nightmare of complex morphological paradigms that simply have to be memorized, e.g. the conjugations of irregular verbs. For this CG and the usage-based approach have no magic cure. They do, however, suggest the reasonableness of what usually occurs in practice. What typically does not occur is that a student thoroughly learns all the forms of a complex paradigm—e.g. all the person, number, tense, and mood inflections of an irregular verb—and instantaneously retrieves them as needed in actual use. Instead, students tend to do what children presumably do in learning a language natively: the forms they learn first and learn best are those which occur most frequently. Aiding the learning process are many low-level generalizations (e.g. several verbs forming their past tense in analogous fashion). Eventually an awareness develops of all the dimensions represented in paradigms, patterns (morphological schemas) emerge for constructing any desired regular form, and a large number of irregular forms are learned with different degrees of thoroughness. This is not to say that paradigms should never be studied as such. But that should not be thought of as the primary means of learning what is needed for fluent speech.

The opposite extreme, that of full productivity and regularity, is far less prevalent than theoretical attitudes would lead one to expect. Much of our knowledge of grammar resides in intermediate cases: patterns usable with multiple lexical items, perhaps even an open-ended set, but not with every member of a basic category. A well-known construction of this sort is the English ditransitive, where a verb has two object-like complements, e.g. *She gave her brother a watch*. Naturally, the verbs occurring in this pattern are limited to those involving three central participants. A further restriction is that the verbal action has a causal relationship in regard to the situation of the first object possessing or having access to the second (e.g. the giving results in her brother having a watch). Observe that this causal relationship may be negative rather than positive (*She denied them permission to interview me*), and instead of actually bringing about the situation it may represent only a commitment to do so (*She promised her brother a watch*). Quite a number of verbs satisfy this schematic characterization. Yet not every verb which does is conventionally used in ditransitives. For instance, while *get* appears in this construction (*She got her brother a watch*), *obtain* does not (*She obtained her brother a watch*). Also excluded are *provide, supply, donate, contribute, deprive*, etc.

Hence the distributional facts do not lend themselves to a single, fully predictive generalization. But neither is the picture one of randomness or complete idiosyncrasy. If the construction cannot be adequately described by means of a global generalization, promising absolute predictability, it nonetheless exhibits considerable regularity in the form of local generalizations, which offer degrees of motivation for the observed distribution (Goldberg 1992, 1995). In other words, the ditransitive construction represents a complex category whose full description consists in a network of related variants centered on a prototype. The prototypical pattern is for the verb to profile an act of transfer from agent to recipient (e.g. *give, send, hand, mail, throw, bring*). In another basic pattern, the agent creates an object with the intent of the recipient having access to it (*cook, bake, knit, build, make, write*). Somewhat more peripheral are verbs of commitment, either positive (*promise, owe, permit, allow, guarantee*) or negative (*refuse, deny*). Alternate groupings may of course be proposed, as well as various subgroups. The point, however, is that the distribution is anchored by particular, fairly frequent verbs well established in the construction. These verbs form clusters on the basis of semantic similarity, and certain clusters give rise to constructional subschemas capable of being used productively.

This organization provides the basis for devising pedagogical strategy. The obvious suggestion is to start with the prototype and then move on to other major clusters, in each case focusing initially on the most frequent and basic verbs. Full mastery of the construction, with native-like knowledge of the conventional range of usage, will come about only gradually through long-term practice with the language. But the same is true of its learning by native speakers.

The ditransitive is not atypical of the pedagogical challenge posed by grammar overall. Fully general and exceptionless rules are themselves the exception. Instead of being monolithic, most constructions exist in multiple variants, with schemas abstracted to represent what is common to different sets of them. At the lowest level are constructional variants that incorporate a particular lexical item well established in the pattern. Such units thus include both specific and schematic elements, providing one argument against any sharp distinction between lexicon and grammar. Thorough knowledge of a construction resides in the entire network of variants (rather than any single unit), and lower-level structures are often the most important in determining conventional usage.

This leads to a final but possibly crucial pedagogical implication of the usage-based approach. A substantial proportion of what is needed to speak a language fluently tends to be ignored because it is part of neither lexicon nor grammar as these are traditionally conceived. What I have in mind are the countless units representing normal ways of saying things. Native speakers control an immense inventory of conventional expressions and patterns of expression enabling them to handle a continuous flow of rapid speech (Langacker 1987a: 35–36, 2001d). While they can certainly be included, I am not referring to lexical items of the sort found in dictionaries, nor even to recognized idioms. At issue instead are particular ways of phrasing certain notions out of all the ways they could in principle be expressed in accordance with the lexicon and grammar of the language. These units can be of any size, ranging from standard collocations to large chunks of boilerplate language. They can be fully specific or partially schematic, allowing options in certain positions.

In fluent speech, piecing together these prefabricated chunks is at least as important as productively invoking lexical and grammatical units. Native speakers cannot avoid using them—here are some examples from the previous paragraph: *leads to; a substantial proportion; speak a language fluently; tends to be ignored; as . . . traditionally conceived; what I have in mind; continuous flow; rapid speech; I am not referring to; nor even; at issue; out of all the . . .; in principle; in accordance with; of any size; ranging from . . . to . . .; large chunks of . . .; boilerplate language.* Given the prevalence of conventional expressions, as well as their critical role in fluency and idiomaticity, finding effective ways to facilitate their learning would seem essential.

4 Conclusion

Of necessity (given its source), this discussion has been long on theory and short on practical recommendations. Nor have the sample descriptions been anything more than fragmentary. If we nevertheless suppose that CG concepts and descriptions are relevant for language instruction, a basic question remains to be addressed: Just who are they relevant to? The main possibilities are the student, the instructor, and those responsible for designing curricula or developing teaching materials. Assuming their validity, explicit awareness of CG notions would seem most clearly helpful for the latter. With effective materials and a sensible curriculum, an instructor with lesser awareness of CG insights can nonetheless still exploit them. And students would hopefully benefit even if they are never exposed to theoretical concepts or explicit analyses. I cannot help thinking, however, that the cognitive linguistic view of language is a matter of universal interest, and that its conceptual descriptions of linguistic phenomena are sufficiently natural and revealing to be widely appreciated. In some form, I can imagine these ideas being an integral part of general education or first language instruction. I can further imagine them as being useful in second language learning, especially at more advanced levels.

Bibliography

Achard, M. (2004). Grammatical instruction in the natural approach: A cognitive grammar view. In M. Achard and S. Niemeier (Eds.), *Cognitive linguistics, second language acquisition, and foreign language teaching* (pp. 165–194). Berlin and New York: Mouton de Gruyter. Studies on Language Acquisition 18.

Allwood, J. (2003). Meaning potentials and context: Some consequences for the analysis of variation in meaning. In H. Cuyckens, R. Dirven, & J. R. Taylor (Eds.), *Cognitive approaches to lexical semantics* (pp. 29–65). Berlin and New York: Mouton de Gruyter. Cognitive Linguistics Research 23.

Barlow, M., & Kemmer, S. (Eds.) (2000). *Usage-based models of language*. Stanford: CSLI Publications.

Brugman, C. (1981). *The story of over*. Berkeley: University of California masters thesis.

Chafe, W. (1994). *Discourse, consciousness, and time: The flow and displacement of conscious experience in speaking and writing*. Chicago and London: University of Chicago Press.

Dapremont, E. M. (2001). Assembled data, mounting evidence: Conceptual contrasts between past and present participle based change. Paper presented at the 7th International Cognitive Linguistics Conference, Santa Barbara.

Fauconnier, G. (1985). *Mental spaces: Aspects of meaning construction in natural language*. Cambridge, MA and London: MIT Press.

Fauconnier, G. (1997). *Mappings in thought and language*. Cambridge: Cambridge University Press.

Fauconnier, G., & Sweetser, E. (Eds.) (1996). *Spaces, worlds, and grammar*. Chicago and London: University of Chicago Press.

Fauconnier, G., & Turner, M. (2002). *The way we think: Conceptual blending and the mind's hidden complexities*. New York: Basic Books.

Fillmore, C. J., Kay, P., & O'Connor, M. C. (1988). Regularity and idiomaticity in grammatical constructions: The case of *let alone*. *Language, 64*, 501–538.

Givón, T. (1991). Isomorphism in the grammatical code: Cognitive and biological considerations. *Studies in Language, 15*, 85–114.

Goldberg, A. E. (1992). The inherent semantics of argument structure: The case of the English ditransitive construction. *Cognitive Linguistics, 3*, 37–74.

Goldberg, A. E. (1995). *Constructions: A construction grammar approach to argument structure*. Chicago and London: University of Chicago Press.

Goldsmith, J., & Woisetschlaeger, E. (1982). The logic of the English progressive. *Linguistic Inquiry, 13*, 79–89.

Haiman, J. (1980). Dictionaries and encyclopedias. *Lingua, 50*, 329–357.

Haiman, J. (1983). Iconic and economic motivation. *Language, 59*, 781–819.

Haiman, J. (Ed.) (1985). *Iconicity in syntax*. Amsterdam and Philadelphia: John Benjamins. Typological Studies in Language 6.

Kövecses, Z. (2001). A cognitive linguistic view of learning idioms in an FLT context. In M. Pütz, S. Niemeier, & R. Dirven (Eds.), *Applied cognitive linguistics II: Language pedagogy* (pp. 87–115). Berlin and New York: Mouton de Gruyter. Cognitive Linguistics Research 19.2.

Kövecses, Z. (2005). *Metaphor in culture: Universality and variation*. Cambridge: Cambridge University Press.

Kövecses, Z., & Radden, G. (1998). Metonymy: Developing a cognitive linguistic view. *Cognitive Linguistics, 9*, 37–77.

Kurtyka, A. (2001). Teaching English phrasal verbs: A cognitive approach. In M. Pütz, S. Niemeier, & R. Dirven (Eds.), *Applied cognitive linguistics II: Language pedagogy* (pp. 29–54). Berlin and New York: Mouton de Gruyter. Cognitive Linguistics Research 19.2.

Lakoff, G. (1987). *Women, fire, and dangerous things: What categories reveal about the mind*. Chicago and London: University of Chicago Press.

Lakoff, G., and Johnson, M. (1980). *Metaphors we live by*. Chicago and London: University of Chicago Press.

Lakoff, G., and Núñez, R. E. (2000). *Where mathematics comes from: How the embodied mind brings mathematics into being*. New York: Basic Books.

Langacker, R. W. (1986). Abstract motion. *Proceedings of the Annual Meeting of the Berkeley Linguistics Society, 12*, 455–471.

Langacker, R. W. (1987a). *Foundations of cognitive grammar*, vol. 1, *Theoretical prerequisites*. Stanford: Stanford University Press.

Langacker, R. W. (1987b). Nouns and verbs. *Language, 63*, 53–94.

Langacker, R. W. (1990). *Concept, image, and symbol: The cognitive basis of grammar*. Berlin and New York: Mouton de Gruyter. Cognitive Linguistics Research 1.

Langacker, R. W. (1991). *Foundations of cognitive grammar*, vol. 2, *Descriptive application*. Stanford: Stanford University Press.

Langacker, R. W. (1992). The symbolic nature of cognitive grammar: The meaning of *of* and of *of*-periphrasis. In M. Pütz (Ed.), *Thirty years of linguistic evolution: Studies in honour of René Dirven on the occasion of his sixtieth birthday* (pp. 483–502). Philadelphia and Amsterdam: John Benjamins.

Langacker, R. W. (1993). Reference-point constructions. *Cognitive Linguistics, 4*, 1–38.

Langacker, R. W. (1995a). Raising and transparency. *Language, 71*, 1–62.

Langacker, R. W. (1995b). Possession and possessive constructions. In J. R. Taylor

& R. E. MacLaury (Eds.), *Language and the cognitive construal of the world* (pp. 51–79). Berlin and New York: Mouton de Gruyter. Trends in Linguistics Studies and Monographs 82.

Langacker, R. W. (1999a). *Grammar and conceptualization.* Berlin and New York: Mouton de Gruyter. Cognitive Linguistics Research 14.

Langacker, R. W. (1999b). Virtual reality. *Studies in the Linguistic Sciences, 29 (2),* 77–103.

Langacker, R. W. (1999c). Assessing the cognitive linguistic enterprise. In T. Janssen & G. Redeker (Eds.), *Cognitive linguistics: Foundations, scope, and methodology* (pp. 13–59). Berlin and New York: Mouton de Gruyter. Cognitive Linguistics Research 15.

Langacker, R. W. (2000). A dynamic usage-based model. In M. Barlow & S. Kemmer (Eds.), *Usage-based models of language* (pp. 1–63). Stanford: CSLI Publications.

Langacker, R. W. (2001a). Topic, subject, and possessor. In H. G. Simonsen & R. T. Endresen (Eds.), *A Cognitive approach to the verb: Morphological and constructional perspectives* (pp. 11–48). Berlin and New York: Mouton de Gruyter. Cognitive Linguistics Research 16.

Langacker, R. W. (2001b). Dynamicity in grammar. *Axiomathes, 12,* 7–33.

Langacker, R. W. (2001c). The English present tense. *English Language and Linguistics, 5,* 251–271.

Langacker, R. W. (2001d). Cognitive linguistics, language pedagogy, and the English present tense. In M. Pütz, S. Niemeier, & R. Dirven (Eds.), *Applied cognitive linguistics I: Theory and language acquisition* (pp. 3–39). Berlin and New York: Mouton de Gruyter. Cognitive Linguistics Research 19.1.

Langacker, R. W. (2003). Context, cognition, and semantics: A unified dynamic approach. In E. van Wolde (Ed.), *Job 28: Cognition in context* (pp. 179–230). Leiden and Boston: Brill. Biblical Interpretation Series 64.

Langacker, R. W. (2004). Aspects of the grammar of finite clauses. In M. Achard & S. Kemmer (Eds.), *Language, culture and mind* (pp. 535–577). Stanford: CSLI Publications.

Langacker, R. W. (2005a). Construction grammars: Cognitive, radical, and less so. In F. J. Ruiz de Mendoza Ibáñez & M. S. Peña Cervel (Eds.), *Cognitive linguistics: Internal dynamics and interdisciplinary interaction* (pp. 101–159). Berlin and New York: Mouton de Gruyter. Cognitive Linguistics Research 32.

Langacker, R. W. (2005b). Integration, grammaticization, and constructional meaning. In M. Fried & H. C. Boas (Eds.), *Grammatical constructions: Back to the roots* (pp. 157–189). Amsterdam and Philadelphia: John Betjamins. Constructional Approaches to Language 4.

Langacker, R. W. (2006). On the continuous debate about discreteness. *Cognitive Linguistics, 17,* 107–151.

Lindner, S. (1982). What goes up doesn't necessarily come down: The ins and outs of opposites. *Papers from the Regional Meeting of the Chicago Linguistic Society, 18,* 305–323.

Maldonado, R. (1988). Energetic reflexives in Spanish. *Proceedings of the Annual Meeting of the Berkeley Linguistics Society, 14,* 153–165.

Maldonado, R. (1999). *A media voz: Problemas conceptuales del clítico se.* Mexico City: Universidad Nacional Autónoma de México. Instituto de Investigaciones Filológicas, Publicaciones del Centro de Lingüística Hispánica 46.

Matlock, T. (2001). *How real is fictive motion?* Santa Cruz: University of California doctoral dissertation.

Matlock, T. (2004). Fictive motion as cognitive simulation. *Memory and Cognition, 32,* 1389–1400.

Matlock, T., & Richardson, D. C. (2004). Do eye movements go with fictive motion? *Proceedings of the Annual Conference of the Cognitive Science Society, 26,* 909–914.

Matsumoto, Y. (1996a). Subjective motion and English and Japanese verbs. *Cognitive Linguistics, 7,* 183–226.

Matsumoto, Y. (1996b). Subjective-change expressions in Japanese and their cognitive and linguistic bases. In G. Fauconnier & E. Sweetser (Eds.), *Spaces, worlds, and grammar* (pp. 124–156). Chicago and London: University of Chicago Press.

Panther, K.-U., & Radden, G. (Eds.). (2004). *Metonymy in language and thought.* Amsterdam and Philadelphia: John Benjamins. Human Cognitive Processing 4.

Reddy, M. J. (1979). The conduit metaphor—A case of frame conflict in our language about language. In A. Ortony (Ed.), *Metaphor and thought* (pp. 284–324). Cambridge: Cambridge University Press.

Rosch, E. (1978). Principles of categorization. In E. Rosch & B. B. Lloyd (Eds.), *Cognition and categorization* (pp. 27–47). Hillsdale, NJ: Erlbaum.

Rudzka-Ostyn, B. (2003). *Word power: Phrasal verbs and compounds (a cognitive approach).* Berlin and New York: Mouton de Gruyter.

Sandra, D., & Rice, S. (1995). Network analyses of prepositional meaning: Mirroring whose mind—the linguist's or the language user's? *Cognitive Linguistics, 6,* 89–130.

Sweetser, E. (1997). Role and individual interpretations of change predicates. In J. Nuyts & E. Pederson (Eds.), *Language and conceptualization* (pp. 116–136). Cambridge: Cambridge University Press. Language, Culture and Cognition 1.

Talmy, L. (1996). Fictive motion in language and "ception." In P. Bloom et al. (Eds.), *Language and space* (pp. 211–276). Cambridge, MA and London: MIT Press.

Taylor, J. R. (1996). *Possessives in English: An exploration in cognitive grammar.* Oxford: Oxford University Press.

Taylor, J. R. (2004). *Linguistic categorization: Prototypes in linguistic theory* (3rd ed.). Oxford: Oxford University Press.

Tuggy, D. (2003). The Nawatl verb *kiisa*: A case study in polysemy. In H. Cuyckens, R. Dirven, & J. R. Taylor (Eds.), *Cognitive approaches to lexical semantics* (pp. 323–362). Berlin and New York: Mouton de Gruyter. Cognitive Linguistics Research 23.

Turner, M. (1987). *Death is the mother of beauty: Mind, metaphor, criticism.* Chicago: University of Chicago Press.

Tyler, A., & Evans, V. (2003). *The semantics of English prepositions: Spatial scenes, embodied meaning and cognition.* Cambridge: Cambridge University Press.

Wierzbicka, A. (1995). Dictionaries vs. encyclopaedias: How to draw the line. In P. W. Davis (Ed.), *Alternative linguistics: Descriptive and theoretical modes* (pp. 289–315). Amsterdam and Philadelphia: John Benjamins. Current Issues in Linguistic Theory 102.

Zlatev, J. (2003). Polysemy or generality? Mu. In H. Cuyckens, R. Dirven, & J. R. Taylor (Eds.), *Cognitive approaches to lexical semantics* (pp. 447–494). Berlin and New York: Mouton de Gruyter. Cognitive Linguistics Research 23.

5

WORD GRAMMAR, COGNITIVE LINGUISTICS, AND SECOND LANGUAGE LEARNING AND TEACHING

Richard Hudson

1 Linguistic theory and teaching

1.1 A personal introduction

To start on a personal note, this chapter is my first opportunity to bring together two strands of my working life which have so far been quite separate (Hudson, 2002a): building models of language structure (Hudson, 1976, 1984, 1990, 2007), and building bridges between academic linguistics and school teaching (Hudson, 2004; Hudson & Walmsley, 2005). Of course, the two strands have influenced each other in my own thinking but I thought it would merely have confused both goals to combine them. After all, I was arguing that a cognitive model was right for language because it was true rather than because it was useful; whereas the arguments for applying linguistics in school teaching were all about usefulness rather than truth. However, I was always aware that truth and utility are hard to separate: ultimately, the most useful approach to solving a problem must, surely, be one based on a true understanding of the problem, and ultimately, a true theory must apply to the real-world situations that we define as problems. I very much regret the historical trends of the last few decades which, at least in the UK, have pushed "theoretical linguistics" and "applied linguistics" further apart, and welcome the opportunities that Cognitive Linguistics provides for bringing them together again.

Another personal card that I should lay on the table now is that most of my school-oriented thinking and activity has been directed at teaching of the mother tongue (L1) rather than of a second language (L2), and that this is also my first opportunity to write about the learning and teaching of L2 as such. However, I accept the argument of the "Language Awareness" movement that L2 teaching should build on a general "awareness" of how language works (Hawkins, 1999; Renou, 2001; Wray, 1994), so I see L1 and L2 teachers as contributing jointly to a single intellectual area of skill and understanding: "language." Consequently, I believe that an L1 perspective is highly relevant to the topic of this book.

Because of these personal biases, my discussion of L2 learning and teaching will be oriented to the most typical language-learning situation in the UK, where a monoglot English child is learning a foreign language such as French in school. I am of course aware that there are many other L2-learning situations, and I hope that some of the general conclusions of this chapter will extend to them as well.

1.2 Variation in language

L2 learning raises well-known questions for any theory of cognition and language, such as how bilinguals store and access their language, but there are other questions that have hardly been touched on. One such, which I have personally found particularly intriguing in the last few years, is the prowess of "hyperpolyglots," people who know dozens of languages well; for example, the legendary Cardinal Giuseppe Mezzofanti was said to be familiar with 72 languages and fluent in 39 (Crystal, 1997, p. 36; Erard, 2005). If they can do it, why can't the rest of us? More interestingly still, there are communities where every single adult speaks several languages fluently; as far as I have been able to determine through informal email inquiries, the highest number of languages spoken in this way is six. (According to Hilaire Valiquette, this is true of Wirrimanu (Balgo), Western Australia.) Even if hyperpolyglots have very special brains, this cannot be true of whole communities so we all have brains which are capable of holding at least six entire languages. Why do most of us have such difficulty in learning just one or two foreign languages? And how do successful learners cope cognitively with such large numbers?

Such questions go to the heart of our ideas about the nature of language. If we have an innate language module, how can it accommodate more than one language? If we have innate parameters to set, how can bilingual children set them differently for several languages at the same time? What is the difference between a "mother tongue" or "first language" and a second language for a child who learns several different languages simultaneously? How do fluent bilinguals manage to speak in just one language when dealing with a monoglot but to switch effortlessly in mid-sentence when in bilingual company? These questions show the need for a model of language structure and language learning in which it is normal to learn and know more than one language. Most obviously, the model will need a place for the notion "language X" (English, French and so on); but somewhat surprisingly, perhaps, very few theories of language structure satisfy even this modest demand. Even the most modern grammars appear to be torn between the traditional aim of describing "a language" and the modern cognitive aim of describing a speaker; and the result is that we all pretend that these goals are the same. For multilingual speakers they are most certainly different.

Even for monolingual speakers this pretence turns out to be deeply problematic as soon as we consider the details of what typical speakers actually know and do. No speaker's individual competence is neatly limited to what we might want to call a single language. On the one hand, many monoglots know fragments of other languages—loan words, quotations, even personal names—and on the other hand, every individual exhibits what Labov calls "inherent variability"—different ways of saying the same thing which vary systematically with the social context, and which crucially vary within the speech of one individual. For example, a typical English speaker has two pronunciations for the suffix –ing, as in walking: with an alveolar [n] or a velar [ŋ] or [ŋg], called collectively the (ing) variable. The choice between these variants is free, but they are linked symbolically to different social groups and social situations so their relative frequencies can be related statistically to objective social variables (Labov, 1989).

Like a bilingual's choice between two languages, the (ing) variable offers a linguistic choice which is based on social choices and raises the same basic question for linguistic theory: how to accommodate linguistic alternatives in a single individual language system without ignoring relevant social distinctions. Unfortunately, we are still waiting for a fully worked-out answer, but I have made a start (Hudson, 1996, pp. 243–257; Hudson, 1997, 2007) and although the hard work remains to be done, I believe that the basic ideas are relevant and important for the teaching of L1 and L2.

In short, I believe linguistic theory and description are ready to emerge from the isolation that structuralism demanded at the beginning of the twentieth century. At that time it was important for linguists to concentrate on the structure of the language system, ignoring external factors such as the supposed world-view or level of civilization of the speakers. But by the end of the century the focus had shifted from the language system to the individual speaker's cognitive system—a very different object, especially if we consider multilingual speakers. The next step will therefore be to develop theories of language with L2 and internal variation at their centers. Most importantly of all, perhaps, they will have a place for linguistic attitudes—the feelings that different languages and variants evoke. We have a great deal of empirical data about these attitudes, as well as a framework of ideas from social psychology for interpreting them (Giles & Powesland, 1975; Giles & Bradac, 1994), but we are still some way from being able to integrate them into a cognitive model with the rest of language structure, though I shall suggest below that we can already take some steps in this direction. (The same problem arises with emotional language such as swearwords and exclamations, whose emotional content has no place at all in any existing model of language.) This is an unfortunate gap for L2 research, where linguistic attitudes are central, so I hope it will receive more attention in the cognitive-linguistics community than it has so far.

The cognitive enterprise is an ambitious one because any cognitive theory of language has to cover not only language structure but also how it is learned and used and how speakers feel about it. I shall suggest that Cognitive Linguistics in general, and Word Grammar (WG) in particular, are well placed to at least start meeting this challenge, but I am well aware of the work that remains to be done before it is a reality.

2 Language is a network

2.1 Vocabulary is a network

One of the leading ideas of Cognitive Linguistics is that language is a cognitive network of units—meanings, words, sounds and so on (Hudson, 1984; Goldberg, 1995; Langacker, 2000). Indeed, it could be argued that this is also the basic idea behind all structuralism, with its emphasis on interconnections and systems; but it goes beyond mere structuralism because it denies that there is anything else in language. In particular, there are no "rules" as such, although (of course) there are plenty of generalizations. I personally first met the idea that language is nothing but a network in the work of Lamb (Lamb, 1966, 1998), and I now think of it as the main claim of WG (Hudson, 1984, p. 1, 2000, 2007). I also think it is a particularly important idea for L2 researchers, as I shall explain below.

The network idea is particularly obvious when applied to vocabulary. A typical word is at the center of a network of homonyms, synonyms, word classes and collocates, each of which is at the center of another little network. The network for just one word, the adjective FAST, is shown in Fig. 5.1, where the little triangle is standard WG notation for the "isa" relation between a concept and its super-category (e.g. BIG "isa" adjective). I leave it to the reader to imagine this network when expanded by the extra links for the verb FAST, the adjectives BIG and QUICK, and the collocating noun WORKER (as in *fast worker*). But even this expanded network is tiny compared with the total network for any one person's knowledge of English.

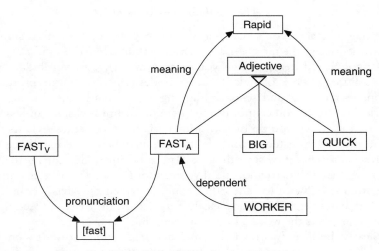

Figure 5.1 A tiny network centered on the adjective FAST.

The research evidence for this network structure is rock solid and virtually beyond dispute. It is based on the fact that when we use some concept we make the node for that concept active by focusing energy on it but, crucially, this process is rather messy as energy spills over onto the neighboring nodes as well. This is called "spreading activation." Take the tiny network in Fig. 5.1 for example, where the concepts include words; if we either say or hear the adjective *fast*, then we must be using the concept labeled FAST$_A$ so this node becomes very active, but all the nodes that are directly connected to it also become more active than they would otherwise be, thanks to the blind spreading of activation. There are two kinds of research evidence for this claim, involving speech errors and "priming." When we accidentally use the wrong word, the word that we use is almost always a "network neighbor" of the target word; for example, when someone used the word *orgasms* when they intended to use *organisms*, the mistake presumably happened because the two words are so close in terms of pronunciation (Aitchison, 1994, p. 20; Harley, 1995, p. 360). This preference for network neighbors obviously presupposes a network structure within which activation can spill over from one word (or other concept) to its neighbors. Similarly for priming, where timing experiments have repeatedly shown that a word is easier to find—for example, in order to decide whether or not it is an English word—if it has just been preceded by a network neighbor; for example, it takes less time to decide that *doctor* is an English word if one has just heard the word *nurse* than after hearing an unrelated word such as *lorry* (Harley, 1995, p. 17).

2.2 The vocabulary network of L2

For the L2 teacher or researcher, the main point of this discussion of networks is that the target—L2—is a network just like this, and not a list of disconnected items. When you learn a new item of vocabulary you add a little network of links to other nodes which define its pronunciation, its meaning, and so on by linking it to items in the existing network. Moreover, you cannot use the item on future occasions unless you can find it, which you do by activating it via the given clues—via its pronunciation when listening and via its meaning when speaking. Since this activation reaches it by spreading from neighboring nodes, the more links it has, the easier it is to find; and if you cannot find it, you have essentially forgotten it. A word (or any other concept) which only has a couple of links is barely integrated and easily forgotten, but a rich collection of links guarantees the word a long and useful life.

Clearly the L2 network will be small and fragmentary to start with, but the L1 network is vast and rich, so the obvious strategy is to build the network for L2 onto the existing one for L1. A translation equivalent provides one such link ("*chat* means 'cat' "), but other anchor-points come from form-based links (e.g. *chat* and *cat* have the same spelling except for one letter). Mnemonics provide further links for the beginner at the point where the main object is simply to make the new word into a permanent part of the network rather than to build links which will be useful in future processing (e.g. *chat* contains the "hat" of the *Cat in the Hat*). Any link is better than no link (Meara, 1998). Fig. 5.2 is meant to model the effect, on an English speaker's language network, of learning the French word CHAT (though I have deliberately simplified the network in some respects and omitted any mnemonic links). The solid lines are links that already existed for the English word CAT, plus the category "French word" which presumably exists for someone who has already started to learn French; in contrast, the dotted links are learned.

This network shows how intimately connected the two languages must be in the learner's mind; in other words, I am assuming a "common-store" model of bilingualism (Harley, 1995, p. 133). Though this is controversial among psychologists, I can see no alternative in a network model because the learner so obviously builds on pre-existing knowledge such as the letters of the alphabet and the meaning. There is also empirical evidence that the word classes are shared even in fluent bilinguals who switch languages in mid-sentence. In such cases, the word classes of the two classes are virtually always respected—a phenomenon known as "categorial equivalence" (Muysken, 2000); for example, if an English verb requires a noun as its object, then whatever the language of the object, it will be a noun. This constraint only makes sense if the two languages share the same word classes so that the language contrast cuts across the

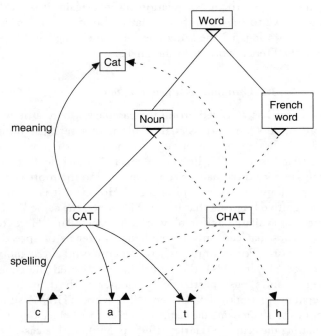

Figure 5.2 An English speaker learns the French word *chat*.

word-class divisions as in Fig. 5.2. Moreover, if different languages share the same word classes even in the mind of a fluent bilingual, how much more likely it is that the same will be true in the mind of a beginner who knows nothing about word classes in the new language.

We can safely assume, therefore, that words from different languages will share the same set of word classes in the mind of the learner— except, of course, where the languages have different structures which require different word classes; for example, only one language may have classifiers. However, another kind of category that the two languages must share is their relations. As the diagrams have already shown, the kind of cognitive network that I am describing is not merely a set of associations but a highly articulated structure where every link belongs to a specified type. In particular, I am advocating what is called a "local" or "symbolic" network, in which every concept corresponds either to a node or to a link, and not a "distributed" or "connectionist" network in which nodes and links are undifferentiated and the distinctive content consists entirely of activity settings. The "isa" relation is fundamentally different from all the others, but the others also fall into categories such as "meaning," "pronunciation," "spelling" and "dependent." (The same is true for all flavors of cognitive linguistics, but I think WG has a particularly well-developed theory of relations.) Once again, it is hard to imagine any alternative to the assumption that L2 builds on the existing categories for L1; so in Fig. 5.2 the same relations "meaning" and "spelling" are found in the French word as in the English one.

2.3 Grammar is a network, too

The discussion so far has revolved around vocabulary, where a network analysis is more or less uncontroversial; a moment's serious thought about the relations among words is enough to show that there is no serious alternative (Aitchison, 1997, Pinker, 1998). It is much less obvious that, or how, the same kind of analysis can be applied to the more general patterns of morphology, syntax and phonology. However, it is common ground among cognitive linguists that it can. Moreover, the same kind of empirical support is available as for networks in vocabulary. Here, too, we find speech errors that can only be explained in terms of spreading activation in a network. For example, when someone said *slicely thinned* (Levelt, Roelofs, & Meyer, 1999), they must have activated the general concepts "adverb" and "past participle," together with their default morphology, separately from the lexical items SLICE and THIN. A similar explanation applies to *I'm making the kettle on*, a blend of *I'm making a cup of tea* and *I'm putting the kettle on* (Harley, 1995, p. 355); in this case, both PUT and MAKE were candidates for expressing the intended meaning, and the general syntactic pattern of direct object followed by ON must have been activated along with PUT so that it could then be combined with the other verb. Moreover, priming experiments also show that general patterns can be activated. For example, *Vlad brought a book to Boris* primes other sentences with the syntactic pattern consisting of a direct object and prepositional phrase (Harley, 1995, p. 356; Bock & Griffin, 2000). All this evidence supports the idea that general patterns are stored and processed in much the same way as more specific patterns.

The conclusion, therefore, must be that cognitive networks contain general concepts as well as specific ones, and that there is some kind of logic which allows us to connect the two—in other words, which allows us to apply generalizations. Cognitive linguists agree in recognizing schematic concepts such as "Word" or "Animal" which carry general properties and are linked to more specific concepts by a special relation which is dedicated to this role. In WG this is the "isa" relation which I have already introduced; for example, CAT isa Noun, CHAT isa French-word. This relation carries the basic logic of generalization called "inheritance," whereby sub-concepts "inherit" properties from their super-categories; for example, if CAT isa Noun, and Noun has a number, then CAT must have a number as well, and if CHAT isa French-word and Noun, and we know that French nouns have a gender, the same must be true of CHAT.

Inheritance is a very powerful mechanism for handling any kind of generalization, and in language it replaces the notion of a "rule." For instance, instead of saying "A verb takes a noun as its subject before it" we define the relation "subject" between Verb and some word W which combines various properties:

- being a noun (W isa Noun)
- being obligatory (the quantity of "subject" is 1)
- preceding Verb

Any word which isa Verb automatically inherits this relation and all its properties as shown in Fig. 5.3, where the dotted properties of *loves* are inherited from the super-category Verb. Incidentally, syntax is particularly simple in WG because it is based on relations between single words; phrases turn out to be redundant when all syntactic relations are made explicit (Hudson, 1990, p. 105, 2007).

The same kind of network translation is possible for morphological rules, although these are usually expressed as processes, e.g. "To form the plural of a noun, take its stem and add the suffix {s}." Once again, we need a general word class (Plural) but this time we also need to invoke an extra level of "forms" which lies between words and sounds. Words are related to forms by the relations "stem" and "word-form" (i.e. the fully inflected form), and special "variants" of forms are defined by relations

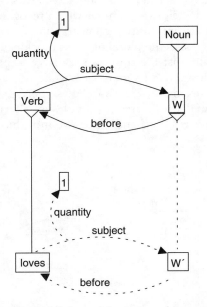

Figure 5.3 Loves inherits its subject properties from Verb.

such as "s-variant." A simple analysis for plural nouns would contain the following:

- A plural noun has a stem S.
- It also has a word-form F.
- F is the s-variant of S.

The "s-variant" relation is a step forward because it is purely morphological, so it can be re-cycled for other syntactic word classes such as singular verbs—in other words, it helps with systematic syncretism. The next step relates s-variants to the morpheme {s}:

- A form has an s-variant V.
- V has two parts, Part1 (A) and Part2 (B).
- A is a copy of the form.
- B isa the morpheme {s}.

These two patterns of generalization are shown in Fig. 5.4, so they are available for inheritance by any plural noun thanks to its isa link to Plural.

The logic of inheritance goes much further than the simple copying of properties because it only copies "by default"—hence the technical name "default inheritance." This is the logic of common-sense reasoning which allows exceptions such as three-legged cats and unusually large birds, and in language it is the logic of every descriptive grammar which recognizes generalizations and exceptions. The exceptions that come to mind first are probably irregular inflections (e.g. *geese* as the plural of *goose*, blocking the default *gooses*), but these are actually just the tip of a very large iceberg which includes most of the complications of syntax such as non-default word order (Hudson, 2003). For example, Fig. 5.3 shows the default subject–verb order, but subject–auxiliary inversion provides an alternative to the default (as in *Are you ready?*). To handle this, we introduce a

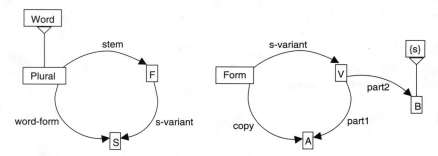

Figure 5.4 The morphology of plural nouns.

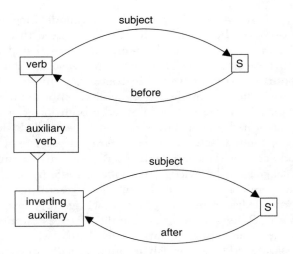

Figure 5.5 Subject–auxiliary inversion in a network.

special "inverting" sub-class of auxiliary verbs with special verb–subject order (as well as the semantics of a question); the analysis is shown in Fig. 5.5. Like a word-order transformation, this captures the important insight that *You are* is "underlying," "unmarked," or "basic" in comparison with *Are you.*

The big generalization that emerges from this discussion is common ground to all cognitive linguists: "the lexicon" (containing vocabulary) and "the grammar" (containing general rules) are just two areas of a single network. The lexicon deals with relatively specific word-types such as CAT, whereas the grammar deals with relatively general categories such as Noun, but both areas have the same network structure and there is no boundary between them. This is probably the point where cognitive linguists part company most clearly with the earlier generative tradition, with its rules and lexical items, and recent psycholinguistic discussions of morphology have tended to contrast unified approaches such as this with a "dual-mechanism" analysis (Pinker, 1998). The debate is important for L2 research because it involves the fundamental nature of what is learned. If vocabulary and rules really are different, they could be learned in quite different ways but, if they are fundamentally the same, we can expect a single mechanism for learning.

2.4 Language and memory

It is not only language that is a network: cognitive psychologists generally agree that the same is true of general long-term memory (Reisberg,

1997, p. 257). How are these two networks related in our minds? Linguists are divided on this question, but cognitive linguists are agreed that the language network is simply the part of long-term memory that deals with language. Given the central role of words in WG, we can define language simply as our memory for words. In contrast, many linguists believe that language is a "mental module" (or a collection of modules) which is clearly separate from the rest of knowledge both in terms of how the knowledge is stored and in terms of how it is used (Fodor, 1983; Chomsky, 1986; Smith, 1999). However, there are good reasons for rejecting the modular view (Hudson, 2002b, 2007), so I shall assume that "knowledge of language is knowledge" (Goldberg, 1995, p. 5). This is not, of course, to deny the variety of knowledge—we still have to distinguish factual knowledge from perceptual knowledge (e.g. images, sounds, smells), motor skills and feelings. But in this classification, language is part of the same gigantic mental network that we use for our social and physical world, and which is often called "long-term memory."

Another traditional boundary separates long-term and short-term memory. The latter is often called "working memory," in recognition of its role in exploiting the contents of long-term memory. One version of modularity is the idea that we have a dedicated working memory for language or even for specific areas of language such as syntax (Lewis, 1996). In this view, working memory is a separate area of the mind, like a workbench, onto which information is copied from long-term memory or perception and then transformed into some kind of output. However, many psychologists now agree that working memory is just a convenient term for the activity—such as spreading activation and inheritance—which is known to take place in long-term memory itself (Miyake & Shah, 1999). This view is much more in harmony with Cognitive Linguistics with its emphasis on the unity of language and the rest of thought.

2.5 Separating different languages in a network

The final question about the formal structures involved in L2 learning is how the two languages are kept separate. As I mentioned earlier, most theories of language are designed to model monolingual speakers who know only one dialect and use only one style. This limitation is left over from the old days when linguistic theories applied to languages rather than to speakers, but is not part of a truly cognitive approach. Indeed, in WG there are several different mechanisms for including variation within the same network analysis.

I have already suggested one mechanism, exemplified by "French-word" in Fig. 5.2. This is what we need for any new generalization about all French words, such as how to relate spellings to pronunciations, which are clearly part of what needs to be learned. For example, grammatical properties of French nouns will be attached to the category "French noun," which isa both Noun and French-word. No doubt those (like me) who learned just one language in early childhood treat this language as the default, so (in my mind) Word and English word are probably the same concept.

Another mechanism involves the notion of "a language" which includes named languages such as English or French, each with whatever properties we may know about it—its name, where it is spoken, and so on. Clearly, languages are part of our knowledge of the world, so there is nothing controversial about this suggestion, but knowing about a language is obviously different from knowing that language and indeed from knowing anything at all about its words. However, if we do know some words of language L, we must have a way of relating each of these words to L, so we have a relation "language" between words and their language, e.g. the language of CHAT is French. As an example, Fig. 5.6 models my knowledge of at least three languages, and shows that I know absolutely no Urdu, just one word of Russian and enough French words to be able to generalize about them.

A third mechanism for handling variability in a person's knowledge of language is the one which is needed for the inherent variability already discussed, where individual items of pronunciation or vocabulary are limited to particular kinds of speaker or situation; for instance, in my experience the word BONNY is limited to Scottish speakers. This mechanism requires a link between a stored word or other pattern and a particular kind of speaker or situation. Situations are still hard to formalize, but speakers are easy because they are already needed for deictic words such as ME, whose referent is the speaker (Hudson, 1990, p. 128). Examples like these make a rather obvious point unavoidable: that the

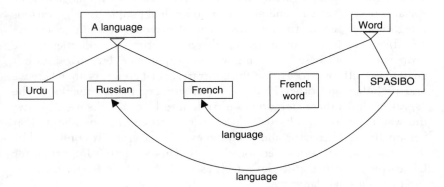

Figure 5.6 Three languages that I know about and the words I know in them.

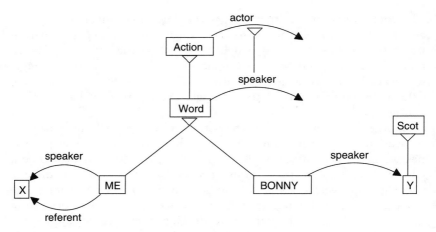

Figure 5.7 What I know about the speaker of two English words.

language structures which we store in our minds are based on our experiences with language, so they may well include details of the situation such as the kind of person who uses them. The two networks in Fig. 5.7 illustrate these two important applications of the "speaker" relation, but they also make the important point that because any word is primarily an action—a general across a range of utterances—rather than marks on a page, it inherits an actor from the general "action" category; and of course the "actor" of a word is its speaker.

The "speaker" link can apply to any portion of language whose speakers we can identify, from individual words to entire languages; for example, if we know that all speakers of Gaelic are Scots, then this is part of the knowledge structure for Gaelic. These links bring together two rich networks of knowledge: what we know about words and what we know about people—our linguistic and social networks. As with language, the social concepts vary in generality from individual people through various categories of people to the most general category, Person (compare: Word); and each concept brings together a collection of properties. These properties are all based, in some way, on experience, but this does not guarantee truth or fairness; on the contrary, social concepts are where we find prejudice and other kinds of social stereotyping, so thanks to the "speaker" links these stereotypes intrude into language. As we all know, the way a person speaks sets up all sorts of expectations about their personality and behavior, and common experience is amply confirmed by the research on attitudes mentioned in 1.1. This research is important for L2 learning because attitudes attach as easily to whole languages as to variants of a single language.

3 How to learn a language network

3.1 From token to type

It should be clear by now that I believe that language is learned, just like any other kind of factual knowledge, rather than "acquired" by the triggering of innate concepts. As I mentioned earlier, although this view is controversial in linguistics, it is more widely accepted by psychologists (whose opinion must surely count for more in this area). In any case, although as a linguist I am of course aware of the standard arguments in favor of innate concepts (e.g. poverty of the stimulus, selective impairments, and critical periods), I find them all quite unconvincing (Hudson, 2007). For lack of space to defend my view I shall simply take it for granted. The main point for L2 is that it can be viewed as a body of knowledge like any other, to be learned and taught by experience. To the extent that it is distinctive, that is just because of its unique place in human life—a matter of function rather than form.

The first step in understanding how we learn a language network is to ask how we use it. How do we apply it to particular experiences, such as hearing and understanding a word such as *cat* in the sentence *Your cat is in our garden*, spoken by a neighbor? To make an obvious point, this uttered word is distinct from the stored word CAT, so they are held mentally as two distinct concepts. In technical terms, the (uttered) "token" is distinct from the (stored) "type." It is all too easy to be misled by the conventions of writing (which do not distinguish types and tokens) into ignoring the difference, but it is actually rather important. For example, in perception we start with a mental representation of the token and its properties, and it takes some processing to work out which type it is an example of. Moreover, we can still link the token to some type even if its properties are slightly different from that type's; for example, we can cope with spelling mistakes, foreign accents, and so on, so we can see the spelling *yelow*, and assign it confidently to the type YELLOW without even noticing the misspelling. In this case we choose the word with the nearest spelling to the token, but this need not be so: we may trade a greater deviance of spelling for the sake of a closer fit in terms of syntax and meaning (e.g. when we read *there* as *their*, or vice versa). The general principle that we seem to follow is to adopt the type which provides the best global fit with the token and the current global scene—what is often referred to as the "best-fit principle." This apparently powerful and mysterious process may be quite easy to model in terms of spreading activation if we assume that the most active candidate type (e.g. in this case, the most active word type) is the one to choose (Hudson, 2007). We shall return to the best-fit principle and its consequences below.

On the other hand, although types and tokens are distinct, they are in some sense "the same." This is precisely the relation covered by the "isa" relation that we find among types: the token *cat* isa the type CAT, which isa Noun, and so on. Furthermore, this is the relation that carries default inheritance so it allows the token to inherit all the stored properties of the type (and of its super-categories right up to the top of the hierarchy)—a wonderfully effective way of applying stored knowledge to new experiences, which allows us to go beyond mere observables. For example, we hear the sounds for *cat*, and inherit its word class and its meaning, just as when we see an unfamiliar cat and inherit the fact that it will enjoy having its tummy stroked. In other words, tokens form a constantly changing "fringe" attached (by "isa" links) to the edge of the permanent network.

Now suppose we consider a token not as a processing experience but as a potential learning experience. Most tokens (of words or of any other kind of experience) are unremarkable, and we may assume that their life in the network is very short indeed—just a second or two before they decay and effectively disappear from memory. This is where the well-known limits of "working memory" apply, so we are doing well if we can remember more than nine or ten words in a sentence that we have just heard. If working memory is merely the currently active part of the network, this limitation must follow from the amount of available activation energy; so we deactivate past tokens as soon as we can in order to make more activation available for future use. But some tokens are so remarkable that we can recall them days or even years later, which shows that this deactivation is not automatic. One plausible explanation for the prolonged life of these tokens is that they were "hyper-active" on first encounter, and one possible reason why extra activation might have been needed is that the usual processes for finding a suitable type ran into trouble. This would be the case if we heard an unfamiliar word, or a familiar word used in an unfamiliar way; in either case there is no existing type, so we have to work out unobservable properties instead of merely inheriting them. In short, we have to guess—a very expensive process in terms of activation. And one effect of all this activation may be that the token node stays active so long that it never disappears.

My suggestion, then, is that hyper-active tokens turn into types; in other words, they become part of the permanent network. This process of "storage" is a combination of remembering and forgetting: remembering the interesting and hyper-active bits, and forgetting uninteresting details such as the time, place and speaker (though any of these may be sufficiently remarkable to be remembered). This is another way of saying that we learn the language system from usage, which is how cognitive linguists generally see language learning (Barlow & Kemmer, 2000; Bybee, 1999; Bybee & Hopper, 2001; Ellis, 2002; Langacker, 2000; Tomasello, 2003). However, it is important to stress that storage can apply to a token even if the best-fit principle has produced an established type for it, provided its properties are sufficiently noteworthy. (For example, the misspelling of *yelow* could produce a stored sub-type linked to the person who wrote it as a mistake to be held against them in the future.) This means that a given word-type (such as CAT) may end up with numerous particular instances stored beneath it as sub-types, together with whatever properties made them stand out. Each stored sub-type reinforces the type in the network by providing extra links, and if a number of sub-types share some property, this may be added to the type's property by the process of induction discussed in 3.3.

This model of storage has two potentially important consequences for L2 learning. The first concerns "frequency." According to this model, we only store tokens with unusual properties—i.e. properties that cannot be inherited from the type. Familiar words already have a rich type that covers all their properties, so they are too boring to remember; but less common word types have had less chance to be enriched by the process outlined above, so their tokens are more likely to be noteworthy because of unpredicted properties. Consequently, there should be a much greater effect of frequency for rare words than for common ones—exactly as predicted by the power law of practice (Ellis, 2002). In the L2 context, hearing a rare word ten times in a lesson should produce much more effect on the learner's knowledge than the same number of repetitions of a frequent word. Moreover, we all know that memories for things such as names and new words are in danger of fading during the following days or weeks (in contrast with the seconds for which a token may survive). For evidence, we only need to consider students who cannot remember technical terms from one class to the next; but psychological studies also confirm that facts are at the greatest risk of being forgotten soon after being learned (Reisberg, 1997, p. 246). The motto for the L2 learner is familiar: Use it or lose it.

The second consequence concerns "distinctiveness." According to this model, a new type is strengthened by the addition of stored sub-types, but this will only happen if the best-fit principle can identify it as the best-fitting type for future tokens. A stored type that never wins the best-fit competition might as well not exist because it can never be retrieved, and it has no prospects of becoming more useful. But if the best fit is decided by spreading activation, a node's chance of success depends on how distinctive it is (along with other factors such as its base level of activation). A new word *zax* should be more memorable than *saf*, as every advertiser knows, provided it has the same number of subsequent repetitions. This is bad news for L2 learners, because one L2 word tends to look to the learner much like another one, so few words are sufficiently distinctive to be memorable in their own right. Fortunately, this is not the end of the story, as there are ways to help a new word to survive even without future tokens; for example, it is possible to explore the word's lexical links to other words. But distinctiveness is clearly an issue for L2 learning and teaching.

3.2 Induction

Another part of learning a network is the induction of generalizations from these low-level stored types. This is a complex process because generalizations feed each other, and a false generalization may lead to a dead end. However, in principle the process is fairly simple, though there are many details that I (at least) don't know.

Generalizations in a network consist of correlated properties, i.e. properties that tend to co-occur. For example, the properties of flying, having a beak, building a nest, and having feathers are strongly correlated in the sense that many different concepts have these properties and few of the properties occur without all the others; so collectively they justify the general concept "bird." Similarly, in language, the properties of combining with *the* or *a*, having an inflection with {s} and referring to a concrete object are correlated and justify "noun." In a network, properties are defined by links to other nodes, so nodes that "share a property" must all have the same relation to some other node, and "correlated properties" are distinct relations that link the same set of nodes to two or more other nodes.

An abstract set of correlated properties is shown in Fig. 5.8. The three arrow styles represent three distinct relations, each pointing at a different concept on the right but each linking this concept to almost the same set of concepts on the left. This congruence justifies the generalization that all three properties apply to A, B, C and D. Admittedly, the generalization is actually not quite true because concept A has a dotted link to W instead of Y, so this concept is an exception; but exceptions can be tolerated thanks to default inheritance.

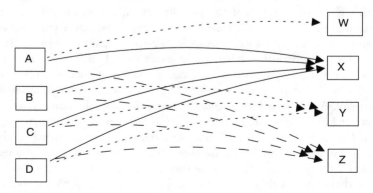

Figure 5.8 An abstract network showing three correlated properties.

According to the WG theory of learning (Hudson, 2007), whenever "we" (i.e. our minds, but well below any kind of consciousness) notice a set of nodes with correlated properties, we record the fact by introducing a new node into the network, giving it the correlated properties, and giving it an isa link to each member of the set of existing nodes. This procedure turns Fig. 5.8 into Fig. 5.9, which now contains the generalization applied to a new node N, though all the original links are still there as well. This is how we manage to combine so many generalizations with so much fine detail: always build generalizations on existing fine detail, and never forget the fine detail.

How do we spot correlated properties? An honest answer is that I don't know, but once again I can speculate, and once again my answer has to involve spreading activation. This time I believe we have to think of low-level activation circulating through our memory in a rather random and undirected way—perhaps during mental "down time" when activation maintains concepts (and which sometimes wakes us in the middle of the night with a name or a word that we failed to find during the day).

I guess that this background activation must also be responsible for inductive generalizations. Take the abstract example in Fig. 5.8. Suppose just one of the right-hand nodes X, Y, or Z becomes active: nothing important happens and the activation just moves elsewhere. But if two of them happen to become active at the same time, activation spreads from both of them to the same set of nodes A–D, signaling a correlation. On the principle of giving more to those who already have most, these nodes receive all the available activation and spread it out to any other properties they may have, thereby increasing the significance of the correlation and possibly collecting even more activation for the sharing nodes. Once

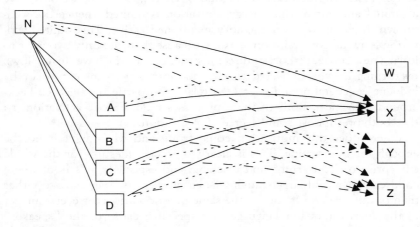

Figure 5.9 A new node carries the default properties.

these nodes have reached some threshold level of activation they spawn a super-category with isa links to them and copies of their shared properties; and the induction is complete.

If this theory is right, it has important implications for theories of L2 learning. First, it presupposes large amounts of initial raw data as the basis for induced generalizations. Second, it presupposes significant amounts of down time for "digesting" these data and finding correlations. But, of course, in the school context, down time is scarce and has to be shared not only with other subjects but also with the multiple demands of the emotional and cognitive life of a child. This may work well for L1 and for learning outside school, but it is unlikely to lead to much spontaneous induction in L2.

3.3 Motivation and attention

The need for motivation is self-evident, but WG theory not only helps to explain why this is so but also why motivation may be in short supply. Once again the mediating variable is activation and the key idea is rather obvious: motivation decides where we channel activation. As I have just suggested, this applies to the background activation which reveals generalizations, but it applies even more obviously on the time-scale of working (alias short-term) memory, where the relevant variable is attention. We are all surrounded by competing calls on our attention, but this is even more true of school-age language learners in a typical classroom situation; so it is hardly surprising that many teachers believe that trying to teach unmotivated students is simply a waste of time.

According to WG, then, motivation decides how we divide attention between competing claims; and what we mean by attention is simply activation. Activation requires some kind of energy, and since we only have a limited amount of this energy, activation is limited—hence the well-known limits on working memory mentioned earlier. This limited activation is a vital constraint on learning because there are only two ways to learn a new concept (short of direct instruction, to which we turn below): by turning a hyper-activated token node into a permanent type or by inducing a general node to carry correlated properties revealed by background activation. Both of these processes require extra activation, so they both presuppose some degree of motivation.

Where does this motivation come from, and why might it not be enough for L2 learning? This is clearly a crucial question for the whole enterprise of L2 learning and teaching, and especially at school where children are by and large studying languages because they have to rather than out of choice. Of course, the same question arises for every subject in the curriculum, but languages are special because of the "speaker" links which bind each language to the social stereotype of its speakers. If we consider the classic distinction between integrative and transactional motivation (Gardner & Lambert, 1972), they require either a very positive social stereotype or the prospect of practical benefits in the near future, neither of which can be taken for granted at all for most school-level language learners. At present the UK is facing a serious crisis in L2 study as decreasing numbers of school children choose to study languages at high school and university and language teachers become harder to recruit (Anon, 2002), and I believe that one of the reasons is that educationalists use transactional arguments (Kelly & Jones, 2003). Fortunately, there is a third motivation to consider alongside the classic pair: "interest." I suspect that this is ultimately the only motivation that will drive English-speaking children to study foreign languages seriously at school, though adults are as open as any to integrative and transactional motivations. How to inspire interest is a topic I shall take up in the last section.

4 How to teach a language network

4.1 General considerations and the implicit/explicit contrast

Suppose cognitive linguists are right about language being a network learned from usage and firmly embedded in general knowledge. What implications should this have for the teaching of L2?

One obvious conclusion is that the school context for L2 is so different from the home context for L1 that we cannot leave anything to Mother Nature. A small child starts from scratch but has vast amounts of richly structured and helpful usage to learn from, and plenty of time to digest it. In contrast, a student at school starts with a richly structured language network for L1 but has much less experience of usage and even less time for digestion. Moreover, a child has devoted and intimate caregivers whereas a student has an expert teacher—a virtual stranger. The two learning situations could hardly be more different.

On the other hand, if language is just knowledge, then language teaching shares at least some features with the teaching of other kinds of knowledge—geography, maths and so on. As in these other subjects, the teacher starts with an explicit syllabus—a planned route through the network—and a repertoire of activities such as exercises to support the learning. There is a very clear content to be learned—the vocabulary, grammar, and pronunciation of L2; and the content has a clear structure. Indeed, the structure of L2 may be easier to understand than that of other subjects precisely because linguists know so much about it. (How many other subjects have a content whose inherent structure is as well understood as language?)

It is true that L2 combines skills—speaking, listening, and so on—with factual knowledge, but the same is true of maths, which is tested in terms of problem-solving abilities much like those of L2 practice. It is also true, as I said above, that L2 faces the learner with a social stereotype and its associated attitudes, which can affect motivation; but the same is true in subjects such as drama and religion. And it is true that L2 is not just a body of knowledge but is itself a tool for communicating knowledge; but the same is obviously true for L1, which the students are still studying alongside L2. In short, a cognitive approach reveals similarities rather than differences between L2 teaching and other school subjects. Indeed, we could even extend the idea of network structure to the school and point to the need for the L2 teacher to "network" with teachers of other subjects.

This view of L2 has important consequences for the choice between implicit and explicit teaching. If the teacher wants students to learn some generalization, is it best to leave them to induce it from usage in which it is implicit, or to tell them the generalization explicitly? If L2 teaching is like other subjects, the question hardly arises. Even L1 teaching (at least in the UK) now favors explicit teaching at all levels (Anon, 1998), and it is self-evidently part of other subjects. Although it was out of favor in L2 teaching for some time it is now much more widely accepted (Norris & Ortega, 2000; Ellis, 1994, 2002; Anon, 2005). If the aim of language teaching is to help rich networks to grow in the learners' minds, the benefits of explicit teaching are very clear. On the one hand, it compensates for the rich input that an L2 learner lacks by guiding the learner to accurate generalizations; and, on the other hand, it provides the richly varied range of experiences that a learner needs to embed each new word in a distinct and rich network.

Incidentally, I notice that the hyperpolyglots discussed in 1.2 learned most of their languages from books, i.e. by learning general patterns explicitly; and indeed these short cuts were presumably essential for their prodigious achievements.

4.2 How to make language interesting

Finally, we come back to the question of motivation. What can schools and teachers do to motivate learners? Everyone knows that this is the crucial variable in L2 teaching, so it deserves attention from all concerned and I believe even theoretical and descriptive linguistics may have something to contribute.

As I have suggested, this problem is especially acute when the learners have neither of the two classic types of motivation, integrative and trans-actional, which is surely the case in the UK and probably in most other English-speaking countries as well. The typical language learner in school is not moved by talk of far-off goals such as being able to get a job or make friends abroad in ten or twenty years' time. No other school subject survives on that basis, so it is hard to see why L2 teaching should be different. To make a child look forward to the next French lesson, the benefits must be much more immediate. One way to ensure this is to offer lots of fun in the lesson, and I certainly applaud anything which achieves this—role play, email exchanges with foreign schools, and so on. But this kind of motivation risks being counter-productive if it channels all of the learners' attention onto the activity and away from the language.

A much better solution is to make the language itself interesting because this guarantees that attention will be on the words and their network connections. If the goal is to enrich network connections, it probably doesn't matter how this is done, and there are many ways of doing it—looking for related words in L2 or etymons in L1, playing games with scrambled letters or words, even solving patterns problems as in the Linguistics Olympiad (http://www.phon.ucl.ac.uk/home/dick/ec/olympiad.htm). The Department for Education and Skills in England has recently produced an impressive list of suggestions for teaching L2 interestingly in primary schools (Anon, 2005), but there are many other sources of ideas—not least academic linguists, as people who almost by definition are driven by interest in language. Even more importantly, every academic linguist I know was already fascinated by language as a school child, so we all have personal experience of what is needed. If every L2 teacher combined Cognitive Linguistics with all the skills and knowledge of a good language teacher, L2 learners would have a really good deal.

Bibliography

Aitchison, J. (1994). *Words in the mind. An introduction to the mental lexicon* (2nd ed.). Oxford: Blackwell.

Aitchison, J. (1997). *The language web.* Cambridge: Cambridge University Press.

Anon (1998). *The grammar papers.* London: Qualifications and Curriculum Authority.

Anon (2002). *Languages for all: languages for life. A strategy for England.* London: Department for Education and Skills.

Anon (2005). *Key Stage 2 Framework for Languages.* London: Department for Education and Skills.

Barlow, M. & Kemmer, S. (2000). *Usage-based models of language.* Stanford: CSLI.

Bock, K. & Griffin, Z. (2000). The persistence of structural priming: Transient activation or implicit learning? *Journal of Experimental Psychology-General, 129,* 177–192.

Bybee, J. (1999). Usage-based phonology. In M. Darnell, E. Moravcsik, F. Newmeyer, M. Noonan, & K. Wheatley (Eds.), *Functionalism and formalism in linguistics. I: General papers* (pp. 211–242). Amsterdam: John Benjamins.

Bybee, J. & Hopper, P. (2001). *Frequency and the emergence of linguistic structure.* Amsterdam: John Benjamins.

Chomsky, N. (1986). *Knowledge of language. Its nature, origin and use.* New York: Praeger.

Crystal, D. (1997). *Cambridge encyclopedia of language* (2nd ed.). Cambridge: Cambridge University Press.

Ellis, N. (1994). *Implicit and explicit learning of languages.* London: Academic Press.

Ellis, N. (2002). Frequency effects in language processing: A review with implications for theories of implicit and explicit language acquisition. *Studies in Second Language Acquisition, 24,* 143–188.

Erard, M. (2005). The gift of the gab. *New Scientist, 2481 (January 8),* 40–44.

Fodor, J. (1983). *The modularity of the mind.* Cambridge, MA: MIT Press.

Gardner, R. & Lambert, W. (1972). *Attitudes and motivation in second language learning.* Rowley, MA: Newbury House.

Giles, H. & Bradac, J. (1994). Speech styles: attitudes and inferences. In R. Asher (Ed.), *Encyclopedia of language and linguistics* (pp. 4,260–4,264). Oxford: Pergamon.

Giles, H. & Powesland, P. (1975). *Speech style and social evaluation.* London: Academic Press.

Goldberg, A. (1995). *Constructions. A construction grammar approach to argument structure.* Chicago: University of Chicago Press.

Harley, T. (1995). *The psychology of language.* Hove: Psychology Press.

Hawkins, E. (1999). Foreign language study and language awareness. *Language Awareness, 8,* 124–142.

Hudson, R. (1976). *Arguments for a non-transformational grammar.* Chicago: Chicago University Press.

Hudson, R. (1984). *Word grammar.* Oxford: Blackwell.

Hudson, R. (1990). *English word grammar.* Oxford: Blackwell.

Hudson, R. (1996). *Sociolinguistic* (2nd ed.). Cambridge: Cambridge University Press.

Hudson, R. (1997). Inherent variability and linguistic theory. *Cognitive Linguistics, 8,* 73–108.

Hudson, R. (2000). Language as a cognitive network. In H. G. Simonsen & R. T. Endresen (Eds.), *A cognitive approach to the verb. Morphological and constructional perspectives* (pp. 49–72). Berlin: Mouton de Gruyter.

Hudson, R. (2002a). Richard Hudson. In K. Brown & V. Law (Eds.), *Linguistics in Britain: personal histories* (pp. 127–138). Oxford: Blackwell.

Hudson, R. (2002b). Word Grammar. In K. Sugayama (Ed.), *Studies in Word Grammar* (pp. 7–32). Kobe: Research Institute of Foreign Studies, Kobe City University of Foreign Studies.

Hudson, R. (2003). Mismatches in Default Inheritance. In E. Francis & L. Michaelis (Eds.), *Mismatch: Form-function incongruity and the architecture of grammar* (pp. 269–317). Stanford: CSLI.

Hudson, R. (2004). Why education needs linguistics (and vice versa). *Journal of Linguistics, 40,* 105–130.

Hudson, R. (2007). *Networks of language: The new Word Grammar.* Oxford: Oxford University Press.

Hudson, R. & Walmsley, J. (2005). The English Patient: English grammar and teaching in the twentieth century. *Journal of Linguistics, 41,* 593–622.

Kelly, M. & Jones, D. (2003). *A new landscape for languages*. London: Nuffield Foundation.

Labov, W. (1989). The child as linguistic historian. *Language Variation and Change*, *1*, 85–97.

Lamb, S. (1966). *Outline of Stratificational Grammar*. Washington, DC: Georgetown University Press.

Lamb, S. (1998). *Pathways of the brain. The neurocognitive basis of language*. Amsterdam: Benjamins.

Langacker, R. (2000). A dynamic usage-based model. In M. Barlow & S. Kemmer (Eds.), *Usage-based models of language* (pp. 1–63). Stanford: CSLI.

Levelt, W. J. M., Roelofs, A., & Meyer, A. S. (1999). A theory of lexical access in speech production. *Behavioral And Brain Sciences*, *22*, 1–45.

Lewis, R. (1996). Interference in short-term memory: The magical number two (or three) in sentence processing. *Journal of Psycholinguistic Research*, *25*, 93–115.

Meara, P. (1998). Second language vocabulary acquisition: A rationale for pedagogy. *Applied Linguistics*, *19*, 289–292.

Miyake, A. & Shah, P. (1999). *Models of working memory. Mechanisms of active maintenance and executive control*. Cambridge: Cambridge University Press.

Muysken, P. (2000). *Bilingual speech. A typology of code-mixing*. Cambridge: Cambridge University Press.

Norris, J. & Ortega, L. (2000). Effectiveness of L2 instruction: A research synthesis and quantitative meta-analysis. *Language Learning*, *50*, 417–528.

Pinker, S. (1998). Words and rules. *Lingua*, *106*, 219–242.

Reisberg, D. (1997). *Cognition. Exploring the science of the mind*. New York: Norton.

Renou, J. (2001). An examination of the relationship between metalinguistic awareness and second-language proficiency of adult learners of French. *Language Awareness*, *10*, 248–267.

Smith, N. V. (1999). *Chomsky. Ideas and ideals*. Cambridge: Cambridge University Press.

Tomasello, M. (2003). *Constructing a language: A usage-based theory of language acquisition*. Cambridge, MA: Harvard University Press.

Wray, D. (1994). *Language and Awareness*. Hodder and Stoughton.

6

SPATIAL LANGUAGE LEARNING AND THE FUNCTIONAL GEOMETRIC FRAMEWORK

Kenny R. Coventry and Pedro Guijarro-Fuentes

1 Introduction

Spatial language, such as asking directions for places in large-scale space, or asking where a misplaced object is in small-scale space, constitutes part of the basic fabric of language. Yet spatial language exhibits problems for the second language learner that provide native speakers with a useful semantic diagnostic tool to identify non-native speakers. Languages carve up space in different ways. For instance, in Spanish the single lexical item *en* maps onto the meanings of both *in* and *on* in English while in Dutch there are two words corresponding to *on* in English; *aan* is used for situations such as *The handle is on the door*, and *op* is used for situations such as *The jug is on the table* (Bowerman, 1996). Moreover, although languages may have the same number of terms to cover a set of spatial relations, they do not always do so in the same way. In Finnish the equivalents of *The handle is on the door* and *The apple is in the bowl* are grouped together using the inessive case (ending *-ssa*), whereas a different case ending (the adessive *-lla*) is used for *The jug is on the table*. When one considers relations other than containment and support, languages differ even more radically from each other. For example, while Indo-European languages use terms for left and right which depend on the reference frame adopted (left from one's point of view versus left based around the intrinsic axis of the object being viewed), several languages, such as Guugu Yimithirr (North Queensland, Australia) and Arandic (Pama-Nyungan, Australia) do not have terms like these at all. Instead these languages use terms associated with an absolute reference frame (e.g., North, South, East, West) in both small-scale (e.g., locating a pencil on a desk) and in large-scale space (Levinson, 1996a, 1996b; Pederson et al.,

1998). So spatial language differs across languages quite radically, thus providing a real semantic challenge for second language learners.

In this chapter we first examine the variables that underpin the comprehension and production of spatial prepositions in English. We overview the results of a body of experimental work conducted since the early 1990s that systematically manipulated properties of visual scenes in order to establish how spatial language and the spatial world co-vary. We then overview the functional geometric framework for spatial language (cf. Coventry & Garrod, 2004) and a computational model (implementation) of the framework that grounds spatial language directly in visual routines (Coventry, Cangelosi, Rajapakse, Bacon, Newstead, Joyce, & Richards, 2005). Finally, we consider the implications of the model for both first and second language acquisition.

2 Spatial language: an experimental natural history

2.1 Precursors to experimental work

Most linguists expressing a research interest in spatial prepositions up until twenty or so years ago in the main assumed that spatial language was about describing the positions of objects in space, and hence was about mapping spatial language onto geometric relations in the real or imagined scene being described. This view culminated in a seminar paper by Landau and Jackendoff (1993) in which they proposed that the distinction in visual science originally made by Ungerleider and Mishkin (1982) between the so-called "what" and "where" systems maps onto differences between syntactic categories in language. They argued that closed class categories such as spatial prepositions relate more to the output of the "where" system while open-class terms such as nouns relate more to the output of the "what" system. In other words, the objects involved in a spatial expression do not play much of a role in defining the spatial relation between the objects in that expression (see also Talmy's discussion of schematisation; Talmy, 1983, this volume).

By tradition the methodology used by linguists researching spatial language has been introspective, taking the form of thinking of examples of sentences and mapping those sentences onto associated spatial scenes. So *The coffee is in the cup* is associated with a relation where the coffee is fully contained in the space occupied by the cup, and one might then be tempted to assume that a containment/enclosure relation underlies the semantics of *in*. However, other examples that come to mind quickly challenge such a belief. *The daisies in the cup* only involves part containment, *The orange is in the fruit bowl* is true even when the orange is placed on top of a high pile of fruit outside the containing space of the fruit bowl, and *The crack is in the cup* is associated with a different spatial relation from the other forms of containment thus far mentioned. These examples (from a large catalogue of such examples; Herskovits, 1986; Coventry & Garrod, 2004) illustrate that coming up with a single unique geometric relation (or core sense) for a spatial preposition is not straight-forward. Acknowledging this problem, some have argued within a cog-nitive linguistic framework that the world is inherently vague and accordingly it is not possible to specify core meanings or definitions for spatial terms. For example, Brugman (1981, 1988) identifies nearly 100 different kinds of uses of *over*, and argued that these represent primary and secondary senses that are radially organized around three prototypical senses in the mind of the language user in the form of image schemata. Others have retained the based tenets of a core sense approach and have added pragmatic principles to bend and stretch these senses to create other senses (also lexicalized) which can themselves be extended by pragmatic principles (Herskovits, 1986).

The accounts of Brugman and Herskovits (among others) document in some detail the diversity of uses of geometric relations associated with individual prepositions, but it is questionable whether their analyses take us much beyond a description of the extensive polysemy of spatial terms. While minimally specified lexical entries for prepositions are associated with the problem of failing to map onto the extensive polysemy apparent with spatial prepositions, fully specified accounts have the mirror image problem of requiring the addition of a set of principles to indicate which sense is being referred to in context (see Coventry, 1998; Coventry & Garrod, 2004; Tyler & Evans, 2003 for more extensive review and dis-cussion). More critically there are two further issues that need to be addressed. First, what exactly are the representations of the geometric relations such as containment, and how does language map onto these representations emanating from perceptual systems? While simple geo-metric constructs, such as *enclosure* or *being higher than*, have intuitive appeal as primitives in the semantics of spatial expressions, the notion that the visual system produces such limited representations can been questioned. Second, the very assumption that spatial prepositions refers to geometric positions of objects in space has been challenged. In the late 1980s several authors began to focus on a range of "extra-geometric" constraints as important elements across a range of prepositions and lan-guages. These constraints have been labeled *extra-geometric* as they do not have to do with the geometry (usually construed) of the spatial relations being depicted in the scenes.

2.2 Spatial language involves more than geometry

While Miller and Johnson-Laird (1976) and Herskovits (1986) recognized interaction between objects as important for the preposition *at* (e.g., *The man is at the piano*), it was Garrod and Sanford (1989) and Vandeloise (1991) who argued for the importance of function for prepositions in English and French respectively while Talmy (1988) raised the issue of force dynamics in language more generally (although he did not apply force dynamics to prepositions directly).

Both Garrod and Sanford (1989) and Vandeloise (1991) pinpointed location control as a key component of the use of *in* and *on*. For an object to be *in* or *on* a reference object entails that the reference object will constrain the location of the located object over time, such that moving the reference object will cause the located object to move with it. So *in* can be regarded as a hybrid relation that involves both the geometric construct of containment and the extra-geometric construct of location control. The recognition of location control as an important element in the meaning of *in* and *on* meant that many of the problematic uses of these terms could be more easily dealt with. While *The daisies in the cup* involves only partial containment, location control is present for this situation (moving the cup will cause the daisies to move with it), as is also the case for *The crack in the cup*. Furthermore, Garrod and Sanford noted that extended uses of spatial prepositions also had the potential to be explained with this analysis (see also Tyler & Evans, 2003). *A person in a queue* means that the person's location is determined by the queue and the movement of the queue rather than by that person's movements alone. *In a bad mood* implies that a person's behavior is being controlled by their mood and *being on social security* implies that financial support is coming from social services. So the claim was made that functional relations between objects is important for spatial language use and also more extended (metaphorical) uses of the same terms.

In the early 1990s empirical evidence for the importance of location control and other extra-geometric variables started to emerge (see below). This body of experimental work led Coventry and Garrod (2004) to develop the functional geometric framework for spatial language comprehension. In the functional geometric framework a distinction is made between three types of information that in combination underpin the comprehension and production of spatial prepositions: geometric routines, dynamic-kinematic routines and specific knowledge of how objects are likely to interact in standard situations. Geometric routines are grounded versions of the types of geometric relations that are present in previous accounts, and two examples of geometric routines are a convex hull routine for *in* (Cohn, 1996; Cohn, Bennett, Gooday & Gotts, 1997) and the attention vector sum model for *above* (Regier & Carlson, 2001). These routines are discussed at length in Coventry and Garrod (2004). Here we focus on dynamic-kinematic routines and specific situational knowledge together with evidence for their existence as these routines provide clues to how spatial language is acquired.

2.2.1 Dynamic-kinematic routines

The first dynamic-kinematic route to be identified was location control which underlies the comprehension and production of *in* and *on*. For a located object to be *in* a container, this entails more than just spatial enclosure/inclusion; containment also entails the notion of location control whereby the reference object constrains the location of the located object over time. Location control is a concept which is amenable to experimental testing, and a number of studies showed just how important location control is for the comprehension of *in* and *on*.

In one series of experiments video images of fruit and balls were shown in various positions in relation to containers. For example, an apple (the located object, marked with a star in Fig. 6.1) was shown perched high on top of a pile of other apples in a bowl (the reference object). The distance between the apple and the bottom and rim of the container was varied so that the apple could be almost touching the bottom of the container in one scene and positioned on top of a large pile of apples high above the rim of the container in another scene. Critically, location control was also manipulated. In the strong location control condition, the whole scene was shown moving from side to side, with all the objects maintaining the same relative positions over time. In contrast, in the weak location control condition the apple was shown wobbling from side to side while the other objects in the scene remained stationary. So in the strong location control condition, location control is seen to hold because the bowl is clearly controlling the location of the apple over time. However, in the weak location control condition the bowl is not seen to control the location of the apple because the apple is

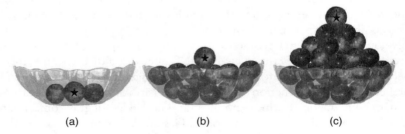

(a)   (b)   (c)

Figure 6.1 Examples of scenes used in video experiments manipulating geometry and location control (Coventry, 1998; Richards, Coventry, & Clibbens, 2004). The object with the star is the located object, and the bowl is the reference object. (a), (b), and (c) illustrate three levels of geometric containment. Location control was manipulated for each level of geometry by either showing the whole scene moving together at the same rate (strong location control), moving the located object independently of the other objects (weak location control), or presenting the scene statically (no movement control).

moving independently of the other objects in the scene. A control (no movement; static scene) condition was also included. If location control is important, it should be expected that *in* would be preferred more in the strong location control condition than in the control condition, and preferred least in the weak location control condition.

Using a range of methodologies including sentence completion tasks (*The located object is* ____ *the reference object*) and sentence acceptability rating tasks (using a Likert scale to rate sentences of the form *The location object is preposition the reference object*), a series of experiments showed the importance of location control as a predictor of preposition use with both adults and children (Coventry, 1998; Richards, Coventry & Clibbens, 2004). *In* was produced most (compared to the production of other prepositions) and was rated as being most appropriate in cases where location control was strongest (where the located and reference objects were moving together at the same rate), and least when the located object was moving of its own accord while the bowl and the rest of the objects remained stationary. Furthermore, Richards, Coventry and Clibbens (2004) found evidence that children's language is initially more sensitive to location control than to the position of the located object. They tested 80 children ranging from 3 years 4 months to 7 years 8 months of age using a naughty puppet scenario where a naughty puppet moved a located object (e.g., an apple) to a new location (e.g., on top of a pile of fruit in a container) and the child had to tell a blindfolded puppet where the located object had been placed. Even in the youngest age group (age range 3;4 to 4;6), children used *in* as first (or only) prepositional phrase most in the scenes where there was evidence of location control and least in the scenes which gave evidence against location control. These results show that children are sensitive to location control not long after they can reliably produce the prepositions *in* and *on*. Moreover, location control impacted more on their choice of language used to describe scenes than the geometric relations in the scene (height of pile). The effects of geometry increased with age but the effect of location control was constant across age groups. These results were also found for scenes involving support (*on*).

A second way in which location control has been manipulated involved static scenes where there were alternative potential sources of location control. Garrod, Ferrier and Campbell (1999) presented participants with video-clips of different arrangements of a pile of Ping-Pong balls and a glass bowl. Much like the scenes in Fig. 6.1, they manipulated the geometric relationship between a black Ping-Pong ball and bowl by varying the distance between the located object and the reference object. The other factor that was manipulated was the degree to which the location of the black Ping-Pong ball could be seen to be controlled by an external source. In half of the scenes the ball was attached to a thin (but visible) piece of wire suspended from above the bowl. According to the extra-geometric routine of location control, viewers' confidence in describing the black Ping-Pong ball as being *in* the bowl should relate directly to the degree to which they see the container (i.e., the bowl) as controlling the location of the located object (i.e., the black Ping-Pong ball). In this study half the participants made judgments regarding the appropriateness of different descriptions of the configuration of ball and bowl. The other half were asked what would happen to the black Ping-Pong ball if the bowl were moved sideways. The proportion of viewers who judged the ball as maintaining its relation to the bowl following the hypothetical movement was taken as an indicator of the degree to which the bowl was seen as controlling the location of the ball. Garrod, Ferrier and Campbell found that location control affected linguistic judgments. Additionally, comparing the two sets of judgments—location control judgments and judgments as to the appropriateness of *in* descriptions—there was a strong correlation between the two sets of judgments.

So there is considerable evidence for the application of what we have termed the dynamic-kinematic routine of location control to *in*. However, there are two points to note. First, location control in the studies thus far mentioned was important only when the containment relation was weak (i.e., when the located object was positioned above the rim of the container). Second, there are many cases where location control does not seem to apply. For example, *The marble in the circle* does not seem to involve location control. Therefore, although this routine is clearly central to the comprehension and production of *in*, and children are very sensitive to it when they are acquiring spatial terms, we need to retain a geometric routine which allows calculation of degree of containment/enclosure independent of the extra-geometric routine of location control (and support independent of location control for *on*).

Just as location control is important for the comprehension and production of *in* and *on*, there is a range of types of evidence that dynamic-kinematic routines are also important for the comprehension and production of projective prepositions. For example, Coventry, Prat-Sala and Richards (2001) set out to examine the effects of functional relations versus geometric routines on the comprehension of *over*, *under*, *above* and *below*. In one experiment they manipulated both geometric and functional relations using objects which have the function of protecting another object (a person) from falling objects (see Fig. 6.2).

Three positions of objects were depicted for each scene representing varying degrees of a higher than relation equivalent to the varying degrees of containment manipulated for *in* and *on*. Additionally, the protecting objects were either shown to protect the person from falling objects (as shown in Fig. 6.2), to fail to protect the person (falling objects were shown to miss the protecting object and hit the person instead), or the falling objects were not present (a control condition). Participants had the task

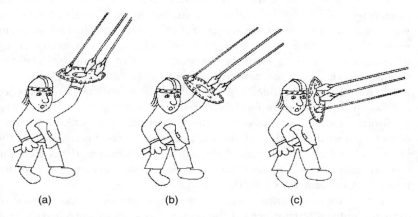

(a)   (b)   (c)

Figure 6.2 Examples of scenes used by Coventry et al. (2001). These pictures, (a), (b), and (c), show three positions of the shield (the located object). All scenes show that the shield is fulfilling its function of protection. The non-functional scenes (not shown) showed the spears missing the shield and striking the Viking. The neutral scenes involved no falling objects.

of rating the appropriateness of sentences of the type *the located object is over/above the reference object* (e.g., *The shield is over/above the Viking*) or *the located object is under/below the reference object* (e.g., *The Viking is under/below the shield*) to describe each picture. First, Coventry et al. (2001) found an effect of geometry as one would expect; rotating the shield, for example, away from the gravitational plane reduced the appropriateness of *over* and *above* (in line with results found by Logan & Sadler, 1996 and Hayward & Tarr, 1995). However, equally strong effects of the functional manipulation were also present. The highest ratings were given to the functional scenes, and the lowest ratings were given to the non-functional scenes. More importantly, effects of function were found even when the protecting objects were in geometrically prototypical positions for those terms (e.g., directly above the center of mass of the reference object for *over*). This indicates that functional factors have an influence even when the geometrical constraints are at their strongest (unlike the results for *in* and *on*). Additionally, this study found evidence that the comprehension of *over/under* and *above/below* is differentially influenced by geometry and functionality. Ratings of *above* and *below* were better predicted by the geometric manipulation than ratings for *over* and *under*, while ratings for *over* and *under* were more influenced by functionality than those for *above/below*.

The same pattern of results is found even when the protection function is not depicted directly. Coventry, Richards, Joyce and Cangelosi (forthcoming) showed static pictures similar to those shown in Fig. 6.2, but the falling objects (e.g., spears) were presented a distance from the protecting objects (e.g., shield) and therefore the success of the protecting function was not directly shown. One group of participants had the task of rating sentences containing *over/under/above/below* as before, and a second group of participants had to estimate the percentage of falling objects they thought would make contact with the person in each picture. Coventry et al. found a strong negative correlation between the percentage of objects that would make contact and the appropriateness of these pre-positions to describe the scene—the greater the percentage of falling objects that would hit the person, the less appropriate it is to describe the shield as being over the Viking, for example. Furthermore, the correlation was stronger for *over/under* than for *above/below*, mirroring the results found by Coventry et al. (2001).

As we have seen, these experiments show important influences of dynamic-kinematic routines on the comprehension and production of a range of projective terms and how weighting given to dynamic-kinematic routines differs across spatial terms and types of objects. We now turn to consider the evidence for the importance of the third component in the functional geometric framework, object knowledge.

2.2.2 *Situational knowledge*

The application of geometric and dynamic-kinematic visual routines is driven by knowledge of the objects involved in the scene and how those objects typically interact in past learned interactions between those objects. Objects are associated with particular routines, both geometric and dynamic-kinematic, and prepositions have weightings for these para-meters. As we have seen above, the comprehension of *over/under* is better predicted by extra-geometric relations than the comprehension of *above/below*, while conversely the comprehension of *above/below* is better pre-dicted by geometric routines than the comprehension of *over/under*. In the functional geometric framework it is how these constraints "mesh" together (Glenberg, 1997) that underpins the comprehension of spatial prepositions. Here we give some examples of how object and situational knowledge impact on spatial language use.

Although containers all have the function of constraining contents over time (location control), some are more appropriately designed for liquids whereas others are only suited to hold solids. Jugs are usually associated with containing liquids, bowls usually contain either liquids or solids, and sieves are designed to contain solids alone. Coventry, Carmichael and Garrod (1994) found that *in* was judged to be more appropriate for a solid (e.g., an apple) in a bowl compared to a solid in exactly the same position in a jug with the same dimensions as the bowl when the solid object was on top of a pile of similar objects.

122

Furthermore, adding liquid to the jug further decreased the use (and rating) of *in* but made no difference in the case of the bowl. Coventry et al. argue that the addition of water appears to make the object-specific function of the jug more salient, further reducing the appropriateness of the jug as a container of solids. This finding is not limited to jugs and bowls, but generalizes to a basic difference between containers that are primarily containers of liquids versus those which are primarily containers of solids (Coventry & Prat-Sala, 2001).

How an object is labeled also influences its perceived function in a scene and in turn influences how one describes the location of an object with reference to that object. Coventry et al. (1994) found that the specific labels given to a reference object influenced the use of prepositions to describe the spatial relation between a located object and that reference object. When the same reference object was labeled a *dish* versus a *plate*, *in* was rated as more appropriate and was used more frequently in the sentence completion task. When the object was labeled *plate*, *on* was preferred and rated more highly. Therefore, objects become associated with particular geometric and/or dynamic-kinematic routines.

The fact that an object may be conceptualized in many different ways leads to situations in which the same object may be processed using different routines, and these may vary according to the language itself. In English a person can be *in* or *on* a bus or plane, but *on* a car would only be appropriate if the person was standing on top of the external shell of the car. Vehicles afford location control, but can be conceptualized as containers or supporting surfaces. For English the application of *on* relates to the size and the length-to-width ratio of such vehicles; large long vehicles are usually regarded as supporting surfaces, but small objects with a low height-to-width ratio are more usually regarded exclusively as containers. In contrast vehicles are all conceptualized as containers in Polish—the equivalent of *in* (the Polish preposition *w*) is appropriate for vehicles but the equivalent of *on* (*na*) is not (Cienki, 1989).

It is not only objects that drive geometric and dynamic-kinematic routines—relations between objects are also important. Carlson-Radvansky, Covey and Lattanzi (1999) asked participants to place an object above a second object, and they varied the association between the two objects. For instance, when the reference object was a toothbrush (with the bristles on the left and the handle of the toothbrush extending to the right), the object to be placed was either a toothpaste tube or a tube of paint. They found that placements of the objects were between the middle (center-of-mass) of the toothbrush and bristles. However, the associated objects (toothpaste tube) were placed nearer the functional part of the reference object (e.g., nearer the head of the toothbrush) than the unrelated objects (the tube of paint). So knowledge of how objects typically interact affects spatial language judgments.

Finally it is important to note that how objects interact is defined in context. Coventry et al. (2001) compared objects that do not have a known protecting function with those that do (e.g., they substituted a *stool* for the *shield* in Fig. 6.2). While an object such as a shield has an obvious protecting function, the function of the stool is as a supporting surface. Although Coventry et al. found that ratings for the inappropriate functional objects (e.g., *The stool is over the Viking*) were lower overall than for the sentences involving appropriate protecting objects, no interactions were found between this variable and any of the other variables examined. In other words, the effects of functionality and geometry were present for the non-stereotypically functioning objects just as they were with the stereotypically functioning objects. This is evidence that how objects are functioning in context is important, irrespective of our stereotypic knowledge about those objects.

2.1.3 The functional geometric framework: Putting multiple constraints together on line

Within the functional geometric framework, dynamic-kinematic routines and the knowledge of the objects involved in the scene and how those objects typically interact in past learned interactions between those objects all come together to establish the situation-specific meaning of spatial language. The meaning of a spatial expression does not simply derive from the addition of the fixed meanings of the preposition together with the meanings of other elements in the sentence (e.g., nouns and verb). Rather, meaning is constructed on-line as a function of how these multiple constraints come together.

The view that meaning is constructed on-line as a result of putting together multiple constraints is consistent with recent work on embodiment, and in particular the work emanating from the labs of Glenberg (e.g., Glenberg, 1997; Glenberg & Robertson, 1999, 2000; Kaschak & Glenberg, 2000), Barsalou (e.g., Barsalou, 1999) and Zwaan (e.g., Zwaan, 2004; Zwaan & Taylor, 2006). Common to these accounts is the notion that words are associated with a range of types of perceptual information. Knowing what an object is requires knowing what one does with it, and therefore its representation should reflect how one can interact with that object, a representation that can prepare you for situated action. For instance Kaschak and Glenberg (2000) have argued that the meaning of a sentence is constructed by indexing words or phrases to real objects or perceptual analog symbols for those objects, deriving affordances from the objects and symbols and then meshing the affordances under the guidance of syntax.

We have developed an implementation of the functional framework using constrained connectionism (see also Regier, 1996, and Regier &

Carlson, 2001 for alternative computational models). Details of the model can be found elsewhere (Coventry, Cangelosi, Rajapakse, Bacon, Newstead, Joyce, & Richards, 2005)—here we confine ourselves to some general observations about this model. The important feature of the model is that it learns spatial language by binding that language directly to visual routines grounded in the processing of visual scenes. Employing a dual-route connectionist architecture, the two input channels to the dual-route connectionist module are separate symbolic input (i.e., expressions of the form NOUN PREPOSITION NOUN) and visual scene information. Visual scenes comprise videos (or still images) of a located object (e.g., a teapot), a reference object (e.g., a cup), and other objects (e.g., tea). The two input systems share hidden-unit resources. Data from participants (from acceptabilty rating studies of the type already described above) is used to train the model to produce the most appropriate spatial expression given the visual input. Training proceeds as follows: the symbolic "half" is trained to auto-associate, establishing representations of symbol–symbol co-occurences (cf. Landauer & Dumais, 1997). The visual "half" is trained similarly. Co-training of both routes then proceeds, enabling a mapping between symbolic and visual domains, resulting in: symbol–symbol processing (co-occurrence of symbols only), and joint visuo-symbol-to-symbol–symbol processing.

The model is able to learn the appropriate NOUN PREPOSITION NOUN combination to describe a given (new) visual input scene. Importantly, the model is also able to utilize predictions about what will happen to objects in scenes which in turn affect the spatial language the model produces to describe those scenes. For instance, training on input videos showing containers pouring substances into other containers in various positions enables the model (using Elman simple recurrent networks; Elman, 1990) to predict what will happen to the pouring substances over time (e.g., whether the tea, for example, will end up inside the cup or not). This information is precisely the dynamic-kinematic information required for *over/under/above/below* judgments. Hence the model is able to run perceptual simulations of events mapping directly onto language judgments about the same scenes, consistent with the functional geometric framework.

3 Learning a first language

3.1 Prelinguistic knowledge of geometric and dynamic-kinematic routines

According to the model developed by Coventry and Garrod (2004) and the implementation of it (Coventry et al., 2005), spatial language involves a combination of grounding symbols directly in perceptual representations as well as learning how symbols co-occur in the language being learned. The goal of the language learner is therefore to bind linguistic and perceptual information (e.g., visual routines) together in order to map language onto meaningful events.

The starting point for learning spatial language is the pre-linguistic perceptual knowledge of the world that is present from the early stages of life. There is good evidence that infants have knowledge of both geometric and dynamic-kinematic routines. In relation to geometric routines, preferential looking studies have established that babies only a few months old can distinguish between a range of relations including *left* and *right* (Behl-Chadha & Eimas, 1995) and *above, below* and *between* (Antell & Caron, 1985; Quinn, 1994; Quinn, Cummins, Kase, Martin & Weissman, 1996; Quinn, Norris, Pasko, Schmader & Mash, 1999). Preferential looking relies on the much replicated finding that infants have a tendency to look longer at novel than at familiar stimuli. For example, Quinn (1994) habituated 3-and 4-month-old infants to a single diamond presented in different positions above a (horizontal) bar. Infants then saw two diamonds in novel positions; one above the bar and one below the bar. Infants consistently showed a visual preference for the diamond presented in the novel position below the bar. This strongly suggests that they had formed a category for *above*.

There is also evidence that infants as young as 2.5 months have expectations about containment events and location control. Hespos and Baillargeon (2001) showed infants an object lowered inside a container with either a wide opening or no opening in its top surface. Infants looked longer at the closed-container event rather than the open-container event indicating the infants have knowledge about containers. In another experiment infants saw an object lowered either inside or behind a container. The container was then moved forward and to the side showing the object visible behind it. Infants looked longer when the object was revealed in the condition where the object was initially placed inside the container than in the condition where it was initially placed behind the container. This was probably as the infants realized that the object could not pass through the wall of the container, and hence should have moved with the container to the new location—an early appreciation of location control.

Infants also have early knowledge of gravity. Kim and Spelke (1992) showed infants videotaped events in which a ball rolled downwards or upwards while speeding up or slowing down. At 7 months infants looked longer at test events with inappropriate acceleration. Similarly, when they were shown a stationary object released on an incline they looked longer when the object moved upwards. In another study Needham and Baillargeon (1993) have shown that 4.5-month infants have expectations that an object will fall towards the ground when it has its supporting surface removed from beneath it. Infants were shown a hand placing a box either on a platform and leaving it there or placing the box beyond the platform and leaving it seemingly floating in mid-air. The impossible event attracted the infants' attention for longer than the possible event.

In summary, before language is learned, infants have developed quite sophisticated knowledge of the spatial world in terms of geometric and dynamic-kinematic routines. But what happens to these conceptual building blocks when language is learned?

3.2 Spatial language acquisition and linguistic relativity

From the pre-linguistic knowledge foundations that the child brings to language learning the child has to acquire the symbol-to-symbol relations in the language and visuo-symbol-to-symbol relations. Given that languages differ in how they carve up the spatial world, one can ask what happens to this pre-linguistic knowledge during language learning.

Comparing English and Korean speakers, Choi and Bowerman (1991) presented evidence to suggest that the first language children are exposed to affects the way in which space is conceptualized and categorized. English expresses path notions (movement into, out of, etc.) in a constituent which is a "satellite" to the main verb (e.g., a particle or preposition), while Korean expresses path in the verb itself (see also section 4.1 below, and Cadierno, this volume). A video cassette is put *in* a video case in English, a lid is put *on* a kettle, a pear is put *in* a bowl, and a glass is put *on* a table. In Korean the verb *kkita* is used for tight-fit path events (e.g., put video cassette in video case / put lid on kettle) whereas *nehta* is used for loose-fit containment relations (e.g., put pear in bowl) and *nohta* is used for loose-fit support relations (e.g., put glass on table). Therefore, Korean carves up the spatial world according to degrees of location control as much as it does according to (geometric) containment and support relations, while English carves up containment and support relations primarily in terms of geometric routines rather than location control. Furthermore, Choi and Bowerman (1991) found evidence that children learning English and Korean respectively extend meanings of terms according to the semantic structure of their input language. English children produced *in* for paths into both tight- and loose-fit containers and extended their use of *in* accordingly, whereas Korean children produced *kkita* for putting objects into tight places, *nehta* for putting objects into loose containers, and extended their use accordingly. Choi, McDonough, Bowerman and Mandler (1999) used a preferential-looking task to assess the generalizations made by children learning either English or Korean. By the age of one-and-a-half to two years the children in both cases spent more time looking at the language-appropriate aspects of spatial relations. English children looked more at containment scenes than non-containment scenes on hearing *in*, whereas Korean children looked more at tight-fit scenes than loose-fit scenes when hearing *kkita*. However, testing even younger children, McDonough, Choi and Mandler (2003) provide evidence that infants have conceptual readiness for learning location control in either language at an earlier age. Testing 9- to 14-month-old Korean and English infants, they found that both groups categorized both tight and loose containment and tight and loose support.

Overall, the data indicate that, prior to the acquisition of L1, prelinguistic infants have information available regarding both geometric and extra-geometric properties of spatial relations (e.g., McDonough et al., 2003), and when language learning gets under way the language learned actually structures how semantic categories are formed (e.g., Bowerman & Choi, 2001).

4 Second Language Acquisition and attention

4.1 Second Language Acquisition: Predictions from the functional geometric framework

We started out this chapter indicating that languages differ in how they carve up the spatial world. Given that one may have acquired a particular language that carves up the world in a particular way, what are the consequences, if any, for the acquisition of a second language? As an example, consider second language learning of English and Spanish.

As discussed earlier, while English has two different lexical items, *in* and *on*, for containment and support events respectively, Spanish has a single term, *en*, to cover both these relations. Furthermore, even where Spanish and English share the same number of prepositions to cover a spatial relation, the weightings given to geometric and dynamic-kinematic routines differ between languages as a function of term. Coventry and Guijarro-Fuentes (2004) compared acceptability ratings for *over/under/above/below* to ratings for the related Spanish prepositions *sobre/encima de/debajo de/bajo* using similar materials to those displayed in Fig. 6.2. For the superior terms *sobre* and *encima de*, the results mirrored the findings for *over* and *above*. Acceptability ratings for *sobre* were more affected by functionality (e.g., whether the shield is shown to fulfil its function or not) than ratings for *encima de*. However, no differences in the influence of functionality and geometry were found for the inferior terms *debajo de* and *bajo*; ratings for both terms were strongly influenced by extra-geometric constraints. Additionally, the influence of the manipulation of geometry for superior and inferior prepositions in Spanish was much weaker than for the equivalent terms in English.

This analysis allows us to enumerate possibilities regarding how Spanish and English may be acquired as L2 as follows:

1   A single dimension is used for L2 learning (either geometric or extra-geometric dimensions), but weightings for this dimension from L1 are not used.

2   A single dimension is used for L2 learning and weightings from L1 are used.

3   Both geometric and extra-geometric dimensions are used to acquire L2, but weightings from L1 are not used.

4   Both dimensions are used to acquire L2, and weightings from L1 are used.

We can illustrate these possibilities with reference to Fig. 6.2, and the difference in weighting for superior and inferior projective terms in English and Spanish. We know that *sobre* and *encima de* behave like *over* and *above* with respect to weightings of extra-geometric and geometric dimensions (*over* and *sobre* are more affected by the position of the rain than the position of the umbrella, and vice versa for *above* and *encima de*). However, for inferior terms, while *under* and *below* mirror *over* and *above* with regard to weighting for these dimensions, *debajo de* and *bajo* are largely unaffected by geometric variables, but both behave like *over/sobre/under* in that they are affected by extra-geometric variables. So if (1) or (2) is the case, then patterns of acceptability rating should only be influenced by a single dimension (i.e., either geometry or function in this case). If (3) or (4) is the case, then both variables should affect acceptability ratings. However, if there is transfer of weightings from L1 to L2, then geometry effects should be found for *debajo de* and *bajo* differentially as well as differential function effects (supporting (4)).

Of course, more basic errors may occur which also allow us to disentangle these possibilities. For example, in case of L2 English learning for L1 Spanish speakers, *in* and *on* may be problematic because *en* covers both these terms in English. It is therefore expected that *in* and *on* maybe confused if (2) or (4) is the case. Furthermore, over-generalization may occur where *in* and *on* are used for spatial relations where another preposition is more appropriate.

We are currently undertaking a large scale study examining these possibilities with regard to spatial prepositions in English and Spanish. However, existing studies suggest that some of these possibilities are more likely than others. To begin with, is there any evidence that transfer occurs at all in the case of spatial language?

With regard to motion events in English and Spanish, there is some evidence that transfer does occur in L2. Talmy has noted that languages package motion events in different ways (see Cadierno, this volume for extensive discussion). Some languages, including English and most Indo-European languages, have been termed "satellite-framed" languages (Talmy, 1985). These languages express path motions (e.g., movement out of, into, on, etc.) using a constituent that is a satellite to the main verb, such as a preposition (in the case of English). Other languages, such as Spanish and Korean (as discussed above), have been termed "verb-framed" languages in that they express path in the verb itself (and in some of these languages, such as Korean, they lack spatial prepositions completely). So the way that languages carve up motion involves a difference in the extent to which particular constituents express motion. This difference allowed a number of authors to examine whether acquiring a verb-framed or a satellite-framed language is affected by whether L1 has the same or a different typology (Cadierno, 2004, this volume; Navarro & Nicoladis, 2005) with somewhat mixed results (see Cadierno, this volume for a review).

In relation to other spatial expressions there are a number of studies providing evidence for L1 to L2 transfer across a range of languages (e.g., Carroll, 1997; Harley, 1989; Ijaz, 1986; Jarvis & Odlin, 2000; Mukattash, 1984; Pavesi, 1987; Schumann, 1986). Although these studies vary methodologically in ways that affect their direct comparison, as well as the reliability and validity of the conclusions drawn in some cases (see Jarvis, 2000; Odlin, this volume, for discussion), they all suggest to some degree that language transfer occurs (though not necessarily conceptual transfer, see Odlin, this volume). For example, Jarvis and Odlin (2000) compared Finnish and Swedish L1 speakers' performance in English as L2. Finnish and Swedish differ in a number of respects with regard to spatial language. Finnish has 15 productive nominal cases (including the nominative, accusative, genitive, partitive cases) that are expressed as agglutinative suffixes on nouns and their modifying adjectives while Swedish, like English, only has the nominative and genitive cases for nouns and these plus the accusative for pronouns. Finnish also has a complex subject–verb agreement system in comparison to Swedish and English. Participants watched a segment of a silent movie, and had the task of writing narrative of the film. The narratives produced some differences between Finnish and Swedish speakers' use of spatial reference in the same spatial contexts. Consistent with the differences between L1s, and the similarities between L1s and L2, Finnish speakers produced different spatial prepositions to Swedish speakers in the same context in L2, and Finnish speakers produced more spatial expressions omitting prepositions than Swedish speakers in L2. Furthermore, the Finnish speakers showed a preference for using *on* while Swedish speakers showed a preference for using *in* (both grammatically correct uses) mapping onto preferences in L1 narrative controls for the same silent movie. So Jarvis and Odlin provide evidence of language transfer for spatial terms consistent with results produced in some other studies spanning a variety of combinations of languages (e.g., Caroll, 1997; Harley, 1989; Mukattash, 1984; Pavesi, 1987; Schumann, 1986).

Overall, there is some preliminary evidence that transfer does occur in the case of spatial language, but what about the more fine-grained predictions made above? One issue in the first and second language learning literature is the extent to which learners use single cues versus multiple cues when learning a language. There is evidence that language learners are selective in the parameters they focus on, at least in the early stages of L2 acquisition. For example, in artificial language learning, it has been shown learners often focus on one cue at a time (e.g., MacWhinney, Pleh & Bates, 1985; Bates & MacWhinney, 1987; see Ellis, 2006a and b for discussion). Consistent with this, in first language acquisition, Richards, Coventry and Clibbens (2004) found that children modified their spatial descriptions more in response to location control changes than to changes in geometry when describing scenes showing containment and support relations in L1 English. Of course, it does not follow that second language learners focus on the same cues when acquiring L2. As we reviewed earlier in the chapter, a natural history of research on spatial language shows that a focus on the importance of extra-geometric relations underpinning the comprehension and production of spatial terms has been a relatively recent development. It is possible that native L1 speakers also focus on geometric relations as a main cue to learning distinctions between spatial terms in L2. Thus far only Munnich (2000) provides any data that speaks to this issue. Hence we will briefly overview his methodology and main results.

Munnich (2000) presented a range of rating and production tests to 60 adults who had learned English as their L2. Half of these were L1 native speakers of Spanish and the other half were L1 native speakers of Korean. These groups were further subdivided into three categories based on age of acquisition—early, mid- and late learners. The tests administered (also given to a control group of English native speakers) included a morphosyntax task (adapted from Johnson & Newport, 1989), and several spatial language tasks presented as both rating tasks and production tasks. Participants were presented with pictures either with sentences to be rated or without sentences where spatial terms were to be freely produced. The spatial materials were more fine-grained than those used in previous studies allowing Munnich (2000) to undertake some preliminary analyses comparing performance on materials varying in geometric and extra-geometric contrasts. The main finding was that age of acquisition effects were found for materials involving function, but not for materials involving geometry. From these data, Munnich proposes that ". . . for those contrasts with little or no functional information required, it appears that even adult learners of English can attain native-like performance" (p. 133). This is the first evidence to suggest that, contrary to the first language acquisition of spatial terms, extra-geometric relations are troublesome for Spanish and Korean speakers in L2 English.

A further issue relates to whether L2 effectively combines lexical items from L1 into a single category, or whether L2 requires finer discrimination than distinctions made in L1. In Spanish the task of moving from *en* in L1 to *in* and *on* in L2 English requires differentiating between containment and support relations that share dynamic-kinematic routines (location control) but differ with regard to geometric routines. For the English speaker learning L2 Spanish *en* can be used for any use of *in* and *on*. So it could be argued that moving from a single lexical category to several is harder than the reverse, a view consistent with previous claims made in the second language acquisition literature (e.g., Stockwell, Brown & Martin, 1965; see also Cadierno, this volume).

To recap, from existing data in the SLA literature we might expect that learners acquiring prepositions in L2 Spanish or English would be likely to focus on minimal cues, either geometric or extra-geometric, and to become sensitive to the subtle interplay between elements of the functional geometric framework only later in acquisition. Preliminary data from Munnich (2000) suggest that extra-geometric variables in L2 may be focused upon later in acquisition, and that this aspect of spatial language is particularly hard to master.

4.2 Second Language Acquisition—further implications and conclusions

The model we have outlined takes us to some more important methodological issues regarding second language acquisition. According to the Coventry el al. (2005) model, language learning involves acquiring symbol–symbol relations and symbol–visuo-symbol relations. Yet much testing of second language ability involves using language alone (e.g., writing a passage, filling in the blanks, etc.) rather than testing how spatial language co-varies with the spatial world. Following the preferential looking work we have briefly reviewed, how language drives attention is a critical part of being a competent speaker of a language in the spatial domain (see Odlin, this volume for discussion of conceptual versus meaning transfer). The use of *in* and *on* in English involves more than knowing which nouns prepositions can co-occur with—these terms should drive how spatial relations are conceptualized in the scene being described. A consequence of this is that when presented with a picture, such as that shown in Fig. 6.3(a), one might expect that English speakers might misremember the shape of the reference object in line with the spatial preposition paired to conceptualize the spatial scene. So if the sentence presented with scene (a) is *The bird is in the dish*, one might expect that (b) would be more likely to be false-alarmed to than (c) on an old-versus-new recognition task. In contrast, we might expect that (c) would be more likely to be false-alarmed to than (b) if *The bird is on the dish* was presented with picture (a). However, one might expect Spanish speakers to false-alarm

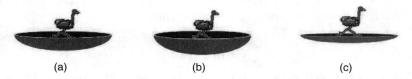

(a) (b) (c)

Figure 6.3 Visuo-spatial scenes illustrating "the bird is in the dish" versus "the bird is on the dish."

equally to (b) or (c) as *en* is appropriate for the dish conceptualized as either a container or supporting surface. Spanish speakers acquiring English as L2 should also exhibit the same pattern as native English native speakers should they truly grasp the symbol–visuo-symbol relation. Hence performance on such tasks may be revealing regarding the extent to which the L2 learner has truly grasped language.

So we have suggested that second language learning research would do well to separate out knowledge of symbol–symbol relations and knowledge of symbol–visuo-symbol relations when considering competence for spatial language. Furthermore, using existing computational models as a means of testing and developing theories of Second Language Acquisition offers much potential for fruitful development in the SLA field in the coming years. Already computational models for spatial language have been shown to operate using the same architecture across a range of languages. For example, Regier's (1996) constrained connectionist model for spatial language has been trained on a range of languages from different language families, including Japanese, Mixtec and Russian as well as English. Using the end states of these training sets to then train on a second language would be an exciting avenue to explore.

A final point to note concerns the current disparity between first and second language learning. First language acquisition clearly involves learning symbol–symbol and symbol–visuo-symbol relations in tandem. Furthermore, there is evidence that learning language with associated images/imagery enhances children's reading comprehension (Glenberg, Gutierrez, Levin, Japuntich, & Kaschak, 2004). However, second language acquisition rarely presents images with language as this knowledge is assumed to be given in first language acquisition and is presented in the form of language (i.e., L1 to L2 language-to-language mappings rather than L2 language—visuo-symbol mapping). It would be worthwhile to examine whether grounding language during second language learning affects the success with which one acquires that second language (see also Tyler & Evans, 2004). Moreover, distinctions between prepositions in language learning guides frequently map spatial prepositions in L2 onto the geometric equivalents in L1. Sensitivity to both geometric and extra-geometric constraints in language teaching may help direct the attention of the second language learner in ways that ground spatial language more directly in line with narrative goals and events.

5 Conclusions

The use of experimental techniques varying the spatial world and measuring linguistic responses to changes in spatial array has produced a comprehensive picture of how spatial prepositions are comprehended and produced in English (and in some other languages). The acquisition of spatial prepositions has been shown to be underpinned by pre-linguistic knowledge of geometric and dynamic-kinematic routines consistent with the functional geometric framework (cf. Coventry & Garrod, 2004) and the acquisition of spatial language across languages is sensitive to components of the framework. Such fine-grained analyses afford fine-grained predictions regarding second language acquisition. We hope that forthcoming experimental work will allow us to establish whether particular constraints dominate the acquisition of spatial prepositions in a second language. The offered model represents the various and extended semantic features associated with the spatial prepositions in both English and Spanish. We believe that this cognitive model gives a more systematic account of the semantics of English and Spanish prepositions than other more traditional accounts, therefore reducing the necessity for rote item learning on Second Language Acquisition. Moreover, we believe that such an analysis has real implications for the classroom context of the different semantic interpretations of each of the spatial prepositions in English and Spanish.

Bibliography

Antell, S. E. G., & Caron, A. J. (1985). Neonatal perception of spatial relationships. *Infant Behavior and Development*, 8, 15–23.

Barsalou, L. W. (1999). Perceptual symbol systems. *Behavioral and Brain Sciences*, *22(4)*, 577–660.

Bates, E., & MacWhinney, B. (1987). Competition, variation and language learning. In B. MacWhinney (Ed.), *Mechanisms of Language Acquisition*, pp. 157–193. Mahwah, NJ: Lawrence Erlbaum Associates.

Behl-Chadha, G., & Eimas, P. D. (1995). Infant categorization of left-right spatial relations. *British Journal of Developmental Psychology*, *13*, 69–79.

Bowerman, M. (1996). Learning how to structure space for language: a cross-linguistic perspective. In P. Bloom, M. A. Peterson, L. Nadel, & M. F. Garrett (Eds.), *Language and space* (pp. 385–436). Cambridge, MA: MIT Press.

Bowerman, M., & Choi, S. (2001). Shaping meanings for language: universal and language-specific in the acquisition of spatial semantic categories. In M. Bowerman & S. C. Levinson (Eds.), *Language acquisition and conceptual development* (pp. 475–511). Cambridge: Cambridge University Press.

Brugman, C. (1981). *The story of "over."* M.A. thesis, University of California at Berkeley. Reprinted by the Indiana University Linguistics Club.

Brugman, C. (1988). *The story of "over": Polysemy, semantics and the structure of the lexicon.* Garland Press.

Cadierno, T. (2004). Expressing motion events in a second languae: A cognitive typological perspective. In M. Achard & S. Niemeier (Eds.), *Cognitive Linguistics, Second Language Acquistion, and Foreign Language Teaching,* pp. 13–49. Berlin: Mouton de Gruyter.

Carlson-Radvansky, L. A., Covey, E. S., & Lattanzi, K. M. (1999). "What" effects on "where": Functional influences on spatial relations. *Psychological Science, 10,* 516–521.

Carroll, M. (1997). The acquisition of English. In A. Becker & M. Carroll (Eds.), *The acquisition of spatial relations in a second language,* pp. 35–78. Amsterdam: John Benjamins.

Choi, S., & Bowerman, M. (1991). Learning to express motion events in English and Korean: the influence of language-specific lexicalization patterns. *Cognition, 41,* 83–121.

Choi, S., McDonough, L., Bowerman, M., & Mandler, J. (1999). Early sensitivity to language-specific spatial categories in English and Korean. *Cognitive Development, 14,* 241–268.

Cienki, A. J. (1989). *Spatial cognition and the semantics of prepositions in English, Polish, and Russian.* Munich: Sagner.

Cohn, A. G. (1996). *Calculi for qualitative spatial reasoning.* Paper presented at the Proceedings of AISMC-3, LNCS.

Cohn, A. G., Bennett, B., Gooday, J., & Gotts, N. M. (1997). Qualitative spatial representation and reasoning with the region connection calculus. *Geoinformatica, 1(3),* 1–42.

Coventry, K. R. (1998). Spatial prepositions, functional relations and lexical specification. In P. Olivier & K. Gapp (Eds.), *The Representation and Processing of Spatial Expressions* (pp. 247–262). Hillsdale, NJ: Lawrence Erlbaum Associates.

Coventry, K. R., Cangelosi, A., Rajapakse, R., Bacon, A., Newstead, S., Joyce, D., & Richards, L. V. (2005). Spatial prepositions and vague quantifiers: Implementing the functional geometric framework. In C. Freksa, B. Knauff, B. Krieg-Bruckner & B. Nebel (Eds.), *Spatial Cognition, Volume IV. Reasoning, action and interaction,* pp. 98–110. Lecture notes in Computer Science. Springer-Verlag.

Coventry, K. R., Carmichael, R., & Garrod, S. C. (1994). Spatial prepositions, object-specific function and task requirements. *Journal of Semantics, 11,* 289–309.

Coventry, K. R., & Garrod, S. C. (2004). *Saying, Seeing and Acting. The Psychological Semantics of Spatial Prepositions.* Essays in Cognitive Psychology Series. Hove and New York: Psychology Press.

Coventry, K. R., & Guijarro-Fuentes, P. (2004). Las preposiciones en español y en inglés: la importancia relativa del espacio y función. *Cognitiva, 16(1),* 73–93.

Coventry, K. R., & Prat-Sala, M. (2001). Object-specific function, geometry and the comprehension of "in" and "on." *European Journal of Cognitive Psychology, 13(4),* 509–528.

Coventry, K. R., Prat-Sala, M., & Richards, L. (2001). The interplay between geometry and function in the comprehension of "over," "under," "above" and "below." *Journal of Memory and Language, 44,* 376–398.

Coventry, K. R., Richards, L. V., Joyce, D. W., & Cangelosi, A. (forthcoming). *Spatial prepositions and the instantiation of object knowledge; the case of over, under, above and below.* Manuscript in preparation.

Ellis, N. C. (2006a). Language acquisition as rational contingency learning. *Applied Linguistics, 27,* 1–24.

Ellis, N. C. (2006b). Selective attention and transfer phenomena in L2 acquisition: contingency, cue competition, salience, interference, overshadowing, blocking and perceptual learning. *Applied Linguistics, 27,* 164–194.

Elman, J. L. (1990). Finding structure in time. *Cognitive Science, 14,* 179–211.

Garrod, S., Ferrier, G., & Campbell, S. (1999). In and on: investigating the functional geometry of spatial prepositions. *Cognition, 72,* 167–189.

Garrod, S. C., & Sanford, A. J. (1989). Discourse models as interfaces between language and the spatial world. *Journal of Semantics, 6,* 147–160.

Glenberg, A. M. (1997). What memory is for. *Behavioral and Brain Sciences, 20(1),* 1–55.

Glenberg, A. M., Gutierrez, T., Levin, J. R., Japuntich, S., & Kaschak, M. P. (2004). Activity and imagined activity can enhance young children's reading comprehension. *Journal of Educational Psychology, 96,* 424–436.

Glenberg, A. M., & Robertson, D. A. (1999). Indexical understanding of instructions. *Discourse Processes, 28,* 1–26.

Glenberg, A. M., & Robertson, D. A. (2000). Symbol grounding and meaning: a comparison of high-dimensional and embodied theories of meaning. *Journal of Memory and Language, 43,* 379–401.

Harley, B. (1989). Transfer in the written compositions of French immersion students. In H. Dechert & M. Raupach (Eds.), *Transfer in language production,* pp. 3–19. Norwood, NJ: Ablex.

Hayward, W. G., & Tarr, M. J. (1995). Spatial language and spatial representation. *Cognition, 55,* 39–84.

Herskovits, A. (1986). *Language and Spatial Cognition. An interdisciplinary study of the prepositions in English.* Cambridge University Press.

Hespos, S. J., & Baillargeon, R. (2001). Reasoning about containment events in very young infants. *Cognition, 78,* 207–245.

Ijaz, H. (1986). Linguistic and cognitive determinants of lexical acquisition in a second language. *Language Learning, 36,* 401–451.

Jarvis, S. (2000). Methodological rigor in the study of transfer: Identifying L1 influence in the interlanguage lexicon. *Language Learning, 50,* 245–309.

Jarvis, S., & Odlin, T. (2000). Morphological type, spatial reference, and language transfer. *Studies in Second Language Acquisition, 22,* 535–556.

Johnson, J., & Newport, E. (1989). Critical period effects in second language learning: the influence of maturational state on the acquisition of English as a second language. *Cognitive Psychology, 21,* 60–99.

Kaschak, M. P., & Glenberg, A. M. (2000). Constructing meaning: the role of affordances and grammatical constructions in sentence comprehension. *Journal of Memory and Language, 43,* 508–529.

Kim, I. K., & Spelke, E. S. (1992). Infants' sensitivity to effects of gravity on visible object motion. *Journal of Experimental Psychology: Human Perception and Performance, 18*, 385–393.

Landau, B., & Jackendoff, R. (1993). "What" and "where" in spatial language and cognition. *Behavioural and Brain Sciences, 16(2)*, 217–265.

Landauer, T., & Dumais, S. (1997). A solution to Plato's problem: the latent semantic analysis theory of acquisition, induction and representation of knowledge. *Psychological Review, 104*, 211–240.

Levinson, S. C. (1996a). Frames of reference and Molyneux's question. In P. Bloom, M. A. Peterson, L. Nadel, & M. F. Garrett (Eds.), *Language and space* (pp. 109–169). Cambridge, MA: MIT Press.

Levinson, S. C. (1996b). Relativity in spatial conception and description. In J. J. Gumperz & S. C. Levinson (Eds.), *Rethinking linguistic relativity* (pp. 177–202). Cambridge: Cambridge University Press.

Logan, G. D., & Sadler, D. D. (1996). A computational analysis of the apprehension of spatial relations. In P. Bloom, M. A. Peterson, L. Nadel, & M. F. Garrett (Eds.), *Language and space* (pp. 493–530). Cambridge, MA: MIT Press.

MacWhinney, B., Pleh, C., & Bates, E. (1985). The development of sentence interpretation in Hungarian. *Cognitive Psychology, 17*, 178–209.

McDonough, L., Choi, S., & Mandler, J. M. (2003). Understanding spatial relations: flexible infants, lexical adults. *Cognitive Psychology, 46*, 229–259.

Miller, G. A., & Johnson-Laird, P. N. (1976). *Language and Perception*. Cambridge: Harvard University Press.

Mukattash, L. (1984). Errors made by Arab university students in the use of English prepositions. *Glottodidactica, 17*, 47–64.

Munnich, E. (2000). *Input maturation in the acquisition of second language spatial semantics*. Unpublished PhD thesis, University of Delaware, USA.

Navarro, S., & Nicoladis, E. (2005). Describing motion events in adult L2 Spanish narratives. In D. Eddington (Ed.), *Selected proceedings of the 6th conference on the acquisition of Spanish and Portuguese as first and second languages*, pp. 102–107. Somerville, MA: Cascadilla Proceedings Project.

Needham, A., & Baillargeon, R. (1993). Intuitions about support in 4.5-month-old infants. *Cognition, 47*, 121–148.

Pavesi, M. (1987). Variability and systematicity in the acquisition of spatial prepositions. In R. Ellis (Ed.), *Second language acquisition in context*, pp. 73–82. Englewood Cliffs, NJ: Prentice-Hall.

Pederson, E., Danziger, E., Wilkins, D., Levinson, S., Kita, S., & Senft, G. (1998). Semantic typology and spatial conceptualisation. *Language, 74(3)*, 557–589.

Quinn, P. C. (1994). The categorization of above and below spatial relations by young infants. *Child Development, 65*, 58–69.

Quinn, P. C., Cummins, M, Kase, J., Martin, E., & Weissman, S. (1996). Development of categorical representations for above and below spatial relations in 3- to 7-month-old infants. *Developmental Psychology, 32*, 942–950.

Quinn, P. C., Norris, C. M., Pasko, R. N., Schmader, T. M., & Mash, C. (1999). Formation of a categorical representation for the spatial relation between by 6- to 7-month-old infants. *Visual Cognition, 6*, 569–585.

Regier, T. (1996). *The human semantic potential: spatial language and constrained connectionism*. Cambridge, MA: MIT Press.

Regier, T., & Carlson, L.A. (2001) Grounding spatial language in perception: an empirical and computational investigation. *Journal of Experimental Psychology: General, 130(2)*, 273–298.

Richards, L. V., Coventry, K. R., & Clibbens, J. (2004). Where's the orange? Geometric and extra-geometric factors in English children's talk of spatial locations. *Journal of Child Language, 31*, 153–175.

Schumann, J. (1986). Locative and directional expressions in basilang speech. *Language Learning, 36*, 277–294.

Stockwell, R., Brown, J., & Martin, J. (1965). *The grammatical structures of English and Spanish*. Chicago: Chicago University Press.

Talmy, L. (1983). How language structures space. In H. L. Pick & L. P. Acredolo, (Eds.), *Spatial orientation: theory, research and application*. New York: Plenum Press (pp. 225–282).

Talmy, L. (1985). Lexicalisation patterns: Semantic structure in lexical forms. In T. Shopen (Ed.), *Language typology and syntactic description*, Volume 3, pp. 36–149. Cambridge: Cambridge University Press.

Talmy, L. (1988). Force dynamics in language and cognition. *Cognitive Science, 12*, 49–100.

Tyler, A., & Evans, V. (2003). *The semantics of English prepositions: spatial scenes, embodied meaning and cognition*. Cambridge: Cambridge University Press.

Tyler, A., & Evans, V. (2004). Applying cognitive linguistics to pedagogical grammar: The case of over. In M. Achard & S. Niemeier (Eds.), *Cognitive Linguistics, Second Language Acquisition, and Foreign Language Teaching*, pp. 257–280. Berlin: Mouton de Gruyter.

Ungerleider, L., & Mishkin, M. (1982). Two cortical visual systems. In D. Ingle, M. Goodale, & R. Mansfield (Eds.), *Analysis of visual behavior*. Cambridge, MA: MIT Press.

Vandeloise, C. (1991). *Spatial prepositions. A case study from French*. University of Chicago Press.

Zwaan, R. A. (2004). The immersed experiencer: toward an embodied theory of language comprehension. In B. H. Ross (Ed.), *The Psychology of Learning and Motivation*, Vol. 44 (pp. 35–62). New York: Academic Press.

Zwaan, R. A., & Taylor, L. J. (2006). Seeing, acting and understanding: motor resonance in language comprehension. *Journal of Experimental Psychology: General, 135*, 1–11.

7

LANGUAGE WITHOUT GRAMMAR[1]

William O'Grady

1 Introduction

Sentences have systematic properties. Subjects occur in a structurally higher position than direct objects. Only some word orders are acceptable. Verbs agree with certain nominals but not others. Relative clauses are formed in particular ways. Reflexive pronouns have a narrowly circumscribed set of possible antecedents. And so forth.

It is pretty much taken for granted that such properties are best understood by reference to a mental grammar—a formal system of linguistic rules and principles that, in the words of Jackendoff (2002, p. 57), "describe patterns of elements," however abstractly. It is likewise widely believed that core grammatical properties are innately stipulated by Universal Grammar (UG)—a dedicated, faculty-specific system that includes categories and principles common in one form or another to all human languages.

In recent years, however, these beliefs have been called into question by the development of so-called "emergentist" approaches to language which hold that linguistic phenomena are best explained by reference to more basic non-linguistic (i.e., "non-grammatical") factors and their interaction (see, e.g., Ellis, 1998; Elman, 1999; MacWhinney, 1999; Menn, 2000; O'Grady, 2005). The purpose of this chapter is to outline how this sort of approach works and to illustrate its potential for the study of various classic problems in syntactic analysis.

The factors to which emergentists turn for their explanations vary considerably, ranging from features of physiology and perception, to processing and working memory, to pragmatics and social interaction, to properties of the input and of the learning mechanisms. The particular idea that I will focus on here, following the detailed proposal put forward in O'Grady (2005) and summarized in O'Grady (2001), is that the mechanisms that are required to account for the traditional concerns of syntactic theory (the design of phrase structure, pronoun interpretation, agreement, and so on) are identical to the mechanisms that are independently required to account for how sentences are processed from "left to right" in real time. According to this view then, the theory of sentence processing simply subsumes syntactic theory. This sort of approach offers a way to think about language without grammar. What it basically says is that language and languages are the way they are because of what happens when words with particular properties are assembled in real time in the course of actual speech and comprehension. A preliminary illustration of how this might work involves the design of sentence structure.

2 Structure building

I take as my starting point the widely held idea that at least two cognitive systems are central to language acquisition and use. The conceptual-symbolic system does the work of a lexicon, providing a list of formatives (words and morphemes) and their combinatorial properties. For instance, the lexical entry for *remain* indicates that it is a verb and that it has an argument dependency (requirement) involving a nominal to the left.

(1) *remain*: V,   <N>   (e.g., *Problems remain.*)
                 ↓

In contrast, *study* is a verb with two argument dependencies, one involving a nominal to the left and the other involving a nominal to the right.

(2) *study*: V,   <N N>   (e.g., *Mary studied Russian.*)
               ↓   ↓

Responsibility for the actual mechanics of sentence formation falls to a computational system which operates on words and morphemes drawn from the lexicon, combining them in particular ways to construct phrases and sentences. The computational system corresponds roughly to what one might think of as "syntax."

The particular computational system that I propose is indistinguishable in its structure and functioning from a processor. It operates in a linear manner, it combines elements, and it checks to make sure that lexical requirements are being satisfied. However, unlike classic processors, it is entirely unconstrained by grammatical principles, obeying a single efficiency-related imperative that is independent of language—it must minimize the burden on working memory, the pool of resources that supports operations on representations (e.g., Carpenter, Miyake, and Just, 1994; Robinson, 2002). This entails compliance with the following mandate.

(3) *The Efficiency Requirement*

Resolve dependencies at the first opportunity.

The intuition here is simply that the burden on working memory is lessened by resolving dependencies at the first opportunity rather than storing them for later resolution.

The formation of a sentence such as *Mary studied Russian* takes place in two steps. Working from left to right, the computational system first combines *Mary* and *study*, creating an opportunity for the verb to resolve its first argument dependency. (I indicate that the dependency has been resolved by copying the index of the nominal onto the appropriate symbol in the verb's argument grid.)

(4)   Step 1: combination of the verb with its first argument

In abbreviated form: **[Mary$_i$ studied]**
$<N_i \ N>$

In the next step, the computational system combines *study* and *Russian*, creating an opportunity to resolve the verb's second argument dependency. Once again, this opportunity is immediately exploited, in accordance with the Efficiency Requirement.

(5)   Step 2: combination of the verb with its second argument

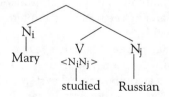

In abbreviated form: [Mary$_i$ **[studied Russian$_j$]**]
$<N_i \ N_j>$

As I see them, "syntactic structures" are nothing but a fleeting residual record of how the computational system goes about combining words—one at time, from left to right, and at the first opportunity. The structure in (4) exists only as a reflex of the fact that the verb first combines with the nominal to its left. And the structure in (5) exists only to represent the fact that the verb then combines with the nominal to its right. A more transparent way to represent these facts might be as follows, with the time line running diagonally from the top down.

(6)   An alternative way to depict formation of *Mary studied Russian*:

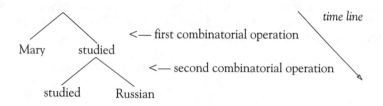

As both notations illustrate, English sentences formed by the proposed computational system have properties very similar to those that traditional approaches attribute to them. In particular, their internal organization manifests a binary-branching design, with a subject–object asymmetry (that is, the subject is structurally higher than the direct object). Crucially, however, these properties are not stipulated by grammatical mechanisms—there are no phrase structure rules or X-bar schema. Rather, the design features of sentences emerge from the interaction of the lexical properties of individual words with an efficiency-driven processor, operating from left to right in real time.

A metaphor may help clarify this point. Traditional UG-based approaches to language focus on the ARCHITECTURE of sentences, positing principles that lay down an intricate innate grammatical blueprint for language. As I see it though, there are no architects. There are just carpenters, who design as they build, limited only by the material available to them (words with particular properties) and by the need to complete their work as quickly and as efficiently as possible.

On this view then, there is no grammar per se. There is a lexicon that includes an inventory of words and information about the particular arguments that they require. And there is a computational system, which is just a processor that combines words one at a time in a linear fashion. The processor is driven by efficiency considerations that are designed to ease the burden on working memory, but it has no special properties beyond this.

This idea runs against long-standing views within linguistics, calling into question one of the few points on which there is a (near) consensus—the existence of grammar. This cannot be taken lightly. After all, grammar—and especially Universal Grammar—offers powerful explanations for a wide and varied range of problems that arise in the study of syntax, typology, acquisition, and other areas central to the field. The remainder of this chapter is devoted to a consideration of these matters.

3 The problem of syntactic description—some agreement puzzles

The first and classic function of a grammar is to deal with the demands of syntactic description—identifying and making sense of the properties of sentences in particular human languages. As is well known, even "simple" phenomena manifest intricacies that challenge the resources of the most sophisticated theories. Verbal agreement in English is a case in point.

3.1 Computing agreement

As a first approximation, English seems to require a match between a verb's person and number features and those of its subject. (For the sake of exposition, I use Roman numerals and upper case for nominal features, and Arabic numerals and lower case for verbal features.)

(7) Third person singular subject, third person singular verb form:

   One remains.
   IIISG   3sg

(8) Third person plural subject, third person plural verb form:

   Two remain.
   IIIPL   3pl

In fact, of course, things are not so straightforward. As the next examples show, there are cases in which the verb agrees with a nominal other than its subject.

(9)a. There is **paper** on the desk.
   3sg IIISG

   b. There are **pencils** on the desk.
   3pl   IIIPL

In fact, in some cases, the nominal triggering agreement is not even an argument of the inflected verb.

(10) There seems [to be **paper** on the desk].
   3sg   IIISG

143

Moreover, there are patterns in which the verb agrees with just part of an NP—the first conjunct of the coordinate NP (Sobin,1997, p. 324).

(11) There is [**paper** and ink] on the desk.
　　　　3sg　IIISG

As explained in much more detail in O'Grady (2005, pp. 90ff.), agreement reflects the interaction of lexical and computational factors. On the lexical side, inflected lexical items can introduce an "agreement dependency"—they carry person and number features that must be matched at some point with features elsewhere in the sentence. The agreement dependencies associated with the inflected form of English verbs are included in the lexical entries that follow.

(12)a. *remains*:　V,　　<N>
　　　　　　　　　3sg　　↓

　　　b. *studies*:　V,　　<N N>
　　　　　　　　　　3sg　　↓ ↓

But how are such dependencies resolved? The lexicon is silent on this matter, and there is of course no agreement "rule" or comparable grammatical device. Rather the problem is left to the computational system to deal with.

Matters are straightforward in a simple sentence such as *One remains*. There, combination of *one* and *remains* creates an opportunity to resolve both the verb's argument dependency (as an intransitive verb, it is looking for a nominal argument) and its agreement dependency. Given the Efficiency Requirement, there is no choice but to resolve both dependencies at once, thereby yielding agreement with the subject NP in this case. (I use a check mark to indicate resolution of an agreement dependency. For simplicity of exposition, I do not represent argument dependencies in what follows.)

(13) Combination of *one* and *remains*; resolution of the agreement dependency
　　　[**One remains**]
　　　　IIISG　　3sg✓

A different result comes about in a pattern such as *There is paper on the desk*, where *be* takes the expletive *there* as its first argument and *paper* as its second argument. Working from left to right, the processor first brings together *there* and *is*, creating an opportunity to resolve the verb's first argument dependency.

(14) **[There is]**
     3sg

However, because *there* lacks number features, no opportunity arises at this point to resolve the verb's agreement dependency, which is therefore held, presumably at some cost to working memory.

In the next step, the computational system combines *is* with the nominal to its right, creating an opportunity not only to resolve the verb's second argument dependency but also to take care of the agreement dependency.

(15) [There [**is paper**]]
     3sg↓ IIISG

Consistent with the Efficiency Requirement, both opportunities are immediately exploited, thereby creating a pattern in which the verb agrees with a non-subject nominal.

It takes even longer to come across an opportunity to resolve the agreement dependency in a sentence such as *There seems to be paper on the desk.*

(16)a. Combination of *there* and *seems*:
    [There seems]
      3sg

   b. Combination of *seems* and *to*:
    [There [**seems to**]]
      3sg

   c. Combination of *to* and *be*:
    [There [seems **[to be**]]]
      3sg

   d. Combination of *be* and *paper*; resolution of the agreement dependency:
    [There [seems [to **[be paper**]]]]
      3sg↓   IIISG

Here again, the computational system does exactly what one would expect an efficiency-driven linear processor to do—it resolves the agreement dependency at the first opportunity, even though this opportunity does not arise with an argument of the inflected verb.

Yet a different result occurs in the case of patterns such as *There is paper and ink on the desk.* Given the linear, efficiency-driven character of the computational system, sentence formation proceeds in the manner summarized below.

(17)a. Combination of *there* and *is*:
[There is]
3sg

b. Combination of *is* and *paper*; resolution of the agreement dependency:
[There [**is   paper**]]
3sg$^\downarrow$ IIISG

c. Combination of *paper* and *and*:
[There [is   **[paper and**]]]
3sg$^\downarrow$ IIISG

d. Combination of *and* and *ink*:
[There [is   [paper   **[and ink]**]]]
3sg$^\downarrow$ IIISG

The key step here is the second one, in which the verb combines with just the first conjunct of the coordinate phrase, the nominal *paper*, creating an opportunity to resolve the agreement dependency. The end result is the phenomenon known as "partial agreement": the verb agrees with a sub-part of one of its arguments. As expected, this phenomenon is only possible when the coordinate NP follows the verb. Where it appears to the left, and is therefore fully formed before the verb is encountered, partial agreement is impossible.

(18) [Paper and ink] are/*is on the desk.

In sum, there is no subject–verb agreement per se in English. There are just dependencies involving person and number features, which, like other dependencies, are resolved at the first opportunity. If the verb's first argument (its "subject") happens to carry features, then the agreement dependencies are resolved right away—giving the appearance of subject–verb agreement. But when the first argument carries no features, the verb must look elsewhere for a way to resolve its agreement dependencies.

As a result, English ends up with a seemingly exotic system of agreement in which the verb variously agrees with its first argument (the "subject"), its second argument, the argument of an embedded verb, and the first conjunct of its second argument.

(19)a. Agreement with the first argument (the subject)
Paper is on the desk.

b. Agreement with the second argument
There is **paper** on the desk.

146

    c.   Agreement with the argument of an embedded verb
        There seems [to be **paper** on the desk].

    d.   Agreement with the first conjunct of a coordinate NP
        There is [**paper** and ink] on the desk.

Seen from the perspective of "grammar," this range of facts appears to be quite strange. (Lasnik, 1999, p. 126 calls it "superficially bizarre," while Sobin, 1997 attributes it to infection by a "grammatical virus.") In reality, things make perfect sense if there is no grammar per se and if sentences are formed by a linear computational system (a processor) driven by the need to minimize the burden on working memory by resolving agreement dependencies at the first opportunity.

3.2 Some further observations

Although agreement dependencies are always resolved *at the first opportunity*, they are not always resolved *immediately*. In a sentence such as *There is paper on the desk*, for instance, the computational system has to wait until it encounters the verb's second argument before having an opportunity to resolve the agreement dependency.

  (20)a. Combination of *there* and *is*:
        [There is]
          3sg

      b.   Combination of *is* and *paper*; resolution of the agreement dependency:
        [There [**is paper**]]
           3sg$^{\downarrow}$ IIISG

This can't be helped. The computational system has to play the hand that it is dealt, and the lexicon is the dealer. If the verb provided by the lexicon has a featureless first argument, there is no opportunity for immediate resolution of the verb's agreement dependency and no choice but to hold the dependency in working memory and to move on.

    Interestingly, there is some evidence of attempts at a "repair strategy" designed to permit immediate resolution of agreement dependencies by endowing *there* with person and number features (third person and singular). This is perhaps most obvious in the widespread use in colloquial speech of contracted *is* in patterns that would normally call for the plural form of the verb (e.g., Sparks, 1984).

  (21)   There**'s** two men at the door.
        (cf. *There is two men at the door)

There may be more radical signs of rebellion in the speech of children. Until my daughter was almost twelve, for example, she insisted on using only the third singular form of *be*, even in its uncontracted form, when the subject was expletive *there*.

(22)   There **is** two men outside.

I've also noted similar examples in the speech of second language learners. The following two sentences were produced by Arnold Schwarzenegger (cited in *The New Yorker*, June 26, 2004, pp. 80 & 85.)

(23)a.   The next thing we know, **there is** injured or there is dead people.
   b.   **There is** a certain amount of people meant to be leaders . . .

Patterns such as those in (22) and (23) are not widely accepted by adult native speakers, but it seems to my ear that the acceptability of "singular *there*" improves with the distance between the verb and the postverbal nominal whose features would otherwise resolve the agreement dependency. Thus the following sentences strike me as far more acceptable than (22).

(24)a.   ?There seems [to be two of them].
   b.   ?There is likely [to be two of them].

Contrasts along these lines have in fact been documented for the English of New Zealand and the Falkland Islands (Britain & Sudbury 2002, pp. 228–229) as well as for the English of York (Tagliamonte 1998, p. 173): the likelihood of "singular *there*" in these speech varieties increases with the number of lexical items intervening between the verb and the noun carrying number features.

A possibly more extreme situation is found in Appalachian English, for which Wolfram and Christian (1976, pp. 78 & 82) report the use of singular *there* even in monoclausal sentences such as (25) at rates exceeding 90 percent. Also of potential relevance is their observation (pp. 125–126) that speakers of Appalachian English often replace expletive *there* by the inherently singular *it*.

(25)a.   . . . the deadliest snake *it* is. [. . . the deadliest snake there is.]
   b.   *It*'s rapids down there. [=There's rapids down there.]
   c.   *It* was a fly in it. [=There was a fly in it.]

A second point where the English system of verbal agreement is less than robust occurs in *there* patterns where the second argument is a conjoined NP. As observed earlier, such patterns routinely manifest "partial agreement," with the verb's agreement dependency being resolved by the first conjunct of the coordinate NP.

(26)　There is [**paper** and ink] on desk.

As already noted, there are good computational reasons for resolving the verb's agreement dependency in this way. Nonetheless, the end result is a somewhat uncomfortable paradox—a verb carrying *singular* inflection takes a *plural* argument (the coordinate phrase *paper and ink*), which can itself serve as antecedent for a plural pronoun.

(27)　There is [paper and ink]$_i$ on desk. I put **them**$_i$ there.

It is presumably not a coincidence that this state of affairs triggers a variety of reactions, as many commentators have observed (e.g., Schmidt & McCreary, 1977 and the references cited in Morgan & Green, 2005). Based on a survey of 18 native speakers of English, Morgan and Green (p. 468) report that "among speakers who otherwise appear to speak the same variety of the language, there is [a lot of] variation in number marking" in sentences in which the agreement trigger is a postverbal coordinate NP. Some speakers have the verb agree with the nearer conjunct, whereas others insist on the plural if either conjunct is plural. There is also variation depending on the choice of conjunction (*and* versus *or*) and on whether the coordinate NP is definite or indefinite.

It is often suggested that language is a "dynamic system" that is in a constant state of flux (e.g., Ellis & Larsen-Freeman, 2006). Indeed, Hopper (1998, p. 157) goes so far as to suggest that language is "always provisional, always negotiable." This is surely somewhat of an exaggeration if we consider language as a whole, but it is perhaps applicable to certain sub-phenomena within language—including, as we have seen, aspects of verbal agreement in English.

An advantage of a processing-based approach to agreement is that it provides independent computational grounds for identifying places where the resolution of agreement dependencies is more likely to be in flux. As we have just seen, one such case involves patterns such as *There seems to be two of them*, in which no nearby opportunity to resolve the agreement dependency presents itself. Another is exemplified by patterns like *There is paper and ink on the desk*, where resolution of the agreement dependency at the first opportunity yields a paradoxical result (singular agreement for an argument that turns out to be plural once the second conjunct is in place). The fact that these are the very points where variation and instability are observed fits well with the general approach to agreement that I have been outlining.

4 The problem of markedness—relative clauses

One of the most important and enduring discoveries in syntactic analysis is the observation that particular patterns are "marked" in the sense of being somehow less expected and more difficult than certain alternatives. This asymmetry has a remarkably broad range of consequences extending from typology to language acquisition and loss, to processing.

A classic example of markedness involves the contrast between subject and direct object relative clauses.

(28)a. Subject relative clause:
the student [who saw the woman]

b. Direct object relative clause:
the woman [who the student saw]

A wide range of phenomena suggests that subject relative clauses are less marked than their direct object counterparts. As shown in the groundbreaking work of Keenan and Comrie (1977), for instance, languages that permit direct object relatives also have subject relatives, but the converse is not true: there are languages like Malagasy which allow only subject relatives.

(29)a. Relativization of the subject:
ny mpianatra [izay nahita ny vehivavy]
the student   that saw   the woman
"the student who saw the woman"

b. Relativization of the direct object:
*ny vehivavy [izay nahita ny mpianatra]
the woman   that saw   the student
"the woman who the student saw"

There is also ample evidence that subject relatives are easier to acquire, in the case of both first language acquisition (e.g., O'Grady, 1997, pp. 175ff.) and second language learning (e.g., Hamilton, 1994). In addition, it is well known that patients suffering from agrammatic aphasia find it far easier to understand subject relative clauses than direct object relatives (e.g., Grodzinsky, 1989). Finally, there is a great deal of evidence that subject relatives are easier to process than their direct object counterparts (e.g., Wanner & Maratsos, 1978; Gibson, 1998; Caplan & Waters, 2002).

Why should things work this way? The answer, I believe, lies in a difference in the demands made on working memory in the course of forming the two types of structure. As illustrated below, a typical relative clause begins with a relative pronoun (e.g., *who*) that must be associated with a position in the verb's argument grid—the first position in the case of the subject relative and the second position in the case of the direct object relative.

(30)a. Subject relative clause:
the student [**who**$_i$ saw the woman$_j$]
    $<$**N**$_i$ N$>$

   b. Direct object relative clause:
the student [**who**$_j$ the woman$_i$ saw]
    $<$N$_i$ **N**$_j>$

A useful way to think about the relationship between the relative pronoun and the corresponding position in the verb's argument grid is to assume that *wh* words introduce a dependency that is resolved with the help of an "open" position in a verb's argument grid (see O'Grady, 2005, pp. 113ff. for details).

Like other dependencies, *wh* dependencies must of course be resolved at the first opportunity. Crucially, as the contrast in (30) illustrates, that opportunity arises sooner in the case of subject relative clauses, in which the relative pronoun occurs next to the verb, than in direct object relatives, where the relative pronoun is separated from the verb by the intervening subject. This in turn suggests that object relative clauses may make comparatively greater demands on working memory. Evidence from processing studies offers striking support for this idea.

In a classic experiment, Wanner and Maratsos (1978) displayed sentences containing relative clauses on a screen one word a time, interrupting the presentation after the fourth word with a list of names.

(31)a. Subject relative clause:
The witch [*who* despised sorcerers] frightened little children.
            ↓
        interruption point

   b. Direct object relative clause:
The witch [*who* sorcerers despised] frightened little children.
            ↓
        interruption point

Recall of the names and comprehension of the relative clauses were both significantly poorer in the direct object relative clauses than in the subject relatives.

This is just what one would expect if establishing the link between the *wh* word and the verb taxes working memory. Because subject relative pronouns occur adjacent to the verb, the relationship can be established immediately, before the interruption point in (31)a.

(32) Subject relative clause:
The witch [*who* despised sorcerers] frightened little children.
     ↓ ↓

     wh dependency interruption point
     is resolved here

In contrast, the object relative pronoun in (31)b. is more distant from the verb and establishment of the link between the two is impeded by the intervening interruption, with negative consequences both for recall of the intruding names and for interpretation of the sentence.

(33) Direct object relative clause:
The witch [*who* sorcerers despised] frightened little children.
      ↓ ↓

    interruption point *wh* dependency
          is resolved here

If all of this is on the right track, then the door is open for a new approach to markedness. As Hawkins (2004) suggests, marked patterns are simply the ones that create the greater processing demands on working memory. They therefore appear less frequently across languages, they are harder to acquire, and they are more susceptible to loss in the case of various language disorders.

There is no reason for appeal to an autonomous grammatical system such as Universal Grammar. The burden of explanation lies entirely on the processor. Languages have the properties that they do and are acquired the way that they are because of how they are processed—by an efficiency-driven linear computational system whose overarching concern is to minimize the burden on working memory.

5 The problem of underdetermination—inversion and structure dependence

A dominant theme in the literature on syntactic theory since the early 1960s is the idea that speakers know far more about their language than they could possibly have learned. (This is sometimes referred to as "underdetermination" or the "poverty-of-stimulus problem.")

A simple example of this—and its far-reaching consequences—comes from the syntax of English *yes-no* questions. As the following examples help illustrate, such patterns appear to be formed by a process of subject–verb inversion.

(34)a. Kitty is hungry.
 b. Is Kitty hungry?

Interestingly, this seemingly simple fact has been turned into a major argument in favor of Universal Grammar—an argument that has, in the words of Levine (2002, p. 326), been "incessantly repeated in the literature" since it was first put forward by Chomsky (1975, pp. 30ff.).

5.1 Inversion and grammar

Chomsky's key observation is that the sorts of simple *yes-no* questions that abound in children's experience—patterns such as the one above—provide insufficient information about the workings of inversion. This is because such sentences are consistent with two very different generalizations:

(35)a. The structure-dependent generalization:
In question structures, *the verb in the main clause* moves to the beginning of the sentence.

b. The linear generalization:
In question structures, *the first verb* moves to the beginning of the sentence.

We can't tell which of these generalizations is right by looking at sentences like (34)b., in which there is only one clause and only one verb. In such cases, fronting the verb in the main clause gives exactly the same result as fronting the first verb. The crucial test case involves how we question a sentence such as (36), in which the first verb is not in the main clause.

(36) Americans [who are rich] are happy too.

$$\downarrow \qquad\qquad \downarrow$$

first verb   verb in main clause

Here the two generalizations yield different results, as (37) shows.

(37)a. The fronted element is the verb from the main clause (structure-dependent):
Are [Americans who are rich] _ happy too?

b. The fronted element is the first verb (not structure-dependent):
*Are [Americans who _ rich] are happy too?

As can be seen here, only the structure-dependent generalization gives the right result.

Crain and Nakayama (1987) offer experimental evidence that even very young children realize this. In Crain and Nakayama's experiment,

30 children aged 3;2 to 5;11 were given prompts such as "Ask Jabba if the boy who is watching Mickey is happy."

(38) Ask Jabba if the boy [who is watching Mickey] is happy.
$$\downarrow \qquad\qquad\qquad\qquad \downarrow$$
first verb   *verb in main clause*

By seeing whether the children responded by saying (39)a. or (39)b., Crain and Nakayama were able to determine which inversion "rule" was being used.

(39)a. The structure-dependent response:
Is [the boy who is watching Mickey] _ happy?

    b. The non-structure-dependent response:
*Is [the boy who _ watching Mickey] is happy?

The results were clear—no errors of the type in (39)b. were found. Clark (2002) reports similar results for adult second language learners.

So how do children figure this out, the proponent of UG asks. The standard answer, as Pullum and Sholz (2002, p. 17) note, is that there are only two possibilities. Either the relevant principle is given in advance as part of a genetically endowed Universal Grammar, or it must be acquired through trial and error based on experience.

Chomsky dismisses the idea of learning from experience in this case by appeal to the "argument from poverty of stimulus." In order to *learn* that the inversion rule acts on the verb in the main clause—and not just the first verb in the sentence, children would need to encounter sentences such as (39)a., in which the verb in the main clause is not also the first verb in the sentence. But, Chomsky (1980, p. 40) argues, sentences of this sort are vanishingly rare. In fact, he suggests, "a person could go through much or all of his life without ever having been exposed to [such sentences]." Hence, the learner has to rely on UG to correctly formulate the inversion rule.

Sampson (1989) and Pullum (1996) adopt a different approach, suggesting that Chomsky is wrong about the poverty of the stimulus and that the input does in fact contain the types of sentences needed to induce structure dependence from experience. Among the examples from actual speech offered by Pullum are the following:

(40)a. Is [the boy who was hitting you] _ still here?
(cf. [The who was hitting you] **is** still here.

    b. Is [what I am doing] _ in the shareholder's best interest?
(cf. [What I am doing] **is** in the shareholder's best interest.

In each of these sentences, the fronted verb is from the main clause, even though it is not the first verb in the sentence. Pullum suggests that such sentences may in fact be relatively frequent, constituting perhaps 1 percent of the interrogative patterns and more than 10 percent of the *yes-no* questions in at least certain types of discourse.

Crucially, however, MacWhinney (2004, p. 890) reports that sentences such as these actually appear very rarely in speech to *children* (perhaps once in three million utterances). He tries to save the input hypothesis by suggesting that a different type of pattern supports induction of the right generalization—namely *wh*-questions such as (41), which he suggests are more common in speech to children.

(41)   Where's [the other dolly [that was in here]]?
       (cf. [The other dolly [that was in here] **is** where])

As can be seen here, the fronted verb comes from the main clause, consistent with the structure-dependent inversion rule. Nonetheless, there is reason to doubt the general availability of sentences of this sort as well: Legate & Yang (2002) report just 14 instances in the 20,651 questions in the CHILDES database for Nina and just four examples in the 8,889 questions in the database for Adam.

Sentence counting aside, there is perhaps a more fundamental issue at stake here: does anyone on either side of the debate really believe that children who were not exposed to sentences such as (41) would be unable to figure out how inversion works? Would such children really be incapable of choosing between (42)a. and (42)b.?

(42)a.   The structure-dependent response:
         Is [the boy who is watching Mickey] _ happy?

    b.   The non-structure-dependent response:
         *Is [the boy who _ watching Mickey] is happy?

I don't think so—my intuition is that children would still make the right choice. This brings us to the question of how an emergentist approach to language might deal with the problems associated with inversion.

5.2 Inversion without grammar

On the lexical side, I assume that certain English verbs (in particular, copulas and auxiliaries) have the special property of being able to look to either the left or the right for their first argument. Thus whereas the verb *study* has the properties repeated in (43)a., looking only leftward for its first argument, the verb *be* has the additional option of being able to look to either the left or the right. (For ease of exposition, I assume that the second argument of *be* is an adjective, as in *Grass is green*, even though various other types of categories can appear in this position as well.)

(43)a. *study:* V, <N N>
               ↓ ↓

   b. *be:* V, <N A>
             ↓ ↓

Copulas look rightward for their first argument in *yes-no* questions as well as in certain other non-realis contexts. Take, for example, the sentence *Is grass green?*, which is formed as follows. (See O'Grady, 2005, pp. 189–190 for details.)

(44)a. First step: The copula combines to the right with its first argument.

[**Is**   **grass**$_i$]
<N$_i$ A>

   b. Second step: The copula combines to the right with its second argument.

[**Is**   [grass$_i$] **green**$_j$]
<N$_i$ A$_j$>

On this view then, *yes-no* questions have a copula or auxiliary verb in initial position not because there is a grammatical rule that moves it there but simply because verbs of this type look rightward for their first argument in question patterns.

Now let us turn to the problematic case represented by the contrast in (45).

(45)a. "Inversion" affects the verb in the main clause:
      Are [Americans who are rich] happy too?

   b. "Inversion" affects the first verb:
      *Are [Americans who rich] are happy too?

The formation of (45)a. is straightforward. To begin, *are* combines to the right with the nominal *Americans*, resolving its first argument dependency.

(46) [**Are**   **Americans**$_i$]
    <N$_i$ A>

Next the relative clause is formed and integrated into the sentence.[2]

(47) [Are [Americans **who are rich**]$_i$]
    <N$_i$ A>

At this point sentence-initial *are* can finally combine with its second argument, the adjective *happy*—exactly parallel to what happens in simple question structures such as *Are Americans happy?* or *Is grass green?*

(48) [**Are** [Americans who are rich]$_i$ **happy**$_j$]
      <N$_i$ A$_j$>

However, things do not go so smoothly in the case of (45)b., in which the "wrong" copula appears at the beginning of the sentence. The problem lies in the fact that the full NP to the right of the verb (its intended first argument) is ill-formed for independent reasons. (Predicative adjectives such as *rich* do not take direct arguments in English; a copula is required.)

(49) [Are *[**Americans who rich**]$_i$]
      <N$_i$ A>

This, presumably, is the reason why utterances of this type are not heard in the speech of children (or anyone else for that matter).

In sum, the syntax of *yes-no* questions is not directly learned from experience. Nor is it given by Universal Grammar. The facts simply follow from the interaction of an efficiency-driven computational system with the properties of the words on which it operates.

6 The problem of language acquisition—rethinking explanatory adequacy

"Language acquisition" is a cover term for a wide and varied range of developmental phenomena that includes everything from learning that English [t] is alveolar rather than dental to figuring out when it is appropriate to say "Excuse me." Somewhere between these two extremes are the challenges associated with acquiring a 60,000- to 100,000-word lexicon, thousands of phrasal expressions and idioms, and hundreds of structural patterns, each with their own characteristics and idiosyncrasies. The search for a unified theory of language acquisition is therefore daunting, to say the least, and perhaps not even practical, at least for the time being.

A more realistic goal is to focus on particular narrowly circumscribed questions and puzzles that arise in the study of the acquisition of specific phenomena. For example, within the class of phenomena that make up "complex syntax" (for lack of a better term), it makes sense to ask whether there are contrasts and constraints that cannot be learned from experience and must therefore follow from inborn mechanisms of some sort. In fact, this question has been at the heart of linguistic theory since the early 1960s, and has been the subject of extensive but inconclusive debate almost from the outset.

My take on the debate is substantially different from that of many opponents of UG in that I do not deny the existence of a learnability (poverty-of-the-stimulus) problem. That is, in contrast to (say) Mac-Whinney (2004), I do not believe that experience, even on the most generous estimate of its richness, is sufficient to support induction of complex syntax. The properties of binding, quantifier scope, and island phenomena (to take three examples at random) are simply too complex, the relevant input too sparse, and mastery too rapid and error-free to be the product of induction.

Interestingly, I know of no actual dissent on this point. There is of course a good deal of opposition to the *idea* of inborn grammatical principles. And there are many accounts for the acquisition of phenomena that are either unrelated or only peripherally related to proposed UG principles—lexical properties, word order, the expression of inflection, the development of function words, and so on. There are even occasional attempts to offer alternatives to some of the simpler phenomena for which poverty-of-stimulus claims have been made (the debate over "structure dependence" in the case of inversion, for instance; see section 5). But I know of no induction accounts for structural constraints on pronoun interpretation (the "binding principles"), for constraints on quantifier scope, or for subjacency effects that look at an even remotely representative set of facts associated with these phenomena.

How, then, is it possible to maintain, as I do, that very significant facts about language are underdetermined by experience and at the same time hold, as I also do, that UG does not exist? The answer is that something other than UG is responsible for bridging the gap between experience on the one hand and knowledge of the intricacies of natural language syntax on the other. The burden of explanation, I suggest, falls on the processor—the efficiency-driven linear computational system that I take to lie at the heart of the human language faculty.

6.1 *The role of the processor in language acquisition*

As I see it, the role of the processor in language acquisition is twofold. First, it helps define an initial state for the language learner by seeking to minimize the burden on working memory—thereby ensuring resolution of dependencies at the first opportunity. As explained in detail in O'Grady (2005), a surprisingly wide range of intricate facts follow, including core properties of co-reference, control, agreement, contraction, extraction, and other phenomena that have long been offered as prima facie evidence in support of UG. I suspect and believe that many additional phenomena work this way.

158

The second role for the processor involves the creation of "routines" consisting of the operations and sequences of operations needed to form and interpret the many different types of utterances that are used in the course of communication. Here are some simple routines in English:

- A verb looks to the left for its first argument.
- A verb looks to the right for its second argument.
- A preposition looks to the right for its nominal argument.
- A determiner looks to the right for a nominal.

As these examples help illustrate, the routines required for a particular language typically include details not covered by the processor's general mandate to minimize the burden on working memory. Even though the processor is compelled to resolve dependencies at the first opportunity, language-particular factors determine (for example) whether the opportunity to resolve a verb's first argument dependency will occur to the left (as in English *I ran*) or the right (as in Tagalog *Tumakbo ako* "ran I"). They likewise determine whether the verb will introduce agreement dependencies (as happens in English but not Mandarin) and, if so, how those dependencies will be expressed (as suffixes in English but as prefixes in Swahili).

I assume that the learning of these details is "usage-based" (e.g., Tomasello, 2003). More specifically, I assume that as particular routines are executed over and over again, they are gradually strengthened. In the words of Anderson (1993, p. 181), routines "gather strength as they prove useful." Over time, they become established to the point where their use is automatic and seemingly effortless.

Because usage-based learning is input-dependent, its developmental course is sensitive to external factors such as frequency, recency, contextual contingencies, perceptual salience, attention, and the like, as well as to internal factors such as working memory (e.g., Ellis, 2006a, 2006b). Of these various considerations, the one that stands out in my mind as particularly crucial is the efficiency-driven character of the processor, particularly its propensity to reduce the burden on working memory.

The development of pronouns is a case in point. As is well known, reflexive pronouns are mastered first in the course of language acquisition (see O'Grady, 1997, pp. 226ff. for a review of the literature). Interestingly, however, the frequency facts strongly favor plain pronouns: a search in the CHILDES database of maternal speech to Adam, Eve, and Sarah turned up 17 instances of *himself*, compared to 487 instances of *him*; there was one instance of *themselves* and 717 of *them*. There is no reason to think that salience seriously diminishes children's access to plain pronouns in object position, which, unlike their counterparts in subject position, are rarely dropped inappropriately in child language (Ingham, 1993/1994; Theakston, Lieven, Pine & Rowland, 2001).

Crucially, however, there is good reason to think that the referential dependencies introduced by reflexive pronouns are easier to resolve in the course of processing. As explained in detail in O'Grady (2005, pp. 28ff.), reflexive pronouns differ from plain pronouns in being immediately interpretable. In a sentence such as (50), for instance, the reflexive pronoun can be interpreted the instant it is added to the sentence, since its referential dependency can be resolved by the index of *John* in the grid of the verb with which the pronoun combines.

(50) [John$_i$ [overestimates himself$_x$]].
        $<N_i\ N_x>$
          $\downarrow$ <resolution of the referential dependency>
          i

In contrast, a plain pronoun in the same position must be linked to a referent mentioned previously in the discourse or somehow evident from the context.

(51) [John$_i$ [overestimates him$_x$]].
        $<N_i\ N_x>$
   ?< .... |

Independent experimental work by Piñango, Burkhardt, Brun and Avrutin (2001) and Sekerina, Stromswold and Hestvik (2004) confirms the increased processing difficulty associated with plain pronouns (see also O'Grady, 2005, pp. 166ff.).

Or take relative clauses. As observed in O'Grady (1997, pp. 175), children do better on subject relatives in experiment after experiment. Yet, direct object relatives occur far more frequently in the input: 57.9 percent of all relative clauses produced by the mothers of four English-speaking children studied by Diessel (2004) were direct object relatives, while an average of 34.3 percent were subject relatives (pp. 145–146).

Diessel and Tomasello (2005, p. 899) speculate that children's success on subject relatives stems from the fact that these constructions are "similar to non-embedded simple sentences." But this ignores psycholinguistic evidence that points in a quite different direction: as the classic work by Wanner and Maratsos, cited in section 4, shows, the processing of direct object relatives taxes working memory because of the need to link the relativized element to a non-adjacent verb.

The explanation for these and countless other facts about language lies (I claim) not in the input but in the nature of the processor that analyzes the input. That processor is surprisingly simple, but it does more than just track frequency, create associations, and record distributional contin-gences. If I am right, an equally important property is the mandate to minimize the burden on working memory. This has far-reaching con-sequences both for the structure of language and for the manner in which it is acquired, as the extensive discussion in O'Grady (2005) attempts to demonstrate.

6.2 A note on Second Language Acquisition

Second language learning presents an even more complicated situation than does first language acquisition, thanks to the relevance of additional factors—prior knowledge of another language, type of instruction, pos-sible critical period effects, and individual differences in motivation, among others. Once again though, it makes sense to address specific ques-tions involving particular phenomena. One such question, which has long been central to research in this area, has to do with "transfer"—the influence of learners' first language on their interlanguage.

The best known UG-based theory of transfer, dubbed "Full Transfer/Full Access," holds that the parameter settings of the native language are initially carried over to the second language but that continued access to UG eventually permits them to be reset in response to the appropriate triggers (e.g., Schwartz & Sprouse, 1996). What might an emergentist approach claim?

In recent work (O'Grady, 2007), I have suggested that the idea behind the Full Transfer/Full Access theory is in some sense right, but only if we rethink what is transferred and what is accessed. In particular, what is transferred in the case of syntax is not a set of parametric values, and what is accessed is not Universal Grammar. Rather, transfer applies to the native language processing routines, and the cognitive system that is accessed is simply the processor, which determines the cost and calculates the strength of those routines.

Space does not permit a detailed discussion of this idea here, but it is nonetheless worth noting the type of phenomena that might be used to test it against the claims of the UG-based theory. As in the case of paral-lel work on first language acquisition, the UG thesis can be properly confronted only through the analysis of phenomena that are governed by abstract constraints for which there is a paucity of relevant data in the input (the poverty of stimulus problem). And, of course, in order to investigate transfer effects, it is crucial that the phenomena in question have somewhat different properties in the L1 and L2.

I believe the quantifier scope is one such phenomenon. Of particular interest is the fact that languages such as English and Japanese differ with respect to the interpretation of sentences such as (52) and (53).

(52) Someone stroked every cat.

(53) Dareka-ga dono neko-mo nadeta.
someone-Nom every cat stroked
"Someone stroked every cat."

Whereas English permits the two readings paraphrased below, Japanese allows only the first of these interpretations.

(54)a. There is a particular person who stroked every cat.

b. For every cat, there is a (possibly different) person who stroked it.

Moreover, the principles governing this phenomenon are apparently both highly abstract and sensitive to extremely limited forms of experience. For instance, in their survey of maternal input to 42 children (age 18 months to 5 years), Gennari and MacDonald (2005/2006, p. 146) found only 14 instances of *every* + noun in a total of 27,804 adult utterances (and about half of these were time phrases such as *every time* and *every day*).

Important work by Marsden (2004) outlines a UG-based account of this phenomenon and of its acquisition in Japanese as a second language by English-, Korean-, and Chinese-speaking learners. O'Grady (2007) proposes an emergentist alternative, focusing on the role of the processor in explaining the character of the scope phenomenon, the nature of cross-linguistic differences in its properties, and the manner in which L1 transfer effects are manifested—and ultimately suppressed.

6.3 Rethinking explanatory adequacy

If these ideas are on the right track, then the key to understanding the nature of the human language faculty lies in the workings of a simple efficiency-driven processor. As explained in detail in O'Grady (2005), the processor contributes to two crucial explanatory endeavors.

On the one hand, the processor has a crucial role to play in understanding why language has the particular properties that it does—why reflexive pronouns appear to seek a local, c-commanding antecedent, why verbs agree with subjects rather than direct objects, why direct object relative clauses are more marked than their subject counterparts, and so forth.

On the other hand, the processor also has a vital role to play in understanding how language is acquired. In particular, it is responsible both for bridging the gap between experience and ultimate proficiency in a language and for forming the particular routines that underlie the formation and interpretation of the actual sentences of a language—with their particular word order, agreement patterns, and so forth.

It is widely believed, both by proponents and by opponents of UG, that "explanatory adequacy"—the gold standard against which the success of linguistic analysis is to be assessed—should be defined with respect to language acquisition, following an early suggestion by Chomsky (1965, pp. 25–26). In a more recent formulation, Chomsky (2002, p. 129) puts it this way: "Explanatory adequacy [is] achieved when a descriptively adequate analysis is completed by a plausible hypothesis about its acquisition."

While such an approach brings language acquisition to the forefront of contemporary linguistics, this may not be the right place for it—regardless of its great practical and emotional importance. On the view I have put forward, language acquisition is simply something that happens when a processor of a certain type interacts with experience of a particular type—certain preferences are implemented and particular routines emerge. If this is right, then processing, not language acquisition, is THE central linguistic phenomenon and the one whose understanding should define the achievement of explanatory adequacy.

7 Conclusion

There is no disagreement in linguistics over the explanatory potential of processing considerations, even among proponents of grammar-based approaches to language (e.g., Newmeyer, 1998). Indeed, as Chomsky (2005, p. 10) acknowledges, explanations of the properties of language that refer to "general considerations of computational efficiency and the like" are highly desirable. Ideas along these lines have in fact been pursued for many years, and there is a sizable literature devoted to processing explanations for specific syntactic phenomena (see O'Grady, 2005, p. 12 for a brief review).

The real question is whether theories of sentence formation need to refer to a grammar in addition to a processor. In particular, if one posits the right type of processor, is there anything left for a grammar to do?

As we have seen, an efficiency-driven linear processor designed to minimize the burden on working memory can account both for the sorts of facts that fall under UG and for the sorts of facts that must be attributed to language-particular grammars. It explains why the subject is structurally higher than the direct object in a transitive clause. It explains intricate facts about verbal agreement in English. It explains why only a verb in the main clause undergoes inversion in *yes-no* questions. And it explains why direct object relatives are more marked and therefore harder to acquire and use than subject relatives. Many additional examples are discussed in O'Grady (2005), all pointing toward the need to shift the burden of explanation in linguistic analysis from an autonomous grammatical system to a processor whose properties seem to follow from the effects of working memory.

The empirical challenges associated with this shift are daunting, it must be admitted. The phenomena that constitute the primary concern of syntactic description (binding, control, agreement, quantification, and so forth) do not simply disappear. The fundamental questions raised by language acquisition, language loss, and language change remain as vital as ever. And data from psycholinguistics, much of it quite puzzling to begin with, becomes even more important than before.

In other words, the problems don't get easier. The hope is simply that new insights can be uncovered, eventually allowing a deeper understanding of how language works.

Notes

1 I am grateful to Nick Ellis, Kevin Gregg, Michael Long, and an anonymous referee for comments, and to Kamil Deen and Jun Nomura for technical assistance involving the CHILDES database.
2 In fact, of course, this happens in the step-by-step manner illustrated below.

  (i)   Combination of *Americans and who*:
        [Are [**Americans who**]]

  (ii) Combination of *who* and *are*:
        [Are [Americans [**who are**]]]

  (iii) Combination of *are* and *rich*:
        [Are [Americans [who [**are rich**]]]]

Bibliography

Anderson, J. R. (1993). *Rules of the Mind*. Hillsdale, NJ: Lawrence Erlbaum.

Britain, D., & Sudbury, A. (2002). There's sheep and there's penguins: Convergence, "drift" and "slant" in New Zealand and Falkland Island English. In M. Jones & E. Esch (Eds.), *Language change: The interplay of internal, external and extra-linguistic factors* (pp. 211–240). Berlin: Mouton de Gruyter.

Caplan, D., & Waters, G. (2002). Working memory and connectionist models of parsing: A reply to MacDonald and Christiansen 2002. *Psychological Review*, 109, 66–74.

Carpenter, P., Miyake, A., & Just, M. (1994.) Working memory constraints in comprehension: Evidence from individual differences, aphasia, and aging. In M. Gernsbacher (Ed.), *Handbook of psycholinguistics* (pp. 1075–1122). San Diego: Academic Press.

Chomsky, N. (1965). *Aspects of the theory of syntax*. Cambridge, MA: MIT Press.

Chomsky, N. (1975). *Reflections on language*. New York: Pantheon.

Chomsky, N. (1980). On cognitive structures and their development: A reply to Piaget. In M. Piatelli-Palmarini (Ed.), *Language and learning: The debate between*

Jean Piaget and Noam Chomsky (pp. 35–52). Cambridge, MA: Harvard University Press.

Chomsky, N. (2002). *On nature and language.* New York: Cambridge University Press.

Chomsky, N. (2005). Three factors in language design. *Linguistic Inquiry, 36,* 1–22.

Clark, M. (2002). Performance errors in yes/no questions by adult second language learners: A replication of Nakayama (1987). In K. Hales & A. Terveen (Eds.), *Selected Papers from the Sixth College-Wide Conference for Students in Languages, Linguistics, and Literature* (pp. 126–133). Honolulu: National Foreign Language Resource Center.

Crain, S., & Nakayama, M. (1987). Structure dependence in grammar formation. *Language, 63,* 522–543.

Diessel, H. (2004). *The acquisition of complex sentences.* Cambridge: Cambridge University Press.

Diessel, H., & Tomasello, M. (2005). A new look at the acquisition of relative clauses. *Language, 81,* 882–906.

Ellis, N. (1998). Emergentism, connectionism and language learning. *Language Learning, 48,* 631–664.

Ellis, N. (2006a). Language acquisition as rational contigency learning. *Applied Linguistics, 27,* 1–24.

Ellis, N. (2006b). Selective attention and transfer phenomena in SLA: Contingency, cue competition, salience, overshadowing, blocking and perceptual learning. *Applied Linguistics, 27,* 164–194.

Ellis, N., & Larsen-Freeman, D. (2006). Language emergence: Implications for applied linguistics. *Applied Linguistics, 27*(4): 558–589.

Elman, J. (1999). The emergence of language: A conspiracy theory. In B. MacWhinney (Ed.), *The emergence of language* (pp. 1–27). Mahwah, NJ: Erlbaum.

Gennari, S., & MacDonald, M. (2005/2006). Acquisition of negation and quantification: Insights from adult production and comprehension. *Language Acquisition, 13,* 125–168.

Gibson, E. (1998). Linguistic complexity: Locality of syntactic dependencies. *Cognition, 68,* 1–76.

Grodzinsky, Y. (1989). Agrammatic comprehension of relative clauses. *Brain and Language, 37,* 430–499.

Hamilton, R. (1994). Is implicational generalization unidirectional and maximal? Evidence from relativization instruction in a second language. *Language Learning, 44,* 123–157.

Hawkins, J. (2004). *Efficiency and complexity in grammars.* Oxford: Oxford University Press.

Hopper, P. (1998). Emergent grammar. In M. Tomasello (Ed.), *The new psychology of language* (pp. 155–175). Mahwah, NJ: Erlbaum.

Jackendoff, R. (2002). *Foundations of language.* New York: Oxford University Press.

Ingham, R. (1993/1994). Input and learnability: Direct-object omissibility in English. *Language Acquisition, 3,* 95–120.

Keenan, E., & Comrie, B. (1977). Noun phrase accessibility and Universal Grammar. *Linguistic Inquiry, 8,* 63–100.

Lasnik, H. (1999). *Minimalist analysis.* Oxford: Blackwell.

165

Legate, J., & Yang, C. (2002). Empirical re-assessment of stimulus poverty arguments. *The Linguistic Review, 19*, 151–162.

Levine, R. (2002). Review of *Rhyme and reason: An introduction to minimalist syntax,* by J. Uriagarecka. *Language, 78,* 325–330.

MacWhinney, B. (1999). Preface. In B. MacWhinney (Ed.), *The emergence of language* (pp. ix–xvii). Mahwah, NJ: Erlbaum.

MacWhinney, B. (2004). A multiple process solution to the logical problem of language acquisition. *Journal of Child Language, 31,* 883–914.

Marsden, H. (2004). Quantifier scope in non-native Japanese: A comparative interlanguage study of Chinese, English, and Korean-speaking learners. Unpublished Ph.D dissertation, University of Durham, U.K.

Menn, L. (2000). Babies, buzzsaws and blueprints: Commentary on review article by Sabbagh & Gelman. *Journal of Child Language, 27,* 753–755.

Morgan, J., & Green, G. (2005). Why verb agreement is not the poster child for any general formal principle. In S. Mufwene, E. Francis, & R. Wheeler (Eds.), *Polymorphous linguistics: Jim McCawley's legacy* (pp. 455–478). Cambridge, MA: MIT Press.

Newmeyer, F. (1998). *Language form and language function.* Cambridge, MA: MIT Press.

O'Grady, W. (1997). *Syntactic development.* Chicago: University of Chicago Press.

O'Grady, W. (2001). An emergentist approach to syntax. Available at http://www.ling.hawaii.edu/faculty/ogrady/.

O'Grady, W. (2005). *Syntactic carpentry: An emergentist approach to syntax.* Mahwah, NJ: Erlbaum.

O'Grady, William. (2007). The syntax of quantification in SLA: An emergentist approach. In M. O'Brien, C. Shea, & J. Archibald (Eds.), *Proceedings of the 8th Generative Approaches to Second Language Acquisition Conference (GASLA 2006): The Banff Conference* (pp. 98–113). Somerville, MA: Cascadilla Press.

Piñango, M., Burkhardt, P., Brun, D., & Avrutin, S. (2001). The psychological reality of the syntax-discourse interface: The case of pronominals. Paper presented at the workshop "From sentence processing to discourse interpretation: Crossing the borders," Utrecht University.

Pullum, G. (1996). Learnability, hyperlearning and the poverty of stimulus. *Proceedings of the Berkeley Linguistics Society, 22,* 498–513.

Pullum, G., & Scholz, B. (2002). Empirical assessment of stimulus poverty arguments. *Linguistic Review, 19,* 9–50.

Robinson, P. (2002). Effects of individual differences in intelligence, aptitude and working memory on incidental SLA. In P. Robinson (Ed.), *Individual differences and instructed language learning* (pp. 211–221). Philadelphia: John Benjamins.

Sampson, G. (1989). Language acquisition: Growth or learning? *Philosophical Papers, 18,* 203–240.

Schmidt, R., & McCreary, C. (1977). Standard and super-standard English: Recognition and use of prescriptive rules by native and non-native speakers. *TESOL Quarterly, 11,* 415–429.

Schwartz, B., & Sprouse, R. (1996). L2 cognitive states and the Full Transfer/Full Access model. *Second Language Research, 12,* 40–72.

Sekerina, I., Stromswold, K., & Hestvik, A. (2004). How do adults and children process referentially ambiguous pronouns? *Journal of Child Language, 31*, 123–152.

Sobin, N. (1997). Agreement, default rules, and grammatical viruses. *Linguistic Inquiry, 28*, 318–343.

Sparks, R. (1984). Here's a few more facts. *Linguistic Inquiry, 15*, 179–183.

Tagliamonte, S. (1998). *Was/were* variation across generations: View from the city of York. *Language Variation and Change, 10*, 153–191.

Theakston, A., Lieven, E., Pine, J., & Rowland, C. (2001). The role of performance limitations in the acquisition of verb-argument structures: An alternative account. *Journal of Child Language, 28*, 127–152.

Tomasello, M. (2003). *Constructing a language: A usage-based theory of language acquisition.* Cambridge, MA: Harvard University Press.

Wanner, E., & Maratsos, M. (1978). An ATN approach to comprehension. In M. Halle, J. Bresnan, & G. Miller (Eds.), *Linguistic theory and psychological reality* (pp. 119–161). Cambridge, MA: MIT Press.

Wolfram, W., & Christian, D. (1976). *Appalachian speech.* Arlington, VA: Center for Applied Linguistics.

8

CHILDREN'S FIRST LANGUAGE ACQUISITION FROM A USAGE-BASED PERSPECTIVE[1]

Elena Lieven and Michael Tomasello

1 Introduction

Children learn language from their language experiences—there is no other way.

There are, however, major debates as to what they bring to this language learning: do they come with innate, specifically syntactic skills or, rather, with more general cognitive and interactive skills? In this chapter, we will argue for the latter and suggest that children's language development can be explained in terms of species-specific learning and intentional communication. We argue that the child learns language from actual "usage events," i.e. from particular utterances in particular contexts, and builds up increasingly complex and abstract linguistic representations from these.

This contrasts with the nativist-linguistic perspective which argues for innate grammatical knowledge, encapsulated in a "syntax" module. This provides the child with an abstract Universal Grammar (UG) which they use in conjunction with the language they hear to arrive at the grammar of that language. In this approach, abstract representations are present from that outset and the particularities of the language are learned on the basis of this abstract knowledge. In the usage-based approach, by contrast, abstract representations arise from these particularities.

In usage-based theory, children start by learning low-scope constructions based around specific words or morphemes. These constructions become more complex and abstractions build up (for instance, of tense, agreement, subject and transitive). Initially a child may have no understanding of the internal structure of a construction (e.g. that the *'s* in *what's that?*[2] is a form of the verb BE) but uses it as a whole with a specific

168

meaning. As development proceeds, distributional analysis based on the relation between a form and (child-identified) functions, leads to linguistic representations developing internal structure. Patterns of relationships build up between constructions and their parts, in a process of increasing complexity and schematization. Constituency develops as a result of functionally-based distributional analysis, the identification of repeated items in strings of speech and the attempt to find a function for each identified item. Over time, this becomes increasingly less item-based and more schematic and the child will learn to express communicative functions (e.g. reference, foregrounding and backgrounding) in increasingly complex ways.

We first give a brief outline of how grammatical development proceeds according to a usage-based approach. From this perspective, the learning of language will be critically dependent on factors in the environment that have been shown to affect learning more generally, namely frequency, consistency, and complexity, and we next discuss these factors. Following this, we look at the processes involved in building linguistic representations using examples from morphological development, the development of the English transitive, and the development of complex syntax. Finally, we consider the issue of differing task demands in both comprehension and production and how this might interact with the nature of linguistic representations in a usage-based model.

We will be almost exclusively concerned with the development of syntax and morphology, but it is important to remember that before children show evidence of approaching the task of syntax learning, they have been immersed in a language-rich environment from before birth. There are a large number of studies that document the infant's progressive development of segmentation, pattern recognition and word recognition skills during the first 12–18 months of life (Jusczyk, 1997; Gomez & Gerken, 1999). Infants also make major developmental strides in cognitive and social development during this same period, showing developing abilities to categorize (Mandler, 2000) and to understand that others have intentions that may be different from their own (Carpenter, Nagel, & Tomasello, 1998; Tomasello, Carpenter, Call, Behne, & Moll, 2005). Putting these pattern-identifying skills together with the ability to understand intentions provides the basis for the mapping between form and meaning that gives rise to early word learning. However, this is a prolonged process: between 15 and 24 months of age, infants increase the speed with which they can look to the correct object when they hear a matching word that they know. At 15 months, they do not turn to the object until milliseconds after the whole word has been heard. By 24 months they are turning as soon as they hear the first formant (Fernald, Pinto, Swingley, Weinberg, & McRoberts, 1998). Such increases in processing speed reflect a relatively long process of entrenchment and automatization of the

169

relation between form and meaning, something, we would argue, that has to happen over and over again in the learning of language.

1.1 A brief outline of how children's grammar develops

In usage-based theory, utterances are strings of speech for getting things said and understood. From these usage events, children build up an inventory of constructions with relationships between them. Constructions can be utterance-level, for instance the transitive construction, or below utterance-level: morphological constructions are a good example but so, too, is the noun phrase. Each construction has a function (meaning) as a whole. In the adult construction inventory, constructions can range from being fully phonologically specific to fully schematic. It takes time for children to abstract the ways in which the parts of constructions contribute to their meaning and to make links between constructions. Three types of representations are building up: whole constructions, slots in constructions into which strings that match the function of the slot can be substituted, and patterns of distribution both between items in constructions and between constructions. All of these interact in the process of abstraction that builds more schematic constructions. The difference between young children's inventories and those of adults is one of degree: many more, initially all, of children's constructions are either fully lexically-specific or contain relatively low-scope slots. As well as being less schematic than many adult constructions they are also simpler with fewer parts. And, finally, children's constructions exist in a less dense network—they are more "island-like."

As children's grammar develops, they add constructions to their inventory that are increasingly complex (with more parts) and increasingly abstract (in the scope of the slots) (Dąbrowksa, 2004a). It is important to note that children are capable of abstraction from the beginning of language. From the moment that a child is able to name a set of nonidentical objects using the same label, they are already making an abstraction. What changes over development is the scope of the abstraction. Equally, as soon as a child uses a construction that has a schematized slot into which words matching the function of the slot can be placed, they are being productive—and many of these early constructions can be highly productive.

Initially, children's constructions may be fully lexically-specific but some constructions rapidly develop slots into which a range of items can be placed—these constructions are then partially schematic with fixed lexical material as well as slots. If the child can insert a novel item into the slot, this is evidence that a form-function abstraction has been made and schematization has occurred. While schematization may be confined initially to one construction, it may also generalize to others: the early development of a relatively abstract "noun" category is an example of this.

At some point, and for some constructions, children will abstract a fully schematic construction: the English transitive is an example. Evidence that the construction is fully schematic is that the child can correctly use a novel verb in the construction. Two interacting factors may contribute to the development of full schematicity. First the presence of the same form-function mapping across utterances, e.g. the presence of the same noun (I, for instance) before the verb may contribute to the abstraction of a "verb" category (Pine, Lieven & Rowland, 1998). Second, the child may make an analogy between different, more isolated constructions, for instance, I hitting it, Daddy drop cup, Mummy pull box, and abstract form-function relations of the type: Noun-before-verb = "do-er," Noun-after-verb = "do-ee" (Tomasello, 2003, p. 174).

Finally, the child has to abstract the relations between constructions. Evidence that this has occurred is that the child is able to transform an utterance in one construction into another construction, for instance a declarative into a wh-question or an active into a passive. This could be done by forming a semantic representation of the first construction and relating this to a semantic representation of what the speaker wishes to say, thereby allowing the production of the other construction. Whether and when the learner actually maps the form-function mappings of one construction to those of the other is an empirically open question at the moment. It may depend on the metalinguistic expertise and/or educational level of different speakers.

Constructions are ways of saying things and the frequency of all or parts of constructions that children hear or say results in their entrenchment, that is in their increasing representational strength which, in turn, makes them increasingly available for the processing and production of utterances. Constructions can be entrenched at varying levels of lexical specificity and schematicity. Consistency aids learning and complexity impedes it. The entrenchment of constructions provides the child with ways of saying things that are adult-like but if the child has not yet fully learned the adult construction, an already entrenched construction may be used instead and this can give rise to competition between more and less entrenched constructions. If the child has a very well-entrenched way of saying something, this may preempt the learning of new constructions. In some cases this prevents error, in others it leads to error. In the next section we consider the role of frequency, consistency, and complexity in detail.

2 Factors affecting the learning of grammar

2.1 Frequency

Psycholinguistic research demonstrates adult language processing to be sensitive to frequency effects at all levels (Bod, Hay & Jannedy, 2003; Bybee & Hopper, 2001; Ellis, 2002) and this is also true in studies of children's production and comprehension. Experimental studies (e.g. Bates & MacWhinney, 1987) and connectionist and computational simulations (e.g. Morris, Cottrell & Elman, 2000; Chang, Dell, & Bock, 2006; Chater & Manning, 2006) can provide considerable insight into the ways in which frequencies of forms and constructions can interact to produce learning outcomes. As we shall see, a crucial issue is the precise form or structure that is being counted.

Many naturalistic studies of children's speech have found that the more frequently children hear a particular morpheme, word, or construction, all things being equal, the earlier they acquire it. For example, de Villiers (1985), Naigles and Hoff-Ginsberg (1998) and Theakston, Lieven, Pine, and Rowland (2004), have all shown that order of emergence of particular verbs is significantly correlated with the frequency of use in language addressed to the children. All three of these studies found that the range of constructions with which adults used the verbs in talking to children was also correlated with the diversity of these verbs in the children's language. Wilson (2003) has shown frequency effects on the provision of obligatory auxiliaries and copulas, as have Theakston, Lieven, Pine, and Rowland (2005). Huttenlocher, Vasilyeva, Cymerman, and Levine (2002) have shown that frequency effects extend into children's development of complex syntax and that these effects were not only found between the speech of parents and their children's development of complex syntax but also between the complexity of teacher's speech and children's development.

The effects of frequency on children's linguistic representations have also been shown experimentally. In a series of "weird word order" experiments in which children were presented with scenes described in non-canonical word orders, children were significantly more likely to correct to canonical word order with verbs that they knew than with novel verbs (Akhtar, 1999; Abbot-Smith, Lieven, & Tomasello, 2001). Matthews, Lieven, Theakston, and Tomasello (2005) extended this paradigm using verbs of high, medium, and low frequency and found similar results for both English- and, subsequently, for French-speaking children (Matthews, Lieven, Theakston, & Tomasello, 2007).

However, frequency interacts with a number of other factors in affecting learning: the child is not a simple associationist mechanism onto which frequency maps directly. There are two broad factors that have to be considered. First, other aspects of the child's developing language will interact with frequency; and, second, there are many different kinds of frequency and these may have differential effects.

A study by Cameron-Faulkner, Lieven, and Theakston (2007) on the development of early negative constructions with verbs shows the different ways in which frequency can interact with a child's developing linguistic system. The child, Brian, was recorded for five hours per week over a year from 2;0–3;0. His multiword utterances containing both negators and verbs were coded for type of negator and meaning at three-monthly intervals. Initially, at 2;3, all Brian's negative utterances with verbs fell into an ungrammatical **no + verb** pattern. At 2;6, **not + verb** (also frequently ungrammatical) began to account for an increasing proportion of the utterances and continued to do so for the next six months. By 3;0, **no + verb** had disappeared and **can't + verb** and **don't + verb** accounted for just under 20 percent of the utterances. At 3;3, **not + verb** had virtually disappeared, **can't + verb** and **don't + verb** accounted for an increasing proportion, and other **auxn't + verb** structures began to appear: the child's system was now a limited version of the adult's.

How does this pattern of development relate to the structures and functions of negation in Brian's input? *No* is his mother's most frequent negator across single and multiword utterances but, although *no* can be combined with nouns (e.g. *no books, no tea*) and parents and teachers do sometimes say things like *no shouting, no running* and *no hitting*, most **no + verb** utterances are ungrammatical in adult English and, in fact, they are not attested in the speech sample of Brian's mother. So Brian constructed a pattern using *no* followed by whatever he wants to negate. Here, then, the frequency (and salience) of *no* in the adult speech and, of course, in Brian's own speech, has been used in a novel construction that is, in itself, highly infrequent in the input. This is an example of creative structure building at the outset of multiword speech but in complex interaction with the frequency of forms in the input and of Brian's own usage.

The emergence of the other three negators used by Brian with verbs up to age 3;0 (*not, can't* and *don't*) also partially followed input frequencies: after *no* these are the next most frequent negators in the mother's speech, all of them more frequent in her multiword utterances than *no*. However the speed with which **not + verb** takes over from **no + verb** and then, for some functions, **can't + verb** and **don't + verb** take over from **not + verb**, does not just reflect input frequency but also the range of negators that the mother uses for a particular function. Thus, if a particular function is consistently mapped by just one form, Brian uses this form earlier than if the function is expressed by several forms, in which case he seems to utilize his all-purpose construction (**no + verb** earlier, **not + verb** later). This pattern of development seems to accord well with Bates and MacWhinney's (1989) definitions of cue validity and reliability in which

173

the frequency of a form interacts with its consistency to allow learning to take place at greater or lesser speed, an issue that we return to below. Note also that the data suggests a "boot-strapping" between the overall frequency of a negator in the input and the development of the child's ability to identify more specific form-function mappings.

2.1.1 Token and type frequency

A crucial distinction, developed by Bybee (1995) in the context of accounting for diachronic changes in inflectional morphology, is between token and type frequency. Token frequency is the frequency of particular items and entrenches the comprehension and use of concrete pieces of language—items and phrases (collocations). For instance, for many children learning English, "What's that?" is often produced very early, presumably because adults use it to them with high frequency. But children will certainly not have mastery of the internal structure of this utterance—they have learned the utterance as a whole as a result of its frequency. Type frequency is the frequency with which different actual forms occur in the same slot (for instance verbs in the transitive construction or past participles marked with -ed in the past tense). This promotes generalization by demonstrating to the learner that within the context of "the same" construction, different concrete items may serve the same function (at the level of either the whole construction or its constituents). Thus, another very early wh-question produced by children is **Where's X gone** where X is substitutable by a range of referents, for some children, only animate, for others, also including object referents. This is also a highly frequent question in the input but adults use a wide variety of referring expressions with it. As a result, while some children may start with a fully frozen construction, for example, "Where's Daddy gone?," almost all children so far studied rapidly produce the construction with a slot for referents (Lieven, Behrens, Speares, & Tomasello, 2003). So the difference between token and type frequency is between entrenching specific words or phrases and creating slots in which a range of words or phrases can occur.

2.1.1.1 TOKEN FREQUENCY

If a particular word or phrase occurs with very high frequency, it can become entrenched as a whole. An example is Bybee and Scheibmann's (1999) study of I don't know. The authors compared the characteristics of the frequently produced I dunno with other productions of don't know and showed that there were major prosodic and phonological differences between the two. They argued that I dunno is not constructed from constituent parts but produced as a whole in a way similar to partially or fully lexically-specific idioms. The degree of isolation of these item-based constructions from other, more abstract, constructions varies. Some highly idiosyncratic constructions can still be instances of abstract constructions (e.g. X *kick(-ed) the bucket* meaning that X *died* is an instance of the transitive construction). This, then, leads to the theoretical proposal made by many usage-based linguists that, as abstractions develop, they do not replace more item-based instances but that all remain in the inventory of constructions that speakers have created, to be drawn upon at various levels of abstraction depending on the context in which the utterance has to be understood or produced and the resulting ease of access to more or less item-based constructions. Thus, the inventory of constructions consists of constructions ranging from the fully lexically-specific through to the fully abstract.

Until recently, there have been relatively few studies focusing on children's acquisition of concrete phrases as a function of what they hear in the input. Presumably this is because, under a UG approach, these rote-learned fragments are not of interest. But, from a usage-based perspective, they are simply part of the inventory of constructions that children and adults can draw upon and their existence may be important in accounting for various learning outcomes in naturalistic and experimental studies. Recent studies have indicated a pervasive role for token frequency in order of emergence of particular forms and in the explanation of errors and non-errors in children's developing productivity. For instance, Cameron-Faulkner, Lieven, and Tomasello (2003) found significant correlations between the relative frequency with which mothers used particular copula frames (e.g, *There's the* X versus *It's a* X) and the frequency with which their children used the exact same frames.

A number of studies have shown, both for children and adults, that "grammaticality judgments" are dependent on frequency. Thus, in an experiment by Brooks and Tomasello (1999) children overgeneralized the syntactic use of particular English verbs as a function of how frequently they had heard them used previously. The children were more likely to say *He vanished it* than *He disappeared it* because, it was argued, their knowledge of *disappear* was more entrenched than that of *vanish*. Theakston (2004) and Ambridge, Pine, Rowland, and Young (in press) have shown precisely the same effect using a grammaticality judgment task with adults and children, indicating that these lexically-specific frequency effects are indeed involved both in learning the system and its representation in adulthood.

These item-based effects have also been produced experimentally using novel verbs. In a between-subjects design, Theakston, Lieven, and Tomasello (2003) presented children aged 3;0, either with novel verbs in constructions marked for finiteness (*This one tams, Look, it tams*) or in constructions where the same verbs appeared in a non-finite form (*Will this one tam? Should it tam?*). In the test phase in which the children were asked a question pulling for 3rd person singular marking (*What does this one do? It . . .*) the children in the non-finite condition produced significantly more indicative sentences with the novel verbs in the non-finite form in which they had heard it, compared to the children who heard the verb in the finite condition who never produced the non-finite form. The authors suggest that the fact that, in questions, English-speaking children frequently hear "subjects" followed immediately by non-finite verbs may account, in part, for the high proportion of "optional infinitives" that they produce (*It go there, He want that*). In other words, there is a priming effect of repeatedly hearing a particular form of the verb.

The idea that "optional infinitive" phenomena can be explained by characteristics of the input was examined in a crosslinguistic modeling study by Freudenthal, Pine, Aguado-Orea and Gobet (2007). These authors used Dutch, German, and Spanish corpora of adult speech to one child learning each language as input to a computational analyzer that learned strings by starting from the ends of utterances and built novel links based on words that had the same neighbors. The analyzer succeeded in replicating the relative proportions of non-finite, finite, and complex finite verbs in each child's speech at matched MLUs. The explanation lies in the relative frequency with which non-finite verbs appear in utterance-final position (very frequently in Dutch, somewhat less frequently in German, and virtually never in Spanish). Since previous attempts to explain these crosslinguistic differences have been made by an appeal to highly abstract aspects of tense and agreement checking in minimalist grammar (Wexler, 1998), it is striking that they can be replicated by a very simple mechanism which simply analyzes strings of Child Directed Speech.

The learning of particular strings as a result of their frequency in the input can also "protect" the child from error. Rowland and Pine (2000) and Rowland (2007) have shown that English-speaking children's error rate on syntactic questions could be predicted by the relative frequency of initial, lexically-specific strings in their mothers' questions. Children were significantly less likely to make errors in questions requiring inversion when these were exemplified by high-frequency lexical strings in the input (i.e. strings in yes/no questions such as **Do you X?** and in wh-questions such as **What can X?**), even when the frequency of the individual words in the strings was controlled. Thus, the effect cannot be attributed to the fact that children and adults are more likely to make errors on low-frequency words—an explanation that could be incorporated into a non-usage-based account. It is the entrenchment of the frames themselves that is a significant negative predictor of error.

Entrenchment of lexically specific strings, as a result of high frequency, is of considerable theoretical importance in linguistic theory. Idioms, such as *Kick the bucket*, cannot be generated by using the basic meanings of *kick* and *bucket* and then assembling the string. They have therefore to be excluded from "core UG." But idioms form a continuum with other, more productive constructions, and many of them can be altered to some extent using "normal grammar" (Jackendoff, 1996; Culicover, 1999). Within a usage-based perspective, this problem does not arise because the grammar is seen as an inventory of constructions, ranging from simple to complex and from fully lexically-specified to fully abstract. The importance of this for the preservation of exceptions to inflectional paradigms has been accepted by many linguists but precisely the same arguments apply to other strings in language. From the point of view of language development the difference between the child and the adult inventories is in the balance between fully item-based constructions and partially or fully abstract constructions. The development of these more abstract constructions depends on function-based distributional analysis (mapping a meaning to an identified form) in which type frequency plays a critical role.

2.1.1.2 TYPE FREQUENCY

Braine (1987) showed, in a series of artificial language experiments, that subjects found it relatively easy to learn "categories" and rules for combining them provided the "words" instantiating the categories were either preceded or followed by a fixed item. Failing this, the categories were difficult or impossible to learn. In terms of children's language development, the proposal is that children are more likely to work out the presence and function of a slot in a construction, the more frequent the variation in items that fill the slot. There are a number of child language studies which suggest that varying the type frequency of elements within a construction encourages generalization/abstraction.

Wittek and Tomasello (2005) in a study on German-speaking children's ability to form the past participle of novel verbs in the German perfect, showed that productivity developed earlier in constructions with the auxiliary *haben* ("have") than *sein* ("be"). Many more verbs take *haben* in the perfect than take *sein*, thus the type frequency of the past participle slot in perfect constructions is much higher for verbs that take *haben*. In a study using a very dense corpus from one child (Brian), Maslen, Lieven, Theakston, and Tomasello (2004) showed that the child produced over-generalization errors for the English plural (e.g. *foots*) earlier than for the English past tense (e.g. *comed*). Although it is possible that the semantics of plurality may be easier for children to identify than that of past, the results can also be explained in terms of (i) the type frequency of the regular paradigm which is greater for plurals than for pasts, i.e. children hear more different nouns taking *-s* earlier than they hear verbs taking *-ed*, and (ii) the token frequency of irregulars which is greater for pasts than for plurals (see below).

In two training studies, Childers and Tomasello (2001) and Abbot-Smith, Lieven, and Tomasello (2004) found that children aged 2;6 acquired productive use of the transitive construction as a result of hearing over 100 transitive utterances employing 16 different verbs and many different noun phrases—much more than a control group who did not hear these. These studies are interesting in that three slots are being created: noun phrase slots for each of the two argument roles and a "transitive verb" slot. There is plenty of evidence to suggest that by the time children are the age of these two studies they already have a NP construction that is highly flexible and that includes, at the least, some knowledge of determiner use (e.g. *a, the, more*). Since, in this experiment, they acquired the ability to generalize the transitive construction to verbs in which they had never heard it—as the control group did not—this must have been on the basis of (a) the constancy of the abstract NP slots and (b) the type frequency of the verbs. However, Childers and Tomasello also found that the use of pronouns in the NP slots of the training exemplars facilitated acquisition and generalization. So the most effective training was type variation along with some consistency. Pronouns are a highly limited set of consistent forms with very abstract meanings and, as has been suggested by Pine, Lieven, and Rowland (1998), they may therefore act as a kind of "stepping stone" to the formation of more abstract argument slots since they play precisely the role of a consistent form followed by a variable slot described above in relation to Braine's study. This demonstrates that what counts as a fixed item will change over the course of development as children's categories become more abstract.

A good example of the interaction between the child's developing representation of more abstract linguistic structure and frequency is provided by Tomasello's (2000) discussion of the argument structure overgeneralizations reported so extensively by Bowerman (1988) (e.g. *She's giggling me* to mean *She's making me giggle*). Tomasello suggests that, if a verb is highly frequent in the input and used early by the child (e.g. *laugh*), it will become entrenched and protected from overgeneralization (e.g. children will not say *she laughed me* for *she made me laugh*). Verbs that are highly infrequent in the language children hear (e.g. *chortle*) will also be protected from overgeneralization because by the time that children learn them, they will have developed the abstractions that prevent such overgeneralizations. It is the verbs of intermediate frequency (e.g. *giggle*) that are not protected by being well entrenched but are learned before the child has fully made the relevant abstractions that are likely to be overgeneralized. While there has not yet been a direct comparison of children's greater willingness to overgeneralize medium-frequency verbs than lower-frequency verbs, there are a number of experiments which support the idea that both children and adults are affected by the frequency of a verb in their acceptance of overgeneralizations. Brooks, Tomasello, Lewis, and Dodson (1999) found that children were less likely to overgeneralize the strongly entrenched verb of a semantically similar pair of fixed-transitivity verbs (e.g. *disappear–vanish*) than they were the less entrenched (later learned) verb. In the series of experiments by Theakston (2004) and Ambridge, Pine, Rowland and Young (in press) mentioned above, high correlations were found between the frequency with which a form occurred and participants' rating of its acceptability in a non-grammatical context. The more infrequent the form, the more acceptable the subjects found the ungrammatical context (though the sentences were always rated as ungrammatical by both adults and older children.)

Token and type frequency go together in complex ways, and determining what is a type depends on how a construction is defined. Type frequency measures items that are similar in some way and the degree of complexity defines which items and structures will be identified as similar at a particular developmental stage such that frequency can be calculated over them. We are a long way from understanding all the ways in which similarity is identified and changes with development and how this interacts with externally derived definitions of complexity and consistency (discussed below). For instance, Maslen, Theakston, Lieven and Tomasello (2004) could not easily account for the fact that some verbs, e.g. *come*, continue to be overgeneralized (to *comed*) after literally thousands of examples of the correct form (*came*). Another example is the fact that a further training study employing differences in type frequency (Ambridge, Theakston, Lieven, & Tomasello, 2006) did not find an effect of type frequency on the children's capacity to abstract the transitive construction. This experiment did, however, yield the interesting result that children make generalizations more readily as a result of distributed rather than massed exposure in the input—a finding that fits in with a large literature on learning that shows distributed input to be better than massed. We take this as an indication that learning grammar has much in common with learning in general.

2.2 Consistency

From the outset of comprehending and producing language, children create and learn form-function mappings. Both the forms identified and the functions that they are mapped to may not initially be those of the adult language. However, the process of arriving at adult form-function mappings is likely to depend to some considerable extent on how consistent this mapping is in the ambient language. Consistency can probably operate at many levels: for instance, at the level of phonological form as well as that of semantic function. Thus, if one function maps to many forms or vice versa, this is likely to make the child's task harder. Slobin (1973) was the first to discuss this in detail when, in outlining his "operating principles" for learning a language, he identified "one form-one function" as a major aid to "cracking the code" and gave a number of examples including the relative difficulty, in a range of languages, of learning to mark the direct object of transitive verbs. But, of course, if we want to compare the relative ease of particular form-function mappings within and across languages, we need a metric. In their "competition model," Bates and MacWhinney (1989) provide one. They focus on form-function relations, and how they are signified in the languages that children are hearing, using measures of cue availability and cue reliability. Cue availability refers to the consistency with which a particular form is present when the child understands that the speaker is attempting to express a certain function, e.g. how consistently **word+-ed** is present when the speaker intends to indicate past tense. Cue reliability refers to the consistency with which a particular function is present when the child hears a particular form, e.g. how consistently a speaker intends to indicate the past tense when she uses **word+-ed**. Putting the two measures together, we get cue validity: a measure of how consistent a form-function mapping is, considering both directions of fit. Other terms used in the model are cue strength, which incorporates frequency, and cue cost, which deals with issues of complexity as outlined below (see also Kempe & MacWhinney, 1998).

The role of relative cue validity in acquisition has been demonstrated many times by the Bates and MacWhinney group. In particular, studies reported in Bates et al. (1984) and in Bates and MacWhinney (1989) showed that syntactic devices for indicating the agent and patient in transitive utterances (e.g. word order, case marking) facilitate acquisition in different languages as a function of their cue validity in the particular language. Maslen et al.'s (2004) results, outlined above, can also be explained in terms of cue validity. A major reason that the plural is generalized and even overgeneralized earlier than the past tense marker is that the plural marker -s has far fewer exceptions than does the -ed past tense marker. Thus when the speaker is intending to indicate plural, -s is highly available, by contrast with -ed which has to compete for availability in the marking of past with all the irregular verbs. Despite the fact that -s is less reliable in marking plural than -ed is in marking past tense (more other functions are also marked with -s than are marked with -ed), the maths shows that it is a more valid cue of plurality than -ed is of past tense.

There is frequently more than one cue that indicates a particular function. An example is the marking of argument roles in transitive utterances in German which we have been researching (Dittmar, Abbot-Smith, Lieven, & Tomasello, in press). The majority of transitive utterances in German show SVO word order but other orders, for instance OVS, are possible and, indeed, occur about 22 percent of the time in German CDS. Case marking in German is mainly indicated on the determiner (and of course, pronouns) but this is only contrastive for masculine nouns (*Der*-NOM *Hund* vs. *Den*-ACC *Hund*, "the dog"). Children were shown two pictures each with one animal doing something to another. The pictures contained the same animals but differed in which animal was the actor and which the patient. The children were asked to point to the picture that matched the sentence they heard, thus to the picture with the correct animals as agent and patient. The study shows that children aged 2;7 can only reliably point to the correct of two pictures with reversed agents and patients if both the SVO word order and contrastive case-marking are present. They are at chance with OVS word order despite the presence of contrastive case-marking and also at chance with SVO utterances with non-contrastive case-marking. Five-year-olds could point reliably to the correct picture when only the canonical word order cue was present but it was only the children aged 7;0 who could solve the task correctly with OVS word order but contrastive case-marking. Clearly, in a situation in which more than one cue indicates a function, then, what Bates and MacWhinney call "cue coalitions" can occur. But in this study the youngest children cannot do the task on the basis of one cue alone, despite the fact that both are valid (the cue validity of contrastive case-marking is 86 percent and of SVO word order is 68 percent, using Kempe and MacWhinney's method of calculation). They seem to have built up a representation of a "prototypical transitive construction" which contains both cues and they can only do the task when they encounter sentences with both.

Again we take the fact that the consistency of form-function mappings affects their acquisition in similar ways to that in which the contingency of cue-outcome pairs determines learning throughout animal and human cognition as evidence that much of grammar acquisition can be understood as the application of general learning mechanisms to the particular problem of language (Ellis, 2006; Shanks, 1995).

2.3 Complexity

Many factors contribute to the syntactic complexity of a construction and, as a result, how easy it is to learn. Of major importance is how many parts the construction has. Thus a rote-learned construction with no analyzed parts will be less complex than a schematic construction with a slot and this, in turn, will be more complex than constructions with greater numbers of slots (Lieven, Behrens, Speares, & Tomasello, 2003). Other candidates for greater complexity are (a) whether cues are local or distributed and (b) how far a construction is from others the child has already mastered.

2.3.1 Local and distributed cues

Slobin has shown in many analyses of naturalistic data that distributed cues are more difficult for children to learn than local cues (e.g. Slobin, 1985). For instance, in Turkish, subjects and direct objects are marked on the relevant nouns with analytic morphemes which are almost perfectly regular. This contrasts with agent- and patient-marking using word order (e.g in English) and with the somewhat more complex situation in which both word order and case-marking are more partial cues as outlined for German above. Word order requires that the arguments are related to the whole sentence rather than being directly indicated on the argument itself. Slobin demonstrates that Turkish children learn to mark agent and patient roles earlier than in English and with few errors.

Another example of a distributed construction is the German perfect. As mentioned above, this is formed using an auxiliary (either *haben* or *sein*) and a past participle. While the finite auxiliary fills the position of second constituent in the sentence (the German "V2" rule), the past participle comes in sentence final position: *Ich habe das gemacht* ("I have this done"). In an experiment using novel verbs, Wittek and Tomasello (2005) showed that children acquire elements of the German perfect productively (e.g., the past participle, **ge-verb-t**) before they acquire the entire construction including both auxiliary verb and past participle with material in between.

Much the same explanation may apply to the difficulty children have with center-embedded relative clauses (Correa, 1995). These have often been shown to be more difficult to acquire than right-branching relative clauses which are not embedded in this way. The explanation may be that center-embedding divides parts of the main clause from each other and means that parsing the main clause for its arguments cannot go through until after the center-embedded clause has been heard.

2.3.2 The relation of known constructions to the learning of new ones

The usage-based approach represents linguistic structure at both abstract and concrete levels and emphasizes that children learn from concrete exemplars. Abbot-Smith and Behrens (2006) have used these ideas to show how acquisition of the German passive could rely on the prior learning of related constructions. They call this, after Morris, Cottrell, and Elman (2000, see also Mintz, 2003), a "construction conspiracy." They argue that the *sein*-passive is learned before the *werden*-passive because children already know and use a number of constructions using either *sein* or a past participle (which is identical to the passive participle) while they have not learned constructions using *werden* before they start to produce the *werden*-passive.

The idea that children use already known constructions to work out the form-function mappings of more complex constructions may also be relevant to the question of how children finally come to be able to deal with center-embedded relative clauses. In an elegant demonstration, Lewis and Elman (2001) showed that a model trained on a set of utterances exemplifying various types of constructions including actives, passives, questions, and right-branching relatives but, crucially, not on utterances containing center-embedded relative clauses, could learn to parse the agreement between the discontinuous elements of the main clause. This is, of course, only a model and the precise nature of the sentences and the order in which they were fed to the model did affect its success. Even so, the authors demonstrate that training on the simpler structures provides the model both with the distributional information governing agreement and the distributional information governing NP constituency and that these together allow it to deal with the more complex, interrupted structure.

In this section we have reviewed a number of factors that have been shown to influence the learning of different aspects of morphology and syntax. In passing we have referred to a number of different levels and types of linguistic representation. We now address more fully the nature of children's linguistic representations and how they arrive at them.

3 Building linguistic representations

In the adult inventory, constructions exist at all levels of abstractness from rote-learned through to fully abstract. What changes is the complexity of constructions (the number of parts), the extent of abstractness in constructions (the scope of the slots) and the network of relationships between them. An example is Theakston, Lieven, Pine, and Rowland's (2002) study of the development of the verb GO in 11 of the children in the Manchester corpus. The authors examined the different forms of GO (*goes, go, going, gone, went*) in terms of the constructions in which they occurred and their semantics. They showed that initially the different forms of GO appeared in very different constructions with different meanings (e.g. *X gone* = disappear; *X went Y* = something made a noise; *X goes Y* = belongs). The different constructions varied in terms of the numbers of slots that occurred and the scope of the slots. Towards the end of their third year, some of the children showed evidence of starting to develop a more complete representation of the verb GO, for instance by using different forms in the same construction or by tense or agreement alternations in discourse. What contributed to this development? In part it may be the direct influence of hearing adults use different forms of GO in the same construction. But it may also be due to the development of a morphological tense construction in which a more abstract verb category together with its past tense inflection has been abstracted. Since the past of GO is irregular, the use of *goed* rather than *went* in some constructions would be evidence that this has taken place. Note that, in turn, this tense construction may not initially cover all verbs. Indeed, there is considerable evidence that, when children start to mark verbs in the past tense, they only do so for a subset of verbs with punctual aspect (Clark, 1996; Li & Shirai, 2000). In this section we will use three examples to look at these processes in more detail: (i) morphological development, (ii) the development of the transitive construction, and (iii) the development of complex sentences.

3.1 Morphological development

As Slobin (1973, 1985) and Peters (1983, 1997) pointed out in their pioneering work on children's learning of morphology, English morphology is so impoverished that English does not make a good language for understanding the development of morphology. It has been claimed that children learning inflectionally richer languages learn productive morphology early and often with little or no error. This has been used as evidence for the existence of pregiven abstract categories.

One central issue is how to measure productivity. This is usually done by counting the number of inflections that appear on a given form and the number of different forms that occur with a different inflection. But choosing the criterion for these numbers is, of course, arbitrary and it is still possible, when dealing with naturalistic corpora, that they hide a considerable amount of rote learning—particularly if the numbers of forms and inflections in the child's corpus are rather small. On the other hand, it is important to compare the child's morphological use with that of adults. If the adult's productivity is no greater than the child's, there is clearly no development to explain.

Pizzuto and Caselli (1992) for Italian and Rubino and Pine (1998) for Portugese did this for aspects of verbal morphology and, in both cases, found that the children's productivity was lower than that of adults and based in considerable part on the rote-learning of particular verbs with particular inflections. In his Ph.D. dissertation Aguado-Orea (2005) developed these ideas by using richer corpora (from two Spanish-speaking children) and a more sophisticated methodology. He directly compared adult and child productivity by counting the number of inflections per verb controlling for the number of tokens produced and only for verbs and inflections used by both adult and child. He found that there was a significant difference between each child and his/her parents. Although at first sight this result might not seem that surprising, it is, in fact, a powerful demonstration precisely because adult and child are compared on exactly the same verbs and inflections and on the same number of tokens.

When Aguado-Orea examined the children's errors to further analyze the nature of the their productivity, he found that although the overall error rate of person-marking on the verbs for the two children was low at around 4.5 percent, there were pockets of very high error rates (for instance the marking of 3rd person plural was wrong 31 percent of the time for one child and 67 percent for the other). If the data was analyzed verb by verb, the error rate went up inversely with the relative frequency of each verb form. Thus, the overall error rate for the 58 verbs requiring 1st person singular was 4.9 percent. However *quiero* and *puedo* accounted for around 60 percent of the child's usage. Once these two correctly marked verbs were taken out, the error rate climbed to 10.4 percent. Thus, in these early stages, the children were incorrectly using forms they had learned as wholes when they did not know the correct form.

How does a morphological system build up? Dąbrowska (2004b) provides the basis for an account of this for Polish case-marking. Genitive and dative case-marking in Polish is variably regular and predictable depending largely on the gender of the noun and, for parts of the masculine paradigm, there is no obvious default. She suggests that children initially learn forms with their inflections by rote—they provide the inflection but do not know what it is (i.e. it is not related to other linguistic representations like the 's in *What's that?* cited earlier and the correctly marked verbs in Aguado-Orea's study). Low-level schemas start to build up and, once these schemas are in place, this helps with the learning of new lexical entries. Dąbrowska argues that these low-level schemas are clustered on the basis of phonology or semantics and the effects of frequency are seen only over clusters that are "psychologically real." In some cases there may be no progress from low-level schemas to higher-level schemas, if there is little phonological or other basis for generalizing across densely populated pockets of systematicity. It may also be that generalization to these higher-level schemas only occurs with explicit grammatical training at school or as a result of high levels of literacy. When children or adults are asked to generalize to novel nouns, they will do so in a variety of ways depending on the current state of their linguistic representations and the precise characteristics of the nouns with which they are presented. Importantly, Dąbrowska also shows that the extent to which adults are able to generalize to novel nouns is quite variable, with a tendency for highly educated speakers to show a higher degree of generalization, presumably due to greater literacy. A similar result was obtained by Indefrey (2003) in an experiment using the weak noun declension in German. This is a small group of about 100 masculine nouns ending in a schwa. Unlike the "strong" noun declensions, these nouns add *-n* in the accusative, dative, and genitive singular (e.g. *der Lowe*-NOM, "the lion"; *Er gibt den Lowen*-ACC *auf dem Affen*-DAT, "he gives the lion to the monkey"). Using familiar nouns belonging to the declension and novel nouns that were clearly identified as masculine and ended in a schwa, Indefrey tested groups of children aged from 4 to 16 plus two groups of adults, one without higher education and the other a group of university students. In every group he found a range of strategies from rote-learning (those who inflected the familiar nouns perfectly but did not generalize) to productivity (those who "correctly" generalized the -n to all novel nouns in accusative, dative or genitive). What differed was the proportion of subjects in each group using either the rote or the productive strategy. Almost all, but not all, of the youngest children used rote while most, but not all, of the university students were productive.

Finally, some of Dąbrowska's results suggest that different tasks may require different levels of schema strength for success. For instance, adult Polish speakers were more likely to generalize novel nouns in a forced choice task than they were in a production task. Dąbrowska suggests that there are two possible explanations. Either a high-level schema was present but too weak to support production. Alternatively only lower-level schemas were present but in the forced choice task, speakers made the generalization on-line by analogy from already existing representations.

Children's early and rapid morphological learning thus seems more partial and complex than has sometimes been claimed. Where morphology is phonologically consistent and/or semantically transparent, it can indeed be learned relatively easily and rapidly—Slobin's (1985) discussion of Turkish case-marking may be a case in point. But for many languages this is not the case, and here it seems that children are initially building up low-level schemas that capture parts of the system and that higher level schemas emerge more gradually, especially in areas of great complexity and irregularity. These higher-level schemas may only be weakly represented and, indeed, they may sometimes only exist in the formalized grammars of linguists!

3.2 The development of the transitive construction in English

There is a great deal of evidence to suggest that children under the age of about 2;10 show much better comprehension and production on a variety of tasks with verbs that they know than with novel verbs. Thus, children will correct utterances with familiar (high-frequency) verbs in non-canonical word order to canonical word order while they are much less willing to do this for low-frequency or novel verbs (Akhtar, 1999; Abbot-Smith, Lieven & Tomasello, 2001; Matthews, Lieven, Theakston & Tomasello, 2005). An explanation for this was originally formulated as the "verb island" hypothesis (Tomasello, 1992) suggesting that children are initially learning verb-specific constructions. Thus, for the English transitive verb *hit*, children might know that the "hitter" goes before the verb and the "hittee" after. But they do not know initially that this positional pattern applies to all transitive verbs and defines the relation of transitive subject and transitive direct object.

There are a number of reasons to think that a version of the hypothesis that maintains that all verbs remain as separate over a long period and up to around 3;0 is too strong (see Tomasello, 2000, for a review and Fisher, 2002; Tomasello & Abbot-Smith, 2002, for the ensuing discussion). First, in the word-order studies mentioned above, there are considerable numbers of children who show "avoidance" of using the non-canonical word order with novel verbs, indicating that, while they do not yet produce the novel verb in canonical word order, they already know that something is not right with *non*-canonical word order. Second, a study by McClure, Pine, and Lieven (2006) compared the length of children's utterances with verbs that were new in their corpora to the length of utterances that children produced at the same stage with known verbs. Children's utterances with new verbs were shorter, suggesting that they were less able to produce complex utterances with them. However, utterances with new verbs at later stages were longer than utterances with new verbs at earlier stages, suggesting that children knew more about verbs in general at later stages. McClure, Pine, and Lieven argue that children are building up low-scope constructions, for instance around pronouns, and this is providing them with constructions into which they can slot the newly learned verbs. This is supported by findings from the word-order studies outlined above: when children correct to canonical word order, they often use pronouns (*He meek it*) and/or partial sequences such as SV or VO (*Duck meek, Meek it*). If we make a parallel between the building up of the transitive construction and of the morphological constructions discussed above, we can see that children may have a number of low-level schemas that already reflect the transitive, e.g. *Mummy do it*, *I want X*. Thus, at the same time as they are learning more verbs and more about particular verbs, they are also developing constructions such as *I verb-ing it* which will lead to a partial category of progressive verbs mapping to ongoing action (Pine, Lieven, & Rowland, 1998). There is, in fact, good evidence for such a category (Clark, 1996) as well as for these sorts of constructions based around "pronoun islands" (Wilson, 2003). But as soon as a child starts to build up some patterns around subject or object pronouns, as well as NP slots around verbs, they have the beginnings of a subject category.

Another challenge to the idea that the abstract transitive builds up slowly comes from a series of recent experiments by Gertner, Fisher, and Eisengart (2006). These involved presenting children with two scenes in a preferential-looking paradigm. Each scene contains two characters, both known to the child, one acting on the other. The actions are different in the two scenes and the characters reversed. Even the youngest children (aged 21 months) looked statistically significantly longer at the scene in which the agent matched the subject of the sentence that they heard. While there are some potential issues around whether the training may have given the children clues as to word order, these experiments do lead us to ask what children may be sensitized to during the preverbal and one-word stage, for instance animacy or energy transfer in event structures. They also lead us to the issue of precisely what type of representation is required to succeed at different tasks.

In a modeling experiment addressing this issue, Chang, Dell, and Bock's (2006) model used two, interacting, learning routes. One route was based on sequencing the words, the other on binding concepts to thematic roles and their ordering. The model was presented with transitives and intransitives containing novel verbs. Results showed that the model was able to discriminate transitives (e.g. *The bunny is gorping Mary*) that match the semantics of a message from transitives that mismatch it (i.e. where the patient is the subject and the agent is the object) much earlier in training than it was able to produce a correct transitive. The research also showed why novel-verb intransitives using *with* prepositional phrases (e.g. *The bunny is gorping with Mary*) are more error-prone than the transitives. Both results are due to the interaction between the learning carried out by the two routes, which gives rise to representations that are initially based more strongly on the sequencing of words than that of the thematic-role binding. This also generates different behaviors with the intransitive task. Preferential-looking paradigms measure only this discrimination sensitivity—they do not tell us the basis on which the discrimination is being made. But if children do already have some sensitivity to word-order relations in English, independently of verbs that they know, the next tasks are (a) to characterize exactly how this sensitivity arises and how it builds into a more robust and full-fledged representation of the transitive and (b) what kinds of sensitivities are shown by children learning languages with less syntactic dependence on word order.

3.3 The development of complex sentences in English

The final example that we discuss indicates that the process of starting with constructions that are lexically-specific and of low scope and building up towards abstractness is not confined to the learning of morphology or to the early stages of syntactic development. In two studies of complex sentences (relative clauses, 2000 and sentences with finite complement clauses, 2001) Diessel and Tomasello show that children's early complex sentences are probably low-scope in nature and monopropositional despite having the formal structure of complex sentences containing two clauses. In the case of complement-taking verbs with finite clauses, Diessel and Tomasello show that the early utterances of children have a monopropositional structure with the main clause consisting of a formulaic "epistemic marker" (*I think X; Look X*), where X, the complement, contains the propositional material. Initially, there are no complementizers and little variation in the main clause. Diessel and Tomasello argue that these structures are very close to children's previous utterances with the epistemic main clause added. Only subsequently do the main clauses become more varied and substantial, complementizers are introduced and complement-taking verbs start to be produced with embedded complements. However, even then, this only occurs for a very few verbs and the authors argue that it is likely that each verb forms a constructional island, rather than being subsumed into a general schema.

In the case of relative clauses, Diessel and Tomasello (2000) also suggest that these are acquired by assimilating a new structure to structures children already have in their construction inventory. Thus, children's early relatives are likely to be attached to the predicate nominals of a copula, with the main clause very frequently being an existential copula construction of the type that children have been producing for many months (*Here's a mouse,*) and the relative clause modifying this (*Here's a mouse go sleep*). Similarly, early object-relatives very frequently have *"look"* as an imperative in the main clause (*Look at dat big truck going some place*), where the main clause construction may have been in the child's inventory for a long time. It may take many years for children to build up a network of related relative clause constructions. For instance, in a task in which they had to repeat back sentences with a variety of heads for relative clauses (Diessel & Tomasello, 2005), both English- and German-speaking children aged 4;3–4;9 tend to convert non-subject relatives to subject relatives, in the case of the English-speaking children by changing the word order while the German-speaking children changed the case-marking on the relative pronoun. There was a clear cline of difficulty as measured by errors: subject relatives were easiest, followed by object, indirect object, and genitive relatives. Clearly, children know a great deal more about some relatives than others. A starting hypothesis of the usage-based approach would be that these different relative clause constructions are being learned separately with the possibility of some more general abstraction for some speakers at later stages. However, this does not fully capture the data since, by and large, the children retain a relative clause in their repetitions. It may be that, side by side with the differential entrenchment of specific relative constructions, earlier relative constructions are providing some affordance for the learning of later, more complex constructions. The precise nature of this affordance requires investigation: it could be a cognitive abstraction, for instance, the possibility of modifying a noun with a clause, or, at a more lexical level, to do with the distributional probabilities that are built up during the processing and production of simpler relative clauses. A training study that investigated these different possibilities would be of considerable interest.

Both of the above studies also bring us back to centrality of usage to learning. *I think* was by far the most frequent matrix verb in complement clauses used in the input to children, and predicate nominals are among the most frequent early constructions used by children and by adults in talking to them and therefore provide an early basis for relativization. However, as we have pointed out, it is very important to determine the forms over which frequency should be measured. In the Diessel and Tomasello (2001) study on complementation, the critical frequency was that of the matrix verb in the construction, not of the verb across the whole corpus—a result that has been replicated in a recent experimental study on complementation (Kidd, Lieven & Tomasello, 2006).

4 Using linguistic representations

When children are faced with a task involving language, there will be a number of important factors involved in how they solve it. In a here-and-now interaction, the child may be able to successfully interpret utterances using context and limited knowledge of some words, in a way that might not be possible in a less context-bound situation or one where crucial words are not known. This is, of course, the reason that we test for linguistic abstractions using novel items, for instance verbs. But, even here, the logic of constructions existing at different levels of sche-maticity means that children may be more successful at interpreting utterances where novel verbs are embedded in constructions with pro-nouns, such as ***He's verb-ing it***, than they are if two full nouns are used. The results reported earlier for our study of children's ability to utilize word-order and case-marking cues in interpreting German transitives (Dittmar, Abbot-Smith, Lieven, & Tomasello, in press) suggest strongly that at the earlier ages children have only weak form-function mappings for word order and for case-marking and need both together for correct matching. The results at later ages also suggest that these two mappings build up at different rates for SVO word order and for case marking. Since constructions exist in a relational network, the relative level of entrenchment of constructions at different levels of schematicity and how these interact will also influence how successfully children can understand any particular utterance.

In production, children are mainly concerned with being understood and they will use whatever they have available. We have shown that, in both morphology and in syntax, the use of highly entrenched strings can give rise to the impression that the child's system is more abstract than it really is. The use of these strings makes the child's language seem relatively error-free, while detailed examination indicates that there are pockets of high error where these entrenched strings are used in place of the correct form. While children are productive from the outset of multiword speech, we would argue that much of this early productivity is of relatively low scope and depends on the use of lexically-specific constructions with highly productive slots. For instance Lieven, Behrens, Speares and Tomasello (2003) showed that 74 percent of the novel utterances in one child's corpus could be accounted for by schematic constructions with just one slot, usually for a noun-referent (see also Dąbrowksa & Lieven, 2005, who performed a similar analysis for four children's syntactic questions at 2;0 and 3;0).

Thus, the strength and nature of representations that different tasks draw on may differ. For instance, as discussed above, looking significantly longer at a picture that matches the order of agent and patient in a transitive utterance may require much weaker or more partial representations than acting out a transitive with a novel verb. Similarly, as also discussed, making a forced choice between morphological options may require a schema of weaker strength than having to produce a generalization.

5 Conclusions

Nativist linguists, committed to UG, would claim that the child starts out with highly abstract linguistic categories and both parses and generates utterances on the basis of these abstract categories. From this perspective, learning the particularities of the language, maturation of parts of the grammar and performance limitations including processing constraints would be used to account for differences in children's performance on different tasks. It is not always easy to distinguish the predictions that ought to follow from this type of theory from those of usage-based theory for which the ideas of partial productivity and initially limited scope are central. For instance, the frequency effects cited by usage-based theorists as evidence for limited productivity are accounted for in terms of processing constraints by UG theorists. Children already possess the abstract grammar but accessing items of lower frequency will be more difficult than accessing more familiar items. One explanation is in terms of learning, the other in terms of limits on production. How can we distinguish these two positions?

From a usage-based perspective, there are a number of phenomena that support the idea of abstraction building up slowly and variably for different constructions. First, children show limited productivity with pockets of high error, even when linguistic knowledge is controlled for. Second, there seems to be a clear developmental pattern in the strength of linguistic representations and in their relationship over time. If these results are to be explained by performance limitations, these need to be clearly specified and tested. Third, different speakers, even in adulthood, seem to have differing levels of schematicity in their linguistic representations, which would not be predicted if all speakers possessed a modular Universal

Grammar that unfolded over the first three to four years of life. However, that said, usage-based theories of language development have a great deal of work to do in specifying the precise interrelation between the level of schematicity in constructions, their entrenchment strength, and how these interact with the requirements of different communicative tasks.

Notes

1 We are grateful to Danielle Matthews and Caroline Rowland who provided us with very useful comments on an earlier draft of this chapter.
2 Constructions that are fully lexically specific are indicated in italics; those that are partially or fully schematic are indicated in bold and italics.

Bibliography

Abbot-Smith, K. & Behrens, H. (2006). How known constructions influence the acquisition of new constructions: the German periphrastic passive and future constructions. *Cognitive Science, 30*, 995–1026.

Abbot-Smith, K., Lieven, E., & Tomasello, M. (2001). What pre-school children do and do not do with ungrammatical word orders. *Cognitive Development, 16*, 679–692.

Abbot-Smith, K., Lieven, E., & Tomasello, M. (2004). Training two-year-olds to produce the transitive: the role of frequency, semantic similarity and shared syntactic distribution. *Developmental Science, 7*, 1, 48–55.

Aguado-Orea, J. (2005). The acquisition of morpho-syntax in Spanish: implications for current theories of development. Unpublished Ph.D. thesis, University of Nottingham.

Akhtar, N. (1999). Acquiring basic word order: evidence for data-driven learning of syntactic structure. *Journal of Child Language, 26*, 339–356.

Ambridge, B., Pine, J. M., Rowland, C. F., & Young, C. R. (in press). The effect of verb semantic class and verb frequency (entrenchment) on children's and adults' graded judgements of argument-structure overgeneralisation errors. *Cognition.*

Ambridge, B., Theakston, A., Lieven, E. V. M., & Tomasello, M. (2006). The distributed learning effect for children's acquisition of an abstract grammatical construction. *Cognitive Development, 21*, 174–193.

Bates, E. & MacWhinney, B. (1987). Competition, variation, and language learning. In B. MacWhinney (Ed.) *Mechanisms of language acquisition.* Mahwah, NJ: Lawrence Erlbaum (pp. 157–193).

Bates, E. & MacWhinney, B. (1989). Functionalism and the competition model. In B. MacWhinney & E. Bates (Eds.) *The crosslinguistic study of sentence processing.* Cambridge: Cambridge University Press (pp. 3–76).

Bates, E., MacWhinney, B., Caselli, C., Devoscovi, A., Natale, F., & Venza, V. (1984). A cross-linguistic study of children's comprehension strategies. *Child Development, 55*, 341–354.

Bod, R., Hay, J., & Jannedy, S. (Eds.) (2003) *Probabilistic linguistics.* Cambridge, MA: MIT Press.

Bowerman, M. (1988). The "no negative evidence" problem: How do children avoid constructing an over-general grammar? In J. A. Hawkins (Ed.), *Explaining language universals*. Oxford: Blackwell.

Braine, M. (1987). What is learned in acquiring word classes—a step towards an acquisition theory. In B. MacWhinney (Ed.), *Mechanisms of language acquisition*. Hillsdale, New Jersey: Lawrence Erlbaum Associates.

Brooks, P. & Tomasello, M. (1999). How children constrain their argument structure constructions. *Language, 75*, 4, 720–738.

Brooks, P., Tomasello, M., Lewis, L., & Dodson, K. (1999). Children's overgeneralization of fixed transitivity verbs: The entrenchment hypothesis. *Child Development, 70*, 1,325–1,337.

Bybee, J. (1995). Regular morphology and the lexicon. *Language and Cognitive Processes, 10*, 425–455.

Bybee, J. & Hopper, P. (Eds.) (2001). *Frequency and the emergence of linguistic structure*. Amsterdam: John Benjamins.

Bybee, J. L. & Scheibmann, J. (1999). The effect of usage on degrees of constituency: the reduction of *don't* in English. *Linguistics, 37*, 575–596.

Cameron-Faulkner, T., Lieven, E., & Tomasello, M. (2003). A construction based analysis of child directed speech. *Cognitive Science, 27*, 843–873.

Cameron-Faulkner, T., Lieven E., & Theakston, A. (2007). What part of *no* do children not understand? A usage-based account of multiword negation. *Journal of Child Language, 34*: 251–282.

Carpenter, M., Nagell, K., & Tomasello, M. (1998). Social cognition, joint attention and communicative competence from 9–15 months of age. *Monographs of the Society for Research in Child Development 255*.

Chang, F., Dell, G. S., & Bock, J. K. (2006). Becoming syntactic. *Psychological Review, 113* (2), 234–272.

Chater, N., & Manning, C. (2006). Probabilistic models of language processing and acquisition. *Trends in Cognitive Science, 10* (7), 335–344.

Childers, J. B. & Tomasello, M. (2001). The role of pronouns in young children's acquisition of the English transitive construction. *Developmental Psychology, 37*, 739–748.

Clark, E. (1996). Early verbs, event types and inflections. In C. E. Johnson & J. H. V. Gilbert (Eds.), *Children's Language, Vol. 9*. Mahwah: New Jersey: Lawrence Erlbaum (pp. 61–73).

Correa, L. (1995). An alternative assessment of children's comprehension of relative clauses. *Journal of Psycholinguistic Research, 24*, 183–203.

Culicover, P. (1999). *Syntactic nuts*. Oxford: Oxford University Press.

Dąbrowska, E. (2004a). *Language, mind and brain*. Washington, DC: Georgetown University Press.

Dąbrowska, E. (2004b). Rules or schemas? Evidence from Polish. *Language and Cognitive Processes, 19* (2), 225–271.

Dąbrowska, E. & Lieven, E. (2005). Towards a lexically specific grammar of children's question constructions. *Cognitive Linguistics, 16*, 3, 437–474.

de Villiers, J. (1985). Learning how to use verbs: Lexical coding and the influence of input. *Journal of Child Language, 12*, 587–596.

Diessel, H. & Tomasello, M. (2000). The development of relative constructions in early child speech. *Cognitive Linguistics, 11*, 131–152.

Diessel, H. & Tomasello, M. (2001). The acquisition of finite complement clauses in English: a usage-based approach to the development of grammatical constructions. *Cognitive Linguistics, 12*, 97–141.

Diessel, H. & Tomasello, M. (2005). A new look at the acquisition of relative clauses. *Language, 81*, 4, 882–906.

Dittmar, M., Abbot-Smith, K., Lieven, E., & Tomasello, M. (in press). Comprehension of case-marking and word-order cues by German preschoolers. *Child Development*.

Ellis, N. C. (2002). Frequency effects in language processing: a review with implications for theories of implicit and explicit language acquisition. *Studies in Second Language Acquisition, 24* (2), 143–188.

Ellis, N. C. (2006). Language acquisition as rational contingency learning. *Applied Linguistics, 27*, (1), 1–24.

Fernald, A., Pinto, J., Swingley, D., Weinberg, A., & McRoberts, G. (1998). Rapid gains in speed of verbal processing by infants in the second year. *Psychological Science, 9*, 228–231.

Fisher, C. (2002). The role of abstract syntactic knowledge in language acquisition: a reply to Tomasello (2000). *Cognition, 82*, 259–278.

Freudenthal, D., Pine, J., Aguado-Orea, J., & Gobet, F. (2007). Modelling the developmental patterning of finiteness marking in English, Dutch, German and Spanish using MOSAIC. *Cognitive Science, 31*, 311–341.

Gertner, Y., Fisher, C., & Eisengart, J. (2006). Learning words and rules: abstract knowledge of word order in early sentence comprehension. *Psychological Science, 17* (8), 684–691.

Gomez, R. L. & Gerken, L. (1999). Artificial grammar learning by 1-year-olds leads to specific and abstract knowledge. *Cognition, 70*, 109–135.

Huttenlocher, J., Vasilyeva, M., Cymerman, E., & Levine, S. (2002). Language input and child syntax. *Cognitive Psychology, 45* (3), 337–374.

Indefrey, P. (2003). Variabilität in Erwerb und Repräsentation der schwachen Substantivdeklination des Deutschen. Paper presented at the 25th annual meeting of the Deutsche Gesellschaft für Sprachwissenschaft, February 2003, München.

Jackendoff, R. (1996). *The architecture of the language faculty*. Bradford: MIT Press.

Jusczyk, P. (1997). *The discovery of spoken language*. Cambridge, MA: The MIT Press.

Kempe, V. & MacWhinney, B. (1998). The acquisition of case marking by adult learners of Russian and German. *Studies in Second Language Acquisition, 20*, 543–587.

Kidd, E., Lieven, E., & Tomasello, M. (2006). Examining the role of lexical frequency in children's acquisition and processing of sentential complements. *Cognitive Development, 21*, 93–107.

Lewis, J. D. and Elman, J. (2001). A connectionist investigation of linguistic arguments from poverty of the stimulus: learning the unlearnable. In J. D. Moore and K. Stenning (Eds.), *Proceedings of the twenty-third annual conference of the cognitive science society*. Mahwah, NJ: Erlbaum.

Li, P. & Shirai, Y. (2000). *The acquisition of lexical and grammatical aspect*. Berlin & New York: Mouton de Gruyter.

Lieven, E., Behrens, H., Speares, J., & Tomasello, M. (2003). Early syntactic creativity: A usage-based approach. *Journal of Child Language, 30*, 333–370.

Mandler, J. (2000). Perceptual and conceptual processes in infancy. *Journal of Cognition and Development*, 1, 3–36.

Maslen, R., Theakston, A., Lieven, E., & Tomasello, M. (2004). A dense corpus study of past tense and plural overregularization in English. *Journal of Speech, Language and Hearing Research*, 47, 1,319–1,333.

Matthews, D., Lieven, E., Theakston, A., & Tomasello, M. (2005). The role of frequency in the acquisition of English word order. *Cognitive Development*, 20, 121–136.

Matthews, D., Lieven, E., Theakston, A. & Tomasello, M. (2007). French children's use and correction of weird word orders: A constructivist account. *Journal of Child Language*, 34 (2): 381–409.

McClure, K., Pine, J. & Lieven, E. (2006). Investigating the abstractness of children's early knowledge of argument structure. *Journal of Child Language*, 33, 693–720.

Mintz, T. (2003). Frequent frames as a cue for grammatical categories in child directed speech. *Cognition*, 90, 91–117.

Morris, W., Cottrell, G., & Elman, J. (2000). A connectionist simulation of the empirical acquisition of grammatical relations. In S. Wermter & R. Sun (Eds.), *Hybrid neural systems*. Heidelberg: Springer-Verlag.

Naigles, L., & Hoff-Ginsberg, E. (1998). Why are some verbs learned before others? *Journal of Child Language*, 25, 95–120.

Peters, A. (1983). *The units of language acquisition*. Cambridge: Cambridge University Press.

Peters, A. (1997). Language typology, prosody and the acquisition of grammatical morphemes. In D. I. Slobin (Ed.), *The crosslinguistic study of language acquisition*, Vol. 5. Hillsdale, N.J.: Lawrence Erlbaum (pp. 135–197).

Pine, J., Lieven, E., & Rowland, C. (1998). Comparing different models of the development of the verb category. *Linguistics*, 36, 4–40.

Pizzuto, E. & Caselli, M. C. (1992). The acquisition of Italian morphology: implications for models of language development. *Journal of Child Language*, 19, 491–557.

Rowland, C. (2007). Explaining errors in children's questions. *Cognition*, 104, 106–134.

Rowland, C. & Pine, J. (2000). Subject-auxiliary inversion errors and wh-question acquisition. *Journal of Child Language*, 27, 1, 157–181.

Rubino, R. B. & Pine, J. M. (1998). Subject-verb agreement in Brazilian Portuguese: what low error rates hide. *Journal of Child Language*, 25, 35–59.

Shanks, D. R. (1995). *The psychology of associative learning*. New York: Cambridge University Press.

Slobin, D. I. (1973). Cognitive prerequisites for the development of grammar. In C. Ferguson & D. I. Slobin (Eds.), *Studies of child language development*. New York: Holt, Rinehart & Winston (pp. 175–208).

Slobin, D. I. (1985). Crosslinguistic evidence for the Language-Making Capacity. In D. I. Slobin (Ed.), *The crosslinguistic study of language acquisition*, Vol. 2. Hillsdale, New Jersey: Lawrence Erlbaum Associates. (pp. 1,157–1,256).

Theakston, A. L. (2004). The role of entrenchment in children's and adults' performance on grammaticality-judgement tasks. *Cognitive Development*, 19 (1) 15–34.

Theakston, A. L., Lieven, E. V. M., Pine, J. M., & Rowland, C. F. (2002). Going, going, gone: the acquisition of the verb "Go." *Journal of Child Language*, *29*, 783–811.

Theakston, A. L., Lieven, E. V. M., Pine, J. M., & Rowland, C. F. (2004). Semantic generality, input frequency and the acquisition of syntax. *Journal of Child Language*, *31*, 61–99.

Theakston, A. L., Lieven, E. V. M., Pine, J. M., & Rowland, C. F. (2005). The acquisition of auxiliary syntax: BE and HAVE. *Cognitive Linguistics*, *16*, 247–277.

Theakston, A. L., Lieven, E. V. M., & Tomasello, M. (2003). The role of the input in the acquisition of third singular verbs in English. *Journal of Speech, Language, and Hearing Research*, *46*, 863–877.

Tomasello, M. (1992). *First verbs: a case study of early grammatical development*. Cambridge: Cambridge University Press.

Tomasello, M. (2000). Do young children have adult syntactic competence? *Cognition 74*, 209–253.

Tomasello, M. (2003). *Constructing a language*. Cambridge, MA: Harvard University Press.

Tomasello, M. & Abbot-Smith, K. (2002). A tale of two theories: response to Fisher. *Cognition*, *83*, 207–214.

Tomasello, M., Carpenter, M., Call, J., Behne, T., & Moll, H. (2005). Understanding and sharing intentions: The origins of cultural cognition. *Brain and Behavioral Sciences*, *28*, 675–735.

Wexler, K. (1998). Very early parameter setting and the unique checking constraint: a new explanation of the optional infinitive stage. *Lingua*, *106*, 23–79.

Wilson, S. (2003). Lexically-specific constructions in the acquisition of inflection in English. *Journal of Child Language*, *30*, 75–115.

Wittek, A. & Tomasello, T. (2005). German-speaking children's productivity with syntactic constructions and case morphology: local cues act locally. *First Language*, *25*, 103–125.

9

CONSTRUCTION LEARNING AND SECOND LANGUAGE ACQUISITION

Adele E. Goldberg [1] *and Devin Casenhiser*

1 Introduction

How do speakers express their ideas in formal strings and how do listeners interpret formal strings as meaningful messages? Children need to learn the way that meaning is expressed formally in order to both produce and comprehend language; that is, they need to learn the form-function correspondences of their language: the *constructions*. Over the past two decades, a new approach to language has been developed in which constructions take center stage as the basic units of language. According to the constructionist perspective, language consists of a network of learned, interrelated form-function correspondences.

Languages differ widely, and each contains hundreds of constructions in the form of idioms and unusual patterns that clearly *must* be learned on the basis of the input together with general cognitive processes. According to the constructionist perspective, more general or abstract constructions are argued to be learned as well, as generalizations over item-specific utterances (Langacker, 1987, Olguin & Tomasello, 1993, Barlow & Kemmer, 2000, Tomasello, 2003). This perspective requires an account of exactly *how* constructions are learned. It is thus a markedly different approach from that based on the Universal Grammar Hypothesis, which assumes that basic aspects of language are unlearnable, and therefore must be prespecified, determined by our biological inheritance (Chomsky, 1965).

Much work within the constructionist tradition has emphasized the item-based nature of early learning. There have been a tremendous number of demonstrations that, with the exception of nouns which are substituted one for another from early on, children's early productions are very conservative: children tend to stick closely to the patterns they have heard (for reviews see Tomasello, 2000, 2003). Moreover, adults as well as children retain a great deal of specific information about how language is used (Barlow & Kemmer, 2000, Garnsey et al., 1997, MacDonald et al., 1994, McRae et al., 1997, Trueswell et al., 1993).

Yet the fact remains that generalization is part and parcel of learning a language: knowledge of language does not consist of a set of unrelated item-based facts but is instead a rich interconnected network, containing both specific and general knowledge. Therefore, the question of how learners form generalizations is of central interest.

The constructionist perspective adopts the position that form-function pairings (*constructions*) are learned on the basis of the input. Studies summarized in this chapter involve training child and adult subjects on a novel construction. Initial experiments strongly indicate that subjects can in fact learn to recognize the form and meaning of a novel construction with quite minimal training. When overall type and token frequencies are held constant, input that is skewed such that one type of example accounts for the preponderance of tokens results in more accurate generalization than input that is more representative. In addition, if the skewed examples are presented first, there is further facilitation in learning the generalization. On the other hand, input that is noisier inhibits generalization.

2 Generalizations over form and meaning

There has been a great deal of fruitful research investigating the role of statistical learning of generalizations in artificial languages (Gomez, 2002, Kam & Newport, 2005, Marcus et al., 1999, Saffran, 2001, 2002, Saffran & Wilson, 2003, Valian & Coulson, 1988). These studies demonstrate that learners are capable of learning particular, purely formal, regularities in the input. Clearly, however, the associations of *functions* with the formal patterns must be learned as well.

Even without knowing the meaning of a novel verb, speakers of a language have some idea what utterances might mean. Consider the examples in (1)–(3):

(1) She blicked him.
(2) She blicked him something.
(3) She blicked him silly.

A speaker could infer that (1) is likely to refer to an asymmetric action in which a female acts as the agent and a male acts as a patient, that (2) is likely to mean that she gave him something, and that (3) means that she did something to cause him to become silly. In fact, in order for children to generalize over the utterances they hear so that they can creatively produce and understand utterances they have never heard before, they need to learn the way meaning is expressed formally in their language, i.e., they need to learn the constructions of their language.[2]

Attention to the function of constructions does not necessarily make learning more difficult. In fact, attention to function or meaning can help learners avoid certain types of errors. For example, erroneous analogies would arise if learners were seeking out purely formal generalizations. For example, after hearing instances like (4) and (5), a form-only generalizer might assume that whenever a sentence like (4) is heard in which the adjective precedes the noun, a sentence with the adjective following the noun is also legitimate. However, such a generalization is clearly not warranted (witness the ill-formedness of (6) despite the well-formedness of (7)).

(4) She hammered the flat metal.
(5) She hammered the metal flat.
(6) She owned the flat metal.
(7) ??She owned the metal flat.

The erroneous analogy is eliminated once we realize that learners associate utterances with intended interpretations. That is, (7) is not generated because the meaning that would be assigned to such a pattern makes no sense (cf. 11).

(8) She hammered the flat metal. → "she acted on the flat metal with a hammer."
(9) She hammered the metal flat. → "she caused the metal to become flat by hammering it."
(10) She owned the flat metal. → "she possessed the flat metal."
(11) ??She owned the metal flat. → "??she caused the metal to become flat by owning it."

Learning to associate formal patterns with meanings is clearly necessary and central to the overall task of learning a language. Yet there is surprisingly little experimental evidence confirming that children *can* indeed *learn* to associate a novel pattern of constituents with a novel meaning. Moreover, there has been virtually no research investigating exactly *how* children learn to assign a novel meaning to a phrasal form. Such research is clearly important from a theoretical perspective as well as from a pedagogical point of view.

Previous work on the acquisition of constructions (or "linking rules") has focused almost entirely on the question of whether the linking rules that exist in a given language have been acquired at a certain age. Findings using the preferential-looking paradigm have been used to argue that children already have certain linking rules at relatively young ages, the implication being that the linking rules are innate and not learned based on the input (Fernandes et al., 2006, Fisher, 1996, Gertner & Fisher, 2005, Gleitman, 1994, Hirsh-Pasek et al., 1996, Naigles 1990, Naigles & Bavin, 2001). That is, linking rules have been claimed to be "near-universal in their essential aspects and therefore may not be learned at all" (Pinker, 1989; cf. also e.g., Baker, 1996; Gleitman, 1994; Levin & Rappaport Hovav, 1995). Other studies, on the other hand, emphasize the early conservatism of children's early language; this research suggests that abstract argument structure constructions of a language are learned late and in an item-specific fashion (e.g., Tomasello, 1992; Akhtar, 1999; Lieven et al., 1997; Tomasello, 2000, 2003).

Training studies are required in order to reconcile the issues involved in this debate, since such studies allow the input and the target construction to be manipulated. As Hauser et al. observe, "Training techniques are a powerful tool to determine if a skill can be developed with practice, experience and attention by an animal" (Hauser et al., 2002).

The few training studies involving both meaning and form that have been done typically require learners to assign familiar meanings to new forms. Thus, there is potential interference or transfer from the existing language when learners try to assign the meaning associated with an already familiar construction to a new formal pattern. When possible, learners may well attempt to assimilate the novel construction to their already known construction, given that speakers rarely, if ever, assign the same meaning to two distinct formal patterns (e.g., Bolinger, 1977, Clark, 1987, Pinker, 1989, Goldberg, 1995, Casenhiser 2004, 2005).

This idea has been used in certain "weird word order" studies (Abbot-Smith et al., 2001, Akhtar, 1999). Children were taught semantically transitive meanings for a few novel verbs. The novel verbs were presented in non-English word orders. The question of interest in these studies was the extent to which children used the new verbs with the word order that they had been taught as opposed to correcting the word order so that the familiar transitive construction was produced. Results demonstrate that, increasingly with age, children produce the familiar English word order instead of the unfamiliar word order used in training. That is, proficiency is demonstrated in this experiment by subjects' production of the already familiar English construction; there is no reason to learn the novel word order as a novel construction once there exists a known construction with the same meaning. These experiments do not attempt to teach subjects a new abstract construction but, rather, they aim to determine how abstract the child's transitive construction already is.

Similarly, Kaschak and Glenberg (2004) have investigated adults' on-line processing of the construction exemplified by *This shirt needs washed*, a construction that was novel to their experimental subjects. They found that speakers were able to read instances of this construction with greater fluency after hearing or reading other instances of the construction. Facilitation was found as well when testing the same pattern with *wants* after training on *needs*, demonstrating that the facilitation transferred to a related verb. The increased fluency, as measured by shorter reading times, was interpreted to indicate that speakers learned to comprehend the construction; however, the target construction contains familiar words semantically identical and formally similar to the familiar construction exemplified by *This shirt needs washing* (Doyle, 2004). There was in fact evidence that subjects were able to comprehend the novel construction from the outset insofar as they demonstrated increased reading times for semantically inconsistent follow-up sentences even in the initial testing trials.

Childers and Tomasello (2001) is another training study that aimed to encourage children at age 2.5 to use the English transitive construction with novel verbs. The researchers demonstrated that training children on the transitive construction with pronominal arguments (*He blicked it*) facilitated the children's use of new novel verbs in the transitive frame at test, when compared with children who learned the novel verbs in sentences containing lexical NP arguments (e.g., *The man blicked the ball*). The target construction again was a construction that children presumably had some familiarity with initially. Abbott-Smith and colleagues (2004) attempted to look for other factors that encourage productive use of the transitive construction, but found null effects of semantic homogeneity and shared syntactic distribution.

Thus, a few training studies exist, and some have required children to learn a novel word order and/or a novel morpheme. However, virtually no previous studies have trained children to map a novel abstract form onto a novel meaning: exactly the task that the child faces when naturalistically learning language. Previous work has used, for example, simple transitivity (e.g., Childers & Tomasello, 2001, Akhtar, 1999, Abbot-Smith et al., 2001), identifiability (in the case of a determiner study by Hudson & Newport, 1999) or no meaning at all (in the case of work on artificial grammar learning). In addition, surprisingly little data has been found that has identified particular facilitory or inhibitory factors in learning constructions, beyond varying overall exposure (Vasilyeva et al., 2006).

Our lab has developed a new experimental paradigm, and we have begun to investigate these gaps in our understanding. Initial experiments strongly indicate that children can in fact learn to recognize a novel construction with quite minimal training. We have also begun to investigate the issue of *how* constructions are learned. It turns out that when overall type and token frequencies are held constant, input that is skewed such that one type of example accounts for the preponderance of tokens results in more accurate generalizations than input that is more representative. In addition, if the skewed examples are presented first, there is further facilitation in learning the generalization.

3 Subjects demonstrate familiarity with a novel construction after minimal exposure

We created a novel construction, and in a series of experiments, exposed children to 16 instances of it: their total exposure to the novel construction was less than three minutes in duration. The meaning assigned to the novel formal pattern was that of APPEARANCE: an entity appears in a location (a meaning novel for English phrasal patterns). Subjects watched a set of short video clips in which they saw objects appear in or on various locations. Each video clip was accompanied by an audio description whose syntactic form was composed as follows:

(12) noun phrase$_{(theme)}$ noun phrase$_{(location)}$ nonsense verb

The audio description was given in the simple present tense at the start of the scene and was repeated in the past tense at the end of the scene. Given a scene where a spot appears on the king's nose, subjects heard, *The spot the king moopos . . . The spot the king moopoed*. The entity named by the first noun phrase appeared in the place named by the second noun phrase. That is, the novel construction involved a non-English word order, Subject Object Verb, together with an abstract meaning that is novel for English constructions: something appears in a location.

In one study, six-year-olds were randomly and equally divided into three conditions: two TRAINING conditions and a CONTROL condition (Casenhiser & Goldberg, 2005). In both training conditions, subjects heard a total five different novel verbs in eight instances of the construction. Each scene was repeated exactly twice in each condition. (The difference between the two training conditions involves the distribution of different novel verb types and is discussed below). Subjects in the control condition saw the same film but heard no language. Any difference between groups can only be attributed to a difference in the linguistic input, as both conditions watched exactly the same video.

Following training, we had the children perform a forced-choice comprehension task; they were asked to match an audio description to one of two video clips displayed simultaneously on a computer screen. One scene showed an object appearing in or on a particular location and the other showed the same object interacting with or acting on that location. For example, given the audio description *the sailor the pond naifoed*, one scene showed a sailor sailing his boat onto a pond (i.e., he begins off camera and sails into the scene) while the second scene showed the sailor sailing his boat around the pond (having been on camera the entire time).

The audio description used the novel appearance construction, so the correct answer would be the first scene. The task is reminiscent of the preferential-looking paradigm, the main difference being that our subjects provided an unambiguous behavioral response, pointing to the matching scene instead of simply looking longer at one scene than another.

Results supported the hypothesis that children are able to learn something about the novel construction, even after minimal exposure. Children in the training conditions outperformed those in the control; moreover, the training conditions demonstrated above-chance performance, while the control condition was no different than chance. Since instances at test involved *new* novel verbs and *new* novel scenes, children had to generalize beyond their input in order to match the novel utterance to the novel scene.

In other work using the same basic paradigm, we have found that four-year-old children can learn to generalize beyond their exposure to identify new instances of a novel construction, and, as we will see in section 4.1, so can adults (Goldberg et al., 2004, Goldberg et al., to appear).

The finding that a novel mapping between a phrasal form and meaning can be generalized so quickly, with so little input, appears to run counter to the large body of evidence that indicates that children are very conservative learners (for reviews see Tomasello, 2000, 2003). It is possible that the ability to learn constructions quickly is a developmental achievement; to date, all of our subjects have been older than the children used to establish early conservatism. However, the reason for conservative learning has been claimed to be that children—and adults—operate with a usage-based model of language (Tomasello, 2003). Usage-based accounts emphasize that generalizations are made over learned instances. Thus, the difference between children and adults has been thought to involve a difference in the amount of experience with the ambient language. Therefore, we would not expect to find quicker generalizations in older children than younger children, nor in adults than in children, if all are exposed to the same amount of input. In fact, in work to date in this paradigm, younger learners and older learners have shown equivalent ability to generalize.

Therefore, it is plausible to conclude that the reason for well-documented conservative learning in earlier studies and the quick generalization evident when our paradigm is used is task-dependent. Studies that have documented conservative learning have used a variety of methods including (1) spontaneous production, (2) elicited production, and (3) act-out tasks. These tasks require *recall* of at least aspects of the pairing of form and meaning. Clearly this is true in the case of production, since in order to produce an utterance, the child must be able to recall its form correctly and use it appropriately. In act-out tasks, children are encouraged to act out scenes that they hear verbal descriptions of; this also requires the child to recall the relevant meaning associated with the given form. The task outlined here, on the other hand, only requires that children *recognize* the relevant meaning from among two given alternatives. This is more akin to the preferential-looking paradigm that has been argued in fact to demonstrate early generalizations (Gleitman, 1994, Naigles & Bavin, 2001, Gertner & Fisher, 2005).

Our results suggest that tentative generalizations are formed quickly. These findings are evidence of a type of "fast mapping," in construction-learning, akin to that previously found for words (Carey & Bartlett 1978). In both cases, the meaning of the novel item (word or construction) was recognized within a contrastive context (in the former, children were asked to choose the "*chromium* tray, not the red one, the chromium one"). In neither case is it clear that children were able to associate an unambiguous meaning with the novel item. In our experiments, children had only to distinguish a relational meaning for the novel phrasal pattern that was distinct from that already associated with other familiar constructions (intransitive or transitive), just as children had only to identify *chromium* as distinct from familiar color categories. Clearly, just as in the case of fast mapping of words, a thorough mastery has not been demonstrated. Indeed, it is likely that more than three minutes of training are required in order for children to fully command the new construction. That is, tentative generalizations would facilitate comprehension; it is quite possible that stronger generalizations are required for production (see also Abbot-Smith & Tomasello, 2006).

4 What is learned?

4.1 Learners are able to distinguish the novel construction from novel instances of the transitive construction at test

In the test phase of experiments on four-year-olds, six-year-olds and adults, subjects heard *either* a new instance of the novel construction *or* an instance of the already familiar transitive construction. Both instances of the novel construction and the transitive construction involved new novel verbs, so each utterance was unfamiliar to the learner. Each test item included both a scene of appearance and a semantically transitive scene. Subjects' task was to choose the scene that matched the description they heard; if they heard the novel construction, the accurate choice was the scene of appearance; if they heard a transitive construction, the accurate choice was the semantically transitive scene. Subjects at all ages demonstrated that they were able to distinguish new instances of the novel construction, involving new novel verbs and new scenes of appearance, from new instances of the transitive construction, also involving new novel verbs (Casenhiser & Goldberg, 2005, Goldberg et al., 2007).

That is, performance on both the novel construction and on the transitive construction was above chance in the training conditions.[3] In order to distinguish the novel construction from the transitive construction in training conditions, learners had to recognize something about both the form and meaning of the novel construction.

4.2 The learning is not simply an effect of priming "appearance"

In our early work, we used a control condition in which subjects watched the same training film without sound. However, it is conceivable that simply hearing language may serve to focus attention on the relevant entities in the scenes during training, and that this increased attention may lead to better performance at test without subjects actually noticing the form of the construction. This is highly unlikely, given the fact that subjects only demonstrated a tendency to choose scenes of appearance when they heard new instances of the novel construction at test, and not when they heard new instances of the transitive construction at test; nevertheless it is a possibility that cannot be dismissed out of hand.

For this reason, in a more recent experiment with adult subjects, we included two new control conditions in addition to using the no-sound control. In one condition, subjects heard just the two NPs (the theme and the location) in randomized order during the training. In the second new control condition subjects heard instances of the familiar intransitive motion construction used with nonsense verbs (e.g., *The sun vaks in the sky*) during training (Goldberg et al., 2007). The first control condition is useful to determine whether hearing any language serves to focus attention sufficiently on scenes of appearance; the second control condition encourages subjects to notice that scenes of appearance are involved insofar as the intransitive motion construction can readily be used to describe just such scenes (e.g., *The sun appears in the sky*).

In all control conditions, the test items (including transitives) remained the same as in the experiments described above. If subjects in the non-control training conditions are truly learning the form of the novel construction on the basis of exposure to the construction during training, neither exposure to two noun phrases nor exposure to novel instances of a familiar construction should facilitate the identification of the novel construction at test. This is in fact what was found: subjects in none of the control conditions performed significantly differently from chance, nor did either of the control conditions that received linguistic input perform significantly differently than the no-sound control condition.

These control conditions need to be run on children as well as adults. However, performance is unlikely to be enhanced in children, since any benefit that may have been expected to accrue from including the (irrelevant) language during training would presumably stem from a general increase in attention to the training stimuli, and/or to an increased aware-ness that all of the scenes during training were appearance scenes. The null hypothesis is that adults would be at least as likely as children to attend to the films and to notice the semantic similarity among the exem-plars. Moreover, we have found that adults' performance in our novel construction-learning experiments is qualitatively the same as children's. Thus, we conclude that subjects are actually learning the construction in the training conditions, and are not simply being primed to choose scenes of appearance at test.

4.3 Morphology is not necessary for learning

In several studies, the novel construction used in training and at test had a stable bit of morphology, as constructions often do cross-linguistically. In these studies, an -o morpheme was suffixed on all novel verbs during training and on all of the novel verbs used in the novel construction at test. This raises the possibility that children attended only to the -o mor-pheme and not to the order of the words in the construction. This possi-bility has been addressed in another study, in which we eliminated the -o morpheme from the novel verbs in training and at test in an experiment with six-year-olds. Subjects still demonstrated recognition of the novel construction (Casenhiser & Goldberg, 2005, experiment #2). Since in this experiment no morphological cue was present, subjects had to learn to distinguish the novel construction from the transitive construction based on word order alone. The novel verbs could not have been respon-sible since they were different in training and at test. From this body of work, we can conclude that children and adults are able to learn to recog-nize a novel construction after only minimal exposure.

5 Skewed input facilitates learning

What causes children to categorize the distinct utterances they hear into a constructional generalization? That is, what makes subjects create a cat-egory instead of treating each utterance as a distinct unrelated idiom? Research on general, non-linguistic categorization processes has empha-sized the fact that learners do not generalize randomly or completely. One factor that has been shown to encourage the learning of abstract categor-ies is shared concrete similarity. In particular, when instances share con-crete attributes, learners are more likely to categorize them together, and moreover are more likely to attend to their more abstract common-alities (Gentner et al., 2002 Ms., Gentner & Medina, 1998, Markman & Gentner, 1993).

To test the idea that shared concrete similarity might encourage the learning of an abstract construction, we distinguished two training conditions. In both conditions, overall type and token frequency of the novel verbs used was held constant. In the BALANCED FREQUENCY TRAINING condition, subjects heard five different novel verbs, each with a relatively low token frequency of 1 or 2 (1–1–2–2–2). The SKEWED FREQUENCY condition was designed to test the hypothesis that children's learning of a novel construction would be aided if a single verb appeared in a disproportionately large number of instances of the novel construction. Therefore, in this skewed frequency condition, subjects again hear the same five novel verbs, but this time one novel verb had an especially high token frequency of four, while the other novel verbs were recorded once each (4–1–1–1–1). Each scene was repeated exactly twice in each condition, so that a total of 16 clips were witnessed. Any difference among groups can only be attributed to a difference in the linguistic input that subjects were exposed to, as all three conditions watched exactly the same video.

Results supported the hypothesis. Children in the skewed frequency condition performed better than children in the balanced condition. Children in the BALANCED FREQUENCY training group outperformed those in the CONTROL group as well, suggesting that skewed frequency *facilitates*, but is not *necessary* for learning a novel construction. Both the scores of the balanced and the skewed frequency groups were significantly greater than would be expected from chance performance, while the scores of the control group did not differ significantly from chance. These same findings have been demonstrated both with six-year-old children (Casenhiser & Goldberg, 2005, experiment #1) and with adults (Goldberg et al., 2004). The finding that learning is possible even without skewed input is important since recent work indicates that there may not always be a single token with exceptionally high frequency (Sethuraman & Goodman, 2004).

The reason we chose to vary token frequencies of particular novel verbs in this way is that the actual input children receive tends to be skewed in just this way. That is, the language input children receive tends to be skewed disproportionately towards a single example or type of example. In this way, tokens of individual constructions are typically centered around a small number of words (often a single word), or around a semantic prototype, even when they potentially occur with a much broader range of words or meanings (Brenier & M.is, 2004, Cameron-Faulkner, Lieven, & Tomasello, 2003, Diessel, 2002, Goldberg, 1995, 1996, 1999, 2006, Hunston & Francis, 1999, Scheibman, 2002, Thompson & Hopper, 2001, Gries et al., 2005). For example, Goldberg et al. (2004) investigated speech from mothers to young children in the Bates corpus from CHILDES (Bates, Bretherton, & Snyder, 1988, in MacWhinney, 1995). We reported that a particular construction is typically dominated by the use of that construction with one particular verb. For example, *go*

Table 9.1 Corpus study (Goldberg et al., 2004): 15 mothers' most frequent verb and number of verbs types for three constructions in Bates et al. (1988) corpus

Construction	Mothers	Total Number of Verb Types
1. Subj V Obj	39% go (136/353)	39 verbs
2. Subj V Obj Obl	38% put (99/259)	43 verbs
3. Subj V Obj Obj2	20% give (11/54)	13 verbs

accounts for a full 39 percent of the uses of the "intransitive motion" construction ((Subj) V Obl$_{path/loc}$) in the speech of mothers addressing 28-month-olds in the Bates corpus. This high percentage is remarkable since this construction is used with a total of 39 different verbs in the mother's speech in the corpus; the figures for three constructions are given above in Table 9.1.

Clear motivation exists for speakers to use certain verbs more frequently than others. If we compare for example, go with amble, or put with shelve, it is clear that go and put are more frequent because they apply to a wider range of arguments and therefore are relevant in a wider range of contexts (Bybee et al., 1992, Heine, 1993, Zipf, 1935).

It is not claimed that any particular verbs are necessarily the very first verbs uttered. Longitudinal studies have suggested that they might be (Ninio, 1999); but see Campbell and Tomasello (2001) for evidence that they are not always the very first verbs.

6 Other factors that encourage or inhibit formation of a constructional category

6.1 Noisy input inhibits learning

Given that adults and children appear to generalize the novel construction beyond their very limited training, it seemed relevant to test whether more noisy input would also yield evidence of learning. In an unpublished study, we investigated whether six-year-old children who witnessed novel instances of a familiar construction (the transitive construction) interspersed among instances of the novel construction during training would still demonstrate evidence of having learned the novel construction at test. In order to do so, learners would have to systematically distinguish instances of the novel construction during training, categorizing these instances together as a distinct abstract construction. As in previous studies, subjects were exposed to 16 instances of the novel construction, involving five novel verbs. They additionally witnessed 16 semantically transitive clips with corresponding novel transitive utterances (involving five novel verbs). Thirty children (mean age 6;1) were tested in the training (20 children) or the no-sound control (10 children) conditions. Despite the fact that the children in both groups performed significantly above chance at assigning semantically transitive meaning to the transitive construction at test, neither of the groups was above chance at recognizing the *novel* construction at test. That is, there was no difference between children who received the noisy input and the no-sound control group (M=3.0[=chance performance] in the training condition and M=3.1 in the no-sound control on the novel construction; M=4.5 in the training condition and M=4.3 in the no-sound control on the familiar transitive construction).

We had consistently found above-chance performance on the novel construction after training when the training included 16 instances of the novel construction and no other "distracter" construction. It thus appears that including instances of other constructions during training, even instances of a familiar construction, inhibits learning of the novel pattern. At the same time, it is likely or at least possible that additional training would have led to better than chance performance. In naturalistic circumstances, learners do of course hear multiple constructions interwoven in discourse. Future work is required to determine the ways in which learners manage to untangle such "messy" input.

6.2 Skewed input first further facilitates learning

As noted above, research in general categorization processes has revealed that categories are more likely to be formed when new instances remind learners of old instances in that the new instances share concrete similarities with old instances.

Ellis and Anderson (1984) have demonstrated a related effect in nonlinguistic category learning: the order of presentation plays a role in subjects' accuracy at test. In their CENTERED condition, subjects were initially trained on more frequently represented members of a category with the study sample growing gradually to include more members of the category. (The study involved descriptions of people belonging to one of two clubs, with members' descriptions varying on five 4-valued dimensions.) In the REPRESENTATIVE condition, subjects were trained on a fully representative sampling from the start. In both conditions, subjects were eventually trained on the full range of instances. Categories were learned more accurately in the centered condition, yielding better typicality ratings and accuracy judgments during the test phase on new instances. Elio and Anderson observe, "The superiority of the centered condition over the representative condition suggests that an initial, low-variance sample of the most frequently occurring members may allow the learner to get a 'fix' on what will account for most of the category members."

We have completed an experiment in which 54 undergraduates were randomly placed in one of three conditions: subjects in the skewed-frequency first (SFF) condition witnessed all eight examples of the novel construction with a single novel verb before the other eight instances involving four other novel verbs; the skewed-frequency random (SFR) condition witnessed the same 16 instances involving five novel verbs in a random order. As predicted, the SFF condition significantly outperformed the SFR condition, indicating that presenting the skewed exemplars first facilitates generalization (Goldberg et al., 2007).[4]

7 Conclusion

Initial findings confirm that adults and children can learn to recognize a novel construction after only three minutes of training; moreover, learners can successfully distinguish a novel construction from the familiar transitive construction at test and they do not require stable morphology to do so. We have also found that both adults' and children's learning is facilitated by input that is skewed such that one type of example accounts for the preponderance of the input (holding overall type and token frequencies constant) (Goldberg et al., 2004, Casenhiser & Goldberg, 2005). Since actual natural input learners receive strongly tends to be skewed in just the relevant way, the input is, to this extent, tailor-made to support generalizations.

At the same time, the learning of the constructional category appears to be further enhanced by training in which exemplars that are similar to one another—in sharing the same novel verb—are presented first, a situation which is not found in naturalistic input. In addition, the learning of the category is inhibited when the minimal training includes non-members of the category: again, a deleterious effect that clearly is relevant to naturalistic input.

The studies discussed in this chapter have clear, but as yet untested, implications for second language learning and pedagogy. Collectively, they suggest that it is advantageous to supply targeted input that includes ample prototypical instances early in training. But, of course, there are other factors that play a role in a classroom setting. It is possible that focused training exclusively on a narrow subtype of a pattern could lead to excessive boredom. Only classroom testing can determine how laboratory findings such as those summarized here are best adapted in order to maximize learning.

A defender of the Universal Grammar Hypothesis might respond that, although these experiments suggest that argument structure constructions can be learned, they do not demonstrate that they actually are learned. It has been suggested that basic patterns of argument structure are universal, and true universals require an explanation. It turns out, however, that legitimate universals of argument structure realization are quite modest and are naturally accounted for by domain-general attentional and pragmatic (Gricean) principles (see Goldberg, 2006, chapters 7–9, for discussion).

The studies presented here offer confirming evidence of the usage-based perspective on language learning that argues that variations in the tokens presented as input lead to different outcomes. In addition, this constructionist approach offers a perspective that can in principle address pedagogical as well as theoretical issues, insofar as the perspective emphasizes manipulable aspects of the input.

Notes

1 We would like to acknowledge support for this work provided to the first author by NSF, grant BCS-0613227.
2 In the case of argument structure patterns, the correspondences have been variously described as *linking rules* projected from the main verb's specifications (e.g., Bresnan & Kanerva, 1989, Dowty, 1991, Grimshaw, 1990, Jackendoff, 1983, Pinker 1989) or as *lexical templates* overlain on specific verbs (Rappaport Hovav & Levin, 1998). Constructional terminology is used below, but the research can naturally be construed as an investigation into how children learn linking rules or learn the semantics associated with various lexical templates.
3 As expected, performance on the transitive construction (only) was above chance in the control condition, since subjects already knew the transitive construction and were not exposed to the novel construction.
4 We are currently investigating whether the critical factor is actually that the skewed examples be presented first or whether presentation of these exemplars in a "clump" during the middle or at the end of the training is equally facilitory.

Bibliography

Abbot-Smith, K., Lieven, E., & Tomasello, M. (2001). What children do and do not do with ungrammatical word orders. *Cognitive Development 16*, 1–14.

Abbot-Smith, K., Lieven, E., & Tomasello, M. (2004). Training 2–6-year-olds to produce the transitive construction: the role of frequency, semantic similarity and shared syntactic distribution. *Developmental Science 7*, 48–55.

Abbot-Smith, K., & Tomasello, M. (2006). Exemplar-learning and schematization in a usage-based account of syntactic acquisition. *The Linguistic Review 23*(3): 275–290.

Akhtar, N. (1999). Acquiring word order: Evidence for data-driven learning of syntactic structure. *Journal of Child Language 26*, 339–356.

Baker, M. (1996). On the structural positions of themes and goals. In J. Rooryck and L. Zaring, (Eds.), *Phrase structure and the lexicon*, pp. 7–34. Dordrecht: Kluwer.

Barlow, M, & Kemmer, S. (2000). *Usage-based models of grammar*. Stanford: CSLI Publications.

Bates, E., Bretherton, I., & Snyder, L. (1988). *From first words to grammar: individual differences and dissociable mechanisms.* New York: Cambridge University Press.

Bolinger, D. (1977). *Meaning and form.* London: Longman.

Brenier, J., & M.is, L. A. (2004). Prosodic optimization by copula doubling in conversational English. Paper presented at *Linguistic Society of America,* Boston.

Bresnan, J., & Kanerva, J. (1989). Locative inversion in chichewa. A case study in the factorization of grammar. *Linguistic Inquiry 20,* 1–50.

Bybee, J., Perkins, R., & Pagliuca, W. (1992). *The evolution of grammar: tense, aspect, and modality in the languages of the world.* Chicago: University of Chicago Press.

Cameron-Faulkner, T., Lieven, E., & Tomasello, M. (2003). A construction-based analysis of child directed speech. *Cognitive Science 27,* 843–873.

Campbell, A., & Tomasello, M. (2001). The acquisition of English dative constructions. *Applied Psycholinguistics 22,* 253–267.

Carey, S., & Bartlett, E. (1978). *Acquiring a single new word.* Unpublished manuscript, Stanford: CA.

Casenhiser, D. (2004). Soft constraints on learning form-meaning mappings, University of Illinois, Ph.D. in linguistics.

Casenhiser, D. (2005) Children's resistance to homonymy: an experimental study of pseudohomonyms. *Journal of Child Language 32*(2), 319–343.

Casenhiser, D., & Goldberg, A. E. (2005). Fast mapping of a phrasal form and meaning. *Developmental Science 8*(6): 500–508.

Childers, J. B, & Tomasello, M. (2001). The role of pronouns in young children's acquisition of the English transitive construction. *Developmental Psychology 37,* 739–748.

Chomsky, N. (1965). *Aspects of the theory of syntax.* Cambridge, MA: MIT Press.

Clark, E. (1987). The principle of contrast: a constraint on language acquisition. In B. MacWhinney (Ed.), *Mechanisms of language acquisition,* pp. 1–34. Hillsdale, NJ: Lawrence Erlbaum Associates.

Diessel, H. (2002). The development of complex sentence constructions in English. A usage-based approach, University of Leipzig: Habilitation thesis.

Dowty, D. (1991). Thematic proto-roles and argument selection. *Language 67,* 547–619.

Doyle, G.. (2004). The "Needs Washed" Construction. Ms. Princeton University.

Ellis, R., & Anderson, J. R. (1984). The effects of information order and learning mode on schema abstraction. *Memory and Cognition 12*(1), 20–30.

Fernandes, K. J., Marcus, G. F., Nubila, J. A. Di, and Vouloumanos, A. (2006). From semantics to syntax and back again: argument structure in the third year of life. *Cognition,* 1–11.

Fisher, C. (1996). Structural limits on verb mapping: the role of analogy in children's interpretations of sentences. *Cognitive Psychology 31,* 41–81.

Garnsey, S. M., Pearlmutter, N. J., Myers, E., & Lotocky, M. (1997). The contributions of verb bias and plausibility to the comprehension of temporarily ambiguous sentences. *Journal of Memory and Language 37,* 58–93.

Gentner, D., & Medina, J. (1998). Similarity and the development of rules. *Cognition 65,* 263–297.

Gentner, D., Loewenstein, J., & Hung, B. T. (2002). Comparison facilitates learning part names. Ms.

Gertner, Y., & Fisher, C. (2005). How does word order guide sentence comprehension? Ed. Proceedings of the Boston Child Language Conference.

Gleitman, L. (1994). The structural sources of verb meanings. In P. Bloom (Ed.), *Language Acquisition: core readings*. Cambridge, MA: MIT Press.

Goldberg, A. E. (1995). *Constructions: a construction grammar approach to argument structure*. Chicago: Chicago University Press.

Goldberg, A. (1996). Optimizing constraints and the Persian complex predicate. *Berkeley Linguistics Society 22*, 132–146.

Goldberg, A. (1999). The emergence of the semantics of argument structure constructions. In B. MacWhinney (Ed.), *The emergence of language*, pp. 197–212. Hillsdale, NJ: Lawrence Erlbaum.

Goldberg, A. E. (2006). *Constructions at Work: the nature of generalization in language*. Oxford University Press.

Goldberg, A. E., Casenhiser, D., & Sethuraman, N. (2004). Learning argument structure generalizations. *Cognitive Linguistics 14*, 289–316.

Goldberg, A. E., Casenhiser, D., & White, T. (2007). Constructions as categories of language: the role of order on construction learning. *New Ideas in Psychology*.

Gomez, R. (2002). Variability and detection of invariant structure. *Psychological Science 13*, 431–436.

Gries, S. Th., Hampe, B., & Schonefeld, D. (2005). Converging evidence: bringing together experimental and corpus data on the association of verbs and constructions. *Cognitive Linguistics 16*, 4, 635–676.

Grimshaw, J. (1990). *Argument Structure*. Cambridge, MA: MIT Press.

Hauser, M. D., Chomsky, N., & F. W. Tecumseh. (2002). The Faculty of Language: What is it, who has it, and how did it evolve? *Science 298*, 1,569–1,579.

Heine, B. (1993). *Auxiliaries: cognitive forces and grammaticalization*. New York: Oxford University Press.

Hirsh-Pasek, K., Golinkoff, R. M, & Naigles, L. (1996). Young children's use of syntactic frames to derive meaning. In K. Hirsh-Pasek and R. M. Golinkoff (Eds.), *The Origins of grammar: evidence from early language comprehension*. Cambridge, MA: MIT Press.

Hudson, C. L., & Newport, E. (1999). Creolization: Could adults really have done it all? Paper presented at Proceedings of the 23rd Annual Boston University Conference on Language Development, Boston.

Hunston, S., and Francis, G. (1999). *Pattern Grammar, a corpus-driven approach to the lexical grammar of English*: Studies in Corpus Linguistics. Amsterdam: John Benjamins.

Jackendoff, R. (1983). *Semantics and cognition*. Cambridge, MA: MIT Press.

Kam, C., Hudson, L. & Newport, E. L. (2005). Regularizing unpredictable variation: the roles of adult and child learners in language formation and change. *Language Learning and Development 1*, 151–195.

Kaschak, M. P., & Glenberg, A. M. (2004). This construction needs learned. *Journal of Experimental Psychology: General 133*, 450–467.

Langacker, R. (1987). *Foundations of cognitive grammar* (Vol. I). Stanford: CA: Stanford University Press.

Levin, B., & Rappaport Hovav, M. R. (1995). *Unaccusativity*. Boston: MIT Press.

Lieven, E. V. M., Pine, J. M., & Baldwin, G. (1997). Lexically-based learning and early grammatical development. *Journal of Child Language 24*, 187–219.

MacDonald, M. C., Pearlmutter, N. J., & Seidenberg, M. S. (1994). Lexical nature of syntactic ambiguity resolution. *Psychological Review 101*, 676–703.

MacWhinney, B. (1995). *The CHILDES Project: Tools for analyzing talk*. Hillsdale, NJ.: Lawrence Erlbaum Associates.

Marcus, G. F., Vijayan, S., Bandi Rao, S., & Vishton, P. M. (1999). Rule learning by seven-month-old infants. *Science 283*, 77–80.

Markman, A. B., & Gentner, D. (1993). Structural alignment during similarity comparisons. *Cognitive Psychology 25*, 431–467.

McRae, K., Ferretti, T. R., & Amyote, L. (1997). Thematic roles as verb-specific concepts. *Language and Cognitive Processes 12*, 137–176.

Naigles, L. (1990). Children use syntax to learn verb meanings. *Journal of Child Language 7*, 357–374.

Naigles, L. R., & Bavin, E. L. (2001). Generalizing novel verbs to different structures: evidence for the early distinction of verbs and frames. Paper presented at BU Conference of Language Acquisition, Boston.

Ninio, A. (1999). Pathbreaking verbs in syntactic development and the question of prototypical transitivity. *Journal of Child Language 26*, 619–653.

Olguin, R., & Tomasello, M. (1993). Twenty-five-month-old children do not have a grammatical category of verb. *Cognitive Development 8*, 245–272.

Pinker, S. (1989). *Learnability and cognition: the acquisition of argument structure*. Cambridge, MA: MIT Press.

Rappaport Hovav, M., & Levin, B. (1998). Building verb meanings. In M. Butt & W. Geuder (Eds.), *The projection of arguments: lexical and compositional factors*. Stanford: CSLI Publications.

Saffran, J. R. (2001). The use of predictive dependencies in language learning. *Journal of Memory and Language 44*, 493–515.

Saffran, J. R., and Wilson, D. P. (2003). From syllabus to syntax, multilevel statistical learning by 12-month-old infants. *Infancy 4*, 273–284.

Scheibman, J. (2002). *Point of view and grammar: structural patterns of subjectivity in American English conversation*. Amsterdam: John Benjamins.

Sethuraman, N., & Goodman, J. (2004). Paper presented at Stanford Child Language Research Forum, Stanford.

Thompson, S. A., & Hopper, P. J. (2001). Transitivity, clause structure and argument structure: evidence from conversation. In J. Bybee and P. J. Hopper (Eds.), *Frequency and the Emergence of Linguistic Structure*, pp. 27–60. Amsterdam: John Benjamins.

Tomasello, M. (1992). *First verbs: a case study of early grammatical development*. Cambridge: Cambridge University Press.

Tomasello, M. (2000). Do young children have adult syntactic competence? *Cognition 74*, 209–253.

Tomasello, M. (2003). *Constructing a language: a usage-based theory of language acquisition*. Cambridge, MA: Harvard University Press.

Trueswell, J. C., Tanenhaus, M. K., & Kello, C. (1993). Verb-specific constraints in sentence processing: separating effects of lexical preference from garden-paths. *Journal of Experimental Psychology: Learning, Memory and Cognition 19*, 528–553.

Valian, V., & Coulson, S. (1988). Anchor points in language learning: the role of marker frequency. *Journal of Memory and Language 27*, 71–86.

Vasilyeva, M., Huttenlocher, J., & Waterfall, H. (2006). Effects of language intervention on syntactic skill levels in preschoolers. *Developmental Psychology 42*, 164–174.

Zipf, G. K. (1935). *The psycho-biology of language*. Boston: Houghton Mifflin.

10

USAGE-BASED GRAMMAR AND SECOND LANGUAGE ACQUISITION

Joan Bybee

1 Introduction and background

The structuralist theories that dominated the field of linguistics during the twentieth century advocated a separation of language use from the more abstract knowledge of language structure. For Saussure this distinction went under the labels of *langue* (knowledge of language) and *parole* (speech) (de Saussure, 1915/1966). In Chomskian theory the distinction is made between *competence* (tacit knowledge of language structure) and *performance* (the actual use of language) (Chomsky, 1965). Because knowledge of structure was taken to be the main object of study, there was little interest in the potential effects that usage might have on cognitive structures. However, common sense tells us that for second language learners, repeated exposure and practice are essential to the development of the cognitive structures that lead to fluent and grammatical speech.

More recently developed Usage-Based Theories of language recognize the impact of usage on the cognitive representation of language (Bybee, 1985, 2001, 2006; Langacker, 1987, 2000). Many empirical studies have now appeared relating frequency of use to various structural phenomena. In addition, many recent studies have revealed the extent to which language users retain specific information about their experience with language (for reviews see Bod, Hay, & Jannedy, 2003; Bybee & Hopper, 2001; Ellis, 2002). From these studies there is now emerging a new theory of language in which grammar is viewed as the cognitive organization of one's experience with language (Bybee, 2006). In this view, as users of language experience tokens of language use, they categorize them at varying degrees of abstractness. This categorization process creates a vast network of phonological, semantic and pragmatic associations that range over what

216

has traditionally been designated as lexicon and grammar. The network resulting from these categorized experiences is affected by repetition (frequency of use) in the ways that will be outlined below. In addition, it contains both specific and generalized information about form, meaning, and context of use of words and constructions.

In this chapter I will review this evidence and its theoretical implications both for native speakers' grammars and for a theory of second language acquisition. This theory, in which usage impacts grammar, has particular relevance for second language teaching and learning.

Some of the discussion will be phrased in terms of constructions, which are stored pairings of form and function that range over units at the level of the word up to and including complex sentences. Several versions of grammar in terms of constructions have been discussed in the literature with proposals being made by Fillmore and Kay (e.g. Fillmore, Kay & O'Connor, 1988; Fillmore & Kay, 1994), Goldberg (1995, 2003), Lakoff (1987), Langacker (1987) and Croft (2001). In all of these proposals, the following constitute constructions (see Goldberg, 2003):

1 simple lexical words: *table, decide, pretty*
2 grammatical morphemes and the items they appear with: VERB + Past Tense; *the* + NOUN.
3 Idioms with fixed lexical content: *go great guns*
4 Idioms that are partially filled: *jog* <someone's> *memory*
5 Constructions with some fixed material: *he made his way through the crowd*
6 Fully abstract constructions: *they gave him an award.*

Almost all constructions contain some explicit morphological material, tying them fairly concretely to specific words or morphemes (e.g. Past Tense *-ed*, the determiner *the*, or *way* and the possessive pronoun in (5)). The ditransitive construction in (6) contains no specific morphological material that identifies it as the ditransitive. Only the word order signals this. However, it should be noted that only a small class of verbs can occur in this construction so that it also has a grounding in particular lexical items.

Taking constructions as the basic unit of grammatical analysis has two advantages: on the one hand with constructions we can see the continuum from lexicon to grammar (as shown in (1) through (6)), and on the other hand constructions allow us to represent the interactions of specific lexical units with specific grammatical configurations (as seen in the relations between *jog* and *memory* or between *give* and the ditransitive construction).

When constructions are combined with a Usage-Based model the result is a theory that proposes that grammatical structures are built up through experience with specific examples of constructions which are categorized in memory by a mapping process that matches strings for similarity and difference. The resulting cognitive representations are abstractions over one's cumulative experience with language. However, as mentioned above, there is evidence that knowledge of specific instances of language use is not entirely lost in this abstraction process and especially with reinforcement through repetition, specific instances of constructions can have memory representations. In this view of grammar, then, frequency of use plays an important role in determining cognitive structures. In the next section I will discuss the particular frequency effects that have been discovered in recent research.

2 Frequency effects

Recent research has shown that repetition of linguistic units has an impact on cognitive representations. To demonstrate this, a distinction must be made between token and type frequency. **Token frequency** counts the number of times a unit appears in running text. Any specific unit, such as a particular consonant [s], a syllable [ba], a word *dog* or *the*, a phrase *take a break*, or even a sentence such as *You know what I mean* can have a token frequency. **Type frequency** is a very different sort of count. Only patterns of language have type frequency because this refers to how many distinct items are represented by the pattern. Type frequency may apply to phonotactic sequences; it would be the count of how many words of the language begin with [sp] versus how many begin with [sf]. It may apply to morphological patterns, such as stem + affix combinations. For instance, the English past tense pattern exemplified by *know, knew; blow, blew* has a lower type frequency than the regular pattern of adding the *-ed* suffix. Syntactic patterns or constructions also have type frequencies: the ditransitive pattern in English, exemplified by *He gave me the change* is used with only a small set of verbs, while the alternate pattern *He gave the change to me* is possible with a large class of verbs (Goldberg, 1995). In this section we treat the three known effects of token frequency and the effect of type frequency, as well as their interaction.

2.1 Token frequency: three effects

The first effect of token frequency to be discussed, which we can call the **Conserving Effect**, depends upon the fact that repetition strengthens memory representations for linguistic forms and makes them more accessible. Accessibility in this sense refers to the fact that, in experiments where subjects are asked to say whether a string of letters or sounds is a word of their language, they respond much more quickly to high-frequency words than to low-frequency words. This greater accessibility suggests that each token of use strengthens the memory representation for a word or phrase (Bybee, 1985).

The strength of representation of higher frequency forms explains why they resist reformation on the basis of analogy with other forms (thus the name, Conserving Effect). For instance, for English irregular verbs, there is a general trend diachronically towards regularization, a trend also witnessed in child language development. However, the higher-frequency verbs resist this trend; thus *keep, sleep, weep, leap*, and *creep* and other verbs of this shape acquired irregular past forms when the vowel was shortened in early Middle English, giving *kept, slept, wept, leapt*, and *crept*. Only the lower-frequency verbs of this class have sub-sequently developed regularized pasts *weeped, leaped*, and *creeped* (still used alongside the irregulars). The mechanism behind this type of change (analogical reformation) is that a new past form is created by accessing the base/present form and adding the suffix *-ed* (in this case its allomorph [t]) to it. For those verbs of high frequency, the greater accessibility of the irregular past makes such a reformation unlikely. For this reason, the lower-frequency paradigms tend to regularize before the higher-frequency paradigms.

This effect of repetition should play out in Second Language Acquisition in a very straightforward way: the more exposure a learner has to irregular forms, the greater the chance that he/she will produce them correctly. Less frequent irregular forms are more likely to be treated by the learner as regular. *[handwritten: How can this help with Spanish verbs?]*

The second effect of token frequency, **Autonomy**, can be thought of as an extreme case of the preceding effect. Sequences are autonomous when they are frequent enough to be learned by rote and are not associated with the units that comprise them. For instance, children may learn to say *gimme* without realizing that is consists of *give* + *me*. For second language learners, they may be autonomous if they are learned before the know-ledge of the language has developed enough to allow analysis. For instance, I learned the Spanish word *ándale* which I assumed meant "hurry up" from exposure to Spanish speakers, but I figured out that it consisted of the verb *andar* "to walk" plus a pronoun *le* only after several years of formal study. *[handwritten: Adios / Hasta luego]*

The third effect, the **Reducing Effect**, refers to the common observation that oft-repeated phrases, such as greetings (*God be with you > goodbye, how are you > hi*) and titles, tend to reduce phonetically. The same observation applies to much-used grammatical items, such as auxiliaries, modals, negatives, and pronouns, and phrases such as *be going to*. In addition, it has recently been fully documented that reductive sound change applies probabilistically across all frequency levels, affecting high-frequency items more quickly and radically than low-frequency items (Bybee, 2002b). The reason for this trend is that repetition of neuromotor sequences leads to greater overlap and reduction of the component gestures. As articulation becomes more efficient, the output appears more and more to have been affected by assimilation and reduction.

The Reducing Effect presents an enormous challenge to second language learners in both production and perception. A phrase such as *going to* when used with a verb in its future sense can be produced as [gɔɪŋtu], [gə̃nə] or with "I" as [aɪmənə]. It is very difficult for students to acquire good approximations of these native variants as the phonetics of their native languages would most likely have different reduction and coarticulation effects.

2.2 Grammar as automatized behavior

These well-documented effects of token frequency point strongly to grammatical knowledge as automatized behavior. All language use involves procedural knowledge, as distinct from declarative knowledge, which is a knowledge of a fact, such as "whales are mammals." Procedural knowledge is bound up with neuromotor events and is knowledge of how to do something, such as drive a car or stir pancake batter. While these kinds of actions are learned through the mastery of a sequence of actions, with practice they are repackaged into a single action. Once automatized, it is difficult to unpack them again. The linguistic routines that make up the grammar and lexicon of a language are like these procedures: they develop over time with practice, they are difficult to unpack and native speakers are often unaware of their component parts and, at times, even their meaning. In contrast, one might want to say that the meanings of lexical items, particularly nouns, is a matter of declarative knowledge, but while this is the case in part, procedural knowledge is also necessary to access lexical items and put them in an appropriate context.

Ellis (1996) discusses the importance of "chunking" for L2 acquisition. Chunking is a property of procedural knowledge; sequences of actions that occur together repeatedly are chunked into a single action. Chunking is possible with sequences of just two actions or it could occur with very long sequences of actions. However, the probability that a smaller number of actions recur is much greater than the probability that a long sequence will recur, so the degree of fusion within small chunks is greater than within larger ones. In Bybee (2002a) I argue that the embedding of small chunks within larger ones is what gives us the grammatical notion of hierarchies or tree structures. In Usage-Based Theory, constructions are chunks—neuromotor routines—with movable parts. They are established through practice and processed as single units. Since chunking occurs naturally and unconsciously with practice, even adults easily learn new chunks in their own language. It is an ability that is necessary and fortunately available for L2 learning. Of course, the difference between

L1 and L2 speakers is that the L1 speakers already have the necessary components of the chunks automatized and ready for re-use in new chunks.

The downside of the fact that repetition leads to chunking is fossilization in Second Language Acquisition: a learner repeats a sequence frequently but incorrectly and it is very difficult to change the internal structure of this chunk once it has become automatized (see Ellis, 2006a; Long, 2003).

2.3 Type frequency

As mentioned above, type frequency is a property of patterns or constructions and refers to the number of distinct items that can occur in the open slot of a construction or the number of items that exemplify a pattern, such as a phonotactic sequence. Type frequency is a major factor determining the degree of productivity of a construction (Bybee, 1985; Guillaume, 1927/1973; MacWhinney, 1978). That is, constructions that apply to a large number of distinct items also tend to be highly applicable to new items. In determining productivity, however, factors other than type frequency must also be taken into account: often the member items that occur with a construction must also belong to certain phonological or semantic categories. The verbs of the *string, strung* class must end in a nasal or a velar (Bybee & Moder, 1983); the adjectives that can be used in the construction [X drives me (or someone) ADJ], (as in *it drives me mad, it drives me crazy*) must suggest some degree of insanity, either literally or figuratively (Boas, 2003).

The contribution of type frequency to productivity is due to the fact that, when a construction is experienced with different items occupying a position, it enables the parsing of the construction. If *happiness* is learned by someone who knows no related words, there is no way to infer that it has two morphemes. If *happy* is also learned, then the learner could hypothesize that *-ness* is a suffix, but only if it occurs on other adjectives would its status as a suffix become established. Thus, a certain degree of type frequency is needed to uncover the structure of words and phrases. In addition, a higher type frequency also gives a construction a stronger representation, making it more available or accessible for novel uses. Hay and Baayen (2002) have proposed several other factors that facilitate parsing and thus influence productivity.

The implications of these findings for second language learning is obvious: if a learner is to apply a pattern productively to forms not necessarily encountered before, he/she must have encountered the pattern with a number of different items in it. We will refine this prediction in the next section.

we aren't teaching morphemes, we just hope that they pick that up on their own

2.4 Interactions of type and token frequency

One result of the interaction of type and token frequency has already been mentioned: a very high-frequency instance of a pattern might be learned and stored as if it were autonomous from the more general pattern. Moder (1992) experimented with the English irregular verb classes, such as *string/strung, fling/flung* and *write/wrote, ride/rode, steal/stole*. She made up nonce verbs that fit these patterns and asked subjects what their past tense forms would be. If she first presented them with a real member of the class that was medium-frequency, then that made the subjects more likely to give a past tense with a vowel change that fit the pattern. However, if she presented them with a very high-frequency verb in the class, they were less likely to respond with a form that fitted the pattern. A similar result on phonotactics is reported by Bailey and Hahn (2001): English-speaking subjects rated nonce phonotactic patterns for how acceptable they would be in English. They tended to prefer phonotactic patterns that were similar to dense groups of similar words (dense neighborhoods). However, the very high-frequency words and the very low-frequency words did not contribute to this effect.

A very different effect of token frequency on productivity of patterns is found with instances of constructions that are relatively high in frequency, but not so high as to cause the autonomy effect just discussed. As I said above, if a construction (either within a word, such as VERB + Past Tense or across words, as the ditransitive construction (*I gave Jim the rest of the stew*)) can occur with lots of different items (in both of these examples, many different verbs), then it is likely to be productive, that is, applicable to new items. One could thus conclude that, in acquiring productivity, exposure to many different types in a construction would be more helpful than exposure to many identical tokens. Actually, recent results of an artificial language learning task by Casenhiser and Goldberg (2005) shows that both type and token frequency are important to learning productive constructions (see also Goldberg, this volume; Goldberg, Casenhiser & Sethuraman, 2004). They taught English-speaking children, aged five to seven, novel verbs in a novel construction. The construction contained a subject, verb, and object, but the word order was non-English—the verb was final in the sentence. In one condition the subjects heard the sentences (while watching a video that represented the meaning of the sentences) with three verbs twice and two other verbs only once. In this condition, then, type frequency was emphasized. In the other condition, one nonce verb was presented in the construction four times while the others were presented only once. It was in the latter condition that the subjects performed better in learning the construction.

As Casenhiser and Goldberg point out, it is a general property of categorization that there will be one higher-frequency member of the category and that this member will be considered prototypical. In a non-linguistic task, Kotovsky and Gentner (1996) have shown children do better extending a simple relational similarity to a more complex one if they have lots of practice on the simple relation. These studies suggest that while varying the types in a construction is important to learning, holding the type constant over some repetitions facilitates learning, probably by increasing general familiarity with the relations in the construction. Note that the mechanism of extension of a grammatical construction assumed here is analogy. Analogy as a basic mechanism for linguistic production has received new attention in the psycholinguistic and modeling literature recently, including connectionist models (Rumelhart & McClelland, 1986), as well as various analogical models (Eddington, 2000; Krott et al., 2001; Skousen, 1989). That is, we are assuming that on the basis of some instances of exposure a structure is built up that can then be used in a new context by analogy with the stored instances. Examples from morphology and syntax will be provided in the next two sections.

3 Morphology: how usage affects the structure of paradigms

The frequency effects discussed above reveal themselves in the structure of morphological paradigms; indeed, in my own work their importance was made clear to me through the cross-linguistic study of morphology (Bybee, 1985). A full treatment of these phenomena with respect to First and Second Language Acquisition can be found in Bybee (1991).

3.1 Token frequency

First consider the Conserving Effect. Mańczak (1980) has pointed out that the forms of a paradigm that are most frequently used are the ones that resist change and serve as the basis of change when new forms are created. To take our example above, when *weep/wept* regularizes to *weep/weeped*, it is the infinitive or present form, *weep*, that is taken as the basis for the new form, *weeped*, rather than a potential but very implausible regularization that would use the past base, *wep*, to create a new present.

Because of this strong tendency across languages, it is often the case that the most frequent form of a paradigm either has no affix or has a simple and short affix, and many of the other forms of the paradigm can be derived from it. Consider a regular present indicative paradigm of Spanish verbs:

	Singular	Plural "sing"
1st	*cánto*	*cantámos*
2nd	*cántas*	*cantáis*
3rd	*cánta*	*cántan*

(I have marked the stress on these forms even though the orthographic conventions would not normally write them on any form but the 2nd plural. Stress will become important in our discussion of the preterite and imperfective forms.) Note here that the stem could be regarded as *canta* and from this form all the forms except 1st singular can be derived by adding an affix. It turns out that the 1st and 3rd singular of the present tense are the most frequently used verb forms in Spanish (Bybee & Brewer, 1980).

A similar set of relations is evident in the imperfect, which indicates past imperfective—a habitual or progressive situation in the past.

	Singular	Plural "sing"
1st	*cantába*	*cantábamos*
2nd	*cantábas*	*cantábais*
3rd	*cantába*	*cantában*

Here we see that both the 1st and 3rd singular are lacking in person/number marking and thus can serve as the base upon which other affixes are added.

Not all verbs in all languages follow this pattern, but the pattern reflects common tendencies towards change, that is, reformation of paradigms based on 1st or 3rd singular forms. Of course, languages are conventional systems and change only slowly, so not all systems nor all verbs would succumb to the pressures of change. The importance of the tendencies towards change is that they give evidence for the types of cognitive representations speakers have. In this case, the tendencies for change demonstrate that the more frequent forms of the paradigm have stronger representations in memory and thus can be used as the basis for constructing the other forms. The frequency skewing in the experience of speakers is reflected in cognitive representations: higher-frequency forms have relatively stronger representations that are easy to access; lower-frequency forms have weaker, less accessible representations.

Second language learners can benefit from the natural frequency skewing in the input in the same way. The higher-frequency forms will have stronger representations (or can be presented first) and the lower-frequency forms can be learned as derivations from the higher-frequency forms.

Special evidence for this property of morphology comes from cases where an unexpected form is highly frequent. In these cases, we find a greater tendency towards irregularity. Thus, the English nouns that have irregular plurals are for the most part nouns that designate entities often referred to in the pairs or groups: *feet, teeth, mice, geese, men*, etc.

Also from morphology we have the lesson that high-frequency items can preserve older patterns longer than low-frequency items. The nouns just mentioned represent only a few members of an older class of nouns that had vowel changes (from earlier umlaut) in Old English: for instance, the older plural of *book* would be modern *beech*, *brother* had earlier *brethren*, *daughter* had a plural *dehter*, and *friend* had a singular *freond* with a plural *friend*. Thus, the surviving members of this class have preserved the archaic patterns.

As mentioned above, more extreme levels of frequency lead to high autonomy. Examples are the copula verbs in most languages, which are usually highly irregular: English *am*, *is*, *are*, *was*, *were*; Spanish *soy*, *eres*, *es*, *somos*, *son*, etc. In such cases, where each form is very highly frequent, each form is likely to be autonomous from every other form, though their meanings remain very closely related. Autonomy is evident in second language learners who use high-frequency irregular past tenses correctly despite not yet being at a stage of consistent application of the regular past tense (Bayley, 1994, 1996).

To summarize this point: token frequency plays a role in morphology by making the higher-frequency forms of a paradigm the anchoring points for the other forms. Lower-frequency forms can be analyzed and learned in terms of these more robust forms, creating a relationship of dependency. In paradigms where several or all forms are of high token frequency, we have less dependency inside the paradigm and more autonomy of individual forms. Since these patterns arise from the natural occurrence of inflected forms in discourse, exposure to natural patterns of use should set up native-like representations in the L2 learner. However, because L2 learners in the classroom have so much less exposure to the target language than children in a natural environment, some measures will likely be necessary to ensure that these paradigmatic relations that depend upon relative frequency are established.

3.2 Type frequency

As mentioned above, type frequency plays an important role in the determination of productivity. In order for the L2 learner to acquire native-like patterns of productivity, regular patterns must be taught by methods that mirror to some extent natural exposure to the L2 patterns. As mentioned above, Casenhiser and Goldberg (2005) found that while type frequency was important to the acquisition of a new pattern, repeated exposure to a single type also facilitated acquisition. In terms of teaching productive morphology, the most effective method would have two stages: first, focus on a single lexical paradigm that exemplifies the productive pattern, and, only after this is quite familiar, advance to a second stage in which the pattern is exemplified with other lexical types. The repeated type provides familiarity with the relations in the pattern, while the range of different types aids parsing and provides practice of the analogical extension of the pattern.

225

4 Syntactic constructions: "become" verbs in Spanish

The effects of frequency just discussed in the context of morphology can be extended to syntax though work in this domain has only just begun (Bybee, 2006; Bybee & Thompson, 1997). For instance, we find the Conserving Effect in syntax in the preservation of older constructions within high-frequency collocations or with high frequency lexical items. For instance, the question *how goes it?* uses the inversion of the main verb with the subject which was the general pattern up until the mid-sixteenth century. Now the more general, productive pattern uses an auxiliary: *how does it go?* (which does not mean the same thing!).

The older pattern of negation evident in phrases such as *She saw no one, he does nothing, we have no aspirin* are retained only with certain high-frequency verbs and in certain collocations, such as *that proves nothing*. Otherwise we use the more productive pattern exemplified by *she didn't see anyone, he doesn't do anything, we don't have any aspirin, that doesn't prove anything* (Tottie, 1991). Often when two patterns are competing in a language, one is older and preserved only in certain contexts, often the more frequent contexts, and the other is newer and more productive, being used in a wider range of contexts, including those of lower frequency.

Usage-Based Theory holds that the properties of constructions can best be studied in corpora of naturally-occurring discourse. Very often, linguists' intuitions about the range of occurrence of constructions do not match what is actually found in language use (Biber, Conrad, & Reppen, 1998; Biber & Reppen, 2002; Sinclair, 1991). By studying the use of constructions in discourse we can learn more about the way they are represented in the speaker's mental grammar. What we find is that the interaction of type and token frequency discussed above also applies to syntactic constructions.

Languages have thousands of constructions, tens of thousands if we include inflected words and idioms. But even restricting our count to constructions that contain an open slot, there are thousands that have to be learned. For instance, in Spanish (as in many other languages) there are a large number of verb + preposition combinations that are conventionalized and have to be learned individually. Examples are *pensar en* + NP "think about NP," *empezar a* + verb "to begin to + verb," *soñar con* + NP "to dream about NP," and *insistir en* + NP "to insist on NP." Each of these can be considered a construction with an open position. Continuing with Spanish examples, there is a very general construction for the placement of an NP direct object (after the verb) and a different one for the placement of pronominal direct objects (before the inflected verb). The way constructions can be effectively taught may depend upon their distribution in natural discourse.

Consider a set of constructions whose distribution in natural corpora has been studied for the purpose of understanding their cognitive representations (Bybee & Eddington, 2006). Spanish has various ways of expressing the notion of entering a state. In particular, there are four verbs that can be used with an adjective with roughly the meaning of "become + adjective." The verbs are all reflexive in form, and are given here with the glosses of the related non-reflexive form: *ponerse* "to put (reflexive)," *volverse* "to turn (reflexive)," *quedarse* "to remain (reflexive)," and *hacerse* "to make (reflexive)." Despite their etymological differences, all four verbs are now used with adjectives with a sense of becoming, for instance *ponerse nervioso* means "to get nervous" and *quedarse sorprendido* means "to be(come) surprised." The problem for the linguist and the learner of Spanish is which verb to use with which adjective. We hoped that a corpus study might shed some light on this question.

We studied these four constructions as used with animate subjects in a spoken corpus of 1.1 million words and a written corpus of just under one million words. One important finding of the study was that very few adjectives occurred with more than one verb. That is, the verbs were not used very often to give special nuances of meaning to the description of the process of becoming. Rather, verb + adjective combinations seemed to be conventionalized. For two of the verbs (*quedarse* and *ponerse*) a very interesting pattern emerged from the data. Certain combinations of verb + adjective had a high token frequency, i.e. they seemed to be conventionalized pairings or prefabs (Erman & Warren, 2000). Here are some examples:

(1) *quedarse solo*   to end up alone
    quedarse quieto   to become still, quiet
    quedarse sorprendido   to be surprised
    quedarse embarazada   to get pregnant

    ponerse nervioso   to get nervous
    ponerse furioso   to get angry
    ponerse pesado   to become annoying

These pairings seem somewhat arbitrary in the sense that, for example, it is difficult to find a semantic feature that characterizes all the collocations listed here with *quedarse*. Many authors have tried to find general features that characterize all the adjectives used with one verb, but these analyses have not been completely successful. Because each of these collocations occurred at least five times in the corpus, we took the view that they were conventionalized and stored in memory.

The other property of the corpus data that supported this view is that there were many single instances of verb + adjective combinations that could be grouped around these prefabs as semantically similar. Thus, along with 28 instances of *quedarse solo* "to end up alone" we found three instances of *soltera* "single, unmarried," two of *aislado* "isolated," and one each of *a solas* "alone" and *sin novia* "without a girlfriend," all used with *quedarse*. No adjectives with a sense of "alone" were used with any other verb. Thus, we argue that the conventionalized prefab *quedarse solo* serves as the central member of a set of tokens with similar meanings that also use *quedarse*.

The same type of pattern emerged for all the collocations or prefabs listed in (1). Here is another example: *ponerse furioso* occurred five times and *agresivo* "aggressive," *bravo* "angry, aggressive," and *enojadísimo* "very angry" occurred once with *ponerse*. In this case, *ponerse furioso* serves as the central member of the category.

 What we propose is that the tokens that are more frequent have stronger representations in memory and serve as the analogical basis for forming novel instances of the construction. These novel instances are also represented in memory (although not so robustly) and may have an effect on the category, causing it to extend in new directions.

Note how the distribution in the corpus mirrors the distribution that Casenhiser and Goldberg (2005) found to be most effective in teaching children a novel construction. Their most effective condition had the construction used with several different verb types, but with one type repeated several times and the others presented only once. If one were learning the use of *quedarse* + adjective or *ponerse* + adjective from natural exposure, this is exactly the pattern that would be presented—certain instances would be of high frequency and other, semantically related instances of low frequency.

This convergence suggests that children's learning patterns and adults' usage patterns are both traceable to the nature of categorization: members of categories that are more frequent in the environment are taken to be the central members of categories; they are more accessible and in many cases more generalized in their meaning. When children are forming categories, frequent exposure helps them to set up the category with a central member. When adults are using language, the more accessible, more generalized member of the category is used more often.

So far the discussion has focused on two of the four verbs studied. The constructions with the other two verbs did not show the same type of categorization as that just discussed. In the case of *volverse* there is one very high frequency collocation, *volverse loco* "to go crazy," but in the corpus we did not find that it had spawned other semantically related collocations. *Volverse loco* occurred 16 times in the corpora, but the other 14 adjectives that occurred once each did not form a semantically coherent set. *Hacerse* did not have any high-frequency uses (with animate subjects—it certainly has some conventionalized uses with inanimate subjects, such as *hacerse tarde* "to get late"). It was used with 18 different adjectives and none more than three times. These adjectives form a miscellaneous set, e.g. *aburrido* "boring," *cursi* "tacky," *consciente* "aware of," etc. Some of the adjectives used with *hacerse* were judged to be similar in an experiment we conducted. These were the positive adjectives *rico* "rich," *bueno* "good," *famoso* "famous," and *fuerte* "strong," which are not synonyms, but may be used together in some contexts. I do not know why the constructions with these two verbs behave differently from the first two we discussed. It appears that the latter two verbs may be used when the stronger patterns with *quedarse* and *ponerse* are not available, that is, with adjectives that do not fit into the more coherent categories. It is worth noting that the tokens that fit into the categories used with *quedarse* and *ponerse* constituted 87 percent of the 453 tokens found in the corpora.

The implications for L2 acquisition seem clear. Efficient learning should occur when the central members of categories are presented early and often. The extensions of the categories should also be modeled, but the learner's natural ability to analogize can be relied on to help him/her produce combinations not experienced before, just as native speakers do. However, this method depends upon good corpus analyses of constructions. Without good information about the type and token frequency of constructions in natural language use, this method cannot be implemented with confidence.

5 Grammaticization

Another linguistic phenomenon that is highly usage-driven is the process of grammaticization (or grammaticalization). Grammaticization is a gradual process taking place in all languages at all times; it is the process by which new grammatical morphemes within grammatical constructions are developed out of lexical items or combinations of grammatical and lexical items (Meillet, 1912/1958; see Hopper & Traugott, 2003). Thus, the English perfect tenses, such as *have done*, *had done* developed from the possessive verb plus the past participle; the future auxiliary *will* was once a verb meaning "to want"; *be going to*, used as future, came from the progressive phrase with *go* and *to*. In French and Spanish, the auxiliary *habere* Latin "to have" after an infinitive form of the verb gives rise to the future and conditional suffixes, as in Spanish *cantaré* from *cantar* + *he*. Cross-linguistic studies have shown that grammaticization is the major force that creates grammar and the processes involved are very similar across all languages (Bybee et al., 1994).

As lexical items become grammatical markers, we see huge increases in frequency, since grammatical elements are much more frequent than lexical ones. This frequency increase is instrumental in many of processes that drive grammaticization. On the phonetic level, grammaticizing phrases undergo massive reduction as the articulatory gestures are reduced and overlap. This produces the variation we find in *be going to*, which we mentioned before is pronounced as [gənə], or in the case of *I'm gonna* we often hear an even more reduced form [aimənə] High-frequency words and phrases tend to reduce more than low-frequency ones, and material undergoing grammaticization usually reduces quite radically (Bybee, 2002b, 2003). As mentioned above, the reason is that neuromotor sequences that are repeated come to be processed as a single unit. The individual gestures are reinterpreted as part of a single routine, leading to the overlap and reduction of the movements. Interestingly, during the process of grammaticization a great deal of phonetic variation is tolerated.

On the semantic side, grammaticizing phrases are said to become semantically bleached—that is, they lose specific features of their earlier meaning. Thus, *have* in the perfect construction does not signal possession; *will* as a future marker shows only faint traces of its earlier meaning of volition (such traces remain in contexts such as *Give them the name of someone who will sign for it* or *If you'll help, we can finish sooner* where willingness is signaled). *Be going to* as a future no longer signals movement in space. Some of this bleaching is due to habituation—the more an item is used, the less force it has.

The other important source of meaning change in grammaticization is change by pragmatic inference (Traugott, 1989). When we communicate with one another, we are constantly making inferences about what the other party means. If a certain inference occurs frequently with a particular construction, then that inference can become conventionalized as part of the meaning of the construction. Thus, if we hear *I'm going to mail this letter* as a person walks out the door, the basic meaning might be movement in space, but a strong inference is that the person intends to mail the letter. The repetition of this inference with *be going to* + verb can lead to the meaning of intention as part of the meaning of this construction. This is apparently what happened around the time that Shakespeare was writing and that started the course of development that led to the intention and future meaning that the construction has today (Hopper & Traugott, 2003).

On the syntactic level, grammaticizing items change category and this affects the constituent structure. The main verb *willan* eventually became the auxiliary *will*; the main verb *have* also became an auxiliary in the perfect construction. *Be going to* has also changed from being a main verb. It will not take on the properties of the established auxiliaries, but it is already functioning like an auxiliary because it does not affect the selectional restrictions between the subject and the now main verb. Thus, entities that are immobile can be the subject of *be going to*, as in *That tree is going to need more fertilizer soon.* The change from main verb status also implies a change from a complex clause with two main verbs to a simple clause with an auxiliary and a main verb. This downgrading in the status of the first verb is related to its loss of meaning.

Grammaticization helps us understand the ranges of variation that we see in both meaning and form and it helps us understand why languages have grammar. However, the variation found in phrases or constructions that are undergoing grammaticization present a real challenge to the L2 learner. On the one hand, such phrases are of very high frequency in the input, which helps with their acquisition. On the other hand, the more grammaticized a form becomes, the less salient it is in running discourse and the more redundant it is given the construction it appears in. In fact, highly grammaticized forms such as agreement markers, tense, aspect, and case inflections, have such a reduced communicative value that they seem to remain in the language largely for convention's sake. Thus, if an L2 learner's main goal is to communicate rather than assimilate the conventions of the society, such items seem dispensable, as evidenced by the fact that many fairly proficient L2 learners in a natural setting fail to use many of the grammatical markers of the target language (see Ellis, 2006b).

6 Low frequency: prefabs

Conventionalized sequences do not have to be of high frequency. Apparently, a few repetitions is enough to establish the conventionality of a sequence for native speakers. For instance, the prefabricated sequence *experience delays* is not very high in frequency, but it is the conventionalized way of expressing a certain notion. Pawley and Syder (1983), Schmitt (2004), Wray (2002) and others have noted the importance of prefabs for success with a second language. As Pawley and Syder point out, selection of pre-formed word sequences provides not only native-like word combinations but also enables native-like fluency since words are selected more efficiently in groups rather than individually.

From a theoretical point of view, prefabs represent an important argument for usage-based grammar. In order for a native speaker to know that a certain sequence of words is a prefab, she or he must remember that they have been experienced before. This means that even completely predictable word combinations such as *experience delays* or *choose one's words carefully* are registered in memory (Bybee, 1998, 2006; Erman & Warren, 2000). This fact points to a highly redundant, experienced-based cognitive storage and access system for language. This system must intertwine grammar and lexicon, as constructions contain both grammatical and lexical material. Such a theory stands in rather dramatic contrast to the generative proposals of an abstract grammatical system with a redundancy-free lexicon.

A number of studies have demonstrated that prefabs are quite common in both written and spoken language. Erman and Warren (2000) count word choices in natural texts, both written and spoken, and find that 55 percent of word choices are determined lexically by occurrence in prefabs. Given the high level of use of prefabs in constructing native-like utterances, it makes sense to suggest that the learning of prefabs should constitute an important part of the SLA curriculum. The lexical approach, originated by Lewis (1993) and also described in Richards and Rodgers (2001, Chapter 12), focuses on these conventionalized word sequences as the center of SLA. If embedded in an approach that also teaches general morphosyntactic constructions, attention to prefabs seems quite appropriate (Biber, Conrad, & Cortes, 2004; Simpson & Ellis, 2005; Simpson & Mendis, 2003).

7 The role of the first language

As Usage-Based Theory views linguistic knowledge as a set of automatized patterns which are schematic to varying degrees, the first language must be viewed as both a help and a hindrance to Second Language Acquisition. To the extent that the constructions in the second language are similar to those of the first language, the L1 constructions can serve as the basis for the L2 constructions, with only the particular lexical or morphological material changed. However, since even similar constructions across languages are likely to differ in detail, the acquisition of the L2 pattern in all its detail is hindered by the L1 pattern (see Odlin, this volume, Robinson & Ellis, this volume).

Despite these difficulties, Usage-Based Theory would predict that with sufficient input and practice, any morphosyntactic pattern can be acquired, though specific productive lexical distributions will present persistent problems. Of course, in addition to exposure, motivation and ability, both of which differ from one situation to the next, are required. The child learner acquires language as part of learning how to be a human being in the culture in which he/she is being raised. Children assimilate the language, gestures, postures, facial expressions of their culture in minute detail. The L2 learner already is a human being and is trying to communicate. He or she may or may not want to fit into the target culture. In my view, this factor is a strong determinant of the degree to which the grammar of the target language is successfully acquired.

8 Usage and pedagogy: controlling frequency in the input

In the foregoing I have pointed out the numerous ways that experience with language impacts its cognitive representation. In some ways this is bad news for the L2 learner, because it is difficult for the adult learner or the classroom learner to get completely native-like exposure to the target language. In addition, many adults lack the plasticity needed to set up native-like neuromotor routines for the new language. On the other hand, there is some good news. The natural frequency distributions do not have to be exactly reproduced in the classroom. In natural frequency distributions, the high-frequency items are much higher in frequency than they would have to be to be learned well and any language material the learner is exposed to will naturally contain this high-frequency material. Exposure to the lower-frequency constructions and prefabs, however, will take more effort.

The other piece of good news for the L2 learner that comes from Usage-Based Theory is that the analogical mechanisms that we use every-day to produce and decode language are just what is needed to use the L2 productively. Similarly, the categorization mechanisms that we use every day for language, as well as for non-linguistic categorization, are available for use in the task of learning a new language. The only requirement is sufficient exposure to the categories of the L2. And finally, the chunking and automatization processes needed to gain fluency occur naturally with practice of both linguistic and non-linguistic tasks.

A great advantage of Usage-Based Theory over Generative Theories is that it does not rely on innateness to explain linguistic categories but rather proposes that much of grammar can be explained on the basis of the domain-general abilities of humans that were mentioned in the previous paragraph. Given these very generalized cognitive abilities, usage factors themselves become part of the explanation for the properties evident in human language.

Bibliography

Bailey, T. M., & Hahn, U. (2001). Determinants of wordlikeness: Phonotactics or lexical neighborhoods? *Journal of Memory and Language, 44*, 568–591.

Bayley, R. (1994). Interlanguage variation and the quantitative paradigm: past tense marking in Chinese-English. In E. Tarone, S. M. Gass, & A. D. Cohen (Eds.), *Research methodology in second-language acquisition* (pp. 157–181). Hillsdale, NJ: Lawrence Erlbaum.

Bayley, R. (1996). Competing constraints on variation in the speech of adult Chinese learners of English. In R. Bayley, & D. R. Preston (Eds.), *Second language acquisition and linguistic variation* (pp. 97–120). Amsterdam: John Benjamins.

Biber, D., Conrad, S., & Cortes, V. (2004). "If you look at . . .": Lexical bundles in university teaching and textbooks. *Applied Linguistics, 25*, 371–405.

Biber, D., Conrad, S., & Reppen, R. (1998). *Corpus linguistics: investigating language structure and use.* New York: Cambridge University Press.

Biber, D., & Reppen, R. (2002). What does frequency have to do with grammar teaching? *Studies in Second Language Acquisition, 24*(2), 199–208.

Boas, H. C. (2003). *A constructional approach to resultatives.* Stanford: CSLI.

Bod, R., Hay, J., & Jannedy, S. (Eds.) (2003). *Probabilistic linguistics*. Cambridge, MA: MIT Press.

Bybee, J. L. (1985). *Morphology: a study of the relation between meaning and form*. Amsterdam, Philadelphia: John Benjamins.

Bybee, J. L. (1991). Natural morphology: the organization of paradigms and language acquisition. In C. Ferguson, & T. Huebner (Eds.), *Second language acquisition and linguistic theory* (pp. 67–91). Amsterdam: John Benjamins.

Bybee, J. L. (1998). The emergent lexicon. *Chicago Linguistic Society, 34*, 421–35.

Bybee, J. L. (2001). *Phonology and language use*. Cambridge: Cambridge University Press.

Bybee, J. L. (2002). Word frequency and context of use in the lexical diffusion of phonetically conditioned sound change. *Language Variation and Change, 14*, 261–290.

Bybee, J. L. (2002a). Sequentiality as the basis of constituent structure. In T. Givón & B. F. Malle (Eds.), *The evolution of language out of pre-language* (pp. 109–132). Amsterdam: John Benjamins.

Bybee, J. L. (2003). Mechanisms of change in grammaticization: the role of frequency. In B. D. Joseph & R. D. Janda (Eds.), *The handbook of historical linguistics* (pp. 602–623). Oxford: Blackwell.

Bybee, J. L. (2006). From usage to grammar: the mind's response to repetition. *Language, 82*, 711–733.

Bybee, J. L., & Brewer, M. A. (1980). Explanation in morphophonemics: changes in Provençal and Spanish preterite forms. *Lingua, 52*, 201–242.

Bybee, J. L., & Eddington, D. (2006). A usage-based exemplar model approach to Spanish verbs of "becoming." *Language, 82*, 323–355.

Bybee, J., & Hopper, P. (Eds.) (2001). *Frequency and the emergence of linguistic structure*. Amsterdam: John Benjamins.

Bybee, J. L., & Moder, C. L. (1983). Morphological classes as natural categories. *Language, 59*, 251–270.

Bybee, J. L., Perkins, R., & Pagliuca, W. (1994). *The evolution of grammar: tense, aspect and modality in the languages of the world*. Chicago: University of Chicago Press.

Bybee, J. L., & Thompson, S.A. (1997). Three frequency effects in syntax. *Berkeley Linguistics Society, 23*, 378–388.

Casenhiser, D. & Goldberg, A. E. (2005). Fast mapping of a phrasal form and meaning. *Developmental Science, 8*(6), 500–508.

Chomsky, N. (1965). *Aspects of the theory of syntax*. Cambridge, MA: MIT Press.

Croft, W. (2001). *Radical construction grammar: syntactic theory in typological perspective*. Oxford: Oxford University Press.

De Saussure, F. (1915/1966). *Course in general linguistics*. New York: McGraw-Hill.

Eddington, D. (2000). Spanish stress assignment within the analogical model of language. *Language, 76*, 92–109.

Ellis, N. C. (1996). Sequencing in SLA: phonological memory, chunking and points of order. *Studies in Second Language Acquisition, 18*, 91–126.

Ellis, N. C. (2002). Frequency effects in language processing: a review with implications for theories of implicit and explicit language acquisition. *Studies in Second Language Acquisition, 24*(2), 143–188.

Ellis, N. C. (2006a). Language acquisition as rational contingency learning. *Applied Linguistics, 27*, 1–24.

Ellis, N. C. (2006b). Selective attention and transfer phenomena in SLA: Contingency, cue competition, salience, overshadowing, blocking and perceptual learning. *Applied Linguistics, 27,* 164–194.

Erman, B., & Warren, B. (2000). The idiom principle and the open choice principle. *Text, 20,* 29–62.

Fillmore, C. J., Kay, P., & O'Connor, M. C. (1988). Regularity and idiomaticity in grammatical constructions: the case of *let alone. Language, 64,* 501–538.

Goldberg, A. E. (1995). *Constructions: a construction grammar approach to argument structure.* Chicago: University of Chicago Press.

Goldberg, A. E. (2003). Constructions: a new theoretical approach to language. *Trends in Cognitive Science, 7,* 219–224.

Goldberg, A. E., Casenhiser, D. M., & Sethuraman, N. (2004). Learning argument structure generalizations. *Cognitive Linguistics, 15,* 289–316.

Guillaume, P. (1927/1973). The development of formal elements in the child's speech. In C. A. Ferguson and D. I. Slobin (Eds.), *Studies of Child Language Development* (pp. 240–251). New York: Holt, Rinehart and Winston.

Hay, J., & Baayen, H. (2002). Parsing and productivity. In G. Booij & J. van Marle (Eds.), *Yearbook of Morphology 2001* (pp. 203–235). Dordrecht: Klewer Academic.

Hopper, P., & Traugott, E. (2003). *Grammaticalization* (2nd ed.). Cambridge: Cambridge University Press.

Kotovsky, L., and Gentner, D. (1996). Comparison and categorization in the development of relational similarity. *Child Development, 67,* 2,797–2,822.

Krott, A., Baayen, R. H., & Schreuder, R. (2001). Analogy in morphology: modeling the choice of linking morphemes in Dutch. *Linguistics, 39,* 51–93.

Lakoff, G. (1987). *Women, fire and dangerous things.* Chicago: University of Chicago Press.

Langacker, R. (1987). *Foundations of cognitive grammar, Vol. 1: Theoretical prerequisites.* Stanford: Stanford University Press.

Langacker, R. (2000). A dynamic usage-based model. In M. Barlow & S. Kemmer (Eds.), *Usage-based models of language* (pp. 1–63). Stanford: CSLI.

Lewis, M. (1993). The Lexical Approach. Hove: Language Teaching Publications.

Long, M. H. (2003). Stabilization and fossilization in interlanguage development. In C. J. Doughty & M. H. Long (Eds.), *Handbook of Second Language Acquisition* (pp. 487–536). Oxford: Blackwell.

MacWhinney, B. (1978). *The acquisition of morphophonology.* Monographs of the Society for Research in Child Development, no. 174, Vol. 43.

Mańczak, W. (1980). Laws of analogy. In J. Fisiak (Ed.), *Historical morphology* (pp. 283–288). Berlin: Mouton.

Meillet, A. (1912/1958). L'évolution des formes grammaticales. *Scientia 12,* No. 26, 6. Reprinted in Meillet 1958, *Linguistique historique et linguistique générale.* Paris: Champion.

Moder, C. A. (1992). Productivity and categorization in morphological classes. Ph.D. diss., SUNY at Buffalo.

Pawley, A., & Syder, F. H. (1983). Two puzzles for linguistic theory: nativelike selection and nativelike fluency. In J. C. Richards & R. W. Schmidt (Eds.), *Language and communication* (pp. 191–226). Longman: London.

Richards, J. C. and T. S. Rodgers. (2001). *Approaches and methods in language teaching.* (2nd ed.). Cambridge: Cambridge University Press.

Rumelhart, D. E., & McClelland, J. L. (1986). On learning the past tenses of English verbs: implicit rules or parallel distributed processing? In J. L. McClelland, D. E. Rumelhart, & the PDP Research Group (Eds.), *Parallel distributed processing: explorations in the microstructure of cognition* (pp. 216–271). Cambridge, MA: MIT Press.

Schmitt, N. (Ed.) (2004). *Formulaic sequences.* Amsterdam: John Benjamins.

Simpson, R., & Ellis, N. (2005). *An Academic Formulas List (AFL): extraction, validation, prioritization.* Paper presented at the Phraseology, Louvain-la-Neuve, Belgium.

Simpson, R., & Mendis, D. (2003). A corpus-based study of idioms in academic speech. *TESOL Quarterly, 3,* 419–441.

Sinclair, J. (1991). *Corpus, concordance, collocation.* Oxford: Oxford University Press.

Skousen, R. (1989). *Analogical modeling of language.* Kluwer: Dordrecht.

Tottie, G. (1991). Lexical diffusion in syntactic change: frequency as a determinant of linguistic conservatism in the development of negation in English. In D. Kastovsky (Ed.), *Historical English syntax* (pp. 439–467). Berlin: Mouton de Gruyter.

Traugott, E. C. (1989). On the rise of epistemic meanings in English: an example of subjectification in semantic change. *Language, 65,* 31–55.

Wray, A. (2002). *Formulaic language and the lexicon.* Cambridge: Cambridge University Press.

Part III

COGNITIVE LINGUISTICS, SECOND LANGUAGE ACQUISITION, AND L2 INSTRUCTION

11

LEARNING TO TALK ABOUT MOTION IN A FOREIGN LANGUAGE

Teresa Cadierno

1 Introduction and theoretical background

This chapter discusses how cognitive semantics and, in particular, Talmy's typological framework for the expression of motion events (1985, 1991, 2000a & b) provide a fruitful basis for the investigation of how adult language learners from different native languages (L1s) come to talk about motion in a second language (L2). It is argued that this line of inquiry can make an important contribution to our understanding of the processes by which L2 learners establish form–meaning connections during second language acquisition (SLA) by: (a) focusing on a rather neglected area within SLA research, namely, the study of how adult language learners come to express spatial relations in an L2; (b) allowing for the systematic investigation of cross-linguistic influence in SLA; and (c) providing an alternative account of linguistic meaning to that commonly held within SLA research. Furthermore, it is argued that the investigation of Talmy's typological framework within the field of SLA can shed light on the issue of linguistic relativity as formulated by Slobin's (1996a) thinking-for-speaking hypothesis, by examining the ease and difficulty with which adult L2 learners adapt to their thinking-for-speaking in a new language.

The chapter is divided as follows. The first section presents the theoretical background to this line of investigation. This includes a general introduction to cognitive semantics, to Talmy's typological classification of motion events, and to Slobin's thinking-for-speaking hypothesis. The second section reviews empirical research inspired by Talmy's typological framework on first language production and reception. With respect to the former, research has focused on how motion is coded in the oral speech and gestures of monolingual speakers, as well as in novels written in typologically different languages, and in their translation from one language type into another. With respect to the latter, research has examined the extent to which different patterns of production reflect different conceptual structures in the minds of speakers from typologically different languages. This research has looked, then, at possible typological influences on native speakers' memory and categorization of motion events. This second section ends with a brief presentation of some of the refinements to Talmy's typology that have been discussed in the literature. The third and final section discusses the implications of Talmy's and Slobin's work for the study of adult SLA. First, it shows how this research can constitute the basis for theoretically motivated hypotheses on how learners from typologically different L1s talk about motion in L2 and, secondly, it reviews empirical research conducted on the acquisition of motion events in L2. The chapter ends with a discussion of future lines of research on motion events within the typological approach discussed.

1.1 Cognitive semantics

Cognitive semantics, which is part of the larger enterprise of Cognitive Linguistics, is an approach to linguistic meaning which appeared in the 1970s as the result of a dissatisfaction with existing formal semantic theories and of a growing wish to explicitly focus on meaning as a cognitive phenomenon (Allwood & Gärdenfors, 1999). Most formal approaches to semantics assume an objectivist philosophical view of meaning in that semantic structure is seen as a truth-conditional relationship between an utterance and an objective reality. One of the main disadvantages of the truth-conditional model is that it can only account for propositions involving descriptions of states of affairs (Sinha, 1999; Evans & Green, 2006). Other types of frequent non-declarative and "irrealis" expressions such as performatives, metaphors, and counterfactuals cannot adequately been described by truth-conditional semantics.

An important consequence of the view of meaning adopted by formal semantics is that it excludes conceptualization from consideration. In contrast to this view, cognitive semantics places human cognition at the centre of linguistic description, and considers linguistic meaning as a manifestation of conceptual structure. Cognitive semantics does not constitute a unified framework but consists instead of a number of slightly different approaches, which share on the one hand a common focus on the relationship between language, meaning, and cognition, and on the other the following three guiding principles (Evans & Green, 2006)[1]:

1   *Conceptual structure is embodied*. This means that ". . . the structures used to put together our conceptual systems grow out of bodily

experience and make sense in terms of it" (Lakoff, 1987: xiv–xv), a philosophical view named experientalism by this author. For example, our understanding of spatial relations is assumed to be based on kinaesthetic image schemas, which are relatively simple structures that constantly recur in our everyday bodily experience (Johnson, 1987; Lakoff, 1987). Of special relevance here is the Source-Path-Goal schema, which is at the base of our understanding of motion, and which is grounded in the embodied experience of moving from one place to another in specific directions.[2] The goal of cognitive semanticists is, therefore, to build a theory of conceptual structure that is consonant with how we experience the world, how we perceive it, and conceptualize it.

2   *Semantic structure is conceptual structure.* In other words, meaning is equated with conceptualization[3] (i.e. mental experience) which is to be interpreted broadly, including all facets of sensorimotor and emotive experience, and apprehension of the social, linguistic, and cultural context (Langacker, 1996). Cognitive semanticists thus set out to explore the ways in which meaning is motivated by human perceptual and conceptual processes, such as figure-ground organization, meta-phorical and metonymic mappings, idealized cognitive models, view-point, construal, mental spaces, and prototypes, all of which have been referred to as "backstage cognition" by Fauconnier (1994).

3   *Meaning representation is encyclopedic.* That is, everything we know about an entity can be regarded as contributing to the meaning of an expression that designates it. The meanings associated with a given expression draw upon complex bodies of knowledge—called "cognitive domains" by Langacker (1987), "frames" by Fillmore (1975, 1985) and "idealized cognitive models" by Lakoff (1987)—which are mental representations of how the world is organized. This means that a sharp distinction between semantics and pragmatics, as between linguistic and extralinguistic knowledge, is not attainable (Langacker, 1987).

A last—though not least—characteristic of cognitive semantics is that, in contrast to most present-day semantic theories, semantic structure is not viewed as compositional, i.e. the meaning of complex expressions is not thought to be uniquely determined by the meaning of its constituents and the mode of combining them. Semantic non-compositionality is not only thought to apply to idioms (e.g. *spic and span*) but also to ordinary expressions (for examples, see Gruber, 1965 and Fillmore, 1982).

In sum, cognitive semantics—and Cognitive Linguistics in general—view language as intrinsically linked to human cognition and general cognitive processes, and not, therefore, as an autonomous cognitive faculty. Language is seen as symbolic in nature, and consequently all linguistic expressions (i.e. lexical, morphological, and syntactic) are viewed as symbolic units consisting of conventionalized form–meaning mappings used to communicative purposes (Langacker, 1987). This provides semantics with a central role in linguistic description, i.e. linguistic meaning is an essential part of grammar. Semantic structure is not viewed as a truth-conditional relationship between a linguistic expression and an objective reality but as largely reflecting conceptual structure, and as embodied—i.e. grounded—in the shared human experience of bodily existence. Finally, meaning is considered to be encyclopedic and constructional, i.e. non-compositional in nature.

1.2 Motion events: Talmy's typological framework

One researcher whose work on cognitive semantics has been very influential is Leonard Talmy. In his work, compiled and extended in the two volumes of *Toward a cognitive semantics* (2000a & b), Talmy has examined the linguistic representation of conceptual structure and discussed how semantic structure reflects the language user's conceptual system. This system is considered to be made up of two subsystems: the structuring system, which provides the structure or skeleton for the description of particular scenes—events or situations—and the content system, which provides the rich content or details pertaining to the scenes. The structuring system is based upon a limited set of schematic systems, which relate to fundamental aspects of embodied sensory-perceptual experience: (a) the configurational system, which structures the temporal and spatial properties associated with particular scenes (e.g. the division of scenes into parts and the participants involved); (b) the perspectival system, which specifies the spatial and/or temporal perspective from which scenes are viewed; (c) the attentional system, which specifies how the speakers intend the hearers to direct their attention towards the different entities participating in given scenes; and (d) the force-dynamic system, which refers to the way in which objects are conceived relative to the exertion of force.

One particular semantic domain that Talmy has investigated in great detail is the motion domain (Talmy, 1985, 1991, 2000a & b), where he has examined the typological patterns in which the conceptual structure of motion events is linguistically encoded in different languages. In his analysis of motion events, Talmy addresses the systematic relations in language between meaning and surface expression, i.e. between different elements within the domain of meaning and different linguistic forms, including both "open" class elements such as motion verbs (e.g. *go*, *climb*, *run*), and "closed" class elements such as satellites (*up*, *down*, *in*, *out*).[4]

A motion event has been characterized by Talmy (2000b, p. 25) as ". . . a situation containing motion and the continuation of a stationary location alike . . .". With respect to the configurational system of a motion event,

Talmy (2000b) made a distinction between a basic motion event and an associated co-event. The basic motion event consists of four internal components, the first two of which reflect a pattern of attentional distribution described under the schematic attentional system, namely, the "center-periphery" pattern[5]: (a) Figure: the moving or stationary object; (b) Ground: the object in relation to which the Figure moves or is located; (c) Path: the path followed or the site occupied by the Figure with respect to the Ground; and (d) Motion: the presence *per se* of motion or locatedness in the event. The motion component thus refers to the occurrence (MOVE) or non-occurrence (BELOC) of translational motion, i.e. motion where ". . . an object's basic location shifts from one point to another in space." (Talmy, 2000b: 35). In addition to these internal components, a motion event can be associated with an external co-event, which typically includes two components: (e) Manner: the manner in which the motion takes place; and (f) Cause: the cause of its occurrence.

Talmy (2000b) offers the following four examples to illustrate the components: *The pencil rolled off the table*, *The pencil blew off the table*, *The pencil lay on the table*, and *The pencil stuck on the table* (after I glued it). In all sentences *the pencil* functions as the Figure, *the table* as the Ground and the particles *off* and *on* express Path. The verbs in the first two sentences (*rolled, blew*) express motion while the verbs in the last two sentences (*lay, stuck*) express location. In addition, the verbs *rolled* and *lay* express Manner of motion whereas the verbs *blew* and *stuck* express Cause of motion.

According to Talmy (1985, 1991, 2000b), different languages package the semantic components of a motion event in different ways. Based on the lexicalization (also called conflation) patterns that take place, Talmy has proposed a typological classification of the characteristic[6] meaning–form mappings for the expression of motion events in different languages of the world. Talmy (2000b) identified three main typological patterns:

a   Motion + Co-event: this pattern is characteristic of one group of languages, which include all branches of the Indo-European family except Romance languages, as well as Finno-Ugric, Chinese, Ojibwa, and Warlbiri. These languages have been referred to as "satellite-framed languages" (S-languages) by Talmy (1991, 2000b), since the core schema of a motion event, i.e. the path, is characteristically coded in the satellite, whereas the fact of motion and the co-event are coded in the verb root. The following two English examples involving the occurrence of motion (MOVE) illustrate this typological pattern (Talmy, 2000b, p. 28): *The rock slid/rolled/bounced down the hall* (MOVE + Manner) and *The napkin blew off the table* (MOVE + Cause).

b   Motion + Path: this pattern is characteristic of Romance and Semitic languages, as well as Japanese, Korean, Turkish, Tamil, Polynesian, Nez

Perce, and Caddo. These languages have been referred to by Talmy (1991, 2000b) as "verb-framed languages" (V-languages), since the path is characteristically coded in the verb together with the fact of motion. If a co-event of manner or cause is expressed in the same sentence, this is coded in a separate constituent, usually by means of an adverbial or a gerund. The following Spanish example, involving the occurrence of motion (MOVE), illustrates this typological pattern (Talmy, 2000b, pp. 49–50): *La botella entró a la cueva (flotando)* (The bottle MOVED-in to the cave (floating) (lit.) or "The bottle floated into the cave").

c Motion + Figure: this pattern, though characteristic of American Indian languages, is also present in languages such as English, as the following sentences show (Talmy, 2000b, p. 57): *It rained in through the bedroom window* and *I spat into the cuspidor*. In the first sentence, the verb *rain* refers to rain moving, whereas in the second sentence, the verb *spit* refers to causing spit to move.

These lexicalization patterns, however, reflect general tendencies and not absolute differences across languages. As indicated by Talmy (2000b), occasional forms of alternative conflation patterns can occur in a given language, such as the presence in English of Latinate verbs (e.g. *enter, descend, ascend*) which conflate motion and path. In addition, other languages, such as Spanish, evidence a split system of conflation, i.e. two different lexicalization patterns for different types of motion events. The following examples illustrate the Spanish split system in contrast to the consistent English pattern:

> *The bottle floated towards the cave*
> *La botella flotó hacia la cueva*
>
> *Mary ran up to the house*
> *María corrió hasta la casa*
>
> *The bottle floated out of the cave*
> **La botella flotó fuera de la cueva*
> *La botella salió flotando de la cueva*
>
> *Mary run into the house*
> **María corrió dentro de la casa*
> *María entró en la casa corriendo*

According to Aske (1989), the difference between the two languages lies in that English allows manner verbs to appear both with locative phrases, i.e. phrases that predicate a location of the whole proposition (e.g. *towards the cave*), and telic phrases, i.e. phrases that predicate an end-state of the figure (e.g. *into the house*). Spanish, on the other hand, only allows manner verbs to appear with the former type of phrases. Slobin and Hoiting (1994) further note that Aske's telic paths always involved paths that involved the crossing of a boundary on the part of the figure. So in V-languages such as Spanish, a constraint seems to operate by which motion and manner cannot be conflated into the verb in boundary-crossing situations, such as entering, exiting and crossing. In these languages ". . . crossing a spatial boundary is conceived of as a change of state, and (that) state changes require an independent predicate . . ." (Slobin, 1997, p. 441).

According to Talmy (1985, 2000b), one of the main consequences of the typology of motion events is that languages differ with respect to the amount of information and type of information that can be presented in the foreground and in the background. He refers to this cognitive phenomenon as salience, i.e. ". . . the degree to which a component of meaning, due to its type of linguistic representation, emerges into the foreground of attention or, on the contrary, forms part of the semantic background where it attracts little direct attention" (Talmy, 2000b, p. 128). According to Talmy, other things being equal, a semantic element is backgrounded if it is expressed in the main verb root or in any other closed-class element such as a satellite. In any other position, it is foregrounded. Because of the different lexicalization patterns they characteristically use, S- and V-languages crucially differ in the way they present information. In S-languages both manner and path are characteristically expressed using backgrounding constituents, whereas in V-languages it is only the path that is characteristically expressed using a background constituent.

This principle of background according to constituent type has important consequences. Firstly, backgrounded information tends to be more readily expressed than foregrounded information. Secondly, information content that is backgrounded can be included in a sentence at a lower cognitive cost than informational content that is foregrounded. Consequently, languages which can express particular information in a backgrounded fashion (such as conflating motion and manner in English, e.g. *staggered, stumbled*) can easily pack more of such information into a sentence than languages which present that information in a foregrounded fashion.[7] This phenomenon can be attested in the difference with which S- and V-languages pack the different motion components within a sentence. English can accumulate several elements of backgrounded path information accompanying just one verb, such as in *The man ran back down into the cellar*, whereas Spanish can background, in the verb, only one of the four English components, as the following possible translations for the English sentence demonstrate (Talmy, 2000b, p. 130): *El hombre corrió al sótano* ("The man ran to the cellar"), *El hombre volvió al sótano corriendo* ("The man went back to the cellar running"), *El hombre bajó al sótano corriendo* ("The man went down to the cellar running"), and *El hombre entró al sótano corriendo* ("The man went into the cellar running").

1.3 Slobin's thinking-for-speaking hypothesis

As previously discussed, a key principle within cognitive semantics is that semantic structure is thought to reflect the language user's conceptual system. In Langacker's words (1987, pp. 6–7), "the semantic value of an expression does not reside in the inherent properties of the entity or situation it describes, but critically involves as well the way we choose to think about this entity or situation and mentally portray it." Critically, however, the language users' conceptualization of a given situation is often influenced by the particular language that they speak, i.e. by the grammatical and lexical resources that are available for use in given semantic domains. This is so because, as indicated by Slobin (1996b), our experiences of the world are not only filtered into verbalized events through the choice of the individual speakers' perspective but also through the particular set of options provided by the particular language we are speaking. Language thus directs our attention—while speaking—to the dimensions of experience that are coded in grammatical categories.

In his thinking-for-speaking hypothesis, Slobin (1996b, p. 75) claims that ". . . [t]here is a special kind of thinking that is intimately tied to language—namely, the thinking that is carried out on-line, in the process of speaking." Thinking-for-speaking then ". . . involves picking those characteristics of objects and events that (a) fit some conceptualization of the event, and (b) are readily encodable in the language" (Slobin, 1996b, p. 76). Even though Slobin uses the label "thinking-for-speaking," his hypothesis embraces all forms of linguistic production (speaking, writing, signing) and reception (listening, reading, viewing) as well as a range of mental processes, such as understanding, imaging, and remembering (Slobin, 2003).

Slobin's thinking-for-speaking hypothesis constitutes a more cautious and dynamic view of the relation between language and thought than that of Whorf (1940 (1956)), who related language to a particular world-view, and that of contemporary scholars such as Lucy (1992, 1996) and Levinson (2003), who advocate the influence of language on non-linguistic cognition, i.e. on speakers' patterns of categorization and memory. Slobin's hypothesis follows, on the other hand, a tradition in anthropological linguistics which is less deterministic in nature and which is exemplified in the work of Boas (1911) who suggested that ". . . any utterance is a selective schematization of a concept—a schematization that is, in some ways, dependent on the grammaticized meanings of the speaker's particular language, recruited for purposes of verbal expression" (as cited in Slobin, 1996b, pp. 75–76).

According to Slobin (1996b), in acquiring a native language, children learn particular ways of thinking-for-speaking—that is, they learn to pay attention to the specific dimensions of experience which are obligatorily enshrined in the grammatical categories of their language. The language(s) that we speak train us, then, to pay different kinds of attention to particular details of events and situations when talking about them. This is so because, in contrast to the position defended by objectivist semantics and in line with the position adopted by cognitive semantics, the language(s) that we learn as children are not neutral coding systems of an objective reality but ". . . a subjective experience to the world of human experience, and this orientation **affects the ways in which we think while we are speaking**" (Slobin 1996b, p. 91). As pointed out by Slobin himself, this training carried out during childhood could be exceptionally resistant to restructuring in adult second language acquisition, a point that will be discussed in the last section of this chapter.

2 Motion events in first language production and reception

As indicated in the introduction, Talmy's typological framework for the lexicalization patterns of motion events has constituted the basis for a wide variety of empirical research on language use, which has focused on first language production—both oral and written—and reception. This section summarizes the main findings of this research, which is cross-linguistic in nature and which has, for the most part, extended Talmy's sentence level analysis of motion events to the realm of narrative discourse.

2.1 Research on oral production

One research area where Talmy's typological classification on motion events has proved to be extremely fruitful is the investigation of whether the typological patterns found in different languages of the world have an impact on how their native speakers—both children and adults—talk about motion. This research includes analyses of both elicited and spontaneous oral speech.

Central to this line of research is the work of Slobin and his colleagues, who have examined the production of oral narratives elicited by means of the wordless picture book, *Frog, where are you?*, i.e. the so-called "frog story" (Mayer, 1969). A key piece of work is Berman and Slobin (1994) which constitutes an extensive cross-linguistic and developmental investigation of native speakers from three main groups (preschool, school-age, and adults) and from both S-languages (English and German) and V-languages (Hebrew, Spanish, and Turkish). The results of this research, which have been discussed and elaborated on in Slobin

(1996a, 1997, 1998, 2000, 2003), showed that children learning typologically different languages differed strikingly by age three in the way they talked about motion. These differences, which are derived from the characteristic lexicalization patterns involved, resulted in distinct rhetorical styles:

1   Speakers of S-languages used a greater variety of motion verbs as compared to speakers of V-languages, primarily due to the higher variety of manner of motion verbs, a point to be discussed below.
2   Speakers of S-languages exhibited a higher degree of elaboration in their description of path of motion than speakers of V-languages, i.e. they tended to provide richer and more detailed descriptions of path trajectories. This was evidenced by a more frequent mention of ground elements and a more frequent use of the so-called event conflation, i.e. the incorporation of the different composites of locative trajectories (path and ground, including source, medium, and goal) within single clauses (e.g. *The deer threw the boy over a cliff into the pond*), a phenomenon referred to as maximum windowing over the whole path by Talmy (2000b).
3   Speakers of S-languages displayed a relatively higher attention to the dynamics of movement along paths, as compared to speakers of V-languages who exhibited a relatively higher attention to scene setting and static descriptions. Speakers of S-languages tended, therefore, to specify the details of trajectories, i.e. provide rich path descriptions, and leave the settings to be inferred (i.e. *The deer threw him off over a cliff into the water*, where the trajectories described allow the listener to infer that there is a cliff above the water), whereas speakers of V-languages tended to describe aspects of the static scene where the movement took place, leaving trajectories to be inferred (e.g. *Lo tiró. Por suerte, abajo, estaba el río. El niño cayó en el agua* (Slobin, 1996a, p. 204) ([The deer] threw him. Luckily, below, was the river. The boy fell into the water).
4   Speakers of S-languages exhibited a higher degree of elaboration of manner of motion than speakers of V-languages. This was evidenced by a more frequent use of manner of motion verbs (token analysis) and a higher variety of these types of verbs (type analysis). As suggested by Slobin (1997, 2000), languages seem to have a "two-tiered" lexicon of manner verbs: neutral, everyday verbs such as *walk, run*, and *fly*, and more expressive or exceptional verbs such as *dash, swoop*, and *scramble*. S-languages have a more extensive and elaborated second-tier than V-languages. Manner of motion is, then, more salient in S- than in V- languages (Slobin, 1997, 2000) and, consequently, speakers of S-languages are trained to make finer manner distinctions than speakers of V-languages.

The inter-typological differences found on elicited oral narratives have received considerable support by research conducted with alternative methodologies, such as the use of elicited non-narrative tasks and the analysis of naturalistic spontaneous speech. With respect to the former, a couple of studies reported in Naigles, Eisenberg, Kako, Highter, and McGraw (1998) compared the expression of manner and path of motion by English and Spanish adult speakers by means of both picture and videotaped stimuli. The results of the studies were quite consistent with Berman and Slobin's (1994) findings, in that English speakers were found to use more manner verbs than path verbs, whereas Spanish speakers tended to use more path verbs than manner verbs. These results are thus in consonance with the characteristic lexicalization patterns of the two types of languages. Additionally, in line with Talmy's description of Spanish as having a split system of conflation, different types of motion events were more or less likely to elicit path or manner verbs in the Spanish speakers. Events involving telic paths and boundary-crossing situations tended to elicit path verbs, whereas events involving locative paths and non boundary-crossing situations tended to elicit manner verbs, a finding that is consistent with Aske's (1989) and Slobin and Hoiting's (1994) analyses of Spanish.

With respect to the latter, studies by Slobin (1997, 2000), and by Bowerman and her colleagues (e.g. Choi & Bowerman, 1991; Bowerman, de León, and Choi, 1995) examined the spontaneous speech of adults and children from one S-language (English) and several V-languages (e.g. Spanish, Turkish, French, Italian, and Korean). These studies revealed language-specific patterns of talking about motion. For example, the speech of English speakers included many more manner distinctions than the speech produced by speakers of V-languages (Slobin, 1997, 2000). Similarly, English-speaking children relied heavily on path particles for the expression of both spontaneous and caused motion events, whereas Korean-speaking children distinguished strictly between words for the two types of events, a difference which directly corresponds to the way spatial meanings are structured in their respective languages (Choi & Bowerman, 1991; Bowerman et al., 1995). These findings challenge the widespread view that children initially map spatial words to non-linguistic concepts and suggest, instead, the influence of the semantic organization of the input language from the beginning.

In sum, the research presented above provides strong empirical evidence for clear differences in the way in which speakers—both children and adults—of S- and V-languages orally encode motion events in their native languages. As argued by Bowerman and colleagues as well as by Slobin, these findings point to the important part played by the child's input language in his/her organization of the conceptual space for purposes of thinking-for-speaking.

2.2 Research on written production—Analyses of novels and novel translations

In addition to research on oral speech, Talmy's (1985, 1991, 2000a & b) typological classification has constituted the basis for a number of studies (e.g. Slobin, 1996a, 1997, 1998, 2000, 2005b) which have examined the expression of motion events in written speech, both in literary fiction texts written in S- and V-languages, and in translations from and into these two types of languages. The results of this research provides additional empirical evidence for the different ways in which speakers of S- and V-languages lexicalize the various semantic components of a motion event.

With respect to the former, Slobin (1996a) compared the narration of motion events in novels written in English and Spanish. Overall, S-language novels contained a wider variety of manner verbs and a larger amount of ground elements (source, medium, goal) mentioned per clause than Spanish narratives. Furthermore, when examining whether novels written in the two types of languages differed with respect to the use of alternative lexical means of encoding manner of motion (e.g. adverbs of manner, descriptions of the internal state or the physical condition of moving entities that would allow the reader to infer manner of motion, and descriptions of environmental conditions that might affect manner of movement), Özçalişkan and Slobin (2003) found that, overall, S-language writers still provided more manner information than V-language writers. In English, these alternative means of conveying manner information typically accompanied manner of motion verbs, thereby elaborating the manner already encoded in the verb, whereas, in Turkish, they typically qualified non-manner-of-motion verbs, thereby apparently compensating for the characteristic lexicalization pattern of this language.

With respect to the latter, Slobin (1996a, 1997, 2005b) analyzed translations into English and Spanish of Spanish and English novels, as well as translations of one chapter of *The Hobbit* (Tolkien, 1937) into several S- and V-languages (e.g. S-languages: Dutch, German, and Russian; V-languages: French, Portuguese, Spanish). With respect to descriptions of path trajectories, Slobin (1996a) showed that, when moving from an S-language into a V-language, translators tended to translate the original compact path-ground depictions either by analyzing the path in several verbs (English original: . . . she **went** downstairs and out of the house (Fowles, 1969) vs. Spanish translation: . . . ella **bajó** la escalera y **salió** de la casa, (lit.) ". . . she **descended** the staircase and **exited** from the house" (Fowles, 1981)), or by incorporating relative clauses which provided static information (English original: I . . . **climbed** up the path over the cliffs towards the rest of the people (Du Maurier, 1938) vs. Spanish translation: Tomé el sendero **que conducía al lugar donde estaba la gente**, (lit.) "I took the path **that led to the place where the people were**" (Du Maurier, 1959)). When moving from a V-language into an S-language, by contrast, translators followed the opposite strategy, namely, to compact the various directional motion verbs found in the original into a complex path expression, as the following English translation of a Turkish novel shows (Slobin, 1997, p. 440): Turkish original: *Igdir ovasin-dan Basköy-e gecti Ahuri koyagin-a cikti, ora-dan Ahuri yaylasin-a gecti,* (lit.) "Igdir plain Basköy **passed** Ahuri vale **ascended** there Ahuri plateau **passed**" (Kemal 1970, p. 21) vs. English translation: *They swept along the plain of Igdir, on to Bashkoy, though the Ahuri Vale and up to the Ahuri plateau* (Kemal 1975, p. 22).

With respect to descriptions of Manner of motion, Slobin (1996a) revealed that translators moving from an S-language into a V-language tended to omit manner information, whereas translators moving from a V-language into an S-language tended to add manner information to the original. So, for example, *They plunged across the road into the long grass on the other side* (taken from *A proper marriage* by Doris Lessing) was translated as *Cruzaron el camino hacia la hierba alta del otro lado,* (lit.) "They **crossed** the road towards the long grass on the other side." In contrast, the following sentence from Cervantes, *Cuando don Quijote salió de la venta, . . .,* (lit.) "When don Quixote **left** the inn . . .", was translated into German as *Als Don Quijote aus der Schenke ritt,* (lit.) "When Don Quijote **rode** out of the inn . . .", "When Don Quijote **rode** from the inn . . .". Furthermore, the analyses of the translations of *The Hobbit* into different S- and V-languages (Slobin, 1997) revealed that the former were characterized by a wider variety of manner of motion verbs and a higher use of alternative lexical means of expressing this semantic component. These differences provide clear evidence of the differing degree of manner salience in the two types of languages (Slobin, 2005b).

In sum, the analyses of both written speech and oral speech clearly indicate that texts produced in S-languages are richer in path and manner descriptions than texts produced in V-languages. These results have been interpreted to be primarily a consequence of the distinct typological patterns of the two languages. S-languages provide their speakers with a rich set of satellites which encode path, i.e. the motion event core schema, leaving the verb "free" to encode manner of motion. Satellites can be accumulated in relation to a single verb within a clause, allowing for the specification of different backgrounded path information. V-languages, on the other hand, tend to encode path in the main verb, with the result that each type of change of location is expressed by a separate verb in a separate clause. Manner of motion can be backgrounded in the main verb in non boundary-crossing situations. In boundary-crossing situations, by contrast, manner information must be encoded separately in a foregrounded fashion by means of a heavier construction, i.e. a gerundive constituent or a prepositional phrase. As a result, manner information is frequently omitted unless it is explicitly on focus.

As indicated by Slobin (1997, p. 443), each type of lexicalization pattern engenders a type of style, a style that is based on language-specific constraints but which goes beyond them. A case in point is the V-languages' lack of accumulation of several ground elements per verb in non-boundary situations, a pattern that is, in fact, allowed by their syntax. As explained by Slobin (1997), the combined effect in these languages of a lexicon of path verbs and the boundary-crossing constraint would result in a narrative style that becomes a habit or norm, and which would go beyond what specific lexicalization patterns would favor or allow.

2.3 Research on speech and gesture

Talmy's (1985, 1991, 2000b) typological classification, and Slobin's thinking-for-speaking hypothesis have further constituted the point of departure for research examining the simultaneous use of speech and gesture in the semantic domain of motion. In a series of publications, McNeill and his collaborators (e.g. McNeill, 1992, 1997, 2000; McNeill & Duncan, 2000) have stressed the importance of examining gestures in conjunction with speech as these can provide us with "... new insights into the nature of language and communication, how we produce speech, and how we use it in thinking" (McNeill, 1997, p. 255). The thinking-for-speaking process is, therefore, thought to bring together two simultaneous modes of mental representations, namely, the visuo-spatial/actional and the language-like.

In their research, McNeill and collaborators have compared the speech-gesture system used by native speakers of three languages, one S-language—English—and two V-languages—Spanish and Chinese—when describing motion events via storytellings based on previously seen animated cartoons. In line with the results obtained for oral speech, this research has revealed crucial cross-linguistic differences in the gestures used by native speakers—both children and adults—from typologically different languages, differences that involve the semantic components of manner and path of motion.[8]

With respect to manner of motion, English speakers were found to use gestures to modulate lexical manner, either reinforcing it (in cases where manner has an important communicative weight) or downplaying it (when it does not). When reinforcing manner of motion, English speakers' gestures typically encoded path and manner information in synchrony with the manner verb used. When downplaying manner of motion, the gestures lacked any manner content, and did not synchronize with the manner verb, i.e. the gestures only expressed path content and coincided with path satellites. Spanish speakers, on the other hand, were found to use abundant gestural manner without linguistically encoded anchors, creating a sort of "manner fog," i.e. entire motion event descriptions blanketed with repeated manner gestures in the total absence of spoken manner. In English, then, gestural manner functions as a "speech strategy" to modulate the lexical system of this language, which almost obligatorily codes manner information in the verb, whereas in Spanish, gestural manner functions as a "gesture strategy" expanding the encoding resources of this language.

With respect to path of motion, English speakers were found to break curvilinear paths into a series of short straight-line segments, so that each gesture embodied the distinct path segment coded by the satellites. Spanish speakers, in contrast, were found to preserve the curvilinearity of the path, even in cases involving highly complex paths. Additionally, differences were found with respect to paths involving boundary-crossing. English gestures, as in speech, assimilated boundaries to other path segments, while Spanish gestures removed the boundaries from the path representation, either by omitting the boundary altogether and describing the path as going up to the border, or by adding a special gesture which focused on the linguistic reference to the boundary-crossing as such (e.g. *meter* "insert").

Differences in the simultaneous use of speech and gestures by speakers of two typologically different languages—English and Turkish—were also found by Özyürek and Kita (1999) and Kita and Özyürek (2003). For example, speakers of English were found to use more manner-path conflated gestures than speakers of V-languages, whereas speakers of Turkish tended to use more gestures encoding manner-only and path-only than speakers of S-languages.

To conclude, the research on the simultaneous use of speech and gesture reviewed above suggests that different languages embody different models of visuo-spatial representation during speaking. Thinking-for-speaking in typologically different languages, thus, differs with respect to the visuo-spatial representation of manner of motion, path structure, and boundary-crossing. As indicated by McNeill (2000, p. 57), these differences in gesture use "are predictable products of languages at different points in Talmy's satellite- and verb-framed typology."

2.4 Research on linguistic reception: effects of typology on memory and categorization

In addition to the research on linguistic production discussed above, a number of studies have examined whether the lexicalization patterns of S- and V-languages affect the ways in which their speakers remember and classify motion events. This research has attempted to find empirical evidence to show whether the different patterns of production evidenced by speakers of S- and V-languages lead to differences in their conceptualization of motion events, as measured by non-linguistic tasks. The results of this research indicate that the cognitive effects of typology on non-linguistic cognition are not as uniform as those found on linguistic production.

Positive effects of typology on memory have been reported by Slobin (2000, 2003, 2005a). Monolingual native speakers of English and Spanish as well as Spanish–English bilinguals were asked to read short passages from novels—passages with no explicit mentioning of manner of motion—and later asked to describe their mental imagery of the protagonist's manner of motion. The results of the study showed that monolingual English speakers tended to experience more mental imagery of manner of motion than V-language speakers, i.e. they tended to include manner information more frequently and in richer detail. Monolingual Spanish speakers, in contrast, reported richer imagery for the setting in which the movement took place, a result that parallels that found in oral narratives (Slobin, 1996b, 1997, 2000). Interesting as well, bilingual Spanish–English speakers reported different imagery in the two languages, including more manner information in English than in Spanish, although their English reports included less manner information than their monolingual English speakers' counterparts.[9]

Similarly, differences have been found between speakers of typologically different languages in learning tasks involving categorization processes. For example, Naigles and Terrazas (1998) found that when confronted with novel motion verbs in which the verb could refer to either path or manner of motion, English speakers attributed more manner than path meanings to novel verbs, whereas Spanish speakers followed the opposite pattern. Likewise, Kersten, Meissner, Schwartz and Rivera (2003, cited in Slobin, 2005a) found that English speakers were significantly better than Spanish speakers at learning to categorize unnameable paths and manners of motion on the basis of manner of motion. These results suggest that adults of typologically different languages learn to attend to the event attributes that are characteristically encoded in their language and use that knowledge when asked to categorize the meanings of new words or new unnameable motion actions.

The results of these studies, however, contrast with the findings of some other research which has examined the effects of linguistic typology on memory and categorization by means of alternative tasks. For example, Papafragou, Massey and Gleitman (2001) and Gennari, Sloman, Malt and Fitch (2002) investigated whether the different lexicalization patterns of motion events found in one S-language (i.e. English) and two V-languages (i.e. Modern Greek and Spanish respectively) could predict how speakers of these languages performed in (a) a recognition memory task, in which subjects were asked to judge whether given stimuli depicting motion events were the same or different than other stimuli previously shown, the original stimuli having been altered by systematically changing either the path or manner of motion; and (b) a categorization task, in which subjects were shown samples of motion events and then asked to select between two choices (i.e. a same-path variant and a same-manner variant) on the basis of its similarity with the samples.

The results of both studies point to very weak effects of linguistic typology on memory and categorization. Whereas Papafragou et al. (2001) found no significant differences between English and Modern Greek speakers—both children and adults—in either of the two tasks, Gennari et al. (2002) found a language-specific effect only in the categorization task, i.e. Spanish-speaking adults made more same-path choices in the experimental condition requiring verbal encoding than English-speaking adults. Both studies concluded that thinking-for-speaking patterns do not seem to have detectable effects in non-linguistic cognition.

In sum, the effects of linguistic typology on non-linguistic cognition have received mixed empirical support. Conflicting results have been reported with respect to two key areas. As regards memory effects, there are discrepancies between Slobin's positive findings on the one hand, and the negative findings of Papafragou et al. (2001) and Gennari et al. (2002) on the other, a difference which could perhaps be attributed to the use of different methodologies, i.e. whether or not they were linked to prior reading of narrations. Secondly, in relation to categorization processes, there are discrepancies between the positive effects obtained in experiments involving learning to categorize novel words or motion actions (e.g. Naigles & Terrazas, 1998, and Kersten et al., 2003) and the weak effects found in tasks involving a match-to sample format (e.g. Papafragou et al., 2001, and Gennari et al., 2002). Even though no hard conclusions can be offered at this point to explain these conflicting results, the differences found could perhaps be attributed to the different methodologies employed in the different studies.

Overall, the results of the empirical research on language use suggest—so far—weaker empirical evidence for the effects of language typology on non-linguistic cognition than on linguistic production. Whereas crucial differences have been found in the way native speakers from typologically different languages attend to the various components of motion events in speech—oral and written—and gesture as well as in translation activities dealing with motion, the question of whether language typology has an effect on linguistic reception, that is, on native speakers' categorization and memory about motion events still remains unclear. Future research on this topic will, hopefully, help to shed more light on the issue of linguistic relativity, that is, on the relation between language and conceptualization in the semantic domain of motion.

2.5 Talmy's typological classification revisited

As evidenced by the research reviewed above, there are systematic differences in the way in which native speakers of different languages of the world encode motion events, and these differences are generally grounded in their characteristic lexicalization patterns. However, when examining the rhetorical styles that emerge in language use, different authors have pointed to intra-typological differences within a given type of language (e.g. Özçalişkan & Slobin 1998 and 2000a; Engberg-Pedersen & Trondhjem, 2004; Ibarretxe-Antuñano, 2004), as well as to the difficulty of classifying particular languages by means of a strict binary language typology that distinguishes between S- and V-languages (e.g. Bowerman et al. 1995; Brown, 2004; Zlatev & Yangklang, 2004; Ameka & Essegbey, in press). In order to account for these facts, Slobin (2004) has stressed the importance of taking into account a number of additional factors of a morpho-syntactic, psycholinguistic and pragmatic nature, such as the availability of specific linguistic forms in grammar, the speakers' language-processing capacities, their cultural practices, and modality.

Both morpho-syntactic and cultural factors have been suggested as influences behind the differences found between languages belonging to the same typological pattern. In their descriptions of path of motion,[10] researchers such as Özçalişkan and Slobin (1998), Ibarretxe-Antuñano (2004), and Engberg-Pedersen and Trondhjem (2004) have observed that the presence of more complex morphological resources for spatial expression in three V-languages, i.e. Turkish, Basque, and West-Greenlandic, seem to lead to more elaborated path descriptions than those found in other more "prototypical" V-languages such as Spanish. The greater attention to path details in other V-languages such as Arrernte and Walpiri, in contrast, have been explained by Wilkins (2004) and Bavin (2004) as possibly related to cultural factors, i.e. to the culture-specific concern for motion and orientation—journeys—among nomads in Central Australia. The importance of lexico-morpho-syntactic factors has, furthermore, been pinpointed when discussing intra-typological variation with respect to manner of motion—for example, the differences in the amount of manner information included in narratives produced in different S-languages (i.e. Slavic languages such as Russian vs. Germanic languages such as Dutch, German, and English) and in different V-languages (Basque vs. Spanish). These differences have led Slobin (2004) to suggest placing languages on a cline of manner salience rather than on a strict bipartite typology.

The importance of psycholinguistic factors has especially been discussed by Özçalişkan and Slobin (2000b) and Slobin (2004) when examining intra-typological variation within single languages. Ease of processing, which is directly related to the relative accessibility of various means of expression within a given domain, i.e. its degree of codability, seems to be a determining factor that can account for speakers' choice of simpler constructions over more complex ones. For example, Turkish speakers preferred to use single verbs that conflate both manner and path of motion rather than path verbs alone or manner subordinate constructions, conveying in this way the maximum amount of semantic information in the simplest syntactic form. Likewise, Spanish speakers tended not to use complex path–manner expressions such as *salió volando* "(she) exited flying," even though such expressions are allowed by the grammar of the language. Expressions like this are heavy constructions to process, and this added processing load prevents their occurrence unless manner is contextually at issue.

Finally, research into serial-verb languages such as Thai and Mandarin Chinese as well as into sign languages has led to a further questioning of a strict binary typological classification between S- and V-languages. Serial languages have been classified by Talmy as S-languages. However, as indicated by Zlatev and Yangklang, and Slobin (2004), these languages would be more adequately described as pertaining to a third typological pattern, which the latter author refers to as equipollently-framed languages, since these are characterized by the expression of both manner and path by elements that are equal in both formal linguistic terms and in their force or significance.[11] Sign languages are likewise special in that the manual modality allows for specific characteristics: (a) path information is unavoidable, i.e. the hand has to move from one location to another; verbs in sign languages are then inherently path verbs; and (b) the moving hand can also represent the type of figure as well as the manner of motion. As shown by Galvan and Taub (2004), this leads to spatial descriptions in American Sign Language to be richer than the corresponding descriptions in English.

In conclusion, even though Talmy's typological classification has been extremely useful in allowing researchers to compare how speakers of different languages of the world talk about motion, this research into actual language use has evidenced the importance of other factors that need to be taken into consideration. These factors, of morpho-syntactic, psycho-linguistic, and pragmatic nature, can help us explain the intra-typological differences found between languages belonging to the same typological pattern, as well as the difficulty found in classifying certain languages in a strict binary typology. As concluded by Slobin (2004), future research should provide a description of typologies of language use, and examine, in greater detail, the complex interplay between typologically determined lexicalization patterns and the types of factors discussed above.

3 Motion events in Second Language Acquisition [12]

Given that Talmy's typological framework addresses the systematic relations in language between meaning and linguistic expression within the spatial domain of motion, it has recently been suggested by Cadierno (2004) and Cadierno and Lund (2004) that this line of inquiry allows for the systematic investigation of the processes by which adult language learners establish form–meaning mappings in their interpretation and production of L2 motion events, an area that has not received much attention in SLA research (but see, for example, Inagaki, 2000, and Montrul, 2001, for two recent studies from a different theoretical perspective). Specifically, Talmy's framework can shed light on the processes which these mappings must go through before they are fully acquired, namely, the establishment of initial connections, their subsequent processing and strengthening, and their accessing for use (VanPatten, Williams & Rott, 2004).

Additionally, this framework allows for the systematic examination of the intricate relationship between cross-linguistic influence and the degree of similarity and difference between the learners' L1 and L2. This suggestion is in line with Odlin (1989), who advocates the usefulness of research based on linguistic typologies, as it allows for the study of systemic influences, and for a clearer understanding of the relations between transfer and developmental sequences. Finally, and as discussed in the first section of this chapter, cognitive semantics in general, and Talmy's framework in particular, can provide SLA with an understanding of semantic structure that goes beyond the purely real-world referential sense. The understanding of meaning as reflecting conceptual structure and as encyclopedic in nature allows for the establishment of links between linguistic and cognitive approaches to language (Tomasello, 1998) and, consequently, between linguistic and cognitive approaches to SLA.

The two relevant SLA questions to ask in light of Talmy's framework are the following: how do L2 learners with typologically different L1s and L2s acquire the characteristic meaning–form mappings of the L2? And how does the performance of this type of learner compare to learners whose L1 and L2 share the same typological patterns? These two questions can further be rephrased in terms of Slobin's thinking-for-speaking hypothesis, namely, how and to what extent do adult L2 learners adapt to their thinking-for-speaking in an L2 that is typologically different from their L1, and how does the adaptation of this type of learner compare to that followed by learners whose L1 and L2 share the same typological patterns?

If, as stated by Berman and Slobin (1994), children learn particular ways of thinking-for-speaking, i.e. they are trained by their native languages to attend to particular aspects of a motion event, and to relate them verbally in ways that are in consonance with them, then learning an L2 must involve learning another way of thinking-for-speaking, that is, (a) learning which particular aspects of a motion event must be attended to in the input and expressed in the L2 (e.g. attention to location-static descriptions vs. movement-trajectories, and relatively more or less attention to manner of motion), and (b) learning how their semantic components are characteristically mapped onto L2 surface forms. The acquisition of these mapping relations in the domain of motion is rather complex, as it does not involve a one-to-one correspondence between meaning and form. A combination of semantic components can be expressed by a single surface form, as *subir* "go up," that conflates motion + path, and *walk*, that conflates motion + manner. And, as discussed by Sinha and Kuteva (1995), under the rubric of distributed semantics, aspects of a single semantic component can be expressed by more than one surface form, as *caminar lentamente* "walk slowly" where manner is encoded both in the verb and in an adverbial expression.

On the basis of Slobin's thinking-for-speaking hypothesis, a plausible general hypothesis is that the learners' L1 typological patterns will, at least initially, constitute the point of departure for the meaning–form mappings established in the L2, that is, the L2 motion constructions will not be initially connected to the L2 specific lexicalization patterns. This hypothesis is in agreement with claims made in the literature (e.g. VanPatten et al., 2004) that, specially, learners in the early and intermediate stages of language acquisition tend to make partial and non-target-like initial mappings that are often influenced by their L1. For example, Jarvis and Odlin's (2002) research on the acquisition of spatial relations found that Swedish learners of English mapped L2 prepositions onto L1-based spatial meanings.

In line with this general hypothesis, Cadierno and Lund (2004) posited a set of specific hypotheses concerning the initial mappings involved in the interpretation and production of manner of motion by learners with typologically different L1s and L2s, namely, Danish—an S-language—and Spanish—a V-language. For example, given that Danish has a more fine-grained lexicon of manner of motion verbs than Spanish and, consequently, Danish speakers have been trained to categorically distinguish between more different manners of motion than Spanish speakers, it was predicted that Spanish learners of Danish would initially tend (a) not to process the fine-grained manner distinctions present in L2 second-tier manner verbs, and (b) not to use these manner verbs in production, over-generalizing, instead, a single or few first-tier manner verbs to all communicative contexts (e.g, *gå* "to walk" in all walking contexts independent of the manner of walking involved, which in Danish could be expressed as *slentre* "stroll," *spadsere* "go for a short stroll, saunter," *stavre* "trot," *traske* "trudge," or *vakle* "stagger"). In contrast, it was predicted that

Danish learners of Spanish would initially tend to add manner information to their interpretation of Spanish motion verbs, as well as add some
kind of manner information in their descriptions of motion events,
information not commonly expressed in the target language. For example,
in order to express the idea that *Folk strømmede gennem gaderne* "People
streamed through the streets," they might say something like *La gente
pasaba por las calles como un río* "People passed through the streets like a
river."[13]

Likewise, given that Danish allows for the mapping of manner and
motion onto the main verb in both boundary and non boundary-crossing
situations, whereas Spanish only allows this mapping in the latter case,
it was predicted that Spanish learners of Danish would initially tend
to interpret Danish boundary-crossing expressions as non-boundary-
crossing (e.g. *Han løber ind i huset* "He runs into the house" to be wrongly
interpreted as *El corre dentro de la casa* "He runs inside the house")[14] as
well as avoid the conflation of manner and motion in the verb in boundary-
crossing situations. In contrast, it was expected that Danish learners of
Spanish would initially tend to interpret Spanish non-boundary-crossing
expressions such as *Corrió en la casa* "(She) ran inside the house" to refer
to both/either a non-boundary- (e.g. He ran inside the house) and a
boundary-crossing (e.g. He ran into the house) situation. Additionally,
they were also expected to produce non-target-like L2 Spanish expressions conflating manner and motion in boundary-crossing situations, as
in *Ella corrió en la casa* "She ran inside the house" to mean "She ran into
the house."

Cadierno and Lund's (2004) analysis was an attempt to demonstrate
how Talmy's typological classification can constitute the basis for theoretically grounded and testable hypotheses on the types of meaning–form
mappings that learners from typologically different L1 and L2s make
when interpreting and expressing motion events in an L2. The next section reviews some empirical studies that have applied this framework to
the research area of Second Language Acquisition.

3.1 Empirical studies on SLA

The existing empirical research into the expression of motion events in
an L2 is rather scarce as compared to the vast bulk of research which has
examined the acquisition and use of these constructions by native
speakers. This research has focused on the expression of motion events in
oral and written narratives, as well as on the synchronous use of speech
and gesture.

With respect to research on oral and written production, three studies
(Cadierno, 2004; Cadierno & Ruiz, 2006; and Navarro & Nicoladis,
2005) focused on the acquisition of a V-language—Spanish—by adult

learners with L1 S-languages—Danish and English. Cadierno's (2004) study examines how Danish learners of Spanish of two different levels of proficiency—intermediate and advanced—expressed motion events in their L2 as well as in their L1, and how their performance compared to that of a control group of Spanish adult native speakers. The study focused on the analysis of the semantic components of path and ground, and examined possible differences between the two subject groups with respect to (a) the amount of motion verb types; (b) the degree of elaboration of path of motion; (c) the use of event conflation, a construction not commonly used in Spanish; and (d) the relative allocation of attention to movement and setting. In light of the results obtained in first language acquisition (Berman & Slobin, 1994), Danish learners were expected to (a) use fewer Spanish motion verb types than the native speaker group; (b) exhibit a higher degree of complexity and elaboration of path of motion than Spanish native speakers; (c) make use of event conflation to a greater degree than the native speakers; and (d) tend to provide descriptions of trajectories as opposed to static descriptions. Furthermore, it was hypothesized that a certain parallelism would be found between the way in which motion events were expressed in the learners' L1 and L2. That is, it was expected that the L2 patterns mentioned above would also be observed in the learners' L1, thus evidencing a possible transfer of (at least) some of the L1 typological patterns. In this study narrative written data were elicited by means of the "frog story," as previous results of research into interlanguage variability (e.g. Tarone, 1983) have shown more target-like performance in written than in oral tasks, presumably due to the possibility of attending more closely to the language code in this mode.

The results of this study partially supported the hypotheses initially posited. As hypothesized, the Spanish learners used fewer motion verb types than the native speakers. This was expected given that second language acquisition entails a process of progressive vocabulary learning, and, consequently, their use of motion verb types was not expected to be as varied as that exhibited by native speakers.[15] In addition, and again as hypothesized, the learners provided more complex and elaborated path descriptions than the native speaker group. This was evidenced by (a) a "satellization" of the Spanish motion constructions, i.e. the use of inaccurate constructions incorporating redundant and anomalous path particles not found in the Spanish native data (e.g. *El niño fue arriba de una roca, Lit: The boy went on top of a rock "The boy climbed onto a rock")—a pattern of use only found in the intermediate-level group, and (b) a more frequent inclusion of more ground adjuncts accompanying motion verbs. This higher degree of elaboration of path of motion was possibly attributed to the influence of the learners' L1—Danish—given their training to provide such elaboration in their native language.

261

In contrast, the hypotheses concerning the use of event conflation and the relative allocation of attention to movement and setting were not supported by the results of the study. Contrary to what was expected, Danish learners did not use event conflation in their Spanish narratives, a construction not easily allowed in this language but common in Danish. It was argued that this could be due to the learners' psychotypology, i.e. the perceived distance between the characteristic constructions of the two languages (Kellerman, 1978, 1979). Likewise, only half of the learners provided descriptions of trajectories in Spanish; the other half provided static descriptions. Surprisingly, however, the same mix pattern of use was observed in the native speaker data, a result that differed from that of Berman and Slobin (1994), but which agreed with the observations made by other researchers (e.g. Özçalişkan & Slobin, 1998; Ibarretxe-Antuñano, 2004) on Turkish and Basque. This finding suggests that even within more "prototypical" V-languages, such as Spanish, there seems to exist some variability among their native speakers with respect to their preferred patterns of expression, i.e. patterns that overlap across typologies.

In conclusion, the results of this study did not show a consistent picture with respect to the role of the learners' L1 in the expression of motion events in the L2. The influence of the learners' L1 seemed to be present in some aspects of their L2 use but not in others, a pattern of behavior that supports the view of cross-linguistic influence as a complex phenomenon which is constrained by a number of factors such as the learners' perceptions about similarities and differences between the L1 and the general level of proficiency in the L2 (R. Ellis, 1994).

In a subsequent study, Cadierno and Ruiz (2006) also examined the expression of manner of motion by three subject groups. These consisted of two groups of advanced learners, one with L1 and L2 belonging to different typological patterns—Danish learners of Spanish—and one with L1 and L2 sharing the same typological patterns—Italian learners of Spanish—as well as a control group of native speakers. As in Cadierno (2004), data were collected by means of elicited narratives based on the frog story. Based on previous studies (Berman & Slobin, 1994), it was expected that the Danish learner group would exhibit a higher degree of elaboration of manner of motion than the other subject groups, as they were used to paying attention to this domain of experience in their native language. Furthermore, given the difference in Danish and Spanish with respect to the mapping of manner of motion onto the verb in boundary and non-boundary situations, the Danish learners were expected to do this mapping in Spanish in both types of situations.

The results of this study did not, for the most part, support the predictions initially stated. No significant differences were found between the three subject groups with respect to the amount of use of manner of motion verbs. Additionally, when examining whether the groups differed with respect to the use of alternative means of expressing manner of motion (e.g. subordinated manner clauses and adverbial expressions), the Danish group was not found to use these means to a significantly larger degree than the other two groups. In contrast, as predicted, this group of learners differed from the other two groups in the inaccurate production of expressions of mappings of manner onto the verb in boundary-crossing contexts, such as *El perro saltó fuera de la ventana "The dog jumped out of the window." Overall, these results suggest a limited role of the L1 thinking-for-speaking patterns in the acquisition of L2 motion constructions by intermediate and advanced language learners.

The results obtained by Cadierno (2004) and Cadierno and Ruiz (2006) received further empirical support in a study by Navarro and Nicoladis (2005), who also examined the expression of motion events by an advanced group of learners—L1 English–L2 Spanish speakers—and a control group of Spanish native speakers. The aim of this study was to investigate whether English learners of Spanish were able to learn the characteristic conflation pattern of this language, namely, the frequent mapping of path of motion onto the main verb. Data consisted of oral narratives elicited by means of two video films. The results of the study showed that the two subject groups did not significantly differ with respect to the amount of path conflation verbs used. However, the learners were found to use bare path verbs to a lesser degree than the native speakers. This result suggests that these learners had not yet fully acquired the use of bare verbs as a property of Spanish rhetorical style, opting instead for the English pattern of producing motion verbs followed by locative phrases (e.g. Berman & Slobin, 1994). Based on these results, the conclusion reached by these researchers was that even though there were some traces of English in the oral narratives of the advanced group of learners, these learners "had almost fully achieved the L1 Spanish patterns for the description of motion events in oral narratives" (p. 106).

Even though Navarro and Nicholadis' (2005) conclusion may seem to be overstated in terms of the few analyses conducted on the data, the results of this study reveal the same trend as those obtained in Cadierno (2004) and Cadierno and Ruiz (2006). Overall, the empirical evidence gathered so far—admittedly still scarce—seems to point towards a rather limited role of the L1 thinking-for-speaking patterns in advanced second language acquisition. Even though some traces of the L1 patterns still seem to be present in their inter-language, learners at this stage of language acquisition appear to have been able to acquire the L2 characteristic meaning–form mappings, and the general rhetorical style of the L2 when talking about motion.

In addition to research on linguistic production, four studies, to our knowledge, have investigated the simultaneous use of language and gesture by L2 learners. Stam (2001) and Kellerman and Van Hoof (2003) examined the expression of motion events by L2 speakers of English in comparison to that of English native speakers. In the former study, all the L2 speakers had Spanish as a native language. In the latter study, both Spanish and Dutch speakers of English were investigated, and their performance in their L1 and L2 were compared. In Stam's study, the learner group represented two levels of language proficiency, namely, intermediate and advanced. In Kellerman and Van Hoof's study, on the other hand, the Dutch group could be characterized as being high-intermediate to advanced, whereas the proficiency of the Spanish group was uniformly lower than that of the Dutch group (Kellerman, personal communication).

With respect to the results, Stam (2001) found that when expressing manner of motion, the Spanish learners of English tended to follow the L1 patterns. However, when expressing path of motion, some of the learners were able to shift towards the English thinking-for-speaking patterns in that their path gestures were synchronized with satellites. The results obtained by Kellerman and Van Hoof (2003) were more complex. As expected, when talking in their native languages, Spanish and Dutch speakers exhibited language-specific gestural patterns: Spanish speakers tended to place path gestures on the motion verb, whereas Dutch speakers tended to place them on the satellite (phrase) denoting path.[16] With respect to path depictions in L2 gestures, however, some unexpected differences were obtained from the Dutch and the Spanish speakers. Surprisingly, the Dutch group followed the V-language pattern of use, placing most of their path gestures on the verb, an unexpected result that the authors could not provide a definite explanation for until taking a closer look at some other factors involved. The Spanish group, on the other hand, behaved as expected on the basis of Slobin's (1996a) thinking-for-speaking hypothesis. Their gesturing in the L2 reflected the L1 gesture patterns in that the path gestures were placed on the motion verb.

In contrast to the two studies reviewed above, which primarily focused on the speech/gesture interface of learners with an L1 V-language and an L2 S-language, Yoshioka (2005) examined how low-intermediate learners with an L1 S-language—Dutch—and an L2 V-language—Japanese—accomplished animate and inanimate reference introduction and tracking in L1 and L2 narratives. The results from the L2 narratives, however, partially parallel those of the other two studies in that evidence for L1-based gestures were observed in the introduction of inanimate references.

Finally, Negueruela, Lantolf, Jordan and Gelabert (2004) carried out a bi-directional investigation, and examined the extent to which advanced Spanish learners of English and advanced English learners of Spanish were able to shift toward an L2 thinking-for-speaking pattern. The results of this study likewise revealed the reliance on L1 patterns when gesturing in an L2. Shifting to the L2 thinking-for-speaking patterns was particularly difficult for the L1 English group. Given that their L1 contains a much more varied lexicon of manner of motion verbs than the L2, these learners tended to use a high percentage of manner gestures as a compensatory strategy.

In general, the available studies on the simultaneous use of speech and gesture in the semantic domain of motion indicate that, whereas some learners are able to shift towards the L2 pattern (e.g. some learners in Stam's study), others still rely on the L1 gesturing patterns even at the advanced levels of language acquisition. As indicated by Kellerman & Van Hoof (2003), this last finding shows that even though L2 learners can be fluent and error-free in their spoken language, they can still transfer their L1 manual accent to an L2.

In sum, the available empirical research on the L2 expression of motion events indicates that, when examining speech alone, advanced language learners are, to a large extent, able to "retrain" their thinking-for-speaking patterns when talking about motion in a L2 that is typologically different from their L1.[17] However, as the study of the simultaneous use of gestures and speech show, learners' gestures may reveal L1-based thinking patterns that are not detectable in otherwise fluent and target-like L2 speech (Kellerman & Van Hoof, 2003).

In view of these findings, one might hypothesize that the influence of the L1 thinking-for-speaking patterns on speech may be stronger at the initial and intermediate stages of language acquisition, the idea being that with increased exposure to motion constructions in the L2 input, they will gradually learn to pay attention to the L2 relevant aspects of experience, and to establish the appropriate meaning–form mappings. Language proficiency has, after all, been shown to be an important constraint factor on cross-linguistic influence. Even though some studies have shown that L1 influence can increase with language proficiency (e.g. Hyltenstam, 1984, and Klein & Purdue, 1993), other research has evidenced the decrease of L1 influence with respect to lexical and grammatical development (e.g. Ellis & Beaton, 1993; Jiang, 2002; Taylor, 1975; Seliger, 1978) as well as to L2 input processing and parsing (e.g. VanPatten, 2004a & b).[18] Additionally, the claims made in the literature (e.g. VanPatten et al., 2004) about initial form–meaning connections being often partial and non-target-like makes this hypothesis still more plausible. Learners will probably tend to pay attention initially to aspects of a motion event they are used to from their L1, and to establish L1-based meaning–form mappings (Cadierno & Lund, 2004).[19]

Despite the key role of frequency of exposure to target language forms in the input on the subsequent processing and strengthening of the meaning–form connections, the power of frequency may fail if the meaning–form mapping is not salient, if it needs to be processed in a different way, or if it involves complex associations that cannot be acquired implicitly (e.g. N. Ellis, 2004). These factors might explain possible differences in the difficulty in acquiring corresponding motion constructions experienced by learners with an L1 S-language learning an L2 V-language and those with an L1 V-language learning an L2 S-language—a hypothesis awaiting empirical support. For both types of learners, the meaning–form mappings involved in the expression of motion events require complex associations not restricted to a one-to-one meaning–form correspondence. However, their degree of saliency is not uniform. As indicated in the first section of this chapter, more semantic information is presented in a backgrounded fashion in S-languages as compared to V-languages (Talmy, 2000b). Specifically, manner of motion is generally less salient in S-languages than in V-languages given its characteristic lexicalization in the verb root (Slobin, 1997, 2000). Learners of S-languages are, therefore, expected to have greater difficulties in the acquisition of motion constructions than learners of V-languages, especially in the domain of manner of motion. This hypothesis, which is seemingly in agreement with old claims made in the literature (e.g. Stockwell, Brown & Martin, 1965) with respect to the greater acquisitional difficulty in cases of splits as opposed to coalesced forms, leads to the supposition that it will be harder to move from a less discriminating L1 into a more discriminating L2 than the reverse. That is, it will be harder to learn to discriminate among different manners of motion for which the learner has not been trained by his/her native language than to learn to make fewer discriminations than he/she is used to.[20] This is a matter that deserves future investigation.

4 Conclusion

The aim of this chapter has been to demonstrate how one line of inquiry within cognitive semantics, namely Talmy's typological framework on motion events, can constitute a promising research area for the investigation of the ways in which adult language learners from different linguistic backgrounds express spatial relations in relation to motion. This line of inquiry within SLA can, in turn, make a contribution to the issue of linguistic relativity by empirically examining how and to what extent adult language learners with typologically different L1s and L2s adapt to a new thinking-for-speaking in the foreign language.

Given that studies so far have focused on advanced learners with L1 S-languages and L2 V-languages, future research should involve: (a) studies with learners at the early and intermediate stages of language acquisition to examine whether the influence of the L1 thinking patterns at these stages is stronger than at more advanced levels; and (b) bi-directional studies which would compare the expression of motion events by learners of

S-languages (e.g. Spanish learners of English) and learners of V-languages (e.g. English learners of Spanish) in order to determine similarities and differences in both acquisitional processes. Ideally, studies should include comparisons involving intra-L1 homogeneity between learners' L1 and L2 performance, inter-L1 group heterogeneity in learners' L2 performance as well as comparisons between L2 learners and native speakers (Jarvis, 2000).

Notes

1 Evans and Green (2006, p. 162) discuss a fourth principle, *Meaning construction is conceptualization*. According to Blending Theory (e.g. Fauconnier & Turner, 1998), meaning is constructed on the basis of complex mapping operations between reality-based mental spaces which are combined to create new blended spaces.

2 Image-schema conceptual structures can also give rise to more abstract kinds of meanings, such as metaphors. In this way purposes are understood in terms of destinations (e.g. one may *go a long way toward* achieving one's purposes), and achieving a purpose is understood as passing along a path from a starting point to an endpoint (e.g. one may get *sidetracked*, or find something getting in *one's way*) (Lakoff, 1987).

3 As Evans and Green (2006) indicate, this claim does not mean that semantic and conceptual structures are identical. There are concepts in the minds of speakers that are not conventionally encoded in language. For example, the area on our faces below our nose and above our mouth is not conventionally coded in languages such as English or Spanish (Langacker, 1987).

4 A satellite has been defined by Talmy (2000b, p. 102) as ". . . the grammatical category of any constituent other than a noun-phrase or prepositional-phrase complement that is in a sister relation to the verb root." A satellite can be both a bound affix or a free word and can consist of elements such as verb particles (e.g. *up, down, out*) and verb prefixes (e.g. *mis* as in *misfire*).

5 A particular case of the "center-periphery" pattern is Figure-Ground organization, according to which the Figure is the entity in a situation that attracts focal attention and the entity whose characteristics and fate are of concern, and the Ground is the entity in the periphery of attention which functions as a reference point for the Figure.

6 By "characteristic" Talmy (2000b) means that (1) it is colloquial in style, rather than literary; (2) it is frequent in the occurrence of speech; and (3) it is pervasive, in the sense that it covers a wide range of semantic notions.

7 Slobin refers to this issue in terms of codability, i.e. ease of expression. A more codable expression is more accessible in psycholinguistic terms. Slobin (2004) discusses three factors that affect the degree of codability of a given expression: (a) expression by a finite rather than non-finite verb; (b) expression by a high-frequency rather than low-frequency lexical item; and (c) expression by a single word rather than a phrase or clause.

8 For the purpose of the present discussion, I limit myself to including the results involving the comparison between English and Spanish despite the fact that differences were also found between these two languages and Chinese with respect to the types of constituents that gestures focused on.

9 Slobin (2005a) further reports on a doctoral dissertation carried out by Oh

(2003), in which memory reports were obtained from Korean and English monolingual adult speakers. In this study English-speaking adults were also found to be significantly better at recalling details of manner of motion than Korean-speaking adults.

10 Here I limit myself to presenting intra-typological variation concerning the semantic components of path and manner of motion. Intra-typological differences, however, have also been observed in relation to the ground(s) of motion (e.g. Brown, 2004; Engberg-Pedersen & Trondjem, 2004; Ibarretxe-Antuñano, 2004; Ragnarsdóttir & Strömqvist, 2004).

11 Slobin (2004) includes two other sets of languages as examples of equipollently-framed languages, given that the manner and path are also expressed by equipollent elements: (a) the so-called bipartite-verb languages, such as Hokan and Algonguian, i.e. languages where the verb expresses manner and path simultaneously; and (b) the Jaminjungan languages, which are characterized by manner preverb + path preverb + verb.

12 This section focuses on the consecutive L2 acquisition of motion events by adult language learners, and not on the simultaneous acquisition of these events by bilingual children. For existing research on that topic, see, for example Özçalişkan and Slobin (2000b) and Nicoladis and Brisard (2002).

13 Interesting enough, this is, in fact, an example found in a commonly used Danish-Spanish dictionary (Hansen & Gawinski, 1996), written by Danish native speakers.

14 As indicated in Cadierno and Lund (2004), this L1-based interpretation might be reinforced by the fact that Danish utilizes subtle phonetic differences such as +/−glotal stop, +/−stress, and vowel length in order to distinguish between expressions of boundary and non-boundary-crossing (e.g. *ind* "into"—boundary-crossing—vs. *inde* "inside"—non-boundary-crossing).

15 It would be interesting to examine whether the L2 learners would still use fewer motion verb types than native speakers if they were taught task-relevant motion verb types before task completion. Thanks to Peter Robinson for this comment.

16 English speakers differed from Dutch speakers in that they, unexpectedly, tended to place path gestures on a combination of the verb and the satellite rather than exclusively on the satellite.

17 Robinson (2006) refers to this process as learning "rethinking-for-speaking" in a foreign language.

18 This conflicting evidence for the role of L1 influence in relation to language proficiency was reflected in Kellerman's (1995) transfer to nowhere principle.

19 Robinson's (2005) notion that different combinations of learners' cognitive abilities or aptitudes may play a role of varying degrees of importance in different stages of language learning may also explain the hypothesized differential effects of the L1 thinking-for-speaking patterns on L2 learners at various levels of language proficiency. According to Robinson, aptitude factors such as noticing the gap and deep semantic processing pay a relatively bigger role in the early stages of language acquisition. It could be argued that learning which particular aspects of a motion event must be attended to in the L2 input, and learning how their semantic components are characteristically mapped onto L2 surface forms involve the aptitude factors just mentioned.

20 Informal observations of Spanish learners of Danish, including the present researcher, suggest that after having learned Danish and lived in Denmark for more than ten years, we still have not managed to discriminate among the

fine-grained manner of motion distinctions encoded in Danish motion verbs. In fact, this researcher was not aware of such distinctions until she started to do research in this area and began to notice the frequent use of these verbs by Danish native speakers.

Bibliography

Allwood, J. S. & Gärdenfors, P. (Eds.) (1999). *Cognitive semantics: Meaning and cognition*. Amsterdam/Philadelphia: John Benjamins.

Ameka, F. K. & Essegbey, J. (in press). Serialising languages: Satellite-framed, verb-framed or neither. In L. Hyman & I. Maddieson (Eds.), *African comparative and historical linguistics: Proceedings of the 32nd Annual Conference on African Linguistics*. Lawrenceville, NJ: Africa World Press.

Aske, J. (1989). Path predicates in English and Spanish: A closer look. *Proceedings of the 15th Annual Meeting of the Berkeley Linguistics Society* (pp. 1–14). Berkeley, CA: Berkeley Linguistics Society.

Bavin, E. L. (2004). Focusing on "where": An analysis of Warlpiri frog stories. In S. Strömqvist & L. Verhoeven (Eds.), *Relating events in narrative. Typological and contextual perspectives* (pp. 17–35). Mahwah, NJ: Lawrence Erlbaum.

Berman, R. A. & Slobin, D. I. (1994). *Relating events in narrative: A crosslinguistic developmental study*. Hillsdale, N.J.: Lawrence Erlbaum.

Boas, F. (1911). *Introduction to Handbook of American Indian languages*. Bulletin 40, Part I. Bureau of American Ethnology, Washington, DC: Government Printing Office. Reprinted in F. Boas 1966. *Introduction to Handbook of American Indian languages*. In P. Holder (Ed.), *Indian linguistic families of America North of Mexico*. Lincoln: University of Nebraska Press.

Bowerman, M., de León, L. & Choi, S. (1995). Verbs, particles, and spatial semantics: Learning to talk about spatial actions in typologically different languages. In E. Clark (Ed.), *The Proceedings of the 27th Annual Child Language Research Forum* (pp. 101–111). Stanford, CA: Center for the Study of Language and Information.

Brown, P. (2004). Position and motion in Tzeltal frog stories. In S. Strömqvist & L. Verhoeven (Eds.), *Relating events in narrative. Typological and contextual perspectives* (pp. 37–57). Mahwah, NJ: Lawrence Erlbaum.

Cadierno, T. (2004). Expressing motion events in a second language: A cognitive typological perspective. In M. Achard & S. Niemeier (Eds.), *Cognitive linguistics, second language acquisition, and foreign language teaching* (pp. 13–49). Berlin: Mouton de Gruyter.

Cadierno, T. & Lund, K. (2004). Cognitive linguistics and second language acquisition: Motion events in a typological framework. In B. VanPatten, J. Williams, S. Rott, & M. Overstreet (Eds.), *Form-meaning connections in second language acquisition* (pp. 139–154). Mahwah, NJ: Lawrence Erlbaum.

Cadierno, T. & Ruiz, L. (2006). Motion events in Spanish L2 acquisition. *Annual Review of Cognitive Linguistics*, 4, 183–216.

Choi, S. & Bowerman, M. (1991). Learning to express motion events in English and Korean: The influence of language-specific lexicalization patterns. *Cognition*, 41, 83–121.

Ellis, N. (2004). The processes of second language acquisition. In B. VanPatten, J. Williams, S. Rott, & M. Overstreet (Eds.), *Form-meaning connections in second language acquisition* (pp. 49–76). Mahwah, NJ: Lawrence Erlbaum.

Ellis, N. & Beaton, A. (1993). Psycholinguistic determinants of foreign language vocabulary learning. *Language Learning, 43,* 559–617.

Ellis, R. (1994). *The study of second language acquisition.* Oxford: Oxford University Press.

Engberg-Pedersen, E. & Trondhjem, F. B. (2004). Focus on action in motion descriptions: The case of West-Greenlandic. In S. Strömqvist & L. Verhoeven (Eds.), *Relating events in narrative. Typological and contextual perspectives* (pp. 59–88). Mahwah, NJ: Lawrence Erlbaum.

Evans, V. & Green, M. (2006). *Cognitive linguistics: An introduction.* Edinburgh: Edinburgh University Press.

Fauconnier, G. (1994). *Mental spaces. Aspects of meaning construction in natural language.* New York: Cambridge University Press.

Fauconnier, G. & Turner, M. (1998). Conceptual integration networks. *Cognitive Science, 22* (2), 133–187.

Fillmore, Ch. J. (1975). An alternative to checklist theories of meaning. *Proceedings of the First Annual Meeting of the Berkeley Linguistics Society* (pp. 123–131). Berkeley, CA: Berkeley Linguistics Society.

Fillmore, Ch. J. (1982). Frame semantics. Linguistics in the morning calm. *The Linguistics Society of Korea* (pp. 111–137). Seoul: Hanshin.

Fillmore, Ch. J. (1985). Frames and the semantics of understanding. *Quaderni di semantica, 6,* 222–254.

Galvan, D. & Taub, S. (2004). The encoding of motion information in American Sign Language. In S. Strömqvist & L. Verhoeven (Eds.), *Relating events in narrative. Typological and contextual perspectives* (pp. 191–217). Mahwah, NJ: Lawrence Erlbaum.

Gennari, S. P., Sloman, S. A., Malt, B. C., & Tecumseh Fitch, W. (2002). Motion events in language and cognition. *Cognition, 83,* 49–79.

Gruber, J. S. (1965). *Studies in lexical relations.* Unpublished doctoral dissertation. Boston, MA.: MIT.

Hansen, J. W., & Gawinski, B. (1996). *Dansk-spansk ordbog.* Norbok: Munksgaard Ordbøger.

Hyltenstam, K. (1984). The use of typological markedness conditions as predictors in second language acquisition: The case of pronominal copies in relative clauses. In R. Andersen (Ed.), *Second languages: A crosslinguistic perspective* (pp. 39–58). Rowley, MA: Newbury House.

Ibarretxe-Antuñano, I. (2004). Motion events in Basque narratives. In S. Strömqvist & L. Verhoeven (Eds.), *Relating events in narrative. Typological and contextual perspectives* (pp. 89–111). Mahwah, NJ: Lawrence Erlbaum.

Inagaki, S. (2001). Motion verbs with goal PPs in the L2 acquisition of English and Japanese. *Studies in Second Language Acquisition, 23,* 153–170.

Jarvis, S. (2000). Methodological rigor in the study of transfer: Identifying L1 influence in the interlanguage lexicon. *Language Learning, 50* (2), 245–309.

Jarvis, S. & Odlin, T. (2002). Morphological type, spatial reference and language transfer. *Studies in Second Language Acquisition, 22,* 535–556.

Jiang, N. (2002). Form-meaning mapping in vocabulary acquisition in a second language. *Studies in Second Language Acquisition*, 18, 149–169.

Johnson, M. (1987). *The body in the mind: The bodily basis of meaning, imagination, and reason*. Chicago: University of Chicago Press.

Kellerman, E. (1978). Giving learners a break: Native language intuitions as a source of predictions about transferability. *Working Papers on Bilingualism*, 15, 59–92.

Kellerman, E. (1979). Transfer and non-transfer: Where are we now? *Studies in Second Language Acquisition*, 2, 37–57.

Kellerman, E. (1995). Crosslinguistic influence: Transfer to nowhere? *Annual Review of Applied Linguistics*, 15, 125–150.

Kellerman, E. & Van Hoof, A. (2003). Manual accents. *International Review of Applied Linguistics*, 41, 251–269.

Kersten, A. W., Meissner, C. A., Schwartz, B. L., & Riveria, M. (2003). *Differential sensitivity to manner of motion in adult English and Spanish speakers*. Paper presented at the Biennial Conference of the Society for Research in Child Development, Tampa, Florida, April.

Kita, S. & Özyürek, A. (2003). What does cross-linguistic variation in semantic coordination of speech and gesture reveal? Evidence for an interface representation of spatial thinking and speaking. *Journal of Memory and language*, 48 (1), 16–32.

Klein, W. & Purdue, C. (1993). Utterance structure. In C. Perdue (Ed.), *Adult language acquisition: Cross-linguistic perspectives* (pp. 3–40). Cambridge: Cambridge University Press.

Lakoff, G. & Johnson, M. (1980). *Metaphors we live by*. Chicago: University of Chicago Press.

Langacker, R. W. (1987). *Foundations of cognitive grammar, vol. 1: Theoretical perspectives*. Stanford, CA: Stanford University Press.

Langacker, R. W. (1996). Cognitive grammar. In K. Brown & J. Miller (Eds.), *Concise encyclopedia of syntactic theories* (pp. 51–54). Oxford: Pergamon.

Levinson, S. C. (2003). *Space in language and cognition: Explorations in cognitive diversity*. Cambridge: Cambridge University Press.

Lucy, J. A. (1992). *Gramatical categories and cognition: A case study of the linguistic relativity hypothesis*. Cambridge: Cambridge University Press.

Lucy, J. A. (1996). The scope of linguistic relativity: An analysis and review of empirical research. In J. J. Gumperz & S. C. Levinson (Eds.), *Rethinking linguistic relativity* (pp. 37–69). Cambridge: Cambridge University Press.

Mayer, M. (1969). *Frog, where are you?* New York: Dial Press.

McNeill, D. (1992). *Hand and mind: What gestures reveal about thought*. Chicago: Chicago University Press.

McNeill, D. (1997). Imagery in motion event descriptions: Gestures as part of thinking-for-speaking in three languages. *Proceedings of the 23rd Annual Meeting of the Berkeley Linguistics Society* (pp. 255–267). Berkeley: Berkeley Linguistics Society.

McNeill, D. (2000). Analogic/analytic representations and cross-linguistic differences in thinking for speaking. *Cognitive Linguistics*, 11 (1/2), 43–60.

McNeill, D. & Duncan, S. D. (2000). Growth points in thinking-for-speaking.

In D. McNeill (Ed.), *Language and gesture: Window into thought and action* (pp. 141–161). Cambridge: Cambridge University Press.

Montrul, S. (2001). Agentive verbs of manner of motion in Spanish and English as second languages. *Studies in Second Language Acquisition, 23,* 171–206.

Naigles, L. R. & Terrazas, P. (1998). Motion-verb generalizations in English and Spanish: Influences of language and syntax. *Psychological Science, 9* (5), 363–369.

Navarro, S. & Nicoladis, E. (2005). Describing motion events in adult L2 Spanish narratives. In D. Eddington (Ed.), *Selected Proceedings of the 6th Conference on the Acquisition of Spanish and Portuguese as First and Second Languages* (pp. 102–107). Somerville, MA: Cascadilla Proceedings Project.

Negueruela, E., Lantolf, J. P., Jordan, S. R., & Gelabert, J. (2004). The "private function" of gesture in second language speaking activity: A study of motion verbs and gesturing in English and Spanish. *International Journal of Applied Linguistics, 14* (1), 113–147.

Nicholadis, E. & Brisard, F. (2002). Encoding motion in gestures and speech: Are there differences in bilingual children's French and English? In E. V. Clark (Ed.), *Space in language: Location, motion, path, and manner. Proceedings of the 31st Stanford Child Language Research Forum* (pp. 60–68). Stanford: Center for the Study of Language and Information, Stanford University.

Odlin, T. (1989). *Language transfer: Cross-linguistic influence in language learning.* Cambridge: Cambridge University Press.

Oh, K-j. (2003). *Language, cognition, and development: Motion events in English and Korean.* Unpublished doctoral dissertation, Department of Psychology, University of California, Berkeley.

Özçalişkan, Ś. & Slobin, D. I. (1998). Learning how to search for the frog: Expression of manner of motion in English, Spanish, and Turkish. In A. Greenhill, H. Littelfield, & C. Tano (Eds.), *Proceedings of the 23rd Annual Boston University Conference on Language Development* (pp. 541–552). Sommerville, MA: Cascadilla Press.

Özçalişkan, Ś. & Slobin, D. I. (2000a). *Climb up* vs. *ascend climbing*: Lexicalization choices in expressing motion events with manner and path components. In S. Catherine-Howell, S. A. Fish, & T. K. Lucas (Eds.), *Proceedings of the 24th Annual Boston Conference on Language Development, vol. 2* (pp. 558–570). Sommerville, MA: Cascadilla Press.

Özçalişkan, Ś. & Slobin, D. I. (2000b). Expression of manner of movement in monolingual and bilingual children's narratives: Turkish vs. English. In A. Göksel & C. Kerslake (Eds.), *Studies on Turkish and Turkik languages* (pp. 253–262). Wiesbaden: Harrasowitz Verlag.

Özçalişkan, Ś. & Slobin, D. I. (2003). Codability effects on the expression of manner of motion in Turkish and English. In A. S. Özsoy, D. Akar, M. Nakipoślu-Demiralp, E. Erguvanli-Taylan, & A. Aksu-Koç (Eds.), *Studies in Turkish linguistics* (pp. 259–270). Istanbul: Bośaziçi University Press.

Özyürek, A. & Kita, S. (1999). Expressing manner and path in English and Turkish: Differences in speech, gesture, and conceptualizations. In M. Hahn & S. C. Stoness (Eds.), *Proceedings of the 21st Annual Conference of the Cognitive Science Society* (pp. 507–512). Mahwah, NJ: Lawrence Erlbaum.

Papafragou, A., Massey, C., & L. Gleitman. (2001). Motion events in language and cognition. In A. H.-J. Do, L. Domínguez, & A. Johansen (Eds.), *Proceedings of the 25th Annual Boston University Conference on Language Development* (pp. 566–574). Sommerville, MA: Cascadilla Press.

Ragnarsdóttir, H. & Strömqvist, S. (2004). Time, space, and manner in Swedish and Icelandic: Narrative construction in two closely related languages. In S. Strömqvist & L. Verhoeven (Eds.), *Relating events in narrative. Typological and contextual perspectives* (pp. 113–141). Mahwah, NJ: Lawrence Erlbaum.

Robinson, P. (2005). Aptitude and second language acquisition. *Annual Review of Applied Linguistics, 25,* 46–73.

Robinson, P. (2006). *Second language speech production research: Processing stages, task demands, individual differences and re-thinking-for-speaking in an L2.* Paper presented at the American Association of Applied Linguistics Conference, Montreal, June 17–20.

Seliger, H. (1978). On the evolution of error type in high and low interactors. *Indian Journal of Applied Linguistics, 4,* 22–30.

Sinha, C. (1999). Grounding, mapping and acts of meaning. In T. Janssen and G. Redeker (Eds.) *Cognitive Linguistics: Foundations, Scope and Methodology* (pp. 223–255). Berlin: Mouton de Gruyter.

Sinha, C. & Kuteva, T. (1995). Distributed spatial semantics. *Nordic Journal of Linguistics, 18,* 167–199.

Slobin, D. I. (1996a). Two ways to travel: Verbs of motion in English and Spanish. In M. Shibatani & S. A. Thompson (Eds.), *Grammatical constructions: Their form and meaning* (pp. 195–220). Oxford: Clarendon Press.

Slobin, D. I. (1996b). From "thought and language" to "thinking for speaking." In J. Gumperz & S. Levinson (Eds.), *Rethinking linguistic relativity. Studies in the social and cultural foundations of language, vol. 17* (pp. 70–96). Cambridge: Cambridge University Press.

Slobin, D. I. (1997). Mind, code, and text. In J. Bybee, J. Haiman, & S. A. Thompson (Eds.), *Essays on language function and language type: Dedicated to T. Givón* (pp. 437–467). Amsterdam/Philadelphia: John Benjamins.

Slobin, D. I. (1998). A typological perspective on learning to talk about space. In H. Ragnarsdóttir & S. Strömqvist (Eds.), *Learning to talk about time and space. Proceedings of the 3rd NELAS Conference* (pp. 1–30). Reykjavík & Göteborg: University College of Education and Department of Linguistics, University of Göteborg.

Slobin, D. I. (2000). Verbalized events: A dynamic approach to linguistic relativity and determinism. In S. Neimeier & R. Dirven (Eds.), *Evidence for linguistic relativity* (pp. 107–138). Amsterdam/Philadelphia: John Benjamins.

Slobin, D. I. (2003). Language and thought online: Cognitive consequences of linguistic relativity. In D. Gentner & S. Goldin-Meadow (Eds.), *Language in mind: Advances in the study of language and thought* (pp. 157–192). Cambridge, MA: MIT Press.

Slobin, D. I. (2004). The many ways to search for a frog: Linguistic typology and the expression of motion events. In S. Strömqvist & L. Verhoeven (Eds.), *Relating events in narrative. Typological and contextual perspectives* (pp. 219–257). Mahwah, NJ: Lawrence Erlbaum.

Slobin, D. I. (2005a). Linguistic representations of motion events: What is signifier and what is signified? In C. Maeder, O. Fischer, & W. Herlofsky (Eds.), *Outside-in–inside-out: Iconicity in language and literature 4* (pp. 307–322). Amsterdam/Philadelphia: John Benjamins.

Slobin, D. I. (2005b). Relating narratives events in translation. In D. Ravid & H. B. Shyldkrot (Eds.), *Perspectives on language and language development: Essays in honor of Ruth. A. Berman* (pp. 115–129). Dordrecht: Kluwer.

Slobin, D. I. & Hoiting, N. (1994). Reference to movement in spoken and signed languages: Typological considerations. *Proceedings of the 20th Annual Meeting of the Berkeley Linguistics Society* (pp. 487–503). Berkeley, CA: Berkeley Linguistics Society.

Stam, G. (2001). *Gesture and second language acquisition.* Paper presented at TESOL Convention, St Louis, Missouri, March.

Stockwell, R., Brown, J., & Martin, J. (1965). *The grammatical structures of English and Spanish.* Chicago: Chicago University Press.

Talmy, L. (1985). Lexicalization patterns: Semantic structure in lexical forms. In T. Shopen (Ed.), *Language typology and syntactic description, vol. 3: Grammatical categories and the lexicon* (pp. 36–149). Cambridge: Cambridge University Press.

Talmy, L. (1991). Path to realization: A typology of event conflation. *Proceedings of the 17th Annual Meeting of the Berkeley Linguistics Society* (pp. 480–519). Berkeley, CA: Berkeley Linguistics Society.

Talmy, L. (2000a). *Toward a cognitive semantics: Concept structuring systems.* Cambridge, MA.: MIT Press.

Talmy, L. (2000b). *Toward a cognitive semantics: Typology and process in concept structuring.* Cambridge, MA: MIT Press.

Tarone, E. (1983). On the variability of interlanguage systems. *Applied Linguistics, 4,* 142–163.

Taylor, B. (1975). The use of overgeneralization and transfer learning strategies by elementary and intermediate students of ESL. *Language Learning, 25,* 73–107.

Tomasello, M. (1998). *The new psychology of language: Cognitive and functional approaches to language structure.* London: Lawrence Erlbaum.

VanPatten, B. (2004a). Input processing in SLA. In B. VanPatten (Ed.), *Processing instruction: Theory, research, and commentary* (pp. 5–31). Mahwah, NJ: Lawrence Erlbaum and Associates.

VanPatten, B. (2004b). Input and output in establishing form-meaning connnections. In B. VanPatten, J. Williams, S. Rott, & M. Overstreet (Eds.), *Form-meaning connections in second language acquisition* (pp. 29–47). Mahwah, NJ: Lawrence Erlbaum.

VanPatten, B., Williams, J., & Rott, S. (2004). Form-meaning connections in second language acquisition. In B. VanPatten, J. Williams, S. Rott, & M. Overstreet (Eds.), *Form-meaning connections in second language acquisition* (pp. 1–26). Mahwah, NJ: Lawrence Erlbaum.

Whorf, B. L. (1940). Linguistics as an exact science. *Techonology Rreview, 43,* 61–63. Reprinted in 1956, *Language, thought and reality: Selected writings of Benjamin Lee Whorf* by J. B. Carroll (pp. 220–232). Cambridge, MA: MIT Press.

Wilkins, D. P. (2004). The verbalization of motion events in Arrernte. In S. Strömqvist & L. Verhoeven (Eds.), *Relating events in narrative. Typological and contextual perspectives* (pp. 143–157). Mahwah, NJ: Lawrence Erlbaum.

Yoshioka, K. (2005). *Linguistic and gestural introduction and tracking of referents in L1 and L2 discourse*. Unpublished doctoral dissertation. The University of Groningen.

Zlatev, J. & Yangklang, P. (2004). A third way to travel: The place of Thai in motion-event typology. In S. Strömqvist & L. Verhoeven (Eds.), *Relating events in narrative. Typological and contextual perspectives* (pp. 159–190). Mahwah, NJ: Lawrence Erlbaum.

12

GESTURES AND SECOND LANGUAGE ACQUISITION

Marianne Gullberg

1 Introduction

When we speak, we regularly gesture as an integral part of communicating. For example, my colleague just explained how her husband backed into another car this morning (she banged her right fist against her flat left hand). One of the hubcaps came off at the impact and disappeared off down the lane (her right hand traced a circling trajectory off to the right). Throughout, she used two modes of expression to convey meaningful elements of the visual scene described: speech and gesture. This chapter presents an overview of why gestures like these are relevant to the cognitive linguistics of Second Language Acquisition (SLA) and, specifically, what gestures can tell us about the processes of SLA. The chapter focuses on two key aspects: (a) gestures and the developing language system and (b) gestures and learning. It further discusses some implications of an expanded view of language acquisition that takes gestures into account.

The first section gives a brief introduction to gesture studies. It demonstrates how gestures are systematically related to speech and language at multiple levels, and reflect linguistic activities in non-trivial ways. It also outlines the current views on the relationship between gesture, speech, and language, and exemplifies cross-linguistic systematicity and variation in gestural repertoires. The second section illustrates what gestures can contribute to the study of a developing second language (L2)—both to a particular L2 and to the developing L2 system in general. With regard to particular L2s, gestures open new avenues for exploring cross-linguistic influences in that learners' gestures allow us to glean information about L1–L2 interactions at the level of semantic-conceptual representations. With regard to L2 development generally, evidence of systematically parallel change in gesture and speech at a given point in development allows for the investigation of how communicative and cognitive constraints influence learner varieties. The third section reviews findings that suggest that both the perception and production of gestures have learning benefits. The chapter concludes by discussing some implications of these findings for L2 acquisition, specifically regarding the relationship between underlying representations and surface forms, and the notion of native-likeness.

2 An introduction to gestures

2.1 The basics

Gestures are typically defined as symbolic movements related to ongoing talk or to the speaker's expressive intention (cf. Kendon, 2004; McNeill, 1992). This definition excludes functional actions like cutting paper with a pair of scissors, self-regulatory movements such as scratching or playing with strands of hair (Ekman & Friesen, 1969), and more traditional types of nonverbal behavior like posture, blushing, etc. (cf. Poyatos, 2002). These behaviors are not without communicative relevance but are not typically part of the message the speaker is trying to convey. The definition still includes a wide range of behaviors: movements like the "victory" gesture, movements depicting properties of objects or events (e.g. bringing the extended index and middle finger together repeatedly as if moving the legs of a pair of scissors), movements pointing to real or imagined things, and simple rhythmic movements. All these behaviors are gestures.

Gestures can be described in terms of their formal, structural properties such as the configuration of the articulators (hands, arms, etc.), the place of articulation (gesture space), and the form of the movement (cf. Stokoe, 1980). Gestures also have internal structure. During the preparation phase the hands move into a particular part of gesture space. The stroke is the core of the gesture where the spatial excursion of the limb reaches its maximum. During the retraction phase the hands fall back to a resting position. These three phases can be separated by holds when the hands are temporarily immobile in gesture space before they move on to the next phase. A whole gesture unit can thus consist of a preparation, a pre-stroke hold, a stroke, a post-stroke hold, and a retraction (Kendon, 1972; Kita, Van Gijn, & Van der Hulst, 1998; Seyfeddinipur, 2006). Gesture phase analysis and the identification of the stroke is crucial to issues of temporal gesture-speech alignment, which in turn underpins the theorizing about the relationship between speech and gesture.

A number of categorization and classification schemes for gestures have been proposed. Many are based on a combination of semiotic and functional distinctions (for an overview, see Kendon, 2004). All systems identify a class of conventionalized, language- and culture-specific gestures that constitute fixed form–meaning pairs with standards of well-formedness. These are often called emblems (Efron, 1941/1972; Ekman

& Friesen, 1969), exemplified by the "victory" gesture mentioned. The conventional nature of these gestures is illustrated by the different meanings attributed to the same gesture form. For instance, the "ring" gesture (thumb and index joined in a circular form) alternatively means "OK," "good," "worthless," "money," and "body orifice" depending on where you are in the world. The victory gesture (index and middle finger in a V-shaped configuration with palm turned outwards) demonstrates the importance of correct form. The outward orientation of the palm is crucial to distinguish it from a similar insulting British gesture with the palm turned towards the speaker. All schemes also recognize gestures with no formal standards of well-formedness that are instead created on the fly. These movements are labeled simply (speech-associated or co-speech) gestures, or gesticulation. In this class further distinctions are made between representational and rhythmic gestures. These represent, depict, illustrate, or emphasize some aspect of what is being conveyed. A current influential classification scheme for speech-associated gestures is based on four not mutually exclusive categories where iconic, metaphoric, and deictic gestures constitute representational gestures, and beats are rhythmic (McNeill, 1992).

Gestures thus vary on a range of dimensions—sometimes referred to as *Kendon's continua* (Kendon, 1988; McNeill, 1992, 2000). They are to varying degrees "language-like," meaning that they are more or less arbitrary, segmentable and combinatorial. Gestures are more or less conventionalized or "lexicalized"; performed with varying degrees of awareness; and are more or less dependent on accompanying speech. These multiple and gradient properties yield very complex form–function relationships in gestures. Gestures are deeply multi-functional and have both communicative and self-directed, cognitive functions, sometimes simultaneously. Gestures are sensitive to communicative and contextual factors such as visibility between interlocutors (Alibali, Heath, & Myers, 2001; Bavelas, Chovil, Lawrie, & Wade, 1992), and the spatial distribution of interlocutors (Özyürek, 2002a). As visuo-spatial phenomena they constitute an important communicative resource for speakers who deliberately draw on them to convey certain aspects of their message (Holler & Beattie, 2003; Melinger & Levelt, 2004). Other clearly interactional functions include turn regulation, feedback eliciting, agreement marking, attention direction (pointing), etc. The self-directed functions are somewhat more controversial but are all related to the relationship between gestures, speech, language, and thought.

2.2 Gestures, speech, and language

The link between gesture, speech, and language is evident in a number of ways. First, gestures are mainly a speaker-phenomenon. People typically gesture when they speak, not when they are silent. Second, gestures serve linguistic functions. For instance, gestures provide propositional content to many deictic expressions. The referents of expressions like "that one" and "there" in (1) are provided by deictic gestures, marked by square brackets. Without the gestures indicating the item and the location, the utterance would have little meaning. Gestures can also occupy structural slots in an utterance and function as a part of speech ("mixed syntax," Slama-Cazacu, 1976). In (2) a zig-zagging gesture functions as a verb. Gestures also serve as entire speech acts or modify other spoken speech acts (cf. Kendon, 2004). A speaker holding up the fist to the ear with thumb and pinkie extended, as in (3), is performing a speech act, namely promising to telephone.

(1) Put [that one] [there].
(2) She [ ] down the slidebar.
(3) [ ].—Sure, call me at home after five.

The link is also evident in the semantic and temporal co-ordination between the modalities observed at various levels of granularity. Gestures and speech often express the same or closely related meaning at the same time (Kendon, 1972; McNeill, 1992). Temporally, the most meaningful part of a gesture, the stroke, will typically be coordinated with the co-expressive part of speech. The sophisticated temporal alignment can be observed in the detailed adaptation of gesture to speech: the preparation phase of a gesture is timed such that the hand is in place for the stroke to co-occur with the relevant speech element; pre-stroke holds make gestures "wait" for speech (Kita, 1993), and stroke onsets shift depending on changes in speech onset (Levelt, Richardson, & La Heij, 1985) and contrastive stress (De Ruiter, 1998). Regarding meaning, gestures generally reflect the information selected for expression in speech. For instance, a speaker may perform a gesture with extended index and middle finger doing a cutting movement saying "she cut the rope." The gesture redundantly depicts the cutting event. However, many gestures also express additional but related information to speech, particularly spatial or imagistic information such as size, shape, and directionality (e.g. Beattie & Shovelton, 2002; Kendon, 2004). If the cutting gesture is performed with the palm facing downwards, this suggests that the rope was vertically oriented, perhaps hanging from the ceiling.

Further, the integration between the modalities is reflected in the parallel development of the modalities in childhood (e.g. Mayberry & Nicoladis, 2000), the parallel breakdown in disfluency (Seyfeddinipur, 2006), stuttering (Mayberry & Jaques, 2000), and in aphasia (McNeill, 1985; but see Goodwin, 2000; Lott, 1999 for aphasics' communicative use of some gesture types).

The tight connection between gesture and speech also extends to reception. Interlocutors or addressees do not only draw on gestures under special circumstances to improve understanding in problematic cases but process gesture and speech information in parallel and as a default. The evidence comes from studies showing that information that has only been present in gesture resurfaces in speech or gesture or both. Moreover, if speech and gesture express conflicting information, the modalities interfere with each other in both directions (Cassell, McNeill, & McCullough, 1999; Langton, O'Malley, & Bruce, 1996). Finally, neurocognitive evidence suggests that the brain processes gesture and speech together in similar ways to how it processes speech alone (Kelly, Kravitz, & Hopkins, 2004; Willems, Özyürek, & Hagoort, 2005; Wu & Coulson, 2005). If a gesture does not match speech or the preceding context, the brain is as surprised as when speech is inconsistent, as revealed by N400 effects in electrophysiological measures of brain responses (EEG, ERP).

Various theories attempt to account for the relationship between speech and gesture, and to specify the role gestures play for speakers. One set of theories sees gestures as an auxiliary system to speech (cf. Kendon, 2004). These either consider gestures to facilitate lexical retrieval (e.g. Krauss, Chen, & Gottesman, 2000), or the representation and packaging of content to be verbalized (e.g. Alibali, Kita, & Young, 2000; Freedman, 1977). Another set of theories views gestures and speech as equal partners and considers gestures to be an integral part of an utterance. These theories either assume that gestures and speech share the same cognitive origin (e.g. Kita & Özyürek, 2003; McNeill, 2005) or that a common communicative intention drives output in two modalities (De Ruiter, 2000; Kendon, 2004).

Existing theories also differ in their view on the nature and the location of the link between gesture and speech. The Lexical Retrieval Model (e.g. Krauss et al., 2000) proposes that gestures are linked to speech at the level of speech formulation (cf. Levelt, Roelofs, & Meyer, 1999). Gestures only occur when a speaker experiences a word-finding problem to help activate lexical entries. In this perspective gestures are an epiphenomenon. Interestingly, advocates of this view also argue against any communicative relevance of gestures for interlocutors (e.g. Krauss, Chen, & Chawla, 1996; see Kendon, 1994 for an overview of the debate). Others have suggested that gestures and speech are linked at the conceptual level, arguing that speech and gesture must be planned together to allow for the detail and flexibility of the temporal and semantic co-ordination. For instance, the Growth Point Theory states that speech and gesture form a fully integrated system where the modalities interact throughout planning and speaking (McNeill, 2005; McNeill & Duncan, 2000). A growth point is the newsworthy element of thought containing both imagistic and linguistic content. It serves as the starting point of an utterance. As the thought is expressed, gesture and speech convey the information for which they are best suited. Under this view, gestures transpose abstractions back into the concrete and help internalize the abstract via the concrete, and therefore play an important role for the embodiment of cognition. This line of thinking has been influential in studies of cross-linguistic conceptualization and for metaphor in gesture and speech (e.g. Cienki, 1998; Núñez & Sweetser, 2006). A related view, the Interface Hypothesis, holds that gestures are shaped by linguistic thinking but also by visuo-spatial properties, labeled spatial thinking (Kita & Özyürek, 2003). Crucially, the two modes of thinking interact and influence each other online. The Sketch Model, finally, also assumes that gestures are planned with speech at the conceptual level (De Ruiter, 2000). In contrast to other models, it states that the actual realization of a gesture is driven by the communicative intent of the speaker as much as by the linguistic and spatial properties of the message alone. This model is the only one to attempt to account for all gesture types and also for the fact that speakers do not always gesture.

In sum, although the details of the relationship between gestures, language, and speech are not yet fully understood and the theories differ in their views on the mechanics, the actual link remains undisputed.

2.3 Cross-linguistic gestural repertoires

Although gestures are subject to individual variation (cf. Alibali, 2005), there is also uniformity in gesturing within groups. Individuals appear to differ with respect to how many gestures they perform, whereas speakers within a speech community and culture are remarkably consistent in when and how they gesture when communicative content and situation are kept constant. There seem to be gestural repertoires whose characteristics are motivated both by culture and by language.

Cultural norms concern "appropriate" gesture usage, typically suggesting that the less you gesture, the better (Schmitt, 1991). Cultural conventions also affect gestural form, most clearly reflected in the sets of culture-specific gestures (emblems) sometimes set down in dictionaries (for inventories, see Morris, Collett, Marsh, & O'Shaughnessy, 1979; Payrató, 1993). More spontaneous forms of gesturing are also subject to cultural conventions such as back-channel signals like nodding and head-shaking (cf. Kendon, 2002; Maynard, 1990; McClave, 2000), pointing (e.g. Haviland, 1993; Sherzer, 1972; Wilkins, 2003), and use of gesture space (e.g. Müller, 1994).

Systematic differences between and uniformity within gestural repertoires also appear to be motivated by language. For instance, the organization of information structure in speech is reflected in gesture. A number of studies have shown that gestures tend to co-occur with elements in speech that represent new or focused information (e.g. Levy & McNeill, 1992; McNeill, Levy, & Cassell, 1993). Cross-linguistic differences in how information is organized and implemented in discourse therefore lead to language-specific gesture patterns (e.g. McNeill & Duncan, 2000). For instance, Dutch, Swedish, and French speakers treat actions as news-worthy, whereas Japanese speakers are more interested in locations and settings for actions. These different linguistic foci are instantiated in different structures in speech: transitive constructions centering on actions on the one hand, and existential constructions introducing entities and settings on the other. These different constructions in turn yield different gesture patterns, with Dutch, French, and Swedish speakers gesturing more about actions, aligning gestures with verbal elements, and Japanese speakers gesturing more about entities forming the setting, aligning gestures with nominal expressions (Gullberg, 2003; 2006a; Yoshioka, 2005; Yoshioka & Kellerman, 2006).

Moreover, there is a growing body of work demonstrating that language-specific lexicalization patterns are reflected in gesture as a result of the semantic and temporal co-ordination between speech and gesture (e.g. Duncan, 1994; Gullberg, submitted; Kita & Özyürek, 2003; McNeill & Duncan, 2000; Müller, 1994). Speakers must constantly make choices about what aspect of reality to talk about and how to talk about it. This selection is alternatively referred to in the literature as linguistic conceptualization, event construal, or perspective taking. Factors that guide the choices include communicative intent (Lakoff & Johnson, 1980, p. 163), the underlying *quaestio* to be answered (Von Stutterheim & Klein, 2002), and shared knowledge or common ground (e.g. Clark, 1996). It has also been suggested that speakers' choices are guided by the linguistic categories afforded by a language, specifically the categories that are habitually used to express events (e.g. Berman & Slobin, 1994; Carroll & Von Stutterheim, 2003; Slobin, 1996). This latter idea is known as the Thinking for Speaking Hypothesis (Slobin, 1996).[1] Linguistic categories are assumed to guide attention to certain types of information that are then selected for expression. In this way language-specific rhetorical styles or event perspectives arise (Slobin, 2004, Talmy, this volume).

Gestures seem to reflect such rhetorical styles or perspectives both in terms of the information selected for expression and the way in which this information is subsequently encoded in speech. Gesture studies have often focused on expressions of voluntary motion, drawing on Talmy's typological distinction between satellite- and verb-framed languages (Talmy, 1985, see also Cadierno, Odlin, this volume). For instance, gestures accompanying motion expressions in English look different from the corresponding Turkish and Japanese gestures (Kita & Özyürek, 2003; Özyürek, Kita, Allen, Furman, & Brown, 2005).

(4) the ball [rolled down] the street
(5) [yuvarlan-arak] [cadde-den iniyor]
roll-Connective street-Ablative descend.present
"(s/he) descends on the street, as (s/he) rolls" (Kita & Özyürek, 2003, p. 22)

English speakers express manner (*roll*) and direction of motion or path (*down*) in one spoken verbal clause, as in (4). They also tend to perform one single gesture that encodes both the manner and the path in one movement (a circling gesture moving in some direction, marked by square brackets in (4)). The tight syntactic packaging of manner and path components into one spoken verbal clause is reflected in a tight, conflated gesture. In contrast, Turkish speakers use two lexical verbs in two verbal clauses, as in (5): one verb expressing the manner (*yuvarlan*) and the other the downward motion (*iniyor*). Turkish speakers are also more likely to perform two accompanying gestures, one expressing the manner only and another path only. The looser syntactic connection between the manner and path components in speech is reflected in separate gestures. Kita and Özyürek (2003) have argued that the distinct gesture patterns hinge on the linguistic lexicalization patterns: a tight one-clause-one-gesture pattern vs. a looser two-clauses-two-gestures pattern. This claim is supported by the observation of within-language variation depending on what structures speakers actually use (Özyürek et al., 2005). When English speakers use a two-clause construction, they too are more likely to produce two gestures.

Verb semantics also influence gestures even in the absence of overt syntactic differences. When talking about caused motion or placement speakers of Dutch and French gesture differently (Gullberg, submitted). Both languages use transitive constructions followed by locational phrases of the type "she put the cup on the table." But French typically uses a general placement verb, *mettre*, "put," whereas Dutch uses a set of fine-grained semi-obligatory posture verbs, *zetten*, *leggen*, "set," "lay." Critically, the choice of verb hinges on properties of the object being placed and its final disposition with respect to the goal ground. The importance of the object for verb choice in Dutch is reflected in gestural handshapes that incorporate the object. French speakers instead focus only on the direction of the placement movement, mirrored in gestures that only express path.

Other factors also contribute to forming gestural repertoires. Situation and context, level of formality and familiarity with the interlocutor, education, mood, what is being talked about, genre, didactic intent, etc., all modulate gestural behavior. This said, language remains a fundamental influence. Speakers of different languages have different gestural repertoires partly for linguistic reasons. Speakers do not necessarily do what they see but rather what they say. Gestures reflect linguistic choices both at the level of information structure and at the level of lexical choices as instantiated in both syntax and semantics.

3 Gestures in Second Language Acquisition

3.1 Gestures and the development of a particular L2

The linguistic influences on gestural repertoires open up new methodological possibilities for examining effects of cross-linguistic influence or transfer on the route and the speed of acquisition of a particular target language given a certain first language (cf. Odlin, 2005, this volume). Because gestures reflect linguistic choices, they can be useful for examining language-specific aspects of linguistic conceptualizations. A cross-linguistic difference in event construal can be evident in gesture, either in terms of where gestures fall (what is newsworthy) or in terms of how gestures look (what meaning elements are taken into account). Moreover, meaning elements relevant to the event construal that are not readily expressible in speech may nevertheless be visible in gesture as additional spatial information.

Shifting perspectives on events in an L2 is likely to be difficult for several reasons. Many cross-linguistic differences in this domain are more a matter of preferential patterns than of grammaticality (cf. Carroll, Murcia-Serra, Watorek, & Bendiscoli, 2000). Although it is possible to say in English that "the ball descended the street while rolling," it is not the typical way of doing it. Kellerman's "transfer to nowhere" principle outlines the challenge in discovering differences not clearly marked as ungrammatical and difficulties in re-directing attention to new information elements. "[L]earners may not look for the perspectives peculiar to [the L2] language; instead, they may seek the *linguistic* tools which will permit them to maintain their L1 perspective. Such cases represent transfer to nowhere, an unconscious assumption that the way we talk or write about experience is not something that is subject to between-language variation" (Kellerman, 1995, p. 141, orig. emphasis). A substantial body of literature, conveniently summarized in Odlin (2005), documents these difficulties. It is equally challenging for the analyst to uncover the details of the perspective a learner actually operates with at a given point in time. A few studies investigate learners' gestures to uncover how the L1 and the L2 interact at the level of semantic-conceptual representations and their interface with information structure. The logic in these studies is the following. Under the theoretical view that gestures reflect linguistic conceptualization, two languages with different event construals should display different gesture patterns. If learners have acquired the L2 conceptualization, then their gestures should look L2-like. Any shift in learners' gestures reflects a shift in underlying representation.

One line of research focuses on the timing of gestures to examine what aspects of an event speakers regard as most newsworthy. In the domain of motion, studies have examined with what speech elements speakers of Spanish, English, and Dutch align their gestures. Native speakers of Spanish overwhelmingly coordinate their path gestures with path verbs like *salir*, "go out," whereas English speakers show a more varied pattern, aligning their path gestures with path particles like "down," with particles and verbs together, with verbs alone, and with expressions of ground (Kellerman & Van Hoof, 2003; McNeill & Duncan, 2000; Negueruela, Lantolf, Rehn Jordan, & Gelabert, 2004). Stam (2006) investigated Spanish learners of English at different proficiency levels. Many learners continued to align their path gestures in L2 with verbs in the L1 fashion, suggesting that they still considered the path (and the verb) to be the most newsworthy element of the motion event. Although some learners *did* align their path gestures with verbs and particles in English style— suggesting a beginning shift of focus—these gestures tended to accompany general motion verbs like "go" more often than in native English discourse, where verbs typically express manner information. Similarly, Kellerman and Van Hoof (2003) found that Spanish learners of English placed their path gestures on verbs in L2 and interpreted this as a case of L1 transfer. However, Dutch learners of English unexpectedly also placed their gestures mainly on verbs, although Talmy's typology suggests that their L1 Dutch should favor an English-like focus on (verbs and) particles. The authors cautiously refrain from explaining this finding, but the gesture data raise the possibility that learners consider path as the most newsworthy element of motion regardless of their L1. If so, this would suggest a possible language-neutral stage of event construal in acquisition.

Another strand of research focuses more on the shape, form, and content of gestures, examining what information is packaged together and how. In a set of beginning, intermediate, and advanced Turkish learners of English, only the advanced group was capable of expressing manner and path in one clause in spoken L2 English ("roll down") (Özyürek, 2002b). Interestingly, this group nevertheless produced Turkish-like gestures expressing only manner or only path at least half of the time, rather than both manner and path in one gesture. Although L2 speech was reasonably target-like, suggesting a perspective shift, Özyürek argues that these learners still conceptualized the motion events in a Turkish manner, focusing either on manner or path components separately. Similar evidence for lingering L1 patterns of event construal is found in the expression of ground elements. Yoshioka and Kellerman (2006) examined Dutch learners of Japanese, i.e. learners moving from a satellite-framed L1 to a verb-framed L2. As already seen, native Dutch speakers introduce grounds with mention of the action and gesture mainly about the action. Native Japanese speakers instead introduce grounds in chains of existential clauses with separate gestures for each ground mentioned. The Dutch learners of L2 Japanese continued to introduce ground together with action in both L2 speech and L2 gesture. These two studies indicate that L1 influences are sometimes visible in both modalities simultaneously, and sometimes only in one.

Other research focuses on the distribution of meaning components across speech and gesture in L2. Two studies have found that Spanish learners of English tend not to express manner in L2 speech but only in gesture (Negueruela et al., 2004; Wieselman Schulman, 2004). Negueruela et al. also found the same pattern for English learners of Spanish. The absence of manner in spoken L2 English is assumed to be due to cross-linguistic influence. Because manner of motion is not a core part of the learners' L1 Spanish event construal, they are assumed to have difficulties encoding it in L2 English speech. The absence of manner in spoken L2 Spanish is of course accurate since manner of motion is not compulsory in Spanish. But why should both groups express manner in L2 gesture? Interestingly, the accounts differ for the two groups. McNeill and Duncan (2000) have suggested that gestures modulate the communicative relevance of manner in native English speech. The presence of manner gestures foregrounds it and their absence backgrounds it. In native Spanish, in contrast, manner gestures regularly occur even when manner is absent from speech in so called "manner fogs." Here it is argued that, because Spanish has no simple (verbal) encoding option for manner in speech, gestures regularly convey the information. The consequence for the L2 data is that Spanish learners of English may continue to rely on gesture for expressing manner as part of an L1-based procedure, i.e. as a form of transfer. For English learners of Spanish, in contrast, manner gestures may instead be a compensatory strategy. English speakers are used to encoding manner in L1 speech. Because Spanish is poor in manner verbs, they cannot find an outlet in L2 speech, and therefore instead rely on gesture.

These findings highlight the common assumption that abandoning an L1 category with no L2 equivalent is easier than creating an L2 category with no L1 equivalent. That is, splitting categories is difficult, but merging two existing categories is assumed to involve mere re-labeling. However, if linguistic categories reflect particular event construals, all transitions should involve adjustments of representations regardless of whether they involve splitting or merging. Gesture data can provide some information on the elusive processes underlying merging. Dutch learners of French accurately use the French placement verb, *mettre*, "put," in L2 as they move from their two finer-grained L1 categories, *zetten*, "set," and *leggen*, "lay" (Gullberg, forthcoming). However, to "mean" the same thing by *mettre* as native speakers of French, they must shift interest away from objects and towards a path-only-oriented perspective. Their gestures reveal both French-like, Dutch-like, and mixed patterns suggesting that different learners operate with different representations for their L2 surface forms. Moreover, the gesture evidence indicates that re-organization of perspective or representations in L2 acquisition is a gradual process with intermediate stages where both L1 and L2 perspectives come into play. Nevertheless, full adjustment is not beyond the realm of the possible since some learners do gesture in a French-like fashion.

Cross-linguistic influences may also operate from L2 to L1 in that an emerging L2 may influence an established L1 (cf. Cook, 2003; Pavlenko & Jarvis, 2002). This is not necessarily a matter of language loss or attrition, nor indeed an effect of advanced bilingualism, but rather the normal result of processing more than one language regardless of proficiency. Such bi-directional influences are amply documented in the literature on lexical processing (e.g. Costa, 2005; Dijkstra, 2005). There is also preliminary evidence for such effects in lexicalization. Native Japanese speakers with intermediate knowledge of English speak and gesture differently about motion events in their L1 than monolingual Japanese speakers (Brown, 2007). They introduce more path elements in L1 Japanese speech, notably expressions of source and goal. Interestingly, in gesture they also adopt more observer-viewpoint perspectives on events than monolingual Japanese speakers who prefer a character-viewpoint perspective (cf. McNeill, 1992). This means that monolingual Japanese speakers perform enacting gestures as if they themselves were the protagonists in a story. Japanese speakers who know some English instead typically represent entities or events in gestures as seen from a distance and not as if they themselves were performing them. Although the speech and gestures are perfectly grammatical, the gesture data in particular suggest that Japanese speakers with knowledge of English construe motion events differently from monolinguals. Observations like these have theoretical and methodological implications, bringing SLA and bilingualism studies closer.

To summarize, gesture analyses of learner production allow additional information to be gleaned on how L2 learners adjust representations and perspectives on events as they go from a certain L1 to a certain L2. Both the timing and form of gestures provide information about gradual changes and intermediate shifts in L2 linguistic conceptualization that may go undetected especially where speech is formally, if not distributionally, target-like. The combined analysis of gesture and speech reveal more about the difficulties learners have in shifting linguistic conceptualization than speech alone. The findings suggest two typical L2 patterns, one where gestures and speech indicate a unified (wholly L1-like) event construal, and one disjoint construal where the modalities show discrepancies. Note, however, that most gesture studies to date tend to assume that any L2 pattern that does not conform to the target is solely due to properties of the L1. This is both theoretically and methodologically ill-founded. Transfer can only be established when learners with different L1s learning the same target L2 are examined. Only then can alternative explanations such as general learner effects be ruled out (cf. Jarvis, 2000).

3.2 Gestures and L2 development in general

SLA research is not only restricted to comparisons of interlanguage against L1 and L2 norms but also focuses upon interlanguage as a systematic and regular variety in its own right, a learner-variety (cf. Bley-Vroman, 1990; Klein & Perdue, 1997). Gestures contribute to this line of study as well. Systematically parallel changes in gesture and speech at a given point in development allow us to investigate interactions between communicative and more process-related constraints on learner varieties.

3.2.1 L2 gestures as indicators of expressive difficulties

It has frequently been observed that L2 learners produce more gestures when speaking the L2 than when speaking their L1 (e.g. Gullberg, 1998; Sherman & Nicoladis, 2004; for exceptions, see e.g. Wieselman Schulman, 2004). One of the presumed reasons for this is proficiency, or more precisely, the notion that gestures reflect increased difficulties and that learners' gestures compensate for speech problems. The view of gestures as a compensation device in production and comprehension is popular in studies of aphasia (cf. Rose, 2006) and specific language impairment (Fex & Månsson, 1998). Although it is clear that not all L2 gestures are motivated by compensatory needs, it is equally clear that L2 learners can and do use gestures as part of their cognitively and interactionally motivated communication strategies (CSs) to overcome various expressive problems (Gullberg, 1998). L2 learners use gestures strategically for three main purposes: to compensate for lexical shortcomings, to alleviate grammatical difficulties, and to manage fluency-related problems.

First, learners use gestures to solve lexical dilemmas. Contrary to popular expectation, these gestures do not replace speech but typically occur *with* speech, often a spoken strategy such as an approximation or circumlocution. These are also joint solutions since learners use gestures to elicit lexical help from the interlocutor. Such gestural solutions work equally well for concrete and abstract items in that abstract concepts are given concrete properties in representational gestures (e.g. Gullberg, 1998; McCafferty, 1998).

Second, learners also use gestures to overcome grammatical difficulties such as those related to tense and temporality. By mapping time onto space metaphorically, learners can gesturally refer to spatial time axes to establish temporal relationships quite precisely even in the absence of adequate temporal morphology in speech (Gullberg, 1999). Again, the use of gestures is closely linked to the use of temporal lexical items that help clarify the relationship between locations on the time axes.

Finally, the troublesome interaction that results from accumulated difficulties and non-fluency yields the most frequent type of gesture in L2 production: metapragmatic gestures (Gullberg, 1998). In speakers of Western-European languages these gestures frequently involve circling movements of the wrist or wriggling fingers. They often occur during communicative breakdowns and they flag the fact of an ongoing word search, but not its content. En route, they also serve efficiently to hold the learner's turn and to elicit clarification or confirmation (cf. Duncan, 1972; Schegloff, 1984; Streeck & Hartege, 1992). These gestures are interactional glue that help sustain and facilitate positive interaction between the non-native and native participants (Bavelas et al., 1992; McCafferty, 2002).

To simply equate higher gesture rate with more difficulty is clearly not sufficient. Different types of difficulties affect different types of gestures. Much more information can be gained if these differences in types and functions are considered. For instance, a shift in reliance on a particular gesture type can shed light on shifts in different interlanguage domains. Taranger and Coupier (1984) showed how, with growing proficiency, Moroccan learners of French changed from using mainly representational gestures complementing the content of speech towards more emphatic or rhythmic gestures related to discourse. Similar development is reported for Japanese learners of French residing in France (Kida, 2005). This suggests a transition from essentially lexical difficulties and lexically based production to more grammatical problems related to discourse. More careful charting of what gestures are produced by learners with particular proficiency profiles has potential pedagogical and diagnostic applications.

3.2.2 Constraints on learner varieties

A different approach takes spoken learner phenomena as the starting point for examining gestural correlates with a view to improving our understanding of learner varieties. For example, many early L2 learners of different L1s and L2s have similar difficulties maintaining reference in discourse. They often use full lexical noun phrases (NPs) instead of pronouns to refer back to an entity just mentioned, leading to clause chains like "the woman . . . the woman . . . the woman" instead of "the woman . . . she . . . ø." Such chains form over-explicit, ambiguous, and non-cohesive speech since new and given information cannot be distinguished (e.g. Givón, 1984; Hendriks, 2003). The over-explicitness in speech is mirrored in the gestures of Swedish, French, and Dutch learners at low levels of proficiency (Gullberg, 2003; 2006a; Yoshioka, 2005; Yoshioka &

Kellerman, 2006). Learners anchor entities talked about in space with gesture at their first mention, and then anaphorically refer back to that same location at the immediate next mention if labeled by a lexical NP in speech. This gestural behavior changes with grammatical development in speech (Gullberg, 2003). Once pronouns are used for maintained reference, the number of anaphoric gestures drops significantly. Importantly, the properties of L2 speech do not depend on the presence of disambiguating anaphoric gestures. Learners' speech remains over-explicit whether their interlocutors can see their disambiguating gestures or not (Gullberg, 2006a). Further, the gestures do no disappear when interlocutors cannot see them, indicating that their presence is not motivated by concerns of ambiguity. Interestingly, however, the gestures are less spatially distinct when they cannot be seen. This suggests that if visible, learners do tailor their gestures for the interlocutor such that they can be exploited for disambiguation. But, overall, the core properties of both speech and gesture seem to depend on development and not to be motivated by communicative concerns, even if communication influences the actual articulation of gestures.

Gestures can thus enrich the analyses of general properties of L2 development illuminating the interplay between cognitive constraints and communicative pressures. Both factors shape learner production when situated in interaction and the combined analysis of speech and gesture contributes to more fine-grained accounts of how their relative weight plays out.

4 Gestures and (language) learning

4.1 Gestures as input—does seeing gestures help?

Interlocutors are known to attend to and make use of gestural information, for instance to improve comprehension in noise (Rogers, 1978). A natural assumption is therefore that gestures that convey speech-related meaning should improve language learners' comprehension and possibly also learning (cf. Harris, 2003; Kellerman, 1992). Instructors or competent speakers seem to sense this. Almost all forms of "instructional communication" or didactic talk have gestural correlates characterized by an increased use of representational and rhythmic gestures (Allen, 2000; Gullberg, 1998). This has been observed in foreigner talk (Adams, 1998), teacher talk (e.g. Hauge, 2000; Henzl, 1979; Lazaraton, 2004), caregiver talk (e.g. Garnica, 1978; Iverson, Capirci, Longobardi, & Caselli, 1999), and academic lectures (e.g. Corts & Pollio, 1999). There is some support for the notion that gestures improve comprehension in L2 contexts. Sueyoshi and Hardison (2005) found that low-proficiency learners did understand a lecture on ceramics in L2 English better when gestures were present. They also benefited more from gestures than more proficient learners. Tellier (2006) shows that French five-year-olds understand the main events of a story told in English, a completely unknown language, if accompanied by iconic gestures. However, the broad claim that gestures improve comprehension may be too general. Musumeci (1989) tested tense assignment in L2 English by beginner EFL learners with different L1s. Three cues to tense were available: temporal adverbials, verb morphology, and gestures indicating temporal reference (past behind, present in front of, and future away from speaker). All learners relied on temporal adverbials, with advanced learners also exploiting morphology. In no group did gestures have a significant effect. The facilitative effect of gestures may depend on the nature of the linguistic units illustrated and be more evident for lexical than grammatical material. Moreover, different gesture types clearly have different effects. While speech-associated gestures may help, culture-specific, conventionalized gestures will not confer comprehension benefits unless they have been explained, as suggested by studies showing that learners do not understand foreign emblems well (e.g. Mohan & Helmer, 1988; Wolfgang & Wolofsky, 1991) without instruction (Jungheim, 1991).

Gesture input also seems to promote actual learning. Children learning about mathematical equivalence (Singer & Goldin-Meadow, 2005) and the concept of symmetry (Valenzeno, Alibali, & Klatzky, 2002) all benefit from their teachers' gestures, especially when these convey more information than speech. In the domain of language, English three-year-olds learn new adjectives such as "spongy" better if they are taught the adjective while shown a descriptive squeezing gesture, than if the adjective is introduced with only a pointing gesture (O'Neill, Topolovec, & Stern-Cavalcante, 2002). For SLA, the available evidence is scarce but indicative of similar benefits. Allen (1995) showed that learners who received explanations of French vocabulary with emblematic gestures learned more and forgot significantly fewer words than learners who had not received gesture input with the explanations.

Accounts for why gestural input is helpful typically suggest that gestures capture attention, provide semantic redundancy, and generally engage more senses by grounding speech in the concrete, physical experience (cf. Hostetter & Alibali, 2004). A possible neurocognitive account pertains to mirror neurons, suggesting that the same areas in motor cortex are activated when observing others' actions and (presumably) gestures as when performing them yourself (e.g. Rizzolatti & Craighero, 2004). Similarly, recent work on "embodied cognition" (e.g. Glenberg & Kaschak, 2002) suggests that comprehension is grounded in action. Words like *doorknob* activate knowledge of the hand shape in clenching (Klatzky, Pellegrino, McCloskey, & Doherty, 1989). Seeing gestures might therefore improve comprehension and learning because sensori-motor experience is evoked. These various explanations need not be mutually exclusive. However, some options could be explored experimentally for the full pedagogical implications for SLA to become clearer. It is an empirical challenge to determine which gestures may help with what both inside and outside the language classroom.

4.2 Gestures as output—does producing gestures help?

It has recently been suggested that gestures not only help listeners but also speakers themselves. For instance, children who gesture while learning about math perform better than children who do not (Alibali & DiRusso, 1999). Adult learners also benefit from gesturing as they reason about novel concepts in science (e.g. Crowder, 1996; Roth, 2003), and medicine (Alac, 2005; Koschmann & LeBaron, 2002). Very few studies actually test learning effects of gesturing in SLA. The majority of studies instead rely on indirect measures. Scholars working within a socio-cultural theory perspective argue that producing gestures helps language learners internalize new knowledge related to various domains in the L2 through enactment or processes of embodiment (e.g. Negueruela et al., 2004). For example, McCafferty (2004; 2006) proposes that a learner's rhythmic gestures may support the acquisition of L2 prosodic structure. He argues that beats may help learners parse and structure the rhythmic pulse of an L2 as they attempt to master syllable structure. This highly interesting suggestion could and should be empirically tested. The input and output perspectives have also been combined to examine measurable effects on comprehension and lexical learning in the teaching of English as a foreign language to French children (Tellier, 2006). Children who receive gestural input with vocabulary explanations retain significantly more items than those who do not. Importantly, children who also reproduce the gestures themselves perform even better than children who do not even if they have had gestural input.

Why should producing gestures help learning? One account is essentially communicative. In many cases, children and adults talking about new and poorly mastered notions convey additional or redundant information in gestures compared to speech (sometimes called "mismatches," cf. Alibali & Goldin-Meadow, 1993; Goldin-Meadow, 2003). In developmental psychology this discrepancy between speech and gesture has been interpreted as an indication of transitional knowledge states. Interestingly, speakers displaying such discrepancies seem to be ready to learn and benefit most from instruction (Church & Goldin-Meadow, 1986; Goldin-Meadow, 2003). Adults and teachers are sensitive to these discrepancies and tailor their own speech-gesture production to the learners' levels (Goldin-Meadow, 2003). In this sense, learners help themselves by gesturing because their gestures influence their interlocutors, prompting these to create optimal input for the learners (cf. the Comprehensible Input Hypothesis, Krashen, 1994). In addition, learners' gestures generate positive attitudes between them and their addressees (McCafferty, 2002), which may increase the opportunities for using the L2 further and promote continued output (cf. the Output Hypothesis, Swain, 2000). This is also assumed to promote language learning. The positive interactional effects of learners' gestures carry over to assessment. Learners who are seen to gesture are often more positively evaluated on proficiency than those who are not (Gullberg, 1998; Jenkins & Parra, 2003; Jungheim, 2001).

Alternative cognitive explanations tend to focus on general cognitive gains of gesturing without making specific claims about learning. For instance, cognitive psychology has demonstrated an effect of enaction on memory. Enacted action is better recalled than action phrases without enactment (Engelkamp & Cohen, 1991) and self-enactment improves recall more than seeing someone else enacting (Frick-Horbury, 2002). More generally, the gestural Information Packaging Hypothesis proposes that gestures help speakers plan what to say. By performing a gesture, speakers can explore aspects of their communicative intentions and more easily select, package, and linearize spatial information into verbalizable units (cf. Alibali et al., 2000). Such facilitation in conceptual and linguistic planning may help learning. A more process-oriented proposal is that gesturing reduces cognitive load on working memory (Goldin-Meadow, Nusbaum, Kelly, & Wagner, 2001). In a task where speakers have to memorize word lists while they explain a math problem, those speakers who gesture during the math explanation subsequently recall more words than those who do not. The argument is that by gesturing speakers unload cognition onto an external representation, thereby liberating processing resources which can be re-assigned to memorization, planning, or other working-memory intense operations. This account is particularly tempting for SLA since it could explain why learners produce so many gestures when they are barely fluent, even when their interlocutors cannot see their gestures. It is possible that L2 learners' gestures reflect their attempts to reduce the processing load of keeping words, grammar, and the relationships between entities in mind at the same time as planning what to say next. In this sense, gestures may help learners to keep talking. Again, in and of itself this is not a direct explanation for actual learning but fits in well with the effects to be gained from producing sustained output and from influencing your interlocutors positively. As before, the communicative and cognitive explanations need not be mutually exclusive.

5 The gesture challenges

The analysis of L2 gestures raises some important theoretical questions regarding the relationship between surface forms, representations and conceptualization, as well as about the status of gestures as mediating between them. L2 gesture data in fact put both gesture and L2 theories under pressure. In native contexts gestures are assumed to tap semantic or conceptual representations (and implicit knowledge) more directly than speech. They are also influenced by surface form such as the actual syntactic constructions chosen to encode semantic components (e.g. Özyürek et al., 2005). Generally, the link to conceptualization is believed to be stronger than to speech by virtue of the fact that gestures can be "ahead" of speech and express knowledge states and information not yet available for linguistic or explicit expression (cf. Goldin-Meadow, 2003). This predicts that representations should change first, followed by gestures and then speech. L2 data pose problems for all of the above. Learners' gestures display a dissociation between surface form and gesture and therefore potentially also between surface form and representations. Learners often continue to align their gestures with spoken elements that reflect L1- rather than L2-typical foci. They can also express meaning in gesture that reflects semantic or conceptual material from the L1 even as they are expressing other semantic elements in the spoken L2. They gesture one thing, and say another. Strikingly, in the L2 studies reviewed speech is overall more likely to be target-like than gestures; L2 speech appears to change towards the target before gestures do. Very few attempts have been made to account for this L2-specific form of speech-gesture discrepancy. It prompts questions, however, regarding what kind of representations actually underpin L2 surface forms. When L2 surface form and gesture both look L1-like, the relationship is clear. However, when L2 speech looks target-like and gesture does not, it is unclear on what representations the spoken L2 forms are based. How can Turkish learners use accurate constructions like "roll down" in speech if they underlyingly still focus on path or on manner separately? More generally, the looser link between spoken and gestural form begs the question of how great the overlap in meaning between the modalities must be in order to be considered a match in representation or conceptualization. Answers to these questions will contribute in important ways to theories of gesture as well as of SLA.

A view of Second Language Acquisition that takes gestures into account also ups the stakes for notions like native-likeness and ultimate attainment (Birdsong, 2004; 2005). Gestures expand the scope of inquiry by providing more dimensions along which learners' utterances and discourse can vary. With this extra information ever more subtle details about the speech production process can be explored and gauged against native speakers. Equally, evidence that gesture patterns typical of the L2 find their way into the L1 also challenges the notion of a monolithic, monolingual native standard (cf. Davies, 2003). Moreover, gestures push the boundaries further if viewed as a modality to which judgments of target likeness apply per se. Under the assumption that language consists of speech and gestures as a "composite signal" (Clark, 1996), learning a new language also entails learning a new gesture repertoire (e.g. Antes, 1996; Von Raffler-Engel, 1980). The acquisition of L2 gesture can be studied in a product-oriented way just like speech, to determine "cross-gestural" influences between L1 and L2, for example. The L1 use of gesture space, small or large, may carry over to L2 production (cf. Kida, 2005). Culture-specific emblems may cause similar trouble in L2 comprehension and production as idiomatic expressions (e.g. Jungheim, 2006). Moreover, new ways of back-channeling or pointing are probably hard to acquire given their semi-conventional but highly automatized nature. The extent to which L2 learners actually acquire any aspect of L2 gestures is a sorely understudied area both in comprehension and production for conventional and speech-associated gestures alike (cf. Gullberg, 2006b).

Clearly, the acquisition of gestural repertoires represents an enormous challenge to language learners and educators. Very little is known about gestural repertoires—forms, usage patterns—beyond what is described in this chapter. What might be learnable and indeed teachable (and therefore assessable) is entirely unknown regardless of the definition of implicit and explicit knowledge and learning. Conversely, it is not known whether non-native-like gesturing, "foreign gesture," is as disruptive to interlocutors as foreign accent. While anecdotally plausible, it remains an open empirical question until a perceptual foreign gesture study is undertaken. Much work lies ahead to expand our knowledge of culture- and language-specific gestural repertoires, form–function relationships in more linguistic domains, contexts, and settings, and the range of variation in native repertoires. Methodological rigor and replicability is fundamental to these endeavors and precise procedures and descriptions are needed that carefully consider the multifunctional nature of gestures. Since gestures can be motivated by many different underlying mechanisms and processes—especially in L2 production where lexical, syntactic, conceptual, and interactive difficulties converge—rigorous criteria must be applied to ensure that relevant gesture types are considered.

6 Conclusions

This chapter set out to demonstrate why gestures are relevant to SLA. The grand answer is that gestures enable us to study the interactions between communicative and cognitive, process-related constraints on L2 development in novel detail. Gestures are at once interactive, spatio-visual phenomena and also closely tied to sophisticated speaker-internal, linguistic processes. They therefore allow a richer perspective to be taken on the processes of language acquisition in which the learner's individual cognition is situated in a social, interactive context. Gestures can be studied in their own right as external representations of meaning and communicative intentions. They also offer new possibilities as a tool to examine old L2 issues in novel ways. For example, differences between tutored and untutored learners and early simultaneous bilinguals may be explored in more detail, considering acquisition both as a product and as a process. Gestures open new ways to examine the SLA of meaning to complement and expand the current predominant focus on form, allowing issues of broad conceptualization, categorization, *and* syntactic form to be fruitfully brought together. Because the distribution of meaning components in gesture and speech is not necessarily one-to-one, gesture may also promote a focus on broader units of analysis, like utterance or discourse, which enable a fuller picture of the learner's language activity to be gleaned. The ultimate challenge is to integrate gestures, as communicatively and cognitively relevant entities, into the wider field of SLA such that they can feed into and inform cognitive, linguistic, and cognitive linguistic theories of L2 learning and L2 use.

Notes

I am indebted to David Birdsong and Nick C. Ellis for helpful comments on an earlier draft. All remaining nonsense is my own.

1 Notice that the Thinking for Speaking Hypothesis (TFS) differs in scope from traditional linguistic relativity (Gumperz & Levinson, 1996; Sapir, 1951). The TFS hypothesis specifically targets linguistic conceptualization whereas linguistic relativity proper assumes that linguistic categories affect general cognition outside language. Gestures have been used to support arguments of linguistic relativity, too, for instance in the domain of spatial frames of reference (Haviland, 1996; Levinson, 2003).

Bibliography

Adams, T. W. (1998). *Gesture in foreigner talk.* Unpublished PhD diss., University of Pennsylvania.

Alac, M. (2005). From trash to treasure: Learning about brain images through multimodality. *Semiotica*, 156(1–4), 177–202.

Alibali, M. W. (2005). Gesture in spatial cognition: Expressing, communicating, and thinking about spatial information. *Spatial Cognition & Computation*, 5(4), 307–331.

Alibali, M. W., & DiRusso, A. A. (1999). The function of gestures in learning to count: More than keeping track. *Cognitive Development, 14*(1), 37–56.

Alibali, M. W., & Goldin-Meadow, S. (1993). Gesture-speech mismatch and mechanisms of learning: What the hands reveal about a child's state of mind. *Cognitive Psychology, 25,* 468–523.

Alibali, M. W., Heath, D. C., & Myers, H. J. (2001). Effects of visibility between speaker and listener on gesture production: Some gestures are meant to be seen. *Journal of Memory and Language, 44*(2), 169–188.

Alibali, M. W., Kita, S., & Young, A. J. (2000). Gesture and the process of speech production: We think, therefore we gesture. *Language and Cognitive Processes, 15*(6), 593–613.

Allen, L. Q. (1995). The effect of emblematic gestures on the development and access of mental representations of French expressions. *Modern Language Journal, 79*(4), 521–529.

Allen, L. Q. (2000). Nonverbal accommodations in foreign language teacher talk. *Applied Language Learning, 11,* 155–176.

Antes, T. A. (1996). Kinesics: The value of gesture in language and in the language classroom. *Foreign Language Annals, 29*(3), 439–448.

Bavelas, J. B., Chovil, N., Lawrie, D. A., & Wade, A. (1992). Interactive gestures. *Discourse Processes, 15*(4), 469–489.

Beattie, G., & Shovelton, H. (2002). An experimental investigation of some properties of individual iconic gestures that mediate their communicative power. *British Journal of Psychology, 93*(2), 179–192.

Berman, R., & Slobin, D. I. (1994). Filtering and packaging in narrative. In R. Berman & D. I. Slobin (Eds.), *Relating events in narrative: A cross-linguistic developmental study* (pp. 515–554). Hillsdale, NJ: Erlbaum.

Birdsong, D. (2004). Second language acquisition and ultimate attainment. In A. Davies & C. Elder (Eds.), *Handbook of Applied linguistics* (pp. 82–105). London: Blackwell.

Birdsong, D. (2005). Nativelikeness and non-nativelikeness in L2A research. *International Review of Applied Linguistics, 43*(4), 319–328.

Bley-Vroman, R. (1990). The logical problem of foreign language learning. *Linguistic Analysis, 20,* 3–49.

Brown, A. (2007). *Crosslinguistic influence in first and second languages: Convergence in speech and gesture.* Unpublished PhD diss., Boston University, Boston.

Carroll, M., Murcia-Serra, J., Watorek, M., & Bendiscoli, A. (2000). The relevance of information organization to second language acquisition studies: The descriptive discourse of advanced adult learners of German. *Studies in Second Language Acquisition, 22*(3), 441–466.

Carroll, M., & Von Stutterheim, C. (2003). Typology and information organisation: perspective taking and language-specific effects in the construal of events. In A. G. Ramat (Ed.), *Typology and second language acquisition* (pp. 365–402). Berlin: Mouton.

Cassell, J., McNeill, D., & McCullough, K.-E. (1999). Speech-gesture mismatches: Evidence for one underlying representation of linguistic and nonlinguistic information. *Pragmatics & Cognition, 7*(1), 1–33.

Church, R. B., & Goldin-Meadow, S. (1986). The mismatch between gesture and speech as an index of transitional knowledge. *Cognition, 23*(1), 43–71.

Cienki, A. (1998). Metaphoric gestures and some of their relations to verbal metaphoric expressions. In J.-P. Koenig (Ed.), *Discourse and cognition. Bridging the gap* (pp. 189–204). Stanford, CA: Center for the Study of Language and Information Publications.

Clark, H. H. (1996). *Using language*. Cambridge: Cambridge University Press.

Cook, V. (2003). Introduction: The changing L1 in the L2 user's mind. In V. Cook (Ed.), *Effects of the second language on the first* (pp. 1–18). Clevedon: Multilingual Matters.

Corts, D. P., & Pollio, H., R. (1999). Spontaneous production of figurative language and gesture in college lectures. *Metaphor & Symbol, 14*(2), 81–100.

Costa, A. (2005). Lexical access in bilingual production. In J. F. Kroll & A. M. De Groot (Eds.), *Handbook of bilingualism. Psycholinguistic approaches* (pp. 308–325). Oxford: Oxford University Press.

Crowder, E. M. (1996). Gestures at work in sense-making science talk. *Journal of the Learning Sciences, 5*(3), 173–208.

Davies, A. (2003). *The native speaker: myth and reality*. Clevedon: Multilingual Matters.

De Ruiter, J.-P. (1998). *Gesture and speech production*. Unpublished PhD diss., University of Nijmegen.

De Ruiter, J.-P. (2000). The production of gesture and speech. In D. McNeill (Ed.), *Language and gesture: Window into thought and action* (pp. 284–311). Cambridge: Cambridge University Press.

Dijkstra, T. (2005). Bilingual visual word recognition and lexical access. In J. F. Kroll & A. M. De Groot (Eds.), *Handbook of bilingualism. Psycholinguistic approaches* (pp. 179–201). Oxford: Oxford University Press.

Duncan, S. (1994). *Grammatical form and "thinking-for-speaking" in Mandarin Chinese and English: An analysis based on speech-accompanying gesture*. Unpublished PhD diss., University of Chicago, Chicago.

Duncan, S. J. (1972). Some signals and rules for taking speaking turns in conversation. *Journal of Personality and Social Psychology, 23*(2), 283–292.

Efron, D. (1941/1972). *Gestures, race and culture* (First edition 1941 as Gestures and environment. New York: King's Crown Press. ed.). The Hague: Mouton.

Ekman, P., & Friesen, W. V. (1969). The repertoire of nonverbal behavior: Categories, origins, usage, and coding. *Semiotica, 1*(1), 49–98.

Engelkamp, J., & Cohen, R. L. (1991). Current issues in memory of action events. *Psychological Research, 53*, 175–182.

Fex, B., & Månsson, A.-C. (1998). The use of gestures as a compensatory strategy in adults with acquired aphasia compared to children with specific language impairment (SLI). *Journal of Neurolinguistics, 11*(1–2), 191–206.

Freedman, N. (1977). Hands, words, and mind: On the structuralization of body movements during discourse and the capacity for verbal representation. In N. Freedman & S. Grand (Eds.), *Communicative structures and psychic structures: A psychoanalytic approach* (pp. 109–132). New York: Plenum Press.

Frick-Horbury, D. (2002). The use of hand gestures as self-generated cues for recall of verbally associated targets. *American Journal of Psychology, 115*(1), 1–20.

Garnica, O. K. (1978). Non-verbal concomitants of language input to children. In N. Waterson & C. Snow (Eds.), *The development of communication* (pp. 139–147). New York: Wiley.

Givón, T. (1984). Universals of discourse structure and second language acquisition. In W. E. Rutherford (Ed.), *Language universals and second language acquisition* (pp. 109–136). Amsterdam: John Benjamins.

Glenberg, A. M., & Kaschak, M. P. (2002). Grounding language in action. *Psychonomic Bulletin & Review, 9*(3), 558–565.

Goldin-Meadow, S. (2003). *Hearing gesture: How our hands help us think.* Cambridge, MA: The Belknap Press.

Goldin-Meadow, S., Nusbaum, H., Kelly, S. D., & Wagner, S. (2001). Explaining math: Gesturing lightens the load. *Psychological Science, 12*(6), 516–522.

Goodwin, C. (2000). Gesture, aphasia, and interaction. In D. McNeill (Ed.), *Language and gesture* (pp. 84–98). Cambridge: Cambridge University Press.

Gullberg, M. (1998). *Gesture as a communication strategy in second language discourse. A study of learners of French and Swedish.* Lund: Lund University Press.

Gullberg, M. (1999). Communication strategies, gestures, and grammar. *Acquisition et Interaction en Langue Etrangère, Numéro spécial: Eurosla8. A selection of papers (ed. Perdue, C. & Lambert, M.) (2),* 61–71.

Gullberg, M. (2003). Gestures, referents, and anaphoric linkage in learner varieties. In C. Dimroth & M. Starren (Eds.), *Information structure, linguistic structure and the dynamics of language acquisition* (pp. 311–328). Amsterdam: John Benjamins.

Gullberg, M. (2006a). Handling discourse: Gestures, reference tracking, and communication strategies in early L2. *Language Learning, 56*(1), 155–196.

Gullberg, M. (2006b). Some reasons for studying gesture and second language acquisition (Hommage à Adam Kendon). *International Review of Applied Linguistics, 44*(2), 103–124.

Gullberg, M. (forthcoming). What learners mean. What gestures reveal about semantic reorganisation of placement verbs in advanced L2.

Gullberg, M. (submitted). Language-specific encoding of placement events in gestures. In E. Pederson & J. Bohnemeyer (Eds.), *Event representations in language and cognition.* Cambridge: Cambridge University Press.

Gumperz, J. J., & Levinson, S. C. (1996). Introduction: Linguistic relativity re-examined. In J. J. Gumperz & S. C. Levinson (Eds.), *Rethinking linguistic relativity* (pp. 1–18). Cambridge: Cambridge University Press.

Harris, T. (2003). Listening with your eyes: The importance of speech-related gestures in the language classroom. *Foreign Language Annals, 36*(2), 180–187.

Hauge, E. (2000). *The role of gesture in British ELT in a university setting.* Unpublished PhD diss., University of Southampton, Southampton.

Haviland, J. B. (1993). Anchoring, iconicity and orientation in Guugu Yimithirr pointing gestures. *Journal of Linguistic Anthropology, 3*(1), 3–45.

Haviland, J. B. (1996). Projections, transpositions, and relativity. In J. J. Gumperz & S. C. Levinson (Eds.), *Rethinking linguistic relativity* (pp. 271–323). Cambridge: Cambridge University Press.

Hendriks, H. (2003). Using nouns for reference maintenance: a seeming contradiction in L2 discourse. In A. G. Ramat (Ed.), *Typology and second language acquisition* (pp. 291–326). Berlin: Mouton.

Henzl, V. M. (1979). Foreigner talk in the classroom. *International Review of Applied Linguistics, 17*(2), 159–167.

Holler, J., & Beattie, G. (2003). Pragmatic aspects of representational gestures. Do speakers use them to clarify verbal ambiguity for the listener? *Gesture, 3*(2), 127–154.

Hostetter, A. B., & Alibali, M. W. (2004). On the tip of the mind: Gesture as a key to conceptualization. In K. D. Forbus, D. Gentner & T. Regier (Eds.), *The 26th Annual Conference of the Cognitive Science Society* (pp. 589–594). Chicago: Cognitive Science Society.

Iverson, J. M., Capirci, O., Longobardi, E., & Caselli, M. C. (1999). Gesturing in mother-child interactions. *Cognitive Development, 14*(1), 57–75.

Jarvis, S. (2000). Methodological rigor in the study of transfer: Identifying L1 influence in the interlanguage lexicon. *Language Learning, 50*(2), 245–309.

Jenkins, S., & Parra, I. (2003). Multiple layers of meaning in an oral proficiency test: The complementary roles of nonverbal, paralinguistic, and verbal behaviors in assessment decisions. *Modern Language Journal, 87*(1), 90–107.

Jungheim, N. O. (1991). A study on the classroom acquisition of gestures in Japan. *Ryutsukeizaidaigaku Ronshu, 26*(2), 61–68.

Jungheim, N. O. (2001). The unspoken element of communicative competence: Evaluating language learners' nonverbal behavior. In T. Hudson & J. D. Brown (Eds.), *A focus on language test development: Expanding the language proficiency construct across a variety of tests* (Vol. 21, pp. 1–34). Honolulu: University of Hawai'i, Second Language Teaching and Curriculum Center.

Jungheim, N. O. (2006). Learner and native speaker perspectives on a culturally-specific Japanese refusal gesture. *International Review of Applied Linguistics, 44*(2), 125–142.

Kellerman, E. (1995). Crosslinguistic influence: Transfer to nowhere? *Annual Review of Applied Linguistics, 15*, 125–150.

Kellerman, E., & Van Hoof, A.-M. (2003). Manual accents. *International Review of Applied Linguistics, 41*(3), 251–269.

Kellerman, S. (1992). "I see what you mean": The role of kinesic behaviour in listening and implications for foreign and second language learning. *Applied Linguistics, 13*(3), 239–257.

Kelly, S. D., Kravitz, C., & Hopkins, M. (2004). Neural correlates of bimodal speech and gesture comprehension. *Brain and Language, 89*(1), 253–260.

Kendon, A. (1972). Some relationships between body motion and speech: An analysis of an example. In A. W. Siegman & B. Pope (Eds.), *Studies in dyadic communication* (pp. 177–210). New York: Pergamon.

Kendon, A. (1988). How gestures can become like words. In F. Poyatos (Ed.), *Crosscultural perspectives in nonverbal communication* (pp. 131–141). Toronto: Hogrefe.

Kendon, A. (1994). Do gestures communicate?: A review. *Research on Language and Social Interaction, 27*(3), 175–200.

Kendon, A. (2002). Some uses of the head shake. *Gesture, 2*(2), 147–182.

Kendon, A. (2004). *Gesture. Visible action as utterance.* Cambridge: Cambridge University Press.

Kida, T. (2005). *Appropriation du geste par les étrangers: Le cas d'étudiants japonais apprenant le français.* Unpublished PhD diss., Université de Provence (Aix-Marseille I), Aix-en-Provence.

Kita, S. (1993). *Language and thought interface: A study of spontaneous gestures and Japanese mimetics.* Unpublished PhD diss., University of Chicago, Chicago.

Kita, S., & Özyürek, A. (2003). What does cross-linguistic variation in semantic coordination of speech and gesture reveal?: Evidence for an interface representation of spatial thinking and speaking. *Journal of Memory and Language, 48*(1), 16–32.

Kita, S., Van Gijn, I., & Van der Hulst, H. (1998). Movement phases in signs and co-speech gestures, and their transcription by human coders. In I. Wachsmuth & M. Fröhlich (Eds.), *Gesture and sign language in human-computer interaction*, pp. 23–35. Berlin: Springer.

Klatzky, R. L., Pellegrino, J. W., McCloskey, B. P., & Doherty, S. (1989). Can you squeeze a tomato? The role of motor representations in semantic sensibility judgments. *Journal of Memory and Language, 28*(1), 56–77.

Klein, W., & Perdue, C. (1997). The basic variety (or: Couldn't natural languages be much simpler?). *Second Language Research, 13*(4), 301–347.

Koschmann, T., & LeBaron, C. (2002). Learner articulation as interactional achievement: Studying the conversation of gesture. *Cognition & Instruction, 20*(2), 249–282.

Krashen, S. D. (1994). The input hypothesis and its rivals. In N. C. Ellis (Ed.), *Implicit and explicit learning of languages* (pp. 45–78). London: Academic Press.

Krauss, R. K., Chen, Y., & Gottesman, R. F. (2000). Lexical gestures and lexical access: a process model. In D. McNeill (Ed.), *Language and gesture* (pp. 261–283). Cambridge: Cambridge University Press.

Krauss, R. M., Chen, Y., & Chawla, P. (1996). Nonverbal behavior and nonverbal communication: What do conversational hand gestures tell us? *Advances in Experimental Social Psychology, 28*, 389–450.

Lakoff, G., & Johnson, M. (1980). *Metaphors we live by*. Chicago: Chicago University Press.

Langton, S. R. H., O'Malley, C., & Bruce, V. (1996). Actions speak no louder than words: Symmetrical cross-modal interference effects in the processing of verbal and gestural information. *Journal of Experimental Psychology: Human Perception and Performance, 22*(6), 1,357–1,375.

Lazaraton, A. (2004). Gesture and speech in the vocabulary explanations of one ESL teacher: A microanalytic inquiry. *Language Learning, 54*(1), 79–117.

Levelt, W. J. M., Richardson, G., & La Heij, W. (1985). Pointing and voicing in deictic expressions. *Journal of Memory and Language, 24*(2), 133–164.

Levelt, W. J. M., Roelofs, A., & Meyer, A. S. (1999). A theory of lexical access in speech production. *Behavioral and Brain Sciences, 22*(1), 1–37(75).

Levinson, S. C. (2003). *Space in language and cognition. Explorations in cognitive diversity*. Cambridge: Cambridge University Press.

Levy, E. T., & McNeill, D. (1992). Speech, gesture, and discourse. *Discourse Processes, 15*(3), 277–301.

Lott, P. (1999). *Gesture and aphasia*. Bern: Peter Lang.

Mayberry, R. I., & Jaques, J. (2000). Gesture production during stuttered speech: Insights into the nature of gesture-speech integration. In D. McNeill (Ed.), *Language and gesture* (pp. 199–214). Cambridge: Cambridge University Press.

Mayberry, R. I., & Nicoladis, E. (2000). Gesture reflects language development: Evidence from bilingual children. *Current Directions in Psychological Science, 9*(6), 192–196.

Maynard, S. K. (1990). Conversation management in contrast: Listener response in Japanese and American English. *Journal of Pragmatics, 14,* 397–412.

McCafferty, S. G. (1998). Nonverbal expression and L2 private speech. *Applied Linguistics, 19*(1), 73–96.

McCafferty, S. G. (2002). Gesture and creating zones of proximal development for second language learning. *Modern Language Journal, 86*(2), 192–203.

McCafferty, S. G. (2004). Space for cognition: Gesture and second language learning. *International Journal of Applied Linguistics, 14*(1), 148–165.

McCafferty, S. G. (2006). Gesture and the materialization of second language prosody. *International Review of Applied Linguistics, 44*(2), 195–207.

McClave, E. (2000). Linguistic functions of head movements in the context of speech. *Journal of Pragmatics, 32*(7), 855–878.

McNeill, D. (1985). So you think gestures are nonverbal? *Psychological Review, 92*(3), 271–295.

McNeill, D. (1992). *Hand and mind. What the hands reveal about thought.* Chicago: Chicago University Press.

McNeill, D. (2000). Introduction. In D. McNeill (Ed.), *Language and gesture* (pp. 1–10). Cambridge: Cambridge University Press.

McNeill, D. (2005). *Gesture and thought.* Chicago: University of Chicago Press.

McNeill, D., & Duncan, S. D. (2000). Growth points in thinking-for-speaking. In D. McNeill (Ed.), *Language and gesture* (pp. 141–161). Cambridge: Cambridge University Press.

McNeill, D., Levy, E. T., & Cassell, J. (1993). Abstract deixis. *Semiotica, 95*(1/2), 5–19.

Melinger, A., & Levelt, W. J. M. (2004). Gesture and the communicative intention of the speaker. *Gesture, 4*(2), 119–141.

Mohan, B., & Helmer, S. (1988). Context and second language development: Preschoolers' comprehension of gestures. *Applied Linguistics, 9*(3), 275–292.

Morris, D., Collett, P., Marsh, P., & O'Shaughnessy, M. (1979). *Gestures, their origins and distribution.* London: Cape.

Müller, C. (1994). Semantic structure of motional gestures and lexicalization patterns in Spanish and German descriptions of motion-events. In K. Beals, J. M. Denton, R. Knippen, L. Melnar, H. Suzuki, & E. Zeinfeld (Eds.), *Papers from the Annual Regional Meeting of the Chicago Linguistic Society. The main session* (Vol. 30, pp. 281–295). Chicago, IL: Chicago Linguistic Society.

Musumeci, D. M. (1989). *The ability of second language learners to assign tense at the sentence Level: A crosslinguistic study.* Unpublished Ph.D diss., University of Illinois at Urbana-Champaign.

Negueruela, E., Lantolf, J. P., Rehn Jordan, S., & Gelabert, J. (2004). The "private function" of gesture in second language speaking activity: A study of motion verbs and gesturing in English and Spanish. *International Journal of Applied Linguistics, 14*(1), 113–147.

Núñez, R. E., & Sweetser, E. (2006). With the future behind them: Convergent evidence from Aymara language and gesture in the crosslinguistic comparison of spatial construals of time. *Cognitive Science, 30*(3), 401–450.

O'Neill, D. K., Topolovec, J., & Stern-Cavalcante, W. (2002). Feeling sponginess: The importance of descriptive gestures in 2- and 3-year-old children's acquisition of adjectives. *Journal of Cognition and Development, 3*(3), 243–277.

Odlin, T. (2005). Crosslinguistic influence and conceptual transfer: What are the concepts? *Annual Review of Applied Linguistics*, *25*, 3–25.

Özyürek, A. (2002a). Do speakers design their cospeech gestures for their addressees? The effects of addressee location on representational gestures. *Journal of Memory and Language*, *46*, 688–704.

Özyürek, A. (2002b). Speech-language relationship across languages and in second language learners: Implications for spatial thinking and speaking. In B. Skarabela (Ed.), *BUCLD Proceedings* (Vol. 26, pp. 500–509). Somerville, MA: Cascadilla Press.

Özyürek, A., Kita, S., Allen, S. E. M., Furman, R., & Brown, A. (2005). How does linguistic framing of events influence co-speech gestures? Insights from crosslinguistic variations and similarities. *Gesture*, *5*(1/2), 219–240.

Pavlenko, A., & Jarvis, S. (2002). Bidirectional transfer. *Applied Linguistics*, *23*(2), 190–214.

Payrató, L. (1993). A pragmatic view on autonomous gestures: A first repertoire of Catalan emblems. *Journal of Pragmatics*, *20*(3), 193–216.

Poyatos, F. (2002). *Nonverbal communication across disciplines* Amsterdam: John Benjamins.

Rizzolatti, G., & Craighero, L. (2004). The mirror-neuron system. *Annual Review of Neuroscience*, *27*(1), 169–192.

Rogers, W. T. (1978). The contribution of kinesic illustrators toward the comprehension of verbal behavior within utterances. *Human Communication Research*, *5*(1), 54–62.

Rose, M. L. (2006). The utility of arm and hand gesture in the treatment of aphasia. *Advances in Speech-Language Pathology*, *8*(2), 92–109.

Roth, W.-M. (2003). From epistemic (ergotic) actions to scientific discourse: The bridging function of gestures. *Pragmatics and Cognition*, *11*(1), 141–170.

Sapir, E. A. (1951). The unconscious patterning of behavior in society. In D. G. Mandelbaum (Ed.), *Selected writings of Edward Sapir in Language, Culture, and Personality* (pp. 544–559/556). Berkeley: University of California Press.

Schegloff, E. A. (1984). On some gestures' relation to talk. In J. M. Atkinson & J. Heritage (Eds.), *Structures of social action* (pp. 266–296). Cambridge: Cambridge University Press.

Schmitt, J.-C. (1991). The rationale of gestures in the West: Third to thirteenth centuries. In J. Bremmer & H. Roodenburg (Eds.), *A cultural history of gesture* (pp. 59–70). Ithaca, NY: Cornell University Press.

Seyfeddinipur, M. (2006). *Disfluency: Interrupting speech and gesture*. Unpublished PhD diss., Radboud University, Nijmegen.

Sherman, J., & Nicoladis, E. (2004). Gestures by advanced Spanish-English second-language learners. *Gesture*, *4*(2), 143–156.

Sherzer, J. (1972). Verbal and nonverbal deixis: The pointed lip gesture among the San Blas Cuna. *Language and Society*, *2*(1), 117–131.

Singer, M. A., & Goldin-Meadow, S. (2005). Children learn when their teacher's gestures and speech differ. *Psychological Science*, *16*(2), 85–89.

Slama-Cazacu, T. (1976). Nonverbal components in message sequence: "Mixed syntax". In W. C. McCormack & S. A. Wurm (Eds.), *Language and man: Anthropological issues* (pp. 217–227). The Hague: Mouton.

Slobin, D. I. (1996). From "thought and language" to "thinking for speaking". In

J. J. Gumperz & S. C. Levinson (Eds.), *Rethinking linguistic relativity* (pp. 70–96). Cambridge: Cambridge University Press.

Slobin, D. I. (2004). How people move. Discourse effects of linguistic typology. In C. L. Moder & A. Martinovic-Zic (Eds.), *Discourse across languages and cultures* (pp. 195–210). Amsterdam: John Benjamins.

Stam, G. (2006). Thinking for Speaking about motion: L1 and L2 speech and gesture. *International Review of Applied Linguistics, 44*(2), 143–169.

Stokoe, W. C. (1980). Sign language structure. *Annual Review of Anthropology, 9,* 365–390.

Streeck, J., & Hartege, U. (1992). Previews: Gestures at the transition place. In P. Auer & A. di Luzio (Eds.), *The contextualization of language* (pp. 135–157). Amsterdam: John Benjamins.

Sueyoshi, A., & Hardison, D. M. (2005). The role of gestures and facial cues in second language listening comprehension. *Language Learning, 55*(4), 661–699.

Swain, M. (2000). The output hypothesis and beyond: Mediating acquisition through collaborative dialogue. In J. P. Lantolf (Ed.), *Sociocultural theory and second language learning* (pp. 97–114). Oxford: Oxford University Press.

Talmy, L. (1985). Lexicalization patterns: Semantic structure in lexical forms. In T. Shopen (Ed.), *Language typology and syntactic description* (Vol. 3, pp. 57–149). Cambridge: Cambridge University Press.

Taranger, M.-C., & Coupier, C. (1984). *Recherche sur l'acquisition des langues secondes. Approche du gestuel.* Paper presented at the Acquisition d'une langue étrangère. Perspectives et recherches, Aix-en-Provence.

Tellier, M. (2006). *L'impact du geste pédagogique sur l'enseignement/apprentissage des langues étrangères: Etude sur des enfants de 5 ans.* Unpublished PhD diss., Université Paris VII–Denis Diderot, Paris.

Valenzeno, L., Alibali, M. W., & Klatzky, R. (2002). Teachers' gestures facilitate students' learning: A lesson in symmetry. *Contemporary Educational Psychology, 28,* 187–204.

Von Raffler-Engel, W. (1980). Kinesics and paralinguistics: A neglected factor in second language research and teaching. *Canadian Modern Language Review, 36*(2), 225–237.

Von Stutterheim, C., & Klein, W. (2002). Quaestio and L-perspectivation. In C. F. Graumann & W. Kallmeyer (Eds.), *Perspective and perspectivation in discourse* (pp. 59–88). Amsterdam: John Benjamins.

Wieselman Schulman, B. (2004). *A crosslinguistic investigation of the speech-gesture relationship in motion event descriptions.* Unpublished PhD diss., University of Chicago, Chicago.

Wilkins, D. P. (2003). Why pointing with the index finger is not a universal (in socio-cultural and semiotic terms). In S. Kita (Ed.), *Pointing: Where language, culture, and cognition meet* (pp. 171–215). Mahwah, NJ: Erlbaum.

Willems, R. M., Özyürek, A., & Hagoort, P. (2005). The comprehension of gesture and speech. *Journal of Cognitive Neuroscience, 17* (Supplement), 231.

Wolfgang, A., & Wolofsky, Z. (1991). The ability of new Canadians to decode gestures generated by Canadians of Anglo-Celtic backgrounds. *International Journal of Intercultural Relations, 15*(1), 47–64.

Wu, Y. C., & Coulson, S. (2005). Meaningful gestures: Electrophysiological indices of iconic gesture comprehension. *Psychophysiology, 42*(6), 654–667.

Yoshioka, K. (2005). *Linguistic and gestural introduction and tracking of referents in L1 and L2 discourse*. Unpublished PhD diss., Rijksuniversiteit Groningen, Groningen.

Yoshioka, K., & Kellerman, E. (2006). Gestural introduction of Ground reference in L2 narrative discourse. *International Review of Applied Linguistics*, 44(2), 171–193.

13

CONCEPTUAL TRANSFER AND MEANING EXTENSIONS

Terence Odlin

1 Preliminaries

As early as Wilhelm von Humboldt (1767–1835) some linguists have seen the mutual relevance of Second Language Acquisition (SLA) and linguistic relativity. As will be described, von Humboldt believed that the relation between language and thought is so highly specific to the native language that full attainment of another language is impossible. Relativistic analyses do not, however, compel this pessimistic stance on ultimate attainment in SLA. Indeed, another famous relativist, Benjamin Lee Whorf (1897–1941), took a decidedly more optimistic stance—even though, ironically, he is often labeled a "linguistic determinist." In decades of intensive SLA research (from the mid-1960s to the present), many linguists have pondered just how far learners of a second language may attain the competence and performance capacities of native speakers, and the question remains controversial (Han & Odlin 2006). Nevertheless, there has been only a belated recognition of the implications of the views of von Humboldt and Whorf for acquisition.

SLA discussions invoking linguistic relativity are not new, but the focus on this problem was sporadic until about ten years ago. Since the mid-1990s, researchers have more intensively studied effects of the native language even though many had already recognized the need to study cross-linguistic influence, also known as language transfer. (This recognition prevailed despite a strong current of skepticism about in the 1970s—cf. Ringbom 1987, Odlin 1989). From the mid-1990s onward several researchers have attempted to incorporate linguistic relativity into their analyses of transfer, and the intertwining of these two areas seems likely to continue for a long time to come. This research area is now frequently designated with the phrase *conceptual transfer*, which can be defined as cross-linguistic influence involving relativistic effects. The mutual relevance of SLA and relativity lies clearly in this area. If the "binding power" (to use Whorf's term) of the native language is even greater than he deemed it to be, full attainment of another language may be theoretically impossible, as von Humboldt claimed. On the other hand, there is no clear evidence that Whorf was wrong in believing that linguistics itself can help to overcome any binding power.

Apart from the attainment question, there is also a need to understand just how different the binding power of two typologically distinct languages may be when the meaning system of one of the languages more closely resembles the system of the target language. For instance, Spanish has a tense system rather similar to that in English, whereas Burmese is analyzed as having no tense system at all (Comrie 1985). Although there does not yet seem to be any research directly addressing this hypothetical example, such an investigation is warranted, and there does exist research on the relative difficulty that speakers of typologically different languages encounter with tense and other verb categories. For a variety of reasons, then, understanding the transfer of meaning is a major research challenge. Success will depend on an accurate assessment of the relation between cognition and language, specifically of the interactions between concepts and meanings in the acquisition of a second (or subsequent) language. This chapter will survey work on the transfer of meanings involving space, time, and motion in a wide range of SLA contexts. Moreover, the chapter will analyze evidence that such meanings in the L1 often involve additional meanings which can and do affect acquisition (as where, for instance, the expression of both motion and purpose involves a semantic extension in the native language system). Before the main survey and analysis, however, it will help to look more closely at the views of von Humboldt and Whorf and also to look at some recent work on relativity.

1.1 The pessimist and the optimist

Von Humboldt's widely cited analysis of relativity is a book-length preface (1836/1960, 1988) written for his three-volume linguistic and cultural investigations of Kawi, a literary language in Java (1836–1839). In the first volume von Humboldt said quite little about Kawi; virtually all of the preface concerns diversity in human language and the putative consequences of such diversity for cognition. In Chapter Nine his pessimism about full attainment in SLA is manifest. However, he does concede that learning a foreign language can result in somewhat new perspectives in one's existing world-view, "Weltansicht" in the original (1836/1960, p. 75). Indeed von Humboldt sees SLA as the sole means by which anyone may escape from the conceptual world constructed through the native language. Even so such escape is never entirely successful, since "one always more or less carries over ("hinüberträgt") one's own world-, indeed one's own language-view ("Welt- . . . Sprachansicht"), this success will not be felt [to be] pure and complete" (1836/1960, p. 75, my translation). The verb *hinüberträgt* represents an early instance of the metaphor of *transfer* (the Latin sources of which likewise mean carrying over), and the phrasing of *Welt-* . . . *Sprachansicht* indicates that von Humboldt thought of transfer as conceptual as well as linguistic, a position similar to a recent one taken by Slobin (1996)—who quotes von Humboldt and who likewise voices pessimism: "It seems that once our minds have been trained in taking particular points of view for the purposes of speaking, it is exceptionally difficult for us to be retrained" (1996, p. 91).

As already noted, Whorf looked at SLA more optimistically. In an article written around 1940, he considered the problems of an English-speaking learner of French who is not aware of first language structures that interfere with learning. With a confidence that seems characteristic of many structuralists, Whorf considers a hypothetical scenario with this learner:

> If, however, he is so fortunate as to have his elementary French taught by a theoretic linguist, he first has the patterns of the English formula explained in such a way that they become semi-conscious, with the result that they lose their binding power over him which custom has given them, though they remain automatic as far as English is concerned. Then he acquires the French patterns without inner opposition, and the time for attaining command of the language is cut to a fraction.
>
> (1956, pp. 224–225)

Whorf's own efforts with Hopi no doubt helped shape this view. During the mid-1930s he considered Hopi to be a language with three tenses: "factual or present-past, future, and generalized or usitative" (1956, p. 51). Two years later, however, he revised his analysis where the same categories do not involve tense but rather modality or evidentiality ("reportive," "expective," and "nomic"), which he deemed "distinct realms of validity" (1956, p. 113) that are "mutually exclusive" (p. 115). From this arose his oft-cited conviction that the Hopi verb is "timeless." Like many second language learners, Whorf revised his analysis drastically yet still not correctly, if a very detailed analysis by Malotki (1983) of the tense system of Hopi is sound. Even so, the conclusions that Whorf drew from his experience heightened his awareness of the analytical pitfalls of spurious interlingual identifications: ". . . Hopi categories are just enough like Indo-European ones to give at first a deceptive impression of identity . . ." (p. 112).

Certain claims Whorf made have few if any defenders nowadays, as the one on the supposedly "timeless" Hopi verb. Moreover, it will be seen (section 3) Whorf underestimated the similarity of time in Hopi and time in English in another important respect. Still a further reason for skepticism is that some subsequent work on relativity has proven inconclusive at best (e.g., Maratsos, Katis, & Margheri 2000). Not surprisingly, then, prominent linguists such as Pullum (1991) and Pinker (1994) have had serious doubts about the legacy of Whorf.

1.2 A look at relativity in spatial concepts

Despite continuing skepticism, empirical research in the last two decades has made it ever clearer that Whorf is not so easy to dismiss (e.g., Lucy 1992a, Levinson 2003). Indeed, Levinson characterizes his own work as "neo-Whorfian" (2003, p. 301). Since this chapter focuses on SLA research, a wider survey of important relativistic work is beyond that scope, but investigations by Levinson and colleagues are especially relevant.

In the last ten years or so, relativistic analyses have challenged some key assumptions underlying a universalist analysis of spatial concepts. Before the 1990s many linguists found it easy to believe that languages do not differ very much in the semantics of space despite considerable cross-linguistic variation in the grammatical realizations of spatial meanings. For instance, Lyons (1977) and Levelt (1989) accepted the analysis of Clark (1973), who propounded a neo-Kantian interpretation of space grounded in the canonical orientation of a standing human. However, this universal phenomenology has been called into question by empirical work on how non-linguistic spatial cognition co-varies with the structuring of spatial meanings in different languages. For instance, Levinson et al. (2003) detected hardly any cross-linguistic uniformity in the meanings of the adpositions in nine typologically distinct languages, as seen in the performance of speakers who were given a picture description task (a task designed to minimize any skewing toward particular linguistic or cultural groups). These results are consistent with earlier studies (e.g., Pederson et al. 1998) which found that speakers of typologically distinct languages differed in their memory of the location of objects in spatial arrays, with the performances co-varying by language. Thus, in contrast to speakers of Dutch, who relied on their deictically-based system of left and right to recall the location of objects, speakers of Arandic (an Australian language) recalled the same spatial array with the aid of the Arandic system of absolute locations (comparable to the cardinal points of north, south, etc.). Speakers of Arandic and other languages that heavily rely on absolute systems generally had more success in recalling the spatial arrays than did speakers of languages relying heavily on a speaker-centered spatial deixis as in Dutch.

Such findings clearly support relativistic analyses and will no doubt help to rehabilitate much of Whorf's reputation. Even so, there are still good reasons to take universalism seriously and to reject any extreme pendulum swing. Whorf himself viewed some kinds of human experiences as independent of culturally-specific influences (1956, p. 158), and another early relativist, Franz Boas, affirmed that "the occurrence of the most fundamental grammatical concepts in all languages must be considered proof of the unity of fundamental psychological processes" (1911/1966, p. 67). This stance seems absolutely necessary for the study of transfer. In many cases including spatial concepts the cross-linguistic correspondences are inexact and can occasion the type of influence that von Humboldt and Whorf hypothesized. For such transfer to occur, however, learners must be able to make interlingual identifications, and such identifications seem impossible in the absence of universals or typological commonalities across languages.

2 Conceptual and meaning transfer

The recent work on spatial concepts reflects two methodological practices now widely accepted in relativity research. First, there should be at least two groups of monolingual speakers whose languages are different enough to provide meaningful comparisons of possible effects of language upon cognition. Second, investigations of such effects should compare performance on tasks with a strong non-verbal component, which will help to assess language-specific effects on cognitive capacities to notice, to categorize, or to recall some experience. Tasks with a verbal component do not necessarily compromise approaches that also have a strong non-verbal component, and some of these tasks have proven useful, e.g., describing pictures and recalling events in a film. The non-verbal element in such tasks can be strong enough to make a case for relativity when performance differences between different language groups are found.

The practices of comparing groups and providing non-verbal tasks should be viewed as prerequisites for work on conceptual transfer. In addition, there must also be individuals showing some knowledge of a second language, and for the strongest possible verification of transfer it is very helpful to have at least two groups of second language learners with different native languages (cf. Jarvis 2000, Odlin 2003). Very few existing studies meet all of these conditions, but the evidence in several is striking enough to support at least some cautious inferences about conceptual transfer.

Evaluating such evidence requires a distinction to be made between *meaning transfer* and *conceptual transfer*. The former includes any type semantic or pragmatic influence from the first language (or from a second in L3 acquisition); although the term *meaning* is obviously very general, it has the advantage of being neutral between semantic and pragmatic influence. An occurrence of meaning transfer does not necessarily constitute a case of conceptual transfer, and the following example of an interlanguage English pronoun use makes clear the need to distinguish the two types of transfer. Polish has a first-person plural inflection (-*my*) that can sometimes serve as a marker of first person singular reference:

Wczoraj byliśmy z bratem w teatrze
Yesterday were-1ˢᵗ PL with brother-INS at theatre-LOC
= My brother and I went to the theatre yesterday.
(INS = instrumental; LOC = locative)

The form *byliśmy* normally indicates more than one referent, but in comitative constructions such as the above example the reference can be singular. This comitative construction seems to be a ready candidate for transfer, where *We were at the theatre with my brother yesterday* would be used to indicate a singular, not a plural, first-person referent. This very example is discussed (presumably to help English speakers understand comitatives) in a textbook on Polish which observes:

> You may notice Poles who speak otherwise excellent English carrying this pattern over into English. You are told that "we" did something with someone else . . . and then a character in a story seems to go missing. That is because "We . . . with X" should really have been "X and I."
>
> (Gotteri and Michalak-Gray 1997, pp. 180–181)

This instance of transfer (note the "carrying over" metaphor also used by von Humboldt) certainly indicates semantic and pragmatic influence, but no one could seriously cite this example as evidence that Poles fail to grasp the conceptual difference between singular and plural referents.

In light of the Polish example the following conclusion seems unavoidable: all conceptual transfer involves meaning transfer but not all meaning transfer involves conceptual transfer. The conclusion thus implies that the relation of conceptual to meaning transfer is one of subset to superset. This analysis thus entails something quite different from the "fairly massive conceptual transfer" discussed by MacWhinney (1982, p. 377), who seems to equate such transfer with meaning transfer, as does Ijaz (1986). Making the distinction between the two types of transfer is, however, consistent with analyses such as that of Levinson (1997), who distinguishes between "semantic representations" and "conceptual representations." The latter presumably constitute much of the foundation for the kind of universals that Boas postulated (as noted above) even while the former may show both language-specific and universal dimensions.

2.1 Grammar, cognitive effects, and some complications

Conceptual transfer could *underlie* patterns of meaning transfer either in lexis or grammar. Cognitive psychology has long provided evidence of effects of lexical choice in monolingual contexts as in a classic study of Loftus and Palmer (1974) that produced different patterns of recall depending on the words in the question asked of participants. Furthermore, SLA research reviewed by Jarvis and Pavlenko (2006) has identified cases of lexical transfer that may also constitute conceptual transfer. However, the transfer of meaning categories in grammar poses an especially interesting research challenge in regard to the "binding power" that Whorf contemplated. For him and for Boas, grammar helped construct language-specific frameworks of cognitive orientation.

As Boas put it, "It [grammar] determines those aspects of experience that *must* be expressed" (1938, p. 132, emphasis in the original). Illustrating his point with the English sentence *The man killed the bull*, Boas observes that definiteness, time, and number are categories of meaning that get mapped onto obligatory morphemes in the English sentence. He stresses, though, that many other languages often do not code such meanings in obligatory categories. The example Boas provides to make this point involves a category required in other languages (though not in English), namely, evidentiality, which can be defined as stating the basis for one's knowledge in making an assertion (Aikhenvald & Dixon 2003). Boas reworks his example sentence in the following way: *This man (or men) kill (indefinite tense) as seen by me that bull (or bulls)*, where the expression of visual experience is obligatory (to confirm how solid the speaker's knowledge is) and where the markers of time, definiteness, and number that are obligatory in English are optional in many languages (p. 133). As will be seen (in section 3.5), SLA research has identified cases of transfer involving not only obligatory verb tense but also obligatory evidentiality categories.

While obligatory grammatical categories seem likely to be especially strong influences on cognition, the nature of such influences also requires close scrutiny. The distinction made between meaning transfer and conceptual transfer implies that investigations of the latter will require tasks having a non-verbal component to help assess language-specific effects on cognitive abilities, which include capacities to notice, to categorize, or to recall experience. The verbs *notice, categorize*, and *recall* all seem sound starting points for research, but there are certainly theoretical and empirical complications. For one thing, each of the three verbs has more than one meaning, and what "noticing" might entail, for instance, has led to a large body of second language research (e.g., Schmidt 1990, DeKeyser 2003, Hulstijn 2003, and Robinson 2003).

Along with the ambiguities of *notice, categorize*, and *recall* there is the problem of how far-reaching relativity effects may be, especially in regard to mental states such as belief, certainty, and emotion, which are, if anything, even harder to define. Lucy (1992b) includes mental states as well as behavior in the nonlinguistic domain: "An adequate study of the relation between language and thought should . . . provide clear evidence of a pattern of nonlinguistic belief and behavior" (p. 259). He faults most anthropological research after Whorf, saying that it "typically did not provide clear evidence of a nonlinguistic correlate with grammatical patterns" (p. 259). In contrast to such research he cites the psycholinguistic study of Bloom (1981), which focused on a hypothesized cognitive difference between Chinese and English speakers in the interpretation of counterfactual statements. Elsewhere in his discussion Lucy is quite critical of Bloom's methodology (cf. Au 1983, Birdsong & Odlin 1983), but he clearly sees the mental states involved in counterfactual reasoning as an instance of something that may involve "nonlinguistic belief."

Lucy's stance has at least two implications. First, nontemporal meanings of verb tenses become highly relevant (cf. Tyler & Evans 2000, 2001). As Bloom observed, the locus of the difference in the expression of counterfactual states between English and Chinese lies in grammatical contrasts also involving the coding of time. Thus, there is a possible cognitive interaction in English between tense marking and counterfactual modality, an intersection somewhat like the cases of evidentiality and tense marking to be discussed.

A second implication of Lucy's notion of nonlinguistic domains is that other types of grammatical polysemy are also candidates for meaning transfer and perhaps also for conceptual transfer. One such case that will be discussed involves the influence of allative case marking in the native language of Kaytetye speakers in the use of a Pidgin English form *bilong* (belong) to mark both purpose and physical goals (Koch 2000).

Ultimately such complications will have to be unraveled if the problem of conceptual transfer is to be well understood, and only some of them can be explored in this chapter. The diffuse nature of mental states is a problem that Slobin (1996) had in mind in a critique of Whorfian thinking: "The [relativity] hypothesis has always run into trouble in attempts to determine the mental structures that underlie perception, reasoning, and habitual behavior, as measured *outside* the contexts of verbal behavior" (p. 75, emphasis in the original). Slobin offers a more specialized approach, termed "thinking for speaking," which he characterizes as "a special form of thought that is mobilized for communication" (p. 76). Thinking for speaking reflects, in Slobin's approach, considerable cross-linguistic variation since obligatory categories such as evidentials and tense vary from one language to the next—and he cites the quotation of Boas (1938) on obligatory categories given above. Slobin considers this approach as "more cautious" (p. 75), but he also recognizes that it is an operational compromise, a way to get at certain relativity problems empirically by narrowing the field of enquiry. The thinking-for-speaking approach has been foregrounded by Kellerman (1995) and by Jarvis and Pavlenko (2007) in their characterizations of conceptual transfer, and a number of the studies discussed in this section can be seen as evidence for thinking-for-speaking effects. Even so, the results of other relativistic research such as by Levinson (section 1.2) hold out the possibility that other kinds of effects of conceptual transfer will sooner or later be demonstrated empirically.

2.2 Space

As noted above, Ijaz (1986) seems to equate meaning transfer with conceptual transfer, and so caution is certainly necessary in drawing inferences from her study. Nevertheless, she did succeed in showing how Urdu and German influenced native speakers of those languages in their choice of English spatial prepositions. Sometimes the prepositional choices of the two groups differed little in the same linguistic context, but in other cases where the context was also identical the choices reflected Urdu or German influences. The method Ijaz used did not allow her to address the problem of relativity very directly since the cloze test procedure she adopted allows only for inferences about the meanings learners opted for, and not about any cognizing of nonlinguistic spatial arrays (as in Levinson's work). Even so, the findings of Ijaz offer valuable insights about how Urdu and German speakers do not always choose the same preposition in an identical linguistic context, and so whatever degree of conceptual transfer may have been at work in learners' responses, meaning transfer definitely was.

In contrast to the Ijaz study, one by Carroll (2000) has a strong nonlinguistic component and provides intriguing evidence that spatial cognition varies on a picture-description task given to native speakers of German, on the one hand, and to English and Spanish speakers using L2 German on the other. The contrast was not in formal accuracy: the L2 users showed high control of the morphosyntactic patterns of German. However, they differed from the native speakers of German in that they produced few coadverbials such as *daneben* (beside there) as in *Auf dem Platz ist ein Kiosk; daneben is[t] ein Farbandständer* (On the square is a kiosk; beside there is a bicycle stand). As Germanic languages English and German both have coadverbials, as seen in *dazu* (thereto) and *darin* (therein), where *da* is cognate with *there*. The common inheritance does not result in wholly equivalent structures, however. For one thing, the English coadverbials have undergone much semantic bleaching so that *there* meanings involve discourse pragmatics much more than space, whereas the German forms still have a clear spatial sense as well as a textual function. Moreover, English coadverbials seem to be less important systemically in English. Yet despite these differences, some positive transfer (i.e. convergences) may occur. In some cases the English speakers performed more like the native speakers than did the group of Spanish speakers. Even so, the contrast between the non-native (whether L1 English or Spanish) and the native speakers of German in using coadverbials is consonant with von Humboldt's position on difficulty of achieving a fully new *Welt-* . . . *Sprachansicht* (world and language view).

Although there do not yet seem to be any studies of transfer using the methods of the Levinson team (but see Bongaerts, Kellerman, and Bentlage 1987), the transferability of an absolute frame of reference may actually be manifest in some pidgins and creoles. One recent description of a Pacific creole offers an intriguing hint: "Spatial orientation on Norfolk Island appears to follow a system of absolute reference points with two main axes (a) away from centre (b) away from coast upwards" (Mühlhäusler 2004, p. 799). The creole known as Norfolk is closely related historically to the more famous variety called Pitkern, which was created mainly by Tahitian women and British seamen who had taken part in the legendary mutiny aboard H.M.S. Bounty and had then settled on Pitcairn Island. The influence of Tahitian and other Pacific languages on Pitkern and Norfolk seems clear in some structures as in the personal pronoun system with dual, inclusive and exclusive categories, which also appear in Tahitian (Lazard & Peltzer 2000). Indeed, such forms are characteristic of other cases of substrate influence in creoles of the region (Keesing 1988, Crowley 1990). Since Mühlhäusler provides only a few examples and no information about the spatial system of Tahitian or other substrate languages, the evidence for conceptual transfer cannot be called abundant. Nevertheless, the likelihood of substrate influence on the spatial reference system of Pitkern seems strong in light of the analysis of Peltzer (1996) of Tahitian spatial reference as more of an absolute ("lococentrique" in her terminology) than a relative ("égocentrique") system. While developed independently, Peltzer's analysis is compatible with the work of Levinson and colleagues and thus makes conceptual transfer in the history of Pitkern and Norfolk a plausible inference.

An interesting example of how obligatory categories can affect transfer in spatial meanings comes from research on the French of Ewe speakers in Togo by Lafage (1985). Like Ewe, French has locative particles that follow nouns that are also marked with a demonstrative as in *Appelle ces enfants-ci* (Call these/those children-here) and in *Appelle ces enfants-là* (Call these/those children-there). However, such particles are not obligatory in French and are used mainly "pour souligner une opposition" (to stress an opposition) (p. 261). In contrast, the meanings of proximal and distal location in Ewe are "indispensable" (p. 261), and not surprisingly the postnominal demonstratives *-ci* and *-là* show up a great deal in interlanguage French both in instances of positive transfer (i.e., convergence between Ewe and French) and negative transfer (i.e., divergence), one example of the latter being *L'auto-là, c'est bien joli* (the auto-there, it's very nice), where the use of the definite article before the noun instead of a demonstrative (e.g., *cet*) is one marker (among others) of interlanguage French in the sentence (p. 262). Lafage's conclusions about transfer in her analysis of NP constituent structure are corroborated by numerous studies of articles in interlanguage (references are given in Odlin 1989, 2003 and Jarvis 2002). What makes the Lafage examples especially significant, though, is the spatial deixis, especially in regard to the obligatory character of the Ewe structures and to possible implications for thinking-for-speaking effects, where Ewe speakers may pay especially close attention to proximal/distal contrasts when speaking either native language or L2 French.

Since deictic reference entails the notion of verbal pointing, it is natural to wonder how much any language-specific characteristics of gesture constitute part of the influence on spatial reference in interlanguage. Recent work by Kellerman and van Hoof (2003) explores this question, but the results so far have proven ambiguous in some ways (cf. Odlin 2005, Cadierno, this volume, Gullberg, this volume). In any case, a full account of conceptual transfer in spatial reference will certainly unravel the complexities of interaction between language and paralanguage.

2.3 Time

The method of verification by IL comparisons discussed in section 2 helps to establish the transferability of verb tenses, and an investigation by Collins (2002) shows an extension of the method. Although Collins focused on only one group of learners of English, (all native speakers of French), she used a testing procedure identical to what Bardovi-Harlig and Reynolds (1995) employed in an earlier study of learners of English who were not native speakers of French. The cloze test used in both studies assessed how well learners distinguish the simple past and present perfect. Collins found that the Francophones frequently overused the present perfect in contexts where the simple past was required, a behavior fully consistent with the influence of the French *passé composé*. In contrast, the individuals studied by Bardovi-Harlig and Reynolds did not often supply present perfects erroneously in the same discourse contexts, and this result is not surprising since the native languages of these learners did not have tense forms comparable to the French *passé composé*.

The Collins study helps enormously in establishing the transferability of tense and aspect, but it would be mistaken to consider transfer as the only relevant factor in the acquisition of temporal meanings. Collins found that Francophone learners did behave in some ways like non-Francophones in the study of Bardovi-Harlig and Reynolds as well as in other research exploring the Aspect Hypothesis (e.g., Bardovi-Harlig 2000, Anderson & Shirai 1996). According to the Aspect Hypothesis, learners associate forms that mark time (whether tense or aspect or both) with the lexical aspect inherent in the meaning of a verb. For instance, individuals acquiring English will associate progressive forms (e.g., *I was flying to Istanbul*) with atelic (i.e., unbounded) meanings, and they will associate past forms (e.g., *I flew to Istanbul*) with punctual meanings. Several studies indicate that such associations develop regardless of native language, and proponents of the Aspect Hypothesis see cognitive simplicity and prototypicality as factors encouraging such associations. In this sense, the Aspect Hypothesis is universalist even while it does not adopt a Chomskyan framework where aspect is considered to be a parameter (cf. Slabakova 1999).

While the Aspect Hypothesis offers strong evidence for a universalist approach, proponents such as Shirai and Nishi (2003) do not rule out possible influences from the native language, and their position is certainly supported by the results of the Collins study. Further support comes from an investigation by Rocca (2003) of the acquisition of L2 English by Italian-speaking children and of L2 Italian by English-speaking children. Rocca's longitudinal data can also be seen as evidence for the developmental predictions of the Aspect Hypothesis, and both the Collins and Rocca studies emphasize developmental readiness as a prerequisite for transfer (cf. Wode 1983, Zobl 1980). That is, the influence of L1 temporal meanings did not arise in the Rocca study until learners had succeeded in making the canonical associations emphasized in the Aspect Hypothesis (and a similar inference seems viable in the cross-sectional study of Collins). In Rocca's investigation, one likely case of transfer is evident in the identification Italian children seem to have made between a past imperfective form such as *voleva* (was wanting) and a one-word progressive such as *wanting* as in *Bunny wanting to catch the little devil.*

Along with Rocca's study, there is other evidence of IL temporal meanings that indicates influence from the native language. Wenzell (1989) studied the alternation of past and non-past forms in the interlanguage of Russian speakers of English who apparently associated past forms in English with perfective meanings in Russian and non-past forms with imperfective meanings. As in Rocca's analysis of *wanting* as an imperfective instead of a progressive form, Wenzell's analysis foregrounds the importance of taking into account what learners mean, which can be something quite different from what the form means for native speakers (cf. Bunte & Kendall 1981, Bley-Vroman 1983).

In some cases the interlanguage form can actually contradict the normal native speaker meaning. In a study of Tamil speakers having an intermediate proficiency English, Sastry-Kuppa (1995) found that *will* is used to mark habitual aspect in past as well as non-past contexts. Habitual *will* does appear in American, British, and other native speaker varieties, as in Mr. X *will never give you the time of day*. However, its more common use as a future tense marker generally precludes use in past contexts by native speakers and also, Sastry-Kuppa found, by non-native speakers with high proficiency. However, speakers with very limited proficiency were recorded using examples such as the following (A and R are conversational partners, and the gloss provided by Sastry-Kuppa is in italics):

A: oh/ okay/ ya/ ya/ so a lot of people in kodaikanal watch films?/
R: yes/ see/ this uh/ see everybody-/ you know-/ see I am not going there/ iz- film/ see ten years I am not going the theatre/
 I don't go there [to watch] films. See, for ten years I have not gone to the theatre.
A: why?/
B: I am not like that/ see before/ you know the corsock here?/
 I don't like it. See, before—do you know Corsock [a church-related organization]?
A: ya/
R: <u>he will give</u> the one projector/ I <u>will show</u> all the f-film/ all the pla-education film/
 They used to give [us] a projector. I used to show [a lot of?] films, all educational films.
A: in the school/
R: no/ town and uh
 No, in the town and
A: town/ oh/
R: munjikal and uuuh pallangi
 In Munjikal and Pallangi [outlying areas of town]

Influence from Tamil seems the best explanation for the use of *will give* and *will show* in the past-tense context of the above passage. Asher (1982, p. 162) provides an example of where future verb forms in Tamil can mark habitual aspect regardless of whether the context is present or past. Obviously in past contexts, the future meaning is neutralized and the habitual meaning alone applies. Intermediate-level speakers of English construct a congruent pattern in their interlanguage where *will* functions as a marker of aspect and not of tense.

Although it has often been claimed that bound morphology is non-transferable (e.g., Eubank 1993, Eubank et al. 1997), such assertions are far too broad, as Jarvis and Odlin (2000) observe, and the use of *will* in the English of some Tamil speakers also calls the claim into question since Tamil marks tense and aspect with bound morphemes. Formal similarities or dissimilarities between languages do matter in cross-linguistic influence, but the similarities interact with meaning in a variety of ways. In fact, the association between future forms and habitual aspect is not unusual typologically speaking (Bybee, Pagliuca, and Perkins 1991, p. 20), and so the transfer of a future-cum-habitual marker may not be rare either. Another use of habitual *will* occasioned by transfer is evident in a detailed study by Sabban (1982) of the English of speakers of Scottish Gaelic. Gaelic relies heavily on periphrastic verb phrases, and the speech of the bilingual (B) in the following excerpt shows an alternation between the present simple and what superficially seems to be a future progressive:

A: And what else are some of the things that you do when you're in Oban?
B: Well, *I'll be staying* in the hotel with my auntie . . . we go out at nights . . . well she stays in and *I'll be going out* dancing. (p. 281, emphasis in the original)

In this example the present simple also marks habituality, but the periphrastic future is clearly an alternative. The less frequent use of the present simple in Hebridean English seems related both to the fact that future forms in Gaelic double as habituals and to the fact that apart from copular forms there are no present simple verb forms (Mark 1986, p. 33).

The use of habitual *will* in India and Scotland is just one case of where transfer leads to similar patterns in different language contact settings. Another instance is where *after* marks perfective aspect as in this example from Hebridean English: *The stone is after going through, he says* (Sabban 1982, p. 155), which can be paraphrased as *The stone has gone through*. In such cases the formal marking of perfective aspect is quite different from what was seen in the Collins study, but such constructions are frequent in some Irish as well as Scottish varieties of English, and virtually all specialists on the contact variety concur that influence from Irish and Scottish Gaelic led to the *after* perfect even while it is also used now by monolinguals (McCafferty 2004). Although Celtic varieties seem to be the only ones where a verb participle follows *after* in the perfective construction, the English of speakers in Poland sometimes uses *after* to mark perfectivity. One example that I myself have heard is *I am after lunch*, where the bilingual speaker was indicating that he had already eaten lunch (the Polish version would be *Jestem po obdiedze*), with the prepositional phrase *po obdiedze* marking the perfective in combination with the present-tense first-person copula *jestem*. The difference between the IL studied by Collins and the Scottish and Polish examples shows that very different forms can mark perfective meanings. In section 3.5, the converse possibility will be explored where learners using the same periphrastic perfect that native speakers use can signal more than just tense and aspect.

None of the studies of tense and aspect considered so far attempted to address the problem of conceptual transfer. Even so, recent work by von Stutterheim (2003) has used a film-narration task to focus on effects consistent with Slobin's notion of thinking for speaking. Her results indicate that native speakers of German and native speakers of English differ in how they tend to frame events in the film. The German speakers normally provided endpoints giving closure to the events while English speakers did not usually provide such endpoints. A typical English description of native speakers was thus *Two nuns are walking down a road* whereas for German speakers, a characteristic description was *Zwei Nonnen laufen auf einem Feldweg Richtung eines Hauses* (Two nuns walk along a lane towards a house), with the house constituting the endpoint of the event frame. Native speakers of English seem to transfer their L1 pattern of framing into L2 German. Those in the study frequently did not state an endpoint in their German descriptions as in *Zwei Nonnen laufen auf der Strasse lang* (Two nuns walk the street along), which makes no reference to the house. According to von Stutterheim, this difference in framing reflects the systemic prominence of progressive aspect in English; although German can express progressive meanings, this aspectual marking occupies only a marginal place in German grammar. The typological difference has cognitive implications in the analysis of von Stutterheim, who concludes that the English progressive induces native speakers to frame events more analytically, while German speakers frame events more holistically (with German speakers thus being more disposed to mention not only the transit of the nuns but also the destination reached). Yet even such transfer would be indirect as von Stutterheim herself suggests. As in the study of Carroll (section 2.2), the apparent cross-linguistic influence here does not manifest itself in grammatical or semantic errors, but a difference persists between the performance of the native and non-native speakers.

2.4 Motion

While motion obviously presupposes space and time, it can still be viewed as a conceptual domain in its own right. As with concepts of space and time, motion concepts permeate the meanings of human languages and also vary cross-linguistically in semantic structure. Cadierno (this volume) explores in detail implications of the distinction made by Talmy (1985, 2000, this volume) between satellite-framed languages (e.g., English and Chinese) and verb-framed languages (e.g., Spanish and Japanese), as illustrated in the different structure of the English and Spanish motion predicates such as in *floated into the cave/entró en la cueva flotando*. It is also worth noting a parallel between Japanese and Spanish—despite their different word orders—evident in the following examples, both of which correspond (albeit in different ways) to English *John returned* (Kuno 1973, p. 30):

John-ga katte   kita
John   returning came
John-ga katte   ita
John   returning went

The similarity noted by Talmy and Cadierno between Chinese and English as head satellite languages makes it natural to wonder if the acquisition of motion predicates in English will differ for Chinese and Japanese speakers. In fact, a dissertation by Yu (1996) addresses this question and indicates that the typological contrast leads to different patterns of acquisition. Yu found that the similarity between Chinese and English facilitated the acquisition of motion verbs by Chinese speakers, who outperformed their Japanese counterparts. The variety of motion verbs produced by Chinese speakers was greater, and their choices often mirrored those of native speakers of English. The likelihood seems high that thinking-for-speaking effects are involved in the results since one of the tasks given to the learners involved picture description (along with story-retelling and translation tasks).

One other notable result of Yu's study is that the Japanese often over-relied on the verb *go* in their motion productions. For instance, while the verb *climb* was by far the most common choice of Chinese speakers in describing a picture of a squirrel climbing down a tree (1996, p. 147), hardly any Japanese speakers chose this verb and for them the most popular choice by far was the verb *go* (often used with *down*). The avoidance of *climb* among the Japanese appears to be related to the directionality of the closest translation equivalent, *noboru*, which denotes, according to Yu, motion in only an upward path. Thus, while the heavy reliance on *go* might seem merely attributable to a pattern of overgeneralization independent of the native language, the semantic constraints of the L1 actually help to foster the overreliance. Similar patterns appear in the use of *go* in the English pidgin of speakers of the Australian language Kaytetye (Koch 2000).

Not surprisingly, Yu's results indicate that the choices of learners depend heavily on the semantic constraints of individual words, but these words also help constitute larger *constructions*, the latter a term used by Goldberg (1995; this volume) to analyze a wide range of predications. The co-occurrence of verbs and prepositions in certain interlanguage patterns shows an interdependence of motion and spatial constructions in cases of transfer. For instance, Jarvis (1998) determined some clear-cut divergences between Swedish and Finnish speakers' descriptions in their native languages of scenes in the Charlie Chaplin film *Modern Times*, with the differences sometimes involving motion constructions. These differences also characterized the interlanguage English of native speakers of both languages. Thus, Jarvis found that the L1 Swedish group frequently opted for the prepositional verb *run on* while such use was much less common among the L1 Finnish group (and when cases did arise, they invariably came from learners who had some knowledge of Swedish).

The transfer of motion constructions is also evident in two studies by Helms-Park (2001, 2003) which focused on verbs of causation, with a number of motion predicates in both investigations. In her 2003 study, Helms-Park found that speakers of Vietnamese, a language that relies heavily on serial verbs, produced several periphrastic causative expressions involving motion verbs, e.g., *She has managed to rise the kite fly over the tallest building* and *The man dropped the can of paint fell*. The effects of transfer are clear since a comparable group of speakers of Hindi and Urdu never produced such constructions. In her 2001 study she obtained similar results, identifying a particularly strong difference between the Vietnamese and the Hindi/Urdu groups in periphrasis involving verbs of forced motion. As Helms-Park observes, the transferability of language-specific argument structures found in her research concurs with work on cross-linguistic influence in studies of pidgins and creoles. Indeed, many analyses have invoked substrate influence to account for serial verbs in creoles (e.g., Holm 1989, Migge 2003, Crowley 1990, Keesing 1988), as has some other language contact research (e.g., Ho & Platt 1993).

In some cases the transfer of meanings involving space and motion is straightforward, but in other instances ambiguities arise. Using the same database employed by Jarvis (1998), Jarvis and Odlin (2000) found another divergence in descriptions of certain episodes in *Modern Times*. For one scene with Chaplin and Paulette Goddard seated on a lawn, several Finnish speakers used the preposition *to* as in the phrase *sat to the grass*, a choice not made by any Swedish speakers. The source of the Finnish speakers' choice of *to* is no doubt the allative case inflection in Finnish as in one description from a native speaker: *tyttö ja Charlie istuvat nurmikolle* (Girl and Chaplin sit to the grass), where the *-lle* ending marks the allative case on *nurmikko* (grass), which also undergoes a stem change (degemination). Although there is definitely a semantic influence from Finnish in this instance, the evidence for conceptual transfer is ambiguous. Two prepositions that both speakers of Finnish and Swedish often used were *on* and *in*, and while *to* can be viewed as a clear case of a motion construction, the other two prepositions may combine with *sit* to mean either static location or a change of location. Thus, while the cases of *to the grass* might suggest a thinking-for-speaking effect whereby the Finnish speakers are more likely to register the dynamic character of the event, this interpretation is open to challenges unless the uses of *in* and *on* can be disambiguated and tallied according to the L1 groups.

Meanings involving motion can interact with temporal as well as spatial meanings, and transfer involving such interaction is likewise possible. In a study of Melanesian Pidgin, Keesing (1991) documents several cases of collocations with *kam* and *go* as calques of constructions in Oceanic languages such as Kwaio. Among the examples is one where reduplicated *go* signals a passing of time:

Olketa lukat-em   mifala go-go olketa kas-em sam-fala
They   search-TRS   us   go-go they   catch-TRS some-ADJ
They searched for us and eventually caught some (people) . . .
(1991, p. 324) (TRS=transitive suffix)

The use of *go-go* corresponds to a Kwaio pattern *leeleka*, which can be reduplicated iconically to indicate a long passage of time (p. 123). The interactions of motion and time meanings can also involve aspect or tense marking in the interlanguage. Ho and Platt (1993) consider influence from Chinese serial verbs to be highly characteristic of substrate influence in Singaporean English, and one of the examples they provide is:

And den we have a total of half year study leave—which is about—two, t(h)ree weeks so we go—*go attend* lah course full time (p. 108).

Ho and Platt see the absence of tense marking of *go* as in this example as a consequence of its non-punctual status in this serial verb construction.

3 Meaning extensions and other forms of polysemy

The research reviewed so far shows ample evidence of meaning transfer in the domains of space, time, and motion. As stated before, such work on meaning transfer does not in itself constitute evidence of conceptual transfer, but it does show that spatiotemporal meanings are often transferable. Moreover, some of the research (e.g., von Stutterheim 2003) suggests relativistic effects based on the L1, i.e., conceptual transfer.

It is now necessary to consider in more detail the relation between spatiotemporal meanings and mental states akin to what Lucy (1992b) has called "nonlinguistic belief" (p. 259). Whorf sensed that certain meanings in English were metaphoric extensions or, in his term, "surrogates" of spatial meanings:

We see things with our eyes in the same space forms as the Hopi, but our idea of space has also the property of acting as a surrogate of nonspatial relationships like time, intensity, tendency, and as a void filled with imagined formless forms, one of which may even be called "space." Space as sensed by the Hopi would not be connected mentally with such surrogates, but would be comparatively pure and unmixed with extraneous notions (p. 159).

Subsequent work by Malotki (1983, pp. 58–81) indicates that Whorf was mistaken in claiming that Hopi did not have extensions of spatial meanings into temporal ones. Indeed, such polysemy appears to be very widespread in human languages. In Tahitian, for example, temporal extensions sometimes closely resemble those of French and English, and Ewe likewise employs spatial morphemes to indicate temporal meanings (Peltzer 1996, Heine, Claudi, and Hünnemeyer 1991).

Yet although Whorf underestimated the similarity of Hopi and English, his more general point about cross-linguistic differences does get support in work on spatial meanings in various languages. That is, the metaphoric extensions of space are far from uniform across languages. For instance, demonstrative pronouns in Tahitian can also serve as personal pronouns—and without any person-marking on the verb or elsewhere (Peltzer 1996, p. 302). Although the system itself shows principles of personal and spatial deixis not altogether different from European languages (Lyons 1977), the semantic extension from spatial to personal reference is clearly language-specific.

Polysemy relations with language-specific characteristics are transferable, and some of the studies already described constitute evidence of such influence. For example, the use of *will* by Tamil speakers as a past habitual marker (Sastry-Kuppa 1995) reflects an extension in Tamil of a future marker into a marker where tense marking is neutralized in favor of habitual aspect compatible with past time reference. There are some other languages where similar patterns of grammaticalization occur (Sankoff 1991), but the Tamil pattern is unusual enough to provide clear evidence of L1-influence and to show that transfer of meaning extensions can involve grammar as well as lexis. This section will look at instances of transfer which involve spatiotemporal meanings but which also involve mental states such as intention.

Before considering the specific cases, it will help to consider similarities and differences in three terms used already and also needed in the following analyses: *metaphor*, *grammaticalization*, and *polysemy*.

3.1 Metaphor

Work on metaphor by cognitive linguists such as Lakoff and Johnson (1980, 1999) has had an impact on transfer and other areas of SLA research (e.g., Zimmermann 2006, Tyler, this volume). Notions of core meaning and prototypicality have long been invoked to account for interlingual identifications or leaners' reluctance to make them (e.g., Kellerman

1978, Ijaz 1986). Moreover, other investigations of idioms and their transferability have attempted to identify conditions where figurative language in L1 may be adopted in interlanguage (e.g., Kellerman 1977, Odlin 1991, Abdullah & Jackson 1998, Cieslicka 2006). Such work is relevant to two concerns for work on conceptual transfer:

- *Transferability.* Widespread (and perhaps universal) metaphoric relations (e.g., between space and time) probably facilitate interlingual identifications and thus make transfer seem viable even in cases where it leads to something non-targetlike, often where learners wrongly assume certain constructions to be universal when in fact they involve language-specific meaning extensions.
- *Cognitive effects.* Citing a wide range of empirical studies, Vervaeke and Kennedy (2004) affirm the facilitating effects of spatial analogies and metaphors for abstract thinking (even while they express reservations about certain cognitivist claims about metaphors). They do not address the question of cross-linguistic variation in meaning extensions, yet since extensions involving space or other domains can indeed be language-specific (as in the Tahitian demonstrative example), there is a real possibility that the extensions will lead to specific thinking-for-speaking effects in the native language and thus also to conceptual as well as meaning transfer.

Heine and Kuteva (2003) use the term *conceptual transfer* in their discussion of certain metaphoric extensions that are common in grammaticalization, but in their analysis this term applies to shifts of meaning within a language as well as to influences on other languages (which they call "replica grammaticalization" as discussed below). The use of *conceptual transfer* by Heine and Kuteva is clearly different from the sense of the term in this chapter, but their use is not surprising. Dechert (2006) has pointed to the same etymology for *metaphor* and *transfer*, both implying motion. In fact, one criticism of the term *transfer* in second language research has been that it suggests motion where something quite different may actually be at work (Corder 1992, Cook 2000, Ellis this volume). (Apart from SLA concerns, the same critique is applicable to *metaphor* and, for that matter, to *translate*, whose Latinate morphemes are etymologically related to those of *transfer*.) Yet whatever problems the motion metaphor may bring, its use in the metalanguage of SLA does clarify a need that learners have. As Lakoff and Johnson suggest more generally, metaphors help humans to try to understand new problems in terms of existing cognitive resources. In language transfer the "carrying across" of linguistic and (sometimes) conceptual resources helps learners to make sense of the new problems that another language presents, even if some of what is carried across would have better stayed at home.

325

3.2 *Grammaticalization*

Although used in various ways, the term *grammaticalization* most commonly designates cases where an ordinary lexical term develops new denotations, at least one of which is a grammatical meaning (Heine, Claudi, & Hünnemeyer 1991; Traugott & Hopper 2003). One common example is the development of the French negator *pas* from the word *pas* meaning "step" (Givón 1984, Jespersen 1917). In other cases, there may also be a formal divergence only faintly hinting at a historical connection, as between the dervational suffix *-ly* and the word *like* (Pyles & Algeo 1993).

Although grammaticalization need not always involve metaphoric extension it frequently does. The form *like* is an abstraction of an earlier word for the body in a number of Indo-European languages (Pokorny 1959, s.v. *leig-*). Body parts are likewise frequent candidates for words that evolve from localized denotation (a head or back, for instance) to more generalized terms for spatial reference (Heine, Claudi, and Hünnemeyer 1991, Chapter Five). Not surprisingly, semantic extensions sometimes find their way into another language through cross-linguistic influence. For instance, a spatial construction in the South American creole Srnan corresponds, as Bruyn (1996) observes, to the Ewe body-part term for back, *megbé*, which also functions as a postposition which can denote the spatial relation "in back of" and which can occur in many constructions (Heine, Claudi, and Hünnemeyer 1991, p. 134). The Srnan construction adopted the English form *back* but tailored it to the postpositional phrase structure of languages such as Ewe, resulting in patterns such as *na a oso baka* "behind the house" (Bruyn 1996, p. 33).

For Heine and Kuteva (2003, p. 558) this case is "a canonical instance" of what they call "replica grammaticalization," which they define thus:

a   Speakers of language R [in this case, Srnan] notice that in language M [here, Ewe] there is a grammatical category Mx.

b   They develop an equivalent category Rx using material available in their own language (R).

c   To this end they replicate the grammaticalization process they assume to have taken place in language M, using an analogical formula of the kind $[My > Mx] = [Ry > Rx]$.

d   They grammaticalize category Ry to Rx.
     (Heine and Kuteva 2003, p. 539, emphasis added).

While precise in some ways, this formulation cannot account for all cases of transfer involving L1 grammaticalization. For one thing, it suggests that the replication process must happen in real time, i.e., where second language learners must first use the Ry form (e.g., the body-part term *baka*) before they use the Rx (postpostion). Considering that the language contact involving Srnan occurred some three centuries ago, there is no way to verify or falsify a real-time scenario. Moreover, it is not clear whether influences involving the transfer of an L1 grammaticalization will always be as transparent as in the Srnan case. For instance, English learners of German may manage to establish accurate interlingual identifications of the suffixes in *freundlich* and *friendly* without any awareness at all of the historical relation of the forms or of the process of semantic bleaching that led to the *-lich* and *-ly* suffixes. Moreover, making an interlingual identification in this case need not entail any knowledge of the German lexical item *Leiche* (corpse), which represents some continuity (though also narrowing) of the earlier Indo-European meaning.

The Heine and Kuteva formulation seems to require more metalinguistic awareness (including awareness of word histories) than seems realistic, and their emphasis on a recapitulatiory process appears to incur the same liabilities that Slobin (2002) has seen in claims in child language research that "ontogeny recapitulates phylogeny." Yet, despite the limited explanatory value of replica grammaticalization, the example given by Bruyn does indeed show how cross-linguistic influence can involve multiple meanings showing a real grammaticalization relation regardless of how much or how little learners apprehend of the relation. A somewhat similar spatial relation will be discussed involving the transfer of allative case meanings found in Kaytetye.

3.3 Polysemy

In cases of metaphoric extension and grammaticalization, there is an identifiable relation between the multiple meanings, even if the meaning is accessible only to linguists. Yet there are other cases where the coexistence of two meanings in the same construction is real but also historically opaque as in the Turkish inflections *-mis* and *-müs* that code both tense and evidentiality (the use of which is illustrated in section 3.5). These allomorphs, which follow the rules of Turkish vowel harmony, have long been part of the verb system (and are indeed found in some other Turkic languages), but their etymology is unknown (Johnson 2003). Whatever the history of the *mis/müs* inflections, their polysemy is undisputed.

3.4 Motion and purpose

As discussed in section 2.4, the allative case in Finnish involves meanings related to motion toward something, which for Blake (1994) is the prototypical use of this case panlinguistically (and he notes that the source of allative case marking is frequently verbs of motion). The influence of the Finnish allative led to non-targetlike uses of *to* in collocations such as *sat to the grass* as detailed by Jarvis and Odlin (2000), but no meaning extensions involving the Finnish allative were investigated. On the other hand, Koch (2000) provides examples of transfer involving the polysemy which allative constructions sometimes show. In his study, the L1 is the Australian language Kaytetye (a branch of Arandic) and the L2 is Central Australian aboriginal English (CAAE). He provides detailed examples of both languages, and his analysis offers strong evidence of cross-linguistic influence in many instances. Prepositions in CAAE often reflect meaning categories of Kaytetye case inflections. One such instance involves the allative marker -*warle*, which in CAAE is realized as a preposition pronounced in various forms such as *longa, bilonga, belonginto* (Koch does not suggest that there are significant meaning differences among these forms). In Kaytetye -*warle* can mark purpose, as in the following example, where a native speaker provides a CAAE translation, with Koch's translation of the whole passage appearing below it:

> Alie*warle* r-apeke. Alie*warle*-apeke. Might <u>belonginto</u> fight . . .
> Alie*warle*. <u>belonginto</u> fight . . . *alararenge* <u>belonginto</u> fight, them spear now. *Eryarte ngwerangkwerre.*
> "Or they [the spears] are for fighting . . . <u>For</u> fighting. They are <u>for</u> fighting, these spears, the other spears" (Koch 2000, p. 48, emphasis in the original).

Examples of -*warle* and *longa* in motion constructions also appear in the study, e.g., *they bin come back and they bin come back leavem old fella longa same place again*, which Koch translates as "they returned and (after getting back) left the old man in the same place" (p. 51). Whatever the historical facts may be about Kaytetye, the relation between the allative in motion constructions and in purpose constructions is consistent with a widespread pattern of grammaticalization (Heine, Claudi, and Hünnemeyer 1991, pp. 161–162).

The patterns of transfer from Kaytetye to CAAE are even more complex since *longa* is a form corresponding to other case markers as well and can denote other abstractions such as possession. Nevertheless, the relation between its use in motion and purposive constructions reflects the widespread event-structure metaphor "Purposes are Destinations" discussed by Lakoff and Johnson (1999, pp. 191–192). Such an instance may well involve conceptual transfer, but it should be noted that at least part of any such transfer would involve convergence since concepts such as the purposes/destination event structure are widespread if not universal.

3.5 Time and evidentiality

One common way of marking evidentiality contrasts is to use different grammatical morphemes that also indicate tense (Aikhenvald & Dixon 2003). Guler (2005) provides the following example from Turkish, where a death, which is indicated by the verb stem öl- (die), has to be characterized as an event known from experience (Ali öldü "Ali died—I saw it") or from inference or hearsay (Ail ölmüs, "Ali died—I inferred/ heard"). As noted in section 3.3, the etymology of the -müs morpheme is unknown, but even so it is an instance of polysemy that is transferable. Guler asked Turkish students to write two essays in English, one describing their own experiences during a summer vacation and the other describing the experiences of a friend. She found a striking difference in tense choices in the two essays. In the paper describing their own experiences, students overwhelmingly preferred the past simple tense. However, in the essay describing a friend's holiday, they frequently chose the past perfect since the writers' knowledge of the events described was only indirect.

These results suggest, of course, that evidentiality contrasts such as between öldü and ölmüs affect the choice of English tenses, and a study by Odlin and Alonso-Váquez (2007) supports this interpretation. Spanish-speaking students in Castile were given the same writing task that Guler's students had, but the pattern of the tense choices was quite different, and the choices usually reflected the considerable similarity between forms and meanings of the past perfect in Spanish and English.

Although the past perfect does not code evidential meanings in Castilian Spanish, it does so in nonstandard Peruvian Spanish. Klee and Ocampo (1995) illustrate the inferential meanings of the past perfect with speech samples such as the following:

> Entonces así, y por allá, dice así arriba se 'bía estao yendo el loco, con su rivista . . . y dos guardias, dice, bajaban de arriba. Media vuelta el loco! Así, dice, le ha tirado con la revista y qué pasa? Mi hija había creído que le estaba tirando con piedra. Faijssmas . . . Se había asustado . . . Se le había venido (p. 63).

Their translation inserts in brackets past perfect calques of the Spanish forms (which in the above example usually have the auxiliary había or its contraction bía).

> Then that way, over there, it is said, that way up the madman was [had been] going with his magazine . . . and two guards, it is said, were coming down from up there. Half a turn the madman! That way, it is said, he threw [has thrown] the magazine at her and what happens? My daughter thought [had thought] that he was

throwing a stone. Faijssmas she became [had bcome] frightened. He [the baby] came [had come] (p. 63).

Like Turkish, Quechua past tense markers code evidentiality contrasts. However, the evidentiality system of Quechua appears to be even more complex since future tense forms can have similar functions and can also lead to transfer in the Spanish of the Andes (Escobar 1997).

The Turkish and Peruvian cases are consistent with the thinking-for-speaking position of Slobin (1993, 1996) on conceptual transfer. However, it may also be wondered if evidentiality contrasts also have other cognitive effects such as remembering differently an event known from a verbal report as opposed to one known from direct experience. Memory is often constructive; people can and do create memories with sensory details for events not directly experienced. A classic experiment of Loftus and Palmer (1974) demonstrated that simple lexical coding of events as either *hit* or *crash* could affect the reconstruction of an event, a scene in a film where a car strikes a wall, in terms of the estimates of the speed of the car. If the obligatory grammatical coding of knowledge source (i.e., evidentiality) likewise plays a role in how people remember events, the possibilities for conceptual transfer may go beyond thinking for speaking. However, any such possibility remains only speculative at this point.

3.6 Time and focus

While linguists have proposed many definitions of the term *focus*, Carston (1996) provides an especially useful one, which is grounded in relevance theory: "focus is the syntactic constituent in which dominates all the information that contributes directly to relevance" (p. 311). Concurring with Wilson and Sperber (1993), she sees the focused constituent as, in effect, a bridge between the information of the utterance with the focused element and background information which may be either implicit or explicit in the discourse context. Carston's approach is similar to certain other approaches grounded in schema theory (e.g., Doherty 1999, 2001), and she also sees the structural characteristics of focus constructions as important for psycholinguistic processing. In the area of language contact or Second Language Acquisition several studies indicate that focus constructions are frequently transferable (e.g., Filppula 1986, Sankoff 1993, Odlin 1997, Odlin & Jarvis 2004), even though varied factors may constrain such influence at times (cf. Odlin 2005, 2006). In most documented cases of such transfer, the syntactic or lexical forms serving as focus markers do not show any close correspondence (at least synchronically) to forms expressing spatial or temporal reference. However, a study by Keesing (1991) of Melanesian Pidgin describes two constructions, one marking aspect and the other focus, which are influenced by a Kwaio grammatical morpheme that doubles as a perfect-ive and focus particle (the latter meaning being one which he considers to be a grammaticalization of the former). The morpheme used for both meanings in Melanesian Pidgin is *nao*, which also has uses like those of the adverb *now*. However, when *nao* functions as an aspect particle, it can denote actions already completed as in *hem i-ranawe nao*, which Keesing translates as "She has run away" (p. 330). The sentence closely matches a Kwaio example also given: *e akwa no'o*, also glossed as "She has run away," where *e* is the pronoun, *akwa* the verb, and *no'o* the aspect marker. Keesing sees the phonetic similarity between *no'o* and *now* as the basis for the Pidgin form *nao*.

When *nao* follows a verb, it serves as a perfective marker (and Keesing glosses all his Kwaio and Pidgin examples having *no'o* or *nao* with verbs in the present perfect as above). However, when *nao* follows a noun, it serves as a focus marker, as in:

> *hem nao i save*
> him TOP he know
> "He's the one who knows" (p. 331).

Keesing also cites Kwaio examples showing the same pattern, including the following:

> *ngai ne-e aga-si-a*
> him TOP he see-TRS-it
> "He's the one who saw it" (p. 331).

In this example, the morpheme *si* is a transitive marker, and the *ne-e* is an allomporph of *no-o*, functioning as a focus marker (where Keesing uses the term *TOP* (topicalizer) in the example but *focus* in his discussion).

One special advantage of Carston's definition given above is that it can help explain how a perfective marker could eventually become a focus marker in the history of Kwaio, a type of grammaticalization that Keesing explicitly refrains from attempting to discuss (p. 340). Although the relation between perfect and perfective constructions is complex, their meanings frequently overlap as the Kwaio and Pidgin examples given by Keesing show. Since the core meaning of the perfect is often designated as "current relevance" or, as Comrie (1976) puts it, "the continuing present relevance of a past situation" (p. 52), relevance factors seem crucial in explaining the pattern in Kwaio and probably in languages in other regions showing a similar pattern such as Nupe and Malay (Heine, Claudi, and Hünnemeyer 1991, p. 240).

The use of *nao* in Melanesian Pidgin constitutes at the very least a case of semantic and pragmatic transfer involving different types of meaning.

However, there is also reason to believe that its use as a focus construction may constitute conceptual transfer. Although Carston's analysis does not cite any empirical research on processing of focus constructions, there is recent evidence that supports her position (e.g., Birch, Albrecht, and Myers 2000, Klin et al. 2004). For instance, the study of Birch, Albrecht, and Myers found that individuals better remembered information occurring in focus constructions than in sentences having only ordinary determiners. Such evidence has concentrated so far on variations of syntactic structure within English, but it seems likely that research on focus on other languages would yield similar results. More intriguing still is the possibility—albeit speculative—that language-specific variations in focus structure (Doherty 2001) could have somewhat different effects on processing. In such a case then, the L1-specific characteristics could result in conceptual transfer as well as meaning transfer.

The types of polysemy discussed in section 3 constitute just a few of what may well be many possibilities. For example, the English progressive indicates an aspectual category, but it can also indicate a speaker's emotional involvement where, for instance, the statement *Thousands of people are dying from smoking every year* seems more emotionally charged than *Thousands of people die from smoking every year*. Dewaele and Edwards (2004) have provided empirical support for this intuition and also for comprehension differences between native and non-native speakers: the former consistently apprehended the affective loading of the progressive, something that the non-native speakers in their study often did not do. However, Dewaele and Edwards did not investigate whether speakers of languages that also use the progressive a great deal (e.g., Spanish) would differ from speakers of languages such as German where progressive meanings play only a marginal grammatical role. In view of the research of Sabban (1982) and von Stutterheim (2003), progressive structures seem to be highly transferable. The possibility of facilitating influence seems all the more likely in light of the positive transfer found among Spanish speakers by Odlin and Alonso-Váquez (2007) with another periphrastic tense (the perfect).

4 Conclusion

This chapter has surveyed several cases of meaning transfer involving space, time, and motion, and it has provided examples of transfer of polysemous constructions involving motion and purpose (the Central Australian Aboriginal English of Kaytetye speakers), tense and evidentiality (the English of Turkish speakers and the Spanish of Quechua speakers), and aspect and focus (the Melanesian Pidgin of Kwaio speakers). These examples thus demonstrate not only the transferability of spatial and temporal meanings but of language-specific patterns of polysemy.

As discussed earlier, not all meaning transfer should be considered conceptual transfer: the latter is a subset of the former. A major question confronting future researchers is just how large the subset is. Jarvis and Pavlenko (2007) tend to view the subset as very large even while they also agree that not all meaning transfer is conceptual transfer. Whether their position or a more conservative one proves to be correct, there is a need to refine methods of verification and doing so will also require further work on defining what Lucy called patterns "of nonlinguistic belief and behavior." If, for example, there are L1-specific effects on memory of focus constructions, it will still be necessary to determine how such effects are evident in non-verbal memory traces.

Since the study of conceptual transfer abounds more in questions than in answers, it seems premature to espouse either the optimism of Whorf or the pessimism of von Humboldt regarding Second Language Acquisition. The continuing progress of linguistics (including SLA research) makes it possible to agree with Whorf that there is no inherent "binding power" of one's native language that well-informed language pedagogy could not address. On the other hand, the binding power may actually be much greater than what Whorf envisioned. The patterns of language-specific polysemy identified here may entail a complexity of entrenchment of neural organization and learned attention (Ellis 2006, this volume) that is impossible to overcome even with sufficient time, instruction, and motivation (cf. Long 2003, Han 2004). It may be possible to model such complexity through connectionist approaches (e.g., Ellis 2003), since their emphasis on strength of connection might shed greater light on the obligatory grammatical categories deemed so important by Boas. Studies of the connections involved in grammatical polysemy might help clarify how polysemous categories orient the linguistic and cognitive activity occurring in interlingual identifications. In any case, however strong or weak the binding power of cross-linguistic influence may prove to be, the efforts to comprehend its strength will be crucial for understanding linguistic relativity as well as Second Language Acquisition.

Bibliography

Abdullah, K., & Jackson, H. (1998). Idioms and the language learner: Contrasting English and Syrian Arabic. *Languages in Contrast*, 1, 83–107.

Aikhenvald, A., & Dixon, R. (Eds.) (2003). *Studies in evidentiality*. Amsterdam: John Benjamins.

Andersen, R., & Shirai, Y. (1996). The primacy of aspect in first and second language acquisition: The pidgin-creole connection. In W. Ritchie (Ed.), *Handbook of second language acquisition* (pp. 527–570). New York: Academic Press.

Asher, R. (1982). *Tamil*. Amsterdam: North Holland.

Au, T. (1983). Chinese and English counterfactuals: The Sapir-Whorf hypothesis revisited. *Cognition*, 15, 155–187.

Bardovi-Harlig, K. (2000). *Tense and aspect in second language acquisition: Form, meaning and use.* Oxford: Blackwell.

Bardovi-Harlig, K., & Reynolds, D. (1995). The role of lexical aspect in the acquisition of tense and aspect. *TESOL Quarterly, 29,* pp. 107–31.

Birch, S., Albrecht, J. & Myers, J. (2000), Syntactic focusing structures influence discourse processing. *Discourse Processes, 30,* 285–304.

Birdsong, D., & Odlin, T. (1983). If Whorf was on the right track, a review essay on *The linguistic shaping of thought: a study in the impact of language and thinking in China and the West* by Alfred Bloom. *Language Learning, 33,* 401–412.

Blake, B. (1994). *Case.* Cambridge: Cambridge University Press.

Bley-Vroman, R. (1983). The comparative fallacy in interlanguage studies: the case of systematicity. *Language Learning, 33,* 1–17.

Bloom, A. (1981). *The linguistic shaping of thought.* Hillsdale, NJ: Erlbaum.

Boas, F. (1911/1966). *Introduction to handbook of American Indian languages.* Lincoln: University of Nebraska Press.

Boas, F. (1938). Language. In F. Boas (Ed.), *General anthropology* (pp. 124–145). Boston: Heath.

Bongaerts, T., Kellerman, E., & Bentlage, A. (1987). Perspective and proficiency in L2 referential communication. *Studies in Second Language Acquisition, 9,* 171–200.

Bruyn, A. (1996). On identifying examples of grammaticalization in creole languages. In P. Baker & A. Syea (Eds.), *Changing meanings, changing functions, Westminster creolistics series 2.* (pp. 29–48). London: University of Westminster Press.

Bunte, P., & Kendall, M. (1981). When is an error not an error? Notes on language contact and the question of interference. *Anthropological Linguistics, 23,* 1–7.

Bybee, J., Pagliuca, W., & Perkins. R. (1991). Back to the future. In E. Traugott & B. Heine (Eds.), *Approaches to grammaticalization. Volume 2* (pp. 17–58). Amsterdam: John Benjamins.

Carroll, M. (2000). The relevance of information organization to second language acquisitions studies: The descriptive discourse of advanced adult learners of German. *Studies in Second Language Acquisition, 22,* 441–466.

Carston, R. (1996). Syntax and pragmatics. In K. Brown & J. Miller (Eds.), *The concise encyclopedia of syntactic theories* (pp. 306–313). New York: Pergamon.

Cieslicka, A. (2006). On building castles in the sand, or exploring the issue of transfer in the interpretation and production of L2 fixed expressions. In J. Arabski (Ed.), *Cross-linguistic influence in the second language lexicon* (pp. 226–245). Clevedon, UK: Multilingual Matters.

Clark, H. (1973). Space, time, semantics, and the child. In T. E. Moore (Ed.), *Cognitive development and the acquisition of language.* (pp. 27–63). New York: Academic Press.

Collins, L. (2002). The roles of L1 Influence and lexical aspect in the acquisition of temporal morphology. *Language Learning, 52,* 43–94.

Comrie, B. (1976). *Aspect.* Cambridge: Cambridge University Press.

Comrie, B. (1985). *Tense.* Cambridge: Cambridge University Press.

Cook, V. (2000). Is *transfer* the right word? Paper presented at International Pragmatics Association, Budapest, July 11, 2000.

Corder, S. (1992). A role for the mother tongue. In S. Gass & L. Selinker (Eds.), *Language Transfer in language learning* (pp. 18–31). Amsterdam: John Benjamins.

Crowley, T. (1990). *Beach-la-Mar to Bislama: the emergence of a national language in Vanuatu*. Oxford: Oxford University Press.

Dechert, H. (2006). On the ambiguity of the notion "transfer". In J. Arabski (Ed.), *Cross-linguistic influence in the second language lexicon* (pp. 3–11). Clevedon, UK: Multilingual Matters.

DeKeyser, R. (2003). Implicit and explicit learning. In C. Doughty & M. Long (Eds.), *Handbook of second language acquisition* (pp. 313–348). Oxford: Blackwell.

Dewaele, J., & Edwards, M. (2004). Tense/aspect, verb meaning and perception of emotional intensity by native and non-native users of English. *EUROSLA Yearbook, 4*, 231–252.

Doherty, M. (1999). Clefts in translation between English and German. *Target, 11*, 289–315.

Doherty, M. (2001). Discourse theory and translation of clefts between English and German. In I. Kenesei & R. Harnish (Eds.), *Perspectives on semantics, pragmatics, and discourse* (pp. 273–292). Amsterdam: John Benjamins.

Ellis, N. (2003). Constructions, chunking, and connectionism: The emergence of second language structure. In C. Doughty & M. Long (Eds.), *Handbook of second language acquisition* (pp. 63–103). Oxford: Blackwell.

Ellis, N. C. (2006). Selective attention and transfer phenomena in SLA: Contingency, cue competition, salience, interference, overshadowing, blocking, and perceptual learning. *Applied Linguistics, 27*(2), 1–31.

Escobar, A. (1997). From time to modality in Spanish in contact with Quechua. *Hispanic Linguistics, 9*, 64–99.

Eubank, L. (1993). On the transfer of parametric values in L2 development. *Language Acquisition, 3*, 183–208.

Eubank, L., Bischof, J., Huffstutler, A., Leek, P., & West, C. (1997). "Tom eats slowly cooked eggs": Thematic-verb raising in L2 knowledge. *Language Acquisition, 6*, 171–199.

Filppula, M. (1986). *Some aspects of Hiberno-English in a functional sentence perspective*. Joensuu, Finland: Joensuu Publications in the Humanities.

Givón, T. (1984). *Syntax. Volume 1*. Amsterdam: John Benjamins.

Goldberg, A. (1995). *Constructions: a construction grammar approach to argument structure*. Chicago: University of Chicago Press.

Gotteri, N., & Michalak-Gray, J. (1997). *Polish*. London: Teach Yourself Books.

Guler, N. (2005). Transfer of Turkish evidentiality. M.A. report, Ohio University.

Han, Z. (2004). *Fossilization in second language acquisition*. Clevedon, UK: Multilingual Matters.

Han, Z., & Odlin, T. (2006). Introduction. In Z. Han & T. Odlin (Eds.) *Studies of fossilization in second language acquisition* (pp. 1–20). Clevedon, UK: Multilingual Matters.

Heine, B., Claudi, U., & Hünnemeyer, F. (1991). *Grammaticalization: A conceptual framework*. Chicago: University of Chicago Press.

Heine, B., & Kuteva, T. (2003). On contact-induced grammaticalization. *Studies in Language, 27*, 529–572.

Helms-Park, R. (2001). Evidence of lexical transfer in learner syntax: The acquisition of English causatives by speakers of Hindi-Urdu and Vietnamese. *Studies in Second Language Acquisition, 23*, 71–102.

Helms-Park, R. (2003). Transfer in SLA and creoles: The implications of causative serial verbs in the interlanguage of Vietnamese ESL learners. *Studies in Second Language Acquisition, 25*, 211–244.

Ho M., & Platt, J. (1993). *Dynamics of a contact continuum: Singaporean English.* Oxford: Oxford University Press.

Holm, J. (1989). *Pidgins and creoles. Volumes 1–2.* Cambridge: Cambridge University Press.

Hulstijn, J. (2003). In C. Doughty & M. Long (Eds.), *Handbook of second language acquisition* (pp. 349–381). Oxford: Blackwell.

Humboldt, W. von (1836/1960). *Über die Verschiedenheit des menschlichen Sprachbaues und ihren Einfluss auf die geistige Entwickelung des Menschengeschlechts.* [On the diversity of human language construction and its influence on human development]. Bonn: Dümmler.

Humboldt, W. von (1836–1839). *Über die Kawi-sprache auf der insel Java.* [On the Kawi language on the island of Java]. Berlin: Royal Academy of Science.

Humboldt, W. von (1836/1988). *On language.* Cambridge: Cambridge University Press.

Ijaz, I.H. (1986). Linguistic and cognitive determinants of lexical acquisition in a second language. *Language Learning, 36*, 401–451.

Jarvis, S. (1998). *Conceptual transfer in the interlanguage lexicon.* Bloomington: Indiana University Linguistics Club.

Jarvis, S. (2000). Methodological rigor in the study of transfer: Identifying L1 influence in the interlanguage lexicon. *Language Learning, 50*, 245–309.

Jarvis, S. (2002). Topic continuity in L2 English article use. *Studies in Second Language Acquisition, 24*, 387–418.

Jarvis, S., & Odlin, T. (2000). Morphological type, spatial reference, and language transfer. *Studies in Second Language Acquisition, 22*, 535–556.

Jarvis, S., & Pavlenko, A. (2007). *Cross-linguistic influence in language and cognition.* Mahwah, NJ: Erlbaum (in press).

Jespersen, O. (1917). Negation in English and other languages. *Historisk-filologiske Meddelelser 1.* Copenhagen.

Johnson, L. (2003). Evidentiality in Turkic. In A. Aikhenvald & R. Dixon (Eds.), *Studies in evidentiality* (pp. 273–290). Amsterdam: John Benjamins.

Keesing, R. (1988). *Melanesian Pidgin and the Oceanic substrate.* Stanford, California: Stanford University Press.

Keesing, R. (1991). Substrates, calquing, and grammaticalization in Melanesian Pidgin. In E. Traugott & B. Heine (Eds.), *Approaches to grammaticalization. Volume 1* (pp. 315–342). Amsterdam: John Benjamins.

Kellerman, E. (1977). Towards a characterisation of the strategy of transfer in second language learning. *Interlanguage Studies Bulletin, 2*(1), 58–145.

Kellerman, E. (1978). Giving learners a break: native language intuitions about transferability. *Working Papers in Bilingualism, 15*, 59–92.

Kellerman, E. (1995). Crosslinguistic influence: Transfer to nowhere? *Annual Review of Applied Linguistics, 15*, 125–150.

Kellerman, E., & van Hoof, M. (2003). Manual accents. *IRAL, 41*, 251–269.

Klee, C., & Ocampo, A. (1995). The expression of past reference in Spanish narratives of Spanish–Quechua bilingual speakers. In C. Silva-Corvalán (Ed.), *Spanish in four continents* (pp. 52–70). Washington, DC: Georgetown University Press.

Klin, C., Weingartner, K., Guzman, A., & Levine, W. (2004). Readers' sensitivity to linguistic cues in narratives: How salience influences anaphor resolution. *Memory and Cognition, 32*, 511–522.

Koch, H. (2000). Central Australian aboriginal English: In comparison with the morphosyntactic categories of Kaytetye. *Asian Englishes, 23*, 32–58.

Kuno, S. (1973). *The structure of the Japanese language.* Cambridge, MA: MIT Press.

Lafage, S. (1985). *Français écrit et parlé en pays éwé* [Spoken and written French in the Ewe-speaking region]. Paris: Société d'études linguistiques et anthropologiques de France.

Lakoff, G., & Johnson, M. (1980). *Metaphors we live by.* Chicago: University of Chicago Press.

Lakoff, G., & Johnson, M. (1999). *Philosophy in the flesh: The embodied mind and its challenge to Western thought.* New York: Basic Books.

Lazard, G., & Peltzer, L. (2000). *Structure de la langue tahitienne* [Structure of the Tahitian language]. Paris: Peeters.

Levelt, W. (1989). *Speaking: From intention to articulation.* Cambridge, MA: MIT Press.

Levinson, S. (1997). From outer to inner space: Linguistic categories and non-linguistic thinking. In J. Nuyts & E. Pederson (Eds.), *Language and linguistic categorization.* Cambridge: Cambridge University Press, 13–45.

Levinson, S. (2003). *Space in language and cognition.* Cambridge: Cambridge University Press.

Levinson, S., Meira, S., & The Language and Cognition Group (2003). "Natural concepts" in the spatial topological domain—adpositional meanings in cross-linguistic perspective: An exercise in semantic typology. *Language, 79*(3), 485–516.

Loftus, E., & Palmer, J. (1974). Reconstruction of automobile destruction: An example of the interaction between language and memory. *Journal of Verbal Learning and Verbal Behavior, 13*, 585–589.

Long, M. (2003). Stabilization and fossilization in interlanguage development. In C. Doughty & M. Long (Eds.), *Handbook on Second Language Acquisition* (pp. 487–535). Oxford: Blackwell.

Lucy, J. (1992a). *Grammatical categories and cognition.* Cambridge: Cambridge University Press.

Lucy, J. (1992b). *Language diversity and thought.* Cambridge: Cambridge University Press.

Lyons, J. (1977). *Semantics. Volumes 1–2.* Cambridge: Cambridge University Press.

MacWhinney, B. (1982). Transfer and competition in second language learning. In R. Harris (Ed.), *Cognitive processing in bilinguals* (pp. 371–390). Amsterdam: North Holland.

Malotki, E. (1983). *Hopi time: A linguistic analysis of the temporal concepts in the Hopi language.* Berlin: Mouton.

Maratsos, M., Katis, D., & Margheri, A. (2000). Can grammar make you feel different? In S. Niemeier & R. Dirven (Eds.), *Evidence for linguistic relativity* (pp. 53–70). Amsterdam: John Benjamins.

Mark, C. (1986). *Gaelic verbs*. Glasgow: Department of Celtic Languages, Glasgow University.

McCafferty, K. (2004). Innovation in language contact. *Diachronica, 21*, 113–160.

Migge, B. (2003). *Creole formation as language contact*. Amsterdam: John Benjamins.

Mühlhäusler, P. (2004). Norfolk Island-Pitkern English (Pitkern Norfolk): Morphology and syntax. In B. Kortmann & E. Schneider (Eds.), *A handbook of varieties of English. Volume 2: Morphology and syntax* (pp. 789–801). Berlin: Mouton de Gruyter.

Odlin, T. (1989). *Language transfer*. Cambridge: Cambridge University Press.

Odlin, T. (1991). Irish English idioms and language transfer. *English World-Wide, 12*, 175–193.

Odlin, T. (1997). Bilingualism and substrate influence: A look at clefts and reflexives. In J. Kallen (Ed.), *Focus on Ireland* (pp. 35–50). Amsterdam: John Benjamins.

Odlin, T. (2003). Cross-linguistic influence. In C. Doughty & M. Long (Eds.), *Handbook of second language acquisition* (pp. 436–486). Oxford: Blackwell.

Odlin, T. (2005). Cross-linguistic influence and conceptual transfer: What are the concepts? *Annual Review of Applied Linguistics, 25*, 3–25.

Odlin, T. (2006). Could a contrastive analysis ever be complete? In J. Arabski (Ed.), *Cross-linguistic influence in the second language lexicon* (pp. 22–35). Clevedon, UK: Multilingual Matters.

Odlin, T., & Jarvis, S. (2004). Same source, different outcomes: A study of Swedish influence on the acquisition of English in Finland. *The International Journal of Multilingualism, 1*, 123–140.

Odlin, T., & Alonso-Vázquez, C. (2007). Meanings in search of the perfect form: a look at interlanguage verb phrases. *Rivista di psicolinguistica applicata* (in press).

Pederson, E., Danziger, E., Wilkins, D., Levinson, S., Kita, S., & Senft, G. (1998). Semantic typology and spatial conceptualization. *Language, 74*, 557–589.

Peltzer, L. (1996). Représentation et structuration de l'espace en tahitien [Representation and structuring of space in Tahitian]. *Bulletin de la Societé Linguistique de Paris, 91*, 297–321.

Pinker, S. (1994). *The language instinct: How the mind creates language*. New York: Morrow.

Pokorny, J. (1959). *Indogermanisches etymologisches Wörterbuch* [Indo-European dictionary]. Bern: Francke.

Pullum, G. (1991). *The great Eskimo vocabulary hoax, and other irreverent essays on the study of language*. Chicago: University of Chicago Press.

Pyles, T., & Algeo, J. (1993). *The origins and development of the English language*. New York: Harcourt Brace Jovanovich.

Ringbom, H. (1987). *The role of the first language in foreign language learning*. Clevedon, UK: Multilingual Matters.

Robinson, P. (2003). Attention and memory during SLA. In C. Doughty & M. Long (Eds.), *Handbook of second language acquisition* (pp. 631–678). Oxford: Blackwell.

Rocca, S. (2003). Lexical aspect in child second language acquisition of temporal morphology: A bidirectional study. In R. Salaberry & Y. Shirai (Eds.) *The*

L2 acquisition of tense–aspect morphology (pp. 249–284). Amsterdam: John Benjamins.

Sabban, A. (1982). *Gälisch-Englischer Sprachkontakt*. Heidelberg: Julius Groos.

Sankoff, G. (1991). Using the future to explain the past. In F. Byrne & T. Huebner (Eds.) *Development and structure of creole languages* (pp. 61–74). Amsterdam: John Benjamins.

Sankoff, G. (1993). Focus in Tok Pisin. In F. Byrne & D. Winford (Eds.), *Focus and grammatical relations in creole languages* (pp 117–140). Amsterdam: John Benjamins.

Sastry-Kuppa, S. (1995). *That's why he will talking for English*: The expression of habitual aspect in the English of untutored and low-level tutored Indian speakers. Presentation at the Ninth International Conference on Pragmatics and Language Learning, University of Illinois, Urbana, Illinois, March 3, 1995.

Schmidt, R. (1990). The role of consciousness in second language learning. *Applied Linguistics, 11*, 129–158.

Shirai, Y., & Nishi, Y. (2003). Lexicalisation of aspectual structures in English and Japanese. In A. Giacaolone-Ramat (Ed.), *Typology and second language acquisition* (pp. 267–290). Berlin: Mouton de Gruyter.

Slabakova, R. (1999). The parameter of aspect in second language acquisition. *Second Language Research, 15*, 283–317.

Slobin, D. (1993). Adult language acquisition: A view from child language study. In C. Perdue (Ed.), *Adult language acquisition: Cross-linguistic perspectives. Volume 2: The results*, (pp. 239–252). Cambridge: Cambridge University Press.

Slobin, D. (1996). From "thought and language" to "thinking for speaking". In J. Gumperz & S. Levinson (Eds.), *Rethinking linguistic relativity* (pp. 97–114). Cambridge: Cambridge University Press.

Slobin, D. (2002). Language evolution, acquisition and diachrony: probing the parallels. In T. Givón & B. Malle (Eds.), *The evolution of language out of pre-language* (pp. 375–392). Amsterdam: John Benjamins.

Stutterheim, C. von (2003). Linguistic structure and information organisation: The case of very advanced learners. *EUROSLA Yearbook, 3*, 183–206.

Talmy, L. (1985). Lexicalization patterns: Semantic structure in lexical forms, In T. Shopen (Ed.), *Language typology and syntactic description. Volume 3*, (pp. 57–149). Cambridge: Cambridge University Press.

Talmy, L. (2000). *Toward a cognitive semantics. Volume 2*. Cambridge, MA: MIT Press.

Traugott, E. & Hopper, P. (2003). *Grammaticalization*. Cambridge: Cambridge University Press.

Tyler, A. & Evans, V. (2000). My first husband was Italian (and he still is): "Exceptional" uses of English tense and pedagogical grammar. Essen University Linguistic Agency Series B: Applied and Interdisciplinary Papers (ISSN 1435–481). Paper Number 285.

Tyler, A. & Evans, V. (2001). The relation between experience, conceptual structure and meaning: Non-temporal uses of tense and language teaching. In M. Putz, S. S. Niemeier, & R. Dirven (Eds.), *Applied cognitive linguistics I: Theory and language acquisition* (pp. 63–105). Berlin: Mouton de Gruyter.

Vervaeke, J., & Kennedy, J. (2004). Conceptual metaphor and abstract thought. *Metaphor and Symbol, 19*, 213–231.

Wenzell, V. (1989). Transfer of aspect in the English oral narratives of native Russian speakers. In H. Dechert & M. Raupach (Eds.), *Transfer in language production* (pp. 71–97). Norwood, New Jersey: Ablex.

Whorf, B. L. (1956). *Language, thought, and reality*, J. Carroll (Ed.). Cambridge, MA: MIT Press.

Wilson, D., & Sperber, D. (1993). Linguistic form and relevance. *Lingua, 90*, 1–25.

Wode, H. (1983). On the systematicity of L1 transfer in L2 acquisition. In H. Wode (Ed.), *Papers on language acquisition, language learning and language teaching* (pp. 144–149). Heidelberg: J. Groos.

Yu, L. (1996). The role of cross-linguistic lexical similarity in the use of motion verbs in English by Chinese and Japanese learners. Unpublished Ed. D. dissertation, University of Toronto.

Zimmerman, R. (2006). Metaphorical transferability. In J. Arabski (Ed.), *Cross-linguistic influence in the second language lexicon* (pp. 193–209). Clevedon, UK: Multilingual Matters.

Zobl, H. (1980). The formal and developmental selectivity of L1 influence in L2 acquisition. *Language Learning, 30*, 43–57.

14

A UNIFIED MODEL

Brian MacWhinney

1 Introduction

There are three obvious differences between first and second language learners. First, infants who are learning language are also engaged in learning about how the world works. In contrast, second language learners already have a full understanding of the world and human society. Second, infants are able to rely on a highly malleable brain that has not yet been committed to other tasks (MacWhinney, Feldman, Sacco, & Valdes-Perez, 2000). In contrast, second language learners have to deal with a brain that has already been committed in various ways to the task of processing the first language. Third, infants can rely on an intense system of social support from their caregivers (Snow, 1999). In contrast, second language learners are often heavily involved in social and business commitments in their first language that distract them from interactions in the new language.

Together, these three differences might suggest that it would make little sense to try to develop a Unified Model of first and second language acquisition. In fact, many researchers have decided that the two processes are so different that they account for them with totally separate theories. For example, Krashen (1994) sees L1 learning as involving "acquisition" and L2 learning as based instead on "learning." Others (Bley-Vroman, Felix, & Ioup, 1988; Clahsen & Muysken, 1986) argue that Universal Grammar (UG) is available to children up to some critical age, but not to older learners of L2.

Despite these differences, there are good reasons to want to develop a Unified Model. First, many of the tasks faced by L1 and L2 learners are identical. Both groups of learners need to segment speech into words. Both groups need to learn the meanings of these words. Both groups need to figure out the patterns that govern word combination in syntactic constructions. Both groups have to work to interleave their growing lexical and syntactic knowledge to achieve fluency. For both groups, the actual shape of the input language of the community is roughly the same.

341

Thus, both the overall goal and the specific subgoals involved in reaching that goal are the same for both L1 and L2 learners.

Furthermore, the fact that L2 learning is so heavily influenced by transfer from L1 means that it would be impossible to construct a model of L2 learning that did not take into account the structure of the first language. Thus, rather than attempting to build two separate models of L1 and L2 learning, it makes more sense to consider the shape of a Unified Model in which the mechanisms of L1 learning are seen as a subset of the mechanisms of L2 learning. Although some of these learning mechanisms are more powerful in L1 than in L2, they are still accessible to both groups (Flynn, 1996). Therefore, it is conceptually simpler to formulate a Unified Model. We can use this same logic to motivate the extension of a Unified Model to the study of both childhood and adult multilingualism.

A first attempt at a unified account can be found in MacWhinney (2005a). The current chapter attempts to further systematize that account, relying on the Competition Model (Bates & MacWhinney, 1982; MacWhinney, 1987a) as its basic starting point. In particular, the Unified Model adopts the core Competition Model insight that, for the adult native speaker, cue strength is a direct function of cue validity. In the Unified Model, forms are stored in associative maps for syllables, lexical items, constructions, and mental models. During processing, the selection of forms is governed by cue strength within a competitive central syntactic processor.

Learning is grounded on self-organization within the associative maps. The processes of buffering, chunking, and resonance further modulate learning in these maps. Buffering works to provide short-term storage of material to allow the processor to compare competing forms and to extract consistent patterns as inputs to learning. Chunking works to facilitate the fluent integration of information between maps. Resonance works to consolidate representations within maps. The next sections explain the structuring of the associative maps, the operation of competition, and the roles of buffering, chunking, and resonance.

2 Self-organizing maps

The Unified Model views long-term linguistic knowledge as organized into a series of self-organizing maps (SOMs) (Kohonen, 1990; Li, Farkas, & MacWhinney, 2004). Self-organizing maps base their computation on a two-dimensional square lattice with a set of neurons or units. These neurons are all fully connected to the input, so that, on a given processing trial, every neuron receives the same pattern of featural input. Within the sheet, neurons are only connected to their nearest neighbors. On a given trial, some input features will be active and others will be turned off. For example, when the learner hears the syllable /pa/, the feature for labiality of the consonant will be active and the feature for affrication will not. Learning involves three phases. In the first phase, all units receive activation from the input and each unit computes its current activation. In the second phase, units compete through local inhibition of their neighbors. The best matching unit then emerges as the winner in this competition. In the third phase, the weights of the responding units are adjusted to increase the precision of activation in future trials. An important result of the weight adjustment procedure is that neighboring units become increasingly responsive to similar input patterns. As a result, similar inputs tend over time to activate neighboring units in the map. This adjustment feature gives SOMs their self-organizing properties.

Fig. 14.1 shows how the SOM used in the DevLex model of Li, Farkas, and MacWhinney shows increasing organization of activity bubbles for specific parts of speech over time. In this figure the upper left map shows the network after learning 50 words; the upper right shows the network after learning 100 words; the lower left shows the network after 250 words; and the lower right shows the network after it has learned 500 words. These figures show how, particularly during the first stages of

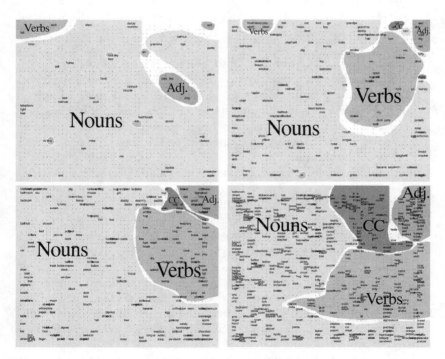

Figure 14.1 Part of speech organization in the DevLex network after learning 50 words (upper left), 100 words (upper right), 250 words (lower left), and 500 words (lower right). Adj = adjectives, CC = closed class.

learning, there is great plasticity with verbs moving from one edge of the sheet to the other. This movement occurs because, at first, particular areas are only weakly committed to particular parts of speech. For example, verbs may have made an initial beachhead in several areas. However, each of these beachheads is only weakly organized and lightly entrenched. Over time, one of these beachheads becomes the strongest and then ends up attracting all verbs to this area. As the network becomes more entrenched, less movement occurs. At the same time, the recall precision of the network increases, as does the size of the vocabulary it has learned.

Kohonen (1990) has shown that a two-dimensional SOM can accurately compute associations in a multidimensional space. Furthermore, the SOM has several structural and processing properties that correspond closely to those found in the brain.

1   SOMs rely on lateral inhibition during the competition of the winner with its nearest neighbors. The shape of this inhibition corresponds closely to the "Mexican hat" function observed in actual neural lateral inhibition.
2   SOMs maximize local connectivity. This corresponds to the observed preference for short connections in the brain.
3   SOMs provide an emergent form of localist representation. Over time, individual neurons come to become responsive to highly specific inputs, down to the level of the individual word or morpheme. This localist organization makes lexical items and parts of speech available for syntactic computation. However, this localism is emergent. If a particular unit is destroyed, the sheet may still be able to respond properly, although somewhat less accurately, to the input preferred by that unit.
4   SOMs demonstrate increased entrenchment and decreasing plasticity over time. As local organization progresses, it becomes more and more difficult to reverse or modify.
5   SOMs learn through unsupervised self-organization, rather than back-propagation. This corresponds to the observed pattern of unidirectional local connectivity in the cortex.

The two-dimensional structure of SOMs corresponds well with the sheetlike nature of cortical regions. Moreover, many cortical regions have been shown to possess a spatial organization (retinotopic, tonotopic, somatotopic) that corresponds in a SOM-like way to the physical structure of the input space.

The Unified Model postulates the existence of SOMs at the level of the syllable, the lexical item, and the construction. Let us look now in greater detail at how each of these maps functions in the Unified Model.

2.1 Syllabic maps

At the level of the syllable, there are initially two maps. The first map organizes recurring auditory input to auditory syllabic patterns, and the second organizes recurring motor sequences to articulatory syllabic patterns. During babbling, the child learns the equivalence between syllables organized in these two alternative ways. Once these equivalences are established, the system can be represented as a conjunction of two sets of inputs to a single central map. In accord with the models of Gupta and MacWhinney (1997) and Li and MacWhinney (2002), syllables are represented as serial chains with positions encoding syllable onset, nucleus, and coda. This representation allows the articulatory processor to convert syllables to a series of articulatory gestures. It also allows the auditory processor to detect formant changes through time across the syllable.

Languages differ markedly in the range of syllables encoded in these maps. Japanese uses no more than 70 different syllables. Mandarin Chinese has about 400 syllables. However, because a given syllable can be produced with up to five tones, the total inventory is about 1,600. English has even more possible syllables, reaching perhaps 3,000. It is likely that the syllabaries of languages like Japanese require no more than one level of SOM organization. However, systems like those for English or Mandarin can rely on hierarchicalization within SOMs, as suggested by Dittenbach, Rauber, and Merkl (2002). In a hierarchically-organized SOM, an area of high local competition projects to a full subordinate feature map which can then be used to further resolve the competition.

These properties of syllable-level SOMs help us understand the challenges faced by L2 learners at the level of phonology. Werker (1995), Kuhl (1991), and others have argued that during the first year children lose their ability to distinguish phonemic contrasts not present in their L1. This effect will arise in SOMs as a result of focusing on highly predictive features in the input at the expense of less predictive features (Regier, 2006). A classic case of this type of loss is the inability of many Japanese speakers to distinguish between English /r/ and /l/ in perception. To perceive this contrast, English speakers rely on third formant (F3) transitions to the following vowel. However, because there is no role for F3 transitions in the smaller Japanese syllabary, native Japanese speakers are not even listening for this cue. Moreover, since production uses this cue to guide subtle aspects of tongue positioning, Japanese L1 speakers also have problems learning to distinguish these consonants in production.

This example illustrates how L1 entrenchment blocks effective L2 learning. In fact, adults can learn to recognize and produce this contrast (Bradlow, Akahni-Yamada, Pisoni, & Tokhura, 1999; Flege, Takagi, & Mann, 1995). The relevant features are still available in the auditory input (Lotto, Kluender, & Holt, 1997); learning just involves allowing these features to have their impact on the auditory SOM. The Competition Model holds that, in order to restructure the syllable maps, L2 learners must rely on repeated focused trials to link changes in the auditory syllabary with changes in the articulatory syllabary. Methods for inducing these changes include presenting clear cases (McCandliss, Fiez, Protopapas, Conway, & McClelland, 2002), facial visual feedback, and diagrams of tongue positions.

The influence of L1 syllabaries on L2 acquisition is not restricted to Japanese speakers learning /r/ and /l/. Even for languages as close as German and English, the transfer of L1 syllabaries to L2 words can lead to strong L1 accents in L2. Consider the pronunciation by German learners of English of the word "German" as "Tsherman" or the use of German guttural /r/ for English flapped /r/. In general, L2 articulatory learning begins with massive transfer of L1 articulatory patterns to L2 (Flege & Davidian, 1984; Hancin-Bhatt, 1994). This transfer is at first successful in the sense that it allows for a reasonable level of communication. However, it is eventually counter-productive, since it embeds L1 phonology into the emergent L2 lexicon. In effect, the learner treats new words in L2 as if they were composed of strings of L1 articulatory units. This method of learning leads to short-term gains at the expense of long-term difficulties in correcting entrenched erroneous phonological transfer.

Forms that are unmarked in L1 transfer much more strongly than forms that are marked in L1 (Demuth, 1995; Eckman, 1991; Major, 2001). This is exactly the type of pattern we would expect to emerge from the operation of a cue-based SOM model. For example, if your goal as an L2 learner of English is to articulate an /r/, and your native Spanish language uses both a marked trilled /r/ and an unmarked tap /r/, you are most likely to make use of the unmarked tapped /r/, even in initial position with English words like "rich," rather than relying on the marked trilled /r/. This pattern of reliance on the unmarked form extends also to lexicon and syntactic constructions, as we will see below.

Some researchers (DeKeyser, 2000; Long, 2005) have attributed these effects not to transfer and entrenchment but to the operation of a biologically determined critical period (Lenneberg, 1967). Critical periods arise when presence or absence of a certain input causes irreversible deviations in the normal course of development (Waddington, 1957). These periods require a sharply defined age of termination, after which normal development is no longer possible. Extending this notion to cover the effects of entrenchment in cortical maps is problematic. We know that synapses and neurons are continually created and lost in most cortical regions, even including segments of the motor system (Yamamoto, Hoffman, & Strick, 2006). Given this, it is better to talk about the persistence of L1 accent in terms of entrenchment of particular features, rather than the end of some global critical period (Hurford, 1991).

Children who are exposed to two languages from birth are able to separate out two syllabaries early on. This separation relies on both segmental and prosodic cues (Mehler & Christophe, 1994). For example, it is easy to use even foot length to distinguish Spanish from English or to use tone to distinguish Chinese from Portuguese. Children learning two languages have up to 14 months of experience in distinguishing their languages by the time they come to saying their first words. The fact that languages can be consistently separated in audition as early as six months (Sebastián-Galles & Bosch, 2005) makes findings of early language separation in production (De Houwer, 2005) understandable in Competition Model terms.

When the child's two languages are roughly equal in dominance or strength, each system generates enough system-internal resonance to block excessive transfer. However, if one of the languages is markedly weaker (Döpke, 1998), then it will not have enough internal resonance to block occasional transfer. The situation is very different for L2 learners, since the balance between the languages is then tipped heavily in favor of L1. In order to permit the growth of resonance in L2, learners must apply additional learning strategies that would not have been needed for children. These strategies focus primarily on optimization of input, promotion of L2 resonance, and avoidance of processes that destroy input chunks.

2.2 Lexical maps

In the DevLex model of Li, Farkas, & MacWhinney (2004), lexical items (words) are represented as links between sounds and meanings. The lexical map encodes the phonological shape of words as a sequence of syllables. The semantic map encodes the meaningful side of words as a series of embodied images (Barsalou, 1999). Basically, words are viewed as associations between forms and functions.

The DevLex model (Li, Farkas, & MacWhinney, 2004; Li, Zhao, & MacWhinney, 2007) has been used to model a wide variety of phenomena in early lexical learning, including the vocabulary spurt, acquisition of parts of speech, semantic association, early lexical confusions, and the age of acquisition effect. It has also been used to model early lexical modularity in simultaneous bilingual acquisition (Hernandez, Li, & MacWhinney, 2005; Li & Farkas, 2002). Unlike most models of early lexical development, DevLex models use realistic parental input gathered from the CHILDES database for English and Chinese corpora. This input is coded using the PatPho system (Li & MacWhinney, 2002) for phonology, the HAL system for lexical co-occurrence (Li, Burgess, & Lund, 2001), and the WordNet system (Harm, 2002) to provide additional semantic detail.

In the DevLex simulations of the simultaneous learning of Chinese and English, the emergent feature maps show a clear separation between the two languages with Chinese words organized to one side of the map and English words organized to the other. L2 learning in DevLex takes a very different form. The L2 learner can achieve rapid initial progress by simply transferring the L1 conceptual world en masse to L2. This amounts to an intermingling of L2 forms in a basically L1 map. When learners first acquire a new L2 form, such as "silla" in Spanish, they treat this form as simply another way of saying "chair." This means that initially the L2 system has no separate conceptual structure and that its formal structure relies on the structure of L1. Kroll and Tokowicz (2005) review models of the lexicon that emphasize the extent to which L2 relies on L1 forms to access meaning, rather than accessing meaning directly. In this sense, we can say that L2 is parasitic on L1, because of the extensive amount of transfer from L1 to L2. The learner's goal is to reduce this parasitism by building up L2 representations as a separate system. Learners do this by strengthening the direct linkage between new L2 forms and conceptual representations. Given the fact that connectionism predicts such massive transfer for L1 knowledge to L2, we might ask why we do not see more transfer error in second language lexical forms. There are four reasons for this:

1   A great deal of transfer occurs smoothly and directly without producing error. Consider a word like *chair* in English. When the native English speaker begins to learn Spanish, it is easy to use the concept underlying "chair" to serve as the meaning for the new word *silla* in Spanish. The closer the conceptual, material, and linguistic worlds of the two languages, the more successful this sort of positive transfer will be. Transfer only works smoothly when there is close conceptual match. For example, Ijaz (1986) has shown how difficult transfer can be for Korean learners of English in semantic domains involving transfer verbs, such as *take* or *put*. Similarly, if the source language has a two-color system (Berlin & Kay, 1969), as in Dani, acquisition of an eight-color system, as in Hungarian, will be difficult. These effects underscore the extent to which L2 lexical items are parasitic on L1 forms.

2   Learners are able to suppress some types of incorrect transfer. For example, when a learner tries to translate the English noun *soap* into Spanish by using a cognate, the result is *sopa* or "soup." Misunderstandings created by "false friend" transfers such as this will be quickly detected and corrected. Similarly, an attempt to translate the English form *competence* into Spanish as *competencia* will run into problems, since *competencia* means competition. Dijkstra (2005) notes that, in laboratory settings, the suppression of these incorrect forms

is incomplete, even in highly proficient bilinguals. However, this transfer effect may be less marked in non-laboratory contexts in which language-internal L2 associations are more fully activated by concurrent reciprocal activation.

3   Error is minimized when two words in L1 map onto a single word in L2. For example, it is easy for an L1 Spanish speaker to map the meanings underlying "saber" and "conocer" (Stockwell, Bowen, & Martin, 1965) onto the L2 English form "know." Dropping the distinction between these forms requires little in the way of cognitive reorganization. On the other hand, it is difficult for the L1 English speaker to acquire this new distinction when learning Spanish. In order to control this distinction correctly, the learner must restructure the concept underlying "know" into two new related structures. In the area of lexical learning, these cases should cause the greatest transfer-produced errors.

4   Learners tend to avoid the transfer of marked lexical forms, just as they avoid the transfer of marked phonological forms. In the lexicon, this often means that learners will use generic forms and superordinates rather than more specific terms. For example, an English speaker learning Spanish will refer to a creek as a "river" using the Spanish word "río" rather than the more specific form "riachuelo." This pattern of learning will minimize error, although it fails to achieve full expressivity.

2.3 Construction maps

The combination of lexical items into sentences is controlled by constructions (Goldberg, this volume; Lieven & Tomasello, this volume). In the Competition Model, constructions are patterns that specify how a predicate (verb, adjective, preposition) can combine with its arguments. MacWhinney (1975, 1982) characterized the child's initial learning of syntax in terms of the acquisition of item-based constructions (Hudson, this volume). These are specific constructions linked to specific individual predicates. For example, we can say that the verb "pour" is linked to the construction: pourer + "pour" + thing_poured + receptacle. Or we can say that the adjective "nice" is linked to the construction: "nice" + thing_described. Although these item-based constructions are limited in scope, they can be combined recursively to produce full productivity in language. For example, constructions based on "nice," "for," and "my" can be combined to produce "for my nice kitty." For recent explications of the details of item-based learning, see MacWhinney (2005b). For older, more detailed accounts, see MacWhinney (1987a, 1987b).

Although we have not yet implemented a SOM-based model for the learning of constructions, we can sketch out the general way in which it will work. Constructions that are linked to individual items can be learned as features of items on the current DevLex semantic map. These additional features encode the expectations of individual predicates for arguments. Because the DevLex map uses co-occurrence information for training, this type of information is already available. For item-based constructions, we just have to add semantic role information to the input vector. In other words, instead of just telling the network that "nice" goes with "kitty," we will also tell it that "kitty" is functioning as "thing described." In addition, the map will encode the other semantic features of the "thing described." This information will then be sufficient for the syntactic processor to activate plausible nouns after the predicate "nice" during comprehension or to relate the predicate to its arguments positionally during production.

Building on the information acquired during the learning of item-based patterns, learners can then organize groups of item-based constructions into lexical group constructions. The extraction of this second level of constructions requires encoding in a separate map that associates groups or types of predicates to types of arguments. For example, verbs such as "pour" or "throw" use the construction Agent + V + Object + Goal as in "Bill poured the water into the tub." Other verbs such as "fill" or "paint" use the construction Agent + V + Goal + Transferred, as in "Bill filled the tub with water." The impact of lexical group constructions on processing has been examined in a variety of recent studies in sentence processing (Holmes, Stowe, & Cupples, 1989; MacDonald, 1994; MacDonald, Pearlmutter, & Seidenberg, 1994; McRae, Spivey-Knowlton, & Tanenhaus, 1998; Trueswell & Tanenhaus, 1994; Trueswell, Tanenhaus, & Garvsey, 1994; Trueswell, Tanenhaus, & Kello, 1993). This work has yielded results that are closely in accord with Competition Model claims regarding cue validity and competition (Elman, Hare, & McRae, 2005).

There is a third level of argument generalization, above the levels of the item-based pattern and the group-based construction. This is the level of the global construction. Whenever group-based constructions can be generalized across predicate groups, global constructions can emerge. In English, the SV and VO global patterns work together to produce prototypical SVO order (MacWhinney, Bates, & Kliegl, 1984). Other languages promote different combinations of global patterns. In Hungarian and Chinese, for example, SV, OV, and VO orders operate to express alternative varieties of object definiteness, producing SVO and SOV orders. Italian combines SV and VO patterns with secondary, but significant use of VS (Dell'Orletta, Lenci, Montemagni, & Pirelli, 2005) to produce SVO and VSO orders.

Among the various global patterns, there are two that seem to be nearly universal. The first is the ordering of the topic before the comment to produce Topic + Comment order. This pattern is used extensively in languages as typologically diverse as Hungarian (É.-Kiss, 1981), Italian (Moro, 2006), and Chinese (Barry, 1975). The second universal global cue is the global animacy cue. All other things being equal, nearly all languages tend to prefer animate subjects. This cue reflects the fact that there is a consistent association of the grammatical subject with the agential, human perspective (MacWhinney, 2005c). However, from the viewpoint of the child acquiring language, the association of animacy or topicality with the role of the subject can be induced directly from the statistical fact that subjects are typically agential and topical.

Thus, animacy is a strong cue to SV interpretation of NV in English but also a strong cue to VS interpretation of VN in Welsh. Second, the marking of agentiality or perspective is typically cued most strongly by the contrast between animate and inanimate nouns. Third, the semantics of the perspective varies across the specific verb or verb group involved. Most verbs treat the perspective as the animate causer, but some verbs like "frighten" treat the cause as the perspective, even when it is not animate. Other verbs, such as those in the passive, create perspectives that are neither causal nor agential.

2.3.1 Transfer in comprehension

There are now over a dozen Competition Model studies that have demonstrated the transfer of a "syntactic accent" in sentence interpretation (Bates & MacWhinney, 1981; de Bot & van Montfort, 1988; Frenck-Mestre, 2005; Gass, 1987; Harrington, 1987; Kilborn, 1989; Kilborn & Cooreman, 1987; Kilborn & Ito, 1989; Liu, Bates, & Li, 1992; McDonald, 1987a, 1987b; McDonald & Heilenman, 1991; McDonald & MacWhinney, 1989). These studies have shown that the learning of global constructions in a second language is a gradual process. The process begins with L2 cue weight settings that are close to those for L1. Over time, these settings change in the direction of the native speakers' settings for L2. The Competition Model view of language interaction is further supported by evidence of effects from L2 back to L1. Sentence processing studies by Liu, Bates, and Li (1992) and Dussias (2001) have demonstrated the presence of just such effects. Although the Competition Model requires that the strongest transfer effects should be from L1 to L2, the view of competition as interactive leads us to expect some weaker amount of transfer from L2 back to L1.

2.3.2 Transfer in production

Pienemann et al. (2005) claim that "only those linguistic forms that the learner can process can be transferred to L2." They argue that this view of transfer contrasts sharply with the Competition Model view that every L1 structure that can find an L2 match will transfer. Pienemann et al. present the case of the learning of the German V2 rule by speakers of L1 Swedish as evidence in favor of their analysis. The V2 rules in Swedish and German allow speakers to front adverbs like "today" or "now." This produces sentences with the verb in second position with forms such as "Today likes Peter milk." The surprising finding is that Swedes do not produce this order from the beginning, starting instead with "Today Peter likes milk" and "Peter likes milk today."

This finding is only surprising, if one believes that learners transfer whole syntactic frames for whole sentences. However, this is not the position of the Competition Model. Instead, the Competition Model holds that individual predicate-argument constructions are transferred one by one. Moreover, transfer will begin with unmarked forms. In this case, the unmarked form produces "Peter likes milk today." Later, when learners attempt to transfer the marked form, they begin with the movement of "today" to first position and then adjust the position of the subject as a second step.

The opposite side of this coin is that, when L2 structures can be learned early on as item-based patterns, this learning can block transfer from L1. Pienemann et al. present the example of learning of Japanese SOV order by speakers of L1 English. These learners almost never generalize English SVO to Japanese. Of course, the input to L2 learners consistently emphasizes SOV order and presents no VO sequences, although these do occur in colloquial Japanese. As a result, learners view Japanese verbs as item-based constructions with slots for objects in preverbal position marked by the postposition "o" and topics in initial position marked by the postpositions "wa" or "ga." After learning a few such verbs, they construct a "feature-based" construction for SOV order. This is positive learning based on consistent input in L2. If L1 were to have a transfer effect at this point, it would be extremely brief, since L2 is so consistent and these item-based constructions with their associated case marking postpositions are in the focus of the learner's attention.

2.4 Morphological maps

Learning of the morphological marking or inflections of a second language is very different from learning of the other areas we have discussed. This is because, in morphosyntax, it is typically impossible to transfer from L1 to L2. For example, an English learner of German cannot use the English noun gender system as a basis for learning the German noun gender system. In German, the sun (*die Sonne*) is feminine and the moon (*der Mond*) is masculine. The spoon (*der Löffel*) is masculine and the fork (*die Gabel*) is feminine. There is nothing in English that tells us how these nouns should be assigned to gender. If a learner of German has an L1 with a real gender system, such as Spanish, there can be transfer. But if the L1 is English, then transfer will be marginal. Similarly, a Spanish learner of Chinese cannot use L1 knowledge to acquire the system of noun classifiers, because Spanish has no noun classifiers. Also morphophonological alternations such as the shift of final /f/ to /v/ in "knives" are immune to transfer. For example, there is nothing in English that can help us decide that the plural of *tükör* (mirror) in Hungarian is *tükrök*, rather than the more regular form *tükörök*.

Although arbitrary forms and classes cannot transfer between languages, the grammatical functions underlying affixes can. For example, the underlying concept for words like "with" (comitative), "for" (benefactive), and "by" (agential) can be used in acquiring affixes and grammatical markings in L2. However, not all concepts are available for transfer to all languages. Consider the learning of article marking in English by speakers of Chinese, Japanese, or Korean. These languages have no separate category of definiteness, instead using classifiers and plurals to express some of the functions marked by the English definite. For learners from these languages, the semantic complexity of the subcomponents of definiteness in English constitutes a major learning barrier.

Earlier models using the back propagation algorithm showed how children could learn the morphology of German (MacWhinney, Leinbach, Taraban, & McDonald, 1989) and English (MacWhinney & Leinbach, 1991). However, these models failed to treat derivational suffixes as separate lexical items (MacWhinney, 2000). A recent extension of this model by Goldsmith and O'Brien (2006) explicitly models learning as the association between stems and affixes. However, that model relies on stems and affixes that have been hand-extracted by the researcher. To solve this analytic problem Pirelli and Herreros (2006) used two-layer SOMs to extract affixes in English, Italian, and Arabic without hand analysis of the input forms. If the SOM is given input that matches the actual token frequencies of Italian, it learns to separate participles of the -tto class like stato and fatto from participles of the -sto class like visto and chiesto. For English, their model serves to extract both regular /-ed/ and the various irregular patterns such as *lend–lent* or *sing–sang*. For Arabic, they demonstrate extraction of a variety of non-concatenative patterns the alter the vowels and consonants of the stem. A next step in this work will be to show how the extraction of these alterations can be linked to learning of the stems as lexical items. Forms extracted in this way could then serve as input to models of the type developed by Goldsmith and O'Brien. In the DevLex framework, this learning would occur in the main lexical map, but connections would be maintained between that map and the extraction of affixes in this secondary map.

3 Competition

We have now completed our examination of the role of SOMs in the learning of both L1 and L2. However, by themselves, these maps do not produce vocal output or conceptual interpretations. Rather, SOMs are repositories in long-term memory of associations and forms that can be used through the online processor to produce and comprehend the patterns of speech. The actual work of integrating information yielded by the SOMs is placed on the shoulders of the competitive processor. In comprehension, the competitive processor combines the patterns and cues used by constructions to derive a directed graph with labeled grammatical relations (Sagae, MacWhinney, & Lavie, 2004) that can then guide final interpretation. In production, the competitive processor receives activations from constructions and lexical items that it uses to structure the form of the output phonological buffer (Dell, Juliano, & Govindjee, 1993)

The competitive processor continually integrates information from both the lexical and phonological level during recognition (Elman & McClelland, 1988). Similarly, it adjudicates incrementally (Kempen & Hoenkamp, 1987; O'Grady, 2005) between conflicting grammatical relation attachment decisions (MacWhinney, 1987b), guided continually by lexical expectations (MacDonald, Pearlmutter, & Seidenberg, 1994). The Competition Model account of sentence processing is extremely close in many details to that developed by O'Grady (this volume).

The study of the process of resolution of competing grammatical attachments has been the chief focus of experimental work in the Competition Model tradition. This work has focused on measurement of the relative strength of various cues to the selection of the agent, using a simple sentence interpretation procedure. Subjects listen to a sentence with two nouns and a verb and are asked to say who was the actor. In a few studies, the task involves direct-object identification (Sokolov, 1988, 1989), relative clause processing (MacWhinney & Pléh, 1988), or pronominal assignment (MacDonald & MacWhinney, 1990; McDonald & MacWhinney, 1995), but usually the task is agent identification. Sometimes the sentences are well-formed grammatical sentences, such as *the cat is chasing the duck*. Sometimes they involve competitions between cues, as in the ungrammatical sentence **the duck the cat is chasing*. Depending on the language involved, the cues varied in these studies include word order, subject–verb agreement, object–verb agreement, case-marking, prepositional case marking, stress, topicalization, animacy, omission, and pronominalization. These cues are varied in a standard orthogonalized ANOVA design with three or four sentences per cell to increase statistical reliability. The basic question is always the same: what is the relative order of cue strength in the given language and how do these cue strengths interact?

In English, the dominant cue for subject identification is preverbal positioning. For example, in the English sentence *the eraser hits the cat*, we assume that *the eraser* is the agent. However, a parallel sentence in Italian or Spanish would have *the cat* as the agent. This is because the word order cue is not as strong in Italian or Spanish as it is in English. In Spanish, the prepositional object marker "a" is a clear cue to the object and the subject is the noun that is not the object. An example of this is the sentence *el toro mató al torero* (The bull killed to-the bullfighter). No such prepositional cue exists in English. In German, case marking on the definite article is a powerful cue to the subject. In a sentence such as *der Lehrer liebt die Witwe* (The teacher loves the widow), the presence of the nominative masculine article *der* is a sure cue to identification of the subject. In Russian, the subject often has a case suffix. In Arabic, the subject is the noun that agrees with the verb in number and gender and this cue is stronger than the case-marking cue. In French, Spanish, and Italian, when an object pronoun is present, it can help identify the noun that is not the subject. Thus, we see that Indo-European languages can vary markedly in their use of cues to mark case roles. When we go outside of Indo-European to languages like Navajo, Hungarian, or Japanese, the variation becomes even more extreme.

Cue strength is a psychological construct measured in Competition Model experiments in which cues are set in conflict with each other. To measure cue strength, Competition Model experiments rely on sentences with conflicting cues. For example, in *the eraser push the dogs* the cues of animacy and subject–verb agreement favor "the dogs" as agent. However, the stronger cue of preverbal positioning favors "the eraser" as agent. As a result, English-speaking adult subjects strongly favor "the eraser" even in a competition sentence of this type. However, about 20 percent of the participants will choose "the dogs" in this case.

Cue validity, availability, and reliability are properties of the linguistic input. To measure the validity of cues in the various languages we have studied, we rely on text counts where we list the cues in favor of each noun and track the relative availability and reliability of each cue. A fully available cue (availability = 1.0) is always there when you need it, although it may or may not be always reliable. Cue availability can be further defined to refer to the presence of the cue in some contrastive form. For example, if both of the nouns in a sentence are animate, then the animacy cue is available, but not contrastively available. A fully reliable cue (reliability = 1.0) is always correct when you use it, although it may or may not be always available. Of course, the best cue is one that is fully available and fully reliable. Thus, we can talk about cue validity as the product of availability and reliability, since perfect availability and reliability will yield perfect validity. A fully valid cue would always be present when you need it and always give you the right answer.

By looking at how children, adult monolinguals, and adult bilinguals speaking about 18 different languages process these various types of sentences, we have been able to reach these conclusions regarding sentence comprehension:

1   When given enough time during sentence comprehension to make a careful choice, adults assign the role of agency to the nominal with the highest cue strength.
2   When there is a competition between cues, the levels of choice in a group of adult subjects will closely reflect the relative strengths of the competing cues.
3   When adult subjects are asked to respond immediately, even before the end of the sentence is reached, they will tend to base their decisions primarily on the strongest cue in the language.
4   When the strongest cue is neutralized, the next strongest cue will dominate.
5   The fastest decisions occur when all cues agree and there is no competition. The slowest decisions occur when strong cues compete.
6   Children begin learning to comprehend sentences by first focusing on the strongest cue in their language.
7   As children get older, the strength of all cues increases to match the adult pattern with the most valid cue growing most in strength.
8   As children get older, their reaction times gradually get faster in accord with the adult pattern.
9   Compared to adults, children are relatively more influenced by cue availability, as opposed to cue reliability.
10 Cue strength in adults and older children (8–10 years) is not related to cue availability (since all cues have been heavily encountered by this time), but rather to cue reliability. In particular, it is a function of conflict reliability, which measures the reliability of a cue when it conflicts directly with other cues.

This list of highly general findings from Competition Model research underscores the heuristic value and scope of the concepts of cue strength, cue validity, and competition.

4 Buffering

Self-organizing maps provide long-term storage for linguistic forms. However, the information that is retrieved from these maps during online processing can often involve ambiguities and competitions. Although there is usually one form or interpretation that is dominant, a second or third interpretation may also be viable and competitive. Such secondary forms may end up as the correct selections, once all the information is fully integrated. To permit this integration, the brain has to have mechanisms for preserving competitors in short-term storage.

Each SOM is associated with a buffer that preserves the activation of current competitors. These buffers allow for short-term storage of the auditory signal, activated lexical items, and competing grammatical role attachments. Baddeley (1992) and others have characterized lexical working memory in terms of a phonological loop or store. Gupta and MacWhinney (1997) showed how phonological storage can facilitate the learning of forms in the lexical map. Several authors (Ellis & Sinclair, 1996; Harrington, 1992; Service & Craik, 1993) have shown how working memory buffers of this type can facilitate the learning of new linguistic forms.

It is not yet clear whether how closely this acquisitional function of working memory is linked to its role in the online processing of specific syntactic structures (Gibson, Pearlmutter, Canseco-Gonzalez, & Hickok, 1996; MacWhinney & Pléh, 1988). However, in a lexically-driven processing model such as the Competition Model, the same processes that facilitate SOM storage during word learning can also operate during sentence processing to preserve lexical activation in maps. During online processing, storage would not involve full vocal rehearsal; rather, it would involve achieving a precise level of control for continued access to competing forms on the lexical maps.

The operation of short term buffering modulates the role of cue validity during both processing and acquisition. For example, the processing of subject–verb agreement for inverted word orders in Italian is not fully learned until about age eight (Devescovi, D'Amico, Smith, Mimica, & Bates, 1998), despite its high cue validity and high cue strength in adult speakers. One of the core findings of Competition Model research has been that, when adult subjects are given plenty of time to make a decision, their choices are direct reflections of the cumulative validity of all the relevant cues. In this sense, we can say that off-line decisions are optimal reflections of the structure of the language. However, when subjects are asked to make decisions on-line, then their ability to sample all relevant cues is restricted. In such cases, we say that "cue cost" factors limit the application of cue validity. These cue cost factors can involve various aspects of processing. However, the most important factors are those that require listeners to maintain agreement cues and distant role-binding cues in working memory.

It is easy to interfere with normal language processing by imposing additional loads on the listener or speaker. Working within a standard Competition Model experimental framework, Kilborn (1989) has shown that even fully competent bilinguals tend to process sentences more slowly than monolinguals. However, when monolinguals are asked to listen to sentences under conditions of white noise, their reaction times are identical to those of the bilinguals. Similarly Blackwell and Bates (1995) and Miyake, Carpenter and Just, (1994) have shown that, when subjected to conditions of noise, normals process sentences much like aphasics. Gerver (1974) and Seleskovitch (1976) report parallel results for the effects of noise on simultaneous interpretation.

5 Chunking

Chunking plays a major role in general models of cognition, such as Newell's SOAR model (Newell, 1990) or Anderson's ACT-R model (Anderson & Lebiere, 1998). It also figures heavily in accounts that emphasize the role of implicit learning (Cleermans & McClelland, 1991). Ellis (1996, 2002) has argued that chunking can help us understand the growth of fluency in second language learning. However, the exact way in which this operates has not yet been fully described. One way in which chunking can operate is by the simple composition of units into a new whole. For example, in Spanish, L2 learners can chunk together the plan for *buenos* with the plan for *días* to produce *buenos días*. They can then combine this chunk with *muy* to produce *muy buenos días* "very good morning."

Second language learners often fail to pick up large enough phrasal chunks. For example, if learners of German often learn the word *Mann* "man" in isolation. If, instead, they would learn phrases such as *der alte Mann*, *meines Mannes*, *den jungen Männern*, and *ein guter Mann*, then they would not only know the gender of the noun, but would also have a good basis for acquiring the declensional paradigm for both the noun and its modifiers. If they analyze a phrase like *der alte Mann* into the literal string "the + old + man" and throw away all of the details of the inflections on "der" and "alte," then they will lose an opportunity to induce the grammar from implicit generalization across stored chunks. If the learner stores larger chunks of this type, then the rules of grammar can emerge from analogic processing of the chunks stored in feature maps (Bybee & Hopper, 2001; Ellis, 2002; MacWhinney, 1982; Tomasello, 2003).

Although the formation of chunks through composition is certainly an important process, this process by itself cannot produce full fluency. There are simply too many possible chunks to learn. One solution to this problem is to extend the original formulations of chunking theory (Chase & Simon, 1973; Newell, 1990) to allow for the formation of more schematic chunks (Gobet, 2005). The theory of Construction Grammar fits in well with this new emphasis, since high-level constructions are schematic in just this flexible way. In addition to retrieving constructions as chunks, learners must work out methods that produce new constructional chunks on the fly in real time. Thus, instead of storing Spanish *muy buenos días* (very good day) as a rote chunk, learners must be able to smoothly integrate the combination of *buenos días* with the additional predicate *muy* without hesitation or delay. Thus, rather than thinking of chunking as only a method for creating new long term memory units, we need to think of it as a method for integrating phrases on line.

Practice in producing combinations can be either fairly limited or quite general. For example, the chunk *muy buenos días* only generalizes to a few other forms such as *muy buenas noches* (very good night), *muy buenas tardes* (very good afternoon) or, perhaps, *muy poco dinero* (very little money). However, a phrase such as *quisiera comprar* (I would like to buy . . .) can be used with any manner of noun to talk about things you would like to buy. In each of these cases, production of one initial combination, such as *quisiera comprar una cerveza* (I would like to buy a beer), may be halting at first. However, soon the result of the creation process itself can be stored as a chunk. In this case, it is not the actual phrase that is chunked but rather the process of activating the predicate combination (*quisiera comprar*) and then going ahead and filling the argument. In other words, we develop fluency by repeated practice in making combinations.

Once we have developed fluency in the combination of well-learned words, we can still experience disfluency when we try to integrate newly-learned words into established constructions. For example, even if we have learned to use the frame *quisiera comprar* fluently with words such as *una cerveza* (a beer) or *un reloj* (a clock), we may still experience difficulties when we need to talk about "a round trip ticket to Salamanca" (*un billete de ida y vuelta para Salamanca*). In this selection, we might have particular problems when we hit the word "para" since the English concept of "for, to" can be expressed in Spanish using either *por* or *para* and our uncertainty regarding the choice between these two forms can slow us down and cause disfluency or error. In general, for both L1 and L2 learners, disfluencies arise from delays in lexical access, misordering of constituents, and selection of agreement markings. Fluency arises through the practicing of argument filling and improvements in the speed of lexical access and the selections between competitors.

6 Resonance

Since the days of Ebbinghaus (1885), we have understood that the learning of the associations between words requires repeated practice. However, a single repetition of a new vocabulary pair such as *mesa—table* is not enough to guarantee robust learning. Instead, it is important that initial exposure be followed by additional test repetitions timed to provide correct retrieval before forgetting prevents efficient resonance from occurring (Pavlik, in press). Because robustness accumulates with practice, later retrieval trials can be spaced farther and farther apart (Pimsleur, 1967). This is the principle of "graduated interval recall." The Unified

Model argues that the success of this method can be attributed to its use of resonant neural connections between cortical areas. While two cortical areas are coactive, the hippocampus can store their relation long enough to create an initial memory consolidation. Repeated access of this trace (Wittenberg, Sullivan, & Tsien, 2002) can serve to further consolidate the memory. Once the initial consolidation has been achieved, maintenance only requires occasional reactivation of the relevant retrieval pathway. This type of resonance can be used to consolidate new forms on the phonological, lexical (Gupta & MacWhinney, 1997), and construction levels.

A fuller form of resonance occurs during covert inner speech. In the case of inner speech, we are using resonance not to acquire new forms, but to activate conceptual interpretations and plan actions. Vygotsky (1934) observed that young children would often give themselves instructions overtly. For example, a two-year-old might say, "pick it up" while picking up a block. At this age, the verbalization tends to guide and control the action. By producing a verbalization that describes an action, the child sets up a resonant connection between vocalization and action. Later, Vygotsky argues, these overt instructions become inner speech and continue to guide our cognition. L2 learners go through a process much like that of the child. At first, they use the language only with others. Then, they begin to talk to themselves in the new language and start to "think in the second language." At this point, the second language begins to assume the same resonant status that the child attains for the first language.

Once a process of inner speech is set into motion, it can also be used to process new input and relate new forms to other forms paradigmatically. For example, if I hear the phrase "ins Mittelalter" in German, I can think to myself that this means that the stem "Alter" must be "das Alter." This means that the dative must take the form "in welchem Alter" or "in meinem Alter." These resonant form-related exercises can be conducted in parallel with more expressive resonant exercises in which I simply try to talk to myself about things around me in German, or whatever language I happen to be learning. Even young children engage in practice of this type (Berk, 1994; Nelson, 1998).

Resonance also helps us understand code-switching. If a language is being repeatedly accessed, it will be in a highly resonant state. Although another language will be passively accessible, it may take a second or two before the resonant activation of that language can be triggered by a task (Grosjean, 1997). Thus, a speaker may not immediately recognize a sentence in a language that has not been spoken in the recent context. On the other hand, a simultaneous interpreter will maintain both languages in continual receptive activation, while trying to minimize resonant activations in the output system of the source language.

Like La Heij (2005), I would argue that multilingual processing relies more on activation and resonance than on inhibition (Green, 1986). We know that the brain makes massive use of inhibitory connections. However, these are typically local connections that sharpen local competitions in SOMs. Inhibition is also important in providing overt inhibitory control of motor output, as in speech monitoring. However, inhibition by itself cannot produce new learning, coactivation, and inner speech. For these types of processing, resonant activation is more effective.

Resonance can facilitate the sharpening of contrasts between forms. Both L1 and L2 learners may have trouble encoding new phonological forms that are close to words they already know. Children can have trouble learning the two new forms "pif" and "bif" because of their confusability, although they can learn "pif" when it occurs along with "wug" (Stager & Werker, 1997). This same phonological confusability effect can impact second language learners. For example, when I came to learn Cantonese, I needed to learn to pay careful attention to marking with tones, lest I confuse *mother*, *measles*, *linen*, *horse*, and *scold*, as various forms of /ma/.

Resonant mappings can rely on cues generated by synaesthesia (Ramachandran & Hubbard, 2001), onomatopoeia, sound symbolism, postural associations (Paget, 1930), lexical analysis or a host of other provisional relations. It is not necessary that this symbolism be in accord with any established linguistic pattern. Instead, each learner is free to discover a different pattern of associations. This nonconventional nature of resonant connections means that we cannot use group data to demonstrate the use of specific connections in lexical learning. However, we do know that constructive mnemonics provided by the experimenter (Atkinson, 1975) greatly facilitate learning. For example, when learning the German word *Wasser*, we can imagine the sound of water running out of a faucet and associate this sound with the /s/ of *Wasser*. For this word, we can also associate the sound of the German word to the sound of the English word *water*. At the same time, we can associate *Wasser* with additional collocations, such as *Wasser trinken*, which themselves resonate with *Bier trinken* and others. Together, these resonant associations between collocations, sounds, and other words help to link the German word *Wasser* into the developing German lexicon. It is likely that children also use these mechanisms to encode the relations between sounds and meanings. Children are less inhibited than are adults in their ability to create *ad hoc* symbolic links between sounds and meanings. The child learning German as an L1 might associate the shimmering qualities of *Wasser* with a shimmering aspect of the sibilant; or the child might imagine the sound as plunging downward in tone in the way that water comes over a waterfall. The child may link the concept of *Wasser* tightly to a scene in which someone pours *ein Glas Wasser* and then the association between the sound of *Wasser* and the image of the glass and the pouring are primary. For the first language learner, these resonant links are woven together with the entire nature of experience and the growing concept of the world.

A major dimension of resonant connections is between words and our internal image of the human body. For example, Bailey, Chang, Feldman, and Narayanan (1998) characterize the meaning of the verb "stumble" in terms of the physical motion of the limbs during walking, the encountering of a physical object, and the breaking of gait and posture. As Tomasello (1992) has noted, each new verb learned by the child can be mapped onto a physical or cognitive frame of this type. In this way, verbs and other predicates can support the emergence of a grounded mental model for sentences. Workers in L2 (Asher, 1977) have often emphasized the importance of action for the grounding of new meanings. The new literature in Cognitive Grammar exemplified in this Handbook provides good theoretical support for that approach. Item-based constructions are central in this discussion, since they provide a powerful link between the earlier Competition Model emphasis on processing and cue validity and the newer theories of grounded cognition (MacWhinney, 1999).

Orthography provides a major source of resonance in L2 learning. When an L2 learner of German learns the word *Wasser*, it is easy to map the sounds of the word directly to the image of the letters. Because German has highly regular mappings from orthography to pronunciation, calling up the image of the spelling of *Wasser* is an extremely good way of activating its sound. When the L2 learner is illiterate or when the L2 orthography is unlike the L1 orthography, this backup system for resonance will not be available. L2 learning of Chinese by speakers of languages with Roman scripts illustrates this problem. In some signs and books in Mainland China, Chinese characters are accompanied by romanized pinyin spellings. This allows the L2 learner a method for establishing resonant connections between new words, their pronunciation, and their representations in Chinese orthography. However, in Taiwan and Hong Kong, characters are seldom written out in pinyin in either books or public notices. As a result, beginners cannot learn from these materials. In order to make use of resonant connections from orthography, learners must focus on the learning of Chinese script. This learning itself requires a large investment in resonant associations, since the Chinese writing system is based largely on radical elements that have multiple resonant associations with the sounds and meanings of words.

7 Age-related effects

At this point, it may be helpful to review how the Unified Competition Model accounts for age-related changes in language learning ability. As DeKeyser and Larson-Hall (2005) note, the default account in this area has been the Critical Period Hypothesis (CPH) which holds that, after some time in late childhood or puberty, second languages can no longer be acquired by the innate language acquisition device but must be learned painfully and incompletely through explicit instruction.

Following Birdsong (2005), the Unified Competition Model attributes the observed facts about age-related changes to very different sources. The model emphasizes the extent to which learning in SOMs produces ongoing entrenchment. This entrenchment operates differentially across linguistic areas, with the strongest entrenchment occurring in output phonology and the least entrenchment in the area of lexicon, where new learning continues to occur throughout the life span. To overcome entrenchment, learners must rely on resonant processes that allow the fledgling L2 to resist the intrusions of L1, particularly in phonology (Colomé, 2001; Dijkstra, Grainger, & Van Heuven, 1999). For languages with familiar orthographies, resonance connections can be formed between writing, sound, meaning, and phrasal units. For languages with unfamiliar orthographies, the domain of resonant connections will be more constrained. This problem impacts older learners severely because they have become increasingly reliant on resonant connections between sound and orthography. Because learning through resonant connections is highly strategic, L2 learners will vary markedly in the constructions they can control or which are missing or incorrectly transferred (Birdsong, 2005). In addition to the basic forces of entrenchment, transfer, and resonant learning, older learners will be affected by problems with restricted social contacts, commitments to ongoing L1 interactions, and declining cognitive abilities. None of these changes predicts a sharp drop at a certain age in L2 learning abilities. Instead, these effects predict a gradual decline across the life span.

8 Conclusion

This concludes our examination of the Unified Competition Model. This model relies on a particular version of Construction Grammar that emphasizes the role of storage in lexical maps and the online integration of constructional chunks during both L1 and L2 processing. In accord with other functionalist accounts in this volume, the model emphasizes the role of cue availability and reliability in determining the course of acquisition. The model views age-related changes in L2 learning in terms of entrenchment, competition, and transfer, rather than the expiration of a critical period. Because of this, the model can provide a unified account for learning both L1 and L2.

Many of the pieces of this model rely on separate theories that have been worked out in some detail. For example, we have a good model of cue competition in syntax for both L1 and L2. We have good models of

L1 lexical acquisition in SOMs. We have good data on phonological and lexical transfer in L2. We have clear data and models regarding the ways in which processing load impacts sentence processing in working memory. We are even learning about the neuronal bases of this load (Booth et al., 2001). Other areas provide targets for future work. In particular, we need to link the item-based construction approach outlined here to the broader theory of embodied cognition (MacWhinney, 2005c; Pecher & Zwaan, 2005). The Unified Model provides us with a high-level road map to guide our ongoing explorations of these topics.

Bibliography

Anderson, J., & Lebiere, C. (1998). *The atomic components of thought*. Mahwah, NJ: Erlbaum.

Asher, J. (1977). Children learning another language: A developmental hypothesis. *Child Development, 48*, 1,040–1,048.

Atkinson, R. (1975). Mnemotechnics in second-language learning. *American Psychologist, 30*, 821–828.

Baddeley, A. (1992). Working memory: The interface between memory and cognition. *Journal of Cognitive Neuroscience, 4*, 281–288.

Bailey, D., Chang, N., Feldman, J., & Narayanan, S. (1998). Extending embodied lexical development. *Proceedings of the 20th Annual Meeting of the Cognitive Science Society*, 64–69.

Barry, R. (1975). Topic in Chinese: An overlap of meaning, grammar, and discourse function. In J. S. R. Grossman & T. Vance (Eds.), *Papers from the Parasession on Functionalism*. Chicago: Chicago Linguistic Society.

Barsalou, L. W. (1999). Perceptual symbol systems. *Behavioral and Brain Sciences, 22*, 577–660.

Bates, E., & MacWhinney, B. (1981). Second language acquisition from a functionalist perspective: Pragmatic, semantic and perceptual strategies. In H. Winitz (Ed.), *Annals of the New York Academy of Sciences conference on native and foreign language acquisition* (pp. 190–214). New York: New York Academy of Sciences.

Bates, E., & MacWhinney, B. (1982). Functionalist approaches to grammar. In E. Wanner & L. Gleitman (Eds.), *Language acquisition: The state of the art* (pp. 173–218). New York: Cambridge University Press.

Berk, L. E. (1994). Why children talk to themselves. *Scientific American, November*, 78–83.

Berlin, B., & Kay, P. (1969). *Basic color terms: Their universality and evolution*. Berkeley: University of California Press.

Birdsong, D. (2005). Interpreting age effects in second language acquisition. In J. F. Kroll & A. M. B. DeGroot (Eds.), *Handbook of bilingualism: Psycholinguistic approaches*. New York: Oxford University Press.

Blackwell, A., & Bates, E. (1995). Inducing agrammatic profiles in normals: Evidence for the selective vulnerability of morphology under cognitive resource limitation. *Journal of Cognitive Neuroscience, 7*, 228–257.

Bley-Vroman, R., Felix, S., & Ioup, G. (1988). The accessibility of universal grammar in adult language learning. *Second Language Research, 4*, 1–32.

Booth, J. R., MacWhinney, B., Thulborn, K. R., Sacco, K., Voyvodic, J. T., & Feldman, H. M. (2001). Developmental and lesion effects during brain activation for sentence comprehension and mental rotation. *Developmental Neuropsychology, 18*, 139–169.

Bradlow, A., Akahni-Yamada, R., Pisoni, D., & Tokhura, Y. (1999). Training Japanese liseners to identify English /r/ and /l/: Long-term retention of learning perception and production. *Perception and Psychophysics, 61*, 977–985.

Bybee, J., & Hopper, P. (2001). *Frequency and the emergence of linguistic structure.* Amsterdam: John Benjamins.

Chase, W., & Simon, H. (1973). Perception in chess. *Cognitive psychology, 4*, 5–81.

Clahsen, H., & Muysken, P. (1986). The availability of UG to adult and child learners: A study of the acquisition of German word order. *Second Language Research, 2*, 93–119.

Cleermans, A., & McClelland, J. L. (1991). Learning the structure of event sequences. *Journal of Experimental Psychology: General, 120*, 235–253.

Colomé, A. (2001). Lexical activation in bilinguals' speech production: Language specific or language independent. *Journal of Memory and Language, 45*, 721–736.

de Bot, K., & van Montfort, R. (1988). "Cue-validity" in het Nederlands als eerste en tweede taal. *Interdisciplinair Tijdschrift voor Taal en Tekstwetenschap, 8*, 111–120.

De Houwer, A. (2005). Early bilingual acquisition: Focus on morphosyntax and the Separate Development Hypothesis. In J. F. Kroll & A. M. B. de Groot (Eds.), *Handbook of bilingualism: Psycholinguistic approaches.* New York: Oxford University Press.

DeKeyser, R. (2000). The robustness of critical period effects in second language acquisition studies. *Studies in Second Language Acquisition, 22*, 499–533.

DeKeyser, R., & Larson-Hall, J. (2005). What does the critical period really mean? In J. F. Kroll & A. M. B. de Groot (Eds.), *Handbook of bilingualism: Psycholinguistic approaches.* Oxford: Oxford University Press.

Dell, G., Juliano, C., & Govindjee, A. (1993). Structure and content in language production: A theory of frame constraints in phonological speech errors. *Cognitive Science, 17*, 149–195.

Dell'Orletta, F., Lenci, A., Montemagni, S., & Pirelli, V. (2005). Climbing the path to grammar: A maximum entropy model of subject/object learning. In *Proceedings of the second workshop on psychocomputational Models of Human Language Acquisition*, pp. 72–81. Ann Arbour, MI: Association for Computational Linguistics.

Demuth, K. (1995). *Markedness and the development of prosodic structure.* Paper presented at the Proceedings of the North East Linguistic Society (NELS), Amherst.

Devescovi, A., D'Amico, S., Smith, S., Mimica, I., & Bates, E. (1998). The development of sentence comprehension in Italian and Serbo-Croatian: Local versus distributed cues. In D. Hillert (Ed.), *Syntax and semantics: Vol. 31. Sentence processing: A cross-linguistic perspective* (pp. 345–377). San Diego: Academic Press.

Dijkstra, T. (2005). Bilingual visual word recognition and lexical access. In J. F. Kroll & A. M. B. de Groot (Eds.), *Handbook of bilingualism: Psycholinguistic approaches*. New York: Oxford University Press.

Dijkstra, T., Grainger, J., & Van Heuven, W. J. B. (1999). Recognizing cognates and interlingual homographs: The neglected role of phonology. *Journal of Memory and Language, 41,* 496–518.

Dittenbach, M., Rauber, A., & Merkl, D. (2002). Uncovering the hierarchical structure in data using the growing hierarchical self-organizing map. *Neurocomputing, 48,* 199–216.

Döpke, S. (1998). Competing language structures: The acquisition of verb placement by bilingual German-English children. *Journal of Child Language, 25,* 555–584.

Dussias, P. E. (2001). Bilingual sentence parsing. In J. L. Nicol (Ed.), *One mind, two languages: Bilingual sentence processing* (pp. 159–176). Cambridge, MA: Blackwell.

É.-Kiss, K. (1981). Topic and focus: The basic operators of the Hungarian sentence. *Folia Linguistica, 15,* 305–330.

Ebbinghaus, H. (1885). *Über das Gedächtnis.* Leipzig: Duncker.

Eckman, F. R. (1991). The structural conformity hypothesis and the acquisition of consonant clusters in the interlanguage of ESL learners. *Studies in Second Language Acquisition, 13,* 23–41.

Ellis, N. (1996). Sequencing in SLA: Phonological memory, chunking and points of order. *Studies in Second Language Acquisition, 18,* 91–126.

Ellis, N. (2002). Frequency effects in language processing. *Studies in Second Language Acquisition, 24,* 143–188.

Ellis, N., & Sinclair, S. (1996). Working memory in the acquisition of vocabulary and syntax: Putting language in good order. *Quarterly Journal of Experimental Psychology, 49,* 234–250.

Elman, J., Hare, M., & McRae, K. (2005). Cues, constraints, and competition in sentence processing. In M. Tomasello & D. I. Slobin (Eds.), *Beyond nature nurture: Essays in honor of Elizabeth Bates*, pp. 111–138. Mahwah, NJ: Lawrence Erlbaum.

Elman, J. L., & McClelland, J. L. (1988). Cognitive penetration of the mechanisms of perception: Compensation for coarticulation of lexically restored phonemes. *Journal of Memory and Language, 27,* 143–165.

Flege, J. E., & Davidian, R. (1984). Transfer and developmental processes in adult foreign language speech production. *Applied Psycholinguistics, 5,* 323–347.

Flege, J. E., Takagi, J., & Mann, V. (1995). Japanese adults can learn to produce English "r" and "l" accurately. *Language Learning, 39,* 23–32.

Flynn, S. (1996). A parameter-setting approach to second language acquisition. In W. C. Ritchie & T. K. Bhatia (Eds.), *Handbook of second language acquisition* (pp. 121–158). San Diego: Academic Press.

Frenck-Mestre, C. (2005). Second language sentence processing: Which theory best accounts for the processing of reduced relative clauses? In J. F. Kroll & A. M. B. de Groot (Eds.), *Handbook of bilingualism: Psycholinguistic approaches*. New York: Oxford University Press.

Gass, S. (1987). The resolution of conflicts among competing systems: A bidirectional perspective. *Applied Psycholinguistics, 8,* 329–350.

Gerver, D. (1974). The effects of noise on the performance of simultaneous interpreters: Accuracy of performance. *Acta Psychologica, 38,* 159–167.

Gibson, E., Pearlmutter, N., Canseco-Gonzalez, E., & Hickok, G. (1996). Recency preference in the human sentence processing mechanism. *Cognition, 59,* 23–59.

Gobet, F. (2005). Chunking models of expertise: Implications for education. *Applied Cognitive Psychology, 19,* 183–204.

Goldsmith, J., & O'Brien, J. (2006). Learning inflectional classes. *Language Learning and Development, 2,* 219–250.

Green, D. W. (1986). Control, activation, and resource: A framework and a model for the control of speech in bilinguals. *Brain and Language, 27,* 210–223.

Grosjean, F. (1997). Processing mixed languages: Issues, findings and models. In A. M. B. de Groot & J. F. Kroll (Eds.), *Tutorials in bilingualism: Psycholinguistic perspectives* (pp. 225–254). Mahwah, NJ: Lawrence Erlbaum.

Gupta, P., & MacWhinney, B. (1997). Vocabulary acquisition and verbal short-term memory: Computational and neural bases. *Brain and Language, 59,* 267–333.

Hancin-Bhatt, B. (1994). Segment transfer: a consequence of a dynamic system. *Second Language Research, 10,* 241–269.

Harm, M. (2002). Building large-scale distributed semantic feature sets with WordNet. *CNBC Tech Report.*

Harrington, M. (1987). Processing transfer: language-specific strategies as a source of interlanguage variation. *Applied Psycholinguistics, 8,* 351–378.

Hernandez, A., Li, P., & MacWhinney, B. (2005). The emergence of competing modules in bilingualism. *Trends in Cognitive Sciences, 9,* 220–225.

Holmes, V., Stowe, L., & Cupples, L. (1989). Lexical expectations in parsing complement-verb sentences. *Journal of Memory and Language, 28,* 668–689.

Hurford, J. (1991). The evolution of the critical period for language acquisition. *Cognition, 40,* 159–201.

Ijaz, H. (1986). Linguistic and cognitive determinants of lexical acquisition in a second language. *Language Learning, 36,* 401–451.

Kempen, G., & Hoenkamp, E. (1987). An incremental procedural grammar for sentence formulation. *Cognitive Science, 11,* 201–258.

Kilborn, K. (1989). Sentence processing in a second language: The timing of transfer. *Language and Speech, 32,* 1–23.

Kilborn, K., & Cooreman, A. (1987). Sentence interpretation strategies in adult Dutch-English bilinguals. *Applied Psycholinguistics, 8,* 415–431.

Kilborn, K., & Ito, T. (1989). Sentence processing in Japanese-English and Dutch-English bilinguals. In B. MacWhinney & E. Bates (Eds.), *The crosslinguistic study of sentence processing* (pp. 257–291). New York: Cambridge University Press.

Kohonen, T. (1990). The self-organizing map. In *Proceedings of the IEEE* (Vol. 78, pp. 1,464–1,480).

Krashen, S. (1994). The Input Hypothesis and its rivals. In N. C. Ellis (Ed.), *Implicit and explicit learning of languages* (pp. 45–78). San Diego: Academic.

Kroll, J., & Tokowicz, N. (2005). Bilingual lexical processing. In J. F. Kroll & A. M. B. de Groot (Eds.), *Handbook of bilingualism: Psycholinguistic approaches.* New York: Oxford University Press.

Kuhl, P. K. (1991). Human adults and human infants show a "perceptual magnet effect" for the prototypes of speech categories, monkeys do not. *Perception and Psychophysics, 50*, 93–107.

La Heij, W. (2005). Selection processes in monolingual and bilingual lexical access. In J. F. Kroll & A. M. B. de Groot (Eds.), *Handbook of bilingualism: Psycholinguistic approaches.* New York: Oxford University Press.

Lenneberg, E. H. (1967). *Biological foundations of language.* New York: Wiley.

Li, P., Burgess, C., & Lund, K. (2001). The acquisition of word meaning through global lexical co-occurrences. *Proceedings of the 23rd Annual Meeting of the Cognitive Science Society,* 221–244.

Li, P., & Farkas, I. (2002). A self-organizing connectionist model of bilingual processing. In R. Heredia & J. Altarriba (Eds.), *Bilingual sentence processing* (pp. 59–85). Amsterdam: North Holland Elsevier.

Li, P., Farkas, I., & MacWhinney, B. (2004). Early lexical development in a self-organizing neural network. *Neural Networks, 17,* 1,345–1,362.

Li, P., & MacWhinney, B. (2002). PatPho: A Phonological Pattern Generator for Neural Networks. *Behavior Research Methods, Instruments, and Computers, 34,* 408–415.

Li, P., Zhao, X., & MacWhinney, B. (2007). Dynamic self-organization and early lexical development. *Cognitive Science, 31*(4), 581–607.

Liu, H., Bates, E., & Li, P. (1992). Sentence interpretation in bilingual speakers of English and Chinese. *Applied Psycholinguistics, 13,* 451–484.

Long, M. (2005). Problems with supposed counter-evidence to the Critical Period Hypothesis. *International Review of Applied Linguistics, 43,* 287–317.

Lotto, A., Kluender, K., & Holt, L. (1997). Perceptual compensation for coarticulation by Japanese quail. *Journal of the Acoustical Society of America, 102,* 1,134–1,140.

MacDonald, M. (1994). Probabilistic constraints and syntactic ambiguity. *Language and Cognitive Processes, 9,* 157–201.

MacDonald, M. C., & MacWhinney, B. (1990). Measuring inhibition and facilitation from pronouns. *Journal of Memory and Language, 29,* 469–492.

MacDonald, M. C., Pearlmutter, N. J., & Seidenberg, M. S. (1994). Lexical nature of syntactic ambiguity resolution. *Psychological Review, 101*(4), 676–703.

MacWhinney, B. (1975). Pragmatic patterns in child syntax. *Stanford Papers And Reports on Child Language Development, 10,* 153–165.

MacWhinney, B. (1982). Basic syntactic processes. In S. Kuczaj (Ed.), *Language acquisition: Vol. 1. Syntax and semantics* (pp. 73–136). Hillsdale, NJ: Lawrence Erlbaum.

MacWhinney, B. (1987a). The Competition Model. In B. MacWhinney (Ed.), *Mechanisms of language acquisition* (pp. 249–308). Hillsdale, NJ: Lawrence Erlbaum.

MacWhinney, B. (1987b). Toward a psycholinguistically plausible parser. In S. Thomason (Ed.), *Proceedings of the Eastern States Conference on Linguistics.* Columbus, Ohio: Ohio State University.

MacWhinney, B. (1999). The emergence of language from embodiment. In B. MacWhinney (Ed.), *The emergence of language* (pp. 213–256). Mahwah, NJ: Lawrence Erlbaum.

MacWhinney, B. (2000). Lexicalist connectionism. In P. Broeder & J. Murre (Eds.), *Models of language acquisition: Inductive and deductive approaches* (pp. 9–32). Cambridge, MA: MIT Press.

MacWhinney, B. (2005a). A unified model of language acquisition. In J. F. Kroll & A. M. B. de Groot (Eds.), *Handbook of bilingualism: Psycholinguistic approaches* (pp. 49–67). New York: Oxford University Press.

MacWhinney, B. (2005b). Item-based constructions and the logical problem. *Association of Computational Linguistics 2005*, 46–54.

MacWhinney, B. (2005c). The emergence of grammar from perspective. In D. Pecher & R. A. Zwaan (Eds.), *The grounding of cognition: The role of perception and action in memory, language, and thinking* (pp. 198–223). Mahwah, NJ: Lawrence Erlbaum Associates.

MacWhinney, B., Bates, E., & Kliegl, R. (1984). Cue validity and sentence interpretation in English, German and Italian. *Journal of Verbal Learning and Verbal Behavior, 23,* 127–150.

MacWhinney, B., Feldman, H. M., Sacco, K., & Valdes-Perez, R. (2000). Online measures of basic language skills in children with early focal brain lesions. *Brain and Language, 71,* 400–431.

MacWhinney, B., & Leinbach, J. (1991). Implementations are not conceptualizations: Revising the verb learning model. *Cognition, 29,* 121–157.

MacWhinney, B., Leinbach, J., Taraban, R., & McDonald, J. (1989). Language learning: Cues or rules? *Journal of Memory and Language, 28,* 255–277.

MacWhinney, B., & Pléh, C. (1988). The processing of restrictive relative clauses in Hungarian. *Cognition, 29,* 95–141.

Major, R. (2001). *Foreign accent: The ontogeny and phylogeny of second language phonology.* Mahwah, NJ: Lawrence Erlbaum Associates.

McCandliss, B. D., Fiez, J. A., Protopapas, A., Conway, M., & McClelland, J. L. (2002). Success and failure in teaching the /r/–/l/ contrast to Japanese adults: Test of a Hebbian model of plasticity and stabilization in spoken language perception. *Cognitive, Affective, and Behavioral Neuroscience, 2,* 89–108.

McDonald, J. L. (1987a). Assigning linguistic roles: The influence of conflicting cues. *Journal of Memory and Language, 26,* 100–117.

McDonald, J. L. (1987b). Sentence interpretation in bilingual speakers of English and Dutch. *Applied Psycholinguistics, 8,* 379–414.

McDonald, J. L., & Heilenman, K. (1991). Determinants of cue strength in adult first and second language speakers of French. *Applied Psycholinguistics, 12,* 313–348.

McDonald, J. L., & MacWhinney, B. (1989). Maximum likelihood models for sentence processing research. In B. MacWhinney & E. Bates (Eds.), *The crosslinguistic study of sentence processing* (pp. 397–421). New York: Cambridge University Press.

McDonald, J. L., & MacWhinney, B. J. (1995). The time course of anaphor resolution: Effects of implicit verb causality and gender. *Journal of Memory and Language, 34,* 543–566.

McRae, K., Spivey-Knowlton, M., & Tanenhaus, M. (1998). Modeling the effects of thematic fit (and other constraints) in on-line sentence comprehension. *Journal of Memory and Language, 37,* 283–312.

Mehler, J., & Christophe, A. (1994). Language in the infant's mind. *Philosophical Transactions of the Royal Society of London B, 346*, 13–20.

Miyake, A., Carpenter, P., & Just, M. (1994). A capacity approach to syntactic comprehension disorders: Making normal adults perform like aphasic patients. *Cognitive Neuropsychology, 11*, 671–717.

Moro, A. (2006). Copular sentences. In M. Eveart & H. Van Riemsdijk (Eds.), *The Blackwell Companion to Syntax, Volume II*, pp. 1–23. Oxford: Blackwell.

Nelson, K. (1998). *Language in cognitive development: The emergence of the mediated mind.* New York: Cambridge University Press.

Newell, A. (1990). *A unified theory of cognition.* Cambridge, MA: Harvard University Press.

O'Grady, W. (2005). *Syntactic carpentry.* Mahwah, NJ: Lawrence Erlbaum Associates.

Paget, R. (1930). *Human speech.* New York: Harcourt Brace.

Pavlik, P. (in press). Timing is an order: Modeling order effects in the learning of information. In F. E. Ritter, J. Nerb, T. O'Shea & E. Lehtinen (Eds.), *In order to learn: How the sequences of topics affect learning.* New York: Oxford University Press.

Pecher, D., & Zwaan, R. (Eds.) (2005). *Grounding cognition.* Cambridge: Cambridge University Press.

Pienemann, M., Di Biase, B., Kawaguchi, S., & Håkansson, G. (2005). Processing constraints on L1 transfer. In J. F. Kroll & A. M. B. de Groot (Eds.), *Handbook of bilingualism: Psycholinguistic approaches* (pp. 128–153). New York: Oxford University Press.

Pimsleur, P. (1967). A memory schedule. *Modern Language Journal, 51*, 73–75.

Pirelli, V., & Herreros, I. (2006). Learning morphology by itself. *Linguistica Computazionale, 22*, 14–19.

Ramachandran, V. S., & Hubbard, E. M. (2001). Synaesthesia: A window into perception, thought and language. *Journal of Consciousness Studies, 8*, 3–34.

Regier, T. (2006). The emergence of words: Attentional learning in form and meaning. *Cognitive Science, 29*, 819–865.

Sagae, K., MacWhinney, B., & Lavie, A. (2004). Automatic parsing of parent-child interactions. *Behavior Research Methods, Instruments, and Computers, 36*, 113–126.

Sebastián-Galles, N., & Bosch, L. (2005). Phonology and bilingualism. In J. F. Kroll & A. M. B. de Groot (Eds.), *Handbook of bilingualism: Psycholinguistic approaches.* New York: Oxford University Press.

Seleskovitch, D. (1976). Interpretation: A psychological approach to translating. In R. W. Brislin (Ed.), *Translation: Application and Research.* New York: Gardner.

Service, E., & Craik, F. I. M. (1993). Differences between young and older adults in learning a foreign vocabulary. *Journal of Memory and Language, 32*, 608–623.

Snow, C. E. (1999). Social perspectives on the emergence of language. In B. MacWhinney (Ed.), *The emergence of language* (pp. 257–276). Mahwah, NJ: Lawrence Erlbaum Associates.

Sokolov, J. L. (1988). Cue validity in Hebrew sentence comprehension. *Journal of Child Language, 15*, 129–156.

Sokolov, J. L. (1989). The development of role assignment in Hebrew. In B. MacWhinney & E. Bates (Eds.), *The crosslinguistic study of sentence processing* (pp. 158–184). New York: Cambridge.

Stager, C. L., & Werker, J. F. (1997). Infants listen for more phonetic detail in speech perception than in word learning tasks. *Nature, 388,* 381–382.

Stockwell, R., Bowen, J., & Martin, J. (1965). *The grammatical structures of English and Spanish.* Chicago: University of Chicago Press.

Tomasello, M. (1992). *First verbs: A case study of early grammatical development.* Cambridge: Cambridge University Press.

Tomasello, M. (2003). *Constructing a first language: A usage-based theory of language acquisition.* Cambridge: Harvard University Press.

Trueswell, J., & Tanenhaus, M. (1994). Toward a constraint-based lexicalist approach to syntactic ambiguity resolution. In C. Clifton, L. Frazier, & K. Rayner (Eds.), *Perspectives on sentence processing,* pp. 155–179. Hillsdale, NJ: Lawrence Erlbaum.

Trueswell, J., Tanenhaus, M., & Garvey, S. (1994). Semantic influences on parsing: Use of thematic role information in syntactic ambiguity resolution. *Journal of Memory and Language, 33,* 285–318.

Trueswell, J., Tanenhaus, M., & Kello, C. (1993). Verb-specific constraints in sentence processing: Separating effects of lexical preference from garden-paths. *Journal of Experimental Psychology: Learning, Memory and Cognition, 19,* 528–553.

Vygotsky, L. (1934). *Thought and language.* Cambridge: MIT Press.

Waddington, C. H. (1957). *The strategy of the genes.* New York: MacMillan.

Werker, J. F. (1995). Exploring developmental changes in cross-language speech perception. In L. Gleitman & M. Liberman (Eds.), *An Invitation to Cognitive Science. Language: Vol. 1* (pp. 87–106). Cambridge, MA: MIT Press.

Wittenberg, G., Sullivan, M., & Tsien, J. (2002). Synaptic reentry reinforcement based network model for long-term memory consolidation. *Hippocampus, 12,* 637–647.

Yamamoto, K., Hoffman, D. S., & Strick, P. (2006). Rapid and long lasting plasticity of input/output mapping. *Journal of Neurophysiology, 96,* 2797–2798.

15

USAGE-BASED AND FORM-FOCUSED LANGUAGE ACQUISITION

The associative learning of constructions, learned attention, and the limited L2 endstate

Nick C. Ellis

1 Introduction

Cognitive Linguistics proposes that First Language Acquisition (L1A) involves the acquisition from language usage of constructions that map linguistic form and function. In this view, competence and performance both emerge from the dynamic system that is the frequency-tuned conspiracy of memorized exemplars of use of these constructions, with competence being the rationally integrated sum of prior usage and performance being its dynamic contextualized activation. L1A tunes the ways in which learners attend to language.

This chapter gives a psychological slant on the associative learning of linguistic constructions. The first part describes the aspects of associative learning that affect both usage-based L1A and L2A: frequency, contingency, competition between multiple cues, and salience. Each of these is taken in turn, its processes are explained from within associative learning theory, and its effects are illustrated with examples from language learning. This section concludes by illustrating the combined operation of these factors in First and Second Language Acquisition of English grammatical morphemes, a particular illustration of a broader claim that they control the acquisition of all linguistic constructions.

However, usage-based Second Language Acquisition (L2A) is typically much less successful that L1A, with naturalistic or communicatively-based L2A stabilizing at end-states far short of nativelike ability. Why? What is it that limits construction learning in L2A in comparison to L1A? The second half of the chapter considers the apparent irrationalities of L2A, the shortcomings where input fails to become intake. It describes how "learned attention" explains these effects. The fragile features of L2A, those aspects of the second language that are not typically acquired, are those which, however available in the input, fall short of intake because of one of the factors of contingency, cue competition, salience, interference, over-shadowing, blocking, or perceptual learning, all shaped by L1 entrench-ment. Each phenomenon is explained within associative learning theory and exemplified in language learning. The second section concludes with evidence of L1/L2 differences in morpheme acquisition order, illustrating these processes as they contribute to transfer and "learned attention."

That the successes of L1A and the limitations of L2A both, paradoxic-ally, derive from the same basic learning principles provides a non-age-invoked biological explanation for why usage-based L2A stops short while L1A does not. These processes also explain why form-focused instruction is a necessary component of L2A, and why successful L2A necessitates a greater level of explicit awareness of the L2 constructions, a dialectic tension between the conflicting forces of the learner's current stable states of interlanguage and the evidence of explicit form-focused feedback, either linguistic, pragmatic, or metalinguistic, that allows socially scaffolded development.

2 Factors affecting usage-based L1A and L2A

2.1 Frequency

The past 50 years of research in psycholinguistics demonstrates that lan-guage processing is rational in that it is exquisitely sensitive to prior usage. Fluent language processing reflects frequency of usage at all sizes of grain: phonology and phonotactics, reading, spelling, lexis, morpho-syntax, formulaic language, language comprehension, grammaticality, sen-tence production, and syntax (N. C. Ellis, 2002a, 2002b). The words that we are likely to hear next, their most likely senses, the linguistic construc-tions we are most likely to utter next, the syllables we are likely to hear next, the graphemes we are likely to read next, and the rest of what's coming next across all levels of language representation, are made more readily available to us by our language-processing systems. Consider, for example, that while you are conscious of words in your attentional focus, you certainly did not consciously label the word "focus" just now as a noun; yet this sentence would be incomprehensible if your unconscious language analyzers did not treat "focus" as a noun rather than as a verb or an adjective. Nor, on reading "focus," were you aware of its nine alter-native meanings or of their rankings in overall likelihood, or of their rankings in this particular context, rather than in different sentences where you would instantly bring a different meaning to mind. A wealth of psycholinguistic evidence suggests that this information is available unconsciously for a few tenths of a second before your brain plumps for the most appropriate one in this context. Most words have multiple meanings, but only one at a time becomes conscious. This is a fundamental fact about consciousness (Baars, 1988, 1997). In these ways our unconscious language mechanisms present up to consciousness the constructions that are most likely to be relevant next.

Consider the particular constructions "Wonderful!," "One, two, three," "Once upon a time," and "Won the battle, lost the war." We have come to learn these sequential patterns of sound simply as a result of repeated usage. All perception is fundamentally probabilistic: every stimulus is ambiguous, as is any utterance or piece of language. Each of these formulaic constructions begins with the sound "wʌn." At the point of hearing this initial sound, what should the appropriate interpretation be? We perceive the most probable thing. Psycholinguistic analyses demonstrate that fluent language users are sensitive to the relative probabilities of occurrence of different constructions in the speech stream. Since we have experienced many more tokens (particular examples) of "one" than they have "won," in the absence of any further information, we favor the unitary interpretation over that involving gain or advantage.

Not only do we know the constructions that are most likely to be of overall relevance (i.e. first-order probabilities of occurrence), but we also predict the ones that are going to pertain in any particular context (sequential dependencies), and the particular interpretations of cues that are most likely to be correct (contingency statistics). Thus, in the context of "Alice in . . .," "wonderland" comes to the fore well ahead of "one"; we stop counting and sense wonder instead. These predictions are rational and normative in that they accurately represent the statistical covariation between events (N. C. Ellis, 2006). There is good evidence that human implicit cognition, acquired over natural ecological sampling as natural frequencies on an observation by observation basis, is rational in this sense (J. R. Anderson, 1990, 1991a, 1991b; Gigerenzer & Hoffrage, 1995; Sedlmeier & Betsc, 2002; Sedlmeier & Gigerenzer, 2001).

This evidence of rational language processing implies that language learning, too, is an intuitive statistical learning problem, one that involves the associative learning of representations that reflect the probabilities of occurrence of form–function mappings. Learners have to figure language out: their task is, in essence, to learn the probability distribution P(interpretation | cue, context), the probability of an interpretation given a formal cue in a particular context, a mapping from form to meaning conditioned by context (Manning, 2003). In order to achieve optimal processing, acquisition mechanisms must have gathered the normative evidence that is the necessary foundation for rationality. To accurately predict what is going to happen next, we require a representative sample of experience of similar circumstances upon which to base our judgments, and the best sample we could possibly have is the totality of our linguistic experience to date. The systematicities of language competence, at all levels of analysis from phonology, through syntax, to discourse, emerge from learners' implicit tallying of the constructions in their usage history and the implicit distributional analysis of this lifetime sample of language input.

2.2 Contingency and ΔP

2.2.1 Learning theory

But it is not just the frequency of encounter of a construction that determines its acquisition. The degree to which animals, human and other alike, learn associations between cues and outcomes depends upon the contingency of the relationship as well. In classical conditioning it is the reliability of the bell as a predictor of food that determines the ease of acquisition of this association (Rescorla, 1968). In language learning it is the reliability of the form as a predictor of an interpretation that determines its acquisition (MacWhinney, 1987). The last 30 years of psychological investigation into human sensitivity to the contingency between cues and outcomes (Shanks, 1995) demonstrates that when given sufficient exposure to a relationship, people's judgments match quite closely the contingency specified by ΔP (the one-way dependency statistic, Allan, 1980) which measures the directional association between a cue and an outcome, as illustrated in Table 15.1.

Table 15.1 A contingency table showing the four possible combinations of events showing the presence or absence of a target cue and an outcome

	Outcome	No Outcome
Cue	a	b
No cue	c	d

a, b, c, d represent frequencies, so, for example, a is the frequency of conjunctions of the cue and the outcome, and c is the number of times the outcome occurred without the cue.

$$\Delta P = P(O/C) - P(O/-C) = a/(a+b) - c/(c+d).$$

ΔP is the probability of the outcome given the cue (P(O/C)) minus the probability of the outcome in the absence of the cue (P(O/-C)). When these are the same, when the outcome is just as likely when the cue is present as when it is not, there is no covariation between the two events and $\Delta P = 0$. ΔP approaches 1.0 as the presence of the cue increases the likelihood of the outcome and approaches −1.0 as the cue decreases the chance of the outcome—a negative association.

2.2.2 Language learning

Consider for example the acquisition of English grammatical morphemes in these terms. In the 25 years following Brown's (1973) descriptions of child L1A, the "morpheme order studies," classic milestones in the history of SLA theory, investigated the L2A of the grammatical functors, progressive -ing, plural -s, possessive -s, articles a, an, the, third person singular present -s, and past tense. These studies showed a remarkable commonality in the L2 and L1 orders of acquisition of these grammatical functors[1] (Bailey, Madden, & Krashen, 1974; Brown, 1973; Dulay & Burt, 1973; Pica, 1983), broadly:

1 plural "-s"   "Book s"
2 progressive "-ing"   "John go ing"
3 copula "be"   "John is here" / "John 's here"
4 auxiliary "be"   "John is going" / "John 's going"
5 articles "the/a"   "The books"
6 irregular past tense   "John went"
7 third person "-s"   "John like s books"
8 possessive " 's"   "John 's book"

Clearly, there are no 1:1 mappings between these cues and their grammatical interpretations. Plural -s, third person singular present -s, and possessive -s, are all homophonous with each other as well as with the contracted allomorphs of copula and auxiliary "be." Therefore, if we evaluate -s as a cue for one particular of these functional interpretations, there are many instances of the cue being present but that outcome not pertaining, b in Table 15.1 is of high frequency, and ΔP accordingly low. View the mappings from the other direction too: plural -s, third person singular present -s, and possessive -s all have variant expression as the allomorphs [s, z, əz]. Therefore, if we evaluate any one of these, say [s], as a cue for a particular outcome, say plurality, there are many instances of that outcome in the absence of the cue, c in Table 15.1 is inflated, and ΔP concomitantly reduced. Thus, a contingency analysis of these cue-interpretation associations suggests that they will not be readily learnable.

So much for the unreliable mappings between -s and its interpretations as plural, or third person plural, or copula. Most high-frequency grammatical functors are similarly highly ambiguous in their interpretations. The semantic analysis of definite and indefinite reference shows its meaning to be highly variable and complicated (Diesing, 1992; Faurud, 1990; Hawkins, 1978, 1991; Lyons, 1999), as evidenced by the many pages of explanation given to *the* in a grammar of English (Biber, Johansson, Leech, Conrad, & Finegan, 1999; Celce-Murcia & Larsen-Freeman, 1999). The fuzziness and complexity of these mappings surely goes a long way to making ESL article acquisition so difficult. Finally, consider how the low ΔP for possessive *-s* compounded by interference from contracted "it is" ensures, as experience of undergraduate essays attests, that the apostrophe is opaque in it's [sic] function and that native language learners can fail to sort out this system even after 18 years of experience. These are no 1:1 form to meaning mappings.

2.3 Multiple cues, the PCM, and Cue-Competition

2.3.1 Learning theory

Normative ΔP theory describes associative learning where learners have to acquire the relationship between a cue and an outcome and where the cue is the only obvious causal feature present. In such situations contingency is easy to specify and human learning is shown to be rational in that it accords with the normative ΔP rule. However, it is rarely if ever the case that predictive cues appear in isolation, and most utterances, like most other stimuli, present the learner with a set of cues which co-occur with one another, with the learner's task being to determine the ones that are truly predictive. In such cases of multiple cues to interpretation, the predictions of normative analysis using the ΔP rule are muddied by *selection effects*: learners selectively choose between potential causal factors. Thus, in some circumstances the cue may be selected for association with an interpretation while in other circumstances it may not, depending on the presence and status of other cues.

Cheng and Holyoak (1995) and Cheng and Novick (1990) have proposed an extended version of contingency theory, which they termed the Probabilistic Contrast Model (PCM), as a descriptive account of the use of statistical regularity in human causal induction. The model, which applies to events describable by discrete variables, assumes that potential causes are evaluated by contrasts computed over a "focal set." The focal set for a contrast is a contextually determined set of events that the reasoner *selects* to use as input to the computation of that contrast. The focal set consists of all trials on which the target cue is present as well as all those trials that are identical to the target present trials except for the absence of the target, the PCM in this way approximating the logic of classical scientific method. Because the focal set is not the universal set of events, the results of this reasoning appear irrational when measured unconditionally against ΔP theory applied to the whole learning set. Shanks (1995) reviews the evidence of human reasoning in situations of multiple cues, concluding that the results are well accommodated by the PCM.

2.3.2 Language learning

There is considerable redundancy in language (Shannon, 1948), with the same meaning or intention potentially expressible in a wide variety of ways. So language is a prime example of a stimulus environment rich in multiple cues. The Competition Model (MacWhinney, this volume, MacWhinney & Bates, 1989; MacWhinney, Bates, & Kliegl, 1984) was explicitly formulated to deal with competition between multiple linguistic cues to interpretation. The Competition Model is language's own PCM. Its algorithm for probability contrast is somewhat different in detail to that of the PCM, but its result is similar in that it first selects the most valid cue using statistical contingency analysis and then introduces cues thereafter on the basis of their potential to decrease error.

Experiments using miniature artificial languages have shown that, in the initial stages of acquisition, learners tend to focus on only one cue at a time (Blackwell, 1995; MacWhinney & Bates, 1989; Matessa & Anderson, 2000; McDonald, 1986; McDonald & MacWhinney, 1991). For example, when cues for determining the agent in sentences include word order, noun animacy and agreement of noun and verb, learners typically decide to focus attention on only one of these as the predictor of interpretation. MacWhinney, Pleh, and Bates (1985) demonstrated that the cue that children first focus upon is that which has the highest overall validity as measured by its availability (its frequency or probability of occurrence) times its reliability (its probability of correctly indicating the interpretation, broadly equivalent to its ΔP). The effect is that a cue with high availability but low reliability may initially be used over a cue that is of lower availability, even though it is in fact more reliable. Learners focus on one cue alone to begin with. Later on, after having tracked the use of this first cue, they will add a second cue to the mix and begin to use the two in combination, and, as development proceeds, so additional cues may be added if they significantly helped reduce errors of understanding, as measured by the statistic "conflict validity" which relates to how the cue affords extra predictive accuracy when its interpretation conflicts with that of a co-occurring cue. This variable by variable incremental sequence is as predicted by the probability contrast model and the Competition Model both.

2.4 Salience

2.4.1 Learning theory

The phenomena summarized by the PCM are qualified by other additional factors of associative learning, those relating to salience of cue and importance of outcome.[2] Experimental investigations of learning in situations of multiple cues illustrate robust phenomena of *selective attention*. In such experiments two cues, C1 and C2, are always presented together during training and they jointly predict an outcome. In the test-phase, the strength of conditioning to C1 and C2 presented individually are measured. The typical outcome is that the strength of conditioning to each cue depends on their relative physical intensity. If C1 is a dim light and C2 a bright light then, after conditioning to the C1–C2 combination, the learned response to the bright light is very strong while the dim light alone produces little or no reaction (Kamin, 1969). The general perceived strength of stimuli is commonly referred to as their *salience*. Although it might in part be related to the physically measurable intensity of stimuli, salience refers to the intensity of the subjective experience of stimuli, not of the objective intensity of the stimuli themselves. Salience, as subjective experience, varies between individuals and between species. Rescorla and Wagner (1972) presented a formal model of conditioning which expresses the capacity any cue has to become associated with an outcome at any given stage of learning:

$$dV = ab(L - V)$$

The associative strength of the outcome to the cue is referred to by the letter V, the change in this strength which occurs on each trial of conditioning is called dV, a is the salience of the outcome, b is the salience of the cue and L is the amount of processing given to a completely unpredicted outcome. The more a cue is associated with an outcome, the less additional association the outcome can induce.

The Rescorla–Wagner model pulled together the findings of hundreds of experiments each designed with an empirical rigor unsurpassed outside animal learning research. Its generality of relevance makes it arguably the most influential formula in the history of conditioning theory. It encapsulates the phenomena that the salience of the cue and the importance of the functional outcome are essential factors in any associative learning. A language learner might never get round to noticing low salience cues, particularly when the interpretation accuracy afforded by the other more obvious cues does well enough for everyday communicative survival. The Rescorla and Wagner 1972 model predicts that for low salience cues whose redundancy denies them any more than low outcome importance, dV on any learning trial will be negligible, and thus they may never become integrated into a consolidated construction.

2.4.2 Language learning

Many grammatical meaning–form relationships, particularly those that are notoriously difficult for second language learners like grammatical particles and inflections such as the third person singular -*s* of English, are of low physical salience in the language stream. The reason for this is the well-documented effect of frequency and entrenchment in the evolution of language: grammaticalized morphemes tend to become more phonologically fused with surrounding material because their frequent production leads to lenition processes resulting in the loss and erosion of gestures (Bybee, in press, this volume; Jurafsky, Bell, Gregory, & Raymond, 2001; Zuraw, 2003). As Slobin (1992, p. 191) put it: "Somehow it's hard to keep languages from getting blurry: speakers seem to 'smudge' phonology wherever possible, to delete and contract surface forms, and so forth."

In informal and rapid speech, this tendency to give short shrift to function words and bound morphemes, exploiting their frequency and predictability, deforms their phonetic structure and blurs the boundaries between these morphemes and the words that surround them. Clitics, accent-less words or particles that depend accentually on an adjacent accented word and form a prosodic unit together with it, are the extreme examples of this: the /s/ of "he's," /l/ of "I'll" and /v/ of "I've" can never be pronounced in isolation. Thus, grammatical function words and bound inflections tend to be short and low in stress, even in speech that is produced slowly and deliberately (Bates & Goodman, 1997) and in speech directed to children (Goodman, Nusbaum, Lee, & Broihier, 1990), with the result that these cues are difficult to perceive. When grammatical function words are clipped out of connected speech and presented in isolation, adult native speakers can recognize them no more than 40% to 50% of the time (Herron & Bates, 1997). If fluent native speakers can only hear these grammatical functors from the bottom-up evidence of input 40%–50% of the time, what chance have second language learners to hear them and thence learn their function?

Fluent language processors can perceive these elements in continuous speech because their language knowledge provides top-down support. But this is exactly the knowledge that learners lack. It is not surprising, therefore, that in L1 acquisition young children are unable to acquire grammatical forms until they have a critical mass of content words, providing enough top-down structure to permit perception and learning of those closed-class items that occur to the right or left of "real words" (Bates & Goodman, 1997, pp. 51–52). Nor is it surprising that it is these elements that are difficult for second language learners, with the order of acquisition of these morphemes being pretty much the same in second as in first language learners (Bailey, Madden, & Krashen, 1974; Brown, 1973; Dulay & Burt, 1973; Larsen-Freeman, 1976). Indeed, lenition eventually influences the form of language as a whole, causing some grammatical markers to "wear away" and creating a pressure for the development of others to replace them. McWhorter (2002) tags this a process of "Defining Deviance Downwards": A generation that grows up hearing a sound produced less distinctly gradually comes to take this lesser rendition as the default. In following the general tendency to pronounce unaccented sounds less distinctly, they in turn pronounce their default version of the sound, already less distinct than the last generation's, even less distinctly. Eventually, the default is no sound in that position at all. This erosion has a particularly dramatic effect in sounds such as suffixes or prefixes that perform important grammatical functions. In this way, while Latin had different forms for all six combinations of person and number in the present tense, French has just three different forms for the present tense of *-er* verbs (four for *-ir*, *-re*, and *-oir* type verbs), and modern English has just two. Thus do psycholinguistic and associative learning processes in usage affect both language learning and language change.

2.5 Frequency, salience, and contingency in morpheme acquisition order

A frequency analysis would predict that grammatical functors, as closed class items of the language, are so frequent in the input that their frequency, recency, and context would guarantee their being learned (N. C. Ellis, 2002a). Yet these same items have other properties which moderate their acquisition: each of the above explanations, low ΔP, low salience, redundancy, and low outcome importance, seems to have the potential to make them difficult to acquire. Can we weigh their respective contributions, or indeed know how factors like these might interact? There are many variables and such potential richness of language usage over time that this makes their dynamic interactions complex and difficult to predict. Nevertheless, there are good data which help to inform an answer.

Goldschneider and DeKeyser (2001) performed a detailed meta-analysis of the 12 "morpheme order studies," described above, that investigated the order of L2 acquisition of the grammatical functors, progressive *-ing*, plural *-s*, possessive *-s*, articles *a*, *an*, *the*, third person singular present *-s*, and regular past *-ed*. Although each of the factors of input frequency, semantic complexity, grammatical complexity, phonological form, and perceptual salience has been historically considered within SLA theory for their sufficiency of cause, with input frequency being the favored account (Larsen-Freeman, 1976), nevertheless, as Larsen-Freeman concluded, "[a] single explanation seems insufficient to account for the findings" (1975, p. 419).

Goldschneider and DeKeyser (2001) investigated whether instead a combination of five determinants (perceptual salience, semantic complexity, morphophonological regularity, syntactic category, and frequency) could account for the acquisition order. Their factors of frequency and perceptual salience were much as have been described here, with scores for perceptual salience being composed of three subfactors: the number of phones in the functor (phonetic substance), the presence/absence of a vowel in the surface form (syllabicity), and the total relative sonority of the functor. Their factor of morphophonological regularity relates to contingency since the two subfactors of conditioned phonological variation (for example, the [s, z, əz] allomorphs of plural -s, possessive -s, and third person singular -s) and contractibility both result in multiple forms of the cue, and thus a less clear mapping between the outcome and one particular cue, while the third subfactor of homophony with other grammatical functors results in a less clear mapping between the cue and one particular outcome. Allomorphy and contractibility reduce ΔP by inflating c, homophony by inflating b (see Table 15.1). Oral production data from 12 studies, together involving 924 subjects, were pooled. On their own, each of these factors significantly correlated with acquisition order: perceptual salience $r = 0.63$, frequency $r = 0.44$, morphophonological regularity $r = 0.41$. When these three factors were combined with semantic complexity and syntactic category in a multiple-regression analysis, this combination of five predictors jointly explained 71% of the variance in acquisition order, with salience having the highest predictive power on its own. Each of these factors of frequency, salience, and contingency is a significant predictor independently; together they explain a substantial amount of acquisition difficulty.

We must conclude that, to the extent that the order of acquisition of these morphemes is the same in L1 and L2, these factors play a similarly substantial role in First and Second Language Acquisition. But, the studies meta-analyzed in Goldschneider and DeKeyser pooled L2 learners from a variety of L1 backgrounds and did not concern the ways in which the nature of the first language might have a particular effect on the detailed path or rate of SLA. On top of the effects described in this first section concerning the learner and the language to be learned, there are discernable effects on second language learning resulting from transfer from the first language that the learner has already learned. The next section describes various associative learning processes that are involved in transfer and learned attention before gathering some experimental demonstrations of these particular effects of L1-specific transfer in L2 morpheme acquisition.

3 Factors special to L2

3.1 The limited endstate of usage-based SLA

Children almost invariably eventually acquire nativelike grammatical competence in their first language. Although the acquisition of functional morphology takes many months of input analysis (Brown, 1973; Tomasello, 1992, 2003; Lieven & Tomasello, this volume) and a large critical mass of evidence is necessary for all the subtle generalizations to emerge (Bates & Goodman, 1997), nevertheless, nativelike competence is the norm. In stark contrast, adults almost invariably fail to acquire nativelike competence in a second language from naturalistic exposure. Although second language learners, too, are surrounded by language, not all of it "goes in," and L2A is typically much less successful than L1A. This is Corder's distinction between input, the available target language, and intake, that subset of input that actually gets in and which the learner utilizes in some way (Corder, 1967). Associative L2 learning from naturalistic usage typically falls far short of a nativelike endstate, often stabilizing at a "Basic Variety" of interlanguage which, although sufficient for everyday communicative purposes, predominantly comprises just nouns, verbs, and adverbs, with little or no functional inflection and with closed-class items, in particular determiners, subordinating elements, and prepositions, being rare, if present at all (Klein, 1998). What are the additional associative learning factors which explain this paradox?

3.2 Interference

3.2.1 Learning theory

A hundred years and more ago, Müller and Pilzecker (1900) produced one of the earliest empirical demonstrations of forgetting due to *interference*: people were less likely to recall a memory item if in the interim the retrieval cue that was used to test that item had become associated to another memory. Memory for association A–B is worse after subsequent learning of A–C in comparison with a control condition involving subsequent learning of unrelated material D–E. They called this effect *retroactive inhibition*, highlighting the manner in which the storage of new experiences interferes with memories encoded earlier in time. It is harder to remember the phone number, car registration, or whatever else you had 10 years ago if you have acquired a new phone number, car registration, etc. in the interim. According to classical interference theory, such effects show that it is not the mere passage of time that causes forgetting (as trace decay explanations would hold), but rather it is what happens in that time, the storage of new experiences into memory. The next 50 years of research into interference theory, particularly that in the "verbal learning tradition" (less kindly dubbed "dust bowl empiricism") in the US, demonstrated that it is the interactions of memories, particularly those of highly similar experiences, that are at the root of memory failures. "Response competition theory" (McGeoch, 1942) held that forgetting was a consequence of adding new associative structure, and it attributed interference effects to heightened competition arising from the association of additional traces to a retrieval cue (or to the strengthening of an existing competitor). These ideas continue today in models that emphasize how retrieval of a given item is impeded by competing associations (M. C. Anderson & Bjork, 1994). Quite simply, when multiple traces are associated to the same cue, they tend to compete for access to conscious awareness (M. C. Anderson & Neely, 1996; Baddeley, 1976, chapter 5; 1997; Postman, 1971), and it is not just new memories that interfere with old; the competition runs both ways. So it is harder to learn a new phone number, car registration, or what-have-you because the old ones tend to compete and come to mind instead—this effect of prior learning inhibiting new learning is called *proactive inhibition (PI)*. Much of this work was succinctly summarized in Osgood's "transfer surface" that draws together the effects of time of learning, similarity of material, and retention interval on negative (and positive) transfer of training (Osgood, 1949).

3.2.2 Language learning

Prior proposals for understanding aspects of SLA in terms of transfer from L1 are well known. In the early 1950s Weinreich emphasized the importance of *interference*: "those instances of deviation from the norms of either language which occur in the speech of bilinguals as a result of their familiarity with more than one language" (Weinreich, 1953, p. 1). PI underpins a variety of fundamental phenomena of language learning and language transfer, as Robert Lado proposed in his Contrastive Analysis Hypothesis (CAH) (Lado, 1957): "We assume that the student who comes in contact with a foreign language will find some features of it quite easy and others extremely difficult. Those elements that are similar to his native language will be simple for him, and those elements that are different will be difficult" (Lado, 1957, p. 2). The CAH held that one could predict learner difficulty by reference to an utterance-by-utterance comparison of a learner's L1 and L2.

PI underlies the general negative transfer that makes the learning of second and subsequent language lexis generally difficult. It affords a positive edge to cognates and an extra negativity to *faux ami*. PI, along with its companions, blocking and perceptual learning that I discuss next in this chapter, is a major process by which similarities and differences between languages can influence the acquisition of grammar, vocabulary, and pronunciation, and transfer has a justifiably rich history in the theoretical analysis of second and foreign language learning (C. James, 1980; Odlin, 1989). A survey of the influence of the CAH, made by a simple search of linguistics and language behavior abstracts to see how many articles abstracted in the last 30 years had the keyword descriptor "contrastive analysis," produced a non-trivial 1,268.

Interference theory primarily concerned the transfer of the content of associations. But more recent analyses demonstrate how from content, given enough of it, emerges principle, how form–meaning mappings conspire in biasing attention and process. As a ubiquitous process of learning, transfer pervades all language learning. As we pursue our researches, so we come to believe that the effects that we observe are ours and are special to our domain. In child language acquisition, the problem of referential indeterminacy (Quine, 1960) led researchers to posit word learning constraints that might help limit learners' search space. It has been proposed that they are guided by general heuristics such as a tendency to believe that new words often apply to whole objects (the whole object constraint), that they more likely will refer to things for which a name is not already known (the mutual exclusivity constraint), that they more often relate to things distinguished by shape or function rather than by color or texture, and the like (Bloom, 2000; Golinkoff, 1992; Golinkoff, Mervis, & Hirsh-Pasek, 1994; Gopnik & Meltzoff, 1997; Markman, 1989; Tomasello, 2003). But mutual exclusivity is PI by another name. If a referent already has an associated name, it is harder to attach a new name to it. And so it is the things of the world that are not already labeled that attract new names more readily, in the same way that it is the empty pegs in the coat rack that more likely get hats hung on them next. Kaminsky, Call, and Fischer (2004) tested the use of mutual exclusivity in a border collie named Rico. New objects were placed along with several familiar ones and the owner asked Rico to "fetch it" using a new name Rico had never heard before. He usually retrieved the new object, apparently appreciating that new words tend to refer to objects that don't already have names. A month later, Rico showed some retention of the words he had learned, with abilities comparable to three-year-old toddlers tested who were tested using similar designs.

Recent computational models provide concrete accounts of how such word-learning principles emerge in development from more general aspects of cognition involving associative learning processes such as PI, learned attention, and rational inference, i.e. from prior knowledge of the world and the ways language usually refers to it, and from the learner's existing repertoire of linguistic constructions (MacWhinney, 1989; Merriman, 1999; Regier, 2003). Mutual exclusivity emerges as rational inference in Bayesian Models (Regier, 2003; Tenenbaum & Xu, 2000) and in Competition Models (MacWhinney, 1989; Merriman, 1999) of word learning and these simulations account for a variety of empirically observed mutual exclusivity effects.

3.3 Overshadowing and blocking

3.3.1 Learning theory

The emergence of a learning bias (Mutual Exclusivity) from prior learned content and associations (PI) illustrates how selective attention can be learned, how salience is a psychological property as well as a physical one. Associative learning research describes two general mechanisms that play a particular role in shaping our attention to language: *overshadowing* and *blocking*. In discussing selective attention above, I introduced the phenomenon of overshadowing whereby, when two cues are presented together and they jointly predict an outcome, the strength of conditioning to each cue depends upon their salience, with the most salient cue becoming associated with the outcome and the less salient one being overshadowed so that on its own it evinces little or no reaction (Kamin, 1969). But cues also interact over time. As the Rescorla–Wagner (1972) model encapsulates, the more a cue is already associated with an outcome, the less additional association that outcome can induce. Equally, there is the phenomenon of *latent inhibition* whereby stimuli that are originally varied independently of reward are harder to later associate with reward than those that are not initially presented at all (Lubow, 1973; Lubow & Kaplan, 1997). Forms that have not previously cued particular interpretations are harder to learn as cues when they do become pertinent later. It makes good rational sense that evidence that an event is of no predictive value should encourage the learning system to pay less attention to that event in future. As long as the world stays the same, that is.

Overshadowing as it plays out over time produces a type of learned selective attention known as blocking. Chapman and Robbins (1990) showed how a cue that is experienced in a compound along with a known strong predictor is blocked from being seen as predictive of the outcome. Their experiment, diagrammed in Table 15.2, had undergraduates make predictions about changes in a fictitious stock market. In the first period of the learning phase, whenever stock A rose in price (cue A), the market rose as well (outcome X). The rise or not of stock B during this period had no effect on the market. Thus, A was a good predictor of outcome and B was not. In the second period of the learning phase, on some trials stocks A and C rose together and the market increased, and on other trials stocks B and D rose together and the market again rose. The number of cases of AC cue combination and BD cue combination in period 2 were the same, so they were equally good predictors of market growth. In a final testing phase, the learners were asked to rate on a scale from −100

Table 15.2 The design and outcome of Chapman & Robbins' (1990) cue interaction experiment illustrating "blocking"

Learning Period 1	Learning Period 2	Test Phase	Mean Judgment
A → X	AC → X	C	31
B no prediction of X	BD → X	D	77

(perfect predictor of market not rising) to +100 (perfect predictor of market rising) how well each stock predicted a change in the market.

Even though stocks C and D were associated with a rise in the market on exactly the same number of occasions with an actual ΔP for C and D of 0.57 calculated unconditionally over all trials, nevertheless, the learners judged that cue D was a much better predictor (rating = 77) of market rise than was cue C (rating = 31). The prior learning of cue A "blocked" the acquisition of cue C. Cue A was highly predictive of outcome in learning phase 1, with the result that, in learning phase 2, cue C was to some extent overshadowed and ignored. In contrast, when cues were compounded with others which were not particularly informative (cue B), the target cue (D) received a normal association with the outcome.

The PCM (Cheng & Holyoak, 1995), introduced above, explains the deviations up and down from 57 as follows. The focal set for cue C is just the AC and A trials; that for cue D is just the BD and B trials. ΔP turns out to be 0.0 for cue C because the outcome has the same probability on AC and A trials:

$$\Delta P_C = P(O/C.A) - P(O/ - C.A) = 1.0 - 1.0 = 0.0$$

where $P(O/C.A)$ is the probability of the outcome in the presence of both C and A and $P(O/-C.A)$ is the probability of the outcome in the absence of A and the absence of C. But ΔP turns out to be 1.0 for cue D because the outcome probability differs on AC and A trials:

$$\Delta P_D = P(O/C.B) - P(O/ - C.B) = 1.0 - 0.0 = 1.0$$

These are more extreme results than the 0.31 and 0.77 shown in Table 15.2, suggesting perhaps that the behavioral results had not yet reached asymptote. But the take-home message is clear: human statistical reasoning is bound by selective attention effects whereby informative cues are ignored as a result of overshadowing or blocking. Research shows this to routinely occur even in very simple learning situations like these (Kruschke, 1993, 1996, 2001; Kruschke & Blair, 2000; Kruschke & Johansen, 1999; Shanks, 1995)—they are not restricted to complex learning environments with dozens of cues and outcomes and intricate interactions.

Krushke and Blair's (2000) explanation of blocking as being caused by rapidly shifting learned attention echoes those of Kamin (1969) and Macintosh (1975). When learners are presented with cases of AC →X, since from before A predicts X, C is merely a distraction from a perfectly predictive cue. To avoid this error-inducing distraction, they shift their attention away from cue C to cue A, and consequently learn only a weak association from C to X. In contrast, a new control cue D which co-occurs with a cue which has no prior known significance, becomes associated with its outcome much more strongly. Blocking is a result of an auto-matically learned inattention. But this learned inattention can be per-vasive and longstanding: once a cue has been blocked, further learning about that cue is attenuated (Kruschke & Blair, 2000). Kruschke simulates these processes by building mechanisms of attention into his computa-tional models of associative learning [ALCOVE (Kruschke, 1992), ADIT (Kruschke, 1996) and RASHNL (Kruschke & Johansen, 1999)]. In these models, each cue is gated by an attentional strength, and total attention is limited in capacity. The attention allocated to a cue affects both the associability of the cue and the influence of the cue on response gener-ation. An exemplar unit is recruited for each distinct cue combination, with each exemplar unit encoding not only the presence or absence of cues, but also the attention paid to each cue. Thus, an exemplar unit does not record the raw stimulus, but the stimulus as processed.

3.3.2 Language learning

Not only are many grammatical meaning–form relationships low in sali-ence but they can also be redundant in the understanding of the meaning of an utterance. It is often unnecessary to interpret inflections marking grammatical meanings such as tense because they are usually accom-panied by adverbs that indicate the temporal reference. Terrell illustrated it thus: "If the learner knows the French word for 'yesterday,' then in the utterance *Hier nous sommes allés au cinéma* (Yesterday we went to the movies) both the auxiliary and past participle are redundant past markers. Furthermore, since the adverb *hier* has now marked the discourse as past, the past markers on subsequent verbs are also redundant" (Terrell, 1991, p. 59).

I believe that this redundancy is much more influential in Second rather than First Language Acquisition. Children learning their native language only acquire the meanings of temporal adverbs quite late in develop-ment (Dale & Fenson, 1996). However, the second language expression of temporal reference begins with a phase where reference is established by adverbials alone (Bardovi-Harlig, 1992; Meisel, 1987), and the prior knowledge of these adverbials can block subsequent acquisition of other cues. Schumann (1987) describes how L2 temporal reference is initially made exclusively by use of devices such as temporal adverbials ("tomor-row," "now"), prepositional phrases "in the morning . . ."), serialization (presenting events in their order of occurrence), and calendric reference ("May 12," "Monday"), with the grammatical expression of tense and aspect emerging only slowly thereafter (Bardovi-Harlig, 2000). Second language learners already know about temporal adverbs and narrative strategies for serialization, that these strategies are effective in the com-munication of temporality, and thus the high salience of these means of expression leads L2 learners to attend to them and to ignore the phono-logically reduced tense-markings.

Inflexions for number are similarly often overshadowed by the more obvious singularity of the clear subject of the verb. Pica (1983) describes how naturalistic L2 learners, but not instructed learners, tended to omit plural -s endings on nouns that are premodified by quantifiers. Like Schumann (1978), she observes how this nonredundant marking of plur-ality is characteristic of L2 learners and pidgin speakers alike. There are many such examples. For each of them, take the relevant pair of high- and low-salience co-occurring forms, substitute them for cues A and C in Table 15.2 above, and they readily fit the requirements for the phenomena involving overshadowing. Thus, another pervasive reason for the non-acquisition of low-salience cues in SLA is that of blocking, where redun-dant cues are overshadowed for the historical reasons that the learners' first language experience leads them to look elsewhere for their cues to interpretation. Under normal L1 circumstances, usage optimally tunes the language system to the input; under these circumstances of low sali-ence of L2 form and blocking, all the extra input in the world might sum to naught, and we describe the learner as having "*fossilized*" or, more properly, "stabilized" with a Basic Variety of IL devoid of functional inflections and closed-class items (Klein, 1998).

The usual pedagogical reactions to these situations of overshadowing or blocking involve some means of retuning *selective attention*, some type of form-focused instruction or consciousness raising (Sharwood Smith, 1981) to help the learner to "notice" the cue and to raise its salience. Schmidt summarized it thus: "Since many features of L2 input are likely to be infrequent, non-salient, and communicatively redundant, intentionally focused attention may be a practical (though not theoretical) necessity for successful language learning" (Schmidt, 2001). Terrell characterized explicit grammar instruction as "the use of instructional strategies to draw the students' attention to, or focus on, form and/or structure" (Terrell, 1991), with instruction targeted at increasing the salience of inflections and other commonly ignored features by firstly pointing them out and explaining their structure, and secondly by providing meaningful input that contains many instances of the same grammatical meaning–form relationship. VanPatten is similarly influenced by the fact that L2 speakers allocate more cognitive activation to meanings they consider to be more important to communication in the design of "processing instruction" (VanPatten, 1996) that aims to alter learners' default processing strate-gies, to change the ways in which they attend to input data, thus to maxi-mize the amount of intake of data to occur in L2 acquisition. Likewise Doughty and Williams: "For forms that are frequent in the input and yet still seem to lack salience for learners, it may be that other means are required to induce learners to notice" (Doughty & Williams, 1998, p. 220).

I review the range of mechanisms for the interface of explicit knowledge on implicit language learning in N. C. Ellis (2005); see also Doughty (2001), R. Ellis (2001) and Robinson (2001).

3.4 Perceptual learning

3.4.1 Learning theory

Our perceptual systems change their structure during their history of processing the stimuli to which they are exposed even in the absence of any overt consequences. William James (1890) discusses the case of the novice wine-taster who starts out being unable to distinguish claret and burgundy, but who, after repeated exposure to these wines, comes to find them highly distinct. As a simple consequence of usage, without there being any contingency between the perceptual stimuli they process and any other outcomes or events, perceptual systems alter their sensitivity to stimulus features, becoming more sensitive to those which are psychologically significant dimensions of variation amongst the stimuli, and becoming less sensitive to those redundant characteristics which do not play any role in accurate classification. This tuning which automatically emerges as a result of experience of exemplars is called *perceptual learning* (Fahle & Poggio, 2002; Goldstone, 1998; Seitz & Watanabe, 2003; Watanabe, Sasaki, & Nanez, 2001). Whereas the associative learning effects detailed above relate to specific cues or constructions and their interpretations, perceptual learning is more to do with the organization of the whole system and the dimensions of the underlying psychological space. As more and more instances are processed, so the representations of these exemplars become sorted and positioned in psychological space so that similar items are close together and dissimilar ones are far apart. The dimensions that define this space are to a large degree emergent—as in the statistical techniques of principle component or factor analysis, they come forward in the analysis as the major defining characteristics of the data under scrutiny (Elman et al., 1996; Nosofsky, 1986, 1987). These psychological representation spaces can be charted using the statistical technique of multidimensional scaling (MDS) (Nosofsky, 1992) rather than factor analysis, and the emergence of structure can be simulated using connectionist techniques such as self-organizing maps (SOM) (Kohonen 1998).

Nosofsky (1986) describes animal learning and human categorization research evidencing attention shifts toward the use of dimensions that are useful for the tasks in hand: the dimensions that are relevant for categorizations are psychologically "stretched," with the result that learners become more sensitive to these dimensions and are better able to make discriminations involving them. But in addition to important dimensions acquiring distinctiveness, irrelevant dimensions are psychologically "shrunk," acquiring equivalence and becoming less distinguishable. During category learning, people show a trend toward emphasizing features that reliably predict experimental categories. For example, Livingston and Andrews (1995) showed that in undergraduates' learning to categorize complex schematic drawings: (1) the sequence of encounter of exemplars caused variation in feature salience, with bottom-up perceptual factors being critical to development of hypotheses about a category; (2) variation in feature salience was related to performance on categorization tasks; and (3) nonoptimal feature salience assignments were revised given sufficient experience in the domain; in particular, learners tended to revise faulty hypotheses by adjusting feature salience so as to maximize outcomes, but this revision was much more difficult when it required a complete reassignment of feature salience values.

Goldstone (1994; Goldstone & Steyvers, 2001) presented a range of experiments involving perceptual learning of shapes showing that physical differences between categories become emphasized with training. After learning a categorization in which one dimension was relevant and a second dimension was irrelevant, learners made same/different judgments about whether two shapes were physically identical. Ability to discriminate between stimuli in this judgment task was greater when they varied along dimensions that were relevant during categorization training, and was particularly elevated at the boundary between the categories. Further research showed that category learning systematically distorts the perception of category members by shifting their perceived dimension values away from members of opposing categories (Goldstone, 1995). Goldstone's research thus provides evidence for three influences of categories on perception: (1) category-relevant dimensions are sensitized; (2) irrelevant variation is deemphasized; and (3) relevant dimensions are selectively sensitized at the category boundary.

A related perceptual phenomenon is that of *feature imprinting*. If a stimulus part is important, varies independently of other parts, or occurs frequently, people may develop a specialized detector for that part. Efficient representations are promoted because the parts have been extracted due to their prevalence in an environment, and thus are tailored to that environment. Hock, Webb, and Cavedo (1987) showed that configurations of dots are more likely to be circled as coherent components of patterns if they were previously important for a categorization. Schyns and Rodet (1997) demonstrated that unfamiliar parts (arbitrary curved shapes within an object) that were important in one perceptual task were more likely to be used to represent subsequent categories. Their learners were more likely to represent a conjunction of two parts, X and Y, in terms of these two components (rather than as a whole unit, or a unit broken down into different parts) when they received previous experience with X as a defining part for a different category. Pevtzow and Goldstone (1994) similarly showed how people learn to decompose complex objects based on their experience with component parts: categorization training influences how an object is decomposed into parts. Once you are trained to see the object in that way, that's the way you see it (or that's the way you first see it), and those are the features whose strengths are incremented on each subsequent processing episode.

Goldstone (1998; Goldstone & Steyvers, 2001; Kersten, Goldstone, & Schaffert, 1998) presented a detailed analysis of the ways in which attentional persistence directs attention to attributes previously found to be predictive, elaborated a theory of conceptual and perceptual learning based on these mechanisms, and provided a connectionist model of the processes whereby category learning establishes detectors for stimulus parts that are diagnostic, and these detectors, once established, bias the interpretation of subsequent objects to be segmented (Goldstone, 2000). These cognitive, computational, and neurophysiological results indicate that the building blocks used to describe stimuli are adapted to input history. Feature and part detectors emerge that capture the regularities implicit in the set of input stimuli. However, the detectors that develop are also influenced by task requirements and strategies. In general, whether a functional detector is developed will depend on both the objective frequency and subjective importance of the physical feature (Sagi & Tanne, 1994; Shiu & Pashler, 1992).

3.4.2 Language learning

The sound categories and categorical perception of L1 are subject to perceptual learning (Lively, Pisoni, & Goldinger, 1994). Whether categorical perception effects are found at particular physical boundaries depends on the listener's native language. In general, a sound difference that crosses the boundary between phonemes in a language is more discriminable to speakers of that language than to speakers of a language in which the sound difference does not cross a phonemic boundary (Repp & Liberman, 1987). Speech representations are not at the outset organized around individual speech sounds or phonemic segments; instead, according to the "lexical restructuring hypothesis," only gradually, in early through middle childhood, do they become more fully specified and undergo segmental restructuring (Garlock, Walley, & Metsala, 2001; Metsala & Walley, 1998; Storkel, 2001). This emergent view has it that the words in a young child's lexicon may be relatively distinct with fewer neighbors than the same words in the fully developed lexicon. As a result, children may be able to rely on more holistic representations to uniquely differentiate each word from every other, and these representations may only become more detailed as words are acquired and density increases. So, as more and more similar words are acquired in the child's vocabulary, this drives an increasingly well-specified representation of these words, initially in terms of subunits like onset and rime, and this effect occurs first in dense phonological neighborhoods. It is the learner's knowledge of individual lexical items which drives the abstraction process, with the mental representation of known words only slowly changing to resemble the lexical structure of an adult.

The initial state of the neural stuff involved in language processing is one of plasticity whereby structures can emerge from experience as the optimal representational systems for the particular L1 they are exposed to. Infants between one and four months of age can perceive the phoneme contrasts of every possible language, but by the end of their first year they can only distinguish the contrasts of their own (Werker & Lalonde, 1988; Werker & Tees, 1984). In contrast to the newborn infant, the starting disposition of the neural stuff for SLA is already tuned to the L1 and is set in its ways, it is a *tabula repleta* with L1 entrenchment determining strong negative transfer (Sebastián-Gallés & Bosch, 2005). The L2 learner's neocortex has already been tuned to the L1, incremental learning has slowly committed it to a particular configuration, and it has reached a point at which the network can no longer revert to its original plasticity (Elman et al., 1996, p. 369). English learners of Chinese have difficulty with tones, and Japanese learners of English with the article system, both problems resulting from zero use in the L1. But, as described above, transfer which requires restructuring of existing categories is especially difficult. This is the essence of "perceptual magnet theory" (Kuhl & Iverson, 1995) in which the phonetic prototypes of one's native language act like magnets, or, in neural network terms, attractors (van Geert, 1993, 1994), distorting the perception of items in their vicinity to make them seem more similar to the prototype. What are examples of two separate phonemic categories, /r/ and /l/, for an L1 English language speaker are all from the same phonemic category for an L1 Japanese speaker. And in adulthood the Japanese native cannot but perceive /r/ and /l/ as one and the same. The same form category is activated on each hearing and incremented in strength as a result. And whatever the various functional interpretations or categorizations of these assorted hearings, their link to this category is strengthened every time, rightly or wrongly. Iverson, Kuhl, Akahane-Yamada, Diesch, Tohkura, Kettermann, et al. (2003) present a detailed analysis of how early language experience alters relatively low-level perceptual processing, and how these changes interfere with the formation and adaptability of higher-level linguistic representations, presenting evidence concerning the perception of English /r/ and /l/ by Japanese, German, and American adults. The underlying perceptual spaces for these phonemes were mapped using multidimensional scaling and compared to native-language categorization judgments. The results demonstrate that Japanese adults are most sensitive to an acoustic cue, F2, that is irrelevant to the English /r/–/l/ categorization. German adults, in contrast, have relatively high sensitivity to more critical acoustic cues. Thus L1-specific perceptual processing can alter the relative salience of within- and between-category acoustic variation and thereby interfere with subsequent SLA. Under normal L1 circumstances, usage optimally tunes the language system to the input. A sad irony for an L2 speaker under such circumstances of transfer is that more input simply compounds their error; they dig themselves ever deeper into the hole begun and subsequently entrenched by their L1.

McClelland (2001) presents a connectionist simulation of such effects. A Kohonen self-organizing map network was taught the mappings between phonological input patterns and phonetic representation space. When the model was trained with exemplars from two relatively distinct neighborhoods (representing /r/ and /l/), it learned separate representations and could correctly classify examples into these categories. If, however, the network had previously been trained with exemplars from one wide neighborhood representing the single Japanese alveolar liquid, thereafter it learned to treat the two /r/ and /l/ classes of input as the same and "diabolically maintain[ed] this tendency, even when faced with input that would at first have caused it to represent the classes separately" (McClelland, 2001, p. 112).

Feature imprinting has been clearly exemplified in the first and second learning of Chinese characters. Yeh, Li, Takeuchi, Sun, and Liu (2003) assessed the effect of learning experience upon the perceived graphemic similarity of Chinese characters by comparing results of shape-sorting tasks obtained from various groups of participants with different learning experiences and ages. Whereas both Taiwanese and Japanese undergraduates classified characters in relation to their configurational structures, American undergraduates, Taiwanese illiterate adults, and kindergartners categorized characters based on strokes or components. This trend of developmental changes from local details to more globally defined patterns which culminated in the identification of structure as consistently perceived by skilled readers is clearly the result of learning experience rather than simple maturation.

These various examples illustrate how a plastic, neural *tabula rasa* can become organized by early experience to optimally represent the phonological and orthographic perceptual input of the first language. Sufficient experience of L1 affords fluent accurate processing in this now-tuned and entrenched neural system, and subsequent second language learning is thus faced with maximal transfer and interference from L1, perceiving the L2 through the L1-entrenched *tabula repleta*.

3.5 Transfer effects in L2 morpheme acquisition order

The first half of this chapter culminated with a review of the morpheme acquisition studies which, averaging over L2 learners of different L1s, showed broadly similar orders of acquisition in L1 and L2 learners of English. This second half, therefore, parallels this organization by considering here more focused L2 morpheme acquisition studies which demonstrate clear evidence of L1 transfer.

Hakuta and Cancino (1977) proposed that a second-language learner whose L1 does not make the same semantic discriminations as the L2 target with regard to particular morphemes experiences more difficulty in learning to use these morphemes. There are various studies which support this claim. Hakuta (1976) reported the English language development of a Japanese L1-speaking child who showed particular difficulty with the definite/indefinite contrast, Japanese being a language that does not mark this distinction in the same way as English. Subsequent larger-scale investigations of ESL article use confirm these particular difficulties experienced by ESL speakers whose L1 does not include articles (Master, 1997). Pak (1987), using the same BSM elicitation procedures as did Dulay and Burt (1974), showed that the order of English grammatical morpheme acquisition of a group of Korean-speaking children living in Texas was significantly different from that of Spanish and Chinese L1-speaking children, evidencing greater difficulty with the indefinite article and plural -s, a finding confirmed by Shin and Milroy (1999) who showed that Korean children acquiring English as an L2 in New York City did very well on pronoun case and possessive -s, but very poorly on articles, plural -s, and third person singular -s, a pattern also found in Japanese L1 children. Thus, (1) there are identifiable differences in rank order of acquisition of morphemes between monolingual English-speaking children and second-language learners of English from particular L1 backgrounds, and (2) there is L1 influence on the course of SLA, with clear differences in rank order of acquisition of English morphemes between Spanish-speaking and Chinese-speaking children on the one hand (Dulay & Burt, 1974) and Korean and Japanese speakers on the other (Shin & Milroy, 1999). The fact that Japanese and Korean are morphosyntactically very similar confirms these language-specific influences on SLA: L2 acquisition is clearly affected by the transfer of learners' knowledge of, and attention to, the features and cues that are criterial for their first language.

Finally, though not directly a morpheme order study, the work of Taylor (1975a; 1975b) serves to both contextualize, as a useful reminder that these have been longstanding questions however much they drifted out of vogue, and to serialize, by quantifying the transition from L1 transfer-induced errors to L2 overgeneralization errors in adult SLA. Taylor investigated the English of elementary and intermediate native Spanish-speaking ESL students. He analyzed their errors in the auxiliary and verb phrases of 80 sentences, categorizing them into those errors that resulted from L1 transfer, and those that resulted from overgeneralization of L2 patterns. The errors of the elementary and intermediate students were not strikingly qualitatively different—they were broadly of the same type. However, the rates of these errors were quantitatively different in the two groups, with transfer errors more prevalent among elementary students (40%) than intermediate students (23%), and overgeneralizations more prevalent in intermediate (77%) than elementary students (60%). As Taylor concludes: "Overgeneralization and transfer learning . . . appear to be two distinctive linguistic manifestations of *one psychological process*. That process is one *involving prior learning to facilitate new learning*. Whether transfer or overgeneralization will be . . . dominant . . . for a given learner will depend on his degree of proficiency in the target language" (Taylor, 1975b, p. 87, my emphasis).

4 Conclusions

Many of the chapters in this Handbook concern theories of Cognitive Grammar, cognitive semantics, and the attentional system of language. These analyses illuminate the content of what is learned and transferred. Their necessary complements are theories of associative learning and the ways that prior language knowledge tunes attention to language and cognition about language, thus to understand the processes of acquisition.

Corder (1967) proposed the "error analysis" model in place of Lado's CAH, introducing the notion of the system of interlanguage (IL) at the same time. Errors were no longer viewed simply as an indication of difficulty but instead they illustrated a learner's active attempts at systematic development via intake, a process which involved the construction of an IL, a "transitional competence" reflecting the dynamic nature of the learner's developing system, where every learner sentence should be regarded as being idiosyncratic until shown to be otherwise. Selinker's development of this concept of interlanguage emphasized the wide range of cognitive influences on this complex and often conscious constructive process: language transfer was indeed an integral part of the mix, but it was accompanied by a range of other factors including overgeneralization of L2 rules, transfer of training, strategies of L2 learning, and communication strategies (Selinker, 1971, 1972). Indeed, every sentence is idiosyncratic, as indeed it is systematic, too. Every sentence conspires in the system, but the system is more than the sum of the parts. Every new usage is created dynamically, influenced by interactions among the different parts of the complex system that are unique in time (N. C. Ellis, 2005; Larsen-Freeman, 1997; Ellis & Larsen-Freeman, 2006). The morpheme acquisition studies that I've concentrated upon for illustration here, however comprehensive, provide little more than crude nomothetic summaries of highly variable dynamic systems. Bayley (1994, 1996; Bayley & Preston, 1996) describes detailed variation analyses of the use of past-tense morphology in advanced Chinese learners of English who overtly inflected in obligatory contexts anywhere between 26%–80% of verbs, depending upon (i) the salience of the phonetic difference between inflected and base forms (e.g. suppletive, ablaut irregular, other irregular, regular syllabic, regular nonsyllabic, etc.), (ii) the grammatical aspect (perfective aspect favors (p_i = .68) and imperfective aspect disfavors (p_i = .32) past tense marking), and (iii) phonological factors involving the preceding and following phonetic segments. His studies clearly show how interlanguage is systematically conditioned by a range of usage factors, linguistic, social, and developmental, and that acquisition of past tense marking may best be described as proceeding, not stepwise from unacquired to acquired, but along a continuum. Not a simple continuum though, "not a uni-dimensional or linear one. Rather, it is multidimensional, with the perfective-imperfective aspectual opposition, phonetic saliency, phonological processes (such as -t, d deletion) that converge with particular morphological classes, and social and developmental factors constituting the different dimensions" (Bayley, 1994, p. 178). As explained in the first half of this chapter and demonstrated in Goldschneider and DeKeyser (2001), add to this utterance-by-utterance variability the systematic influences of frequency, contingency, semantic complexity, and broader aspects of salience and syntactic category. Next, as explained in the second half of this chapter and demonstrated in L2 transfer research like that of Shin and Milroy (1999), add the ways first language usage induces interference, overshadowing and blocking, and perceptual learning, all biasing the ways in which learners selectively attend to their second language. These are the associative mechanisms that underlie learned attention as it affects "thinking for speaking" and "thinking for listening," the usage that underpins language learning itself.

Notes

1 Later studies did call for some qualification of this conclusion by demonstrating some variability across L1/L2 that resulted from language transfer. We will consider this in more detail towards the end of this chapter, but for the moment concentrate on the commonalities.

2 In constructional terms, outcome importance is the degree to which successful interpretation of the construction is essential to successful interpretation of the message as a whole.

Bibliography

Allan, L. G. (1980). A note on measurement of contingency between two binary variables in judgment tasks. *Bulletin of the Psychonomic Society, 15*, 147–149.

Anderson, J. R. (1990). *The adaptive character of thought*. Hillsdale, NJ: Lawrence Erlbaum Associates.

Anderson, J. R. (1991a). Is human cognition adaptive? *Behavioral and Brain Sciences, 14*(3), 471–517.

Anderson, J. R. (1991b). The adaptive nature of human categorization. *Psychological Review, 98*(3), 409–429.

Anderson, M. C., & Bjork, R. A. (1994). Mechanisms of inhibition in long-term memory: A new taxonomy. In D. Dagenbach & T. Carr (Eds.), *Inhibitory processes in attention, memory and language* (pp. 265–326). San Diego: Academic Press.

Anderson, M. C., & Neely, J. H. (1996). Interference and inhibition in memory retrieval. In E. L. Bjork & R. A. Bjork (Eds.), *Memory. Handbook of perception and cognition* (2nd ed., pp. 237–313). San Diego, CA: Academic Press.

Baars, B. J. (1988). *A cognitive theory of consciousness*. Cambridge: Cambridge University Press.

Baars, B. J. (1997). *In the theater of consciousness: The workspace of the mind*. Oxford: Oxford University Press.

Baddeley, A. D. (1976). *The psychology of memory*. New York: Harper and Row.

Baddeley, A. D. (1997). *Human memory: Theory and practice*. (Revised ed.). Hove: Psychology Press.

Bailey, N., Madden, C., & Krashen, S. (1974). Is there a "natural sequence" in adult second language learning? *Language Learning, 24*, 235–243.

Bardovi-Harlig, K. (1992). The use of adverbials and natural order in the development of temporal expression. *International Review of Applied Linguistics in Language Teaching (IRAL), 30*, 299–320.

Bardovi-Harlig, K. (2000). *Tense and aspect in second language acquisition: Form, meaning, and use*. Oxford: Blackwell.

Bates, E., & Goodman, J. C. (1997). On the inseparability of grammar and the lexicon: Evidence from acquisition, aphasia and real-time processing. *Language and Cognitive Processes, 12*, 507–586.

Bayley, R. (1994). Interlanguage variation and the quantitative paradigm: Past tense marking in Chinese-English. In E. Tarone, S. M. Gass, & A. D. Cohen (Eds.), *Research methodology in second-language acquisition* (pp. 157–181). Hillsdale, NJ: Lawrence Erlbaum.

Bayley, R. (1996). Competing constraints on variation in the speech of adult Chinese learners of English. In R. Bayley & D. R. Preston (Eds.), *Second language acquisition and linguistic variation* (pp. 97–120). Amsterdam: John Benjamins.

Bayley, R., & Preston, D. R. (1996). *Second language acquisition and linguistic variation*. Amsterdam: John Benjamins.

Biber, D., Johansson, S., Leech, G., Conrad, S., & Finegan, E. (1999). *Longman grammar of spoken and written English*. Harlow, UK: Pearson Education.

Blackwell, A. (1995). *Artificial languages, virtual brains*. Unpublished doctoral dissertation, University of California at San Diego.

Bloom, P. (2000). *How children learn the meanings of words*. Harvard, MA: MIT Press.

Brown, R. (1973). *A first language: The early stages*. Cambridge, MA: Harvard University Press.

Bybee, J. (in press). Mechanisms of change in grammaticalization: The role of frequency. In R. D. Janda & B. D. Joseph (Eds.), *Handbook of historical linguistics*. Oxford: Blackwell.

Celce-Murcia, M., & Larsen-Freeman, D. (1999). *The grammar book: An ESL/EFL teacher's course* (2nd ed.). New York: Heinle & Heinle.

Chapman, G. B., & Robbins, S. J. (1990). Cue interaction in human contingency judgment. *Memory and Cognition, 18*, 537–545.

Cheng, P. W., & Holyoak, K. J. (1995). Adaptive systems as intuitive statisticians: Causality, contingency, and prediction. In J.-A. Meyer & H. Roitblat (Eds.), *Comparative approaches to cognition* (pp. 271–302). Cambridge MA: MIT Press.

Cheng, P. W., & Novick, L. R. (1990). A probabilistic contrast model of causal induction. *Journal of Personality and Social Psychology, 58*, 545–567.

Corder, S. P. (1967). The significance of learners' errors. *International Review of Applied Linguistics, 5*, 161–169.

Dale, P. S., & Fenson, L. (1996). Lexical development norms for young children. *Behavioral Research Methods, Instruments, and Computers, 28*, 125–127.

Diesing, M. (1992). *Indefinites*. Cambridge, MA: MIT Press.

Doughty, C. & Williams, J. (Eds.) (1998). *Focus on form in classroom second language acquisition*. New York: Cambridge University Press.

Doughty, C. (2001). Cognitive underpinnings of focus on form. In P. Robinson (Ed.), *Cognition and second language instruction* (pp. 206–257). Cambridge: Cambridge University Press.

Dulay, H. C., & Burt, M. K. (1973). Should we teach children syntax? *Language Learning, 23*, 245–258.

Dulay, H. C., & Burt, M. K. (1974). Natural sequences in child second language acquisition. *Language Learning, 24*, 37–53.

Ellis, N. C. (2002a). Frequency effects in language processing: A review with implications for theories of implicit and explicit language acquisition. *Studies in Second Language Acquisition, 24*(2), 143–188.

Ellis, N. C. (2002b). Reflections on frequency effects in language processing. *Studies in Second Language Acquisition, 24*(2), 297–339.

Ellis, N. C. (2005). At the interface: Dynamic interactions of explicit and implicit language knowledge. *Studies in Second Language Acquisition, 27*, 305–352.

Ellis, N. C. (2006). Language acquisition as rational contingency learning. *Applied Linguistics, 27*(1), 1–24.

Ellis, N. C. & Larsen-Freeman, D. (Eds.) (2006). Language emergence: Implications for Applied Linguistics. *Applied Linguistics*. Special issue, 27:4.

Ellis, R. (2001). Introduction: Investigating form-focused instruction. *Language Learning, 51*(Supplement 1), 1–46.

Elman, J. L., Bates, E. A., Johnson, M. H., Karmiloff-Smith, A., Parisi, D., & Plunkett, K. (1996). *Rethinking innateness: A connectionist perspective on development*. Cambridge, MA: MIT Press.

Fahle, M., & Poggio, T. (Eds.) (2002). *Perceptual learning*. Cambridge, MA: MIT Press.

Faurud, K. (1990). Definiteness and the processing of noun phrases in natural discourse. *Journal of Semantics, 7*, 395–433.

Garlock, V. M., Walley, A. C., & Metsala, J. L. (2001). Age-of-acquisition, word frequency, and neighborhood density effects on spoken word recognition by children and adults. *Journal of Memory and Language, 45*(3), 468–492.

Gigerenzer, G., & Hoffrage, U. (1995). How to improve Bayesian reasoning without instruction: Frequency formats. *Psychological Review, 102,* 684–704.

Goldschneider, J. M., & DeKeyser, R. (2001). Explaining the "natural order of L2 morpheme acquisition" in English: A meta-analysis of multiple determinants. *Language Learning, 51,* 1–50.

Goldstone, R. L. (1994). Influences of categorization on perceptual discrimination. *Journal of Experimental Psychology: General, 123,* 178–200.

Goldstone, R. L. (1995). Effects of categorization on color perception. *Psychological Science, 6,* 298–304.

Goldstone, R. L. (1998). Perceptual learning. *Annual Review of Psychology, 49,* 585–612.

Goldstone, R. L. (2000). A neural network model of concept-influenced segmentation. In *Proceedings of the Twenty-Second Annual Conference of the Cognitive Science Society* (pp. 172–177). Hillsdale, NJ: Lawrence Erlbaum Associates.

Goldstone, R. L., & Steyvers, M. (2001). The sensitization and differentiation of dimensions during category learning. *Journal of Experimental Psychology: General, 130,* 116–139.

Golinkoff, R. (1992). Young children and adults use lexical principles to learn new nouns. *Developmental Psychology, 28,* 99–108.

Golinkoff, R., Mervis, C. B., & Hirsh-Pasek, K. (1994). Early object labels: The case for a developmental lexical principles framework. *Journal of Child Language, 21,* 125–156.

Goodman, J. C., Nusbaum, H. C., Lee, L., & Broihier, K. (1990). *The effects of syntactic and discourse variables on the segmental intelligibility of speech.* Paper presented at the Proceedings of the 1990 International Conference on Spoken Language Processing, Kobe, Japan.

Gopnik, A., & Meltzoff, A. N. (1997). *Words, thoughts, and theories.* Cambridge, MA: MIT Press.

Hakuta, K. (1976). A case study of a Japanese child learning ESL. *Language Learning, 26,* 321–352.

Hakuta, K., & Cancino, H. (1977). Trends in second language acquisition research. *Harvard Educational Review, 47,* 294–316.

Hawkins, J. (1978). *Definiteness and indefiniteness: A study of reference and grammaticality prediction.* London: Croom Helm.

Hawkins, J. (1991). On (in)definite articles: Implicatures and (un)grammaticality prediction. *Journal of Linguistics, 27,* 405–442.

Herron, D., & Bates, E. (1997). Sentential and acoustic factors in the recognition of open- and closed-class words. *Journal of Memory and Language, 37,* 217–239.

Hock, H. S., Webb, E., & Cavedo, L. C. (1987). Perceptual learning in visual category acquisition. *Memory and Cognition, 15,* 544–556.

Iverson, P., Kuhl, P. K., Akahane-Yamada, R., Diesch, E., Tohkura, Y., Kettermann, A., et al. (2003). A perceptual interference account of acquisition difficulties for non-native phonemes. *Cognition, 87,* B47–B57.

James, C. (1980). *Contrastive analysis.* London: Longman.

James, W. (1890). *The principles of psychology* (Vol. 1). New York: Holt.

Jurafsky, D., Bell, A., Gregory, M., & Raymond, W. D. (2001). Probabilistic relations between words: Evidence from reduction in lexical production. In J. Bybee & P. Hopper (Eds.), *Frequency and the emergence of linguistic structure* (pp. 229–254). Amsterdam: John Benjamins.

Kamin, L. J. (1969). Predictability, surprise, attention, and conditioning. In B. A. Campbell & R. M. Church (Eds.), *Punishment and aversive behavior* (pp. 276–296). New York: Appleton-Century-Crofts.

Kaminsky, J., Call, J., & Fischer, J. (2004). Word learning in a domestic dog: Evidence for "Fast Mapping". *Science, 304,* 1,682–1,683.

Kersten, A. W., Goldstone, R. L., & Schaffert, A. (1998). Two competing attentional mechanisms in category learning. *Journal of Experimental Psychology: Learning, Memory, and Cognition, 24,* 1,437–1,458.

Klein, W. (1998). The contribution of second language acquisition research. *Language Learning, 48,* 527–550.

Kohonen, T. (1998). The self-organization map, a possible model of brain maps. In K. H. Pribram (Ed.), *Brain and values: Is a biological science of values possible?* (pp. 207–236). Mahwah, NJ: Lawrence Erlbaum Associates.

Kruschke, J. K. (1992). ALCOVE: an exemplar-based connectionist model of category learning. *Psychological Review, 99,* 22–44.

Kruschke, J. K. (1993). Human category learning: Implications for backpropagation models. *Connection Science, 5,* 22–44.

Kruschke, J. K. (1996). Base rates in category learning. *Journal of Experimental Psychology: Learning, Memory and Cognition, 22,* 3–26.

Kruschke, J. K. (2001). Toward a unified model of attention in associative learning. *Journal of Mathematical Psychology, 45,* 812–863.

Kruschke, J. K., & Blair, N. J. (2000). Blocking and backward blocking involve learned inattention. *Psychonomic Bulletin and Review, 7,* 636–645.

Kruschke, J. K., & Johansen, M. K. (1999). A model of probabilistic category learning. *Journal of Experimental Psychology: Learning, Memory, and Cognition, 5,* 1,083–1,119.

Kuhl, P. K., & Iverson, P. (1995). Linguistic experience and the "perceptual magnet effect." In W. Strange (Ed.), *Speech perception and linguistic experience: Issues in cross-language research* (pp. 121–154). Timonium, MD: York Press.

Lado, R. (1957). *Linguistics across cultures: Applied linguistics for language teachers.* Ann Arbor: University of Michigan Press.

Larsen-Freeman, D. (1975). The acquisition of grammatical morphemes by adult ESL students. *TESOL Quarterly, 9,* 409–419.

Larsen-Freeman, D. (1976). An explanation for the morpheme acquisition order of second language learners. *Language Learning, 26,* 125–134.

Larsen-Freeman, D. (1997). Chaos/complexity science and second language acquisition. *Applied Linguistics, 18,* 141–165.

Lively, S. E., Pisoni, D. B., & Goldinger, S. D. (1994). Spoken word recognition. In M. A. Gernsbacher (Ed.), *Handbook of psycholinguistics* (pp. 265–318). San Diego, CA: Academic Press.

Livingston, K. R., & Andrews, J. K. (1995). On the interaction of prior knowledge and stimulus structure in category learning. *Quarterly Journal of Experimental Psychology: Human Experimental Psychology, 48A,* 208–236.

Lubow, R. E. (1973). Latent inhibition. *Psychological Bulletin, 79,* 398–407.

Lubow, R. E., & Kaplan, O. (1997). Visual search as a function of type of prior experience with target and distractor. *Journal of Experimental Psychology: Human Perception and Performance, 23,* 14–24.

Lyons, J. (1999). *Definiteness.* Cambridge: Cambridge University Press.

Mackintosh, N. J. (1975). A theory of attention: Variations in the associability of stimuli with reinforcement. *Psychological Review, 82,* 276–298.

MacWhinney, B. (1987). The Competition Model. In B. MacWhinney (Ed.), *Mechanisms of language acquisition* (pp. 249–308).

MacWhinney, B. (1989). Competition and lexical categorization. In R. Corrigan (Ed.), *Linguistic categorization* (pp. 195–242). Amsterdam: John Benjamins.

MacWhinney, B., & Bates, E. (1989). *The crosslinguistic study of sentence processing.* Cambridge: Cambridge University Press.

MacWhinney, B., Bates, E., & Kliegl, R. (1984). Cue validity and sentence interpretation in English, German, and Italian. *Journal of Verbal Learning and Verbal Behavior, 23*(2), 127–150.

MacWhinney, B., Pleh, C., & Bates, E. (1985). The development of sentence interpretation in Hungarian. *Cognitive Psychology, 17*(2), 178–209.

Manning, C. D. (2003). Probabilistic syntax. In R. Bod, J. Hay, & S. Jannedy (Eds.), *Probabilistic linguistics* (pp. 289–341). Cambridge, MA: MIT Press.

Markman, E. (1989). *Categorization and naming in children: Problems of induction.* Boston, MA: MIT Press.

Master, P. (1997). The English article system: acquisition, function, and pedagogy. *System, 25,* 215–232.

Matessa, M., & Anderson, J. R. (2000). Modeling-focused learning in role assignment. *Language and Cognitive Processes, 15*(3), 263–292.

McClelland, J. L. (2001). Failures to learn and their remediation: A Hebbian account. In J. L. McClelland & R. S. Siegler (Eds.), *Mechanisms of cognitive development: Behavioral and neural perspectives. Carnegie Mellon symposia on cognition* (pp. 97–121). Mahwah, NJ: Erlbaum.

McDonald, J. L. (1986). The development of sentence comprehension strategies in English and Dutch. *Journal of Experimental Child Psychology, 41,* 317–335.

McDonald, J. L., & MacWhinney, B. (1991). Levels of learning: A comparison of concept formation and language acquisition. *Journal of Memory and Language, 30*(4), 407–430.

McGeoch, J. A. (1942). *The psychology of human learning: An introduction.* New York: Longman.

McWhorter, J. (2002). *The power of Babel: A natural history of language.* San Franciso, CA: W. H. Freeman & Co.

Meisel, J. (1987). Reference to past events and actions in the development of natural second language acquisition. In C. Pfaff (Ed.), *First and second language acquisition.* New York, NY: Newbury House.

Merriman, W. (1999). Competition, attention, and young children's lexical processing. In B. MacWhinney (Ed.), *The emergence of language* (pp. 331–358). Hillsdale, NJ: Erlbaum.

Metsala, J. L., & Walley, A. C. (1998). Spoken vocabulary growth and the segmental restructuring of lexical representations: Precursors to phonemic awareness and early reading ability. In J. L. Metsala & L. C. Ehri (Eds.), *Word recognition in beginning literacy* (pp. 89–120).

Müller, G. E., & Pilzecker, A. (1900). Experimentalle Beitrage zur Lehre vom Gedächtnis. *Zeitschrift fur Psychologie*, 1, 1–300.

Nosofsky, R. M. (1986). Attention, similarity, and the identification-categorization relationship. *Journal of Experimental Psychology: General*, 115, 39–57.

Nosofsky, R. M. (1987). Attention and learning processes in the identification and categorization of integral stimuli. *Journal of Experimental Psychology: Learning, Memory, and Cognition*, 13, 87–108.

Nosofsky, R. M. (1992). Similarity scaling and cognitive process models. *Annual Review of Psychology*, 43, 25–53.

Odlin, T. (1989). *Language transfer*. New York: Cambridge University Press.

Osgood, C. E. (1949). The similarity paradox in human learning: A resolution. *Psychological Review*, 56, 132–143.

Pak, Y. (1987). *Age difference in morpheme acquisition among Korean ESL learners: Acquisition order and acquisition rate*. Unpublished PhD dissertation, University of Texas, Austin.

Pevtzow, R., & Goldstone, R. L. (1994). Categorization and the parsing of objects. In *Proceedings of the Sixteenth Annual Conference of the Cognitive Science Society* (pp. 717–722). Hillsdale, NJ: Lawrence Erlbaum Associates.

Pica, T. (1983). Adult acquisition of English as a second language under different conditions of exposure. *Language Learning*, 33, 465–497.

Postman, L. (1971). Transfer, interference, and forgetting. In J. W. Kling & L. A. Riggs (Eds.), *Woodworth and Schlosberg's: Experimental psychology* (3rd ed., pp. 1,019–1,132). New York: Holt, Rinehart & Winston.

Quine, W. V. O. (1960). *Word and object*. Cambridge, MA: MIT Press.

Regier, T. (2003). Emergent constraints on word-learning: a computational perspective. *Trends in Cognitive Science*, 7, 263–268.

Repp, B. H., & Liberman, A. M. (1987). Phonetic category boundaries are flexible. In S. Harnad (Ed.), *Categorical perception: The groundwork of cognition* (pp. 89–112). Cambridge: Cambridge University Press.

Rescorla, R. A. (1968). Probability of shock in the presence and absence of CS in fear conditioning. *Journal of Comparative and Physiological Psychology*, 66, 1–5.

Rescorla, R. A., & Wagner, A. R. (1972). A theory of Pavlovian conditioning: Variations in the effectiveness of reinforcement and nonreinforcement. In A. H. Black & W. F. Prokasy (Eds.), *Classical conditioning II: Current theory and research* (pp. 64–99). New York: Appleton-Century-Crofts.

Robinson, P. (Ed.). (2001). *Cognition and second language instruction*. Cambridge: Cambridge University Press.

Sagi, D., & Tanne, D. (1994). Perceptual learning: learning to see. *Current Opinion in Neurobiology*, 4, 195–199.

Schmidt, R. (2001). Attention. In P. Robinson (Ed.), *Cognition and second language instruction* (pp. 3–32). Cambridge: Cambridge University Press.

Schumann, J. H. (1978). *The pidginization process: A model for second language acquisition*. Rowley, MA: Newbury House.

Schumann, J. H. (1987). The expression of temporality in basilang speech. *Studies in Second Language Acquisition*, 9, 21–41.

Schyns, P., & Rodet, L. (1997). Categorization creates functional features. *Journal of Experimental Psychology: Learning, Memory, and Cognition*, 23, 681–696.

Sebastián-Gallés, N., & Bosch, L. (2005). Phonology and bilingualism. In J. F. Kroll

& A. M. de Groot (Eds.), *Handbook of bilingualism: Psycholinguistic approaches*. Oxford: Oxford University Press.

Sedlmeier, P., & Betsc, T. (2002). *Etc.—Frequency processing and cognition*. Oxford: Oxford University Press.

Sedlmeier, P., & Gigerenzer, G. (2001). Teaching Bayesian reasoning in less than two hours. *Journal of Experimental Psychology: General, 130*, 380–400.

Seitz, A. R., & Watanabe, T. (2003). Is subliminal learning really passive? *Nature, 422*, 36–37.

Selinker, L. (1971). A brief reappraisal of contrastive linguistics. *University of Hawaii Working Papers in Linguistics, 3*, 1–10.

Selinker, L. (1972). Interlanguage. *IRAL, International Review of Applied Linguistics in Language Teaching, 10*, 209–231.

Shanks, D. R. (1995). *The psychology of associative learning*. New York: Cambridge University Press.

Shannon, C. E. (1948). A mathematical theory of communication. *Bell Systems Technological Journal, 27*, 623–656.

Sharwood Smith, M. (1981). Consciousness raising and the second-language learner. *Applied Linguistics, 2*, 159–168.

Shin, S. J., & Milroy, L. (1999). Bilingual language acquisition by Korean school children in New York City. *Bilingualism: Language and Cognition, 2*, 147–167.

Shiu, L., & Pashler, H. (1992). Improvement in line orientation discrimination is retinally local but dependent on cognitive set. *Perception and Psychophysics, 52*, 582–588.

Slobin, D. I. (1992). *Psycholinguistics* (2nd ed.). Glenview, IL: Scott, Foresman and Company.

Storkel, H. L. (2001). Learning new words: Phonotactic probability in language development. *Journal of Speech, Language, and Hearing Research, 44*, 1,321–1,337.

Taylor, B. P. (1975a). Adult language learning strategies and their pedagogical implications. *TESOL Quarterly, 9*, 391–399.

Taylor, B. P. (1975b). The use of overgeneralization and transfer learning strategies by elementary and intermediate students in ESL. *Language Learning, 25*, 73–108.

Tenenbaum, J., & Xu, F. (2000). *Word learning as Bayesian inference*. Paper presented at the 22nd Annual Conference of the Cognitive Science Society.

Terrell, T. (1991). The role of grammar instruction in a communicative approach. *The Modern Language Journal, 75*, 52–63.

Tomasello, M. (1992). *First verbs: A case study of early grammatical development*. New York: Cambridge University Press.

Tomasello, M. (2003). *Constructing a language*. Boston, MA: Harvard University Press.

van Geert, P. (1993). A dynamic systems model of cognitive growth: Competition and support under limited resource conditions. In L. B. Smith & E. Thelen (Eds.), *A dynamic systems approach to development: Applications* (pp. 265–331). Cambridge, MA: MIT Press.

van Geert, P. (1994). *Dynamic systems of development: Change between complexity and chaos*. New York: Harvester Wheatsheaf.

VanPatten, B. (1996). *Input processing and grammar instruction in second language acquisition*. New York: Ablex.

Watanabe, T., Sasaki, Y., & Nanez, J. (2001). Perceptual learning without perception. *Nature, 413*, 844–848.

Weinreich, U. (1953). *Languages in contact*. The Hague: Mouton.

Werker, J. E., & Lalonde, C. E. (1988). Cross-language speech perception: Initial capabilities and developmental change. *Developmental Psychology, 24*, 672–683.

Werker, J. E., & Tees, R. C. (1984). Cross-language speech perception: Evidence for perceptual reorganization during the first year of life. *Infant Behavior and Development, 7*, 49–63.

Yeh, S.-L., Li, J.-L., Takeuchi, T., Sun, V. C., & Liu, W.-R. (2003). The role of learning experience on the perceptual organization of Chinese characters. *Visual Cognition, 10*, 729–764.

Zuraw, K. (2003). Probability in language change. In R. Bod, J. Hay, & S. Jannedy (Eds.), *Probabilistic linguistics* (pp. 139–176). Cambridge, MA: MIT Press.

16

CORPUS-BASED METHODS IN ANALYSES OF SECOND LANGUAGE ACQUISTION DATA*

Stefan Th. Gries

1 Introduction

Second Language Acquisition (SLA) is a truly interdisciplinary field at the intersection of psychology, linguistics, applied linguistics, psycholinguistics, and educational science. Given the large number of associated fields and the fact that each of these fields has undergone considerable changes in a time period as short as the last 50 years, it is only natural that SLA is a diverse field in terms of both the theoretical approaches that have been adopted and the data and methodologies that have been applied. The present article looks at SLA at the intersection of the theoretical approach of Cognitive Linguistics—as is obvious from the title of this handbook—and the methodology of Corpus Linguistics—as is obvious from the title of the chapter. After a short introduction, I will first give a very brief overview of those characteristics of Cognitive Linguistics that are relevant in this connection. Then, I will discuss assumptions underlying contemporary Corpus Linguistics and at the same time highlight the large degree of overlap of the two fields. In the main section of this article, Section 4, I will discuss the main three methods of Corpus Linguistics and their application in SLA research. Section 5 will conclude and present some caveats and desiderata.

Let me begin by briefly clarifying a few things. First, some scholars distinguish between second language learning (L2 learning) and foreign language learning (FLL). In such cases, the former is used to refer to the learning of a language other than one's first language that takes place in a geographical/sociological context where the target language is spoken. The latter, by contrast, is used to refer to the learning of a language other than one's first language that takes place in a geographical/sociological context where the target language is not spoken. In the present context, I will not distinguish the two settings because "the underlying learning processes are essentially the same for more local and more remote target languages, despite differing learning purposes and circumstances" (Mitchell & Myles 1998, p. 1). Second, some scholars argue for a strict separation of SLA and language pedagogy, allowing for overlap only when "pedagogy affects the course of acquisition" (Gass & Selinker 2001, p. 2). However, in the present context I will conflate these domains, though I will not be concerned with students' corpus explorations in second/foreign language learning contexts (e.g., data-driven learning).

Among the key questions that researchers in SLA attempt to answer are "how do learners create a new language system with only limited exposure (to the target language)?" and "what is learned, what is not learned, and why so?" Different schools of thought in SLA have proposed different answers to these questions. For example, behaviorist approaches viewed the acquisition of a language as the formation of new habits on the basis of development and reinforcement of stimulus-response pairs.

However, when behaviorist views of language came under attack, a more cognitive perspective was adopted both in psychology, where cognitive developmentalist views gained ground, and linguistics, where Chomsky's review of Skinner's *Verbal behavior* helped usher in a mentalist approach to psychology and linguistic theory by:

1   demonstrating the rule-governed and creative nature of language acquisition;
2   pointing out the role of innate knowledge that aids children's acquisition process on the basis of impoverished input;
3   directing linguists' attention to putative linguistic universals, which also attest to genetically hard-wired linguistic knowledge.

For SLA, this implied a focus on the representation and acquisition of L2s rather than the way in which L2s are actually used (cf. Mitchell & Myles 1998, p. 45), on whether or to what degree L2 learning processes have access to principles and parameters of Universal Grammar, and on transfer, e.g., whether or not parameter settings of L1 influence the acquisition of L2(s).

Most importantly for the purposes of the present volume, there are alternative approaches that could be broadly labeled as cognitively-oriented. These include (adopting the classification of Mitchell and Myles (1998)), but are not limited to, parallel distributed processing, functional models such as the Competition Model by Bates and MacWhinney (1982), and most relevant in the present context, Cognitive Linguistics, which will be discussed in the following section. As will become obvious in Sections 2 and 3, many of the assumptions underlying cognitive-linguistic work—in particular the relevance assigned to frequency of patterns in learners' input—are not only gaining ground in SLA (cf., e.g., Ellis 2002a, 2002b, 2006) but also are often completely analogous to working assumptions in Corpus Linguistics.

2 Cognitive Linguistics

Over the past 25 years, Cognitive Linguistics has matured into one of the most prominent alternatives to the linguistic paradigm of Chomskyan generative grammar. Cognitive Linguistics as such is no single theory but is probably best seen as a family of approaches which share several theoretical and methodological assumptions. The theoretical commitments lying at the heart of Cognitive Linguistics are the Generalization Commitment and the Cognitive Commitment (cf. Lakoff 1990). The former requires cognitive linguists to "characterize the general principles governing all aspects of human language" on all levels of description (e.g., phonology, syntax, semantics, pragmatics); this principle is basically a reformulation of a general scientific commitment to discover knowledge in the form of regularities. The latter Cognitive Commitment requires linguists "to make one's account of human language accord with what is generally known about the mind and the brain, from other disciplines as well as our own" (Lakoff 1990:40). The following exposition of the characteristics of Cognitive Linguistics will focus on the, to my mind, most fully articulated theory within Cognitive Linguistics: Langacker's Cognitive Grammar (cf. Langacker 1987, 1991). For reasons of space, I will restrict my discussion of the central properties of Cognitive Grammar to those that will be relevant for the discussion of corpus-based approaches in SLA.

In Cognitive Grammar, the only kind of element the linguistic system contains are symbolic units. A unit as such is defined as:

> a structure that a speaker has mastered quite thoroughly, to the extent that he can employ it in largely automatic fashion, without having to focus his attention specifically on its individual parts for their arrangement [. . .] he has no need to reflect on how to put it together.
>
> (Langacker 1987, p. 57)

A symbolic unit in turn is a unit that is a pairing of a form and a meaning/function, i.e., a conventionalized association of a phonological pole (i.e., a phonological structure) and a semantic/conceptual pole (i.e., a semantic/conceptual structure). There are essentially no restrictions on the nature and the number of formal elements that constitute the form,

408

and neither are there restrictions on the flexibility of the elements involved in the symbolic unit, but there are two major restrictions that need to be discussed. First, in order for something to attain unit status, the speaker whose linguistic system one is concerned with must have been able to form one or more generalizations (schemas in Langacker's parlance) which sanction the concrete instances. Crucially for our present purposes, the generalizations resulting in symbolic units can be made on the basis of any element from a continuum of increasingly abstract, or schematic, linguistic units. More specifically, generalizations can apply to and, thus, generate:

1   maximally or highly specific elements such as morphemes or words;
2   intermediately specific elements such as partially lexically filled constructions; e.g., the *way*-construction (e.g., *He made his way through the crowd*), the *into*-causative (e.g., *She tricked him into marrying her*), or the conative construction (e.g., *He cut at the bread*);
3   highly abstract/schematic elements such as lexically unfilled constructions; e.g., the intransitive-motion construction (e.g., *The man was swimming in the ocean*), the ditransitive construction (e.g., *He gave her a book*), or linking constructions such as the subject-predicate construction.

Note in passing that this innocuous-sounding definition actually implies something very crucial, namely that Cognitive Grammar does away with a strict separation of syntax and lexis. This is because only symbolic units are allowed in the grammar, and generalizations across encounters of units can be made at the various levels of abstraction mentioned above. Thus, even syntactic patterns are meaningful in their own right, since they must have a semantic pole, which is highly schematic to allow for the diverse ways of how they can be instantiated. All this obviously stands in stark contrast to the various incarnations of transformational-generative grammar.

The second major restriction for something to attain the status of a symbolic unit is that the symbolic unit in question must have occurred frequently enough for it to be entrenched in a speaker/hearer's linguistic system.

These points have important corollaries. The first and most important one is concerned with the fact that Cognitive Linguistics in general and Cognitive Grammar in particular are usage-based approaches. This means that cognitive linguists assume that the use of linguistic elements and structures not only derives from the representation of the linguistic system in the minds of speakers but in turn also influences their representation via mechanisms of routinization, entrenchment, etc. More specifically, the frequency of use of a particular symbolic unit does not only bear on whether some unit is represented in the system or not but also on how the unit is represented and how it is accessed and processed. There are two aspects to this, one concerned with token frequency, one with type frequency. As to the former, the assumption is that high token frequency correlates with strong entrenchment: the more often a speaker/hearer encounters a particular symbolic unit, the more entrenched this symbolic unit becomes in his or her linguistic system and, as indicated in the above quotation from Langacker, the more automatically the symbolic unit is accessed. As to the latter, the assumption is that the type frequency of a particular linguistic expression—the number of different tokens instant-iating a particular symbolic unit—correlates with that particular symbolic unit's productivity. For example, the transitive construction can be argued to be more productive than the ditransitive construction because the former occurs with more and more varied verbs. Both of these aspects also reflect the fact that Cognitive Linguistics is a surface-oriented approach: rather than assuming that, for example, input to L1 acquisition is impoverished (in the sense of not providing the child with clues to the wide variety of empty categories and traces posited by generative lin-guists), cognitive linguists argue that that very same input does not contain all sorts of phonologically null elements but is rather rich in terms of probabilistic correlations or cues. This conception of language is partic-ularly central to the input-driven models of learning and acquisition such as the Competition Model by Bates and MacWhinney (1982, 1989); cf. Ellis (2002a) for a comprehensive review. The acquisition of linguistic elements and structures, therefore, involves extensive frequency-based processing of actual linguistic input, processing that in turn involves pattern matching, bottom-up categorization and inferencing, and storing (of instances/exemplars and/or schemas, as will be described below).

The second major corollary is concerned with the degree of redun-dancy in the representational system. Since frequency of encounter is the only necessary condition for an expression's unit status (or sanctioning the unit status of a more abstract expression it instantiates), we have already seen above that speakers can make generalizations at many differ-ent levels of abstractness or, as Langacker calls it, schematicity. The point to be made here, however, is that these generalizations can be made on several levels *at the same time*. For example, encountering the word *years* will not only reinforce the entrenchment of the word *year* as a symbolic unit, the plural morpheme with [z] as its allomorph, and the schema that allows plural morphemes to be attached to nouns, it will, since *years* is among the most frequent plural nouns,[1] also reinforce the entrenchment of the word *years* as a symbolic unit. More broadly, while many frame-works would rule out such a redundancy in the storage system on grounds of lack of efficiency of storage, Langacker (1987, pp. 29, 42) argues forcefully against this so-called rule-list fallacy, pointing out that *years* can be stored as a symbolic unit itself, too, if it is sufficiently frequent *even though* it could be derived productively from a regular plural formation rule. Crucially, this also applies to multi-word units: if a multi-word expression is encountered frequently enough—e.g., *I don't know*—it will be stored as a unit just like a monomorphemic word. To take a more abstract example, encountering the idiom *to spill the beans* will reinforce the entrenchment of all individual words and morphemes in the expression, the idiomatic unit (with its semantic pole "to reveal a secret"), and the transitive construction, which it also instantiates.

In a nutshell, just like many psycholinguistic models of language, Cognitive Linguistics presumes a variety of frequency effects on various levels. Put differently, there is a widespread recognition that absolute frequencies, relative frequencies (i.e., percentages), conditional probabilities, etc. are represented in the linguistic systems of speakers and, thus, play a primary role on all levels of linguistic analysis.[2] In addition, the last 25 years of both linguistics and psycholinguistics have seen an increasing reliance on the lexicon to investigate syntax (cf. Ellis 2002a, p. 157; Hudson, this volume). Given these two assumptions, it is therefore no surprise that Cognitive Linguistics is the theoretical framework that makes most use of the methodology of Corpus Linguistics. First, corpus linguists discarded a separation of syntax and lexis on independent grounds. Second, Corpus Linguistics is virtually exclusively based on frequency information—in fact, it is "the only reliable source of evidence for features such as frequency" (McEnery & Wilson 1996, p. 12).

3 Corpus Linguistics

The expression *Corpus Linguistics* refers to a method in linguistics which involves the computerized retrieval, and subsequent analysis, of linguistic elements and structures from corpora. The concept of *corpus* in turn is a radial category with a prototypical central element. I will define a prototypical corpus as a machine-readable collection of (spoken or written) texts that were produced in a natural communicative setting, and the collection of these texts is compiled with the intention (i) to be representative and balanced with respect to a particular linguistic variety or register or genre and (ii) to be analyzed linguistically. In this definition, I use *representative* to mean that the different parts of the linguistic variety one is interested in should all be manifested in the corpus. Relatedly, by *balanced* I mean that not only should all parts of which a variety consists be sampled into the corpus but also that the proportion with which a particular part is represented in a corpus reflects the proportion the part makes up in this variety and/or the importance of the part in this variety.[3]

From this characterization of Corpus Linguistics as involving "computerized retrieval," it follows that, strictly speaking at least, the only thing corpora can provide is information on frequency, be it frequency of occurrence (of morphemes, words, grammatical patterns, . . .) or frequencies of co-occurrence of the same kinds of items (as determined by the computerized retrieval). The assumption underlying basically all corpus-based analyses, however, is that formal differences correspond to functional differences such that different frequencies of (co-)occurrences of formal elements are supposed to reflect functional regularities, where functional is meant here in the broadest sense including both semantic and pragmatic aspects of linguistic behavior.

This fact alone—that Corpus Linguistics is basically all about frequencies—would already provide for a strong affinity of Cognitive Linguistics and Corpus Linguistics: Corpus Linguistics provides exactly the kind of data that are at the heart of Cognitive Linguistics. However, the overlap of many of the two approaches' core assumptions and notions is much larger, in fact so large that it is surprising that this is not usually recognized more explicitly (cf. Schönefeld 1999 for a laudable exception). For example, we have seen that the only element in Cognitive Grammar is the symbolic unit, which can take on differently schematic forms. These are in fact perfectly reflected by the main ontological elements in Corpus Linguistics, which I take to be:

1   words, which are symbolic units;
2   phraseologisms, which are often defined as co-occurrences of at least one word form and other elements (i.e., collocations or colligations) which function as a semantic unit and, thus, often correspond to the partially lexically-filled constructions from above;
3   syntactic patterns, which correspond to lexically unfilled, highly schematic symbolic units, which construction grammarians in Cognitive Linguistics refer to as (argument structure) constructions (cf. Gries to appear for a more detailed discussion of these parallelisms).

Just like Cognitive Grammar, corpus linguists also use sufficient frequency of occurrence as the usual definition for something to count as a phraseologism (Hunston 2002: Chapter 6) or a pattern (Hunston and Francis 1999, p. 37). In line with this inventory of elements, corpus linguists have also abandoned the division of syntax and lexis. What is more, we have seen above that the notion of a (symbolic) unit in Cognitive Grammar entails that units are accessed automatically, i.e., fast and without the need to analyze their internal structure. Exactly these notions figure in the formulation of one of the most prominent principles in contemporary Corpus Linguistics, Sinclair's so-called idiom principle. This principle states that "a language user has available to him or her a large number of semi-preconstructed phrases that constitute single choices, even though they might appear to be analyzable into segments" (Sinclair

1991, p. 110) and contrasts with the open-choice principle, which states that "[a]t each point where a unit is completed (a word or a phrase or a clause), a large number of choices opens up and the only restraint is grammaticalness" (Sinclair 1991, p. 109). In other words, corpus linguists share Langacker's rejection of the rule-list fallacy and claim—cf., for example, Pawley and Syder (1983, p. 213, 215ff.)—that speakers' mental lexicons do contain much more than just lexical primitives, namely also probably hundreds of thousands of prefabricated items that could be productively assembled but are, as a result of frequent encounter, redundantly stored and accessed.

4 Three corpus-linguistic methods in SLA

For the purposes of the present review, it is useful to distinguish three different kinds of corpus-linguistic methods. First, there are frequency lists and collocate lists, or collocations. These constitute the most decontextualized methods, with the possible exception of one search expression largely ignoring the context in which an utterance or a sentence was produced. Second, there are colligations and collostructions, in which context is largely reduced to co-occurrences of lexical elements with a particular grammatical element or structure. Finally, there are concordances (of search expressions), which usually provide the occurrence of a match of the search expression in a user-defined context window, often four words to both the left and the right of the match or the whole clause/sentence in which the match occurred.

These methods will be discussed in more detail in the remainder of this section. They can be applied to several different kinds of data of interest to the SLA researcher. Depending on what kinds of corpora are available, one can look at all the kinds of language that will influence the output of the learner:

1   how does the input language pattern?
2   how does the native language of the learners pattern?[4]
3   how does the target language pattern?
4   what are the differences between how the native language and the target language pattern? (That is, all sorts of comparisons between these, cf. contrastive analysis.)

On the other hand, one can directly look at the output of the learner:

1   how does the interlanguage pattern? and/or
2   which (kinds of) errors do the language learners commit (computer-aided error analysis)?

Obviously, in many studies information from various of the above sources will, and actually should, be combined in order to be able to isolate sources of observed effects (cf. Juffs (2001, p. 312) for a similar argument and, e.g., Tono (2004) or Borin and Prütz (2004) for applications).

One final word of caution. Corpus-linguistic methods can basically be applied to symbolic units of all kinds of schematicity, but given the current state of the art in corpus annotation, not all symbolic units are equally amenable to corpus-based analysis. More specifically, symbolic units differ with regard to the precision and the recall with which they can be retrieved for analysis automatically. Symbolic units of low degrees of schematicity—most morphemes and words—are often easy to retrieve automatically and do not even require corpora with specific annotation (cf. Section 5 for some caveats, though). In other words, their retrieval is characterized by high precision and high recall. Symbolic units of intermediate schematicity are more problematic. In the absence of well-annotated corpora, one usually must conduct lexical searches and then weed out false hits manually. This way, the retrieval achieves high precision, but the recall is dependent on how much manual data correction can be done. If the amount of lexically-based hits makes an exhaustive correction impossible, recall will be low—alternatively, recall can be high, but the effort required may increase dramatically, and I know of cases where many thousands of matches were combed through manually. Symbolic units of high schematicity such as argument structure constructions, finally, often require part-of-speech (POS) tagged if not syntactically annotated corpora for automated retrieval. If these are not available, some schematic symbolic units, those that contain at least one lexical element, can be retrieved with high recall, but require extensive manual post-editing to yield acceptable degrees of precision.

4.1 Frequency lists and collocates / lexical co-occurrences

The most basic corpus-linguistic tool is the frequency list. In the most basic sense, a frequency list indicates how frequent words are in a corpus. Usually, a frequency list is a two-column table with all words occurring in the corpus in one column and the frequency with which they occur in the corpus in the other column. Typically, one out of three different sorting styles is used: alphabetical (ascending or descending), frequency order (ascending or, more typically, descending), and first occurrence (each word occurs in a position reflecting its first occurrence in the corpus). While this is certainly the most widespread kind of frequency list, theoretically other frequency lists are conceivable; depending on the corpus makeup and annotation, one can find frequency lists of morphemes, reverse frequency lists of words (to, say, group together all regular adverbs ending in -ly in English), pairs or even larger uninterrupted chains of words, interrupted sequences of words, lemmas (as opposed to word forms), parts of speech, syntactic patterns, constructions, etc.

Frequency lists of various kinds of units or constructions are useful for a variety of purposes in the domain of SLA. In a pedagogy context, frequency lists are mostly built on the assumption that it is more useful for L2 learners to learn first those units that are particularly important in the target register/genre/variety, and not surprisingly in Corpus Linguistics, "particularly important" translates into "particularly frequent." This assumption can be found in virtually all contemporary introductions to Corpus Linguistics and has, for example, been argued for by Sinclair and Renouf (1988, p. 148): "the main focus of study should be on (a) the commonest word forms in the language; (b) the central patterns of usage; (c) the combinations which they usually form"; cf. also Biber and Reppen (2002). However, frequency lists are also theoretically relevant in Cognitive Linguistics because, as outlined above, the more frequent a linguistic expression, the more entrenched it is assumed to be and the more likely it has unit status.

On the basis of the above assumption, the most straightforward application of frequency lists in SLA has been in the area of syllabus or curriculum development, where frequency lists are used to determine how much it is that is to be learned (cf. Hazenberg & Hulstijn 1996), what to attend to first and foremost, and in what order, ideally focusing (first) on what is typical/atypical rather than on what is possible/impossible. The logic is that since frequencies of symbolic units typically exhibit a Zipfian distribution—very few types account for very many tokens—the benefit of learning the most frequent elements first should be enormous (cf. Willis 1990 for some statistics and detailed discussion).[5] For example, Grabowski and Mindt (1995) provide a frequency list of irregular verbs that, if used in L2 teaching, would allow learners to quickly account for more than 80 percent of the verb tokens in the corpora analyzed. Similar proposals have been made for a variety of phenomena: modal verbs (Mindt 1995), markers of epistemic modality (Holmes 1988), progressive aspect (Römer 2005), etc. A more refined strategy—more refined in the sense that this strategy is statistically more sophisticated and allows for register/genre specific lists—is the use of key words, where key words are defined as those words in a corpus which are (significantly) over-represented in this corpus as revealed by a statistical comparison to a (usually much larger and more overall representative) reference corpus (usually by means of chi-square of log-likelihood statistics).

Another relevant aspect in the more teaching-oriented area of the discipline is that of using frequency lists to quantify and/or compare the attainment of language proficiency. The most basic and most frequent statistic employed in this context is certainly the type-token ratio. For example, Cadierno (2004) analyzes how native and non-native speakers express motion events differently in verb-framed and satellite-framed languages on the basis of type-token statistics of motion verbs in L1 and L2 Spanish. However, the problematic nature of this statistic is by now well known (cf. Granger & Wynne 1999) and other, more sophisticated indices of lexical richness such as the Lexical Frequency Profile (cf. Laufer & Nation 1995, and Meara 2005 for a critique) have been developed to serve as indicators of the development of vocabulary (cf. also Read 1997, 2000; Baayen 2001; Chipere, Malvern, and Richards 2004).

As to more theoretical approaches, frequency lists are used as approximations of the frequencies of elements in the input to the L2 learner or in the target language—"approximations" because it is of course unclear to what degree corpus frequencies can in fact reflect actual learner input frequencies (cf. Ellis & Schmidt 1997), and the same applies of course to the reflection of target-language frequencies. Also, frequency lists serve to pick experimental stimuli: for example, Wolter (2001) uses experimental stimuli chosen on the basis of a word-frequency list generated from the Collins Cobuild Bank of English.

While most of the above work focuses on individual lexical words and syntactic patterns, there is also some interesting work involving frequency lists of elements consisting of more than just one word or one syntactic pattern, namely co-occurrences of words, variously referred to as collocations, lexical n-grams (where n refers to the number of words involved), multi-word units, prefabs, and certainly other expressions. For example, De Cock et al. (1998, also De Cock 1998) compare "prefabs" in native-speaker and learner corpora to test the hypothesis that learners tend not to use formulae as frequently as native speakers do. Biber et al (1999, p. 993–994) examine "lexical bundles" in conversation and academic prose. Howarth (1998) reports quantitative results regarding the collocational density and stylistic conventionality of non-native-speaker collocations and idioms as well as qualitative results regarding the errors made, and strategies used, by non-native speakers. Other work is somewhat more abstract. For example, Aarts and Granger (1998) do not focus on n-grams of words but rather compare frequencies of 3-grams of part-of-speech (POS) tags in the ICLE interlanguage corpus with the corresponding frequencies in a corpus of L1 speakers of the target language English, an instance of contrastive interlanguage analysis. Borin and Prütz (2004) go even further and also include n-gram frequencies of POS tags in the native language of the language learners.

Finally, it is worth noting in passing that such raw frequency statistics are often reported at the beginning of results sections to give a feel for the kinds of corpora that were used or the kinds of elicited corpus results that were obtained (cf. Waara's (2004) analysis of the argument structures taken by *get* for an example).

4.2 Colligations and collostructions: lexico-grammatical co-occurrence

The next method includes more contextual information than just frequencies or collocations and bridges the gap to grammatical analysis. Much of the work in Cognitive Linguistics—especially work in Construction Grammar—is concerned with colligations and collostructions, the co-occurrence of lexical and grammatical elements.[6] More specifically, *strong tea*—as opposed to *powerful tea*, to use a famous example—is a collocation as is *hermetically sealed* since the two co-occurring elements, *strong* and *tea* as well as *hermetically* and *sealed*, are all lexical items. By contrast, the fact that the verb *to hem* is usually used in the passive is a colligation or collostruction since only one of the co-occurring elements is a lexical item whereas the other is a grammatical element, the passive construction.[7] Recall, however, that, since Cognitive Grammar does away with a strict separation of syntax and lexis, collocations as well as colligations and collostructions are all co-occurrences of symbolic units, if only at different levels of schematicity, which, as pointed out above, usually goes hand in hand with an increase of the time and effort required for retrieval and annotation. Two perspectives are conceivable: the analysis starts out either from the retrieval of the lexical element of the colligation/collostruction or from the grammatical element. In what follows, examples of both strategies will be discussed.

One of the most important areas of application for colligations and collostructions would obviously be the investigation of grammatical proficiency as such, as well as the knowledge of interdependencies of lexis and syntactic patterns/constructions. The most central domain of study in this area is probably verb subcategorization patterns. A huge research project concerned with charting out the ways in which syntax and lexis interact in the usual target language, English, is Hunston and Francis's pattern grammar project based on the COBUILD project. Interestingly, many of their conclusions could in fact be straight quotations from studies independently arrived at in Construction Grammar, as the following quote exemplifies:

> [. . .] words sharing the same patterns tend to fall into groups based on shared aspects. This in turn suggests that *the patterns themselves can be said to have meanings*, and there is some evidence that the use of a lexical item with a pattern it does not commonly have is a resource for language creativity and, possibly, for language change.
>
> (Hunston & Francis 1998, p. 69; my emphasis, STG)

A study more directly concerned with acquisition patterns is the above-mentioned paper by Tono (2004), who conducts a multifactorial analysis of the factors governing the acquisition of verb subcategorization frame patterns by Japanese learners of English. She uses three corpora: an interlanguage corpus of Japanese L2 learners of English, an L1 speaker corpus of Japanese, and a target language corpus, which is a corpus of textbook English rather than "real, authentic" English, an unfortunate choice in her case, at least from my point of view (but cf. Tono (2004, p. 51f.) for a defense of her choice of a textbook corpus as representing the target language).

An example closer to a Cognitive Linguistics/Construction Grammar approach is Waara (2004). She attempts to compare argument structure constructions of the English light verb lemma *to get* on the basis of two corpora of test interviews—one of L1 speakers of English, one of Norwegian L2 learners of English. She starts out from the forms of the verb and then reports the frequencies with which different argument structure constructions occur with *to get* aiming to explain how learner constructions reflect different transfer, blending, and overgeneralization of the developing L2 system.

Colligations and collostructions also provide approximations to input frequencies and target language frequencies of lexico-grammatical co-occurrences in much the same way as frequency lists and collocations do for words. For example, several central notions of the Competition Model—cue validity, cue availability, and cue reliability—are usually approximated probabilistically on the basis of co-occurrence frequencies of some cue(s) (such as word order, agency, animacy, . . .) and some grammatical structure or some comprehension preference under consideration (cf., e.g., Kempe & MacWhinney 1998); these notions are very similar especially to Hoey's more recent usage of *colligation* (cf. again Note 7).

An interesting approach—from my certainly not unbiased point of view—to verb-subcategorization preferences and constructions of L2 learners is the study by Gries and Wulff (2005). They investigate whether advanced German learners of English have acquired knowledge of the syntax-lexis interface that is similar to that of native speakers of English. They use data from an L1 English corpus (the British component of the International Corpus of English) and verb-subcategorization preferences obtained from a parsed L1 German corpus and correlate these corpus data with results from a syntactic-priming and a sorting experiment conducted with the German learners. Syntactic priming refers to the tendency to re-use syntactic patterns used shortly before. In the syntactic priming experiment, subjects were asked to complete sentence beginnings. Some sentence beginnings served as primes for ditransitive constructions (such as *The racing driver showed the helpful mechanic . . .*) while others served as primes for the prepositional dative (such as *The racing driver showed the torn overall* . . .). The dependent variable was the choice of syntactic construction upon presentation of a non-biasing sentence fragment after the prime (such as *The angry student gave* . . .). In the sorting experiment, the German learners were given 16 cards, each displaying one sentence, and asked to sort these into four groups of four sentences each. The sentences crossed four verbs (*cut*, *get*, *take*, and *throw*) and four argument structure constructions (the transitive, caused-motion, resultative, and ditransitive construction). The dependent variable was whether the subjects adopted a perceptually simpler verb-based sorting style or a more complex construction-based sorting style. Their findings lend support to a conception of L2 learning that involves the development of a probabilistic system from (probabilistic correlations in) actual input and is, thus, fully compatible with a usage-based approach.

First, they find that advanced German L2 learners do not only exhibit overall syntactic priming effects in English comparable to those of native speakers of English but they also exhibit verb-specific priming effects that are (i) very highly correlated with the verbs' subcategorization preferences in native speaker English and (ii) completely unlike the verbs' German translation equivalents' subcategorization preferences in native speaker German. Second, they find that (different) advanced German L2 learners also exhibit a preference for sorting sentences according to the argument structure constructions they instantiate rather than according to the verb they feature. Interestingly, the grouping of constructions conform to a Construction Grammar account of how these constructions are related to each other. What is more, one can now compare the average number of cards one has to move to arrive at purely construction-based sortings (where smaller values indicate a higher degree of construction-based sorting) from several studies: Bencini and Goldberg (2000, p. 645) obtained a value of 3.2 for native speakers; Gries and Wulff's (2005, p. 192) replication with very advanced German learners of English obtained a value of 3.45; Liang's (2002) replication with intermediate Chinese learners of English obtained a value of 4.9. Obviously, the degree of proficiency of the L2 learners of English is well reflected, at least on an ordinal scale, by their recognition of, and sorting based on, argument structure constructions in English; a finding which is not only interesting for the above theoretical reason but also because it at the same time demonstrates the power of converging evidence from different experimental studies and corpus-linguistic data (cf. also Wulff and Gries (2008) for a follow-up).

4.3 Concordances

Concordances are the most comprehensive tool in the sense of providing the most informative context for the matches of the search expression(s). Usually, a user specifies a search expression, which can, depending on the annotation of the corpus, involve information from many different levels of linguistic analysis, e.g., lemmas, POS tags, etc. In addition, the user defines the format of the output by typically either specifying a number of words around the match that should be displayed (usually referred to as window or span) or by setting the concordancer to display the whole sentence in which the match occurred (or even additional sentences). This way, concordances do not miss out on any information and are probably the most universally applicable and widespread method; only a tiny snapshot of what is possible beyond the above examples can be given here.

Cadierno (2004) applies Slobin's notion of thinking-for-speaking as well as Talmy's typology of motion verbs and investigates how native speakers of a satellite-framed language describe events in a verb-framed language, comparing data from narratives elicited from L1 speakers of Spanish and Danish L2 learners of Spanish. She finds how L2 proficiency and cross-linguistic influence interact in the expression of motion events: on the one hand, Danish learners of Spanish "exhibited a relatively higher degree of complexity and elaboration of the semantic component of path of motion," but on the other hand, they "did not transfer the characteristic typical typological pattern of the L1 into the L2" (Cadierno 2004, p. 41ff.).

Nesselhauf (2004) investigates the errors committed by German learners of English in the use of support-verb constructions with *make, have, take,* and *give.* Given that her corpus—a part of the German section of the ICLE—is not annotated syntactically, her retrieval of support-verb constructions was a two-step procedure such that she first retrieved all matches of the verb forms and then manually identified verb-support constructions. Her conclusions are interesting in that she cautions against teaching recommendations exclusively based on the criterion of frequency. A study with a slightly similar focus by Altenberg and Granger (2001) looks at the use of the high-frequency verb *to make,* comparing data from interlanguage and native corpora.

A not yet particularly widespread issue in SLA is that of contrastive semantic prosody. Semantic prosody refers to aspects of typically evaluative meaning words take on from their most frequent collocates; for example *happen* and *set in* usually take collocates referring to unpleasant situations. Accordingly, contrastive semantic prosody refers to the different semantic prosodies of translational equivalents in different languages. For example, Xiao and McEnery (2006) explore concordance data for collocations that reveal semantic prosodies in the target language and the interlanguage to determine the degree to which language learners master semantic prosodies; they also point out the importance of making teachers and learners aware of cross-linguistic and text type-specific differences.

Many other approaches are conceivable since concordances basically impose no limit on the amount of information that can be included. Thus, even issues that superficially seem to be less tied to formally identifiable patterns, for example the polysemy of prepositions, metaphorical uses vs. literal uses of verbs such as *to see*, quantification in L2 (cf. Kennedy 1987), etc.—all of these aspects await more attention from corpus linguists.

5 Caveats, conclusions, and desiderata

This handbook chapter has discussed the intimate relation of Cognitive Linguistics and Corpus Linguistics as well as how many examples of cognitive-linguistic concepts and corpus-based methods are used in SLA research.

While the above discussion has—for expository reasons—treated different methods separately, the theoretical ideal would of course be that, for example, detailed studies of the behavior of any symbolic unit integrate information from all these methods. Hunston (2002, p. 76ff.) gives an excellent example in her textbook discussion of the word *leak*. She first finds that collocates of the verb *to leak* indicate that the verb has at least two broader senses. One is concerned with the movement of a liquid through objects that are supposed to be solid and reflected by collocates such as *oil*, *water*, *gas*, and *roof*; the other, more metaphoric, sense is concerned with making information available as reflected by collocates such as *document(s)*, *information*, *report*, *memo*, and *confidential*. However, she then also shows that the collocation frequencies alone cannot reveal that the metaphoric sense is used both intransitively and transitively, something that can only be noticed by looking at syntactic patterns or the concordance lines.

Also, it is clear that the larger the number of different corpora that are included in one's study, the greater the likelihood of robust and revealing findings: as the work by, say, Tono (2004) shows, including as many as possible of the different kinds of corpora discussed at the beginning of Section 4 into a multiple comparison approach will assist in separating L1-induced variation from L2-induced variation from learner input-induced variation. Finally, it is all too obvious that probably every kind of SLA research can benefit from converging evidence from several methods such as corpus data of various sorts *and* experimentation, and a few such examples were mentioned above.

An advantage of corpus data seems to be that once the required corpora are available, frequency lists, concordances, collocates, etc. seem easy to come by. For example, there are many corpus programs available with which frequency lists of corpora are just a few mouse clicks away;[8] the situation is similar with regard to collocate displays (cf. Wiechmann & Fuhs 2006 for a comparative review). However, there are also some problems that are associated with these methods that tend to be underestimated and not addressed explicitly enough in much recent work. One is concerned with the fact that most of the data retrieval is done by computer programs. For example, frequency lists, collocations, and concordances presuppose that the retrieval is done correctly and that one has a definition of what a word is (and, for the sake of comparison with other work, that this definition is shared by other linguists and their computer programs).[9] However, this may not be so. Concordance programs usually define word forms as a sequence of alphabetic (or alphanumeric) characters uninterrupted by whitespace (i.e., spaces, tabs, and newlines), but some also allow the user to specify what to do with hyphens, apostrophes, and other special characters. For example, concordancers may differ as to how they handle "better-suited" or "ill-defined"; "armchair-linguist," "armchair linguist," and "armchair-linguist's"; "This" and "this"; "1960"; "25-year-old"; and "favor" and "favour." Thus, one needs to exercise extreme caution when comparing frequency lists from different sources. In addition, some corpus files come with a lot of annotation in headers and not every program is equally good at ignoring the words in the header etc.[10]

More often than not, it is the restricted accessibility of SLA corpus data that puts considerable limits on the kinds of studies that are possible or not; however, with regard to those corpus data that actually are widely accessible to date, the very fact that they are so easily accessible may also be problematic. For example, a potential downside of concordances derives from their strongest advantage, namely the fact that they provide the most informative output. This high degree of informativeness can be disadvantageous because it usually goes in hand in hand with not being able to automate (parts of) the analysis. For example, if all one is interested in is the number of different prepositions used after a verb in the same clause, it is easy to retrieve this information largely automatically with a snippet of code of a programming language. However, if one really wishes to exploit all the information available in concordances of, say, a particular verb, then there are many characteristics that computer scripts usually fail to retrieve with a high degree of precision; examples include animacy of participants, clause types, transitivity of the verb, properties of the process denoted by the verb, the metaphoricity of the use of the verb, etc. The number of properties that need to be coded manually or at least semi-manually can easily reach 100,000 or more (cf. Gries 2006 or Divjak & Gries 2006). Thus, often the data to be included in an analysis are reduced such that only every n-th match of an actual concordance output can be investigated in as much detail as would usually be desired. Therefore, adequate sampling strategies are of vital importance in this context. One possibility would be to use stratified sampling on the basis of top-down distinctions, sampling, for example, different speaker groups (e.g., as defined by perceived proficiency), different speakers, different genres, etc. Another possibility, which has so far not been used widely in

Corpus Linguistics, is to apply resampling and/or bootstrapping techniques to better (i) derive the relevant sample groups directly from the data themselves, i.e., in a bottom-up fashion, without necessarily invoking any particular researcher's preconceptions, and (ii) quantify the variability in the data more precisely than simple summary statistics do; cf. Meara (2005) and Gries (2007) for discussion and exemplification.

Yet another issue is concerned with the kind of frequencies that are provided. There are three aspects to this. First, much work using frequencies exhibits a—from my point of view—rather unfortunate preference to use only raw frequencies of occurrence or of co-occurrence in a usually arbitrarily defined span or of a usually arbitrarily defined length. Second and relatedly, the frequencies that are obtained this way are often just reported or evaluated in but the simplest possible ways. Third, it seems as if there is as yet no rigorous operationalization of when something is frequent enough to be considered a unit in the above sense of the term. Rather, different scholars just use subjective impressions of what is frequent enough or not, and, to quote but one example, Hunston (2002, p. 147) even states pessimistically:

> How many examples of a three-, four- or five-word sequence are necessary for it to be considered a phrase [sic! I guess what is meant is "a phraseologism"; STG]? As this is not an answerable question [. . .]

However, there is a lot of research that is just waiting to be exploited in Cognitive Linguistics/Corpus Linguistics in general and in corpus-based SLA in particular. As to the first, there is immensely useful work on, for example, how to determine the ideal span size or slot to investigate in terms of collocations. For example, much work involving collocations is based on the words found in a span of three to five words around the node word that was retrieved. However, this leaves much noise in the data to be filtered out. An interesting refinement is, for example, Mason's (1997, 1999) work on what he refers to as lexical gravity, namely a method to identify those positions around a node word which exhibit the smallest amount of entropy and are, thus, most revealing for the subsequent analysis. Another example is work by Kita et al. (1994) and many others, who have provided interesting proposals concerning the identification of multi-word units in corpora.

As to the second and related aspect of evaluation of frequencies, there is probably even more previous work on how statistical approaches going beyond absolute or relative frequencies allow for a more appropriate analysis of the data. For example, Gries, Hampe, and Schönefeld's (2005, to appear) work on the so-called as-predicative shows that collocational statistics (such as the Fisher-Yates exact test) outperform raw frequencies in terms of their predictive power in experimental setups. For example, work by Evert and his collaborators (cf. Evert & Krenn 2001) investigates which measures of collocational attraction are most useful in terms of reflecting native speaker intuitions, etc. Also, there are quite a few, but not yet enough, studies that exhibit the degree of statistical sophistication that a discipline whose main subject matter is frequencies would lead one to expect; for example, Tono (2004) or Borin and Pütz (2004) are laudable exceptions in this regard, using multifactorial and other significance tests.

As to the third aspect regarding frequency thresholds, I am not in a position to propose a universally applicable frequency criterion for unit status—perhaps some ratio of observed vs. expected frequency of occurrence will be useful—but there is work approaching this issue in interesting ways. For example, studies such as Bybee and Scheibman (1999) or Jurafsky et al. (2001), in which the assumption that particular expressions with high-token frequencies have unit status is supported by additional independent evidence concerning an expression's status as an autonomous unit, namely the readiness of these expressions to undergo, say, processes of grammaticalization and/or phonological reduction (e.g., the reduction of the vowel in *don't* in *I don't* or *why don't you . . .?*). While these are promising steps, this is certainly still a crucial issue that needs to be addressed and developed further if the notion of unit status is to be more than a guesstimate. In addition, while the quoted studies demonstrate the relevance of frequency data at the level of the word forms (e.g., *don't* or *that you*), there may well be occasions on which other levels of granularity—e.g., the lemma—are even more revealing (cf. Harrington & Dennis 2002 on what they call the redescription problem). For example, inspecting spoken American corpus data shows that *you know what I mean?* may be a unit, as may *you know what I'm sayin'?* or *you know what VP?* Especially from an exemplar-based theoretical perspective, speakers/learners may make generalizations with different degrees of predictive power on many levels at the same time. It remains to be hoped that these and other methodological advances will further our use and understanding of frequency data.

In the area of syllabus design, it is not always clear what corpora to choose as reference corpora for the target language (cf. again Tono 2004, p. 51ff. for discussion) and how useful frequency lists that do not take register differences or communicative goals of speaker/writer into account can actually be. Perhaps even more fundamental, however, is the question of if and to what degree frequency-based syllabi are more useful to L2 learners in the first place. While it may seem intuitively obvious that (i) frequent units are more useful to learners than rare units and that (ii) teaching material should resemble authentic speech, there are also several not-so-obvious issues involved that are not always topicalized. First, one has to decide on which level of granularity frequency is supposed to be important. On the one hand, one could go for the most frequent lexical forms (or, of course, syntactic constructions, etc.). On the other hand, one could go for the most frequent lexical lemmas. Yet again, one could go for the most frequent senses of lexical lemmas or for senses in particular syntactic patters, etc. Different level choices may yield different results and it is not immediately obvious which level of granularity is most useful.

Second, even if one decides on a particular level of granularity, it is still not always clear whether the learner benefits more from the exposure to authentic examples. One may argue that the exposure to authentic examples increases the likelihood of the learner developing a network of differently weighted probabilistic connections that approximates that of a native speaker. However, proponents of corpus-based material face several challenges. First, Baugh et al. (1996, p. 43) argue that "[m]ost citations are unsuitable for a learner dictionary because they are too complex grammatically, contain unnecessary difficult words or idioms, or make culture-dependent allusions or references to specific contexts," and many reference works have therefore chosen to carefully edit authentic examples. Second, authenticity does not automatically entail typicality, and it may well be the case that learners benefit equally or more from the careful comparison of, say, minimal-pair-like examples that have been constructed to highlight a particular aspect or contrast to be learned. In other words, the issue is whether the saliency created in constructed examples may outperform the frequency of authentic examples. It is worth pointing out in this connection that authors such as Nesselhauf (2004), Mauranen (2004), and Gabrielatos (2005) underscore the importance of including not just frequency-based factors into attempts at improving teaching material. On these grounds, and because it is my impression that so far even some of the most ardent defenders of the authenticity/ frequency camp—e.g., Glisan and Drescher (1993) or Römer (2004)— have not yet provided experimental evidence to bolster their claims as to the utility or even indispensability of corpus-based curricula, the issue of whether corpus frequency-based materials are necessary or useful is still largely unresolved.

In spite of all these caveats and desiderata, it should be obvious that corpus-based work has a lot to offer to the analyst. I therefore hope and predict that more and more SLA corpora will be developed, annotated, and shared among research groups—especially corpora on interlanguages other than English—and that methods to increase precision and recall of symbolic units of all kinds will be developed to help cognitive- and corpus-linguistics approaches to SLA mature and prosper.

Notes

* I am very grateful to Stefanie Wulff for a lot of advice and discussion. Also, I thank the editors of this handbook for their detailed comments and Beate Hampe for feedback. The usual disclaimers apply.

1 Note, for example, that it is the most frequent word tagged as a plural noun in the British National Corpus World edition.

2 Cf. Bley-Vroman (2002) or Eubank and Gregg (2002) for commentaries that accord frequency a less prominent role for data analysis and theory development.

3 Note how his definition already implies that usually SLA corpora are not prototypical corpora—according to the above definition, that is. This is not meant to imply they are deficient but that they are specialized in one ore more respects. For example, a widely known SLA corpus, the International Corpus of Learner English (Granger, Dagneaux, and Meunier 2002) largely consists of student essays and it is debatable, to say the least, whether essays students write at the request of a language instructor instantiate communication in a natural setting (cf., e.g., Granger 2002, p. 7f. and Stewart et al. 2004: Section 4 for discussion); similar remarks apply to the Longman Learners Corpus (1993). Often, SLA research involves experiments which could be viewed as corpus-generation experiments. For example, van Hest (1996) uses a corpus of self-repairs in Dutch in three different experimental tasks, Bardovi-Harlig (1998) investigates tense-aspect morphology in interlanguage using a corpus of spoken and written narratives elicited by means of a film-retell task; Waara (2004) compares data from corpora of test interviews of pairs of students (in English as their L1 and L2) by teachers using corpus-linguistic methods and software; similar examples abound in the literature. Similarly, in ways reminiscent of the analysis of parallel corpora, Cadierno (2004, this volume) compares Spanish and Danish spoken narratives produced by native speakers and non-native speakers of Spanish who narrate the events unfolding in a picture book story.

4 This is, of course, a slight simplification because, especially in the domain of curriculum planning, what is of interest may be only the patterning in a particular register rather than the language as a whole. However, this does not affect the general argument here.

5 For example, in the British National Corpus World edition, the 100 most frequent word forms (i.e., about 0.015% of all types) account for a staggering 47% of all the tokens. This is also true of forms of word classes. For example, George (1963) showed that the morphological verb forms taught in a typical first-year English course account for only 20% of all verb form tokens whereas if the course covered only the seven most frequent morphological forms, these would account for almost 60% of all verb form tokens in his corpus.

6 I will not be concerned with collocational frameworks here. Collocational frameworks are structures of two usually closed-class words surrounding an open-class word slot; examples include *a* N *of* or *be* ADJ *to*; cf. Renouf and Sinclair (1991) or Butler (1998) for discussion and application.

7 It is worth pointing out that *colligation* is used very differently by different scholars. Originally coined by Firth, it referred to co-occurrences of grammatical elements, i.e., by analogy to collocations as co-occurrences of lexical elements. The majority of corpus linguists seems to use the term as I do here, namely to refer to co-occurrences of lexical elements with grammatical elements. More recently, Hoey (e.g., Hoey 2005) has broadened the scope of

colligation considerably to also include the preference of lexical elements to particular positions in texts, etc. It remains to be seen whether this extension will be accepted in the field. The notion of *collostruction* basically corresponds to the second definition of colligation but, as the blend of *collocation* and *construction* already suggests, is more strongly related to a Construction Grammar approach and comes with a statistically more sophisticated approach than previous work on Pattern Grammar or colligations (cf. Stefanowitsch & Gries 2003 as well as Gries, Hampe, & Schönefeld 2005).

8 The programs reviewed in Wiechmann and Fuhs (2006) are MonoConc Pro 2.2, WordSmith Tools 4, Concordance, Multi-Language Corpus Tool, ConcApp 4, AntConc 1.3, Aconcorde, Simple Concordance Program, Concordancer for Windows 2.0, and TextStat 2.6. Links to these programs can be found on the author's website.

9 This may seem a trivial point but in fact this is more important than one might think. For example, in the study mentioned above, Waara (2004) states "[e]very occurrence of *get* was extracted from the corpora, i.e., *get, got, getting, gotten,* and *to get*," and one wonders whether the fact that *gets* is missing from this list is responsible for the difference of 157 instances in Tables 1 and 2 of that paper.

10 For example, MonoConc Pro 2.2's (build 242) frequency lists of files from the British National Corpus World edition includes all tags and all words from the header (!) in the frequency list even if the makeup of the tags is specified.

Bibliography

Aarts, J. & Granger, S. (1998). Tag sequences in learner corpora: a key to interlanguage grammar and discourse. In: Granger, S. (Ed.). *Learner English on computer*. London and New York: Addison-Wesley. pp. 132–141.

Altenberg, B. & Granger, S. (2001). The grammatical and lexical patterning of MAKE in native and non-native student writing. *Applied Linguistics* 22.2:173–195.

Baayen, R. H. (2001). *Word frequency distributions*. Dordrecht: Kluwer.

Bardovi-Harlig, K. (1998). Narrative structure and lexical aspect: Conspiring factors in second language acquisition of tense aspect morphology. *Studies in Second Language Acquisition*, 20:471–508.

Bates, E., & MacWhinney, B. (1982). Functionalist approaches to grammar. In Wanner, E., & Gleitman, L. (Eds.). *Child language: State of the art*. New York: Cambridge University Press, pp. 173–218.

Bates, E., & MacWhinney, B. (1989). Functionalism and the Competition Model. In MacWhinney, B. & Bates, E. (Eds.). *The crosslinguistic study of sentence processing*. New York: Cambridge University Press, pp. 3–76.

Baugh, S., Harley, A., and Jellis, S. (1996). The role of corpora in compiling the Cambridge Dictionary of English. *International Journal of Corpus Linguistics* 1.1:39–59.

Bencini, G. & Goldberg, A. E. (2000). The contribution of argument structure constructions to sentence meaning. *Journal of Memory and Language* 43.4:640–651.

Biber, D., Johansson, S., Leech, G., Conrad, S., & Finnegan, E. (1999). *Longman grammar of spoken and written English*. Harlow: Pearson Education Limited.

Biber, D. & Reppen, R. (2002). What does frequency have to do with grammar teaching? *Studies in Second Language Acquisition* 24.2:199–208.

Bley-Vroman, R. (2002). Frequency in production, comprehension, and acquisition. *Studies in Second Language Acquisition* 24.2:209–213.

Borin, L. & Pütz, K. (2004). New wine in old skins? A corpus investigation of L1 syntactic transfer in learner language. In: Aston, G., Bernardini, S., & Stewart, D. (Eds.). *Corpora and language learners*. Amsterdam and Philadelphia: John Benjamins, pp. 67–87.

Butler, C. S. (1998). Collocational frameworks in Spanish. *International Journal of Corpus Linguistics* 3.1:1–32.

Bybee, J. & Scheibman, J. (1999). The effect of usage on degrees of constituency: The reduction of *don't* in English. *Linguistics* 37.4:575–596.

Cadierno, T. (2004). Expressing motion events in a second language. In: Achard, M. and Niemeier, S. (Eds.). *Cognitive linguistics, second language acquisition, and foreign language teaching*. Berlin and New York: Mouton de Gruyter, pp. 13–49.

Chipere, N., Malvern, D., & Richards, B. (2004). Using a corpus of children's writing to test a solution to the same size problem affecting type-token ratios. In: Aston, G., Bernardini, S., & Stewart, D. (Eds.). *Corpora and language learners*. Amsterdam and Philadelphia: John Benjamins, pp. 137–147.

De Cock, S. (1998). A recurrent word combination approach to the study of formulae in the speech of native and non-native speakers of English. *International Journal of Corpus Linguistics* 3.1:59–80.

De Cock, S., Granger, S., Leech, G., & McEnery, T. (1998). An automated approach to the phrasicon of EFL learners. In: Granger, S. (Ed.). *Learner English on computer*. London and New York: Addison Wesley Longman, pp. 67–79.

Divjak, D. S. & Gries, S. Th. (2006). Ways of trying in Russian: Clustering behavioral profiles. *Corpus Linguistics and Linguistic Theory* 2.1:23–60.

Ellis, N. C. (2002a). Frequency effects in language processing and acquisition. *Studies in Second Language Acquisition* 24.2:143–188.

Ellis, N. C. (2002b). Reflections on frequency effects in language processing. *Studies in Second Language Acquisition* 24.2:297–339.

Ellis, N. C. (2006). Language acquisition as rational contingency learning. *Applied Linguistics* 27.1:1–24.

Ellis, N. C. & Schmidt, R. (1997). Morphology and longer distance dependencies. *Studies in Second Language Acquisition* 19.2:145–171.

Eubank, L. & Gregg, K. R. (2002). News flash—Hume still dead. *Studies in Second Language Acquisition* 24.2:237–247.

Evert, S. & Krenn, B. (2001). Methods for the qualitative evaluation of lexical association measures. *Proceedings of the 39th Annual Meeting of the Association for Computational Linguistics*, pp. 188–195.

Gabrielatos, C. (2005). Corpora and language teaching: just a fling or wedding bells? *Teaching English as a Second or Foreign Language* 8.4: A1.

Gass, S. & Selinker, L. (2001). *Second Language Acquisition: An Introductory Course*. 2nd ed. Mahwah, NJ: Lawrence Erlbaum.

George, H.V. (1963). *A verb-form frequency count: application to course design*. Hyderabad: Central Institute of English.

Glisan, E. W. & Drescher, V. (1993). Textbook grammar: Does it reflect native speaker speech. *The Modern Language Journal* 77.1:23–33.

Grabowski, E. & Mindt, D. (1995). A corpus-based learning list of irregular verbs in English. *International Computer Archive of Modern English (ICAME) Journal* 19:5–22.

Granger, S. (2002). A bird's eye view of learner corpus research. In: Granger, S., Hung, J., & Petch-Tyson, S. (Eds.). *Computer learner corpora, second language acquisition and foreign language teaching.* Amsterdam/Philadelphia: John Benjamins, pp. 3–33.

Granger S., Dagneaux, E., & Meunier, F. (2002). *The International Corpus of Learner English. Handbook and CD-ROM.* Louvain la Neuve: Presses Universitaires de Louvain.

Granger, S. & Wynne, M. (1999). Optimising measures of lexical variation in EFL learner corpora. In: Kirk, J. (Ed.). *Corpora galore.* Amsterdam and Atlanta: Rodopi, pp. 249–57.

Gries, S. Th. (2006). Corpus-based methods and cognitive semantics: The many meanings of *to run.* In: Gries, S. Th. & Stefanowitsch, A. (Eds.). *Corpora in Cognitive Linguistics: Corpus-Based Approaches to Syntax and Lexis.* Berlin, Heidelberg, New York: Mouton de Gruyter, pp. 57–99.

Gries, S. Th. (2007). Exploring variability within and between corpora: some methodological considerations. *Corpora* 1.2:109–151.

Gries, S. Th. (to appear). Phraseology and linguistic theory: a brief survey. In: Granger, S. & Meunier, F. (Eds.). *Phraseology: an interdisciplinary perspective.* Amsterdam and Philadelphia: John Benjamins.

Gries, S. Th. & Divjak, D. (to appear). Behavioral profiles: a corpus-based approach to cognitive semantic analysis. In Evans, V., & Pourcel, S. S. (Eds.). *New directions in cognitive linguistics.* Amsterdam and Philadelphia: John Benjamins.

Gries, S. Th., Hampe, B. & Schönefeld, D. (2005). Converging evidence: bringing together experimental and corpus data on the association of verbs and constructions. *Cognitive Linguistics* 16.4:635–676.

Gries, S. Th., Hampe, B., & Schönefeld, D. (to appear). Converging evidence II: more on the association of verbs and constructions. In: Newman, J. and Rice, S. (Eds.). *Empirical and Experimental Methods in Cognitive/Functional Research.* Stanford, CA: CSLI.

Gries, S. Th. & Wulff, S. (2005). Do foreign language learners also have constructions? Evidence from priming, sorting, and corpora. *Annual Review of Cognitive Linguistics* 3:182–200.

Harrington, M. & Dennis, S. (2002). Input-driven language learning. *Studies in Second Language Acquisition* 24.2:261–268.

Hazenberg, S. & Hulstijn, J. H. (1996). Defining a minimal receptive second-language vocabulary for non-native university students: an empirical investigation. *Applied Linguistics* 17.2:145–163.

Hoey, M. (2000). A world beyond collocation: new perspectives on vocabulary teaching. In: Lewis, M. (Ed.) *Teaching collocations.* Hove, UK: Language Teaching Publications, 224–243.

Hoey, M. (2005). *Lexical priming: A new theory of words and language.* London: Routledge.

Holmes, J. (1988). Doubt and certainty in ESL textbooks. *Applied Linguistics* 9.1:21–44.

Howarth, P. (1998). Phraseology and second language proficiency. *Applied Linguistics* 19.1:24–44.

Hunston, S. (2002). *Corpora in applied linguistics.* Cambridge: Cambridge University Press.

Hunston, S. & Francis, G. (1999). *Pattern grammar: a corpus-driven approach to the lexical grammar of English.* Amsterdam and Philadelphia: John Benjamins.

Juffs, A. (2001). Verb classes, event structure, and second language learners' knowledge of semantics-syntax correspondences. *Studies in Second Language Acquisition* 23.2:305–313.

Jurafsky, D., Bell. A., Gregory, M., & Raymond, W. D. (2001). In: Bybee, J. & Hopper, P. (Eds.). *Frequency and the emergence of linguistic structure.* Amsterdam and Philadelphia: John Benjamins, pp. 229–254.

Kempe, V. & MacWhinney, B. (1998). The acquisition of case marking by adult learners of Russian and German. *Studies in Second Language Acquisition* 20.4:534–587.

Kennedy, G. D. (1987). Quantification and the use of English: a case study of one aspect of the learner's task. *Applied Linguistics* 8.3:264–286.

Kita, K., Kato, Y., Omoto, T., & Yano, Y. (1994). A comparative study of automatic extraction of collocations from corpora: Mutual information vs. cost criteria. *Journal of Natural Language Processing* 1.1:21–33.

Lakoff, G. (1990). The invariance hypothesis: is abstract reason based on image schemas? *Cognitive Linguistics*, 1:39–74.

Langacker, R. W. (1987). *Foundations of Cognitive Grammar, Volume 1: Theoretical prerequisites.* Stanford, CA: Stanford University Press.

Langacker, R. W. (1991). *Foundations of Cognitive Grammar, Volume 2: Descriptive application.* Stanford, CA: Stanford University Press.

Laufer, B. & Nation, P. (1995). Vocabulary size and use: lexical richness in L2 written production. *Applied Linguistics* 16.3:307–322.

Liang, J. (2002). *How do Chinese EFL learners construction sentence meaning: Verb-centered or construction-based?* M.A. thesis, Guangdong University of Foreign Studies.

Mason, O. (1997). The weight of words: an investigation of lexical gravity. *Proceedings of PALC 1997*, pp. 361–375.

Mason, O. (1999). Parameters of collocation: the word in the centre of gravity. In: Kirk, J. (Ed.). *Corpora galore: analyses and techniques in describing English.* Amsterdam and Atlanta: Rodopi, pp. 267–280.

Mauranen, A. (2004). Speech corpora in the classroom. In: Aston, G., Bernardini, S., and Stewart, D. (Eds.). *Corpora and language learners.* Amsterdam and Philadelphia: John Benjamins, pp. 195–211.

McEnery, T. & Wilson, A. (1996). *Corpus linguistics.* 1st edn. Edinburgh: Edinburgh University Press.

Meara, P. (2005). Lexical frequency profiles: a Monte Carlo analysis. *Applied Linguistics* 26.1:32–47.

Mindt, D. (1995). *An empirical grammar of the English verb: modal verbs.* Berlin: Cornelsen.

Mitchell, R. & Myles, F. (1998). *Second language learning theories.* London and others: Arnold.

Nesselhauf, N. (2004). How learner corpus analysis can contribute to language teaching. In: Aston, G., Bernardini, S., & Stewart, D. (Eds.). *Corpora and language learners.* Amsterdam and Philadelphia: John Benjamins, pp. 109–24.

Pawley, A., & Syder, F. H. (1983). Two puzzles for linguistic theory: nativelike selection and nativelike fluency. In Richards, J., & Schmidt, R. (Eds.). *Language and communication*. New York: Longman, pp. 191–226.

Read, J. (1997). Assessing vocabulary in a second language. In: Clapham, C. & Corson, D. (Eds.). *Language testing and assessment. Encyclopedia of language and education*, Vol. 7. Dordrecht: Kluwer, pp. 99–107.

Read, J. (2000). *Assessing vocabulary*. Cambridge: Cambridge University Press.

Renouf, A. & Sinclair, J. M. 1991. Collocational frameworks in English. In: Aijmer, K. & Altenberg, B. (Eds.). *English corpus linguistics*. London: Longman, pp. 128–143.

Römer, U. (2004). Comparing real and ideal language learner input. In: Aston, G., Bernardini, S., & Stewart, D. (Eds.). *Corpora and language learners*. Amsterdam and Philadelphia: John Benjamins, pp. 151–168.

Römer, U. (2005). *Progressive, patterns, pedagogy*. Amsterdam and Philadelphia: John Benjamins.

Schönefeld, D. (1999). Corpus linguistics and cognitivism. *International Journal of Corpus Linguistics* 4.1:131–171.

Sinclair, J. McH. (1991). *Corpus, concordance, collocation*. Oxford: Oxford University Press.

Sinclair, J. McH. & Renouf, A. (1988). A lexical syllabus for language learning. In Carter, R., & McCarthy, M. (Eds.). *Vocabulary and language teaching*. Harlow: Longman, pp. 197–206.

Stefanowitsch, A. & Gries, S. Th. (2003). Collostructions: investigating the interaction between words and constructions. *International Journal of Corpus Linguistics* 8.2:209–243.

Stewart, D., Bernardini, S., & Aston, G. (2004). 'Introduction'. In Aston, G., Bernardini, S., & Stewart, D. (Eds.). *Corpora and language learners*. Amsterdam/Philadelphia: John Benjamins, pp. 1–18.

Tono, Y. (2004). Multiple comparisons of IL, L1 and TL corpora: the case of L2 acquisition of verb subcategorization patterns by Japanese learners of English. In: Aston, G., Bernardini, S., & Stewart, D. (Eds.). *Corpora and language learners*. Amsterdam and Philadelphia: John Benjamins, pp. 45–66.

Van Hest, E. (1996). *Self-repair in L1 and L2 production*. Tilburg: Tilburg University Press.

Waara, R. (2004). Construal, convention, and constructions in L2 speech. In: Achard, M. & Niemeier, S. (Eds.). *Cognitive linguistics, second language acquisition, and foreign language teaching*. Berlin and New York: Mouton de Gruyter, pp. 51–75.

Wiechmann, D. & Fuhs, S. (2006). Concordancing software. *Corpus Linguistics and Linguistic Theory* 2.1:109–130.

Willis, D. (1990). *The lexical syllabus: a new approach to language teaching*. London: Collins Cobuild.

Wolter, B. (2001). Comparing the L1 and L2 mental lexicon. *Studies in Second Language Acquisition* 23.1:41–69.

Wulff, St. & Gries, S. Th. (2008) *To-* vs. *ing-*complematation of advanced foreign language learners: corpus- and pycholinguistic evidence. Paper presented at the 15th World Congress of Applied Linguistics (AILA 2008). University of Duisburg-Essen; 24–29 August 2008.

Xiao, R. & McEnery, T. (2006). Collocation, semantic prosody, and near synonymy: a cross-linguistic perspective. *Applied Linguistics* 27.1:103–129.

17

TEACHING CONSTRUAL: COGNITIVE PEDAGOGICAL GRAMMAR

Michel Achard

1 Introduction

The kind of grammatical instruction dispensed in the L2 classroom obviously depends on the teacher's view of what grammar is, and how students process it. Virtually every practical decision the instructor makes from the conception of the syllabus (Grundy 2004) to the design of the activities themselves (Achard 2004) implements a set of hypotheses about the nature of grammatical organization and the manner in which its units are learned, whether these hypotheses are explicitly stated or not. This chapter explores some of the practical implications of the adoption of the tenets and principles of Cognitive Grammar [henceforth CG, (Langacker 1987, 1991)] for the teaching of grammar, and more generally for the general orientation of the L2 classroom. It argues that the CG view of linguistic organization presents two major advantages. First, by emphasizing the symbolic nature of all linguistic expressions, it allows the instructor to focus on the meaning of grammatical constructions. This focus on meaning in turn provides useful insights into the form of those constructions, since meaning can be shown to motivate form (Doughty & Williams 1998, VanPatten, Williams, Rott & Overstreet 2004). It also allows the instructor to make explicit the semantic relations that obtain with other related constructions. From a methodological standpoint, the recognition of the meaning of grammatical constructions provides opportunities to teach grammar in a way similar to that of lexical items, which makes grammatical instruction congruent with the principles of most contemporary communicative models of language pedagogy, such as processing instruction, content-based teaching, task-based teaching for example. Secondly, the adoption of the CG principles places the speaker squarely in the center of the communicative act. The specific distribution of linguistic expressions in discourse should therefore be imputed to speaker choice rather than to properties of the system itself. This "teaching of usage" (to be explained in the following sections) reflects the complexity and flexibility of the target system. It also allows the students to understand the choices natives make in specific situations, and exercise their own creativity in similar ways.[1] From a pedagogical point of view, the progression toward native-like flexibility of expression represents the goal of the advanced levels of instruction. This chapter is structured in the following fashion. Section 2 presents some of the issues about the teaching of grammar in L2 most hotly debated in the literature. Section 3 introduces the CG tenets most directly relevant for foreign language instruction. Section 4 illustrates the practical implementation of these positions with an example from French. Section 5 recapitulates the results and concludes the chapter.

2 Grammatical instruction

The teaching of grammar in L2 remains one of the most often debated issues in foreign language education. This chapter cannot even pretend to present an exhaustive overview of the multiple issues discussed in the literature. It merely introduces those for which the adoption of the CG model is most directly relevant. Interested readers will find a more comprehensive overview in Hinkel and Fotos (2002), Nassaji and Fotos (2004), Ellis (2002).

Perhaps the most fundamental question about grammatical instruction is whether or not it should have a place in the L2 classroom, or more specifically, if any attention (in whatever manner) should be paid to the specific form of linguistic expressions. The rise of the communicative models of instruction made instructors so suspicious of undue focus on structure that in the 1980s and early 1990s systematic grammatical instruction was banned from many language classrooms. In particular, Krashen and Terrell's Natural Approach (Krashen & Terrell 1983) strongly argued that a steady stream of comprehensible input in a relaxed atmosphere represents the best possible environment to foster proficiency in the target language. According to their "Monitor Hypothesis," grammatical instruction can only have an effect on the few low-level rules that are accessible to the learner's explicit analysis. It is therefore highly limited in scope and hardly worth the precious classroom time which could be more valuably spent on the kind of input activities that truly promote learning. Even though the Natural Approach continues to be used successfully in the US classrooms, the radical grammarless position of the 1980s and early 1990s has somewhat softened. Data from (mostly Canadian) immersion programs (Swain & Lapkin 1989 among many others) confirmed many practitioners' fears that exclusive focus on communication encourages fossilized production, and convinced them that some form of grammatical

433

instruction is desirable regardless of the methodology selected. Conse-quently, the integration of grammatical activities in communicative models currently constitutes one of the hardest pedagogical challenges foreign language teachers face, especially at the beginning levels of instruction.

If an agreement on the necessity to teach grammar in some form has by now mostly been reached, the debate has turned to the precise nature of grammatical instruction. Opinions on this issue critically depend (among other things) on the theoretical assumptions about the place grammatical concepts occupy in the overall process of language learning, as well as on the global methodological orientation followed in the course. For example, Negueruela (2003), and Negueruela and Lantolf (2006) working within a Vygotsky inspired "concept-based" model of instruction, argue that suc-cessful grammatical instruction must focus on the explicit and coherent presentation of theoretical concepts (the category "perfect" in Spanish for example). Consequently, they advocate the use of "didactic models" such as verbalization charts that explicitly guide the students through each decision-making step that leads to the choice of a particular expression. In their model, grammatical rules are not only explicit, but also "talked through," to ensure successful incorporation in the learner's cognitive system. Other models take a radically different approach. For example, Achard (2004) presents a version of the Natural Approach where the only grammatical instruction congruent with the model's communicative prin-ciples is implicit. Grammatical rules are presented to students inductively by focusing their attention to recurrent linguistic patterns via carefully targeted activities.[2]

In addition to the explicit/implicit debate, the language of instruction has also been much discussed. Here again, specific hypotheses about learning, the overall model of instruction, as well as the students' level of pro-ficiency, constitute the parameters that determine the instructor's choice. To use concept-based learning again as an example, where a clear under-standing of the concepts coded by specific grammatical forms is viewed as providing the key to acquisition, grammatical presentation in the source language will be favored, because it maximizes the learner's chances of fully understanding the new concept. This position, however, may be modified if the students' proficiency in the target language is sufficient to enable them to fully understand the relevant concepts presented in that language. In the Natural Approach, on the other hand, where the processing of comprehensible input is viewed as the motor of acquisition (Krashen & Terrell 1983), the instructors will be more likely to use the target language to describe grammatical constructs (if they are described at all), in an attempt to provide additional comprehensible input.

This very brief exposition of the some of the issues the teaching of grammar in L2 raises should enable us to better understand precisely how the adoption of the CG conception of language might influence this ongoing debate. It should be clear, for example, that nothing in the model itself will direct the instructor toward explicit or implicit instruction. Such decisions will be made outside the CG principles. The adoption of the CG conception of language does not constitute a global teaching methodology, and can therefore not be expected to address the whole range of issues such methodologies address. It will clearly provide the most satisfactory results when used in conjunction with a proven model of instruction within which it will suggest useful directions for the overall conception of grammatical instruction, as well as the specific presentation of individual instructions. The next section briefly presents the CG model in order to illustrate the specific areas where its adoption may benefit language instruction.

3 CG and L2 instruction

A comprehensive overview of CG is obviously beyond the scope of this chapter (see Langacker 1987, 1991, 2000, for a detailed description of the model). This section merely introduces the tenets that most directly influence the presentation of grammar in a L2 classroom.

3.1 Meaning and construal

Perhaps the most fundamental position of CG concerns its attempt to capture the symbolic function of language, namely to allow the symbolization of conceptualizations by means of phonological sequences. A CG grammar takes the form of "a structured inventory of conventionalized linguistic units" (Langacker 2000, p. 8). Only three types of units are posited, namely phonological, semantic, and symbolic units. A symbolic unit consists in the symbolic association established between a semantic unit (its semantic pole) and a phonological unit (its phonological pole). Because symbolic units are by definition meaningful, the description of the meaning of an entity constitutes an essential aspect of a CG investigation. Meaning is equated with conceptualization, to be explicated in terms of cognitive processing. It is thus anthropomorphic and subjective, and includes, beside the objective properties of the described object, the way in which the conceptualizer chooses to present it. Each expression is characterized by the specific profile its presence imposes on a conceptual base, that is to say how precisely it structures that base. The exploration of the meaning of an expression thus consists in eliciting exactly how a given expression construes the scene it describes. For example, the meaning of *Tuesday* is characterized as the appropriate sub-section of our social organization of time. Because they present a different profile on the same base, two competing expressions express alternative construals of that base.

The centrality of construal to the meaning of linguistic expressions clearly points to their conventional nature, as well as to the central role of the speaker in the distribution of linguistic expressions in discourse. Langacker (2000, pp. 9–10 emphasis in the original) squarely places the speaker at the center of a "usage event":

> It is not the linguistic system per se that constructs and understands novel expressions, but rather the language user, who marshals for this purpose the full panoply of available resources. In addition to linguistic units, these resources include such factors as memory, planning, problem solving ability, general knowledge, short- and long-term goals, as well as full apprehension of the physical, social, cultural, and linguistic context. An actual instance of language use, resulting in all these factors, constitutes what I will call a **usage event**.

The central position of the speaker relative to the usage event she participates in clearly shows that the distribution of grammatical constructions in discourse is governed by the speaker's decision to express her conceptualization in specific ways rather than by properties inherent to the system. This might seem trivial, but section 4 will show that it critically shapes the kind of grammatical instruction students are exposed to. At this point, I will simply note that from the learner's perspective this position implies that the most successful integration of a specific expression into her panoply of linguistic resources comes from the observation of the "on-line" conditions that motivate its choice as well as from the knowledge of the specific parameters that guide the selection of competing constructions. Because language is largely a matter of conventionalized choice, maximal exposure to the conditions that favor the selection of a particular expression will in turn lead the students to exercising native-like decisions on their own.[3]

3.2 A structured inventory of conventionalized linguistic units

A direct consequence of the symbolic status of grammar is that the lexicon, morphology and syntax are strictly describable by means of symbolic units. They form a continuum which can not be naturally divided into separate components. Importantly for our purposes, this also applies to grammatical expressions. In the CG model, grammatical constructions have meaning, even though it is usually more abstract than that of lexical items. Langacker (2000, pp. 8–9) describes the presence in the system of the actually occurring expressions (the instances), and the rules that validate their use as follows (emphasis in the original):

In Cognitive Grammar, a language is described as a **structured inventory of conventional linguistic units**. The units (cognitive routines) comprising a speaker's linguistic knowledge are limited to semantic, phonological, and symbolic structures which are either directly manifested as part of actual expressions, or else emerge from such structures by the processes of abstraction (schematization) and categorization (this restriction is called the **content requirement**). In describing these units as an inventory, I am indicating the non-generative and non-constructive nature of a linguistic system. Linguistic knowledge is not conceived or modeled as an algorithmic device enumerating a well-defined set of formal objects, but simply as an extensive collection of semantic, phonological, and symbolic resources which can be brought to bear on language processing.

It follows from the symbolic status of linguistic expressions that all of them are meaningful regardless of their degree of complexity or abstraction. Grammatical constructions, in particular, are also symbolic in nature, only differing from other units by their greater level of abstraction. In CG, grammatical rules take the form of constructional schemas. These schemas can be viewed as templates that generalize over existing expressions and sanction their felicity. Importantly, they are also symbolic in nature, i.e. they have a semantic and a phonological pole. The content of these poles is, however, more abstract than that of the actually occurring expressions which instantiate them. Importantly, these rules or templates cohabitate in the grammar with actually occurring expressions they abstract over. The cohabitation of the schema (the rule) and the occurring expressions validated by the rule is illustrated in Fig. 17.1 by the rule of plural formation (-s) (from Langacker 1988, p. 131).

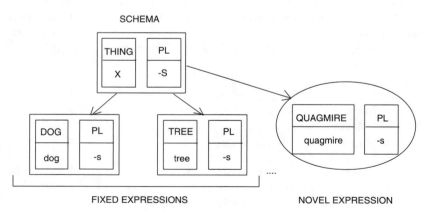

Figure 17.1 Plural formation.

437

Fig. 17.1 represents the cohabitation in the grammar of the schema (the rule), occurring expressions, and novel expressions. In the CG model, the generalization over a set of data (knowledge of the rule) is not incompatible with the specific learning of individual pieces of data. A schema and its instantiation represent two different facets of linguistic knowledge. Their coexistence in the grammar represents different ways for the speaker to access a complex but regular expression with unit status.

The symbolic position of CG presents two major advantages for L2 instructors. First, it allows them to teach syntax in a way similar to lexical items.[4] Syntax is not viewed as a particular level of organization but as a mere facet of their symbolic status. The specific form and syntactic behavior of an expression is motivated (at least partially) by its semantic organization, and thus inseparable from it. The spirit of the CG model is well captured by Wierzbicka (1988, p. 3) who writes: "Grammar is not semantically arbitrary. On the contrary, grammatical distinctions are motivated (in the synchronic sense) by semantic considerations; every grammatical construction is a vehicle of a certain semantic structure; and this is its raison d'être, and the criterion for determining its range of use." Just as the meaning of any lexical item is crucially invoked in learning its form, the semantic import of grammatical constructions constitutes the best insight as to its formal structure. This position provides the L2 instructor with a solid presentational methodology. Since the very form of these constructions represent the linguistic conventions of the specific construal of a conceptualized scene, the teaching of the constructions will investigate in detail precisely how each construction structures the scene it describes. A crucial facet of the presentation involves showing the intricate relation between the form of the expression and its semantic import.

The remainder of this section illustrates this position with an example from French. French causation/perception verbs can participate into two constructions that differ from each other in their word order. These constructions (respectively called VV and VOV in Achard 1996, 1998) are introduced in (1)–(4).

(1) *Marie a fait manger les enfants*
Mary has make-PART eat the children
"Mary made the children eat"

(2) **Marie a fait les enfants manger*
Mary has make-PART the children eat
"Mary made the children eat"

(3) *Marie a laissé les enfants partir*
Mary has let-PART the children leave
"Mary let the children leave"

(4) *Marie a laissé partir les enfants*
      Mary has let-PART leave the children
      "Mary let the children leave"

VV illustrated in (1) exhibits a puzzling discrepancy between the perceived semantic role of the causee (the children) with respect to the subordinate verb (eat), and its syntactic coding. The children perform the act of eating, even though they are forced to do so. In that sense, the noun phrase *les enfants* can be viewed as the logical subject of the verb *manger*. It is, however, realized syntactically as a direct object, as shown by its post-verbal position and its possible cliticization as the plural object pronoun *les* in *Marie les a fait manger* "Mary made them eat." VOV illustrated in (3) does not exhibit the same discrepancy because the logical subject of the infinitive precedes that infinitive. In Achard (1996, 1998), I argued that VV and VOV represent two alternative ways of structuring an induced/perceived scene, and that their specific form (their respective word order) reflects the specific construal each construction imposes on the scene. In a nutshell, VV structures the induced scene as the main subject's sole responsibility, even though the complement process is performed by another entity. Consequently, the causee is not viewed as the initiator of the subordinate process but as a reluctant participant. Its coding as a direct object reflects its non-agentive role. The particular form of the construction, i.e. the unexpected place and coding of the causee, directly follows from its semantics, that is to say the highly specific way in which it construes the induced scene. The specificity of that construal sets VV apart from other causative constructions which structure the induced scene differently, and thus have different syntactic forms.

With VOV, the form of the construction also reflects the construal it imposes on the perceived/induced scene. Even though the responsibility of the occurrence of the complement process ultimately resides in the main subject, the logical subject of the infinitive is nonetheless perceived as the energy source responsible to initiate (or at least sustain) that process. Its position before the verb that codes the process it is responsible for reflects its (limited) agentive role. The meaning of the constructions inter-acts with the semantics of the main verbs to yield the distribution pre-sented in (1)–(4). The semantics of *faire* "make" make it incompatible with VV because this verb in all its French contexts (unlike "make" in English) profiles the accomplishment of its main clause subject (see Achard 1998 for the evidence of this claim). With *laisser* "let" and the perception verbs, the choice of an expression is determined by the speaker's construal of the causee's role relative to the infinitival process. If the latter is viewed as the energy force that initiates it, VOV represents the most obvious choice. In the opposite case, VV stands to be selected.

The recognition of the meaning of the constructions provides several important advantages for the second language instructor. First and most obviously, the relationship between meaning and form (word order in our example) can easily be pointed out. More generally, the consideration of grammatical constructions as symbolic units enables the instructor to pedagogically treat structural learning (the learning of grammatical constructions) in the same fashion as lexical learning. In CG, there are no special devices that interpret grammatical forms and remain invisible to teaching. Nor are there specific rules that yield linguistic expressions as their output. Rather, all linguistic expressions, regardless of their level of complexity, represent a form/meaning pair, with a semantic and phonological pole. Each one is individually learned, and therefore amenable to the same presentational pedagogical techniques.[5] To come back to the French constructions illustrated in (1)–(4), because VV and VOV are meaningful, their form can be accessed through their meaning in a way identical to the meaning of any lexical unit. Activities can thus be designed where students learn to associate VV with situations of low levels of agentivity of the causee, and VOV with situations where the causee is more agentive toward the infinitival process. This pedagogical approach is exactly identical to the one used to present two competing lexical items.

Finally, we can note that this construal-based analysis affords the instructor more flexibility than the more popular approach based on the necessary semantic pairing between verbs and complement forms. VV is usually taught in French by pointing to its necessary occurrence following *faire*, as if this pairing were a property of the system. In the case of *faire*, this approach is quite successful, but the usual specification that this construction is merely optional following *laisser* and the perception verbs provides little help for the students to guide their own usage. Section 4 will consider in more detail the advantages of construal-based approaches versus the more traditional rules stated in terms of co-occurrence restrictions.

3.3 A *usage-based* model

The organization of the vast array of form/meaning pairings that constitute the grammar of a language has been called "usage-based" because: "Substantial importance is given to the actual use of the linguistic system and a speaker's knowledge of its use; the grammar is held responsible for a speaker's knowledge of the full range of linguistic conventions, regardless of whether those conventions can be subsumed under more general statements" (Langacker 1987, p. 494). Importantly for foreign language instructors, the presentation of the "rule" of a construction can never substitute for the presentation of actually occurring instances of that rule, since the rule merely captures the commonalities individual examples share.[6] The usage-based conception of CG is crucial for second language instructors because it posits that learners will most benefit from actual exposure to "real" instances of language use. It is only through exposure to the situations in which the natives select specific constructions that they can gain the necessary confidence and expertise to make similar choices themselves in comparable situations.

4 Teaching construal

The central role of the speaker in the selection of a specific construction makes radical implications for the way in which language instructors should present the distribution of grammatical rules. Although most practitioners would dismiss this focus on the speaker's role as trivial (everyone knows speakers choose what they say!), it seriously alters the way in which grammatical constructions have traditionally been presented. The most casual glance at language manuals suffices to reveal that the grammatical rules offered to L2 learners are usually presented as a property of the target linguistic system, and not a result of the speaker's choice. For example students of Romance languages are taught that the subjunctive mood should be used following a specific list of verbs and adverbials. Beside its specific morphological shape, learning the subjunctive mood therefore amounts to learning the lexical items it occurs with. The fact that a given verb takes the subjunctive is viewed as a lexical property of that verb. Selectional restrictions are thus marked in the lexicon, and the students learn them at the same time as the verb's meaning. Such practices are deeply entrenched in our pedagogical history. They also make the rules easy to state (if not to follow) because they yield a stable system of co-occurring expressions that can be committed to memory. Difficulties only arise when learners become aware of the numerous exceptions that creep into the supposedly regular system, or when the same lexical item occurs in multiple contexts [see examples (3) and (4) for example].

This "system-based" statement of rules is inconsistent with the CG emphasis on the centrality of construal to linguistic production. Recall that it is not the system per se that is responsible for the form of specific constructions just by being in a certain way, but the shape of novel expressions is predominantly determined by speaker choice. For the instructor, focusing on the speaker rather than on the system involves the shift from teaching set patterns of lexical associations to teaching the conventionalized way of matching certain expressions to certain situations, as well as the flexibility of using the available alternatives to express specific semantic nuances. It represents a thorny pedagogical challenge because of the inherent flexibility of construal. The methodological difficulty consists in providing clear guidelines that teach students how to exercise their linguistic choice. In addition to making available to students the whole range of conventionalized options (the target forms), the instructor also

~~needs to be able to show them the precise parameters that determine native usage of each particular construction.~~

It should be noted at this point that from a pedagogical standpoint, two aspects of construal need to be treated separately, especially at the beginning level of instruction. As the following section illustrates, some linguistic choices are socially conventionalized and therefore stable. They represent a privileged entry point into explaining the notion of choice to students because article selection clearly reflects culturally rich conceptual constructs (often organized in the form of schemas) that can easily be identified. The second aspect of construal concerns the more flexible, on-line choices made by specific speakers as they react to the particularities of a given situation. These are more difficult to approach systematically, but should easily be accessible to students if the more stable choices have been well understood. The mastery of on-line creativity represents the ultimate attainment for the L2 learners who not only have incorporated the conventions of the target language but feel confident enough to extend them creatively to convey specific nuances. This chapter is more particularly concerned with the more socially stable linguistic choices, but it will also briefly consider how those conventionalized choices provide useful entry points into the more creative aspects of on-line conceptualization.

4.1 The distribution of French definite and partitive articles

This section illustrates the CG tenets presented above with the example of the competition between the definite and partitive articles in French.[7] More specifically, it shows that a grammatical presentation of the distribution of the two articles in terms of the construal each of them imposes on the entity it precedes is better suited to account for the complexity and flexibility of attested usage than the more traditional rules stated in terms of the co-occurrence restrictions between specific verbs and articles. Unless otherwise specified, the data used in this section come from a corpus of journalistic prose (articles from *Le Monde* and *Agence France Press*) and literary works from the ARTFL database.[8]

In addition to the definite *le, la, les* "the," and indefinite *un, une, des* "a," French has a series of partitive articles *du, de la*, which are often translated in English by unstressed "some," and indicate some idea of quantity. In the overwhelming majority of beginning French textbooks, these articles are formally introduced in the chapter thematically devoted to food and meal preparation. The presentational strategy the authors recommend invariably emphasizes the co-occurrence of a given article form with specific verbs. For example, in *Deux Mondes*, the French textbook that implements the principles of the Natural Approach (Krashen

& Terrell 1983), the students are given the following advice: (Terrell et al. 2001, p. 245 emphasis in the original):

> To choose the appropriate article, look at the kind of verb used in the sentence. With verbs describing likes or dislikes, such as **aimer, adorer, detester, préférer**, use the definite article because you are talking about things in a general sense. Nathalie **aime** beaucoup **les** carottes et **les** petits pois, mais elle **déteste les** épinards "Nathalie likes carrots and peas, but she detests spinach." Je n'**aime** pas **le** café fort "I don't like strong coffee."
>
> On the other hand, if the verb deals with having, obtaining, or consuming, use **du, de la, de l', or des,** because you are talking about some amount of a thing. Such verbs include **avoir, acheter, manger, boire, prendre**, and many others. Les Français **boivent du** café après le dîner "the French drink coffee after dinner." Nous **mangeons de la** pizza tous les vendredi soir "We eat pizza every Friday night."

This quote is addressed to the students, and can therefore be interpreted as a helpful suggestion to take advantage of a general tendency. However, the instructor receives similar advice as to the best kind of presentational technique to use to present article distribution (Terrell et al. 2001, p. 245): "Point out that it is the verb of which the given noun is the object that determines the article choice, e.g., *j'aime le café*, but *j'aime boire du café tous les matins.*"

In a way characteristic of the pedagogical practice observed earlier, *Deux Mondes* presents article selection as a property of individual verbs. This position is clearly untenable in the face of the multitude of examples one can easily find in written and spoken usage alike. The examples in (5)–(10) all violate the presumed co-occurrence restriction between the *manger* "eat" type verbs and the definite article.[9]

(5) *L'invasion des termites. Les petits insectes qui mangent le bois infestent progressivement tout le territoire français.*
"The invasion of termites. The little insects that eat (the) wood are progressively infesting the whole French country."

(6) *Ou bien il est ce sage prisonnier qui attend l'heure de boire la ciguë.*
"Or he is this quiet prisoner waiting for his time to drink the hemlock."

(7) *Et puis, voici trois mois, un paquet est arrivé, du même expéditeur, avec des chocolats et des cigarettes. J'ai fumé les cigarettes et mon voisin de cellule a mangé les chocolats.*
"And then three months ago, a package arrived from the same sender with chocolate and cigarettes. I smoked the cigarettes and my cellmate ate the chocolate."

(8) *Les rats d'argent pendus à la treille qui mangent les raisins sans cesser de me regarder.*

"The silver rats hanging from the vines that eat the grapes while staring at me."

(9) *Les céréales devenant moins chères, les cultivateurs seront tentés de les valoriser, notamment en faisant manger le blé par les vaches ou par les poules.*

"Since cereals are getting cheaper, farmers will be tempted to increase their value, specifically by having the cows and the chickens eat (the) wheat."

(10) *Combien étaient partis, qui s'étaient cassé les reins, faute de ressources suffisantes, et qu'on avait vus revenir au pays, bien contents de manger la soupe, et de bêcher les vignes, comme les camarades.*

"How many had left, who failed for lack of sufficient resources, and came back to their village, happy to be eating (the) soup and tilling the vineyards like everyone else."

(11) *Dom Felletin lâchera ses novices ou nous les amènera et s'il ne déjeune point, il boira au moins le café avec nous.*

"Dom Felletin will abandon his novices or he will bring them to us and if he does not have lunch, he will at least drink (the) coffee with us."

In each of the examples in (5)–(11), the definite article occurs instead of the partitive one would have expected from *Deux Mondes*' selectional restrictions. The collocation *boire le café* in (11) is particularly surprising since *boire* is specifically pointed out as requiring the partitive. It is worth noting that the partitive would be possible (resulting in different meanings) in all the examples. The article selection illustrated in (5)–(11) can therefore not be treated as exceptional, or dismissed as belonging to arcane expressions that the students will not encounter until much later in their studies. Rather, the presence of the definite article reflects a choice to construe the entity coded in the verbal complement in a certain way. The role of the instructor thus consists in making clear to the students what specific construals the presence of the partitive and definite articles respectively reveal. In a nutshell, the students need to appreciate the semantic difference between *boire du café* "drink some café" and *boire le café* "drink (the) coffee."[10]

The first step in explaining article distribution in terms of speaker choice involves the recognition of the meaning of both finite and partitive articles, characterized by the way in which they relate the object nominal to the speech situation.[11] The basic meaning of French articles is well known. The definite article marks generic nouns (as in *J'aime le café*), as well as nouns which are judged identifiable by the hearer. The partitive does not focus on the identifiability of the nominal but on the fact that it represents a certain quantity of the substance referred to by the nominal (*Je bois du café*). Competition between the two articles arises when a given situation can be construed in two alternative ways, namely when a nominal can be considered with respect to its identifiability, or with respect to its mere quantity. In certain contexts, even with the verbs whose lexical meaning usually favor the construal of the nominal as a quantity, some discourse conditions render the alternative construal possible, where the identifiability of the nominal is emphasized. The second step in the pedagogical exposition of article distribution consists in identifying these conditions and illustrating them during specific activities. Fortunately for language instructors, most of these conditions are fairly systematic and convenient to point out. The remainder of this section considers some examples.

The regular uses of the definite article often resist the presence of the *manger* type verbs. This is illustrated in (5) with general statements.[12] Also, entities that can easily be identified can be followed by the definite article even if the verb that they are complement of usually occur with partitives. Unique entities, in particular, confirm this tendency. For example, *boire la ciguë* "drink the hemlock" in (6) is a synonym for officially administered poison. The (necessarily finite) quantity ingested is not viewed as relevant. The expression should therefore be treated as a separate lexical item. This does not represent an isolated case. Other unique nominals also are most frequently preceded by the definite article with *boire*, as illustrated in (12)–(14):[13]

(12) *L'air est frais, ineffablement vif et pur: on croit respirer à même l'azur du ciel, et boire l'ambroisie comme un dieu.*
"The air is fresh, constantly vivifying and pure. It is like breathing the very blue of the sky and drinking (the) ambrosia like a god."

(13) *Il cessa de boire l'air, comme s'il lui était devenu irrespirable.*
"He stopped drinking the air, as if it had become unbreathable to him."

(14) *Le progrès ressemble « à cet horrible dieu païen qui ne voulait boire le nectar que dans le crâne des ennemis tués ».*
"Progress resembles this horrible pagan god who only wanted to drink (the) nectar in the skulls of killed enemies."

Other easily identifiable entities include those that have been previously mentioned, as well as those that can be easily inferred from the immediate context. These cases are respectively illustrated in (7) and (8)–(9). In (7), the previous mention of *chocolats* "chocolates" justifies the presence of the definite article. In (8), *les raisins* "the grapes" are clearly inferable from the presence of the vines. Similarly, *le blé* "the wheat" is accessible in (9),

445

because it represents an instance of the previously mentioned cereal category.

A particular aspect of background knowledge concerns the presence of the entities considered relative to various cultural schemas, and therefore their identifiability within those schemas. The number of those schemas is certainly far too large for an exhaustive survey to be attempted, but I will concentrate on two of them related to food and beverages. The first one concerns the kinds of prepared dishes available in specific cultures. These dishes are well established within their communities and can therefore easily be identified in a store or restaurant, as illustrated in (15):

(15) *Mais en semaine, il faut revenir plus souvent que Georgette ne voudrait à des plats relativement simples, comme le poulet rôti, le pigeon aux petits pois, le gigot d'agneau, le modeste rostbeef.*
"During the week, however, we need to come back more often than Georgette would like to relatively simple dishes, such as (the) roasted chicken, (the) pigeon with green peas, (the) leg of lamb, (the) modest roast beef."

The dishes in (15) are all part of a socially recognized category of "relatively simple" dishes. They are classics, readily identifiable by anyone living in the community. The presence of the definite article reflects their possible identification in a well-known schema of culinary dishes. Some of those dishes have a particular status. Soup, for example, stands out as the symbol of poor and unsophisticated rural life. For instance, *manger la soupe* "eat (the) soup" in (10) can be viewed as a separate lexical item that codes the kind of life the people who had attempted to leave their rural environment ultimately had to settle for. In this context, the use of the partitive would be impossible. Some dishes acquire further notoriety within the specific context of family traditions. This is illustrated in (16) where this notoriety is formally recognized by the quotation marks that surround the famous dish:

(16) *Dînez-vous à la maison? Les Barrès désirent vous voir. Nous aurons "le" poulet rôti.*
"Will you be dining with us? The Barrès would like to see you. We'll be having 'the' roasted chicken."

Finally, it should be noted that the presence of the definite article alone is sufficient to place the dish considered among the culturally determined schema of food preparation. This is illustrated in (17):

(17) *Le sultan, – personne en Europe ne connaît le sultan, monsieur le colonel, personne! Vous-même, qui lui avez été présenté un vendredi,*

*après le sélamlick, et qui avez mangé l'iftar au palais, un soir de
ramadan, vous ne soupçonnez pas l'homme qu'il est.*
"The sultan—No one in Europe knows the sultan, Colonel, no
one! Even you, who have been introduced to him, on a Friday
after Selamlick, and who ate (the) iftar at the palace one evening
during Ramadan, you don't suspect what kind of a man he is."

In (17), even though the reader may not be familiar with Middle Eastern
customs, the presence of the definite article preceding iftar is sufficient to
present the latter as a well-accepted part of the local culinary institutions.

A second conventionalized schema concerns the beverages French
people enjoy at certain times of the day. For instance, *boire le café* in
(11) refers to much more than drinking coffee to encompass the ritualistic
behavior that surrounds the drinking act at different times of the day.
The expression usually covers breakfast time, as well as the periods that
immediately follow lunch and dinner. For example, in (11), the communicative emphasis of the sentence is less on the liquid ingested than on the
time period during which Dom Felletin will be able to join his guests. In
that sense, *boire le café* is much more restricted than *boire du café*. It is also
best analyzed as a separate lexical item that codes a specific part of a large
food and drink schema in which people drink certain beverages at different times of the day. This ritual doesn't only involve coffee. The other
beverages that also mark the social rhythm of the French day also appear
in the same Def. Art. + Noun construction. Some of them are illustrated
in (18)–(22):

(18) *Boire . . . le champagne, ça fait drôle quand on n'en a pas l'habitude,
c'est léger, et puis c'est lourd.*
"To drink . . . (the) champagne; it feels strange when one is not
used to it, it is light, and then it is heavy."

(19) *Dès qu'ils furent devenus les maîtres, on les vit envahir le beau
jardin. Ils y venaient boire l'anisette, cassaient les tables et les bancs,
couvraient d'inscriptions obscènes les murs blancs des kiosques
moresques.*
"As soon as they had become the masters, they invaded the
beautiful garden. They came here to drink (the) aniseed, broke
the tables and benches, and covered the white walls of the
Moorish kiosks with obscene graffiti."

(20) *Il est avec sa tête dans le soleil auquel il n'est plus habitué et il faut
qu'il s'y réhabitue; car c'est beau, mais ça fait mal, et c'est bon, mais
ça brûle. C'est comme quand on fait boire la goutte aux petits
enfants . . .*
"He is with his head in the sun to which he is no longer used,
and he needs to get used to it again; because it is beautiful, but it

hurts, and it is good, but it burns. It is as when you let little children drink (the) liquor . . ."

(21) *Ce lieu harmonieux fut construit pour le plaisir des membres du « syndicat du commerce des haricots et du riz », qui, sans doute, par les nuits de printemps, y viennent boire le thé en regardant briller le bord inférieur de la lune.*

"This harmonious place was built for the pleasure of the members of the "rice and beans trade union," who, most likely during spring nights, come here to drink (the) tea while watching the lower edge of the moon shine."

(22) *« Nous ne sommes pas venus jusqu'ici pour prendre le thé », déclare . . . Carlos Vivoli, régisseur de l'estancia . . . El Maiten, . . . « Nous avons une mentalité d'hommes d'affaires »*

"We didn't come here to drink (the) tea, declares . . . Carlos Vivoli, the manager of the El Maiten ranch . . . 'We think like businessmen'."

The beverages presented in (18)–(22) all correspond to certain times of the French day. Just like *boire le café*, the expressions include the social circumstances that surround the drinking act. For example, *boire (ou prendre) le champagne* in (18) can broadly be construed as celebrating a happy occasion. *L'anisette* in (19) represents the prototypical drink one enjoys during the *apéritif* (i.e., before a meal). *Prendre l'apéritif* represents the social gathering that precedes a meal along with the drinks that are traditionally drunk. *La goutte* in (20) represents the generic term for a post-meal alcohol. Finally, *boire le thé* in (18) refers to a late afternoon small meal during which the warm drink is accompanied by cakes or pastries. The expression can also be used to describe a civil gathering, as in (22). In (22), there is no reference to drinks of any sort. The expression *prendre le thé* strictly refers to the atmosphere of the gathering. The speaker deliberately opposes their business-like attitude to an overly civil tea party.

It seems clear that the data presented in (5)–(22) as well as other numerous examples not mentioned here do not constitute exceptions to a rule of co-occurrence. Rather, they illustrate cases where despite the lexical semantics of the main verb, some aspect of the situation favors the construal of the nominal as an identifiable entity. The overview of these situations where the definite and partitive articles compete is by no means complete but it should suffice to enable us to establish some pedagogical guidelines that will help the students understand the motivation for the presence of the definite article in these unexpected cases.

4.2 *Pedagogical guidelines*

The pedagogical challenge of teaching construal consists in placing students in situations where native speakers are the most likely to exercise a specific choice, so that they can make the same choices the natives make, and enjoy the same flexibility of expression. With respect to article distribution, it is clear that not all the contexts where the examples presented in (5)–(22) occur are equally approachable from the early stages of language learning. An important part of teaching construal therefore consists in selecting the right presentational sequencing of the relevant environments, so that the linguistic choices they motivate appear as transparent as possible to the students.

Perhaps the best place to start is when article selection reflects the presence of a visible cultural schema, or in other words a highly institutionalized social practice. Cultural schemas constitute strong pedagogical assets because they are both meaningful (hence culturally rich) and easily teachable. Communicative activities can be designed to link each *manger/ boire* + definite article expression to the culturally marked episodes which it codes. As a result of this strategy, the students will associate the whole expression (*prendre le café* for example) to a specific social act, and not analyze the verb and article combination as an expected and confusing sequence. Successful activities will focus on the context of the eating/ drinking episode, namely the rhythm of a person's day and its social circumstances rather than on what is actually consumed. For example, a guessing game can be organized with two students working in pairs. One of them reads off a specific set of circumstances that surround the social activity someone is involved in, without mentioning any beverage. The other student guesses what that activity is. A possible sequence could be as follows. Student 1: *M. Dumas est au bar. Il parle avec ses amis. Il est 11 heures et demie du matin* "Mr. Dumas is in a bar, he is speaking with his friends, it is 11:30 a.m." Student 2: *Il prend l'apéritif* "He is taking a drink before lunch."

The same strategy can be followed in the case of other schemas that motivate the use of the definite article with consumption verbs such as a restaurant menu, a shopping list, or a list of regional specialties. The basic idea is to narrow the context of the activity in such a way that it facilitates the identification of the entities considered. For example, menus can be passed to students who are required to order from the selection they propose, hence justifying the use of the definite article. Note that in such tight context (and yet meaningful if the activity is done properly), an answer such as *C'est sur la liste* "It's on the list" to a student's query as to why *la* and not *de la* is used constitutes a legitimate grammatical explanation. I will not present a whole lesson here, but the idea is to associate a particular linguistic usage to its communicative function to show that conveying that function represents the meaning of the construction. Attention to meaning necessarily entails attention to form, because students need to have access to the proper form in order to convey the intended meaning. Teaching the whole range of article distribution is accomplished by targeting separately each condition where the uses of the partitive and definite articles are in competition, clearly identifying the motivating factors for the presence of the definite, and integrating the activities designed to enhance their awareness to the general flow of the lessons.[14]

As indicated earlier, this teaching strategy only addresses the most stable aspects of construal. However, it also provides a starting point from which the other aspect, namely the individual flexibility speakers enjoy in their linguistic expression, can also be approached. Native-like construal flexibility should only constitute a pedagogical focus for the intermediate and advanced levels, but it can be started earlier by using the more stable configuration presented in this section as a springboard.

Speakers routinely minimally depart from well-established usage to express the subtle nuances of their conceptualizations. Consider for instance the examples in (23)–(25):

(23) *Je ne m'ennuie pas, dit-il. Le matin à sept heures et demie on a le café au lait. Pas mauvais. On s'habille; on circule un peu, puis on dit: tout le monde au lit pour la visite du docteur.*
"I am not bored, he said. In the morning, at seven thirty, we have (the) coffee and milk. Not bad. We get dressed, we walk about a little, then someone says: Everyone in bed the doctor is coming."

(24) *Et le soir, pour causer de ce projet, Raspoutine venait quelquefois boire le vin chez Youssoupof.*
"And in the evening, to discuss this project, Rasputin sometimes came to Youssoupof's to drink (the) wine."

(25) *Un pauvre khani nous fournit du lait de chèvre et un café buvable. A-t-il beaucoup changé depuis le passage de Chateaubriand? J'avais mangé l'ours et le chien sacré avec les sauvages; je partageai depuis le repas des bédouins, mais je n'ai jamais rien rencontré de comparable à ce premier khani de Laconie.*
"A poor khani gave us goat milk and some drinkable coffee. Has he changed a lot since Chateaubriand came here? I had eaten (the) bear and (the) holy dog with savages; I had since shared the Bedouins' meals, but I had never experienced anything that compares to this first khani in Laconia."

The presence of the definite article in the examples in (23)–(25) cannot be accounted for in the same manner as earlier, because none of the entities that follow the article squarely fits in any of the previously discussed schemas. Neither the *café au lait* in (23) not the wine in (24) corresponds to one of the socially marked beverages discussed in the preceding section. In both these examples, however, the author chooses to depict them as such. The desired effect is to present the beverages as habitual, stable, and expected elements of the character's life, in order to enhance the feeling of orderliness and regularity the reader can expect from life in a nursing home in (23), or the life of Rasputin in (24). Similarly in (25), the identifiability of the bear and sacred dog cannot be imputed to their repetitive occurrence in the character's diet but to their enhanced status in the social organization of the community the character visited. The regular status of these unusual dishes enhances the exoticism of the author's past experiences, and thus further heightens the memorable nature of the dinner he is currently describing.

The strategy of the authors in (23)–(25) clearly consists in extending the usage of the definite article in well-attested situations to present their conceptualizations in a specific way. Their creative usage therefore minimally departs from established convention. The presentation of such departures to the students who already master the well-established uses will serve to give them a possible range of departure and enable them to gage their own budding creativity. The instructor's role in the process is to carefully choose the examples to present, point out the ways in which they extend conventional usage, and evaluate the communicative results. It is only after sufficient exposure to these creative examples that they will feel confident enough to test the bounds of their own linguistic flexibility.

5 Conclusion

This chapter argued that the adoption of the Cognitive Grammar principles offers two major advantages for the L2 instructor. Firstly, because CG recognizes the symbolic value of grammatical constructions, it provides a way of presenting their meaning to the students. This meaning can in turn be used to motivate their specific form as well as distinguish them from other related constructions. For example, the specific meaning of the two French constructions VV and VOV was shown to motivate their respective word order. The consideration of the meaning of grammatical constructions also allows the instructor to teach lexical and grammatical expressions in similar ways. Because the grammar of a language is strictly composed of a structured inventory of symbolic units, there is no a priori distinction between the teaching of grammar and that of lexical elements. This is particularly welcome because it provides a way of teaching grammar in ways compatible with the principles of most communicative models of instruction.

Secondly, by placing the speaker in the center of the communicative act, L2 instructors can develop methodologies to teach usage, that is to say the flexibility native speakers enjoy for the linguistic description of their conceptualizations. This method was shown to provide better results than the often used lexical association models which treat linguistic distribution as a property of the target system. The distribution of French partitive and definite articles was shown to be determined by the competing motivations to represent the conceived entity as a mere quantity, or as identifiable within a specific domain. The examination of corpora revealed stable socially determined schemas that naturally account for the unexpected presence of the definite article with verbs that seem to demand its partitive counterpart. Finally, these stable configurations were shown to represent valuable pedagogical stepping stones to introduce students to the less stable situations where natives extend the conventional use of the articles to express the subtle semantic nuances of their conceptualizations. By teaching usage, and thus placing the students in the very set of circumstances that motivates the natives' choices, the instructor enables them to fully exercise their own growing expressivity in the target language.

Notes

1 The concept of "usage" as it described in Cognitive Grammar should not be confused with the use of the same term in Widdowson (1978 Chapter 1). Widdowson (1978, p. 3) distinguishes between a language user's knowledge of linguistic "usage," namely her "knowledge of abstract linguistic rules," and her ability to achieve her communicative purposes, which reflects her awareness of language "use." The two terms are contrasted in the following fashion: "Usage, then, is one aspect of performance, that aspect which makes evident the extent to which the language user demonstrates his knowledge of linguistic rules. Use is another aspect of performance: that which makes evident the extent to which the language user demonstrates his ability to use his knowledge of linguistic rules for effective communication." In CG, "usage" refers to specific language events, which reflects at the same time the speaker's knowledge of grammatical and communicative conventions.
2 For recent analyses of the multiple facets of the explicit/implicit debate, see Norris and Ortega (2000), Hulstijn (2005), as well as the other papers in the special review of Studies in Second Language Acquisition (27, 2) devoted to the issue.
3 The centrality of usage events to the CG view of language make this model particularly congruent with the input models of language learning. See Achard (2004) for a discussion of the natural fit between CG and the Natural Approach from that perspective.
4 For related work on formulaic sequences in instructed SLA, see Schmitt (2004).
5 Since not all the rules in a language can be taught explicitly, the instructor will use her experience to determine which ones deserve to be specifically targeted for presentation.
6 As indicated earlier, the CG model is neutral as to the implicit or explicit statement of the rule. The usage-based conception, however, clearly favors an inductive presentation of grammatical constructions where the awareness of the general pattern emerges from exposure to numerous instantiations.
7 Teaching (and learning) articles is notoriously difficult in any language. For

example, Gass and Selinker (2000, p. 323) claim that: "The English article system [. . .] appears to be virtually impermeable to instruction."

8 The use of corpora in this chapter is restricted to the analysis of the different environments where the definite article unexpectedly occurs with verbs that are usually followed by partitives. Because they provide an instant slice of linguistic usage, corpora also represent valuable assets in the L2 classroom, but their use might cause some difficulties. First, some students might not feel sufficiently confident to be exposed to "real" instances of language use without the necessary help from the appropriate context. Secondly, instructors might wonder how to present the attested forms in a way that best fosters the induction of the relevant generalizations. Both learners and native corpora are well attested in the L2 classroom (Granger, Hung & Petch-Tyson 2002 for example), but I will leave their integration within the CG guidelines for grammatical instruction for further research.

9 The constraint most severely violated in the observed data concerns the verbs *acheter* "buy," *manger* "eat," *boire* "drink," and *prendre* "take" with the partitive article. The other one, namely the necessary occurrence of the definite article following the preference verbs, is not so blatantly violated in the corpus considered. However, created examples such as *Moi, ce que j'aime bien, c'est de la confiture avec du pain!* "Me, what I really like is (some) jam with (some) bread" (Achard 2004) show that it can also be violated.

10 The need for the students to understand the meaning difference between such expressions as *boire du café* versus *boire le café* for example is particularly important in the Natural Approach because this method places such strong emphasis on input. The instructor is expected to use the widest possible range of comprehensible expressions in her speech in order to enrich the students' understanding of a given domain. When talking about drinks and socializing, the students are thus likely to hear both *j'aime boire du café* and *j'aime boire le café*. Although their general understanding of the message may not be affected, they may be confused, or simply miss the cultural dimension of the meaning distinction between the two forms (to be considered shortly).

11 An exhaustive characterization of the meaning of both articles is well beyond the scope of this chapter. The remainder of this section merely attempts to show that the flexible notion of speaker construal can be presented systematically, and that students can be pedagogically placed in situations that mirror those in which native speakers predictably exercise specific choices.

12 Other examples of general statement include the following:

(i) *un mouton, s'il mange les arbustes, il mange aussi les fleurs?*
"a sheep, if it eats (the) shrubs, does it also eat (the) flowers?"

(ii) *Asseyez-vous, n'ayez pas peur. Je ne mange pas les petits garçons.*
"Sit down, don't be afraid. I do not eat (the) little boys."

However, other general statements behave differently. Consider for example:

(iii) *Tous les chats boivent du /*le lait*
"All cats drink (some) (*the) milk."

The distinction between these different statements involves different parameters, such as, among others, the respective topicality of the subject and object of the *manger/boire* verb. It will not be considered any further here.

13 When *la ciguë* "the hemlock" is not used in this particular sense but as a mere dangerous substance ingested by accident, the partitive is most likely to be selected, as illustrated in (i):

(i) *Il était mort de longtemps. On a su, parce qu'il en avait encore des brins dans sa petite main, qu'il avait mangé de la ciguë.*
"He had been dead for a long time. We could tell, because he still had some blades in his little hand that he had eaten some hemlock."

14 The success of this activity depends on its integration in the general course of the lesson. For a discussion of the pedagogical integration of grammatical activities into a Natural Approach lesson, see Achard (2004).

Bibliography

Achard, M. (1996). Two Causation/Perception Constructions in French. *Cognitive Linguistics* 7: 315–357.

Achard, M. (1998). *Representation of Cognitive Structures: Syntax and Semantics of French Sentential Complements.* Berlin: Mouton de Gruyter.

Achard, M. (2004). Grammatical Instruction in the Natural Approach: A Cognitive Grammar View. In Achard & Niemeier: 165–194.

Doughty, C., & Williams, J. (1998). *Focus on Form in Classroom Second Language Acquisition.* Cambridge and New York: Cambridge University Press.

Ellis, R. (2002). The Place of Grammar Instruction in the Second/Foreign Curriculum. In E. Hinkel & S. Fotos (Eds.), *New Perspectives on Grammar Teaching in Second Language Classrooms.* Mahwah, NJ: Lawrence Erlbaum Associates: 17–34.

Gass, S., & Selinker, L. (2000). *Second Language Acquisition: An Introductory Course.* Second edition. Mahwah, NJ: Lawrence Erlbaum Associates.

Granger, S., Hung, J., & Petch-Tyson, S. (Eds.). (2002). *Computer Learner Corpora, Second Language Acquisition and Foreign Language Teaching.* Amsterdam and Philadelphia: John Benjamins.

Grundy, P. (2004). The Figure/Ground Gestalt and Language Teaching Methodology. In Achard & Niemeier: 119–142.

Hinkel, E., & Fotos, S. (2002). *New Perspectives on Grammar Teaching in Second Language Classrooms.* Mahwah, NJ: Lawrence Erlbaum Associates.

Hulstijn, J. (2005). Theoretical and Empirical Issues in the Study of Implicit and Explicit Second Language Learning: Introduction. *Studies in Second Language Acquisition* 27, 2: 129–140.

Krashen, S., & Terrell, T. D. (1983). *The Natural Approach: Language Acquisition in the Classroom.* San Francisco: Alemany Press.

Langacker, R. W. (1987). *Foundations of Cognitive Grammar.* Vol. 1: *Theoretical Prerequisites.* Stanford: Stanford University Press.

Langacker, R. W. (1988). A Usage-Based Model. In B. Rudzka-Ostyn (Ed.), *Topics in Cognitive Linguistics.* Amsterdam and Philadelphia: John Benjamins: 127–161.

Langacker, R. W. (1991). *Foundations of Cognitive Grammar.* Vol. 2: *Descriptive Application.* Stanford: Stanford University Press.

Langacker, R. W. (2000). A Dynamic Usage-Based Model. In M. Barlow & S. Kemmer (Eds.), *Usage-Based Models of Language.* Stanford, CSLI: 1–63.

Nassaji, H., & Fotos, S. (2004). Current Developments in Research on the Teaching of Grammar. *Annual Review of Applied Linguistics* 24, 126–145.

Negueruela, E. (2003). *Systemic-Theoretical Instruction and L2 Development: A*

Sociocultural Approach to Teaching-Learning and Researching L2 Learning. Unpublished Doctoral Dissertation: The Pennsylvania State University.

Negueruela, E., & Lantolf, J. P.. (2006). Concept-Based Pedagogy and The Acquisition of L2 Spanish. In R. Salaberry & B. A. Lafford (Eds.), *The State of The Art of Teaching Spanish: From Research to Praxis.* Georgetown University Press: 79–102.

Norris, J., & Ortega, L. (2000). Effectiveness of L2 Instruction: A Research Synthesis and Quantitative Meta-analysis. *Language Learning* 50: 417–528.

Schmitt, N. (Ed.). (2004). *Formulaic Sequences, Acquisition, Processing, and Use.* Amsterdam and Philadephia: John Benjamins.

Swain, M., & Lapkin, S. (1989). Canadian Immersion and Adult Second Language Teaching: What's the Connection? *The Modern Language Journal* 73: 150–159.

Terrell, T. et al. (2001). *Deux Mondes. A Communicative Approach* 4th edition. McGraw Hill Publishers.

VanPatten, B., Williams, J., Rott, S., & Overstreet, M. (2004). *Form-Meaning Connections in Second Language Acquisition.* Mahwah, NJ: Lawrence Erlbaum Associates.

Widdowson, H. G. (1978). *Teaching Language as Communication.* Oxford University Press.

Wierzbicka, A. (1988). *The Semantics of Grammar.* Amsterdam/Philadelphia: John Benjamins.

18

COGNITIVE LINGUISTICS AND SECOND LANGUAGE INSTRUCTION

Andrea Tyler

1 Introduction

During the past 15 years there has generally been a move away from attempts to apply theoretical models of language to issues in second language (L2) pedagogy. Attention has focused on issues of methodology, such as the usefulness of implicit versus explicit instruction, with little regard for the underlying model of language being assumed. In large part this is because the predominant linguistic paradigms have been based on highly abstract, non-usage-based models that offered L2 teachers little in the way of insightful, accessible presentations of grammar or lexis (Larsen-Freeman, 1996). L2 teachers are often hesitant to explore new theoretical approaches. In many cases, even the most cogent theoretical analysis is likely to be seen as having little use to L2 researchers and teachers who are unfamiliar with the theoretical framework or unable to make links between the theoretical analysis and effective teaching materials. Thus, one of the most central challenges for applied cognitive linguists is to provide accessible, precise explanations of various linguistic phenomena to nontheoreticians. A key goal of the present work is to provide a cognitive linguistic presentation of the English modal verbs that is accessible to L2 teachers and to offer evidence that such applications of the theory can form the basis for L2 research and teaching materials.

No matter what method of language teaching one employs, the teacher is best served by a clear, accurate understanding of how grammar and lexis are structured. Even in the most inductive approaches, a fuller understanding of language on the part of the teacher is vital to material and curriculum design. And, as all practicing language teachers know, learners inevitably ask for explanations of various grammar points; the teacher needs to be ready to respond to these queries. Furthermore, as Norris and

Ortega (2000) show in their review of studies which have investigated the effectiveness of implicit versus explicit approaches to L2 instruction, explicit grammar explanations, coupled with more communicative activities, are consistently more effective in the instructed L2 setting than solely inductive approaches in which the learner is given no explicit explanation. In short, L2 teachers are best served by having as complete an understanding of grammar and lexis as possible. I believe Cognitive Linguistics offers the most accurate, systematic, and complete model of language currently available.

Using English modal verbs as a lens, this chapter considers the usefulness of a cognitive linguistic approach to instructed language learning. After presenting a general overview of several key tenets of traditional approaches to language, which form the basis of most English Language Teaching (ELT) grammars and texts, versus key tenets of Cognitive Linguistics, the two general approaches are exemplified by comparative analyses of the English modal verbs. In the course of the comparison, I establish that the cognitive linguistic approach to modal verbs (Sweetser, 1990; Talmy, 1988) provides a more systematic, precise analysis than those offered by English Language Teaching grammars, which take a traditional perspective. The chapter concludes by presenting language teaching materials based on a cognitive linguistic analysis and reporting on the findings of two studies that offer support for the effectiveness of using a cognitive linguistic approach to modals in an instructed L2 classroom situation.

2 Background: Some basic principles

2.1 Traditional view

L2 researchers and teachers have long recognized that the semantics of English modal verbs are one of the most difficult aspects of English for L2 learners to master (e.g., Celce-Murcia & Larsen-Freeman, 1999). While acknowledging that the semantics of modal verbs are subtle, complex, and not completely systematic, I hypothesize that at least part of the difficulty for L2 learners lies in the inadequate analyses provided by current English Language Teaching grammars and texts, which tend to be based either in a structuralist/descriptive paradigm or in a superficial functionalist analysis. These approaches and the materials based on them may very well make the task of the instructed L2 learner more difficult by the fact that important elements of systematicity and precision that exist in the modal verb system have not been captured by these traditional representations of language. The work represented in this volume (e.g., Goldberg's alternative analysis of various grammatical constructions) as well as my previous work in the semantics of English prepositions (e.g.,

Tyler & Evans, 2003; Tyler, 2003) strongly indicates that this is true for language as a whole, not just the modal verbs.

Over the past 50 years, there has been a dizzying array of approaches to L2 teaching. However, in general, the view of the nature and structure of language that underpins these approaches has changed very little in that time. For instance, when we compare many of the exercises and explanations of specific grammar points in Lado's (1957) book, which exemplifies the audiolingual/structuralist approach, to those in Frodesen and Eyring in *Grammar dimensions* (1997), which is oriented with respect to a communicative perspective, we find a startling amount of overlap. This traditional view of language, which underlies most L2 grammars and texts, treats language as a system unto itself, separate from other cognitive and social abilities. Being an isolated system, disconnected from general cognitive processes and conceptual structure, language has traditionally been understood as operating under its own set of rules and properties, most of which have been assumed to be largely arbitrary, idiosyncratic, and mysterious. This view tends to represent language as a set of rules (often attempting to represent "alternating," "synonymous" sentence patterns, such as so-called dative alternation or active-passive alternation, as transforms of a basic pattern), a list of vocabulary items that plug into the rules, and a list of exceptions to the rules. Lexical items with multiple meanings are presented as homophones, with virtually no attempt to demonstrate any motivated connections among the meanings. The approach to language learning that accompanies this view of language emphasizes the need for the learner to memorize forms, master the rules, and memorize the exceptions.[1]

Relatively recently, the traditional approach has acknowledged another layer of the language system that involves functional or pragmatic aspects of language use. Examples of this layer include politeness formulas and their contexts of use, for example, in making a polite request, use of the modal verb *could* instead of *can*, as in *Could I ask a favor?*, and speech act formulas, such as set phrases for offering an apology or making a request. While inclusion of functional aspects of language use represents an important addition to our understanding of how language works, its usefulness is severely limited by the traditional orientation that pragmatics should be largely treated as an "add-on" to the rest of the language system, disconnected from the grammatical structure of the language. Even within more functionally oriented accounts, we find presentations of language in general, and modal verbs in particular, fail to present a holistic, motivated view of the system. In short, the traditional grammars fail to inform the language teacher of significant regularities and systematic connections in the language and hence rely on memorization of seemingly disconnected patterns as the primary mode of learning. (For a fuller explanation, see Tyler and Evans 2001.)[2]

To summarize, the key tenets of the traditional approach include:

1   Language is understood as a separate system made up of a number of compartmentalized subsystems (i.e., phonology, morphology, syntax, and the lexicon). More recent versions of this approach have also assumed an independent pragmatics component. The language system is treated as being uninfluenced by general human cognitive capacity and ordinary human interaction with and experience of the spatio-physical-social world. (By this I do not mean that all previous approaches have ignored the communicative and pragmatic aspects of language use but they do not represent pragmatic aspects, such as the form politeness phenomena actually take, as being a systematic representation of our general understanding of the world.)

2   The many meanings associated with a particular form are largely unrelated and must be learned one by one. This is reflected in the traditional, dictionary view of word meaning in which each meaning is listed, without any attempt to identify recurring patterns of meaning extension. For instance, the following uses of the preposition *over* are seen as arbitrary and largely unrelated:

(1)a. *The picture is over the mantel.*
    b. *Class is over.*
    c. *She played the same song over and over.*

Tyler and Evans (2003) have shown that these meanings are, in fact, connected in systematic ways.

3   Non-literal language is peripheral. Metaphor, that is understanding entities, actions, or events in one domain in terms of entities, actions, or events in another domain, and other figurative language is seen as being part of the poetic use of language, rather than as a fundamental property of human thought, reasoning, and understanding. Thus, under the traditional view, the use of *up* to convey the notion of an increase in amount, as in *The price of gas is up*, is either not addressed at all, or else is treated as arbitrary.

2.2 Cognitive Linguistics

A cognitive linguistic account of language differs radically from traditional perspectives by emphasizing that language is a reflection of general cognitive processes, not a separate, isolated system with its own system of rules. Language is understood as being grounded in lived human experience with the real world and as crucially reflecting the human perceptual system and human understanding of the spatial-physical-social world we inhabit. Moreover, our understanding of the spatial-physical-social world provides structure for our understanding of less external, less

459

perceptually-based experiences. This is the heart of conceptual metaphor, which is seen as pervasive in terms of how humans understand the world and how all aspects of language are structured. From a cognitive linguistic account, the use of *up* in the sentence *The price of gas is up* is a result of humans regularly observing real world situations in which an increase in amount is correlated with an increase in vertical elevation, such as the level of liquid in a glass rising (the vertical elevation) as the amount of liquid increases. Because these two physical phenomena are so closely correlated in real world experience, speakers of English use language from the domain of vertical elevation, *up*, to talk about increases in amount.

[handwritten margin note: embodied experience]

Let's consider the role of one particular conceptual metaphor involving English speakers' use of tense to code non-temporal information. The metaphor we will consider is NOW IS HERE—THEN IS THERE, which maps proximal and distal spatial phenomena and their real world consequences to temporal language. Sweetser (1990) talks about aspects of this metaphor in terms of a proximal-distal distinction. This conceptual metaphor accounts for a wide range of phenomena, such as tense shifts in discourse in which authors often code foregrounded ideas with the present tense and backgrounded ideas with past tense (Riddle, 1985; Tyler & Evans, 2000):

> In November 1859, Charles Darwin's *The Origin of Species* . . . **was** published in London. The central idea in this book **is** the principle of natural selection. In the sixth edition Darwin **wrote** "This principle of preservation of the survival of the fittest, I have called Natural Selection."
>
> Eigen & Winkler, 1983, p. 53

We can understand this use of present tense to indicate what is in focus in a text as drawing on our physical experience in the world. Events that are occurring at the present moment tend to be our focus of attention, rather than events that happened in the past. Similarly, entities and activities that are occurring proximal to us tend to be in foveal vision and to more likely be the focus of our attention than those occurring at a distance.

Another aspect of entities being proximal is that they are potentially under our physical control. If a parent wants to control an unruly two-year-old, physical constraint, and hence physical proximity, is often required. In many situations, humans have learned to use language to assert control in lieu of physical control. In situations of possible imposition, English speakers tend to make requests, offer invitations, etc., using the past tense, even when there is no implication of reference to past time. Following the logic of the conceptual metaphor THEN IS THERE, using the past tense implies that the speaker is physically distant from the addressee and therefore cannot exercise physical control over the addressee. The further implication is that the addressee is free to agree to or reject the imposition. It is always more pleasant to feel one has a choice to agree rather than feeling that one is being forced to agree. (Note this analysis is consistent with Brown and Levinson's (1987) insights into politeness theory and the notion of negative face.) Hence, the metaphor accounts for otherwise puzzling uses of past tense to indicate politeness:

(2) Patient calling a doctor's office:
Receptionist: *Good morning, Doctor X's office.*
Patient: *Yes, I **wanted** to ask you a question.* (Davies, personal communication)

Here the patient is clearly getting ready to ask a question. The wanting is continuing into the present moment. The choice of past tense is a conventionalized polite way to pose the question. Similarly, Fleishman (1990) cites the following as a conventionally polite way to issue an invitation:

(3) *Hi, are you busy? I **was** hoping you **were** free for lunch.*

Again, the typical interpretation is that the hoping continues into the moment of speaking, not that it is in the past. Indeed, it would seem quite odd for a speaker to announce such a hope if it were no longer the case that she/he wanted to invite the addressee to lunch. Both these examples are exploiting the implication of physical distance, cued by the use of past tense, which gives a nod to the polite fiction that the addressee is freer to accept or reject the request. As we will see, this same metaphor also plays an important role in the analysis of modals.

Cognitive Linguistics highlights recurrent, meaningful linguistic patterns and organizing principles found at all "levels" of language. The theory rejects the long-held notion that language is composed of insulated submodules that have their own special organizational systems. For example, Cognitive Linguistics treats both metaphor and knowledge of real world force dynamics as fundamental aspects of human cognition that are pervasively reflected in language. Under a cognitive linguistic account, the same principles of metaphorical extension and knowledge of force dynamics that account for semantic extension of open-class lexical items, such as *head* (e.g., *head of cabbage, head of the table, head the ball, head in the right direction*) and semantic extensions of closed-class lexical items, such as prepositions (Tyler & Evans, 2003), are also central to a systematic, principled account of verb argument structure and the particular syntactic patterns in which individual verbs occur (Goldberg, 1995).

Finally, because Cognitive Linguistics is a usage-based model of language, it does not make a strict divide between synchronic and diachronic grammar. This means that it acknowledges the importance of the history of lexis and grammar, and their vestiges, in the current linguistic system.

This perspective allows for historical "explanations" that allow for accounts of motivated extension, which viewed solely from a diachronic perspective may look arbitrary.

These characteristics suggest that a cognitive linguistic approach may be particularly useful for L2 learners. By viewing language as a function of general interaction with other cognitive abilities and our interaction with the world, Cognitive Linguistics offers explanations that draw on learners' everyday real world experience by tapping into an intuitive reservoir of knowledge that facilitates an understanding of the systematic relationships among the units of language. This is the same reservoir of experiential knowledge of the world which underpins the human conceptual system and hence, language itself. This is not to say that Cognitive Linguistics will magically make learning a second language easy. Learning any language requires committing a vast array of lexical items to memory. All languages have "irregularities," such as irregular past tense marking in English, that will have to be memorized. All languages have certain conventionalized uses that are not straightforwardly open to a systematic explanation. Moreover, each language potentially highlights slightly different aspects of human experience and conceptualization of the spatial-physical world and thus learners will face certain challenges mapping the differences between their L1 and the L2. Nevertheless, Cognitive Linguistics offers important advances in our understanding of language that would appear to be of real benefit to L2 learners.

3 The English modal verbs

3.1 The challenge

English, like many languages, has a system to represent speaker attitude relating to permission, ability, and obligation within social situations when giving advice, suggestions, permission, orders, etc., and commitment to surety in predictions and reasoning. In English these attitudinal colorings are expressed by the modal verbs (as well as adverbial phrases such as *is likely*, *is probable*, etc.) The modal verbs include *can, could, will, would, shall, should, may, might*, and *ought*.

The semantics of modal verbs involve the strength of the speaker's position and aspects of status between the participants in a speech event.

(4)a. *You could eat more vegetables*
  b. *You must eat more vegetables*
  c. *You should eat more vegetables*

Advice using *could* is interpreted as weaker than advice using *must*. Native speakers of English would likely interpret sentence a. as a friendly suggestion rather than directive advice. In contrast, sentence b. carries a strong sense of directive force and could even be considered a command in certain contexts (e.g., *You must finish writing this contract before 5 o'clock or the firm will have to let you go*). The appropriateness of using the stronger form is generally tied to the speaker's status vis-à-vis the addressee, for instance in the case of a boss speaking to an employee. When *should* is used to give advice, as in c., it introduces a moralistic dimension not found with *could* or *must*.

An additional complexity is that almost all English modals exhibit two meanings, one involving the external, physical-social world of ability, obligation, or permission, often called the *root* meaning, and a second meaning involving speaker internal mental reasoning and logical conclusion, called the *epistemic* meaning. Root meaning is illustrated in:

(5) *Mother said I should be home by 10:00.*

Here the speaker is expressing the strong social obligation imposed by her mother. Epistemic meaning is illustrated in:

(6) Doorbell rings. Speaker: *That should be John now.*

Here the speaker is indicating the strong belief in her conclusion that the unseen person at the door is John.

The overview of modals presented here represents a rudimentary outline of the entire system. There are additional modals, so-called paraphrastic modals, and a number of quirks having to do with shifting meanings when modals are negated or used in questions which are not addressed. A review of all these properties represents a book-length discussion.

3.2 Traditional view

All theories of modal verbs must account for the synchronic fact that virtually every modal has two basic senses—a root sense and an epistemic sense. Within traditional or formal linguistic theory, the root and epistemic meanings of modals have often been represented as homophones (Frank, 1972; Lyons, 1977; Palmer, 1986). More recently, several attempts have been made to apply some version of truth-conditional semantics (e.g., Papafragou, 2000) to account for the multiple senses associated with each modal. None of these approaches address any systematic patterning found in the modal system as a whole. Neither do they relate the patterns found in the modal system with potential parallels found in other areas of the language such as verbs of perception or the tense system. None of the more recent formal approaches have made their way into standard ELT grammars or texts.

3.2.1 Speech act presentations

An examination of 10 current ELT texts showed that modals tend to be presented from a superficial functional perspective, focusing on various speech acts in which the modals commonly occur. While such an approach has the appearance of being usage-based, it is important to note that the examples tend to be decontextualized and fail to give a complete representation of modal use. Since several modals can occur in the same speech act and each modal can occur in more than one speech act, under the speech act presentation their distribution and meaning appear to be largely idiosyncratic. Such accounts leave both the teacher and the learner with the impression that the only approach to mastering modals is to memorize formulaic expressions for each speech act, and the particular modals which happen to occur in those expressions. Indeed, Celce-Murcia and Larsen-Freeman (1999) have noted that acquiring modals is one of the most difficult aspects of L2 English precisely because of their seemingly idiosyncratic nature.

A representative approach to the teaching of modals from a speech act perspective is provided in Werner and Nelson (1996) *Mosaics 2: A Content-based grammar*. For instance, *may/might/can/could* are represented as relating to expressing ability and possibility; *may/can* as relating to granting permission; *may/could/can* as relating to asking for permission; *would/could/will/can* as relating to asking for assistance. Other categories include advice, suggestions, lack of necessity, prohibition, and expressing preferences. Even from this brief overview, we can see that *may* falls into three categories—ability and possibility, granting permission, and asking for permission. Note that a slightly different set of modals is listed for granting permission versus asking for permission. Similarly, *could* occurs in the categories of ability and permission, asking for permission and asking for assistance. *Can* appears in all four. No explanation is given for this distribution.

Students are given practice manipulating the forms through short dialogues and fill-in-the-blank exercises. In subsequent lessons on different speech acts, many of the same modals appear again. A consequence of this approach, in which a range of shifting interpretations represented by modals are presented in relation to isolated speech acts, is that there is no attempt to relate the various contextualized interpretations. The issue of tense patterns is not addressed. Moreover, the relationship between the root uses and the epistemic uses is completely ignored. Hence, any systematic patterns of usage remain unexplored. This results in a fragmented picture of the lexical class in question, leaving the learner with the impression that the various uses are arbitrary.

Perhaps even more problematic is the lack of precision introduced by presenting the modals in this particular paradigmatic fashion. The subtle yet fundamental differences in speaker attitude signaled by modal verbs such as *might* versus *could* versus *should* are obscured as the presentations list several modals together as functional equivalents that are essentially interchangeable when giving advice (or performing other speech acts).

The informed teacher, of course, might be able to help her students come to an integrated, accurate account of the modals based on this limited functional approach, but this presupposes the teacher has been able to construct an accurate and systematic understanding of the modal system. Unfortunately, most traditional and pedagogical grammars, even the more recent ones, simply do not provide teachers with such an overview. Consider the representation of modals in the 1999 corpus-based *Longman grammar of spoken and written English* by Biber, Johansson, Leech, Conrad, and Finegan (1999), which is specifically aimed at L2 teachers. Although the important contribution of corpus-based grammars, which can offer detailed description of patterns of language use, is clear, it is important to note that even the fullest description of uses falls far short of accessible analysis. Biber et al. offer copious amounts of information concerning how often particular modals are used in general contexts (spoken versus written discourse) and to perform certain social functions; however, they do not provide an analysis which would lead to insights into the subtle range of meanings among the modals, nor any systematic account of the root-epistemic polysemy associated with each modal.

As with most traditional accounts, Biber et al. (1999) group modals into three major functional categories: 1) permission/**possibility**/ability (*can, could, may, might*), 2) obligation/necessity (*must, should, had better, have got to, need to, ought to*), and 3) volition/**prediction** (*will, would, shall, be going to*). No meaning distinctions are made among modals within these groups; for instance, no meaning distinctions are made among *should* versus *need to* versus *must*. As the following sentences demonstrate, native speakers do have differentiated, albeit subtle, interpretations of these three modals:

(7)a. *The doctor said I should get my blood pressure checked.*
   b. *The doctor said I need to get my blood pressure checked.*
   c. *The doctor said I must get my blood pressure checked.*

Moreover, this initial grouping suggests that we would not find modals from one category participating in the same speech act as modals from another category. Sentences such as the following show clearly that modals from different "functional categories" are used in the same speech acts:

(8) Parent speaking to a reluctant child:

   a. *You must go to swimming lessons this morning* (obligation/necessity category)

    b. *You will go to swimming lessons this morning* (volition/prediction category)

In both these utterances, the parent is interpreted as strongly suggesting or commanding.

Biber et al. (1999) do point out that "each modal can have two different types of meaning, which can be labeled intrinsic [or root] and extrinsic [or epistemic]. Intrinsic modality refers to actions and events that humans (or other agents) directly control: meaning relating to permission, obligations, or volition (or intention). Extrinsic modality refers to logical status of events or states" (p. 485).

There are a number of weaknesses in Biber et al.'s (1999) representation. First, notice that the description of intrinsic and extrinsic seems to contradict the representation of *can, could, may, might* as the modals of "possibility" and *will/would/be going to* as the modals of "prediction," as virtually all modals are used to indicate logical prediction or the speaker's assessment of logical possibility in their epistemic or extrinsic uses. Moreover, Biber et al. offer no explanation as to the relationship between intrinsic and extrinsic uses of the individual modals. Rather, they simply offer examples of utterances which fall into the two categories. In many instances these examples are far from clear:

(9) *You **must** have thought that you **must** have so much time.* (necessity)[3]

Note that the first use of *must* is epistemic in nature, i.e. it is making a logical prediction about the addressee's state of mind, while the second use indicates real-world necessity. These distinctions are not discussed.

The explication notes that the three modals of permission/possibility (*could, may* and *might*) are used predominantly to mark logical possibility. The modals of obligation/necessity (*must/should/have to/need to*) are represented as primarily being used to mark personal obligation rather than logical necessity (except *must* which is primarily used for logical necessity). There is a brief discussion about the strong degree of directive force signaled by *must* as an explanation for its relatively low use for personal obligation in conversation. The problem here is that all these modals (*could, may, might, must, should, will, would*) do have epistemic uses, particularly in certain genres such as legal discourse. The modals of volition/prediction (*will/would/be going to*) are represented as often blurring the distinction between volition and prediction. Sentences illustrating the two uses are provided:

(10)a. *I'll come and show you* (personal volition)
    b. *I would give it back* (personal volition)
    c. *Will my coat be ready tomorrow?* (prediction)
    d. *She would just feel better if she went out* (prediction)

Again, no analysis of the relationship of the uses is offered. Moreover, sentence b. would seem to be functioning as a suggestion (and as part of a conditional construction as in *I would give it back if I were you*) rather than a statement of personal volition. Note that the kinds of "prediction" involved in sentences c. and d. are quite distinct.

The presentation further notes that a limited set of modals (*can/could, may/might, shall/should,* and *will/would*) have past tense forms. However, no discussion of the fact that *could, might, should,* and *would* are regularly used in non-past situations is included. For instance, they offer no discussion as to why the past tense *would* can be used to make predictions about the future (as in b. and d.).

Thus, even though Biber et al. (1999) call on a wealth of data and provide information about the general distribution of the modals, they do not provide a systematic account of the semantic distinctions among modals, regular relations between the root and epistemic meanings, or systematic patterns associated with historic past tense forms. It is my estimation that most language teachers would be at a loss to discern systematic, motivated patterns from this account.

3.3 Cognitive linguistic account

Cognitive linguists Talmy (1988) and Sweetser (1990) developed an alternative analysis of the semantics of modal verbs based on force dynamics. Specifically, they argue that the root meanings of modals have to do with physical forces, barriers, and paths. Further, there is a mapping between our understanding of these physical forces and our understanding of mental "forces, barriers, and paths," which is reflected in the epistemic uses. Here I primarily follow Sweetser's analysis, which emphasizes intentional, directed forces, barriers, and paths.

As noted above, the premise that our spatial-physical-social experiences structure much of our cognition and language is a central tenet of Cognitive Linguistics. Specifically, our "real world" observations of basic force dynamics (such as movement of entities along a path and barriers to forward movement) provide important event schemas we use to reason and talk about the non-physical. This pattern is found in many uses of English, not just the modal verbs. One example of how language from the realm of spatio-physical perceptions is used to describe mental operations involves the use of verbs of perception to talk about the mental operation of understanding.

(11)a. *I see your point*
   b. *I hear what you're saying.*

Lakoff and Johnson (1980) have also pointed out that verbs of physical manipulation are used to talk about mental operations. So when English speakers want to convey their degree of understanding of an issue, they may say something like:

(12)a. *I have a good* **grasp** *of the issues*
    b. *I am well* **grounded** *in the theory*
    c. *I feel like I have only a tenuous* **grip** *on the theory*

English speakers also use general language of physical compulsion, barriers, and paths to talk about internal states of understanding and reasoning:

(13)a. *Her carefully developed argument* **forced** *me* **to move from my original position**
    b. *He* **swayed** *the crowd* **to his side** *with his passionate speech*
    c. *My thoughts were* **racing ahead to the next point** *in the argument*
    d. **Part way through** *his argument, he suddenly* **changed direction**
    e. *Some people seem to face a mental* **block** *when it comes to understanding math*
    f. *This theory has* **run into a major obstacle**

As Sweetser (1990) argues, "a pervasive and coherently structured system of metaphors underlies our tendency to use vocabulary from the external domain in speaking of the internal domain" (p. 49).

Historically, the English modals developed from non-modal lexical items that first expressed physical strength or social obligation; for instance, *may/might* derive from *magan* "be strong" (clearly physical strength) and *must* derives historically from *moste*, the past form of *mot*, meaning "obliged" (clearly social obligation). The general pattern of historical development for modal verbs was that the semantics and usage of the non-modal forms gradually extended to root modal meaning and later broadened to epistemic meaning. Sweetser (1990) argues that these historical changes are systematically motivated by the ubiquitous cognitive pattern of using language from the external world to express aspects of the internal, mental world. She further notes that "Thus, we view our reasoning processes as being subject to compulsions, obligations and barriers just as our real-world actions are subject to modalities of the same sort" (p. 50). Sweetser also emphasizes that physical forces and barriers are not objectively similar to our mental processes, rather that humans' **experience** of physical world and the epistemic domain share a certain amount of common structure which allows metaphorical mapping between the two.

In her analysis, Sweetser (1990) offers distinct root meanings for each of the modals based on different kinds of forces emanating from different sources, as well as barriers to forward motion. Here we will consider her representations of *must, need to, may*, and *can*. The root meaning of *must* is represented as an irresistible force directing the subject or doer towards an act, a positive compulsion imposed by someone else, as in the following, from a high school policy statement:

(14) *You must get your research paper in by the deadline or you will not be allowed to graduate with your class.*

Here the compelling force is the authority of the institution which is imposing the writing of a research paper on the student. In distinction from *must*, Sweetser represents *need to* as a compelling force imposed by something **internal** to the actor. For instance, in *I need to get a hair cut*,[4] the internal force involves the speaker's desire to have a particular, groomed appearance. Sweetser illustrates the semantic distinction in the following sentences:

(15)a. *I **need to** get this paper in, but I guess I'll go to the movies instead*
    b. *?? I **must** get this paper in, but I guess I'll go to the movies instead*
        (p. 54)

Here we can understand the strong internal force is deniable by the speaker/actor thus accounting for the acceptability of a. while the compelling external force is irresistible, thus accounting for the oddity of b.

May is represented as a situation in which an authority figure takes away or keeps away a potential barrier to the doer undertaking some action. The action of keeping the barrier at bay has the result of allowing the doer to undertake the action. Thus, the meaning focuses on lack of restriction imposed on the doer by someone else who has the authority or power to impose the restriction, and hence the interpretation of permission granted by an authority who could potentially block the doer's action. In contrast, *can* is represented as a positive physical or social ability on the part of the doer, analogous to potential energy in physics. The energy or ability emanates from the doer. As Sweetser explains, *can* is the equivalent of a full gas tank in a car and *may* is the equivalent of an open garage door. "These two factors will exert certain similar influences on the situation: neither factor forces the car (or driver) to travel a given path, and yet if either factor were reversed, then travel would be correspondingly restricted. The full tank is a positive enablement, while the open door is a negated restriction; yet the results are similar enough to allow a good deal of overlap in the larger force-dynamic schemata surrounding the two modalities" (p. 53).

Sweetser (1990) argues that if we assume that the domain of reasoning is understood in terms of the social-physical world, we have an accurate, motivated explanation for the systematic polysemy of root and epistemic meaning found with virtually all the modals. (Unfortunately, one of the continuing, unexplained exceptions is *can*'s lack of epistemic extension, but no analysis has been able to satisfactorily explain this). Thus, each epistemic modal usage is metaphorically correlated with that real-world modality which is its closest parallel in force-dynamic structure. In terms of *may*, "we can see why general sociophysical potentiality, and specifically social permission, should be . . . chosen as analogous to possibility in the world of reasoning. *May* is an absent potential barrier in the sociophysical world, and the epistemic *may* is a force-dynamically parallel case in the world of reasoning. The meaning of epistemic *may* would thus be that there is no barrier to the speaker's process of reasoning from the available premises to the conclusion expressed in the sentence qualified by *may* . . ." (Sweetser, 1990, p. 59). Sweetser offers the following examples:

(16)a. John may go = John is not barred by authority from going
     b. John may be at the party = I am not barred by my premises
         from the conclusion that he is there (p. 59)

The epistemic uses of *might, could, will, would, must, shall, should*, etc. all represent parallel extensions of the particular forces and barriers indicated by the modal in the social-physical world to the domain of reasoning and logical prediction.

While Sweetser's analysis goes a long way towards revealing the systematicity of modals, there are still some details of the modals that the analysis does not account for. As noted above, she offers no explanation for the fact that *can* has no epistemic or predictive uses. This must simply be memorized. However, as Sweetser points out, if root modals are understood as referring to functional notions like permission or advice, it is almost impossible to account for their epistemic uses. The *may* of permission, as in *You may leave the table* seems to have little connection to epistemic *may* as in *That may be John now*. For the L2 learner, presentations of modals solely in terms of functional uses have the result that, rather than creating a systematic rubric or schema to understand and learn modal usage, all the various uses of each modal must be memorized piecemeal.

So far we have seen how metaphoric extension of force dynamics into the domain of logic is a key conceptual metaphor for explaining the modal verbs. A second metaphor central in my analysis of modals is the proximal-distal metaphor discussed previously, NOW IS HERE—THEN IS THERE. We have already seen that this conceptual metaphor offers a coherent explanation for politeness phenomenon. The modal verbs reflect this systematic pattern in the uses of the historically past tense modals *could* and *would* as the polite forms of *can* and *will* to make requests, suggestions, etc.

Another important reflex of the proximal-distal metaphor involves the use of present tense to indicate a higher degree of surety, realis, and speaker force in contrast to the use of past tense to indicate a lower degree of surety, realis, and an attenuation of speaker force or control. Experientially, humans are much surer of the reality of that which they can immediately perceive with their physical senses, than that which is out of range of their physical senses. This includes being surer of that which is experienced in the immediate moment than that which we remember. Thus, present tense is used to express higher degrees of surety, realis, and force than past tense. The metaphor explains the systematic lessening of surety and realis indicated by the use of historically past tense modals. Thus in the present/past pairs *will/would, can/could, shall/should* we find the past tense forms consistently indicating less surety on the part of the speaker or less social and/or physical force. For example, in legal discourse *shall* indicates a legally binding circumstance while *should* indicates a preferred, but non-binding circumstance.[5]

An analysis of modals grounded in force dynamics allows Cognitive Linguistics to offer not only a principled, explanatory representation of the semantics of these modals but also a more accurate and complete one. Sweetser (1990) has been able to provide precise, distinct definitions of each of the root meanings and their epistemic counterparts. Drawing on the notion of conceptual metaphor and embodied meaning, Cognitive Linguistics not only offers a systematic account of the relations between the root and epistemic senses but also the historically present and past modal forms. Thus, a cognitive linguistic approach provides a motivated, precise explanation for the patterns of usage that is not captured by the speech acts approach or traditional representations. While the cognitive linguistic analysis goes a long way towards illuminating the semantics of modal verbs, its technical nature may render it difficult for L2 teachers and learners. As one thoughtful, well-read L2 specialist remarked upon reading Sweetser's analysis, "I should certainly not want to be a learner trying to use the gas tank/garage door formulation of *can* and *may* in order to decide which modal to use in *We ____ drive out because the gate's open* or *It ____ rain this afternoon*." Of course, the speaker has missed the important distinction that the first sentence is making a statement about the present state of the world and physical ability to undertake an action while the second sentence is making a prediction about the probability of future events. Nevertheless, the remark is representative of a widespread reluctance on the part of L2 professionals to adopt new explanations and highlights the challenge of converting a coherent theoretical analysis into learner-friendly teaching materials.

471

4 Making theoretical insights accessible to L2 teachers

In this section, I present sample materials that can be used for teaching the modals. There are a number of caveats that must be issued. This is not a full representation of the modals. Meaning shifts that occur when modals are negated or used in questions are not addressed. Little attention is given to the functional uses. I have no doubt that these materials would have to be supplemented. Moreover, these materials were designed for a teacher-fronted lesson aimed at advanced learners enrolled in a US law school. As I noted earlier, using a cognitive linguistic analysis in order to gain a more precise, systematic understanding of the system does not tie the L2 teacher to fronted grammar lessons.

The following chart (Fig. 18.1) attempts to represent Sweetser's analysis of the modals with a minimum amount of jargon or explanation. Because a cognitive linguistic analysis is based on experience in the physical world, it is possible to represent the meaning of each modal diagrammatically, or in terms of scenes, rather than only in terms of linguistic propositions or dictionary definitions. These diagrams can rather straightforwardly capture the nuanced differences among the various modals. This allows for detailed, accurate specification of the meaning of the modals which are at the same time accessible to language learners.

Some explanation is needed in order to interpret the diagrams. The actor is the figure walking forward. Internal force is represented by lines in the actor's head. External force or authority is represented by a larger figure applying various amounts of pressure on the actor's back. Recognition of the external force's legitimate authority is represented by double-headed arrows between the external force and the actor. Historically present tense modals are represented in solid lines. Historically past tense modals are represented in dotted lines.

So, if we take the representation of *will*, in the first column, the actor is moving forward along a path. The double-extended arms are meant to represent strong volition and forward momentum. The lines inside the actor's head indicate that the force is internally generated, coming from the actor's own will or willpower. The solid lines indicate this is the present tense form and thus the stronger form of the modal. The second column offers a metaphoric translation of the root use into the epistemic use. The third column provides examples of epistemic uses and paraphrases of those uses.

ENGLISH MODAL VERBS

Past tense indicates a weakened force of the utterance and less surety on the part of the speaker (move from realis/here & now to irrealis or there/then). Present tense is indicated by solid lines; past tense is indicated by dotted lines.

ROOT Physical/Social reasoning	METAPHORIC EXTENSION	EPISTEMIC Predictive/logical-causal

WILL

Force emanates from doer.

If I let go of this apple, it will fall.
I will finish the paper today.
You will be happy you took this course.
Absolute surety or commitment → future implied.

Just as I am sure about the state of the world & my commitments, the data & premises support the certainty of my conclusion.

The Court will find in favor of our client. =
"I am certain of the Court's ruling; no other ruling is possible."

Very strong certainty.

WOULD

Strong, but lessened commitment.

I think you would like this movie.

Barring any unforeseen contingencies, the data give strong support for my conclusion.

Under these circumstances, the Court would find in favor of our client. =
"I think there is a very good chance the Court will rule this way, but I can't be 100 percent sure. There is a small chance the Court could rule differently."

Figure 18.1 continued overleaf

473

MUST

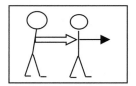

Strong external authority. Irresistible force.

You must pass all your courses in order to graduate. You must be home by 10.

The data & premises force me to the conclusion.

The Court must find in favor of our client. =
"I believe the Court has no choice; it is forced by the law and the facts to find as I predict."

Very high certainty, but because of the strength of claim, sounds slightly emotional or desperate.

SHALL

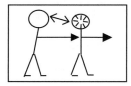

Actor recognizes the authority of powerful external force. Sense of binding obligation.

All the data & premises will follow their appropriate trajectories, or follow the rules, so I can conclude with confidence.

The defendant shall be hanged by the neck until dead.
All parties shall agree to binding arbitration.
"These are binding pronouncements that everyone is forced to abide by."

SHOULD

Lessened sense of the authority or of the power of external force. Lessened sense of binding obligation.

I should finish this project now because the boss wants it soon.

If all the data & premises conform to their appropriate trajectories, or follow the rules, then I can conclude X.

The Court should find in favor of our clients. =
"I believe that if everyone follows the rules and thinks reasonably, the Court will act as I predict."

Strong possibility, with moral overtone.

474

MAY

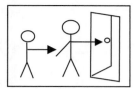

External authority allows action, takes away possible barrier to action.

You may leave whenever you are finished.

Nothing bars me from concluding X (but nothing compels me to conclude this).

The Court may find in our favor. =
"I believe it is possible the Court will rule in our favor, but it is almost as likely it will not."

MIGHT

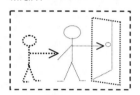

Weakened form.

I might want to take a walk, but I'm really not sure.
You might want to try another approach.

Probably nothing to bar me from concluding, but nothing seems to compel me to conclude this either.

The Court might find in our favor. =
"I believe it is possible the Court will rule in our favor, but it is just as likely it will not. I have no strong reasons to be able to predict the outcome."

CAN

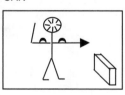

I know I can lift 100 pounds.
Nancy can multiply huge numbers in her head.

CAN*

This is the only modal that specifically relates to ability. Doesn't have an epistemic extension.

PREMISES GIVE ME THE ABILITY OR KNOW HOW TO CONCLUDE?

Figure 18.1 continued overleaf

COULD

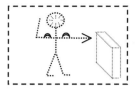

Weakened ability to undertake action. Implies
possibility.

I've been going to the gym so
I think I could lift 100 pounds
now.

You could wash the dishes if
you wanted to help.

The data provide weakened
support to possibly conclude
X, but I see potential barriers.

The Court could find in our
favor. =
"We have a number of good
arguments. The opposition
also has a number of good
arguments. I can't make a
strong prediction about how
the Court will rule."

NEED TO

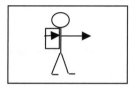

Internal desire to meet
certain (societal)
expectations.

I need to get my hair cut.
I need to get my taxes done
this weekend, otherwise I'll
feel too rushed.

The data internally compel
me to conclude X.

?? That needs to be John.
Doesn't seem to be used to
make predictions in legal
discourse.

Figure 18.1 English modal verbs.

5 Support for the approach

To suggest the usefulness of these cognitive linguistic-based materials, I will outline the results of two classroom-based studies that looked at changes in subjects' use of modals before and after receiving instruction based on the materials presented above.

The two studies were both situated in a Master of the Laws (LL.M.) program at a major law school in the northeastern United States. All subjects had already earned law degrees in their home countries and had been using English in their professional work for several years. All reported to the researcher that they had received traditional instruction on the modals. All had studied English for a minimum of 10 years and scored a minimum of 600 on the TOEFL. Thus, they can all be classified as very advanced learners of English. In spite of their advanced status, they continued to have difficulty producing appropriate modals in their written English discourse.

Appropriate use of modal verbs is particularly important in legal discourse. For instance, in legal memoranda, one of the most common and central legal documents these students are called on to write, the lawyer is required to make predictions about how the court is likely to rule on particular matters and make suggestions about which actions are likely to be most beneficial for the client. The difference in informing a client that: *If the court finds this argument persuasive, it will find in your favor* versus *If the court finds this argument persuasive, it could find in your favor* is crucial. Similarly, telling your client: *Considering all the arguments, both pro and con, I believe the court should find in your favor* versus *Considering all the arguments, both pro and con, I believe the court might find in your favor* may make the difference between the client deciding to pursue the case or not. Precise understanding of the meaning of the modals is also essential in correctly interpreting case law. One example is the absolute binding effect in contracts of the modal *shall* versus the non-binding effect of *should*.

The first study (Abbuhl, 2005) is a quasi-experimental investigation involving 38 subjects, which examined a number of dimensions of written discourse produced by the subjects, modal usage being just one of several. Two groups of LL.M. students were compared: (1) one group (the feedback group) which received 10 weeks of writing instruction that involved a weekly teacher-fronted class and individualized written and oral feedback on both the *content* (e.g., legal argumentation) and *form* (e.g., grammar and lexical choice) of their writing, and (2) a second group which received only one set of written comments on the quality of their legal argumentation (minimal feedback group). For the feedback group, instructors highlighted grammatical problems or inappropriate lexical choices, but did not correct the problem. Students were asked to try to self-correct. In individual feedback sessions, students were free to ask instructors to discuss grammatical and lexis problems. Records of these discussions are not available. Some teachers reported having discussions about the meaning or use of particular modals, but no systematic presentation of the modals was given individually.

For the study, two sets of writing samples were compared for each student: a first draft of a client memo (produced at week 5 of the course) and a final draft (produced at week 10 of the course). For our purposes, two metadiscourse analyses, which examined the use of hedges and boosters to signal the writer's stance towards the strength of the argument being presented and the predictions being made, are of particular interest. The following is an example of a booster:

(17) *Because the issues in the Katz case are similar to our clients' case, even though it is a Delaware case and not a New York case, the judge*

will very likely *find it persuasive. Thus the court* **will most probably** *decide in our client's favor.*

Here we see the choice of the modal *will* indicates the writer's strong prediction about the court's interpretation of the importance of the Katz case and the court's eventual decision. The statement is further strengthened with the phrases *very likely* and *most probably.* The following is a hedged version of this argument:

(18) *Because the issues in the Katz case are similar to our clients' case, even though it is a Delaware case and not a New York case, the judge* **may** *find it persuasive. Thus the court* **might** *decide in our client's favor.*

Here the use of *may* and *might* indicate the writer is less sure how the court will judge the importance of the Katz case and the court's eventual decision.

As exemplified here, modal verbs are one of the primary linguistic elements used to code boosters and hedges. Boosters and hedges are also coded by a number of phrases such as *"is possible" and "is likely."* Frequently modals plus additional phrases are used together, as in the example of the booster.

The purpose of the client memo is to inform senior law partners about the facts of the client's case, provide an overview of the pertinent law, and make predictions about the probable outcome of the case. While the client may also use the memo to help determine if he or she will go forward with the case, the primary use is for the law firm to decide how to advise the client. It is, thus, important that the predictions made in the memo are appropriately nuanced; the lawyer is expected not to overstate the strength of the client's case and to be circumspect about the court's findings. As a result, client memos tend to contain many hedges but not many boosters (Tiersma, 1999).

Both groups received feedback on the first draft—the minimal feedback group received comments on content only; the feedback group received response on grammar in terms of problematic points being highlighted, as well as comments on content. One week after the first draft was turned in, the feedback group received a 30-minute, teacher-fronted presentation on the semantics of the modals. The presentation involved a short discussion of the Proximal-Distal metaphor (i.e., the Now is Here and Then is There metaphor). The heart of the presentation was a discussion of a chart containing the diagrams of the root meanings of the modals and their metaphoric extension into the realm of reasoning and logical prediction, very similar to the chart presented above. The teacher-fronted presentation was followed by pair work; students were given eight excerpts in which modals occurred which were from writing generated by students in the class.

Some of the modals were appropriately used, some were not (Appendix A). The students' task was to determine the appropriateness of each modal and how changing the modal affected the interpretation of the text. The students kept the modal charts and were allowed to use them whenever they chose to. No attempt was made to determine how frequently any of the subjects used the charts after the classroom instruction.

Using a Mann Whitney U test, Abbuhl found that the first drafts written by the two groups did not differ significantly on the use of boosters and hedges. However, on the second drafts, the feedback group, which had received the cognitive linguistic-based instruction on the modals, as well as having inappropriate use highlighted, showed significantly more appropriate uses of boosters and hedges. In order to determine changes in the use of hedges and boosters in the two drafts of the two groups more specifically, Wilcoxon Signed Ranks tests were performed. The results appear on Tables 18.1 and 18.2 and are represented in graphic form in Figs 18.2 and 18.3.

For the minimal feedback group, there was no statistically significant evidence of change for either hedges or boosters. In contrast, for the feedback group, the Wilcoxon Signed Ranks tests indicated that in Draft 2, these writers employed significantly more hedges than in Draft 1 and significantly fewer boosters. Thus, by the time of the final draft, the feedback group's use of boosters and hedges more closely matched those of the target discourse community.

Table 18.1 Wilcoxon Signed Ranks test for minimal feedback group

All measures per T-units	Draft 1		Draft 2		
	M	SD	M	SD	Z
Hedges	.35	.13	.32	.13	−.85
Boosters	.24	.10	.26	.11	−.56

Note: $df = 18$; * = $p < .05$; ** = $p < .01$ (two-tailed)

Table 18.2 Wilcoxon Signed Ranks test for feedback group

All measures per T-units	Draft 1		Draft 2		
	M	SD	M	SD	Z
Hedges	.42	.12	.48	.14	−2.09*
Boosters	.22	.08	.17	.06	−2.66**

Note: $df = 18$; * = $p < .05$; ** = $p < .01$ (two-tailed)

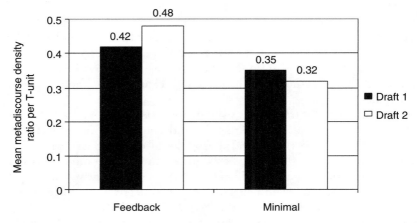

Figure 18.2 Wilcoxon Signed Ranks test for "Hedges" in Drafts 1 and 2 of feedback and minimal feedback groups.

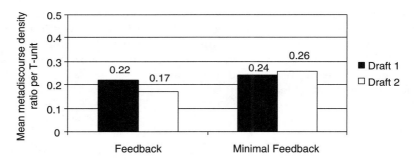

Figure 18.3 Wilcoxon Signed Ranks test for "Boosters" in Drafts 1 and 2 of EL and USLD groups.

Although use of modals was not examined in isolation from hedges and boosters, the findings suggest that the feedback group made important gains in appropriate use of modals. The minimal feedback group, in contrast, in spite of being in an immersion context in which they were required to read an extensive number of US legal documents, including authentic client memos, which used modals to appropriately hedge the argument, showed no gain in this aspect of their English writing. The findings are suggestive that the cognitive linguistic intervention allowed the feedback group to make gains in their appropriate use of modals. However, we must also acknowledge that in addition to the cognitive intervention, some of these students received feedback from their instructors when their use of modals was inappropriate. There was not a third control group which received the same responses to their inappropriate use of modals as the feedback group but without the cognitive linguistic explanation of the modals. Thus, we can only say that these results are suggestive.

The second study (Hama, 2005) involves six case studies. The data come from six students[6] enrolled in a five-day intensive English writing course for lawyers at the same law school as the subjects in Abbuhl's study. As with Abbuhl's subjects, the subjects can all be classified as very advanced learners of English. Again, in spite of their advanced status, they continued to have difficulty producing appropriate modals in their written English discourse.

The class met three hours a day for one week. Students turned in one piece of writing (a client letter) via email prior to the first class. Written feedback was given to each piece of writing and sent to the students prior to class. As with the class in Abbuhl's study, instructors primarily responded with comments and questions about the content of the writing. Problems with modals (and other grammatical aspects) were highlighted, but not corrected. Each day, students met with individual instructors for approximately 30 minutes and discussed various issues in the student's writing. The focus was on clarification of the argument, but if students raised questions about grammar points, the instructor addressed them. The pattern of students submitting writing electronically and receiving written comments prior to class, then having an oral feedback in class was repeated all subsequent days. No records were kept of the oral feedback sessions. The instructors reported that with some students there was some discussion of the use of modals, but no systematic explanation was provided prior to Day 3.

During the first two days of the course, the students produced a total of three documents of 3–4 typed pages in length. Large group presentations and activities addressed the overall structure of a client memo, effective exemplification, and analysis of common law argumentation. No grammar points were discussed.

At the beginning of the third day, a 30-minute, teacher-fronted presentation of the semantics of the modals, very similar to the presentation given in Abbuhl's study, was given. Again the teacher-fronted presentation was followed by pair work in which students examined eight excerpts from writing generated by other students and determined the appropriateness of each modal or how changing the modal affected the interpretation of the text. These discussions were quite lively. The teachers monitoring the discussions observed that the students consistently demonstrated understanding of the meanings of modals they had previously had difficulty producing appropriately in their writing. The students were allowed to keep their copies of the modal charts and refer to them whenever they wished.

In the second half of the class, students worked on revising their writing. Anecdotally, the instructors noticed that some students spontaneously used the modal chart when they had to make a decision about which modal to use as they were discussing their own writing. On Days 4 and 5, the students produced more complete versions of their memos, 4–6 pages in length. Each piece of writing received written feedback. Inappropriately used modals were highlighted. In the oral feedback sessions, teachers discussed problematic modal use if the students had questions, referring the students back to the chart when it was warranted.

The data analyzed for this study consisted of 30 pieces of writing produced by six individuals over a five-day period. All pieces of writing were analyzed for modal usage. The key issue was to determine if and how the students' production of modals changed after the presentation of the cognitive linguistic account of the modals at the beginning of Day 3.

The number of sites where a modal verb was used or required but omitted was determined by two independent coders for all 30 papers. Each site was then coded as 1) modal correctly supplied, 2) inappropriate choice, or 3) modal omitted. Each category is exemplified below:

(19) Examples of modal coding
1. Modal Correctly Supplied: the use of the modal verb is appropriate in the position.
   1a. Therefore the arbitration clause **would** not be likely [to be] considered as an additional term.
   1b. Both of these arguments **could** have been expressly refused on your behalf upon receiving each receipt instead of when the breach of contract occurred.
2. Inappropriate Choice: the use of the modal does not convey appropriate meaning
   2a. Likewise, UCC presumes that between merchants additional terms **will** be included in a contract. (will → can).
   2b. These **would** not apply considering that the confirmations were illegible. (would → may).
3. Modal Omitted: A modal verb is missing.
   3a. It is most likely that the Court of Appeals XXX finds the aforementioned clause binding between the parties. (XXX → would).
   3b. From our case, we know that, even though the company has never expressed its acceptance in writing, the company has performed enough activities which XXX have lead NYSFC to consider that there is an acceptance. (XXX → could).

Table 18.3 Comparison of modal verb usage before and after modal lesson

	Before	After
Modal sites or required site	154	184
Modal correctly supplied	86 (56%)	144 (78%)
Incorrect usage	68 (44%)	40 (22%)

The number of subjects is too small for inferential statistics, but the overall results show that before and after the modal lesson, there was a noticeable difference in the participants' correct modal usage (see Table 18.3). Before the lesson, the participants correctly supplied modals 56% of the time (86 out of 154 required occurrences). In contrast, after the lesson the participants correctly supplied modals 78% of the time (144 out of 184 required occurrences).

Moreover, five out of six (all but number 6) subjects showed an increase in correct usage (average gain in raw numbers of 9.6, range 5–25, average gain in percentages 18%, range –4%–29%), as illustrated in Table 18.4. It is perhaps not too surprising that subject number 6 did not show the gain that the other subjects showed as this subject started out with the highest percentage of correct usage, although one other subject, number 3, finished the week with an even higher percentage of correct uses.

Again, these findings suggest that a cognitive linguistic approach was effective in increasing these very advanced learners' understanding of the semantics of the modals. In addition, in the large class discussion, several of the students stated that after the instruction they understood for the first time differences in the meaning of several of the modals. In particular they noted that they had not previously understood the differences between *should*, *would*, and *could* in making predictions.

Abbuhl's study indicates that more input alone, even massive amounts of contextualized input, is not sufficient for these advanced learners to modify their established use of the modals. The two studies together suggest that a cognitive linguistic approach to the modals has a positive

Table 18.4 Correct modal usage by individual subject

Subject	Before	After
1	3 (23%)	11 (50%)
2	12 (46%)	17 (68%)
3	14 (61%)	24 (80%)
4	24 (80%)	39 (90%)
5	13 (30%)	18 (53%)
6	20 (87%)	25 (83%)

effect on very advanced learners, who despite many years of instruction in English, including traditional instruction on the modals, still have difficulty with using the modal verbs appropriately in written legal discourse.

However, there are a number of limits to the present studies that need to be addressed before we can claim with confidence the usefulness of a cognitive linguistic orientation. In the present studies there were no control groups that received parallel instruction in which the instructor highlighted problems with modals, but who did not receive the teacher-fronted cognitive linguistic intervention. Thus, we cannot claim with confidence that the students in the present studies made these gains because of the cognitive linguistic intervention. A future study that sorts out the effects of instructors drawing the students' attention to inappropriate modal usage versus the effects of the cognitive linguistic instruction is needed. Moreover, in Abbuhl's study, modal use was confounded with phrasal material in boosters and hedges; more studies need to be undertaken which focus solely on learning of modals.

The subjects in these studies were very advanced, adult learners; they all came to the instructed situation with a strong basis in the speech act uses of modals. Future research should investigate the usefulness of language pedagogy based on a cognitive linguistic perspective aimed at learners of varying ages and levels of proficiency. In examining the learning of modals at lower levels of proficiency, it is particularly important to note that the teaching materials in the present study represent a limited set of modal uses. Certainly, attention to speech act uses would be necessary for less advanced learners. Information on some of the quirks of negation and questioning found with modals would also be required for students to acquire a full range of the modal uses. Given the complexity of the modal system, it is impractical to assume that a short intervention would be sufficient; longitudinal studies are clearly called for.

In addition, in order to be able to argue for the clear superiority of a cognitive linguistic orientation, future research is needed in which a cognitive linguistic orientation to teaching modals is directly compared to a traditional orientation. Care should be taken to control a number of possibly confounding variables:

1   Both experimental groups should be presented with the same general pedagogical techniques. For instance, both groups could be presented with a combination of teacher-fronted instruction and task-based materials;
2   The materials should be constructed so that they were comparable in terms of interestingness and relevance. For instance, if the subjects were from a pool such as the LL.M. students in the present studies, the materials would need to be equally applicable to the general educational needs of the subjects;

3   A third control group, whose subjects received no instruction, should again be included.

Clearly the present studies have a number of limitations and a good deal of future research is needed. What can be legitimately recognized is that a fresh perspective, which provided precise definitions for each of the modals and an explanation of the systematicity between root and epistemic uses, as well as proximal and distal uses, seemed to help these very advanced learners move from a stable but defective understanding of the modals to one which resulted in more nativelike production.

6 Conclusion

In this chapter I have argued that L2 researchers and teachers would be well served by reassessing their (often implicit) assumptions about the nature of language and the traditional model of language that forms the basis of most L2 texts and grammars. I have further argued Cognitive Linguistics, which represents a radical departure from the traditional models, is a theoretical model that offers important new insights into grammar and lexis. The focus of this work has been on the English modals, but there are many other areas of grammar that have been insightfully analyzed by cognitive linguists and that the interested reader would find informative. Dirven and Verspoor (2004) have written an introductory textbook of general linguistics that takes a cognitive linguistic approach; Evans and Green (2006) present an accessible, comprehensive introduction to the cognitive enterprise, including a chapter that addresses first language learning. Adele Goldberg's (1995) work in construction grammar provides a particularly promising approach to several key aspects of English syntax. Although there are few experimental studies applying Cognitive Linguistics to second language learning, Achard and Niemeier (2004) have edited a volume of essays on applications of Cognitive Linguistics. In this volume, Frank Boers presents an overview of experimental work using metaphor theory to teach vocabulary acquisition. A number of the essays include valuable bibliographies. Tyler and Evans (2003) provide a detailed analysis of the semantics of English prepositions. Along with several of my graduate students, I have been carrying out a series of experiments focusing on the teaching of the prepositions *over*, *above*, *to*, *for*, and *at* based on this model of prepositions. The preliminary results of these experiments are quite promising.

A major challenge to applied cognitive linguists is to demonstrate to L2 researchers and teachers that Cognitive Linguistics is not only a more complete and accurate theoretical model of language but also one that appears to be of particular benefit to L2 learners. Key to this endeavor is creating and testing language teaching materials that maintain the precision offered by the theoretical model, but that are also accessible to L2 teachers and learners. The examination of English modal verbs and the two studies using cognitive linguistic-based teaching materials represent a promising first step in this process.

Notes

1 With both the communicative approach and task-based approaches there has been a shift in emphasis to implicit learning through rich input, meaning negotiation, and pushed output. These L2 teaching methodologies do not overtly relate to any particular model of language and often do not overtly attempt to explain the patterns of the target language. In theory, learning of the target language takes place implicitly. However, most language teachers do offer explanations for the grammar, and certainly most ELT texts, even those purporting to take a communicative approach, offer rules. These rules are generally based on the traditional view. It is unlikely that the long established practice of explicit presentation of rules will end soon.

2 Criticizing pedagogical grammars for presenting organized systems, such as the multiple functions of tense, in a piecemeal fashion should not be taken as criticizing ELT texts for not presenting students with all aspects of the system in one go, rather than in a selected and graded fashion. The point is that the teacher needs to understand the system in order to make informed choices about appropriate sequencing and materials.

3 Biber et al.'s label.

4 It is possible to say something like *I must get my hair cut*. Following Sweetser's argument, this would indicate a subtle shift in the speaker's stance, perhaps indicating a sense of obligation to meet certain societal expectations about grooming.

5 This understanding of proximal-distal equating with degrees of force and surety may begin to give us an explanation for why the use of *can* is restricted to root meanings. Surety of physical ability or enabling force matches with the current moment. We may not be able to perform tomorrow in the way we can perform today.

6 There were nine students enrolled in the class. The data from two students were eliminated because they missed the day of the modal intervention. The data from the third student was eliminated because she wrote a very long final memo that had 73 modals, a much higher number than the other subjects. Of these 73, 69 were correctly used. Including her data would give an appearance of disproportionate group gain in correct use of modals.

Bibliography

Abbuhl, R. J. (2005). *The effect of feedback and instruction on writing quality: Legal writing and advanced L2 learners.* Unpublished doctoral dissertation, Georgetown University, Washington DC.

Achard, M. & Niemeier, S. (2004). *Cognitive linguistics, second language acquisition, and foreign language teaching.* Berlin: Mouton de Gruyter.

Biber, D., Johansson, S., Leech, G., Conrad, S., & Finegan, E. (1999). *Longman grammar of spoken and written English.* London: Longman.

Brown, P. & Levinson, S. 1987. *Politeness: Some universals in language usage.* Cambridge: Cambridge University Press.

Celce-Murcia, M. & Larsen-Freeman, D. (1999). *The grammar book: An ESL/EFL teacher's course* (2nd ed.). Boston, MA: Heinle & Heinle.

Dirven, R. & Verspoor, M. (2004). *Cognitive explorations of language and linguistics,* (2nd ed.) Amsterdam: John Benjamins.

Eigen, M. & Winkler, R. (1983). *Laws of the game: How the principles of nature govern chance.* Harmondsworth, UK: Penguin.

Evans, V. & Green, M. (2006). *Cognitive linguistics: An introduction.* Mahwah, NJ: Lawrence Erlbaum Associates.

Fleischman, S. (1990). *Tense and narrativity.* London: Routledge

Frank, M. (1972). *Modern English: a practical reference guide.* Englewood Cliffs, NJ : Prentice-Hall.

Frodesen, J. & Eyring, J. (1997). *Grammar dimensions: Form, meaning, and use* (2nd ed., Vol. 4). Boston, MA: Heinle & Heinle.

Goldberg, A. E. (1995). *Constructions: A construction grammar approach to argument structure.* Chicago: Chicago University Press.

Hama, M. (2005). The effects of the minilesson on advanced learners' acquisition of English modals: A case study. Unpublished manuscript, Georgetown University, Washington, DC.

Lado (1957). *Language across cultures: Applied linguistics for language teachers.* Ann Arbor, MI: University of Michigan Press.

Lakoff, G. & Johnson, M. (1980). *Metaphors we live by.* Chicago: University of Chicago Press.

Larsen-Freeman, D. (1996). The role of linguistics in language teacher education. In J. Alatis, C. Straehle, B. Gallenburger, and M. Ronkin (Eds.), *Proceedings of the 1995 Georgetown Roundtable.* Washington, DC: Georgetown University Press.

Lyons, J. (1977). *Semantics.* Cambridge: Cambrige University Press.

Norris, J. M. & Ortega, L. (2000). Effectiveness of L2 instruction: A research synthesis and quantitative meta-analysis. *Language Learning, 50*(3), 417–528.

Palmer, F. (1986). *Mood and modality.* Cambridge: Cambridge University Press.

Papafragou, A. (2000). *Modality: Issues in the semantics-pragmatics interface.* Amsterdam and New York: Elsevier Science.

Riddle, E. (1985). The meaning and discourse function of the past tense in English. *TESOL Quarterly, 20*(2), 267–286.

Sweetser, E. (1990). *From etymology to pragmatics: Metaphorical and cultural aspects of semantic structure.* Cambridge: Cambridge University Press.

Talmy, L. (1988). Force dynamics in language and cognition. *Cognitive Science, 12,* 49–100.

Tiersma, P. (1999). *Legal language.* Chicago: University of Chicago Press.

Tyler, A. (2003). Applying cognitive linguistics to instructed language learning: An experimental investigation. Invited colloquium "Cognitive Linguistics and SLA" organized by Peter Robinson. American Association of Applied Linguistics (AAAL) Annual Conference. Arlington, VA (March 2003).

Tyler, A. & Evans, V. (2000). *My first husband was Italian: Examining "exceptional" uses of English tense.* Linguistic Agency of University of Duisburg (L.A.U.D), Series A: General and Theoretical Papers.

Tyler, A. & Evans, V. (2001). The relation between experience, conceptual structure and meaning: Non-temporal uses of tense and language teaching. In M. Putz, R. Dirven, & S. Niemeier (Eds.), *Applied Cognitive Linguistics I: Theory and language acquisition* (pp. 63–105). Berlin: Mouton de Gruyter.

Tyler, A. & Evans, V. (2003). *The semantics of English prepositions: Spatial scenes, embodied meaning and cognition.* Cambridge: Cambridge University Press.

Werner, P. & Nelson., J. (1996) *Mosaics Two: A Content-based grammar.* McGraw-Hill.

Appendix A

Consider the following excerpts. Are the modals used appropriate? Do you think there are better choices? How does choosing one modal rather than another change the meaning of the sentence? Are there any places where modals are missing?

1   Given these facts, one can wonder if Urbania should/could be sued by the holdouts because of the use of this exit consent.

2   Considering that in our case Urbania is facing serious financial problems, it seems clear that the last good alternative for the bondholders to receive payment is through the exit consent. Given these circumstances, it is probable the bondholders should have agreed to the restructuring.

3   Under the hypothesis that the court would find that the gross-up clause can be amended by the issuer and a certain majority of bondholders, the plaintiff holdouts will almost certainly claim the existence of an implied covenant concerning a contractual obligation of good faith by Urbania. The court can have to decide on the possible existence of wrongful coercion by Urbania.

4   Finally, the potential for a successful lawsuit could be seen in the argument that the cancellation of the gross-up clause has at least an indirect impact on the payment conditions of the bonds and therefore might not be changed without the agreement of all bondholders.

5   The key question we have to ask is, under New York law, should Urbania breach the bond contract due to the deletion of the tax gross-up clause?

6   Urbania is seeking our opinion on a debt restructuring plan . . . In order to encourage all bondholders to exchange their bonds, Urbania will cancel the tax gross-up clause contained in the existing bonds. With this change, the existing bonds will be less attractive than the new bonds, which will provide a new tax gross-up clause.

7   In order to induce the holdouts to accept the new bonds, the existing bonds shall be amended by deleting the tax gross-up clause.

8   For example, one of the students asked if the bank considers the social development that the investment would bring to the country.

19

CONCLUSION: COGNITIVE LINGUISTICS, SECOND LANGUAGE ACQUISITION AND L2 INSTRUCTION— ISSUES FOR RESEARCH

Peter Robinson and Nick C. Ellis

1 Introduction: Language use and language learning

Cognitive Linguistics and usage-based models explain how we learn language using environmentally adaptive, domain-general, cognitive abilities (such as attention scheduling and working memory). We learn language while processing input and *doing* things with words and gesture in socially conventionalized ways (narratives, conversations) to communicate intentions and ideas to others (see Bybee, 2006; Goldberg, 2006; Gullberg, 2006; Hudson, 2007; Langacker, 1999; MacWhinney, 1999; O'Grady, 2005; Talmy, 2000; Tomasello, 2003 and their chapters in this volume). Functionalist and concept-oriented approaches to First and Second Language Acquisition (SLA) share complementary interests in these issues (e.g., Andersen, 1984; Bardovi-Harlig, 2000; Bates, 1976; Bates & MacWhinney, 1982; Becker & Carroll, 1997; Berman, 1987; Berman & Slobin, 1994; Bloom, 1970; Cromer, 1974; Dietrich, Klein & Noyau, 1995; Givón, 1985, 1995; Greenfield & Smith, 1976; Hickman, 2003; Karmiloff-Smith, 1979; Klein, 1986; Li & Shirai, 2000; Mandler, 2004a; Nelson, 1996; Perdue, 1993a, 1993b; Sato, 1990; Schlesinger, 1982; Schumann, 1978; Slobin, 1973, 1985; Snow & Ferguson, 1977; Stromqvist & Verhoeven, 2004; Tomlin, 1990; von Stutterheim & Klein, 1987). Cognitive Linguistics describes how cognitive routines (focusing attention, event construal) and conceptual structure interface with language in the mind, and how the *processes* that give rise to learning are embodied in adaptive responses to communicative contexts and task demands (Coventry & Guijarro Fuentes, this volume; Lakoff & Johnson, 1998; MacWhinney, 1999;

Tomasello, 1999, 2003; Tomasello, Kruger & Ratner, 1993) which mediate, and so variably direct and support them (Ceci, 1996; Dai & Sternberg, 2004; Engestrom & Middleton, 1996; Lave & Wenger, 1991; Snow, 1994; Sternberg & Wagner, 1994; Suchman, 1987).

Cognitive Linguistics and usage-based models therefore emphasize that language is learned from participatory experience of processing input and producing language during *interaction* in social contexts where individually desired non-linguistic outcomes (a bank transfer, another cup of milk) are goals to be achieved (or not) by communicating intentions, concepts and meaning with others. These issues are complementary, too, to pedagogic rationales for adult second language (L2) learner needs analysis, communicative language teaching, and the design of materials and programs that aim to deliver it (Breen & Candlin, 1980; Crombie 1985; Johnson, 1996, 2004; Long, 2006; Long & Doughty, in press; Milanovich & Saville, 1996; Munby, 1978; Norris, Brown, Hudson & Yoshioka, 1998; Van den Branden, 2006; Widdowson, 1978; Wilkins, 1976); to proposals for when and how to intervene in L2 communication to focus attention on form–meaning relationships during classroom interaction (Achard, this volume; Doughty, 2001; Doughty & Williams, 1998; Ellis, 2006b, this volume; Long, 1991, 2007; Long & Robinson, 1998; Tyler, this volume; VanPatten, 2004); and to proposals for task-based language teaching that claim increasing the complexity of the communicative and conceptual demands of tasks directs learner attention to the "code" resources different languages make available to meet them, and that sequencing tasks on this basis thereby promotes "rethinking" for speaking and interlanguage development (Garcia Mayo, 2007; Gilabert, 2004, 2007; Ishikawa, 2007; Kuiken, Moss & Vedder, 2005; Kuiken & Vedder, 2007; Rahimpour, 1999; Robinson, 1996b, 2001a, 2001b, 2003b, 2005a, 2007a, 2007c; Robinson & Gilabert, 2007; Robinson, Ting & Urwin, 1995).

Findings from research into cognitive linguistic, usage-based learning are also important to understanding core issues in cognitive psychology and learning theory such as the nature of the cognitive processes involved in category formation and induction (e.g., Anderson & Lebriere, 1998; Elman, 2004; Gentner, Holyoak & Kokinov, 2001; Holland, Holyoak, Nisbett & Thagard, 1989; Hudson, 2007, this volume; Mandler, 2004b; Murphy & Ross, 2005; Nosofsky, 1986; Palmeri, 1997; Pothos, 2005; Rosch, 1975; Sloman & Rips, 1998; Smith & Medin, 1981; Taylor, 1995, this volume), and the cognitive abilities contributing to implicit and explicit learning and automatization of this (L1, L2, and other) knowledge (Bybee, 2006, this volume; Carlson, 1997; Carroll, 2001; DeKeyser, 1997, 2001, 2007; N. Ellis, 1994, 1995, 2002, 2003, 2005, in press, this volume; Ellis & Schmidt, 1998; Hulstijn, 2001; Hulstijn & Ellis, 2005; Hulstijn & Schmidt, 1994; Knowlton & Squire, 1996; Logan, 1988; MacWhinney, this volume; Perruchet & Vintner, 2002; Reber, 1993;

Reber & Allen, 1978, 2000; Robinson, 2003a, 2004, 2005b; Robinson & Ha, 1993; Schmidt, 1992, 1994, 1995; Speelman & Kirsner, 2005).

The issues raised, and implications drawn, are thus wide in scope since Cognitive Linguistics deals broadly with the relationships between language function, linguistic expression and conceptual structure. The "unit" of description Cognitive Linguistics provides for capturing these relationships during language use and language learning is the "construction" (see, e.g., the chapters by Achard, Ellis, Goldberg & Casenhiser, Gries, Langacker, Lieven and Tomasello, and O'Grady this volume). Goldberg (2006) and Tomasello (2003) have both described in detail how constructions—at various levels of schematicity—and usage-based learning, together, provide the complementary *property* (what knowledge is at point A) and *transition* theories (how it changes to knowledge at point B over time, see Cummins, 1983; Gregg, 2001) that are necessary for explaining *first* language (L1) acquisition. However, *reconstructing* a language, and learning an L2, clearly poses additional issues to those involved in constructing it during child L1 acquisition, and these fall into two broad areas in need of further theory and empirical research.

Firstly, the *input* to L1 and instructed adult L2 learning differs in quantity and consistency, and in acknowledgement of this a number of compensatory pedagogic L2 interventions have already been proposed and researched (see, e.g., Chaudron, 1988; Doughty, 2001, 2003; Gass, 2003; Long, 2007; Mackey & Gass, 2006; Parker & Chaudron, 1987; White, 1998; Yano, Long & Ross, 1994). Research into child language learning described by Goldberg and Casenhiser, this volume, provides experimental evidence of the optimizing effects of manipulating type and token frequencies, and skewing input to speed construction learning which may offer some additional insights of pedagogic value in this regard. How we assess whether second language (L2) learners have constructions, what they are, and how type and token frequency in the input to usage-based learning affects their L2 abstraction, generalizability, and productivity in L2 use throughout development are some of the issues for research that we consider in detail in the third section of this chapter.

Secondly, L1 constructions, their form–meaning pairings, are *entrenched* in the adult L2 learner and so are likely to affect L2 construction learning and the processes of function-form and form-function mapping in comprehension and production in variable ways (see MacWhinney, this volume). Languages differ in the way they "structure concepts" requiring expression during communication, by "windowing attention" to aspects of event structure that are available for coding linguistically (Talmy, 2000, this volume). Consequently, ways of "thinking for speaking" (Cadierno, this volume; Odlin, this volume; Slobin, 1996, 2004) at the conceptualization stage of message production (de Bot, 1992; Kormos, 2006; Levelt, 1989) have to be realigned with L2 syntactic and grammatical encoding options during message formulation and it is not yet clear how revised encoding procedures that follow from "rethinking-for-speaking" could become established in the L2 user during development, or how they are related to the prior stage in message formulation, i.e., L2 lexical encoding and lemma activation. These are issues for research that we consider in the fourth section of this chapter.

Linguistic theory and the descriptions of language it leads to, like findings from research into Second Language Acquisition (SLA), can, but need not, be directly relevant to language instruction. As Langacker, this volume, reminds us, "the impact of linguistic theory on language pedagogy has been less than miraculous and sometimes less than helpful." Over and above *descriptive* and *explanatory* adequacy, a view of language, and the units it characterizes as available for description, must also have *utility* value for pedagogic decision-making at a range of levels, e.g., from dictionary and materials design, to the articulation of portable and accessible classroom explanations, to the assessment of language needs, proficiency and progress (see Achard, this volume: Gries, this volume; Halliday, MacIntosh & Strevens, 1964; Hudson, this volume; Hutchinson & Waters, 1978; Langacker, this volume; Rutherford & Sharwood Smith, 1988; Swales, 1990; Tyler, this volume; Widdowson, 1990 for discussion). These latter, as yet little-explored, utility issues aside, in the following section we describe why we feel, in principle, the *view* of language characterized by Cognitive Linguistics and captured by usage-based models of construction learning, supplements (not supplants) many current educational concerns and practices in L2 pedagogy, before summarizing issues we propose for empirical research into these in the remaining two sections of this chapter.

2 Linguistics, language acquisition and language teaching

Over the last 50 years, as Tyler (this volume) notes, there have been a "dizzying array of approaches to L2 teaching." In part this has been because various characterizations of language (its properties) have been adopted in theories of SLA (see Ritchie & Bhatia, 1996) and often conflicting implications from these have been drawn for L2 instruction. In the 1950s, structural approaches to linguistic description (Fries, 1952) and the Contrastive Analysis Hypothesis of Second Language Acquisition (Lado, 1957) were both drawn on to motivate audiolingual methodology and materials for language teaching (see Howatt & Widdowson, 2004, for review). What all L2 learners had to do, the audiolingual method assumed, was habituate to the L2 "structural patterns" that differed from those in the L1 (what Fries, 1957, called learners' "blind spots"; cf. Ellis' discussion of "learned inattention," this volume), and in these areas of

L1–L2 contrast language production, pattern practice, and explicit negative feedback were provided to jointly facilitate this L2 "learning" process. What Fries (1952, p. 56) called "structural meaning" was emphasized in materials design and methodology, and in order to highlight it, "lexical meaning" and variation were minimized and controlled during instructional exposure. However, this particular co-articulation of property and transition theory, and the pedagogy it gave rise to, were soon called into question.

Supplanting the first element in this equation, in the 1960s "generative" approaches to linguistic theory were proposed, positing "deep" universal properties of human languages underlying apparent "surface structure" differences between them (Chomsky, 1965). Innate knowledge of these purely "formal" properties was invoked to explain how all L1 learners could proceed at the same rate, and with the same guarantee of success, despite variation in, and the "logical" insufficiency of, the amount of input and negative feedback they received, and regardless of the apparent surface-level discrepancies between the languages they learned. Complementary to these proposals, SLA research into "interlanguage" (Selinker, 1972) and "natural" sequences of Second Language Acquisition, which were seemingly shared with child L1 learners and robust despite L1 differences among populations of L2 learners (Dulay & Burt, 1974; Dulay, Burt & Krashen, 1982; Felix, 1981; Lightbown, 1983), led to the non-interventionist "Natural Approach" (Krashen & Terrell, 1983) to L2 instruction and the "Procedural Syllabus" (Prabhu, 1987) for delivering it. These prioritized the provision and pedagogic sequencing of comprehensible input, alone: L2 learners' language production, and negative feedback on it which attempted to direct learners' attention to the formal elements of language, and how they encode meanings, were seen to be of little, if any, importance, and neither was encouraged. But subsequent empirical research into the effects of L2 instruction showed that a focus on meaning alone, as in the Natural Approach, French Canadian immersion, and other non-interventionist programs of instruction (see Long & Robinson, 1998 for review)—while leading to considerable levels of success in activities requiring L2 listening and reading abilities (see Cummins, 1988; Siegel, 2003)—resulted in a limited (not natural) acquisitional endstate, especially as revealed by evidence of the poor oral L2 production abilities of learners after many years in, and upon exiting, bilingual-immersion programs (Day & Shapson, 1991; Gass, 2003; Harley & Swain, 1984; Lightbown, 2000; Swain, 1985).

Many contemporary approaches to L2 instruction, by contrast, are interventionist, allowing a role for a "Focus on Form" (Doughty & Williams, 1998: Long, 1991) during meaningful engagement with the L2, and in some cases adopting task-based approaches to organizing curriculum content (Candlin, 1987; Long, 1985, 2007; Long & Norris, 2000;

Van den Branden, 2006). In these approaches communicative tasks are theorized and designed along dimensions contributing to their information-processing demands on L2 comprehension and production, and also along dimensions contributing to the nature and amount of interaction they encourage and require for successful completion (Bygate, Skehan & Swain, 2001; Cameron, 2001; R. Ellis, 2003; Garcia Mayo, 2007; Crookes & Gass, 1993; Long, 1989, 1996; Mackey & Gass, 2006; Robinson, 2001b, 2007a, in press; Skehan, 1998). Opportunities for communicatively contextualized implicit and explicit negative feedback such instruction provides are matched to options in delivering it methodologically, as these are suitable to learners with a range of strengths in aptitudes, and the cognitive and other abilities contributing to them (Ackerman, 2003; Carroll, 1993; Dornyei, 2002, 2005; Dornyei & Skehan, 2003; Robinson, 2002, 2005c, 2007b; Skehan, 1989, 2002; Snow, 1987, 1994; Sternberg, 2002; Sternberg & Wagner, 1994), the aim being to do this using optimally effective techniques for drawing learner awareness to form–meaning mappings in the L2, and the communicative functions these can help serve. Cognitive Linguistics provides a view of language that is relevant to these aims, in which, as Langacker (this volume) points out, the centrality of meaning, the meaningfulness of grammar, and its usage-based nature are all fundamental assumptions.

2.1 Usage-based models and L2 instruction—Learning by doing and syllabus design

As the chapters in this book have made clear, Cognitive Linguistics describes the properties of language in very different ways than either structuralist or generative approaches. There are no deep "structures" and no formal "rules" that generate permissible "strings" which the lexicon fills out. The product of learning reveals cross-linguistic differences in how languages structure conceptual content for expression, and cognitive linguists describe these differences. But the processes which give rise to them are shared by all language learners. Usage-based models of acquisition argue language is learned from the input, using general cognitive mechanisms, sensitive to type and token frequency, resulting in item-specific knowledge and more abstract categories of form–meaning relationships that are integrated with and supported by conceptual structures, as these become established in the child during cognitive development. There is no Logical Problem (Baker & McCarthy, 1981): language input is sufficient evidence for the general learning processes that give rise to its abstract representation. No innate linguistic knowledge (Pinker, 1994) is needed to supplement these processes.

Usage-based models assume language acquisition is input-driven and experiential. They assume first-person experience of language (by children or adults) during situated, communicative language use provides evidence of *patterns* in the input that carry *meaning*, and that these patterns are learned while doing something with communicative intent, like playing "peekaboo" with mommy, or exchanging currency in a foreign country. A second language classroom providing learners with plentiful exposure to meaningful input, and opportunities to use the L2 while performing realistic communicative activities would be complementary, therefore, to the "input-driven" and "experiential" assumptions of usage-based learning. Content-based (Brinton, Snow & Wesche, 1989), immersion (Harley, Allen, Cummins & Swain, 1990), Natural Approach (Achard, this volume) and task-based (Van den Branden, 2006) programs (while differing in procedures for content selection, and other implementational details) all provide these. The various syllabi adopted in these programs specify instructional units in terms of holistic communicative activities, sequenced using non-linguistic criteria (see Long, 2007; Long & Crookes, 1992; Robinson, 1994, 2001b, in press; White, 1988 for review). Such approaches do not divide up the language to be learned, by presenting grammatical structures, notions and functions, lexical items, or other units of language separately, and serially, for the learner to later "synthesize" and put together during communicative practice (Wilkins, 1976). They require the learner to "analyze" the language used on pedagogic tasks, or during immersion program instruction in domains such as mathematics, physics, etc., in line with their own perceptions of the form–meaning connections that the L2 makes, and that need to be understood and used to achieve communicative goals under real-time operating conditions, and the processing constraints they impose.

Analytic approaches to syllabus design therefore allow for plentiful opportunities for L2 exposure, and provide learners with a "first-person," "participatory" perspective on the language experienced, and its meaningful coordinates in communicative context. In classrooms where such syllabi are followed, language is predominantly learned incidentally while "doing" something else for which it is useful. This is complementary to usage-based approaches to language learning: an approach to instruction which took descriptions of language from Cognitive Linguistics—or any other approach to linguistic description—and used those as a basis for serially delivering explicit instruction in grammar (so promoting third-party, outsider understanding of language taught as object) would not. Educational philosophers (Dewey, 1916), intelligent systems designers (Schank, 1999), SLA researchers (Hatch, 1978), and developmental psychologists (Bruner, 1960) (among others) have all argued that we "learn by doing," and more effectively so than when we are "taught" "facts" for passive absorption.

2.2 Cognitive Linguistics and conceptualization—Case-based reasoning and task-based L2 communication

Learning by doing presents us with problems which we have to resolve using existing systems of knowledge. Early L2 learning, therefore, is influenced by the L1 system (see Ellis, this volume; MacWhinney, this volume; Odlin, this volume). And inevitably, by trying to "do" more than we currently know how to, we must develop the "means" to do it, or we fail. Learning is success-driven, but also failure-driven, as is memory (Schank, 1999). Communication breakdowns, and the resulting failure to accomplish intentions, provide learners of L2s with vivid memories for "cases" of unsuccessful prior experience in using the L2, and from which they can reason towards better scripts, plans, and frames for performance in subsequent efforts to communicate (Ellis, 2005; Fillmore, 1985; Goffman, 1974; Robinson & Gilabert, 2007; Schank, 1999; Schank & Abelson, 1977). We develop, that is, when our own systems of L2 knowledge (how its forms realize meanings) functionally adapt to (and so reorganize under) various pressures to conceptualize and perform communicatively. Where the L1 system constrains and impedes the L2 system's adaptation to these pressures we are prompted to shed its influence.

We learn best by apprenticed, gradual, approximation to the demands placed on knowledge and skilled execution that complex problems in untutored environments pose on our abilities in a domain (landing an aircraft in a blizzard, on an unknown airfield, at night, without a co-pilot; doing simultaneous translation of an important speech, with live air feed, amid conditions of distraction, such as a noisy crowd of demonstrators). In child language learning, apprenticeship—scaffolded by caregivers and the language environment their input provides—is largely guaranteed, and the demands of communication in the L1 unfold slowly, and naturally, in pace with the child's own cognitive, conceptual and social development (Brown, 1973; Cromer, 1991; Nelson, 1996; Ninio & Snow, 1996; Schneider, Schumann-Hengesteler & Sodian, 2005; Slobin, 1973; Tomasello, 1999, 2003). In adult L2 learning, the situation is different. Being cognitively developed, and socially aware, adults often want to communicate more than they can in the L2 right from the start, and the support they have available for doing this is very often lacking. In untutored settings *input* is often not guaranteed, and so has to be sought out, as do interlocutors who may, or may not, adjust their L1 input to the L2 learner's level making it comprehensible, and who may, or may not, sustain engagement in *interaction* and negotiate meaning (out of lack of interest, shared goals, or frustration), or provide *feedback* on the L2 learner's language (or if they do so, not with any useable level of consistency).

Instructional programs aim to offer this support (comprehensible input, scaffolded interaction and usable feedback) by organizing learner participation in, and teacher interventions into, the classroom performance of pedagogic tasks and by facilitating understanding of their conceptual content (Jonassen, 1999). When such tasks are classified and sequenced for learners in an order of increasing conceptual and communicative complexity (Robinson, 2005a, 2007a), which approximates the order in which the child engages in them, it prompts, thereby, the development of the language abilities they need to accomplish them successfully. The mind is a dynamic, complex system, evolved to adapt to a complex environment, and language is one adaptive response to it that the mind has evolved (N. Ellis, 1998, 2002, 2003; Ellis & Larsen-Freeman, 2006; Thelen & Smith, 1994). When the complexity in the target adult language environment is pared down in the scaled world of the L2 language classroom (Ehret, Gray & Kirshenbaum, 2000), consistency with existing L1 systems of thinking and speaking is established. When it is gradually increased, adaptation to the L2 is facilitated. Parents provide this consistency and challenge for children: classrooms aim to provide it for L2 learners.

Cognitive Linguistics offers insights into how such L2 tasks and content can be designed, and sequenced, and production and learning opportunities maximized for learners attempting them, since it is an approach to language description which sees linguistic expression and conceptualization to be mutually dependent, and interfaced with other cognitive and social systems in adult language use and language development. It motivates descriptions of language structure which are psycholinguistically and acquisitionally plausible by drawing on "converging evidence" (see Langacker, 1999) concerning environmental, biological, psychological, developmental, historical, and sociocultural factors—and the domains and methods of inquiry they implicate. SLA researchers, too, consider all of the above factors to impact upon the social and cognitive processes that underlie variation in the rate and extent of language learning, whatever the language being learned, across a range of populations, and social contexts for learning. And in some of the ways, and following some of the rationales, we have discussed briefly above, second language instruction seeks to contrive contexts and interventions that promote the acquisition processes leading to those levels of development that are critical to success in using language for a range of purposes, and across a wide spectrum of personal and institutional settings.

2.3 Overview of areas to be addressed and research issues raised

In what follows we take perspectives on each of these fields and their mutual intersects and areas of overlapping interest, as revealed by the preceding chapters in this volume, placing particular emphasis on issues relevant to the acquisitional and pedagogic underpinnings of effective L2 instruction. There are two broad areas that we address in the remainder of this chapter, raising research topics and questions relevant to each, and we briefly introduce them here. Firstly we address the role of *constructions* in Second Language Acquisition. Both Cognitive Grammar and Cognitive Construction Grammar, as described in the chapters by Langacker, and Goldberg and Casenhiser in the second section of this handbook, assume constructions are the central units of language acquisition. Both assume constructions are stored as a structured inventory of form–meaning pairings, established by learners on the basis of exposure to input during communication, and that constructions are stored in a complex *network* of language knowledge (syntactic, lexical, morphological, phonological, pragmatic, etc.), as Hudson, Taylor and Bybee, this volume, each describe it. Construction Grammar approaches also motivate the description of L1 acquisition put forward by Lieven and Tomasello. The *cognitive processing* issues of how constructions are learned, and from what kind, and quantity of input are important for SLA to address, as well as issues of L2 development over time, and the relationship of construction learning to developmental sequences and acquisition orders that have been observed in SLA (e.g., Becker & Carroll, 1997; Ellis, 2006a; Larson-Freeman, 1976; Perdue, 1993a, 1993b; Pienemann, 1998, 2003; Schumann, 1978).

The issues of which *learning conditions* may be most conducive to construction learning, and the roles of type and token frequency in automatizing and generalizing constructional knowledge under these different conditions, are also important. A number of what Goldberg and Casenhiser call laboratory "training" studies of the effects of different degrees of *awareness* of, and orientations to *form–meaning* relationships during implicit, incidental, intentional, and instructed language learning have been done with adult L2 learner populations. One aim of this research has been to identify whether focusing learner attention on formal characteristics of the L2, or their meanings, or some selective combination of both (Doughty & Williams, 1998; Long, 1991) is most effective in promoting instructed SLA. Many of these studies have involved experimentally controlled exposure to "constructions" in natural L2s (with which learners are in some cases familiar and in others unfamiliar), as well as artificial and semi-artificial language (e.g., de Graaff, 1997; DeKeyser, 1995, 1997; Ellis, 1993; Hulstijn & Ellis, 2005; Robinson, 1995b, 1996a; Williams, 1999, 2005). In some cases constructions (Samoan ergative transitives, incorporated, and locatives; English ditransitives and datives) have been presented with different frequencies, and associative chunk-strengths (Robinson, 1997, 2005b: Robinson & Ha, 1993). In general (see Norris & Ortega, 2000) *explicit* conditions, in which learners are made aware of positional cues to constructional forms, or cues to correspondence between these forms and their meanings, have been found to be more effective in promoting successful post-treatment assessments of construction learning, compared to *implicit* learning conditions where such awareness is not promoted or demonstrated by learners. Many details of these findings remain to be confirmed and explored, but the experimental research into construction learning, and the roles of type and token frequency in this process, described by Lieven and Tomasello, and Goldberg and Casenhiser raise issues that will be important to pursue in future laboratory studies of implicit and explicit learning of L2s, and the effectiveness of techniques for focusing learner attention on form–meaning relationships, and we identify some of these issues in our proposals for future research.

The amount and perceptual salience of input (Ellis, 2006b; Goldschneider & DeKeyser, 2001) and its conceptual and communicative content both cooperate as important (broadly bottom-up, data-driven, and top-down, conceptually-driven) factors determining which constructions are learned, and how abstract, generalizable, and productive they are. The second area we address concerns *conceptualization and communicative content*, and how differences between languages predispose learners to describe events and window attention to them in different ways. This issue takes up many of the ideas about the attention function of language Talmy (this volume) describes, particularly the notion of cross-linguistic similarities and differences in lexicalization patterns for referring to motion events that Cadierno (this volume) explores, in the broader context of factors constraining and promoting conceptual transfer described by Odlin (this volume). Many of such cross-linguistic differences have been described, but the extent of their influence on transfer, at different levels of proficiency and development, is still unclear (Ringbom, 2006). We also consider what pedagogic activities and interventions may facilitate what Slobin (1996) has called "thinking for speaking," or what could be more properly called re-thinking for speaking and writing in the L2, as suggested in the chapters by Achard and Tyler.

Related to these issues, we describe SLA research into the cognitive/conceptual and procedural/performative demands of L2 learning tasks and consider how these may be manipulated with the aim of systematically promoting awareness of L2 lexicalization patterns, and promoting grammaticization of the morphological and grammatical means to express them in the L2, over the time course of instructional programs. Tasks make different demands on our attention, during both comprehension and production as Lieven and Tomasello describe (this volume), and it is especially important to know whether these attentional demands constrain or promote L2 learning in instructed settings (Robinson, 1995c, 2003a; Schmidt, 2001; Skehan, 1998). L2 instruction provides teachers and materials designers with opportunities to guide attention to and "enhance" constructions in the L2 input, while at the same time demonstrating their conceptual and communicative value. Similarly, it is possible to manipulate the frequencies with which, for example, verbs and the frames that various complex constructions require—such as those identified by Diessel (2004)—appear in the written or aural input learners process. Classroom settings also provide many opportunities for L2 interaction and both explicit and implicit negative feedback on L2 production (Allwood, 1993; Doughty, 2001; Ellis, 1999; Mackey & Gass, 2006; Long, 1996, 2007; Tomasello & Herron, 1989) as well as a communicative context for "priming" constructions in the input to learners during interaction and feedback episodes (Bremer, Broeder, Roberts, Simonot & Vasseur, 1993; McDonough, 2006; McDonough & Mackey, 2006; Pickering, Branigan, Cleland & Stewart, 2000).

Throughout our summary of these two broad areas, and in the topics and questions we identify for future research into them, we also address the important issue of *individual differences*. Clearly, differences in the frequency, and type of input affect the extent of language learning, in adults and children, as usage-based approaches predict, and as some research has already confirmed (see e.g., Bates, Bretherton & Snyder, 1988; Bybee, 2006, this volume; Dabrowska & Street, 2006; Ellis, this volume; Goldberg, 2006; Goldberg & Casenhiser, this volume). Cognitive abilities, too, which differ across adult second language learners (as they clearly do across child L1 and adult L2 learner populations), also enable and constrain the cognitive processes which give rise to language learning. But specifically what cognitive abilities contribute to usage-based construction learning, or the ability to re-think for speaking in the L2, and under what pedagogic conditions are differentials in these cognitive abilities most influential on L2 learning? How are these cognitive abilities related to apparent age-related differences in the levels of ultimate attainment reachable by learners (DeKeyser, 2000; Hyltenstam & Abrahamsson, 2003)? How can measures of aptitude (Carroll, 1993; Robinson, 2005c; Skehan, 2002) for second language learning be developed to assess individual differences in these potentially enabling and constraining cognitive abilities, and how could such information be used pedagogically? Important questions, all, to which we still seek answers.

3 Learning second language constructions

The chapters by Lieven and Tomasello and Goldberg and Casenhiser illustrate how, using general cognitive abilities, and the interactive skills they are gradually developing, children begin the process of constructing their language. Starting small, producing first words, then two or three word combinations in which verbs are conservatively used with familiar frames, more complex and abstract constructional schemas develop from the particularities of the language they hear in the input, prompted by the child's growing need to engage in and successfully manage increasingly complex communicative activities at home and at school. Adult expressions typically consist of a number of constructions—conventionalized pairings of form and function: "What did Liza buy Zach?" (Goldberg, 2006, p.10) consists of word level constructions (Liza, Zach, etc.), and others of greater size and complexity (VP, NP construction; subject auxiliary inversion construction; question construction; ditransitive construction). These are combined freely to form utterances in adult language. In the usage-based model of child language learning, instances of language used in specific contexts are the evidence from which the child develops constructions, and the frequency of instances in the input affects speed of language processing, the extent of automatic recognition and retrieval of instances, generalizations over these instances, and abstraction of the linguistic system.

3.1 Token and type frequency in the input

High-token frequency of a construction (a morpheme, word or larger unit) in the input leads to entrenchment, and automatic recognition and fluent production (see Bybee, this volume). Thus, "Where Daddy gone?" uttered frequently by the mother becomes a frozen form or chunk available for use by the child, but unanalyzed initially. Type frequency concerns the number of distinct items that can occur in any of the "slots" in a constructional frame: "Where's Mummy gone?; Where's baby gone?" are instances of the same construction, with different types of referent, demonstrating how the construction can be used productively.

High-type frequency therefore provides the child with evidence of how to "fission" (Peters, 1983) a formulaic chunk, and so generalize it into an abstract schematic frame. Evidence of high-type frequency is also used to abstract the general "combinatorial privileges" (Braine, 1963; Maratsos, 1982) shared by specific lexical items, out of which emerge prototypical grammatical categories (see Taylor, this volume). Form and function conspire in this process. On the one hand, as Maratsos argues "the child constructs grammatical categories such as noun, verb, gender class by analyzing the groups of grammatical uses or operations that groups of terms tend to take in common, thereby learning how uses in such operations predict each other" (1982, p.247). But semantic and pragmatic meaning also provide information that helps co-predict the emergence of grammatical categories (Bates & MacWhinney, 1982; Ninio & Snow, 1996). Combinatorial privileges groups of words share, supplemented by notions of agency and topic, animacy, intention, cause, and others, form the criterial features around which, for example, the prototypical notion of "subject" is constructed.

Second language learners start with much larger units than words in developing constructional knowledge, but input-driven processes likely contribute to their segmentation, and so thereby the subsequent availability for recombination and "fusion" (Peters, 1983) of resulting units in learner speech. There are many documented examples of this segmentation process. For example, Wong Fillmore (1979; cf. Wagner-Gough & Hatch, 1976; and Ellis, 1996 and Wray, 2002, for extensive review) gives an example from the L2 speech of Nora in which an initial unit or formula becomes segmented into three units on the basis of type and token variation in the input, commenting ". . . the analytic process carried out on formula yielded formulaic frames with abstract slots representing constituent types which could substitute in them, and it also freed constituent parts of the formula to function in other constructions either as formulaic units or as wholly analyzed items" (Wong Fillmore 1979, p. 213). In Nora's case, "Iwannaplaywidese" appeared first as a single unit, followed by "Iwanna" used separately from "playwidese" (Iwanna +VP), and then by "playwi" used separately from "dese" (playwi+ NP). As each slot in the initial frame becomes available for independent use, they themselves function as frames for further input-driven learning, and so the network (Hudson, 2007, this volume) of relations between the separate units becomes *elaborated* on the evidence of type frequency, and simultaneously *entrenched*, at various levels of schematicity, as constructional knowledge, on the basis of token frequency. Bracketing and chunking in this fashion provide a link between hierarchical structure and string, so allowing phonology, lexis, and syntax to develop hierarchically by repeated cycles of differentiation and integration of chunks of sequences (Ellis, 1996; Studdert-Kennedy, 1991).

As Hudson and O'Grady, this volume, argue, dependency grammars are well suited to characterizing the linear, real-time processing involved in such item-based input-driven learning, and so have been adopted in a number of "lexicalist" descriptions of first and second language learning of item-specific "valency" information, and item-specific formulae (Bates & Goodman, 1999; Ninio, 2006; Robinson, 1986, 1990). Type frequency establishes membership in the different classes of items that can co-occur in a construction—their categorial "valency": token frequency entrenches and makes automatically available preferred and fixed patterns of co-occurrence between specific items in constructional units of variable degrees of fixedness, automaticity, and productivity, such as collocations, colligations, idiomatic, and other formulaic chunks (N. Ellis, 2001, 2003, this volume; Gries, 2003, this volume; Hoey, 2005; Hunston & Francis, 2000; Myles, Mitchell & Hooper, 1999; Pawley & Syder, 1983; Robinson, 1989, 1993; Schmitt, 2004; Sinclair, 1984; Wray, 2002).

3.2 Consistency and complexity in the input

Combinations of high-type frequency and high-token frequency give rise to the relatively greater *consistency* of some versus other elements provided in the input, and this facilitates acquisition and generalization of a constructional frame (Lieven & Tomasello, Goldberg & Casenhiser, this volume). For example, using pronouns in the ditransitive construction during a training experiment, in which many types of verbs were presented to children (he's <u>kicking/eating/drinking/</u>etc. it) led to acquisition and generalization of the ditransitive construction to novel verbs. In contrast, children trained using a variety of full NPs (<u>the boy, the dog, the sofa, the water</u>, etc.) showed less, though still some, acquisition and generalization (Childers & Tomasello, 2001). The consistency provided by these pronouns (their high-token frequency, as well as their consistent semantic indeterminacy), together with type variation in the verbs (and their greater semantic specificity) led to better generalization and constructional abstraction. The availability of simplified input helps in part to guarantee this consistency for child language learners (pronoun use is an example of linguistic and lexical simplification, i.e., a preference for high-frequency vocabulary, and a feature of motherese) in contrast, often, to much of the input to L2 learners in adulthood where Foreigner Talk (Ferguson, 1971), if used, is more variable (Gass, 1997), and often dispreferred in favor of interactional modifications (Long, 1983).

Consistency of form–function mappings also make constructions easier to learn (MacWhinney, this volume). When a form is consistently available in the input and a function is understood to be being expressed, and when a function can reliably be inferred on hearing a form, then the resulting "cue validity" means faster form–function mapping, cross-linguistically, in child language acquisition. Despite such consistency, for L2 learners, especially at those lower levels of proficiency and with less exposure, existing L1 knowledge may inhibit the L2 mapping of form and function (as both Ellis and MacWhinney, this volume, point out). For example, where the L1 conflates manner with motion on the verb, and encodes path separately on a satellite as in Danish and English, this lexicalization pattern may persist in the L2 production of verb-framed languages like Spanish and Japanese where path is conflated with the verb, and manner encoded separately (see Cadierno, this volume, and Ringbom, 2006; Van-Patten, Williams, Rott & Overstreet, 2004 for general discussion). In such cases, a Focus on Form (Doughty & Williams, 1998; Long, 1991; Long & Robinson, 1998) in communicative context has been argued to facilitate the mapping process between form and function by directing attention to, and promoting "noticing" of (Schmidt, 1990) formal characteristics of the L2 while the meaning they convey is simultaneously being demonstrated.

As children begin to develop more complex constructions—schemas with larger numbers of slots in coordinated and subordinated clauses (see Diessel, 2004)—these, too, are restricted to a few verbs when language is produced (I <u>think/ know</u> . . . he is coming soon) so initially forming complex constructional islands of only gradually developing schematicity—a process Mellow (2006) describes for L2 learners. Acquisition and production of these complex constructions, too, reflects their frequency in the input at home and at school (Tomasello, 2003, p. 266) and establishing gradual control over the use of them is promoted by the need for successful participation in multi-party conversational interactions (involving reference to topics displaced in time and space, of a variety of conceptual content); for organizing and relating events in narrative discourse; and for other complex communicative activities.

Repeated processing of particular constructions facilitates their fluency of subsequent processing, too, and these effects occur whether the learner is conscious of this processing or not. Although you are conscious of words in your visual focus, you definitely did not just now consciously label the word focus as a noun. On reading it, you were surely unaware of its nine alternative meanings, though in a different sentence you would instantly have brought a different meaning to mind. What happens to the other meanings? Psycholinguistic evidence demonstrates that some of them exist unconsciously for a few tenths of a second before your brain decides on the right one. Most words (over 80% in English) have multiple meanings, but only one of these can become conscious at a time. So your reading of focus has primed subsequent reading of that letter string (whatever its interpretation), and your interpretation of focus as a noun has primed that particular subsequent interpretation of it. In this way, particular constructions with high-token frequency are remembered better, recognized faster, produced more readily and otherwise processed with greater facility than low-token frequency constructions (see Ellis, 2002 for review). Each token of use thus strengthens the memory traces of a construction, priming its subsequent use and accessibility following the power law of practice relationship whereby the increase in strength afforded by early increments of experience are greater than those from later additional practice. In these ways language learning involves considerable unconscious "tallying" (Ellis, 2002) of construction frequencies, and native-like fluency and idiomaticity (Pawley & Syder, 1983) in language use requires exploitation of this implicit statistical knowledge (Bod, Hay, & Jannedy, 2003; Bybee & Hopper, 2001; Chater & Manning, 2006; Ellis, in press 2008).

3.3 Skewed input, procedural vocabulary, and argument structure generalization

The consistency that high-token frequency provides works together with the variation that high-type frequency provides to help children abstract patterns from what they hear. Goldberg and Casenhiser show that parental language naturally *skews* the input to children to provide systematic patterns of consistency and variation, and that such skewed input leads them to learn and *generalize* argument structure constructions. In a corpus of mothers' speech to children (Bates, Bretherton & Snyder, 1988), certain "light," "general purpose" verbs are associated with very high proportions of the use of specific constructions (39% of verbs in Subj V Obl are "go"; 38% in Subj V Obj Obl are "put"; 20% in Subj V Obj Obj2 are "give"). The same trends are mirrored in children's production, where one or another of these verbs is used with its associated construction: their high-token frequency in the input thereby likely establishes a correlation between verb meaning and a constructional form for the child. As vocabulary increases new verbs (with more specific, and so narrower ranges of meaning) are assimilated into the pattern, but the "general purpose" verbs remain the prototypical exemplars.

Such verbs (like the pronouns mentioned above which supply the semantically indeterminate, but positional consistency needed to enable pattern abstraction) while having basic meanings are highly indexical (compare "give him credit" and "give him a dollar") and semantically opaque (e.g., "give" versus "fax"). The consequence is that the meaning contributed by the "construction as a whole" and its specific lexical content is needed to supplement the verb semantics. The constructional meaning "fills in" the verb meaning, and is at least as reliable, consequently, as verb meaning in predicting sentence meaning (Goldberg & Casenhiser, this volume). As Bybee (this volume) notes, such highly indexical, typically reduced and semantically "bleached" words serve many grammatical functions, together with other "closed class" grammatical words, and so are highly frequent, entrenched, and automatized in adult production. They have "procedural" value (Robinson, 1989, 1993; Widdowson, 1983) in syntactically organizing the declarative content of more lexically specific words, and are stored in a distinct "procedural" memory system from "declarative" vocabulary, and the meanings it gives rise to (Ullman, 2001).

Talmy (2000) argues that the grammatical meanings carried by such closed class vocabulary, serves a "concept-structuring" function across languages—providing the language learner with a skeletal frame which scaffolds the mapping of conceptual material to constructions (see the following section). What Childers and Tomasello (2001) and Goldberg and Casenhiser show (see also Goldberg, 2006) is the "construction-structuring" function of these words (the consistency provided by pro-forms, "it," "him", and similar highly indexical verbs, "give," "put") for children, and how the skewed frequencies with which they appear in different constructions in parental input make that, in part, possible.

3.4 Issues for research

Do second language learners have constructions? We need to know many details concerning this basic issue. What constructions do L2 learners know, how productive are they, and how is constructional knowledge in the target language affected by *cross-linguistic* influences from the L1, or other languages known? How does constructional knowledge develop with level of *proficiency* in the target language, from beginner to advanced and native-like levels of L2 ability? Two experimental procedures for examining the availability of constructional knowledge in guiding performance on primed-production tasks and comprehension-sorting tasks have provided initial evidence in this area, and provide a basis for further research into the questions raised above. Benicini and Goldberg (2000) asked native English speakers to sort 16 sentences into four piles based on "overall" sentence meaning. The 16 sentences crossed four verbs (took, sliced, got, threw) with four constructions (transitive, ditransitive, caused motion, resultative). Subjects were found to be just as likely to sort on the basis of the meaning provided by the construction, as they were to sort on the basis of verb meaning. In a replication of this study, Liang (2002) found that at lower levels of proficiency L1 Chinese learners of L2 English based their sorts on the four verbs used, but intermediate-level learners based sorts on the construction types, and at the advanced level there was an even greater (than for intermediate, or L1 native speakers of English) preference for construction-based sorting, demonstrating not only the availability of constructional knowledge but increasing reliance on it with developing L2 proficiency. No evidence of how different L1 populations differ, or do not, in their preferences for basing L2 sorts on verbs, or construction types was shown—or intended to be—in these studies, but this procedure is clearly suitable for addressing the extent of cross-linguistic influence on the use of constructional knowledge (of a wide variety of levels of schematicity), and whether, and how, this diminishes over time.

Gries and Wulff (2005) found similar results for sorting to Liang (2002), and also addressed the influence of constructional knowledge on L2 production. There is a tendency towards structural repetition in natural unmonitored speech, and the facilitating effect of prior exposure to a structure (either heard or previously produced) has been examined using a variety of experimental methodologies. Gries and Wulff used a sentence-completion task (Pickering & Branigan, 1998), in which L1 German speakers first completed sentences in fragments that biased them to producing and completing them as ditransitive or prepositional dative constructions. Subsequent to completing each production prime, a shorter sentence fragment was completed, and the results showed that ditransitives were produced in higher quantities following ditransitive construction primes, and vice versa for prepositional datives. As with the sorting procedure for examining the extent of constructional knowledge, further priming studies are also needed to examine the influence of L1, L2 construction type and level of L2 proficiency on the priming effect of prior exposure to L2 constructions on written production (as in Gries & Wulff, 2005) and spoken production, in experimental, and more naturalistic classroom contexts (see McDonough, 2006).

Psycholinguistic techniques can also be brought to bear to investigate second language learner constructions. This is an area of considerable current research activity focusing upon second language learners' sensitivity to the frequency of constructions and the mutual dependency of their elements in processing for recognition, comprehension, and production of collocations (Ellis, Frey, & Jalkanen, 2007a), patterns of semantic prosody (Ellis, Frey, & Jalkanen, 2007b), and formulaic sequences (Ellis & Simpson-Vlach, in preparation; Ellis, Simpson-Vlach & Maynard, in preparation; Schmitt, 2004).

Constructional knowledge, construction use, and cognitive abilities. An interesting question is how related *knowledge* demonstrated by a preference to sort sentences into groups with similar *overall meaning* on the basis of constructions is related to sensitivity to constructional primes, and so *use* of primed constructions in speech and writing. There are two ways to examine this relationship. Developmentally, do priming effects also increase with proficiency, as constructional sorting tendencies seem to do? And at any one point of development do those who show a greater preference for constructional sorting, also show greater sensitivity to, and "uptake" of constructional primes in speech and writing? If so, then it could be argued that there are some learners with a special sensitivity to, and proclivity to use construction knowledge, and the further interesting issue would then be "What cognitive abilities and capacities would predict this 'aptitude' for construction learning and use?"

Analogical mapping, cognitive abilities, and construction learning. Tomasello (2003) and Goldberg (2006) speculate that the abilities drawn on in analogical mapping, together with functional distributional analysis, are likely responsible for childrens' ability to schematize across utterances and develop abstract constructions. In a general sense, analogy is the ability to think about relational patterns, and the structure-mapping or structural alignment it gives rise to is at the heart of many different cognitive processes. What cognitive abilities contribute to analogical mapping across utterances for adult second language learners, and how would they be measured? If they could be measured, would they predict differences in the rate and complexity of construction learning? The words in sentences subtest of the Modern Language Aptitude Test (Carroll & Sapon, 1959) measures the ability to identify the analogous grammatical role of words in pairs of sentences, but this would seem to heavily implicate explicit metalinguistic knowledge. Are more basic, non-metalinguistic abilities for forming analogies drawn on by adults in developing abstract constructions (as they must be in child L1 learners)? How are these abilities related to others involved in language processing, such as phonological working memory, and capacity limits on it? Models of what these combinations of abilities might be, and of their contribution to "aptitude complexes" for language learning under different conditions of exposure to input are proposed in Robinson (2002, 2007b) and Skehan (2002) which could serve as frameworks for initial research into this area of "aptitude for construction learning" and how it interacts with opportunities to process and learn input in different instructional contexts.

Is the course of acquisition of complex constructions the same for adults and children? The cross-sectional studies and experimental methods used by Benicini and Goldberg (2000) and Gries and Wulff (2005), described above, are useful as supplements to longitudinally gathered data concerning the use of constructions, of various degrees of complexity, over time. Although longitudinal studies of L2 speech production are relatively rare, they are as necessary to understanding the course of construction learning and use in SLA as they are in the studies reported in Lieven and Tomasello, this volume (see also Diessel, 2004; Ellis, Ferreira Junior, & Ke, in preparation; Tomasello, 1992). As in child language acquisition research, progress rests upon the acquisition, transcription, and analysis of detailed dense longitudinal corpora (Ortega & Iberri-Shea, 2005).

Diessel (2004) has described the course of acquisition of later learned complex constructions in English, including those consisting of a matrix clause and a subordinate clause, which are of three types: finite and non-finite complement clauses (she said that he would come; she wants him to come); finite and non-finite relative clauses (she bought the bike that was on sale; is that the bike costing 50 dollars?); and finite and non-finite adverbial clauses (he arrived when she was about to leave; she left the door open to hear the baby) and co-ordinate clauses (he tried hard, but he failed). He argues that acquisition of these complex constructions, as Lieven and Tomasello, this volume, also claim, is initially lexically specific, each organized around a few concrete lexical expressions, and so forming complex constructional islands. He also argues that complement and relative clauses emerge by gradually *expanding* simple sentences, and that adverbial and co-ordinate clauses emerge by *integrating* independent constructions into a bi-clausal unit. Mellow (2006) is the first study of the emergence of complex constructions in L2 production, and more studies of this kind are needed to examine the comparability of complex construction learning across child and adult learners.

Is constructional knowledge related to traditionally identified acquisition sequences? Related to this issue is how stages in the emergence of complex constructions, once identified, are related to the architecture of the second language speech processor (see the following section), and in particular to Pienemann's Processability Theory (1998, 2003), which describes a hierarchy of processing stages predicting the emergence of more complex structures at different points in development. How do the processes of expansion and integration Diessel describes for childrens' learning of more complex constructions relate to these L2 processing stages, in development, and in theory? Similarly, could information about the constraints on, and sequence of emergence of constructions in L2 use be used as an index of L2 development?

How do type and token frequency interact in learning SL constructions? The effects of type and token frequency, examined in the experimental child language acquisition studies described above, are also worthy of Second Language Acquisition research. Does increasing type variation in the verb *slot* lead to greater abstraction and generalizability of argument structure constructions? Are the effects of type variation increased by consistency of other elements in the construction, as the study reported by Lieven and Tomasello showed, such that proforms in NP positions increase the salience of type frequency in the verb slot in the ditransitive construction?

Frequency effects of sub and supra lexical units on construction learning. Probabilistic, statistical learning contributes to the effects of manipulating the type and token frequencies of words in constructions in the studies reported by Goldberg and Casenhiser, but cues for generalizing constructions can be at any number of levels, such as phonemes, morphemes, and larger chunks. The same questions raised above can be asked with respect to these sub and supra lexical units, and the effects of their type and token frequency on learning smaller, and complex multi-clausal L2 constructions. What is the effect of manipulating chunks of co-occurring words, and the type and token frequencies contributing to "chunk strength" (Knowlton & Squire, 1996; Robinson, 2005b) on L2 learning and generalization of complex constructions such as pseudo-clefts (Robinson, 1996a) and finite and non-finite complement and relative clauses (Mellow, 2006)?

What is the effect of skewing input, and sequencing skewed input on adult SLA of constructions? Does presenting many instances or tokens of a single verb in a constructional frame first, followed by more varied types of verbs, with lower token frequency in the same constructional frame, result in superior generalizability of the learned argument structure, compared to more balanced input? This was found to be so in the experimental studies reported by Goldberg and Casenhiser (this volume) whereby a skewed experience of exemplars with one exemplar presented much more often that the others led to faster acquisition. So they and others (Bybee, this volume; Ellis, in press 2008; Goldberg, 2006; Morales & Taylor, in press) suggest that the Zipfian structure of natural language presents a usage distribution that optimizes learning.

Zipf's law (1935), describes the distributional properties of the lexicon whereby the frequency of a word decays as a (universal) power function of its rank. The more common words account for many more tokens of our language than do the less common ones (consider *the* at more than 60,000 tokens per million words, *of* 29,000, *and* 27,000, etc.). Goldberg (2006) proposes that Zipf's law applies within individual construction profiles, too, and so the learning of linguistic constructions as categories is optimized because there is one very high-frequency exemplar that is also prototypical of the meaning of the construction, and gives evidence of this for child language acquisition where *put* is the most frequent exemplar of the caused motion construction, *give* of the double object ditransitive, etc. Recent work by Ellis, Ferreira Junior, and Ke (in preparation) has shown this also to apply to naturalistic second language learners of English in the ESF corpus (Perdue, 1993a, 1993b)—the type-token frequency profiles of these constructions in the input to these learners followed a Zipfian distribution and the learners' acquisition of each pattern was seeded by the highest-frequency exemplar which was also prototypical in its meaning.

More research on this topic is needed both in analyses of longitudinal corpora of Second Language Acquisition and in experimental studies investigating the effects of different frequency profiles of construction exemplars upon L2 acquisition. There are clear implications for adult L2 learners—for delivering "floods" of enhanced input (White, 1998), implicit negative feedback via recasts (Doughty, 2001), or other techniques for focus on form during classroom interaction—suggesting that skewing input floods or recasts, by initially presenting high-token frequencies of an important positional element in a flooded or recast constructional frame, should have an advantage over more balanced input floods and recasting (Bybee, this volume; Ellis, in press 2008).

What are the patterns that are present in the input? Proper description of usage-based acquisition and its component constructions requires the proper description and analysis of usage. As Gries (this volume) explains, Corpus Linguistics and Cognitive Linguistics are natural partners in this enterprise. We need dense longitudinal corpora of learner input and of their acquisition (N. Ellis, 1999; MacWhinney, 1995; Ortega & Iberri-Shea, 2005; Tomasello & Stahl, 2004), we need representative corpora for specific genres, e.g., academic speech (e.g., MICASE, 2004), and we need detailed means of marking up these corpora and performing constructional and collostructional analyses (Gries, this volume; Goldberg, 2006).

What are the details of the acquisition process? Usage-based theories of acquisition are exquisitely "bottom-up." They have turned upside down the traditional generative assumptions of innate language acquisition devices, the continuity hypothesis, and top-down, rule-governed, process-ing, replacing these with data-driven, emergent accounts of linguistic sys-tematicities. Constructionist analyses chart the ways in which children's creative linguistic ability, their language system, emerges from their analy-ses, using general cognitive abilities, of the utterances in their usage his-tory, and from their abstraction of regularities within them. In these views, language acquisition is a sampling problem, involving the estimation of the population norms from the learner's limited sample of experience as perceived through the constraints and affordances of their cognitive apparatus, their human embodiment, and the dynamics of social inter-action. There is too much complexity here for researchers simply to "think through." If language emerges from the learners' sample of usage, and all of the types of constructions therein properly represented in terms of token frequencies, then the only way to properly get a handle on these processes is through computer modeling. Recent developments in emergentism, dynamic systems theory, and chaos complexity/complex systems theory inform issues of emergence from usage, from the inter-actions of agents who communicate, of language form and language function, of signals and perceptual systems, of prior knowledge, learned attention, and working memory in processing, of language representa-tions upon signals, of multiple languages in contact, of language aptitude, of networks of social interaction (Ellis & Larsen Freeman, 2006; Holland, 1992, 1998; MacWhinney, 1999; de Bot, Lowie, & Verspoor, 2007). We cannot understand the whole without realizing that it is more than the sum of its parts, or the parts without understanding the whole. We will only fully understand these processes by exploring some of the inter-actions using connectionist simulations of the learning of linguistic con-structions in models exposed to representative samples of usage and in agent-based simulations of language change. Agent-based models are used to study how a population develops and changes, the transient behaviors of a system before it reaches equilibrium. They consider the different social structures in finite populations because recent network studies show that these have a profound influence on system dynamics (Newman, Barabasi, & Watts, 2006). Moreover, agents in a population are not homogenous but often differ in their properties or behaviors. This hetero-geneity is particular true in considering language learning and language use. Children show different trajectories of their language development, and people in different social classes and of different ages differ a lot in their language use. Neural networks, in contrast, are better known for their use in simulating learners' characteristics as they are exposed to a problem space of many learning trials representative in content and statistical distributions to experience in quasi-regular domains. Learning in a neural network is accomplished by changing weights on the inputs to a neuron, using some measure of the usefulness of the neuron's output signal. Categorization and prediction is the forte of neural networks. Because the output of a neuron depends upon the weighted sum of its inputs, it nicely implements conditional actions, hence the tradition of connectionist research in language acquisition and psycholinguistics (Chater & Manning, 2006; Christiansen & Chater, 2001; Elman et al., 1996).

4 Language and conceptualization, thinking for speaking, and L2 production

In Cognitive Grammar, as Langacker and Achard, this volume, describe it, shared meaning results from an interplay of conceptualizations, and constructions are conventionalized linguistic means for presenting different conceptualizations and construals of an event. Achard illustrates this by comparing two causative constructions into which the verb "<u>laisser</u>" (let) can enter in French: the VV construction as in "<u>Marie a laissé</u> (V) <u>partir</u> (V) <u>les enfants</u>," structures the action scene as the main subject's (Marie) agentive responsibility and the causee (les enfants) coded as direct object reflects its non-agentive role. In contrast the VOV construction reflects a different construal of the scene "<u>Marie a laissé</u> (V) <u>les enfants</u> (O) <u>partir</u> (V)," in which the causee (les enfants) is conceptualized as the energy force initiating an action, and its position prior to the verb coding the process it is responsible for reflects its agentive role. The same scene, in other words, can be construed as one in which the causee's role is non-agentive (VV) or one in which the causee is an agentive energy force initiating an action (VOV). Languages make available different constructions for representing these alternative speaker construals of the scene, and the roles of participants in them. The central role of the speaker in selecting constructions which represent alternative construals of events is not captured in purely formal descriptions of pedagogic, structural rules (such as the "structural meanings" of sentence patterns that Fries, 1952, described). Achard argues that learners benefit most from actual exposure to real instances of "use" in "situations" where they can match the choice of construction with the speaker's intended construal of events (so understanding the constructional meaning) and receive opportunities to participate in, and share constructional construals of events with others (this, in contrast to learning the formal properties of constructions in isolation, via decontextualized instruction in grammatical "rules").

512

In their discussion of L2 spatial language, and prepositions, Tyler, and Coventry and Guijarro-Fuentes (this volume) similarly emphasize the necessity of participation in *situated action* to learners' full understanding of their meaning, and communicatively effective L2 use of them. The meaning of spatial language does not simply derive from the addition of fixed meanings prepositions have for "where" an object is to the meanings of other elements in the sentence describing "what" is being located (e.g., nouns and verb) which can be taught by L2 rule and learned by rote. Rather, Coventry and Guijarro-Fuentes argue, meaning is flexibly constructed on-line as a function of multiple constraints involving object knowledge, dynamic-kinematic routines, and functional geometric analyses which come together in contexts that "embody" meaning for language users. Such situations naturally, therefore, involve not only understanding the speaker's intention, and learning how it motivates a particular choice of linguistic expression for referring to spatial location (comprehending the input), but also opportunities for communication which may require reciprocal use of such expressions (output) to convey meaning to others through speech production.

In what follows we take up some of these and other issues involved in understanding how different languages map conceptualization to constructions that are of especial interest to SLA research and language instruction. These include the extent to which these differences may require the learner to "rethink" for L2 speaking in making these mappings; of how structured exposure to "L2 tasks" making different communicative and conceptual demands may facilitate the mapping processes and promote more accurate and complex L2 speech; and of the consequences of this for models of the "psycholinguistic processes" involved in L2 speech production. These are issues, then, of how usage-based *learning* leads to development in productive L2 *use*, and of the mechanisms, and pedagogic interventions that enable and facilitate it.

4.1 *Conceptualization, construal, and speech production*

Choice of one or another construction for describing an entity or situation in the L1 are the result of our unconscious structuring of the aspects of experience we wish to convey. Alternative construals of entities or situations are achieved by a variety of cognitive operations, and constructions are the linguistic reflex of these operations. In terms of Levelt's (1989) model of speech production constructions represent a mapping from the first stage in message formulation, in what Levelt calls the "Conceptualiser" to later stages of lemma activation, and lexical and syntactic encoding. At the conceptualization stage units of content are prepared for expression, drawing on the episodic and semantic memory stores. There is a thought, for example, about a currently observed event scene, or one recently observed and stored in episodic memory. Preparation of this thoughtful content, in Levelt's terms, includes macroplanning, of the communicative intention to be conveyed, and the appropriate discourse mode, and microplanning of the perspective to be taken in conveying the message. In theory one could assume that these preverbal construal processes and cognitive operations are language-independent. But there has been much recent debate about this, and evidence reported to support the claim that in a number of domains languages influence the way events are conceptualized and prepared for verbal expression. There is Talmy's work on how language structures concepts and windows attention to aspects of experience through the options specific language make available to speakers (see Talmy, 2000, this volume), and Berman and Slobin's (1994: Stromqvist & Verhoeven, 2004) cross-linguistic research into how different languages lead speakers to prioritize different aspects of events in narrative discourse. Levinson's (2003) and Coventry and Guijarro-Fuentes' research (this volume) into language and spatial cognition, also suggests this, as does the research into L2 conceptual transfer described by Odlin (this volume).

An example of research in this area is that of Carroll and colleagues (Carroll, von Stutterheim & Nuese, 2004; see also Becker & Carroll, 1997; Perdue, 1993a, 1993b; von Stutterheim & Nuese, 2003) who have investigated the extent to which macro and microstructural planning processes in the Conceptualiser contributing to narrative performance are language-specific, and guided by the meanings which specific languages grammaticize or do not. These conceptual planning processes include *segmenting* static situations into a number of states and property predications, or dynamic situations into events or processes; *selecting* from among the conceptual building blocks (entities, spaces, times, actions, etc.) from which propositions are formed; *structuring* these components with regard to spatial and temporal anchoring, topic, and focus assignment, etc.; and then *linearizing* the selected units. Comparing English L1 and German L1 narrations, Carroll et al. (2004) describe significant cross-linguistic differences in the events selected for mention and in temporal framing at the macrostructural level of conceptualization. Narration in German is based on a temporal sequence of bounded events, which are each related to an endpoint. Narration proceeds by linearly relating succeeding to preceding bounded events through the use of lexical adverbials (he walks and then . . . he sees and then . . . he thinks). In contrast, narrators in English frame events with respect to a deictic point of reference "now," and events are not related to an endpoint but are represented as ongoing (he is walking, and he sees, and he is thinking). They argue this is largely because German has no grammaticized progressive aspect, whereas English does. Consequently English narrators' conceptual planning processes are heavily influenced by the grammaticized means for describing ongoingness of events available in English. "The results . . . show that speakers of different languages prefer one pattern of conceptualization over another in language production" (p. 204), and "processes at this level are language-specific and grammatically driven" (p. 213). The abstract principles of perspective-taking that narrators of different L1s implicitly adopt when conceptualizing and construing the events to be verbalized are rooted in language-specific patterns of grammaticization. There is also evidence, Carroll et al. (2004) report, that L1 speakers of German continue to make use of the L1 preferred pattern of temporally framing events when giving narratives in L2 English. But can these preferences change, and if so, how can second language instruction facilitate such change?

4.2 Lexicalization patterns, focus on form, and thinking for speaking

These are issues, of course, of what Slobin (1996, 2003) calls "thinking-for-speaking," the notion that we access the conceptual contents of our experience of the world in a very "special" way when we access them on-line for the purposes of verbalizing them, in either speech or writing. "Thinking for speaking involves picking those characteristics of objects and events that (a) fit some conceptualization of the event, and (b) are readily encodable in the language . . . In acquiring a native language, the child learns particular ways of thinking for speaking" (1996, p. 76). In L2 speech production these conditions of access change because different languages make available not only different word forms (lexemes) for concepts, and clusters of syntactic and morphological features (lemmas) attached to them in the mental lexicon, during *lexical encoding*, but also preferred ways, or schemata, for assembling these into phrases and clauses during the subsequent stage of message formulation, i.e., *syntactic encoding*.

Slobin argues that "restructuring" the mapping of formal expression and conceptual content while producing L2 utterances may, even if possible, be a prolonged process: "Each native language has trained its speakers to pay different kinds of attention to events and experiences when talking about them. This training is carried out in childhood and is exceptionally resistant to restructuring in adult second-language acquisition" (1996, p. 89). The extent to which this is true, and of the effect of pedagogic interventions in facilitating this remapping and restructuring, are issues for SLA research with theoretical, and important practical consequences. An extreme version of linguistic relativity (see Odlin, this volume) claims the training L1 acquisition involves (see, e.g., the L1 construction learning processes described in section 3 of this chapter) leads to a mapping of language forms to concepts which makes conceptual distinctions not encoded in the L1 unavailable for thought, and so communicative expression, in an L2 in later adulthood. One consequence of this extreme version of linguistic relativity is that native-like ability for adult L2 learners is not attainable. On the whole Odlin (this volume) rejects this pessimistic conclusion as premature, in the absence of basic and needed important research into "conceptual" transfer and its permeability—not the least in response to instructional interventions which aim to make both forms, and the meanings they map to in adult second language learning, clear during second language instruction (see Cadierno, this volume; Ellis, this volume; Doughty & Williams, 1998; VanPatten, 2004). Slobin's (1996) own slightly less pessimistic position is that, while concepts evoked by events and human experience remain available for prelinguistic thought, whatever the L1, the on-line process of speaking in an L2 heavily implicates only the *dispositions* to map forms to preferred patterns of conceptualization for linguistic expression, and so communicative effect, developed in the L1.

Typological differences between satellite-framed (S-framed), and verb-framed (V-framed) languages identified by Talmy (2000) have been influential in examining these claims (see Cadierno, Gullberg, this volume), and are a clear example of the issues involved. It has been shown that typologically different lexicalization patterns for referring to motion events do have consequences for the way narratives are performed throughout development in the L1 (Berman & Slobin, 1994). First language speakers of S-framed languages produce narratives which are often richer in descriptions of manner, conflated with a great variety of verbs of motion (e.g., in English, <u>rushed; fled; staggered</u>) and with more elaborate coding of path in separate satellites (<u>out of</u> and <u>into</u>; <u>from</u> and <u>down</u>; <u>through</u> and <u>along</u>), compared to V-framed language speakers who encode path on a smaller number of motion verb types (e.g., in Japanese, <u>haitta</u> (went in); <u>detta</u> (went out), and deemphasize descriptions of manner in separate adverbials (<u>isoide</u> (hurriedly) <u>haitta</u>; <u>yukkuri</u> (slowly) <u>detta</u>) due to their reduced "codability" and so increased processing "cost" to the language user (two words for expressing the same motion and manner event in Japanese, versus one in English). Consequently, in English "manner comes for free" in construing motions events, but is dispreferred in construing them in Japanese (see Slobin, 2004, p. 237). Examining results of the studies to date researching the L2 expression of motion events, and Slobin's claim that speakers of L2s may be highly resistant to attempts to retrain L1 patterns of thinking for speaking that encoding options in the L1 lead them to prefer in construing events, Cadierno (this volume) reports that, although there are persistent effects of these L1 lexicalization patterns on L2 production (e.g., a tendency by Danish L1 S-framed learners of V-framed Spanish L2 to use fewer verbs conflating path and motion, and to use more elaborative coding of path in external satellites), there is nonetheless evidence that restructuring appears to be possible. Acquisition of L2 constructions for describing motion events, though delayed in the early stages of L2 learning and exposure, becomes increasingly native-like over time in speech production.

4.3 Grammaticization, conceptual domains, and cross-linguistic differences

Another aspect of Talmy's work that has been influential in first language acquisition research into the acquisition of form–function relations, as well as adult SLA in naturalistic settings, is his cross-linguistic analysis of grammaticizable notions. Distinguishing between two universal subsystems of meaning-bearing forms in language, the *open-class*, lexical and the *closed-class*, grammatical subsystems, Talmy (2000; this volume; cf. Coventry and Guijarro-Fuentes, this volume) notes that whereas the meanings that open-class forms (e.g., nouns, verbs, and adjectives) can express are very wide, the meanings of closed-class forms (e.g., verbal inflections, prepositions, determiners) are highly constrained, both with respect to the conceptual domain they can refer to, and as to member notions within any domain. For example, grammaticizable conceptual domains typically marked on verbs include tense, aspect, and person, but never spatial setting (indoors, outside), or speaker's state of mind (bored, interested), etc. And, whereas many languages have closed-class forms indicating the number of a noun referent *within* that conceptual domain, forms can refer to notions such as singular, dual, or plural, but never to even, odd, a dozen, etc. Languages differ in the extent to which they grammaticize forms within this constrained inventory of conceptual domains and individual concepts, and this inventory, Talmy argues, amounts to the fundamental conceptual-structuring system used by language.

Drawing on this work Slobin has argued that "such notions must constitute a privileged set for the child, and that they are embodied in the child's conceptions of 'prototypical events' that are mapped onto the first grammatical forms universally" (1985, p. 1,173). Whether this prelinguistic conceptual basis for form-meaning mappings remains available into adult Second Language Acquisition is an interesting question. However, even if it does, as Slobin again notes, the adult's language-learning task is clearly different from the child's: "For the child, the construction of the grammar and the construction of semantic/pragmatic concepts go hand-in-hand. For the adult, construction of the grammar often requires a revision of semantic/pragmatic concepts, along with what may well be a more difficult task of perceptual identification of the relevant morphological elements" (1993, p. 242). In cases where L2 morphology lacks perceptual salience for learners, or where the semantic/pragmatic concepts contributing to constructional meaning are unfamiliar, additional attention to form in communicative context is likely to be needed in order help learners map forms to meaning. Tyler and Achard, in their chapters in this volume, make various suggestions about how and when cognitive linguistic-motivated interventions can successfully be managed during classroom L2 learning to achieve this.

4.4 Conceptualization, developmental sequences, and L2 task demands

Divergence from target language norms in L2 speech production can be explained by many of the factors influencing "transfer" described by Coventry and Guijarro-Fuentes, MacWhinney and Odlin (this volume). The extent of this divergence, and the conceptual, processing, and cross-linguistic coordinates of why it occurs, are important to explain in theory and to address in pedagogic practice. But parallels between the order of linguistic emergence of available grammaticizable notions do exist in child and naturalistic adult SLA and are described in detail in Perdue, (1993a, 1993b), Becker and Carroll (1997) and Dietrich, Klein, and Noyau (1995). Slobin (1993), in discussing one of these cases, i.e., the order of emergence of prepositions for marking first topological relations of neighborhood and containment, and later, axis-based projective relations of above/below, front/back, in the European Science Foundation (ESF) project data (Perdue, 1993b), comments as follows:

> The parallels, though, cannot be attributed to the same under-lying factors. In the case of FLA (first language acquisition) one appeals to cognitive development: the projective notions simply are not available to very young children. But in the case of ALA (adult language acquisition) all of the relevant cognitive machinery is in place. Why, then, should learners have difficulty in discovering the necessary prepositions for spatial relations that they already command in the L1. There are at least two possibilities: (1) adult learners retain a scale of conceptual complexity, based on their own cognitive development, and at first search the TL (target language) for the grammatical marking of those notions which represent some primordial core of basicness or simplicity; and/or (2) these most basic notions are also used with relatively greater frequency in the TL . . . It is likely that speakers, generally, have less recourse to the encoding of complex notions, and that learners are simply reflecting the relative frequency of occurrence of various prepositions in the input . . . Or it may be that the complex relations are, indeed, communicated above some threshold of frequency, but that learners "gate them out" due to their complexity. In this case cognitive factors play a role in both FLA and ALA, but for different reasons: the complex notions are not

available to very young children, while they are available but not accessed in early stages of ALA.

Slobin, 1993, p. 243

If either of one of these possibilities raised by Slobin is true, then this suggests a pedagogically feasible and potentially useful intervention for promoting L2 acquisition of *some* form-function mappings. This is that pedagogic tasks for L2 learners be designed and sequenced, over time, in such a way as to increase in the complexity of the communicative demands they make in conceptual domains that Talmy has shown to be available for grammaticization processes to operate on. Increasing complexity of task demands in these domains has the potential to direct learners' attentional and memory resources to the way the L2 structures and codes concepts, so leading to interlanguage *development* (see Robinson, 2003b, 2005a, 2007a). For example, tasks which differ along the Here-and-Now/There-and-Then dimension clearly require the learner to distinguish between the temporality of reference (present versus past), and to use distinct deictic expressions (this, that, here, there) to indicate immediately present versus absent objects. As Cromer (1974) and others have noted, this sequence of conceptual and linguistic development takes place in L1 acquisition of English. Children first make reference to the Here-and-Now, and at a later point to the There-and-Then, and a similar sequence of linguistic development has been observed in L2 acquisition (see Behrens, 2001; Meisel, 1987; von Stutterheim & Klein, 1987).

Similarly, tasks which require no causal reasoning to establish event relations, and simple transmission of facts, compared to tasks which require the speaker to justify beliefs, and support interpretations of why events follow each other by giving reasons, also require, in the latter case, expressions, such as logical subordinators (so, because, therefore, etc.). In the case of reasoning about other people's intentions and beliefs, use of psychological and cognitive state verbs (e.g., know, believe, suppose, think) is required. Both of these introduce complex syntactic finite and non-finite clause complementation and prompt the development of complex constructions described by Diessel (2004), Tomasello (2003), and Lieven and Tomasello (this volume). This sequence of conceptual and linguistic development, too, has been observed in L1 acquisition, with psychological state terms emerging in the order, physiological, emotional, and desire terms, and then later, cognitive state terms (Bartsch & Wellman, 2005; Lee & Rescorla 2002; Nixon, 2005). The later emergence of cognitive state terms (and the complex syntactic predication that accompanies them) is associated with the child's development of a "theory of mind" (see Baron-Cohen, 1995; Schneider, Schumann-Hengsteller, & Sodian, 2005; Tomasello, 1999, 2003; Wellman 1990).

Thirdly, in developing the ability to navigate through a complex spatial

location, containing many elements which have to be referred to and distinguished, it has been observed that during childhood a basic *topological*
network of landmarks is first constructed and referred to, in which a
landmark is connected only with the few landmarks that can be seen from
it. This has been called an egocentric, ground level *route map* (see Carassa,
Aprigliano & Geminiani, 2000; Chown, Kaplan, & Kortenkamp, 1995;
Cornell, Heth, & Alberts, 1994; Taylor & Tsversky, 1996). At a later
stage, *survey maps* are developed and used in navigation that make use of
many landmarks, allowing the speaker/child to take multiple perspectives
on a location using *axis-based* relations of betweeness and front/backness.
This same sequence of development, from topological to axis-based reference to spatial location, has been documented during naturalistic adult
SLA as well, in which axis-based referring expressions themselves emerge
in the L2 in the order vertical axis< lateral axis< sagittal axis (see Becker
& Carroll, 1997; Perdue, 1993b).

In each of these three cases it appears that increasing task complexity
during L2 performance involves some recapitulation of a sequence of
conceptual development in childhood, and that the increasingly complex
demands that tasks impose along these dimensions *can* be met by use
of specific aspects of the L2 which code these "familiar" adult concepts.
Increases in cognitive complexity along these dimensions should therefore
represent a "natural order" for sequencing the conceptual and linguistic
demands of L2 tasks. As von Stutterheim has argued, "such conceptual
categories provide an important guideline for the course of acquisition
in a particular domain" (1991, p. 388). Whether such ontogenetically
motivated, incremental changes in task complexity also provide "opti-
mum" contexts for the development of needed (task relevant) function–
form mappings in the L2 is an interesting question in need of research.
The Cognition Hypothesis of adult task-based language learning and task
sequencing (Robinson, 2001b, 2003b, 2005a, 2007c) proposes that they
do, and Slobin's speculation (above) that "adult learners retain a scale of
conceptual complexity, based on their own cognitive development, and at
first search the TL (target language) for the grammatical marking of those
notions which represent some primordial core of basicness or simplicity"
also suggests that this may be so.

Sequencing the cognitive demands of L2 tasks from simple to complex
along conceptual dimensions requiring grammaticized linguistic expression (such as those described above) would therefore be complementary
to adult learners' own initial dispositions, and also helpful in prompting
them to move beyond them. That is, increasingly complex, cognitively
demanding tasks in these conceptual domains should *orient* learners to
their lexical and syntactic encoding L2 prerequisites for communicatively
effective speech, thereby promoting not only greater grammaticization,
and so accuracy, but also greater complexity of production. While *general*

measures of L2 task-based speech production, such as percent error-free T- or C-units, or S nodes or clauses per T- or C-unit (see Bardovi-Harlig, 1992; Ellis & Barkhuizen, 2005; Ortega, 2003; Larson Freeman, 2006; Robinson, 1995a, 2001a; Skehan, 1998; Skehan & Foster, 2001), may capture *global* changes in orientations to accuracy and complexity of speech across one cycle of simple to complex task performance, *specific* measures, as captured by cognitive linguistic descriptions of the *language and conceptualization* interface, may produce equally relevant results over much longer cycles of increasing task demands (i.e., weeks or months of such cycles). These task demands should also lead—the Cognition Hypothesis claims—not only to greater amounts of interaction but also to heightened attention to input and output, causing more noticing (of problematic forms in the output, and forms made salient in the input). Consequently, the conceptual and communicative effort they induce in the learner should additionally cause the formulator to expand, adjust, and reorganize L2 lexical and syntactic encoding processes in line with the conceptual demands of the task and the target L2 system.

4.5 Formulation and the L2 formulator: Cognition, conceptualization, and "rethinking-for-speaking"

An issue of considerable theoretical importance is therefore *how* the adjustment and reorganization of L2 *lexical and syntactic encoding* procedures that follow from "rethinking-for-speaking" (stimulated by attempts to meet complex L2 task demands) become established in the L2 user during development, and how these are related to the prior stage in message formulation, i.e., L2 *lexical encoding* and lemma activation. There are two positions which have been proposed. Firstly, Truscott and Sharwood Smith (2004) propose that during development, where L1 syntactic encoding procedures are highly activated, they are selected to serve L2 production purposes. In this sense the L1 formulator is initially piggybacked to serve the additional demands of L2 production. Secondly, and in some contrast, de Bot (1992) and Pienemann (1998, 2003) argue syntactic encoding processes are language-specific, and that L2 lemmas do not trigger L1 syntactic encoding processes. In this sense the syntactic encoding procedures followed by the L2 formulator are separately constructed, from scratch as it were, and are not piggybacked on the L1 formulator.

A third possibility is that perhaps *both* of these options are drawn on in tandem by the L2 learner, with the second of these, i.e., the L2-formulator-built-from-scratch option winning out in the later advanced stages of fluent L2 speech production over the first of these, the L1-formulator-coopted option. On the one hand, in this dual developmental-process view, consciously learned, and effortfully managed L2 declarative

521

rules at first coexist with highly automatized L1 production rules which consequently have a much lower activation threshold level, leading them to be selected for L2 syntactic encoding early in development. These have to be inhibited or suppressed if accurate L2 production is to occur, but often this does not occur—as Truscott and Sharwood Smith's model suggests. Krashen (1982) laid some well-known constraints on when this successful inhibition of L1 syntactic encoding procedures, and accurate use of L2 syntactic encoding procedures, might happen, i.e., having time, knowing the L2 rules, and being focused on form. One could also add that individuals differ in their ability to inhibit the L1, and control attention, as work on the bilingual lexicon (e.g., Lee & Williams, 2001; Meuter, 2005; Michael & Gollan, 2005) and the L2 processing of relational terms for referring to spatial location (Taube-Schiff & Segalowitz, 2005) has shown, and this would contribute to the variability not only within but also across individuals in their successful syntactic encoding and construction mapping of L2 lemmas.

In tandem with this, on the other hand—in the view being proposed—a new set of syntactic encoding procedures would be being built (or rather, circuits supporting it would be being established) from scratch, resulting at first in utterances that conform, variously, say, to the basic variety, as Klein and Perdue (1997) have described it, or the pragmatic mode that Givón (1995) describes, or, of course, the early stages of speech production described in Pienemann's (1998, 2003) model of L2 development. Since this L2 formulator does not recruit L1 syntactic encoding processes, nothing need be inhibited, and so speech production across learners from a variety of L1s would show a similar developmental trajectory, with little within-learner variation in its use at any one developmental point. Eventually, this becomes the preferred L2 syntactic encoding option, and the early used L2-co-existing-with-L1 syntactic encoding option is abandoned, and the L1 formulator left to do its originally dedicated job. If this were true, then, it would mean that the L2 is much more likely to influence the workings of the L1 formulator in the earlier stages of L2 acquisition, when the two co-operate, than in the later, advanced stages, when the two sets of syntactic encoding procedures are independent. Evidence for this would be L2 intrusions into the L1 speech of early, in contrast to advanced and highly proficient L2 learners. Interestingly, Pavlenko and Jarvis (2002) have found just such evidence of bi-directional transfer, and L2 influence on L1 production for post-puberty Russian L1 learners of L2 English living in the USA for between three and eight years. Clearly these are not learners in the early stages of L2 acquisition, but it is not clear that they are very advanced either. The position just described would predict that very advanced learners would show little or no L2 transfer to L1 speech production. These issues considered, research into the development of L2 speech production ability, and claims about the mechanisms supporting it, needs to look not just at L2 speech production data but also at the reciprocal influence (and of what kind) learning to speak an L2 (at early versus later and very advanced stages) has on L1 speech production, for some of the reasons just given (see also Cook, 2003; Meuter, 2005 for relevant discussion and findings).

4.6 Issues for research

Cross-linguistic influences on language, thought, and L2 development. The research projects described in Berman and Slobin (1994) and Stromqvist and Verhoeven (2004, and in Perdue, 1993a, 1993b) have addressed many of the issues raised above, and produced findings which are an important foundation for future Cognitive Linguistic, SLA research into language, thought, and L2 development. Berman and Slobin describe the similar developmental trajectories for L1 acquisition of narrative ability, and the ways in which typological, cross-linguistic differences between L1s, and constructions at various levels of specificity they make available for performing narratives, lead L1 speakers to filter experience for speaking about it in different ways, with regard to the expression of temporality, motion event conflation, and perspective taking. As children develop cognitively, older established grammaticized forms become the means for expressing new conceptual distinctions and communicative functions that require narrative expression and integration. Carroll et al.'s (2004) findings (described above) are one example of how the L1 predispositions for thinking about and construing events in narratives, developed in child L1 acquisition, persist in adult use of the L2. Cadierno shows (this volume) that L2 transfer of these L1-based ways of thinking for speaking, however, is variable and suggests that instruction may be able to lead adult L2 learners to refilter experience by focusing on form–meaning connections (specifically, lexicalization patterns) in ways the L2 makes available to speakers and listeners. Perdue (1993a), and the work of the European Science Foundation (ESF) project, similarly focuses on the role of cross-linguistic differences between a variety of L1s and L2s in influencing the course of SLA in the domains of reference to space, time, causation, and other conceptual domains, finding evidence for similar developmental trajectories across different L1–L2 pairings (as described earlier in this chapter). These two research projects have resulted in cumulative, interpretable findings as a result of *consistency* in the research questions addressed and their operationalization, both in measures of language *learning,* and the *tasks* chosen to elicit language *use* across the range of ages, and language learned, in the populations studied. Further research into these issues needs to address two questions with regard to the use, consistency, and reliability of elicitation tasks.

Task construal: How do we ensure learners are construing task demands in the way researchers intend? Berman and Slobin (1994, p. 17) claim that a serious weakness of their research project was that it was not possible to control learners' definition of the narrative task they were set, and that in telling the *Frog Story* some learners—especially younger ones—described individual pictures in isolation without attempting to "relate" them in narrative, which was the cognitive, conceptual, and discourse operation of interest. Berman and Slobin (p. 17) claim "our texts show us" this, but the text cannot show that conclusively. On-line measures of what learners are actually attempting to do, such as protocols (Jourdenais, 2001) are one way of ensuring that intended task demands, and efforts at conceptualization and its integration with language, are being met by learners, though there are acknowledged problems with this methodology in that protocols may interfere with and impede the cognitive processes of interest, disrupting concerted effort at conceptualization and linguistic expression. Post-task questionnaires are less intrusive but less faithful to choices learners make in construing task demands on-line. These have been adopted in SLA research into task performance where "difficulty-rating" questionnaires have been used following simple and complex task performance (along dimensions of conceptual complexity), and have shown, to date, that in all cases perceived "difficulty" of the research task performed by the learners, and the researchers' intended-to-be-construed task "complexity," co-vary systematically in the intended and predicted ways (Gilabert, 2004, 2007; Robinson, 2001a, 2005a, 2007c). Variance in production data irrelevant to addressing intended research questions (concerning, in these cases, the relationship of language to conceptualization during task performance) could be minimized by using such measures, and also large group designs. The issue of task "purity" and unintended participant construal of task demands has been addressed extensively in cognitive psychology, where laboratory tasks (e.g., those used in studies of language and spatial cognition by Levinson, 2003, and Majid et al., 2004) make demands which are often under much more researcher control (see, e.g., Stanovitch, 1999 for discussion). The issue is also important to address in assessing the extent to which learners are attempting to make, and articulate through language, conceptual distinctions during tasks requiring language production so as to examine the L2-thought interface during development.

Conceptual demands: How do we design tasks, which differ in the demands on reasoning, reference to time, space, and causation, and perspective-taking? If we want to examine how L2 learner production reflects different efforts at conceptualization (given any one cross-linguistically, typologically similar, or different L1), how do we design tasks that promote, for example, no versus some causal reasoning, or reference to events happening in the present versus the past, or to events requiring just one perspective to be taken on an event, versus multiple second- and third-party perspectives? These are design issues that have been addressed in research into the effects of increasing the conceptual demands of tasks, and their relevant dimensions for increasing pedagogic task complexity (see Robinson, 2007a, for a taxonomy and operational definitions). Some of these conceptual dimensions of task demands on speech production (e.g., here-and-now versus there-and-then, Gilabert, 2007; Ishikawa, 2007; Robinson, 1995a) are fairly unproblematic to manipulate, but others (e.g., reasoning demands) will require more careful, theoretically informed and coordinated design decisions.

SLA research into these issues should at the least be cumulative, and so operationally consistent in choice of task to examine a particular language, conceptualization influence on speech production and comprehension, as was the work of Berman and Slobin (1994) and the ESF project described by Perdue (1993a, 1993b). But narrating the *Frog Story*, while illuminating, is limited, and not exhaustive of adult second language learners' narrative dispositions or abilities, or complementary to their age-related interests and motivations. Arguing acquisition is "pushed by the communicative demands of the tasks of the discourse activities which the learner takes part in" Perdue (1993a, p. 53) describes how the communicative tasks targeting adult L2 learners' acquisitional processes in conceptual and communicative domains were chosen in the ESF project. Continuity with both the above (Berman & Slobin, 1994; Perdue, 1993a) operational choices for elicitation tasks, and as well as with those suggested for application to pedagogy and materials and syllabus design (e.g., Robinson, 2007a, in press; Robinson & Gilabert, 2007) is advisable if future SLA research findings in this area are to be cumulative and also of relevance to possible pedagogic application.

Motion, causation, lexicalization patterns, and L2 task demands. Research needs to motivate not only "choice" of elicitation or comprehension task but also directional hypotheses for how differences in task demands along a conceptual dimension will affect speech production and comprehension. Greater effort at conceptualization, pushed by the communicative demands of tasks that L2 learners undertake, should lead to qualitatively different efforts at encoding these different conceptualizations and communicative demands in speech. Greater functional complexity in discourse, leads to greater structural and "constructional" complexity in speech, Givón (1985) and Rohdenburg (2002) have both claimed, and the cognitive development which leads children to attempt a wider range of more complex functions in communicative interaction is responsible, at least in part, for the changes that take place in first language development (see Slobin, 1973, 1985; Tomasello, 2003).

In what ways, then, does increasing the conceptual complexity of tasks in one of the domains described above lead learners to attempt greater grammaticization and syntacticization of speech, with regard, for example, to lexicalization patterns (Cadierno, this volume) for expressing motion events in the case of reference to space and progress through it in narrative description? Robinson and Nakamura (in preparation) have found that more complex L2 tasks, requiring reference to motion events in English by speakers of both V-framed and S-framed L1s, do lead to greater target-like lexicalization patterns, and more conflation of manner with motion verbs (as is typical in English) compared to performance on less conceptually and communicatively demanding tasks in the same domain. The extent to which increasing the conceptual and communicative demands on this and other dimensions, such as those requiring the use of lexicalization patterns for expressing causation (see Odlin's discussion of causative constructions, this volume), leads learners to attempt increasingly complex and more target-like forms of L2 expression is an area in much need of research, and with many pedagogic implications for the design of developmentally motivated language learning materials, tasks, and task sequences.

Tense, aspect, developmental sequences, and task demands. How might tasks be designed to elicit developmental changes in the ability to code reference to time and duration of activity in the L2, so as to research the influence of conceptualization on language production in this area, and its susceptibility (or not) to L1 influence? Following the reasoning above, one might expect that on simple versions of tasks low in their conceptual and communicative demands in this domain, learners initially restrict past or perfective marking on verbs to achievement and accomplishment verbs, but on more complex versions, over time, they would progressively extend this marking to activities and then states, as the Aspect Hypothesis predicts happens in development (Bardovi-Harlig, 2000; Comajoan, 2006; Li & Shirai, 2000). The measures used to capture this developmental shift, pushed by the complexity of task demands, would be different from the currently used accuracy measures, or measures of complexity such as clauses per C-unit. They would be developmentally motivated measures of the increasing attempt to extend past or perfective marking on verbs, particularly as complex tasks may encourage this. These issues lead to a further issue for future research.

Assessing the accuracy, fluency, and complexity of L2 learner speech. A great deal of current research uses general measures of complexity (T-units, C-units), accuracy (e.g., % error-free C- or T-units) and fluency (ratio measures of pauses per T- or C-unit, see Ellis & Barkhuizen, 2005, for an extensive overview) when assessing classroom L2 learner language, and the influence of tasks or other demands on it. But following the rationale given above, specific measures relevant to the particular conceptual demands tasks make (such as lexicalization patterns for reference to motion events) also need to be used if the effects of these (and not other demands) on speech production are to be assessed. To what extent do such general and specific indices of speech production relate to each other? To what extent do the coding procedures for establishing each differ (if at all) in reliability, and to what extent do they co-predict changes in speech performance under different task conditions?

Individual differences, cognitive and conceptual abilities, and rethinking for speaking. Cadierno (this volume), summarizing her own findings, and those of others on the acquisition of L2 lexicalization patterns for describing motion events, concludes that there seems to be "a rather limited role of the L1 thinking for speaking patterns in advanced second language acquisition." In the select population of second language learners who reach advanced levels, what cognitive abilities could contribute to the capacity for "rethinking for speaking" that learners at lower levels must exercise in order to progress in this area of L2 attainment? It seems unlikely that these capacities are related in any obvious way to the abilities measured by subtests of currently available aptitude tests (e.g., Carroll & Sapon's, 1959, MLAT). The abilities nominated as contributing to the aptitude factor "deep semantic processing" in the *aptitude complex/ability differentiation* model of aptitude (Robinson, 2002, 2007b), i.e., analogizing concepts, and inferring word meaning, may be related to this. The capacity to rethink for speaking may also be related to the ability to break set, as measured by a wide variety of tasks that assess insight into problem-solving (see Sternberg & Davidson, 1994).

Typological differences, relative difficulty, and L2 transfer. As Odlin (this volume) argues, the relative difficulty experienced by speakers from typologically different, versus similar L1 and L2s is important to explore for the light it can cast on whether "conceptual" transfer persists in L2 learners, what late-learned associations between language and L2 conceptualization are, and what levels of ultimate attainment L2 learners can reach in "rethinking for speaking." The issue of identifying to what extent conceptual transfer accompanies meaning transfer—as Odlin describes it—is important but problematic since, as Odlin notes, investigating conceptual transfer involves having tasks with a non-verbal component, in contrast to the tasks described above, to assess language-specific effects on cognitive abilities, such as orienting to spatial location, categorization, and recall. This will involve using a number of the experimental procedures and methodologies for investigating these issues adopted outside those typically used in SLA research (see, e.g., Majid, Bowerman, Kita,

Haun & Levinson, 2004; Levinson, 2003), as well as the development of new ones.

5 Summary and conclusion

Many other issues remain but must go untreated here. Enough issues, and directions for future research, have been described in this, and throughout the preceding chapters, however, to guide research connections between Cognitive Linguistics, SLA and language instruction. Cognitive Linguistics provides a wide overview of language and its cognitive, social, psychological, and pragmatic dimensions, and an opportunity for interdisciplinary collaboration in research into all of these. We trust this volume, and its individual contributions, will contribute to that interdisciplinary inquiry, benefiting deeper theoretical understanding of issues connecting these areas, and useful applications of relevant research into them, alike.

Bibliography

Ackerman, P. (2003). Aptitude complexes and trait complexes. *Educational Psychologist, 38*, 85–93.

Allwood, J. (1993). Feedback in second language acquisition. In C. Perdue (Ed.), *Adult language acquisition: Cross-linguistic perspectives, Vol. 2: The results* (pp. 196–235). Cambridge: Cambridge University Press.

Andersen, R. (1984). The one-to-one principle of interlanguage construction. *Language Learning, 34*, 77–95.

Anderson, J. R., & Lebriere, C. (1998). *The atomic components of thought*. Mahwah, NJ: Erlbaum.

Baker, C., & McCarthy, J. (1981). *The logical problem of language acquisition*. Cambridge, MA: MIT Press.

Bardovi-Harlig, K. (1992). A second look at T-unit analysis: Reconsidering the sentence. *TESOL Quarterly, 26*, 390–395.

Bardovi-Harlig, K. (2000). *Tense and aspect in second language acquisition: Form, meaning and use*. Oxford: Blackwell.

Baron-Cohen, S. (1995). *Mindblindness*. Cambridge, MA: MIT Press.

Bartsch, K., & Wellman, H. (1995). *Children talk about the mind*. Oxford: Oxford University Press.

Bates, E. (1976). *Language and context: The acquisition of pragmatics*. New York: Academic Press.

Bates, E., & Goodman, J. (1999). On the emergence of grammar from the lexicon. In B. MacWhinney (Ed.), *The emergence of language* (pp. 115–152). Mahwah, NJ: Erlbaum.

Bates, E. & MacWhinney, B. (1982). Functionalist approaches to grammar. In E. Wanner & L. Gleitman (Eds.), *Language acquisition: the state of the art* (pp. 173–218). New York: Cambridge University Press.

Bates, E., Bretherton, I., & Snyder, L. (1988). *From first words to grammar:*

Individual differences and dissociable mechanisms. Cambridge: Cambridge University Press.

Becker, A., & Carroll, M. (1997) (Eds.). *The acquisition of spatial relations in a second language*. Amsterdam: John Benjamins.

Behrens, H. (2001). Cognitive-conceptual development and the acquisition of grammatical morphemes: The development of time concepts and verb tense. In M. Bowerman & S. Levinson (Eds.), *Language acquisition and conceptual development* (pp. 450–474). Cambridge: Cambridge University Press.

Benicini, G., & Goldberg, A. (2000). The contribution of argument structure constructions to sentence meaning. *Journal of Memory and Language, 43,* 650–661.

Berman, R. (1987). Cognitive components of language development. In C. Pfaff (Ed.), *First and second language acquisition processes* (pp. 3–27). Cambridge, MA: Newbury House.

Berman, R., & Slobin, D. (1994) (Eds.). *Relating events in narrative: A crosslinguistic developmental study*. Mahwah, NJ: Erlbaum.

Bloom, L. (1970). *Language development: Form and function in emerging grammars*. Cambridge, MA: MIT Press.

Bod, R., Hay, J., & Jannedy, S. (Eds.) (2003). *Probabilistic linguistics*. Cambridge, MA: MIT Press.

Braine, M. D. S (1963). The ontogeny of English phrase structure: The first phase. *Language, 39,* 1–3.

Breen, M., & Candlin, C. (1980). The essentials of a communicative curriculum in language teaching. *Applied Linguistics, 1,* 89–112.

Bremer, K., Broeder, P., Roberts, C., Simonot, M., & Vasseur, M. (1993). Ways of acheiving understanding. In C. Perdue (Ed.), *Adult language acquisition: Crosslinguistic perspectives, Vol. 2: The results* (pp. 154–195). Cambridge: Cambridge University Press.

Brinton, D., Snow, M., & Wesche, M. (1989). *Content-based second language instruction*. Rowley, MA: Newbury House.

Brown, R. (1973). *A first language*. Cambridge, MA: Harvard University Press.

Bruner, J. (1960). *The process of education*. New York: Random House.

Bybee, J. (2006). *Frequency of use and the organization of language*. Oxford: Oxford University Press.

Bybee, J., & Hopper, P. (Eds.) (2001). *Frequency and the emergence of linguistic structure*. Amsterdam: John Benjamins.

Bygate, M., Skehan, P., & Swain, M. (2001) (Eds.). *Researching pedagogic tasks: Second language learning, teaching and testing*. London: Longman.

Cameron, L. (2001). *Teaching languages to young learners*. Cambridge: Cambridge University Press.

Candlin, C. (1987). Towards task-based language learning. In C. Candlin & D. Murphy (Eds.), *Language learning tasks* (pp. 5–22). London: Prentice-Hall.

Carassa, A., Aprigliano, A., & Geminiani, G. (2000). Describers and explorers: A method for investigating cognitive maps. In S. O'Nuallain (Ed.), *Spatial cognition* (pp. 33–43). Amsterdam: John Benjamins.

Carlson, R. (1997). *Experienced cognition*. Mahwah, NJ: Erlbaum.

Carroll, J. B. (1993). *Human cognitive abilities: A factor analytic survey*. New York: Cambridge University Press.

Carroll, J. B., & Sapon, S. M. (1959). *Modern language aptitude test*. Washington, DC: Second Language Testing Incorporated.

Carroll, M., von Stutterheim, C., & Nuese, R. (2004). The language and thought debate: A psycholinguistic perspective. In T. Pechman & C. Habel (Eds.), *Multidisciplinary approaches to language production*. Berlin: Mouton de Gruyter.

Carroll, S. (2001). *Input and evidence: The raw material of second language acquisition*. Amsterdam: John Benjamins.

Ceci, S. (1996) *On intelligence: A bioecological treatise on intellectual development*. Cambridge, MA: Harvard University Press.

Chater, N., & Manning, C. (2006). Probabilistic models of language processing and acquisition. *Trends in Cognitive Science, 10*, 335–344.

Chaudron, C. (1988). *Second language classrooms*. New York: Cambridge University Press.

Childers, J., & Tomasello, M. (2001). The role of pronouns in young children's acquisition of the English transitive construction. *Developmental Psychology, 37*, 739–748.

Chomsky, N. (1965). *Aspects of the theory of syntax*. Cambridge, MA: MIT Press.

Chown, E., Kaplan, S., & Kortenkamp, D. (1995). Prototypes, Location and Associative Networks (PLAN): Towards a unified theory of cognitive mapping. *Cognitive Science, 19*, 1–51.

Christiansen, M. H., & Chater, N. (Eds.) (2001). *Connectionist psycholinguistics*. Westport, CO: Ablex.

Comajoan, L. (2006). The Aspect Hypothesis: Development of morphology and appropriateness of use. *Language Learning, 56*, 201–268.

Cook, V. (2003) (Ed.). *Effects of the second language on the first*. Clevedon: Multilingual Matters.

Cornell, E., Heth, D., & Alberts, D. (1994). Place recognition and way finding by children and adults. *Memory and Cognition, 22*, 633–643.

Crombie, W. (1985). *Process and relation in discourse and language learning*. Oxford: Oxford University Press.

Cromer, R. (1974). The development of language and cognition: The cognition hypothesis. In B. Foss (Ed.), *New perspectives in child development*, (pp. 184–252). Harmondsworth: Penguin.

Cromer, R. (1991). *Language and thought in normal and handicappped children*. Oxford: Blackwell.

Crookes, G. & Gass, S. (1993). *Tasks in language learning: Integrating theory and practice*. Clevedon: Multilingual Matters.

Cummins, J. (1988). Bilingualism and second language learning. *Annual Review of Applied Linguistics, 13*, 51–70.

Cummins, R. (1983). *The nature of psychological explanation*. Cambridge, MA: MIT Press.

Dabrowska, E., & Street, J. (2006). Individual differences in language attainment: Comprehension of passive sentences in native and non-native English speakers. *Language Sciences, 28*, 604–615.

Dai, D., & Sternberg, R. J. (2004). *Motivation, emotion and cognition: Integrative perspectives on intellectual functioning and development*. New York: Cambridge University Press.

Day, E., & Shapson, S. (1991). Integrating formal and functional approaches in language teaching: An experimental study. *Language Learning, 41*, 25–58.

de Bot, K. (1992). A bilingual production model: Levelt's "speaking" model adapted. *Applied Linguistics, 13*, 1–24.

de Bot, K., Lowie, W., & Verspoor, M. (2007). A dynamic systems theory to second language acquisition. *Bilingualism: Language and Cognition, 10*, 7–21.

de Graaff, R. (1997). *Differential effects of explicit instruction on second language acquisition*. The Hague: Holland Institute of Generative Linguistics.

DeKeyser, R. M. (1995). Learning second language grammar rules: An experiment with a miniature linguistic system. *Studies in Second Language Acquisition, 17*, 379–410.

DeKeyser, R. M. (1997). Beyond explicit rule learning: Automatizing second language syntax. *Studies in Second Language Acquisition, 19*, 195–222.

DeKeyser, R. M. (2000). The robustness of critical period effects in second language acquisition. *Studies in Second Language Acquisition, 22*, 499–533.

DeKeyser, R. M. (2001). Automaticity and automatization. In P. Robinson (Ed.), *Cognition and second language instruction* (pp. 125–151). Cambridge: Cambridge University Press.

DeKeyser, R. M. (2007) (Ed.). *Practicing in a second language: perspectives from applied linguistics and cognitive psychology*. New York: Cambridge University Press.

Dewey, J. (1916). *Democracy and education*. New York: MacMillan.

Diessel, H. (2004). *The acquisition of complex sentences*. Cambridge: Cambridge University Press.

Dietrich, R., Klein, W., & Noyau, C. (1995). *The acquisition of temporality in a second language*. Amsterdam: John Benjamins.

Dornyei, Z. (2002). The motivational basis of language learning tasks. In P. Robinson (Ed.), *Individual differences and instructed language learning* (pp. 137–158). Amsterdam: John Benjamins.

Dornyei, Z. (2005). *The psychology of the language learner*. Mahwah, NJ: Erlbaum.

Dornyei, Z., & Skehan, P. (2003). Individual differences in second language learning. In C. Doughty & M. H. Long (Eds.), *Handbook of second language acquisition* (pp. 589–630). Oxford: Blackwell.

Doughty, C. (2001). Cognitive underpinnings of focus on form. In P. Robinson (Ed.), *Cognition and second language instruction* (pp. 206–257). Cambridge: Cambridge University Press.

Doughty, C. (2003). Instructed SLA: Constraints, compensation and enhancement. In C. Doughty & M. H. Long (Eds.), *Handbook of second language acquisition* (pp. 256–310). Oxford: Blackwell.

Doughty, C., & Williams, J. (1998). Pedagogical choices in focus on form. In C. Doughty & J. Williams (Eds.), *Focus on form in classroom second language acquisition*, (pp. 197–262). New York: Cambridge University Press.

Dulay, H., & Burt, M. (1974). Natural sequences in child second language acquisition. *Language Learning, 24*, 37–53.

Dulay, H., Burt, M., & Krashen, S. (1982). *Language two*. New York: Cambridge University Press.

Ehret, B., Gray, W., & Kirschenbaum, S. (2000). Contending with complexity:

Developing and using a scaled world in applied cognitive research. *Human Factors, 2,* 8–23.

Eigen, M., & Winkler, R. (1983). *Laws of the game: How the principles of nature govern chance.* Harmondsworth, UK: Penguin

Ellis, N. C. (1993). Rules and instances in foreign language learning: Interactions of explicit and implicit knowledge. *European Journal of Cognitive Psychology, 5,* 289–318.

Ellis, N. C. (1994) (Ed.). *Implicit and explicit learning of languages.* New York: Academic Press.

Ellis, N. C. (1995). Consciousness in second language acquisition: A review of field studies and laboratory experiments. *Language Awareness, 4*(3), 123–146.

Ellis, N. C. (1996). Sequencing in SLA: Phonological memory, chunking, and points of order. *Studies in Second Language Acquisition, 18*(1), 91–126.

Ellis, N. C. (1998). Emergentism, connectionism and second language learning. *Language Learning, 48,* 631–664.

Ellis, N. C. (1999). Cognitive Approaches to SLA. *Annual Review of Applied Linguistics, 19,* 22–42.

Ellis, N. C. (2001). Memory for language. In P. Robinson (Ed.), *Cognition and second language instruction* (pp. 33–68). Cambridge: Cambridge University Press.

Ellis, N. C. (2002). Frequency effects in language acquisition: A review with implications for theories of implicit and explicit language acquisition. *Studies in Second Language Acquisition, 24,* 143–188.

Ellis, N. C. (2003). Constructions, chunking, and connectionism: The emergence of second language structure. In C. Doughty & M. Long (Eds.), *Handbook of second language acquisition* (pp. 63–103). Oxford: Blackwell.

Ellis, N. C. (2005). At the interface: Interactions of implicit and explicit learning. *Studies in Second Language Acquisition, 27,* 294–356.

Ellis, N. C. (2006a). Language acquisition as rational contingency learning. *Applied Linguistics, 27,* 1–24.

Ellis, N. C. (2006b). Selective attention and transfer phenomena in SLA: Contingency, cue competition, salience, interference, overshadowing, blocking and perceptual learning. *Applied Linguistics, 27,* 164–194.

Ellis, N. C. (in press). Implicit and explicit knowledge about language. In J. Cenoz (Ed.), *Knowledge about language* (Vol. 6, Encyclopedia of Language and Education). Heidelberg: Springer Scientific.

Ellis, N. C. (in press 2008). Optimizing the input: Frequency and sampling in usage-based and form-focused learning. In M. H. Long & C. Doughty (Eds.), *Handbook of second and foreign language teaching.* Oxford: Blackwell.

Ellis, N. C., Ferreira Junior, F., & Ke, J.-Y. (in preparation). Form, function, and frequency: Zipfian family construction profiles in SLA.

Ellis, N. C., Frey, E., & Jalkanen, I. (2007a). *The Psycholinguistic Reality of Collocation and Semantic Prosody—Neighbourhoods of Knowing (1): Lexical Access.* Paper presented at the conference on Exploring the Lexis-Grammar interface, Hanover.

Ellis, N. C., Frey, E., & Jalkanen, I. (2007b). *The Psycholinguistic Reality of Collocation and Semantic Prosody—Neighbourhoods of Knowing (2): Semantic Access.* Paper presented at the conference on Formulaic language, University of Wisconsin Milwaukee.

Ellis, N. C., & Larsen Freeman, D. (2006). Language emergence: Implications for applied linguistics—Introduction to the special issue. *Applied Linguistics, 27,* 558–589.

Ellis, N. C., & Schmidt, R. (1998). Rules or associations in the acquisition of morphology? The frequency by regularity interaction in human and PDP learning of morphosyntax. *Language and Cognitive Processes, 13,* 307–336.

Ellis, N. C., & Simpson-Vlach, R. (in preparation). Native and non-native processing of formulas and collocations: Psycholinguistic analyses.

Ellis, N. C., Simpson-Vlach, R., & Maynard, C. (in preparation). The processing of formulas in native and second-language speakers: Psycholinguistic and corpus determinants. *TESOL Quarterly.*

Ellis, R. (1999) (Ed.). *Learning a second language through interaction.* Amsterdam: John Benjamins.

Ellis, R. (2003). *Task-based language teaching and learning.* Oxford: Oxford University Press.

Ellis, R., & Barkhuizen, G. (2005). *Analyzing learner language.* Oxford: Oxford University Press.

Elman, J. L. (2004). An alternative view of the mental lexicon. *Trends in Cognitive Sciences, 8,* 301–306.

Elman, J. L., Bates, E. A., Johnson, M. H., Karmiloff-Smith, A., Parisi, D., & Plunkett, K. (1996). *Rethinking innateness: A connectionist perspective on development.* Cambridge, MA: MIT Press.

Engestrom, Y., & Middleton, D. (1996). *Cognition and communication at work.* New York: Cambridge University Press.

Felix, S. (1981). The effect of formal instruction on second language acquisition. *Language Learning, 31,* 87–112.

Ferguson, C. (1971). Absence of copula and the notion of simplicity: a study of normal speech, baby talk, foreigner talk and pidgins. In D. Hymes (Ed.), *Pidginization and creolization of languages* (pp. 141–150). Cambridge: Cambridge University Press.

Fillmore, C. (1985). Frames and the semantics of understanding. *Quaderni di Semantica, 6,* 222–254.

Fries, C. C. (1952). *The structure of English.* New York: Harcourt Brace and Company.

Fries, C. C. (1957). Foreword. In R. Lado, *Linguistics across cultures: Applied linguistics for language teachers.* Michigan, MI: Michigan University Press.

García Mayo, M. P. (2006). (Ed.), *Investigating tasks in formal language learning.* Clevedon: Multilingual Matters.

Garcia Mayo, M. P. (2007). (Ed.), *Investigating tasks in formal language learning.* Clevedon: Multilingual Matters.

Gass, S. (1997). *Input, interaction and the second language learner.* Mahwah, NJ: Erlbaum.

Gass, S. (2003). Input and interaction. In C. Doughty & M. H. Long (Eds.), *Handbook of second language acquisition* (pp. 224–255). Oxford: Blackwell.

Gentner, D., Holyoak, K., & Kokinov, B. (2001) (Eds.). *The analogical mind.* Cambridge, MA: MIT Press.

Gilabert, R. (2004). *Task complexity and L2 oral narrative production.* Unpublished

Ph.D. dissertation. Department of Applied Linguistics, University of Barcelona, Spain.

Gilabert, R. (2007). The simultaneous manipulation along the planning time and +/– Here-and-Now dimensions: Effects on oral L2 production. In M. P. García Mayo (Ed.), *Investigating tasks in formal language learning* (pp. 44–68). Clevedon: Multilingual Matters.

Givón, T. (1985). Function, structure, and language acquisition. In D. Slobin (Ed.), *The crosslinguistic study of language acquisition: Vol 1* (pp. 1,008–1,025). Hillsdale, NJ: Erlbaum.

Givón, T. (1995). *Functionalism and language.* Amsterdam: John Benjamins.

Goffman, E. (1974). *Frame analysis: An essay on the organization of experience.* New York: Harper & Row.

Goldberg, A. (2006). *Constructions at work: The nature of argument structure generalizations.* Oxford: Oxford University Press.

Goldschneider, J. M., & DeKeyser, R. (2001). Explaining the "natural order of L2 morpheme acquisition" in English: A meta-analysis of multiple determinants. *Language Learning, 51,* 1–50.

Greenfield, P., & Smith, J. (1976). *The structure of communication in early language development.* New York: Academic Press.

Gregg, K. (2001). Learnability and second language acquisition theory. In P. Robinson (Ed.), *Cognition and second language instruction* (pp. 152–182). Cambridge: Cambridge University Press.

Gries, S. Th. (2003). Towards a corpus-based identification of prototypical instances of constructions. *Annual Review of Cognitive Linguistics, 1,* 1–27.

Gries, S. Th., & Wulff, S. (2005). Do foreign language learners have constructions? Evidence from priming, sorting and corpora. *Annual Review of Cognitive Linguistics, 3,* 182–200.

Gullberg, M. (2006) (Ed.). *Gestures and second language acquisition.* Guest-edited special issue *International Review of Applied Linguistics, 44, (2).* Berlin: Mouton DeGruyter.

Halliday, M. A. K., MacIntosh, A., & Strevens, P. (1964). *The linguistic sciences and language teaching.* London: Longman.

Harley, B., Allen, P., Cummins, J., & Swain, M. (1990). *The development of second language proficiency.* Cambridge: Cambridge University Press.

Harley, B., & Swain, M. (1984). The interlanguage of immersion students and its implications for language teaching. In A. Davies, C. Criper & A. Howatt (Eds.), *Interlanguage* (pp. 291–311). Edinburgh: Edinburgh University Press.

Hatch, E. (1978). Discourse analysis and second language acquisition. In E. Hatch (Ed.), *Second language acquisition: A book of readings.* Rowley, MA: Newbury House.

Hickman, M. (2003). *Children's discourse: Person, space and time across languages.* Cambridge: Cambridge University Press.

Hoey, M. (2005). *Lexical priming.* London: Routledge.

Holland, J. H. (1992). *Hidden order: How adaption builds complexity.* Reading: Addison-Wesley.

Holland, J. H. (1998). *Emergence: From chaos to order.* Oxford: Oxford University Press.

Holland, J. H., Holyoak, K., Nisbett, R., & Thagard, R. (1989). *Induction: Processes of inference, learning and discovery*. Cambridge, MA: MIT Press.

Howatt, A. P., & Widdowson, H. G. (2004). *A history of English language teaching*. Oxford: Oxford University Press.

Hudson, R. (2007). *Language networks*. Oxford: Oxford University Press.

Hulstijn, J. (2001). Intentional and incidental second language vocabulary learning: A reappraisal of rehearsal, elaboration and automaticity. In P. Robinson (Ed.), *Cognition and second language instruction* (pp. 258–286). Cambridge: Cambridge University Press.

Hulstijn, J., & Ellis, R. (2005) (Eds.). *Theoretical and empirical issues in the study of implicit and explicit second-language learning*. Guest edited special issue. *Studies in Second Language Acquisition, 27, (2)*. New York: Cambridge University Press.

Hulstijn, J., & Schmidt, R. (1994) (Eds.). Consciousness and second language learning, *AILA Review, 11*.

Hunston, S., & Francis, G. (2000). *Pattern grammar: A corpus-driven approach to the lexical grammar of English*. Amsterdam: John Benjamins.

Hutchinson, T., & Waters, A. (1978). *English for specific purposes: A learning centered approach*. Cambridge: Cambridge University Press.

Hyltenstam, K., & Abrahamsson, P. (2003). Maturational constraints in SLA. In C. Doughty & M. H. Long (Eds.), *Handbook of second language acquisition* (pp. 539–588). Oxford: Blackwell.

Ishikawa, T. (2007). The effect of manipulating task complexity along the +/– Here-and-Now dimension on L2 written narratve discourse. In M. P. Garcia Mayo (Ed.), *Investigating tasks in formal language learning*. Clevedon: Multilingual Matters.

Johnson, K. (1996). *Language teaching and skill learning*. Oxford: Blackwell.

Johnson, K. (2004). *Designing second language learning tasks*. Oxford: Blackwell.

Jonassen, D. (1999). Designing constructivist learning environments. In C. Reigeluth (Ed.), *Instructional-design theories and models* (pp. 215–239). Mahwah, NJ: Erlbaum.

Jourdenais, R. (2001). Cognition, instruction and protocol analysis. In P. Robinson (Ed.), *Cognition and second language instruction* (pp. 354–376). Cambridge: Cambridge University Press.

Karmiloff-Smith, A. (1979). *A functional approach to child language*. Cambridge: Cambridge University Press.

Klein, W. (1986). *Second language acquisition*. Cambridge: Cambridge University Press.

Klein, W., & Perdue, C. (1997). The basic variety (or: Couldn't natural languages be much simpler?). *Second Language Research, 13*, 301–347.

Knowlton, B., & Squire, L. (1996). Artificial grammar learning depends on acquisition of both abstract and exemplar-specific information. *Journal of Experimental Psychology: Learning, Memory and Cognition, 22*, 169–181.

Kormos, J. (2006). *Speech production and second language acquisition*. Mahwah, NJ: Erlbaum.

Krashen, S. D. (1982). *Principles and practice in second language acquisition*. Oxford: Pergamon.

Krashen, S., & Terrell, T. (1983). *The Natural Approach*. Oxford: Pergamon.

Kuiken, F., & Vedder, I. (2007). Cognitive task complexity and linguistic performance in French L2 writing. In M. P. García Mayo (Ed.), *Investigating tasks in formal language learning* (pp. 117–135). Clevedon: Multilingual Matters.

Kuiken, F., Mos, M., & Vedder, I. (2005). Cognitive task complexity and second language writing performance. In S. Foster-Cohen, M. P. García Mayo & J. Cenoz (Eds.), *Eurosla Yearbook*, Vol. 5 (pp. 195–222). Amsterdam: John Benjamins.

Lado, R. (1957). *Linguistics across cultures: Applied linguistics for language teachers.* Michigan, MI: Michigan University Press.

Lakoff, G., & Johnson, M. (1998). *Philosophy in the flesh.* New York: Basic Books.

Langacker, R. (1999). *Grammar and conceptualization.* Berlin: Mouton DeGruyter.

Larson Freeman, D. (1976). An explanation for the morpheme acquisition order of second language earners. *Language Learning, 26,* 125–134.

Larson Freeman, D. (2006). The emergence of accuracy, fluency and complexity in the oral and written production of five Chinese learners of English. *Applied Linguistics, 27,* 590–619.

Lave, J., & Wenger, E. (1991). *Situated learning.* Cambridge: Cambridge University Press.

Lee, C. E., & Rescorla, L. (2002). The use of psychological state terms by late talkers at age 3. *Applied Psycholinguistics, 23,* 623–641.

Lee, M., & Williams, J. (2001). Lexical access in spoken word production by bilinguals: Evidence from the semantic competitor priming paradigm. *Bilingualism: Language and Cognition, 4,* 233–248.

Levelt, W. (1989). *Speaking: From intention to articulation.* Cambridge, MA: MIT Press.

Levinson, S. (2003). *Space in language and cognition.* Cambridge: Cambridge University Press.

Li, P., & Shirai, Y. (2000). *The acquisition of lexical and grammatical aspect.* Berlin: Mouton de Gruyter.

Liang, J. (2002). Sentence comprehension by Chinese learners of English: Verb-centered or construction-centered (cited in Goldberg, 2006).

Lightbown, P. (1983). Exploring relationships between developmental and instructional sequences. In H. G. Seliger & M. H. Long (Eds.), *Classroom-oriented research in second language acquisition* (pp. 217–243). Rowley, MA: Newbury House.

Lightbown, P. (2000). Classroom SLA and second language teaching. *Applied Linguistics, 21,* 431–462.

Logan, G. D. (1988). Toward an instance theory of automatization. *Psychological Review, 95,* 492–527.

Long, M. H. (1983). Native speaker/non-native speaker conversation and the negotiation of comprehensible input. *Applied Linguistics, 4,* 126–141.

Long, M. H. (1985). A role for instruction in second language acquisition: task-based language teaching. In K. Hyltenstam & M. Pienemann (Eds.), *Modeling and assessing second language acquisition* (pp. 77–99). Clevedon: Multilingual Matters.

Long, M. H. (1989). Task, group, and task-group interactions. *University of Hawaii Working Papers in ESL, 8,* 1–25.

Long, M. H. (1991). Focus on form: A design feature in language teaching methodology. In K. de Bot, R. Ginsberg, & C. Kramsch (Eds.), *Foreign language research in cross-cultural perspectives* (pp. 39–52). Amsterdam: John Benjamins.

Long, M. H. (1996). The role of the linguistic environment in second language acquisition. In W. Ritchie & T. Bhatia (Eds.), *Handbook of second language acquisition* (pp. 413–463). San Diego, CA: Academic Press.

Long, M. H. (2006) (Ed.), *Second language needs analysis*. New York: Cambridge University Press.

Long, M. H. (2007). *Problems in SLA*. Mahwah, NJ: Erlbaum.

Long, M. H., & Crookes, G. (1992). Three approaches to task-based syllabus design. *TESOL Quarterly, 26,* 27–56.

Long, M. H. & Doughty, C. (in press). *Handbook of second and foreign language teaching*. Oxford: Blackwell.

Long, M. H., & Norris, J. (2000). Task-based teaching and assessment. In M. Byron (Ed.), *Encyclopedia of language teaching* (pp. 597–603). London: Routledge.

Long, M. H., & Robinson, P. (1998). Focus on form: Theory, research, and practice. In C. Doughty & J. Williams (Eds.), *Focus on form in classroom second language acquisition* (pp. 15–41). New York: Cambridge University Press.

Mackey, A., & Gass, S. (2006) (Eds.). *Interaction research: Extending the methodological boundaries*. Guest-edited special issue, *Studies in Second Language Acquisition, 28,* (2). New York: Cambridge University Press.

MacWhinney, B. (1995). *The CHILDES project: Tools for analyzing talk (2nd ed.)*. Mahwah, NJ: Erlbaum.

MacWhinney, B. (1999) (Ed.). *The emergence of language*. Mahwah, NJ: Erlbaum.

Majid, A., Bowerman, M., Kita, S., Haun, D., & Levinson, S. (2004). Can language restructure cognition?: The case for space. *Trends in Cognitive Sciences, 8,* 108–114.

Mandler, J. (2004a). *The foundations of mind: Origins of conceptual thought*. Oxford: Oxford University Press.

Mandler, J. (2004b). Thought before language. *Trends in Cognitive Sciences, 8,* 508–513.

Maratsos, M. (1982). The child's construction of grammatical categories. In E. Wanner & L. Gleirman (Eds.), *Language acquisition: the state of the art* (pp. 240–262). New York: Cambridge University Press.

McDonough, K. (2006). Interaction and syntactic priming: English L2 speakers' production of dative constructions. *Studies in Second Language Acquisition, 28,* 179–207.

McDonough, K., & Mackey, A. (2006). Responses to recasts: Repetitions, primed production, and linguistic development. *Language Learning, 57,* 457–481.

Meisel, J. (1987). Reference to past events and actions in the development of natural second language acquisition. In C. Pfaff (Ed.), *First and second language acquisition processes* (pp. 206–224). Cambridge, MA: Newbury House.

Mellow, D. (2006). The emergence of second language syntax: A case study of the acquisition of relative clauses. *Applied Linguistics, 27,* 645–670.

Meuter, R. (2005). Language selection in bilinguals. In J. Kroll & A. M. B. de Groot (Eds.), *Handbook of bilingualism: Psycholinguistic approaches* (pp. 349–370). Oxford: Oxford University Press.

MICASE (2004). from *http://www.hti.umich.edu/m/micase/*

537

Michael, E. & Gollan, T. (2005). Being and becoming bilingual: Individual differences and consequences for language production. In J. Kroll & A. M. B. de Groot (Eds.), *Handbook of bilingualism: Psycholinguistic approaches* (pp. 389–407). Oxford: Oxford University Press.

Milanoic, M., & Saville, N. (1996). *Performance testing, cognition and assessment.* Cambridge: Cambridge University Press.

Morales, F., & Taylor, J. R. (in press). Learning and relative frequency. In C. Zelinski (Ed.), *Memory and language.*

Munby, J. (1978). *Communicative syllabus design.* Cambridge: Cambridge University Press.

Murphy, G., & Ross, B. (2005). The two faces of typicality in category-based induction. *Cognition, 95,* 175–200.

Myles, F., Hooper, J., & Mitchell, R. (1999). Interrogative chunks in French L2: a basis for creative construction? *Studies in Second Language Acquisition, 21,* 49–80.

Nelson, K. (1996). *Language in cognitive development.* New York: Cambridge University Press.

Newman, M., Barabasi, A. L., & Watts, D. J. (2006). *The structure and dynamics of networks.* Princeton, NJ: Princeton University Press.

Ninio, A. (2006). *Language and the learning curve.* Oxford: Oxford University Press.

Ninio, A., & Snow, C. (1996). *Pragmatic development.* Boulder, CO: Westview Press.

Nixon, S. (2005). Mental state verb production and sentential complements in four-year-old children. *First Language, 25,* 19–39.

Norris, J., Brown, J. D., Hudson, T., & Yoshioka, J. (1998). *Designing second language performance assessments.* Honolulu, HI: University of Hawaii Press.

Norris, J., & Ortega, L. (2000). Effectiveness of L2 instruction; A research synthesis and quantitative meta-analysis. *Language Learning, 50,* 417–528.

Nosofsky, R. M. (1986). Attention, similarity and the identification–categorization relationship. *Journal of Experimental Psychology: General, 115,* 39–57.

O'Grady, W. (2005). *Syntactic carpentry: An emergentist theory of syntax.* Mahwah, NJ: Erlbaum.

Ortega, L. (2003). Syntactic complexity measures and their relationship to L2 proficiency: A research synthesis of college-level L2 writing. *Applied Linguistics, 24,* 492–512.

Ortega, L., & Iberri-Shea, G. (2005). Longitudinal research in second language acquisition: Recent trends and future directions. *Annual Review of Applied Linguistics, 25,* 26–45.

Palmeri, T. (1997). Exemplar similarity and the development of automaticity. *Journal of Experimental Psychology: Learning, Memory and Cognition, 23,* 324–347.

Parker, K. & Chaudron, C. (1987). The effects of linguistic simplification and elaborative modification on L2 comprehension. *University of Hawaii Working Papers in ESL, 6,* 102–133.

Pavlenko, A., & Jarvis, S. (2002). Biderectional transfer. *Applied Linguistics, 23,* 190–214.

Pawley, A., & Syder, F. (1983). Two problems for linguistic theory: Nativelike selection and nativelike fluency. In J. Richards & R. Schmidt (Eds.), *Language and communication.* London: Longman.

Perdue, C. (Ed.) (1993a). *Adult language acquisition: Cross-linguistic perspectives, Vol. 1: Field methods.* Cambridge: Cambridge University Press.

Perdue, C. (Ed.) (1993b). *Adult language acquisition: Cross-linguistic perspectives, Vol. 2: The results.* Cambridge: Cambridge University Press.

Perruchet, P., & Vintner, A. (2002). The self-organizing consciousness. *Behavioral and Brain Sciences, 25,* 297–388.

Peters, A. (1983). *The units of language acquisition.* New York: Cambridge University Press.

Pickering, M. J., & Branigan, H. (1998). The representation of verbs: Evidence from syntactic priming in language production. *Journal of Memory and Language, 39,* 633–651.

Pickering, M. J., Branigan, H. P., Cleland, A. A., & Stewart, A. J. (2000). Activation of syntactic information during language production. *Journal of Psycholinguistic Research, 29,* 205–216.

Pienemann, M. (1998). *Language processing and second language development; Processability theory.* Amsterdam: John Benjamins.

Pienemann, M. (2003). Language processing capacity. In C. Doughty & M. H. Long (Eds.), *Handbook of second language acquisition* (pp. 679–714). Oxford: Blackwell.

Pinker, S. (1994). *The language instinct.* Harmondsworth: Penguin.

Pothos, E. (2005). The rules versus similarity distinction. *Behavioral and Brain Sciences, 28,* 1–49.

Prabhu, N. S. (1987). *Second language pedagogy.* Oxford: Oxford University Press.

Rahimpour, M. (1999). Task complexity and variation in interlanguage. In N. O. Jungheim & P. Robinson (Eds.), *Pragmatics and pedagogy: Proceedings of the 3rd Pacific Second Language Research Forum, Vol. 2* (pp. 115–134). Tokyo: PacSLRF.

Reber, A. S. (1993). *Implicit learning and tacit knowledge: An essay on the cognitive unconscious.* Oxford: Clarendon Press.

Reber, A. S., & Allen, R. (1978). Analogy and abstraction strategies in artificial grammar learning: A functionalist interpretation. *Cognition, 6,* 189–221.

Reber, A. S., & Allen, R. (2000). Individual differences in implicit learning: Implications for the evolution of consciousness. In R. Kunzendorf & B. Wallace (Eds.), *Individual differences in conscious experience* (pp. 227–250). Amsterdam: John Benjamins.

Ringbom, H. (2006). *Cross-linguistic similarity in foreign language learning.* Clevedon: Multilingual Matters.

Ritchie, W., & Bhatia, T. (1996). Second language acquisition: Introduction, foundations and overview. In W. Ritchie & T. Bhatia (Eds.), *Handbook of second language acquisition* (pp. 1–49). San Diego, CA: Academic Press.

Robinson, P. (1986). Constituency or dependency in the units of language acquisition? An approach to describing the learner's analysis of formulae. *Linguisticae Investigationes, 10,* 417–438.

Robinson, P. (1989). Procedural vocabulary and language learning. *Journal of Pragmatics, 13,* 523–546.

Robinson, P. (1990). Metaphors for the description of acquisition data: From constituency "trees" to dependency "frames." *International Review of Applied Linguistics, 28,* 273–292.

Robinson, P. (1993). Procedural and declarative knowledge in vocabulary learning:

Communication and the language learner's lexicon. In T. Huckin & J. Coady (Eds.), *Second language reading and vocabulary learning* (pp. 223–259). New York: Ablex.

Robinson, P. (1994). Implicit knowledge, second language learning and syllabus construction: Comments on Rod Ellis' "The structural syllabus and second language acquisition." *TESOL Quarterly, 28*, 161–166.

Robinson, P. (1995a). Task complexity and second language narrative discourse. *Language Learning, 45*, 99–140.

Robinson, P. (1995b). Aptitude, awareness and the fundamental similarity of implicit and explicit second language learning. In R. Schmidt (Ed.), *Attention and awareness in second language learning* (pp. 303–357). Honolulu, HI: University of Hawaii Press.

Robinson, P. (1995c). Attention, memory and the "noticing" hypothesis. *Language Learning, 45*, 283–331.

Robinson, P. (1996a). *Consciousness, rules and instructed second language acquisition.* New York: Lang.

Robinson, P. (Ed.) (1996b). *Task complexity and second language syllabus design: Data-based studies and speculations.* University of Queensland Working Papers in Language and Linguistics (Special issue).

Robinson, P. (1997). Generalizability and automaticity of second language learning under implicit, incidental, enhanced and rule-search conditions. *Studies in Second Language Acquisition, 19*, 223–247.

Robinson, P. (2001a). Task complexity, task difficulty, and task production: Exploring interactions in a componential framework. *Applied Linguistics, 22*, 27–57.

Robinson, P. (2001b). Task complexity, cognitive resources, and syllabus design: A triadic framework for investigating task influences on SLA. In P. Robinson (Ed.), *Cognition and second language instruction* (pp. 287–318). Cambridge: Cambridge University Press.

Robinson, P. (2002). Learning conditions, aptitude complexes and SLA: A framework for research and pedagogy. In P. Robinson (Ed.), *Individual differences and instructed language learning* (pp. 113–133). Amsterdam: John Benjamins.

Robinson, P. (2003a). Attention and memory during SLA. In C. Doughty & M. H. Long (Eds.), *Handbook of second language acquisition* (pp. 631–678). Oxford: Blackwell.

Robinson, P. (2003b). The Cognition Hypothesis, task design and adult task-based language learning. *Second Language Studies, 21*, (2), 45–107.

Robinson, P. (2004). Rules and similarity processes in Artificial Grammar and natural second language learning: What is the "default"? *Behavioral and Brain Sciences, 28*, 33–34.

Robinson, P. (2005a). Cognitive complexity and task sequencing: A review of studies in a Componential Framework for second language task design. *International Review of Applied Linguistics, 43*, 1–32.

Robinson, P. (2005b). Cognitive abilities, chunk-strength and frequency effects in implicit Artificial Grammar and incidental L2 learning: Replications of Reber, Walkenfeld and Hernstadt (1991) and Knowlton and Squire (1996) and their relevance for SLA. *Studies in Second Language Acquisition, 27*, 235–268.

Robinson, P. (2005c). Aptitude and second language acquisition. *Annual Review of Applied Linguistics, 25,* 46–73.

Robinson, P. (2007a). Criteria for classifying and sequencing pedagogic tasks. In M. P. García Mayo (Ed.), *Investigating tasks in formal language learning* (pp. 7–27). Clevedon: Multilingual Matters.

Robinson, P. (2007b). Aptitudes, abilities, contexts and practice. In R. M. DeKeyser (Ed.), *Practice in second language learning: Perspectives from applied linguistics and cognitive psychology* (pp. 256–286). Cambridge: Cambridge University Press.

Robinson, P. (2007c). Task complexity, theory of mind, and intentional reasoning: Effects on speech production, interaction, uptake and perceptions of task difficulty. In P. Robinson & R. Gilabert (Eds.) (in press), *Task complexity, the Cognition Hypothesis and second language instruction.* Guest-edited special issue *International Review of Applied Linguistics.* Berlin: Mouton DeGruyter.

Robinson, P. (in press). Syllabus design. In M. H. Long & C. Doughty (Eds.), *Handbook of second and foreign language teaching.* Oxford: Blackwell.

Robinson, P., & Gilabert, R. (Eds.) (2007). *Task complexity, the Cognition Hypothesis and second language instruction.* Guest-edited special issue *International Review of Applied Linguistics.* Berlin: Mouton DeGruyter.

Robinson, P., & Ha, M. (1993). Instance theory and second language rule-learning under explicit conditions. *Studies in Second Language Acquisition, 15,* 413–438.

Robinson, P., & Nakamura, D. (in preparation). Construing motion on simple and complex second language tasks: Lexicalization patterns, the Aspect Hypothesis and task performance in the Here-and-Now and There-and-Then.

Robinson, P., Ting, S. C.-C., & Urwin, J. (1995). Investigating second language task complexity. *RELC Journal, 26,* 62–79.

Rohdenburg, G. (2002). Processing complexity and the variable use of prepositions in English. In H. Ballerman (Ed.), *Perspectives on prepositions* (pp. 79–101). Tubingen: Gunter Narr.

Rosch, E. (1975). Cognitive representations of semantic categories. *Journal of Experimental Psychology: General, 104,* 192–233.

Rutherford, W., & Sharwood Smith, M. (1988). *Grammar and language teaching: A book of readings.* Rowley, MA: Newbury House.

Sato, C. (1990). *The syntax of conversation in interlanguage development.* Tubingen: Gunter Narr.

Schank, R. (1999). *Dynamic memory revisited.* New York: Cambridge University Press.

Schank, R., & Abelson, R. (1977). *Scripts, plans, goals and understanding.* Hillsdale, NJ: Erlbaum.

Schlesinger, I. M. (1982). *Steps to language.* Hillsdale, NJ: Erlbaum.

Schmidt, R. (1990). The role of consciousness in second language learning. *Applied Linguistics, 11,* 127–158.

Schmidt, R. (1992). Psychological mechanisms underlying second language fluency. *Studies in Second Language Acquisition, 14,* 357–385.

Schmidt, R. (1993). Awareness and second language acquisition. *Annual Review of Applied Linguistics, 13,* 206–226.

Schmidt, R. (1994). Implicit learning and the cognitive unconscious: Of artificial grammars and SLA. In N. C. Ellis (Ed.), *Implicit and explicit learning of languages* (pp. 165–209). London: Academic Press.

Schmidt, R. (1995). A tutorial on the role of attention and awareness in second language learning. In R. Schmidt (Ed.), *Attention and awareness in second language learning* (pp. 1–56). Honolulu, HI: University of Hawaii Press.

Schmidt, R. (2001). Attention. In P. Robinson (Ed.), *Cognition and second language instruction* (pp. 1–32). Cambridge: Cambridge University Press.

Schmitt, N. (2004) (Ed.). *Formulaic sequences: Acquisition, processing and use.* Amsterdam: John Benjamins.

Schneider, W., Schumann-Hengsteler, R., & Sodian, B. (2005) (Eds.). *Young children's cognitive development: Interrelationships among executive functioning, working memory, verbal ability and theory of mind.* Mahwah, NJ: Erlbaum.

Schumann, J. (1978). *The pidginization process: A model for second language acquisition.* Rowley, MA: Newbury House.

Selinker, L. (1972). Interlanguage. *International Review of Applied Linguistics, 10,* 209–231.

Siegel, J. (2003). Social context. C. Doughty & M. H. Long (Eds.), *Handbook of second language acquisition* (pp. 178–223). Oxford: Blackwell.

Sinclair, J. McH. (1984). Naturalness in language. In J. Aarts & W. Meijs (Eds.), *Corpus linguistics* (pp. 203–210). Amsterdam: Rodopi.

Skehan, P. (1989). *Individual differences in second language acquisition.* London: Arnold.

Skehan, P. (1998). *A cognitive approach to language learning.* Oxford: Oxford University Press.

Skehan, P. (2002). Theorizing and updating aptitude. In P. Robinson (Ed.), *Individual differences and instructed language learning* (pp. 69–94). Amsterdam: John Benjamins.

Skehan, P., & Foster, P. (2001). Cognition and tasks. In P. Robinson (Ed.), *Cognition and second language instruction* (pp. 183–205). Cambridge: Cambridge University Press.

Slobin, D. (1973). Cognitive prerequisites for the development of grammar. In C. Ferguson & D. Slobin (Eds.), *Studies of child language development* (pp. 175–208). New York: Holt, Rhinehart & Winston.

Slobin, D. (1985). *The crosslinguistic study of language acquisition, Vol 1.* Hillsdale, NJ: Erlbaum.

Slobin, D. (1993). Adult language acquisition: A view from child language study. In C. Perdue (Ed.), *Adult language acquisition: Crosslinguistic perspectives, Vol. 2: The results* (pp. 239–252). Cambridge: Cambridge University Press.

Slobin, D. (1996). From "thought and language" to "thinking for speaking." In J. Gumperz & S. Levinson (Eds.), *Rethinking linguistic relativity* (pp. 70–96). Cambridge: Cambridge University Press.

Slobin, D. (2003). Language and thought online: Some cognitive consequences of linguistic relativity. In D. Gentner & S. Godlin Meadow (Eds.), *Language in mind: Advances in the investigation of language and thought* (pp. 157–191). Cambridge, MA: MIT Press.

Slobin, D. (2004). The many ways to search for a frog: Linguistic typology and the expression of motion events. In S. Stromqvist & L. Verhoeven (Eds.),

Relating events in narrative, Volume 2: Typological and contextual perspectives, pp. 219–258. Mahwah, NJ: Lawrence Erlbaum.

Sloman, S., & Rips, L. (1998). Similarity as an explanatory construct. *Cognition*, 65, 87–101.

Smith, E. E., & Medin, D. L. (1981). *Categories and concepts*. Cambridge, MA: Harvard University Press.

Snow, R. E. (1987). Aptitude complexes. In R. E. Snow & M. J. Farr (Eds.), *Aptitude, learning and instruction, Vol. 3: Cognitive and affective process analysis* (pp. 11–34). Hillsdale, NJ: Erlbaum.

Snow, R. E. (1994). Abilities in academic tasks. In R. J. Sternberg & R. K. Wagner (Eds.), *Mind in context: Interactionist perspectives on human intelligence* (pp. 3–37). New York: Cambridge University Press.

Snow, C., & Ferguson, C. (1977). *Talking to children*. Cambridge: Cambridge University Press.

Speelman, C., & Kirsner, K. (2005). *Beyond the learning curve: The construction of mind*. Oxford: Oxford University Press.

Stanovitch, K. (1999). *Who is rational? Individual differences in reasoning*. Mahwah, NJ: Erlbaum.

Sternberg, R. J. (2002). The theory of successful intelligence and its implications for language aptitude testing. In P. Robinson (Ed.), *Individual differences and instructed language learning* (pp. 13–44). Amsterdam: John Benjamins.

Sternberg, R. J., & Davidson, J. E. (1994) (Eds.). *The nature of insight*. Cambridge, MA: MIT Press.

Sternberg, R. J., & Wagner, R. (1994) (Eds.). *Mind in context: Interactionist perspectives on human intelligence*. New York: Cambridge University Press.

Stromqvist, S., Nordqvist, A., & Wengelin, A. (2004). Writing the Frog Story: Developmental and cross-modal perspectives. In S. Stromqvist & L. Verhoeven, (Eds.), *Relating events in narrative, Vol. 2: Typological and contextual perspectives* (pp. 359–396). Mahwah, NJ: Erlbaum.

Stromqvist, S., & Verhoeven, L. (2004) (Eds.). *Relating events in narrative, Vol. 2: Typological and contextual perspectives*. Mahwah, NJ: Erlbaum.

Studdert-Kennedy, M. (1991). Language development from an evolutionary perspective. In N. A. Krasnegor, D. M. Rumbaugh, R. L. Schiefelbusch, & M. Studdert-Kennedy (Eds.), *Biological and behavioral determinants of language development* (pp. 5–28). Mahwah, NJ: Erlbaum.

Suchman, L. (1987). *Plans and situated action*. New York: Cambridge University Press.

Swain, M. (1985). Communicative competence: some roles of comprehensible input and comprehensible output in its development. In S. Gass & C. Madden (Eds.), *Input in second language acquisition* (pp. 235–253). Rowley, MA: Newbury House.

Swales, J. (1990). *Genre analysis: English in academic and research settings*. Cambridge: Cambridge University Press.

Talmy, L. (2000). *Towards a cognitive semantics, Vol. 1: Concept structuring systems*. Cambridge, MA: MIT Press.

Taube-Schiff, M., & Segalowitz, N. (2005). Within-language attention control in second language processing. *Bilingualism: Language and Cognition*, 8, (3), 195–206.

Taylor, H., & Tversky, B. (1996). Perspective in spatial description. *Journal of Memory and Language, 35,* 371–391.

Taylor, J. (1995). *Linguistic categorization: Prototypes in linguistic theory* (2nd edition). Oxford: Oxford University Press.

Thelen, E., & Smith, L. B. (1994). *A dynamic systems approach to the development of cognition and action.* Cambridge, MA: MIT Press.

Tomasello, M. (1992). *First verbs: A case study of early grammatical development.* New York: Cambridge University Press.

Tomasello, M. (1999). *The cultural origins of human cognition.* Cambridge, MA: Harvard University Press.

Tomasello, M. (2003). *Constructing a language: A usage-based theory of language acquisition.* Cambridge, MA: Harvard University Press.

Tomasello, M., & Herron, C. (1989). Feedback for language transfer errors: The garden path technique. *Studies in Second Language Acquisition, 11,* 385–395.

Tomasello, M., Kruger, A., & Ratner, H. (1993). Cultural learning. *Behavioral and Brain Sciences, 16,* 495–552.

Tomasello, M., & Stahl, D. (2004). Sampling children's spontaneous speech: How much is enough? *Journal of Child Language, 31,* 101–121.

Tomlin, R. (1990). Functionalism in second language acquisition. *Studies in Second Language Acquisition, 12,* 155–177.

Truscott, J., & Sharwood Smith, M. (2004). Acquisition by processing: A modular perspective on language development. *Bilingualism: Language and Cognition, 7,* 1–20.

Ullman, M. (2001). The neural basis of lexicon and grammar in first and second language acquisition: The declarative/procedural model. *Bilingualism: Language and Cognition, 4,* 105–112.

Van den Branden, K. (2006). *Task-based language education: From theory to practice.* Cambridge: Cambridge University Press.

VanPatten, B. (2004) (Ed.). *Processing instruction: Theory, research and commentary.* Mahwah, NJ: Erlbaum.

VanPatten, B., Williams, J., Rott, S., & Overstreet, M. (2004). *Form-meaning connections in second language acquisition.* Mahwah, NJ: Erlbaum.

von Stutterheim, C. (1991). Narrative and description: Temporal reference in second language acquisition. In T. Heubner & C. Ferguson (Eds.), *Crosscurrents in second language acquisition and linguistic theories* (pp. 385–403). Amsterdam: John Benjamins.

von Stutterheim, C., & Klein, W. (1987). A concept-oriented approach to second language studies. In C. Pfaff (Ed.), *First and second language acquisition processes* (pp. 191–205). Rowley, MA: Newbury House.

von Stutterheim, C., & Nuese, R. (2003). Processes of conceptualisation in language production: Language-specific perspectives and event construal. *Linguistics, 41,* 851–888.

Wagner-Gough, J., & Hatch, E. (1976). The importance of input data in language acquisition studies. *Language Learning, 25,* 297–308.

Wellman, H. (1990). *The child's theory of mind.* Cambridge, MA: MIT Press.

White, J. (1998). Getting the learners' attention: A typographical input enhancement study. In C. Doughty & J. Williams (Eds.), *Focus on form in classroom second language acquisition,* (pp. 85–113). New York: Cambridge University Press.

White, R. (1988). *The ELT curriculum: Design, management, innovation*. Oxford: Blackwell.

Widdowson, H. G. (1978). *Teaching language as communication*. Oxford: Oxford University Press.

Widdowson, H. G. (1983). *Learning purpose and language use*. Oxford: Oxford University Press.

Widdowson, H. G. (1990). *Aspects of language teaching*. Oxford: Oxford University Press.

Wilkins, D. (1976). *Notional syllabuses*. Oxford: Oxford University Press.

Williams, J. N. (1999). Memory, attention, and inductive learning. *Studies in Second Language Acquisition, 21*, 1–48.

Williams, J. N., & Rott, S. (2005). Learning without awareness. *Studies in Second Language Acquisition, 27*, 269–304.

Wong Fillmore, L. (1979). Individual differences in second language acquisition. In C. Fillmore, D. Kempler, & S.-W. Wang (Eds.), *Individual differences in language ability and language behavior* (pp. 203–228). New York: Academic Press.

Wray, A. (2002). *Formulaic language and the lexicon*. Cambridge: Cambridge University Press.

Yano, Y., Long, M. H., & Ross, S. (1994). The effects of simplified and elaborated texts on foreign language reading comprehension. *Language Learning, 44*, 189–219.

Zipf, G. K. (1935). *The psycho-biology of language: An introduction to dynamic philology*. Cambridge, MA: MIT Press.

AUTHOR INDEX

SUBJECT INDEX

References for notes are indexed as, e.g., 60n. References to sample words and constructions are indexed as, e.g. *'fruit'*, *'be like'* or (more abstractly) *'ing'* variable. References to language learners are constructed with the languages in order of acquisition, e.g. a native speaker of Swedish learning English would be entered under 'Swedish-English speakers'. References to phonemes are entered as, e.g., /r/.